# Adaptation Nursing

## ASSESSMENT & INTERVENTION

Beverly J. Rambo, R.N., M.N., M.A.

Formerly Assistant Professor of Nursing
Mount St. Mary's College
Los Angeles, California
Director, Nursing Publications
UCLA Extension, Allied Health Publications
Los Angeles, California

## W.B. Saunders Company

PHILADELPHIA / LONDON / TORONTO / MEXICO CITY / RIO DE JANEIRO / SYDNEY / TOKYO

**W. B. SAUNDERS COMPANY**
**Harcourt Brace Jovanovich, Inc.**

The Curtis Center
Independence Square West
Philadelphia, PA 19106-3399

Listed here is the latest translated edition of this book together with the language of the translation and the publisher.

Japanese (1st edition) Igaku-Shoin/Saunders, Tokyo, Japan

**Library of Congress Cataloging in Publication Data**

Rambo, Beverly J.
    Adaptation nursing.

1. Nursing.     2. Nursing—Psychological aspects.
3. Adaptability (Psychology)     4. Adjustment
   (Psychology)     5. Sick—Psychology.
   I. Title.

RT42.R35   1984     610.73     83–2975

ISBN 0–7216–1048–X

Adaptation Nursing: Assessment and Intervention                    ISBN 0–7216–1048–X

Last digit is the print number:     9     8     7

# Foreword

The use of models for practice to organize and derive nursing knowledge has been one of the greatest developments of the modern era of nursing. Efforts have been directed toward establishing what the nurse contributes to the well-being of patients in all clinical settings. In recent years, a growing body of literature articulates these nursing models and their application to nursing practice. Faculty of schools of nursing, particularly in the 1970s, revised their curricula using models for nursing practice as a major organizing focus. Mount St. Mary's College in Los Angeles has been a leader in this movement by the first implementation of the Roy Adaptation Model in 1970 in the baccalaureate program.

In 1972, the Roy Model was used to establish an associate degree nursing program at the same department of nursing but located on the second campus of Mount St. Mary's College, the Doheny Campus. The author of this text, Beverly Rambo, was one of the faculty who developed the associate degree curriculum. During the next nine years she taught the 600 students who studied nursing according to the Roy Adaptation Model. This experience, in conjunction with that of her colleagues at the Doheny Campus, provided both the motivation and expertise to publish a text that would simplify and present in concrete terms the components of the Roy Adaptation Model of nursing.

This text makes several contributions to the literature on models for nursing practice. First, the author provides a rationale for the use of nursing models by outlining some clear distinctions between the disciplines of medicine and nursing. Second, I believe that she has achieved her central objective of presenting a major nursing model in clear and concrete terms with a focus on clinical practice in acute care hospitals or skilled nursing facilities. The Guide for Nursing Care Plan—Adaptation Approach, at the end of Chapter Three, will be particularly useful for beginning students, nursing faculty, and practicing nurses in organizing nursing care based on the Roy Adaptation Model of nursing.

Another major contribution of the text is the author's alternative approach for obtaining information about the patient's psychosocial integrity. In working with inexperienced students, Mrs. Rambo found it helpful to have them focus the psychosocial assessment on the person's roles. Thus, students obtain information about self-concept by exploring feelings about the person's tasks of life and about interdependence by identifying relationships with others within major roles. The approach found useful with this particular student population may be appropriate for certain levels of nursing education or roles in nursing practice.

The author's presentation of one faculty's synthesis of ideas and of content development that was successful over a period of years will serve to promote the scientific basis of nursing by assisting the teaching and application of one model to nursing practice and by continuing to raise questions to clarify the theoretical and philosophical basis of the Roy Adaptation Model of nursing.

SISTER CALLISTA ROY
MOUNT ST. MARY'S COLLEGE
LOS ANGELES

# *Preface*

Since its inception and implementation, the Roy adaptation model of nursing has gained in popularity. It has been adopted by an increasing number of schools of nursing as their framework for nursing, both in this country and abroad. Historically, the Roy model was first implemented in the baccalaureate nursing program of Mount St. Mary's College in the fall of 1970 and in the associate degree nursing program in 1972. This unique situation of having both programs in the same college afforded the nursing faculty an excellent opportunity to compare the graduates of both programs of study, using the adaptation model. A method of articulation permitted the movement of the A.D. graduate into the baccalaureate program to obtain the bachelor of science degree in nursing. The differences between students of both programs were found to be minimal except for individual differences in level of competence. Based on these findings, the faculty has completed plans to merge the two nursing programs into one, leading to the completion of the basic nursing program by the end of the junior year with public health, leadership skills, and contracts for advanced studies in clinical areas emphasized in the senior year.

The past years have been busy ones for our faculty as we have developed the curriculum to incorporate adaptation nursing theory and refined these theoretical concepts into our actual clinical practice. Few, if any, textbooks were available that offered the integrated view of nursing as a science, so it was necessary to write our own study guides, outlines, assessment tools, care plans, and other materials to present the concepts in a clearer and more concise way for the students. We have drawn information from many disciplines and searched for material that would help us gain a better understanding of people and their behavior.

The textbook Introduction to Nursing: An Adaptation Model, by Roy and members of the faculty, has been used as a guide. Although the book meets a very real need, its approach is more theoretical. The most frequently heard questions after reading it were "Yes, but how?" "Where do I start?" "How do I know what questions to ask?" "Won't the patient (or client) think these questions are too personal?" "Who determines whether behavior is maladaptive or ineffective?" "Isn't that determination just a matter of the nurse's belief or whim?" "What happens to the patient's medical problem?" "Is the medical condition ignored?" "How is it handled?" This book is based on the curriculum course that we have devised to provide some answers to these questions. It is not meant to be the only approach but does represent the work of one faculty group to implement the adaptation model of nursing in a cohesive, logical, and practical way.

This textbook is intended for use by students in a basic nursing program who have had limited or no previous exposure to nursing and who will spend the major part of their clinical practice time in a hospital or skilled nursing facility. Many of the examples refer to patients on the illness end of the Health-Illness Continuum. At Mount St. Mary's College, the material in this book is covered in weekly classes throughout the first year, and disease conditions and medical therapy are taught in another course. Following this basic course in the theory of nursing science, students are able to apply adaptation concepts to patients in any setting: maternal-child health, mental health, community and public health, and intensive care units, as well as those with medical-surgical conditions. The following elements are emphasized in this course:

1. Normal physiological function and behaviors
2. Common disturbances of the basic physiological needs
3. Identifiable patterns of behavior
4. Coping mechanisms most frequently used

5. Coping problems most often encountered
6. Interventions used to change behaviors, both procedural skills and interpersonal skills
7. The nursing process as the problem-solving method.

This content is very practical, and the nursing process is an effective problem-solving method that faculty members and students can use in their own lives. It works well for those who have a problem in coping with changes in their lives. Those who are familiar with the Roy adaptation theory will note that some of the concepts in this book are interpreted in a somewhat different light from that of the purist. This is especially true with the role-function mode, which one nursing faculty found to be confusing to beginning students. They tended to handle all problems of self-concept and interdependence modes as problems in role-function and to intervene by providing role cues, sanctions, and rewards which failed to solve the presenting problems. Using role-function as the means of assessing self-concept and interdependence integrity has been more effective, and, by the second year, students quickly pick up role-function concepts and are able to apply these to parenting and to groups. Roy has carefully monitored the development of her theory and believes that it is flexible enough to permit different interpretations or ways of implementing it in various nursing programs as long as the basic components are intact. In other words, the adaptation model of nursing is adaptable and dynamic.

Throughout this book, the author has sought to simplify the concepts of Roy's adaptation model of nursing and present them in very concrete terms. The content progresses from the simple to the complex and from the known to the unknown, focusing on the individual condition before extending to the family and to groups. The chapters are organized to meet the stated objectives for each by presenting the theory and describing the assessment behaviors and the stimuli for them, the types of coping problems people have that are within the scope of nursing, and the interventions to be used. The overall emphasis is on what the nurse needs to know in order to practice effectively and not on a presentation of every topic in great depth. When time permits, further reading and study in these areas are an excellent source of enrichment and expansion of skills in using the adaptation approach to nursing.

The chapters are divided into sections containing related subjects. Section One consists of an explanation of the adaptation model of nursing and the nursing process as it is used in solving problems and planning nursing care. Special emphasis is given to the assessment phase of the nursing process. Section Two focuses on increasing knowledge and understanding of human behavior because this is a primary concern of nursing. Sensory perception is examined in terms of the nature of stimuli and their meaning. Types of behavior, types of behavioral patterns, and ways in which behaviors are learned or changed are described. The effects of stress and anxiety produce physiological changes through the autonomic nervous system, as well as being expressed in emotional feelings and states. The condition of illness is an important stimulus that strains people's coping mechanisms as they respond to what meaning illness has for them. The expectations of the sick role and the stages of illness provide standards the nurse uses when comparing observed patients and determining whether these are adaptive or not. Section Three is devoted to the assessment of the physiological mode. The assessment factors focus on the normal or adaptive behaviors involved as individuals act to meet their basic physiological needs in order to sustain life. Types of problems are described and interventions are listed to help to meet the basic needs.

Psychosocial functioning is the topic of Section Four. People carry out roles in performing the work of society, and the expectations of their role performance change as they progress from one stage of life to another. The growth and developmental tasks for each stage of life are the basis for role performance. A description of stages illustrates how people mature mentally, intellectually, and emotionally and how they attain the social skills needed to live successfully in the world. The self-concept and interdependence modes are presented with their theory and component parts, which are used to classify the behaviors gained through the assessment of the performance of roles in carrying out the appropriate growth and developmental tasks. The problems associated with these modes are the subject of additional chapters. Section Five concludes by examining several stimuli that are powerful influencing factors on behavior. These influencing factors include the effects of changes related to old age, the persistence of cultural values and beliefs, the constrictions of poverty, and the events in life that lead to a crisis in coping.

The value of the adaptation approach to nursing depends upon its usefulness in improving the quality of care that is given. At the end of each chapter (except Section One), suggestions are made for applying the related theoretical content to nursing practice in the clinical setting. These suggestions form one set of learning objectives for clinical nursing experiences. Appendix A provides a complete assessment tool for the physiological need areas and the assessment of roles for the appropriate growth and developmental tasks. The completed assessment is helpful as a guide for charting observations and nursing care in the patient's record. Appendix B contains two examples of nursing care plans.

It is my hope that this textbook will prove helpful to readers in understanding the adaptation approach to nursing care and its application. As a nurse who originally was educated in the medical model in a diploma program, I am convinced that the adaptation model is superior in teaching nursing students to be effective in handling psychosocial coping problems of people as well as physiological problems. We have a great need for nurses who not only carry out the medical regimen competently and skillfully but also can identify people with coping problems and intervene with sensitivity to assist them in regaining the comfort and ease of an adaptive state. The young women and men who have graduated from our program and entered professional nursing have demonstrated that these are achievable goals.

BEVERLY J. RAMBO

# Acknowledgements

Many people have given me encouragement and support in my efforts to prepare this manuscript, and I am most grateful to them. The nursing faculty at Mount St. Mary's College has provided much insight into the use of the adaptation model through the stimulating and philosophical discussions that occurred whenever we met to clarify various interpretations and plan for the clinical application of the Roy adaptation model of nursing. I am especially grateful to Sister Callista Roy, Joan Hanson, Rita Veatch, Joan Cho, Sheila Driscoll, and Kathryn Casey, among others, who have provided valuable input. My special thanks go to my friend and colleague, Joan Cho, who has been steadfast in her search for utilizing a logical thought process and the application of adaptation concepts and who provided the basic assessment method for the physiological mode. I appreciate the efforts of our many students as they struggled to write their nursing care plans and assessment reports. Some of their material, selected from the hundreds of care plans that I have kept, provided examples to illustrate points under discussion. Through their clinical practice, they have demonstrated the practicality and advantages of an adaptation approach to nursing.

I am indebted to Dr. Miles Anderson of the Allied Health Professions project at the University of California, Los Angeles, who encouraged me to undertake this project. Although the adaptation approach represents a departure from the traditional views of nursing, Dr. Anderson has visions of the future and the willingness to take risks. Thanks also are due to Christine Ford for her efficient and capable handling of the many details in the office and to Ruth Barmettler for her artistic talents in producing illustrations that conveyed the messages I had hoped they would. Katherine Pitcoff, the nursing editor of W. B. Saunders, has been very supportive of my efforts and has shown her understanding of the adaptation nursing concept. I am grateful for her encouragement. Finally, I want to thank my family and friends who understood my need to spend so much time at the typewriter and my desire to complete this work.

Beverly J. Rambo

The Allied Health Publications Program is part of University of California Extension, Education Extension, Los Angeles. It is an outgrowth of a research project, "Development and Validation of Instructional Programs for the Allied Health Occupations," supported by the U.S. Office of Education and conducted by the Division of Vocational Education, now also a part of University of California Extension. The research program generated curriculum materials such as occupational analyses and instructional manuals. These were sold to those who needed them, and the Allied Health Publications Program was set up to print and distribute some of the materials and to work out publication agreements with private publishers for others.

When the original research grant program ended, the Allied Health Publications Program continued, supported entirely by earnings from sales of some publications and royalties on others. As earnings increased, new publications were undertaken, working with outside writers, illustrators, and editors on a contract basis. All of these publications are instructional materials in various health-care fields, produced and distributed for the program by private publishers on a royalty basis.

The educational philosophy exemplified in these materials emphasizes helping the student to perform the tasks of the occupation and to use the basic scientific and technical knowledge related to them. This approach is designed to shorten the learning process so that "more learning in less time with greater retention" can be achieved. If these materials make a significant contribution toward accomplishing this goal, they will help solve the health manpower problems, and we will feel that the hours we labored on the development of this material were not in vain.

Miles H. Anderson, Ed.D., Director (Emeritus)
Allied Health Publications
University Extension
University of California, Los Angeles

# A Note of Explanation

In preparing the manuscript for this book, the author has attempted to avoid using sexist terms. However, certain conventions have been used for convenience and to avoid repetition or awkward construction. For example, the term "man" is occasionally used to refer to all human beings.

This book is intended for students in a basic nursing program who have had limited or no previous exposure to nursing and who will spend the major part of their clinical practice time in a hospital or skilled nursing facility. Many of the examples refer to patients on the illness end of the Health-Illness Continuum, although the adaptation model is equally effective with clients in the community as well as one's self, family, and friends. The concepts apply to all people, regardless of their positions in life or their roles.

# Contents

*Section ONE*

# INTRODUCTION TO THE NURSING PROCESS

The practice of nursing consists of more than following the doctor's orders, carrying out the steps of a procedure, or performing tasks in a routine way. It is a profession engaged in dealing with people as they struggle with the problems of life. Nursing focuses on behavior—how people act and behave. Nurses assist people who are faced with some of the most serious and emotionally upsetting situations in their lives. They are trying to cope with problems that have affected their health and disturbed their ability to continue with the usual pattern of their lives. Because no two people think or act in exactly the same way when they are under stress, nurses see people who respond to their problems with a variety of behaviors. In order to render competent care to people from all walks of life, nurses must be able to understand these behaviors and help people solve their problems.

In this section, you will be introduced to the adaptation approach to nursing and will be given an explanation of the problem-solving method of the nursing process.

The adaptation approach to nursing is based on the theory developed by Sister Callista Roy. Her adaptation model provides a framework for observing people who are in an adapted, or healthy, state. It is a guide to assessment because it determines the type of information and functions needed in order to provide nursing care. The nursing process focuses on assessment, which includes the gathering of information about the person's level of functioning and the identification of behaviors outside the adapted range, followed by a second assessment to determine the stimuli or the causes of these ineffective behaviors. The clusters of maladaptive behaviors are examined, the overall problem in the need area is identified, goals are set, and interventions are planned and carried out. Results are evaluated to determine whether the goals have been met or whether further interventions are needed.

A guide for nursing care plans is given at the end of Chapter Three. This guide represents one method of classifying all possible situations and behaviors that the nurse might encounter when working with people who are ill or people who are having problems in coping with changes in their lives. It is a concise way of examining the functions of biopsychosocial beings and the types of behaviors associated with the basic needs areas, and it is a statement of the problems associated with unmet needs and the types of stimuli that cause the problems.

# Chapter ONE

# Adaptation: A Framework for Nursing

## OBJECTIVES   Information in this chapter will help you to

1. Define *adaptation* and the key concepts related to it as individuals seek to cope with their changing world.
2. Discuss the purposes and the components involved in a model of nursing.
3. Describe the Roy Adaptation Model of Nursing by its beliefs, components, and nursing actions that promote the individual's physiological, psychological, and social adaptation.
4. Define the terms used in an adaptation model of nursing.
5. Compare the model for adaptation nursing with the model for medical practice and define the differences between them.

## DEFINITION OF TERMS

The following terms are defined as they are used in the Roy Adaptation Model of Nursing and throughout this book.

**adaptation** — a positive response to changes in the individual's internal or external environment that maintains integrity.

**behavior** — an action or response of the body that can be observed, perceived, or measured.

**client** — a recipient of nursing services with an adaptation problem located in any setting.

**coping** — use of innate or acquired mechanisms or ways of responding to a stimulus in order to adapt to change.

**health** — successful management of and coping with stressors, characterized by a sense of coherence and ease in life.

**health-illness continuum** — a continuous line that represents the various degrees of health, ranging from a high level of well-being to a low level of poor health and critical illness.

3

**integrity** — the state of being whole, sound, and unimpaired.

**maladaptive** — an action or response that is disruptive or does not promote the individual's integrity.

**need** — a basic requirement within the individual that stimulates a response to maintain integrity — oxygen, food, rest, respect, and meaning in one's life are examples.

**norm** — an accepted standard of behavior.

**patient** — a recipient of nursing services who is located on the illness end of the continuum as a result of a disease causing problems in adaptation.

**patient problem** — a disruption in a need area, related to the patient's activities of daily living, coping with feelings, or dealing with other people that requires the nurse's assistance or intervention.

**stimulus** — a stressor or factor that causes or influences behavior.
   a. *focal stimulus* — the primary or causative stressor provoking the change.
   b. *contextual stimuli* — all other stressors or factors in the situation that contribute to or influence behavior.
   c. *residual stimuli* — an individual's internal characteristics, such as attitudes and beliefs, that may exist but have not been validated in the assessment.

---

Adaptation is the process used to cope with or adjust to changes in one's environment. Today, people are subjected to a constant bombardment of intense stimuli producing changes that affect not only their external physical world but also their internal physiological environment. Changes alter and disturb the usual pattern of how we live so it is increasingly difficult to predict or to rely on a familiar outcome to an action or an event. In effect, one is confronted with strange and unfamiliar situations for which additional energy is needed for coping and adjusting. This time in which we live is so pervaded by the stresses associated with change that it is referred to often as the Age of Stress. This stress has subtle effects on health and well-being that cause psychological as well as physical suffering, ranging from mild discomfort to intense pain.

As in every facet of life, many changes have occurred in nursing during the past century. In the nineteenth century, Florence Nightingale described the goal of nursing as putting patients in the best condition so that nature would heal them. In Nightingale's view, the patient was a passive recipient of care by the nurse, who provided nourishing food and kept the patient clean, warm, and comfortable. The majority of the sick and injured were nursed in the home by a family member or a woman from the community who was skilled in taking care of the sick.

Within the medical profession, doctors were searching for the causes and cures of disease. High priority was given to childhood diseases, pneumonia, and epidemics, which claimed many victims, young and old, each year. At the begin-ning of the twentieth century, infectious diseases were still the leading cause of death in most countries of the world.

Tremendous progress in health care has been made. By the 1950s, most of the acutely sick patients were cared for in hospitals rather than in homes. Medical science had found the cure for many diseases, and a large number of patients survived life-threatening conditions. They were treated with newly discovered "miracle drugs," such as antibiotics and steroids, and by various complex and highly technical medical treatments. Although patients tended to be passive recipients of medical treatment prescribed by the physician, they began to assume a more active role in their nursing care. Virginia Henderson, a nurse educator, wrote that the nurse's role was to do those things for patients that they would do for themselves if they had the strength, will, or knowledge. The nurse supplemented patients' efforts and promoted their return to independence to continue the activities of daily life.

Today, there is a growing trend toward viewing nursing services in relation to patients or clients as they adapt to their changing world. People cope not only with internal changes in their bodies or minds but also with changes in their relationships with others and with the physical environment. When people become ill, they have the same hopes, fears, problems, and responsibilities that they had when they were well but, in addition, they have the added stresses of the illness. The miracle drugs and sophisticated treatments used to cure the illness often have no impact on the other stressors affecting patients.

These stressors interfere with treatment and delay recovery when patients are unable to cope with them effectively and reduce tension. Today, there is a need for nurses to extend the scope of nursing beyond the physical illness and to support patients and clients in their efforts to cope with the psychological and social stresses of their illness.

The adaptation approach to nursing emerged during the late 1960s at a time when nursing theorists were trying to define the science and the practice of nursing. It evolved from the concepts of equilibrium and homeostasis and now provides a framework for the practice of nursing to meet the needs of patients in health care facilities and the needs of clients in a wide variety of community settings.

## WHY A MODEL OF NURSING?

What is a nursing model? A model is defined as a way of presenting a situation in logical terms to show the structure of the original idea or object. It is a representation of the original idea or object that gives direction in much the same way that a dress pattern is a guide and provides instructions for making a dress. Models have been used extensively in other disciplines such as medicine and mathematics, but it has been only in the past 15 years that distinct nursing models have emerged, providing a framework for nursing practice. Prior to this, the nursing approach relied heavily on the medical model as a guide for nursing care.

## *PURPOSES OF A MODEL*

A nursing model serves as a unifying framework in three different areas: nursing education, nursing practice, and nursing research. In nursing education, a model provides a means for organizing information into a meaningful whole. It serves to identify the content needed to achieve the goal of nursing care, the learning objectives, and the criteria for evaluating nursing practice. As nursing education continues to expand, a model provides a way to classify and incorporate relevant data and to delete obsolete material.

In nursing practice, a model gives direction for the assessment process and provides a systematic approach to patient care. It shows the nurse what to look for and how to provide nursing care. A model also stimulates scientific inquiry and research to validate nursing theories and concepts and to improve nursing practice.

## *COMPONENTS OF A MODEL*

The essential components of a model answer the questions Who does What? To whom? Where? How? Why? In the nursing model, these components are

Values on which the model is based
Client or patient as the recipient of the action
Goal of the action or intervention
Intervention or service provided, in terms of the framework, the procedures, the agent, and the source of energy

When described in more detail, these components identify what the nurse will assess and what is to be done about the health problems presented by the client or patient. Because nursing is a service performed for people, values are an important aspect of a model. The goals established for nursing care must be consistent with the cultural values and beliefs of the patient. The manner in which one views the recipient of nursing care is based on one's values about man as a biopsychosocial being, one's beliefs about health and illness, and one's beliefs about the relationship between the nurse and the recipient of nursing care. A model also prescribes the method and the actions used to achieve the goal, the setting in which the nursing care takes place, and the source of energy involved.

## ADAPTATION AND HEALTH

As previously stated, adaptation is the process of coping with changes in one's internal and external environment. To understand the process fully, it is necessary to explore such concepts as stressors or stimuli as agents of change, the adaptive state as health, need states arising within the individual, the coping mechanisms used, and the resources available to help individuals resist the effects of stress.

## *THE STRESS OF CHANGE*

Everything that happens can be defined as change, including the passage of time, aging, conversations, relationships with people, and the weather.

Although change is continuously occurring, the rate of change has been increasing. The rapid expansion of technology and scientific knowledge, the great increase in the world's population, the advancements in mass media, the women's movement for equal rights, the rise of consumerism, and the mobility of people are factors that contribute to changes with which everyone must cope in order to adapt to life in today's world. For example, the use of electronics and computers, while enhancing our way of life, has led to a

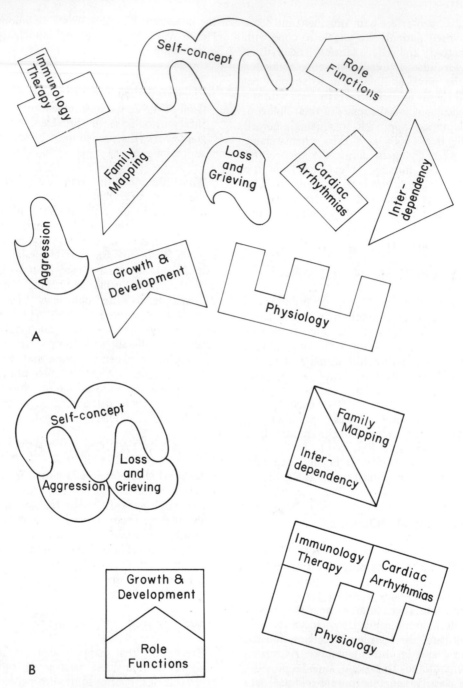

**Figure 1-1.** A, Nurses utilize information about many subjects. B, A model of nursing provides a method of organizing data in a meaningful way.

proliferation of knowledge. Any new information that is useful will produce some sort of change. Often, this knowledge becomes news that is rapidly communicated by television, radio, or other news media to millions of people around the world and affects their lives. Events that occur on the banks of an isolated river in South America could produce dramatic changes in the lives of people halfway around the world.

By its very nature, change is a stressor or stimulus that disrupts the even flow or pattern of life by making life less organized, less familiar, and less predictable. Change can have a ripple effect. One change can lead to others—some can be anticipated, others are unexpected. Each change is a stressor on the body, and when it poses a threat to the person's integrity, it becomes a source of anxiety. The ripple effect of change can be seen in people who become ill with an infection and rest in bed for a few days. As a result, they find that when they get up they are weak, their appetite has diminshed and they have become constipated. In a similar manner, the charge nurse who changes the coffee-break time for staff members may find that this action has far-reaching effects. The cafeteria personnel may complain of overcrowding at the new time, staff members may complain of longer lines and increased traffic on the elevators, some patients may have to have their baths and treatments delayed, and other personnel, such as therapists, may find it necessary to rearrange their schedules.

There are three general categories of stressors in the external environment: (1) those of a cataclysmic nature that are shared by large groups of people, such as changes that result from wars, floods, or earthquakes; (2) those changes shared by one or several individuals such as changes that result from employment, travel, illness, or bereavement; and (3) the stresses or "hassles" of daily living. All these stressors that are caused by the external environment have an effect on the body's internal environment. The body's regulatory function makes continual adjustments on a cellular level to meet fluctuating needs and to ensure survival.

Although everyone tolerates and even needs the stimuli of change to grow and to develop, too much change and stress can cause a breakdown in coping. This causes distress in the individual and, thus, poses a health problem.

## THE ADAPTIVE STATE

In what way does the changing and stressful world relate to health and adaptation? In general usage, *adaptation* means to adjust to something. In this book, adaptation refers to the positive response an individual makes in coping with changes in the internal or external environment. Adaptation is always a positive response that maintains one's biopsychosocial integrity or functioning and promotes well-being. It is the process of responding to all the conditions necessary to meet one's needs.

## WHAT IS HEALTH?

Although most people can easily define illness, they find it difficult to describe health. It is common to define health as the absence of illness. This definition of health allows no middle ground —either a person is entirely well or is ill. In reality, absolute health or illness is uncommon. Is the person who has dental caries or the person who is anxious about a sick child considered healthy or ill? This definition of health focuses on the absence of illness or disease and disregards the multiple causes and contributing factors of illness. Also, it does not explain what health is.

Probably the best known definition of health is that of the World Health Organization (WHO). The preamble of its charter states, "Health is the state of complete physical, mental, and social well-being and not merely the absence of disease or infirmity." It has been difficult to implement this approach to health in terms of the cost of providing the necessary services and resources.

Antonovsky (1979) describes health as adaptation. He states that health involves a high level of confidence, that one's internal and external environment is predictable, and that there is a high probability that all situations will be dealt with as well as can reasonably be expected. Health, or adaptation, is a state of ease in which an individual has a sense of coherence about life and its events.

A useful view of health is to consider it as a condition of life that exists on a continuum ranging from a high level of well-being at one end to extreme illness at the other end, with various stages between the two. Health is the ability to handle stress and change effectively; this occurs in adaptation. Successfully coping with a wide variety of stressors is characteristic of health and adaptation; thus, the words health and adaptation can be used interchangeably.

## THE HEALTH-ILLNESS CONTINUUM

An individual's position on the health-illness continuum is dynamic and changes according to responses to various stresses. These stresses may produce a positive, a neutral, or a negative response. The type of response produced depends on the adequacy and the effectiveness of the coping mechanisms that are used. Positive responses reduce tension and promote the optimum functioning of health. Neutral responses maintain function. Negative responses are ineffective in reducing tension. They tax or exceed an individual's adaptation resources, require the expenditure of additional energy, and lead to breakdown. Breakdown results in developmental and growth problems, coping problems, and pathophysiological illness. The severity of the breakdown can be measured by the following: the degree of functional limitation, whether the problems require definite action to resolve them, the degree of pain, and whether diagnosis and prognosis by a health professional is involved.

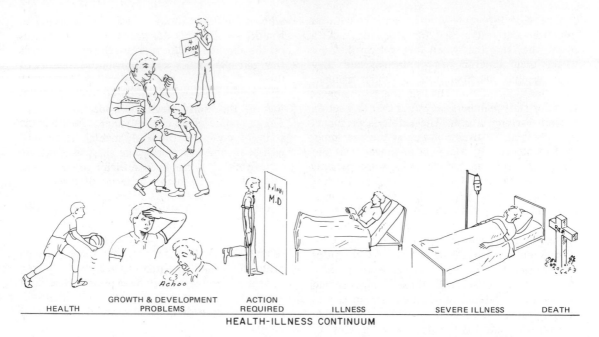

HEALTH    GROWTH & DEVELOPMENT PROBLEMS    ACTION REQUIRED    ILLNESS    SEVERE ILLNESS    DEATH

**HEALTH-ILLNESS CONTINUUM**

**Figure 1–2.** The health-illness continuum envisioned as a progressive range of adaptation, with the high levels in each mode characterized by optimum health, the middle levels characterized by minor disturbances that lead to the lower levels, which are characterized by breakdown in physiological functions that constitute serious illness.

## NEED STATES

In any individual, changes, whether large or small, cause tension and uneasiness that demand attention. This tension is called a need state.

The basic need states of the body were described by Maslow (1970), who envisioned a hierarchy of needs according to their priority and in the form of a pyramid. At the base of the pyramid are the physiological needs that have the highest priority and must be satisfied to maintain life and survival. This level includes the needs for oxygen, fluids, food, elimination of waste products, exercise, movement, and rest. When there is a need in one of these areas, that need assumes a more important position than needs located at other levels in the hierarchy, and it continues to be the primary need until it is met. Even among the basic needs, some have a greater priority than others. One can survive only minutes if deprived of oxygen, but a need to eliminate solid wastes may persist for days when one is constipated.

The next level on the hierarchy includes needs related to safety and sameness, that is, being at ease with familiar people, things, and events. Once survival has been assured by meeting the basic physiological needs, safety needs related to comfort and freedom from distress or pain become important. However, safety from an immediate and obvious danger has higher pri-

ority than the need for food, water, or elimination, which are less immediate.

The need for love, affection, and belonging are at the next level. From infancy, every human being has a need for love and caring. Research studies have shown that infants deprived of "mothering" or affection during the first year or two of life fail to thrive and grow; some even die. Infants who are hospitalized or in institutions are at risk of developing this syndrome, and their care should include suitable interventions to meet their need for belonging.

Higher on Maslow's scale are the needs for social esteem and being valued and respected by others. At the peak are the individual's self-actualizing needs—namely, to create and to understand and appreciate the aesthetic things in life, such as music, art, and beauty. Although highest on the hierarchy, these needs are held in abeyance or deferred when needs of a greater priority occur.

As the basic needs are met, tension occurs in needs higher on the hierarchy and these needs claim the individual's attention and energy. The amount of energy available is limited; however, the body is very efficient at diverting energy to the functions necessary to sustain life and to perform essential activities.

The order of priorities can be determined by examining the various need states to see how

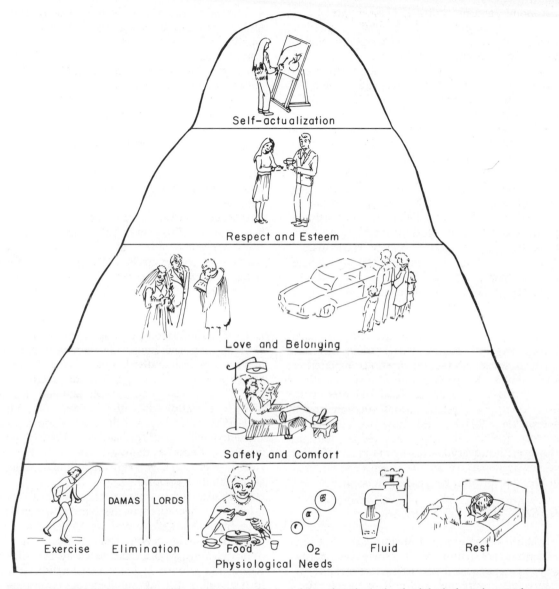

**Figure 1–3.** The hierarchy of needs developed by Maslow shows that the basic physiological needs must be met and that they take precedence over all other needs. Needs for safety and comfort are met next and take precedence over those higher on the pyramid. As needs in each level are met, individuals are able to tend to needs on the next higher level.

long a person could survive if the need were not met. One could live for only a few minutes without oxygen, but one could live for a couple of days without the intake of water and the excretion of wastes. The safety needs may continue for extended periods, as is often seen in the discomfort and pain associated with cancer and chronic diseases. Affection and belonging needs are more difficult to relate to survival; however, fulfilling these needs is essential for psychosocial integrity. There is evidence in the social sciences that persisting needs in this area are associated with emotional problems, social alienation, and suicide. One's need for prestige, self-esteem, and self-actualization may exist partially fulfilled. Some people may never have these needs completely satisfied during their lifetimes.

## COPING MECHANISMS

People respond to a need state through coping mechanisms. When stresses occur in the body's internal environment, certain physiological responses occur. Many of these responses are autonomic and involuntary. The nervous system and the endocrine system perform a regulatory function to maintain the body's stability and to adapt to changes. For example, the level of carbon dioxide ($CO_2$) in the blood stimulates chomoreceptors in major vessels and in the brain to activate the respiratory center. The respiratory drive (a response) causes the person to breathe deeper and more rapidly to bring more oxygen into the lungs. When a person recognizes a danger or threat of any type, the autonomic nervous system is activated by the anxiety and immediately prepares the body for "fight or flight." The amount of epinephrine and norepinephrine hormones in the bloodstream rises instantly to produce this "ready" state of the body, and the formation of antidiuretic hormone is stimulated. These internal coping mechanisms are innate and biological.

Other types of coping mechanisms are cognitive and are acquired through learning and experience. They are used primarily to cope with stresses from the external environment. The individual learns ways of coping with various stressors through social interaction, previous experiences with similar situations, and formal education. One learns how to obtain food and prepare it, how to express anger in various situations and in acceptable manner, and how to cope with anxiety feelings in ways that reduce tension. However, not everyone learns the most effective coping responses to all the stresses encountered in life; thus breakdown and illness occur.

## RESISTANCE TO STRESS

Stimuli in the external environment that provoke stress are so universal that there is no realistic way to escape them. These stresses are sufficient to disorganize, overcome, and destroy people; however, many people, despite numerous stressors, enjoy a relatively high level of health. They have found ways or resources that help them resist the pressures and the damage of the stressors.

Antonovsky (1979) has identified many general resources that increase the individual's ability to resist stress, which are used by nurses in adaptation interventions for clients and patients with coping problems. One of these is simply to avoid stressors. This requires utilizing one's knowledge about possible ill effects from stress. Also, one can rely on attitudes or beliefs that place a value on health and realize that the actions one can take may have a beneficial outcome. Such actions as learning about health, undergoing medical checkups, eating a nutritious diet, and not smoking are ways of avoiding stressors. Adequate material resources, such as food, shelter, clothing,

and money, increase one's resistance to stress. Money provides a protection from stress and anxiety, whereas the lack of money is often a potent stressor.

Cognitive and emotional resources utilize knowledge, intelligence, and one's self-concept to lessen the impact of stress. Knowledge is the storehouse of information about the real world, and intelligence encompasses the skills needed to acquire and use this data. Self-concept is how one feels about oneself. High self-esteem is beneficial; it is characterized by one's sense of an inner person who is integrated and stable yet flexible.

Attitudes and values are other factors that may help reduce stress. One's values are a result of one's particular culture and form the basis for the type of coping mechanism selected to reduce stress. A social support system is another means for defusing stress. Antonovsky (1979) cites mortality studies that show the effectiveness of support systems in terms of survival. Being married is more advantageous to men than to women. Married men live longer than unmarried men; however, marital status is not significant to the life expectancy of women. The key factors for longer life appear to be commitment and attachment to a relationship with individuals or groups that fosters a feeling of cohesiveness and fulfills the individual's needs for belonging. Forming and nurturing support systems are part of the female role. This process begins early in life and continues as the family is established.

Sociocultural resources are related to the various roles and expectations of the world in which one lives. Institutions, customs, laws, and government exist to protect people from stresses. United States citizens, who are protected by the Bill of Rights and who live in an industrial nation with a high standard of living and numerous government assistance programs, are less apt to have the stresses of people who live in less-developed countries besieged by extreme poverty, civil war, tyranny, or famine.

The extent to which these many types of resources are available for use in resisting the effects of stress is a major determinant of how one adapts to changes and one's position on the health-illness continuum.

## THE ROY ADAPTATION MODEL

The adaptation model of nursing is an approach that focuses on individuals who are having difficulty coping with changes in their lives. It uses a problem-solving method to assist and support people in achieving an adaptive state. This model of nursing was developed by Sister Callista Roy

a right to exist and to find meaning in one's life. Although the nurse and patient or client may not have the same values, adaptation nursing is based on an objective assessment of the patient's actual behavior, identifying with the patient those behaviors that are disrupting the patient's integrity, then working cooperatively to change those behaviors. In this method, each recipient of nursing services is treated with dignity and allowed to make decisions. The adaptation approach avoids the pitfalls associated with relating one behavior or problem with one cause that can be reversed by one cure; rather, it ensures that the nurse view man as a biopsychosocial being whose behavior is shaped by many stimuli.

**Goal of Nursing.** The nursing goal is to promote adaptation or a positive coping response to the stimuli and stresses encountered by the patient. It specifies what behavior is to be changed and the direction of the change. Because it is the patient's behavior that is to be altered, the patient must be actively involved in the activities.

**Nursing Interventions.** The interventions and nursing activities are based on a problem-solving approach. In the nursing process, an expanding range of psychomotor procedures and skills are performed by the nurse in diverse settings, including hospitals, offices, clinics, schools, and industrial plants. Both the patient and the nurse are involved to achieve the goal of adaptation—the patient as the doer of the activity, the nurse as the provider of input or assistance. The energy for the activity is supplied by both the nurse and the patient.

## CONTINUED DEVELOPMENT OF THE ROY MODEL

Further development and refinement of the adaptation model of nursing continue as nurses gain more experience in working with and applying the concepts of it to their clinical practice. A basic challenge for nurses using the adaptation approach is to gain further understanding of the behavior of people coping with changes in their lives. People respond differently to the same or similar changes, as is evidenced by the wide range of behavior of people who are coping with illness. Adaptation nurses not only deal with these behaviors, but also analyze the factors involved to determine the stimuli causing or influencing the behavior. New insights and thoughts on the processes involved provide a more definitive view of adaptation as well as guidelines for their application in nursing care.

Randall (1982) and colleagues recently contributed to the Roy adaptation model by introducing several new terms to describe the interaction that takes place between the adapting person and the environment and between the adapting person and the adaptation nurse. Briefly, Randall describes adaptation as the way people respond to their environment. The point at which the person and the environment come together is called the triggering event and results in a transaction consisting of five phases. Randall emphasizes the functions of the regulator and the cognator in the transaction. The regulator is the mechanism governing the physiological adaptation to the environmental impact. The cognator is the intellectual and emotional component that alerts the adapting person to the triggering event and interprets it to give meaning to the experience. Examples show how adaptation nurses make judgments based on the assessed data and their own knowledge to arrive at nursing diagnoses. These diagnoses are classified into three categories that reflect the disruption in the level of adequacy of the response. These concepts enrich the understanding of the Roy model.

The approach presented in this book represents the efforts of one nursing faculty to simplify the complex concepts that are the basis of the adaptation theory. The focus is on how individuals meet their basic needs and cope with changes in the dynamic world in which they live. The content is the synthesis of the ideas of nursing faculty members' various areas of expertise, the responses generated by the questions posed by students as they sought to master the concepts and the practical experiences gained from the application of this knowledge to the nursing process. Subsequent chapters are devoted to presenting the theoretical basis of the adaptation model, the use of the adaptation nursing process with emphasis on assessment, information about standards of behavior or acceptable ranges of behavior that serve as a basis for comparison of the observed behavior, and selected interventions to use when manipulating the stimuli to promote adaptation.

## COMPARISON OF MEDICAL AND NURSING MODELS

Before the emergence of nursing models, the practice of nursing relied heavily on the medical model for direction and values, because both professions deal with people who have health problems. Because nursing attempts to define the value and the uniqueness of nursing with models, it may be advantageous to compare and contrast component parts of the nursing models and the medical model.

**Table 1–1.**  COMPARISON OF THE COMPONENTS OF THE MEDICAL MODEL AND THE ROY ADAPTATION NURSING MODEL

| Components | Medical Model | Roy Adaptation Nursing Model |
|---|---|---|
| Recipient | Sick person, any age | Person, any age, anywhere on the health-illness continuum with coping problem. |
| Approach | Problem-solving method | Problem-solving method |
| Focus of services | Cellular changes and symptoms caused by disease | Coping problems influenced by location on the health-illness continuum |
| Goal | Cure | Promote adaptation in all modes |
| Intervention | | |
|   Setting | Office, clinic, hospital, or other health care agency | Anywhere: home, community, or health care agency |
|   Procedure; process | Medical process to diagnose disease and prescribe treatment | Nursing process to assess behaviors, identify problems, and intervene by manipulating stimuli |
|   Agent for change | Physician | Patient or client as an adaptive being |
|   Source of energy | Physician acts upon patient, with medications and therapy given by others | Patient's coping mechanisms supported by problem-solving nurse |

According to the Roy adaptation model of nursing, recipients of nursing care are people who have a problem coping with their internal or external environment. The medical model provides services primarily for people who are sick. The focus is on changes occurring at the cellular level that can be diagnosed and treated. Preventing disease is a highly desirable social goal; however, most medical practitioners devote little of their time to matters of prevention. The majority of their time and effort is spent treating the sick to cure the illness. In both models, the recipient is the individual; however, the goals of each model differ. In medical practice, the goals is to cure the disease and to restore health. In adaptation nursing, the goal is to promote adaptation.

In general, there are significant differences between the medical model and the adaptation nursing model concerning the way they provide for the care of the recipient. The practice of medicine is based on cellular changes that affect the structure, function, or regulation of various parts or systems of the body. Nursing practice, on the other hand, is concerned with the behavioral responses of the patient or client, who is located at some point on the health-illness continuum. The physician's chief concern is the disease, whereas the nurse sees the person holistically. While medical practice is involved in treating and curing the illness, nursing practice is able to emphasize interventions for preventing further disease and illness.

The behavioral sciences have made progress in identifying some of the more common behavioral patterns and processes that people use in interpersonal relationships. Nurses derive much satisfaction from the study of people and of life as they learn more about why people behave as they do and how people are alike and how they differ from others. Nursing, then, covers a complex and richly varied fabric of life as it deals with the individual as he copes with changes in his body or his environment.

## REFERENCES

Antonovsky, Aaron: Health, Stress, and Coping. San Francisco, Jossey-Bass Inc., Publishers, 1979.

Camooso, Carol, et al.: Students' adaptation according to Roy . . . three masters students describe their adjustment to graduate school. Nurs Outlook, *29*:108–109, (February) 1981.

Cassel, J. C.: The contribution of the social environment to host resistance. Am J Epidemiol, *104*:107–123, 1976.

Coelho, George, Hamburg, David, and Adams, John: Coping and Adaptation. New York, Basic Books Inc., Publishers, 1974.

Farkas, Ludmilla: Adaptation problems with nursing home application for elderly persons: an application of Roy adaptation model. J Adv Nurs, *6*:363–368, (September) 1981.

Harmer, B., and Henderson, V.: Textbook of the Principles and Practice of Nursing. New York, Macmillan Inc., 1955.

Henderson, Virginia: The Nature of Nursing. New York, Macmillan Inc., 1966.

Janelli, Linda M.: Utilizing Roy's adaptation model from a gerontological perspective. J Gerontol Nurs, *6*:140–142, (March) 1980.

Kaplan, B. H., Cassel, J. C., and Gore, S.: Social support and health. Journal of Medical Care, 25 (Supplement), pp. 47–58, 1977.

Lazarus, R. S., and Cohen, J. B.: Environmental Stress. *in* Altman, L. and Wohlwill, J. F. (Eds.): Human Behavior and Environment, Vol. 2. New York, Plenum Publishing Corp., 1977.

Maslow, Abraham: Motivation and Personality, 2nd ed. New York, Harper & Row Publishers, Inc., 1970, pp. 34–40.

Randell, Brooke, Tedrow, Mary Pouch, and Van Landingham, Joyce: Adaptation Nursing: The Roy Conceptual Model Applied. St. Louis, The C. V. Mosby Co., 1982.

Riehl, Joan, and Roy, Sister Callista: Conceptual Models for Nursing Practice, 2nd ed. New York, Appleton-Century-Crofts, 1980.

Roy, C.: Adaptation: a conceptual framework for nursing. Nurs Outlook, *18*(3):42–45, (March) 1970.

Roy, C.: Adaptation: a basis for nursing practice. Nurs Outlook, *19*(4):254–257, (April) 1971.

Roy, C.: Adaptation: implications for curriculum change. Nurs Outlook, *21*(3):163–168, (March) 1973.

Roy, Sister Callista: Introduction to Nursing: An Adaptation Model. Englewood Cliffs, NJ, Prentice-Hall Inc., 1976.

Selye, Hans: The Stress of Life. New York, McGraw-Hill Inc., 1956.

World Health Organization: Constitution of the world health organization. Chronicle of the World Health Organization, *1*:29–43, 1947.

# The Nursing Process: Assessment

**OBJECTIVES**   Information in this chapter will help you to

1. Describe the steps of the nursing process that are used with the Roy adaptation model of nursing.
2. Explain what a behavior is and differentiate it from an inference or an assumption.
3. Discuss the general behavioral patterns classified as moving-toward, moving-away, and moving-against.
4. Describe the first level assessment, the type of information gathered, and the sources used.
5. Discuss the method of organizing data and comparing it with criteria to determine whether behaviors are adaptive or maladaptive.
6. Explain the second level assessment.

## ADAPTATION NURSING AND THE NURSING PROCESS

In the discussion of the adaptation approach to nursing, it was stated that nursing is a valuable social service that is provided for anyone who has a problem coping with changes in the internal or external environment. Changes are defined as stimuli that cause the body to respond with actions referred to as behavior. Behaviors may be involuntary, such as the action of the heart that results in the pulse and the blood pressure, or voluntary, such as speaking, reading a book, or walking. When behaviors fall within the acceptable range, the individual is said to cope in an adaptive way. Problems in coping occur when behaviors fall outside the adaptive range and the internal need state that triggered the coping response is unsatisfied or not met. When one is unable to satisfy one's needs, the result is a lack of integrity in that area and movement toward the illness end of the health-illness continuum.

The goal of adaptation nursing is to promote adaptation in all the modes—physiological, self-concept, role-function, and interdependence. To achieve that goal, it is essential that the nurse identify the patient's need areas, the effectiveness of the patient's coping mechanisms, the patient's position on the health-illness continuum, and plan the nursing care needed to promote adaptation. The method that the nurse uses to achieve the goal is called the nursing process.

## WHAT IS THE NURSING PROCESS?

A crucial element in nursing is recognizing what is wrong with the patient and doing something about it. This is the problem-solving method and the basis for the nursing process.

Without consciously thinking about it, people use the problem-solving technique in their everyday lives. It is used to arrive at a course of action when considering such questions as "What shall I prepare for dinner tonight?", "Is it worth my time and energy to complete the nursing program?", and "What topic should I choose for my term paper?" Members of all professions use their specialized knowledge to solve problems related to their particular field.

- Mathematicians use mathematical equations to solve problems of speed, distance, and gravitational force encountered by a space probe that is sent millions of miles through the universe.
- Geophysics engineers solve innumerable problems involved in tapping oil reserves located thousands of feet beneath the surface of the ocean.
- Lawyers use the problem-solving approach to build a defense for clients to obtain a not guilty verdict.
- Physicians make a diagnosis of a patient's complaints of nausea, vomiting, and abdominal pain by using problem-solving techniques.

The problem-solving method leads to decisions that are more appropriate and produces results that are more successful and more predictable than those produced by any other method. It eliminates the trial-and-error approach to solving problems. The problem-solving method consists of identifying the problem, gathering sufficient information about all aspects of the problem, preparing several plans that could be used to solve the problem, selecting the plan that seems to have the best chance of succeeding, and implementing it. The final stage is evaluating the results—to what degree did the action reduce or solve the problem?

The nursing process has been built on this problem-solving method. It is a logical thought process, involving intellectual skills and knowledge gained from many fields, including anatomy, physiology, chemistry, nutrition, sociology, and psychology. The purpose of the nursing process is to identify the patient's problems and needs for nursing care, then to plan the care. The nursing process serves three functions.

1. *It is a guide to planning.* Planning enables the nurse to anticipate events that might occur with the patient, initiate appropriate actions, and have some control over the outcome, rather than being merely a responder who waits for events to occur.

2. *It is patient-centered.* The nurse's attention is focused on the individual patient and the assessment of the patient's needs, rather than being focused only on devising a routine plan of care for a disease entity such as "nursing care for the appendectomy patient."

3. *It is goal-directed.* When the patient has an adaptation problem, the nursing goals is to restore integrity, repair the breakdown, and help move the patient toward the health end of the health-illness continuum. The nursing process is not complete until there has been an evaluation of how well the nursing plan has solved the patient's problem(s).

## COMPONENTS OF THE NURSING PROCESS

One of the nurse's major tasks is to identify patients' problems and plan the nursing care to solve them. As previously described, patients' adaptation problems derive from unmet needs; these needs arise in the physiological, self-concept, role-function, and interdependence modes. Patients who are ill are unable to do certain things for themselves because of their position on the health-illness continuum, thus, they are in need of nursing care. Frequently, patients are able to tell the nurse what their problems are. For example, "Nurse, I haven't had a bowel movement for four days." However, not all problems are recognized as easily as this problem. The patient may perceive the problem incorrectly; may not know what the problem is, particularly in the case of young children; or may be reluctant to say what the problem is because of fear, anxiety, or embarrassment. The nursing process enables the nurse to assess the patient's condition, identify problems, and plan appropriate care.

A nursing model serves an important function in the nursing process because it helps identify what the nurse will look for and what the nurse will do about the health problems that are found. The way one looks at any situation or object is a major factor in what one will see. For example, although all students in a typical classroom share the same experience, their observations and perceptions may vary greatly, depending upon their points of view. The teacher sees faces; students in the back of the room see heads of hair; students in the front of the room see only the teacher and a few persons on either side of them. Nursing also depends on point of view: The information that is assessed and the nursing care that follows the assessment are the outcome of the approach taken by the nurse. When nurses follow the medical model, the focus is on the patient's pathology and the medications and

**Figure 2–1.** In any situation, what is seen depends on point of view. A model of nursing provides a way of looking at nursing activities and at the recipient of nursing services in a specific way. The use of an adaptation model of nursing provides a rich and varied source of information, such as is seen from the front of a class of interested students.

treatments used to cure the disease. The adaptation model guides the nurse in planning nursing care for patients or clients who are experiencing difficulties in coping with changes in their lives. This approach to nursing results in care that is qualitatively different from care using other methods.

The adaptation approach expands the nursing process by specifying additional steps that complete the logical thought process (Table 2–1). There are six components of the nursing process that are used with the adaptation model. First is the assessment phase, which is divided into two parts: (1) first level assessment, gathering information from various sources about the patient's behavior, and (2) second level assessment, identifying the causes of maladaptive behaviors. The next phase is identifying the patient's problem(s), followed by planning and formulating goals. Next, the problems are arranged according to priorities, and interventions are selected and implemented. Finally, the results are evaluated. (Each of these components is examined in greater detail in this chapter and in following chapters.)

## FIRST LEVEL ASSESSMENT

Before problem-solving can begin, the nurse must know something about the patient and the patient's condition. Assessment is the information-gathering phase of the nursing process. Because the nurse is concerned with the patient's problem(s) in coping with or adapting to changes, the nurse must determine the extent to which the patient is able to meet needs and to adapt. The first level assessment consists of obtaining information about the patient's behavior.

## WHAT IS A BEHAVIOR?

In the adaptation model of nursing, one is seen in constant interaction with changes in one's environment. Each change in one's internal or external environment is a stimulus that is capable of creating a need state and evoking a response. The response is called a behavior; it is either a voluntary or an involuntary action of the body that can be observed and measured in some form, or has been reported by the patient or client. Many internal adjustments to change are under the control of the autonomic nervous system and result in behaviors such as the level of glucose in the blood, blood pressure, heart rate, white blood count, and other physiological responses that can be measured.

All other behaviors are learned responses to stimuli to reduce the need state. This results in purposeful behavior, which is illustrated in Figure 2–2. As the infant grows and develops, smiling at pleasing objects and sensations, learning to eat with a spoon, sitting up, and walking are added to the repertoire of purposeful behavior. The infant also learns the shape and feel of things and the pattern of activities during the day. This learning becomes more complex and abstract as new skills and behaviors are learned.

All behavior has some meaning to the person involved. Even a verbal statement made by a patient, such as "I think I'm going crazy," is a behavior because the patient actually said it, regardless of whether or not the patient is crazy. The statement has a meaning for the patient, and the patient chose to use the statement as a coping mechanism in response to a stimulus.

The process used to establish purposeful behavior begins with a stimulus. This stimulus creates a need state that the patient recognizes as requiring some type of action. The patient mentally reviews the types of actions that could be taken and, on the basis of the available resources and the foreseeable consequences, selects an action and responds to it. If the response is successful, the need is met and the goal has been achieved. Inadequate coping results when the response does not fulfill the need state, which continues to exist and causes tension in the patient.

When a nurse assesses a patient's behaviors, the description should include a verb that states what the body is doing or the action that is observed.

---

**Table 2–1. THE NURSING PROCESS
FOR ADAPTATION**

---

1. **First Level Assessment**
   Describe patient's behaviors in each need area
   Compare behaviors with criteria or norms
   Locate on health-illness continuum

2. **Second Level Assessment**
   Identify factors influencing behavior
   Classify stimuli as focal and contextual (influencing factors)
   Validate with patient

3. **Statement of the Patient's Problem**
   Need areas not met, or unsatisfied
   Probable stimulus or cause of problem

4. **Setting Goals**
   Realistic and reachable
   Acceptable to patient
   State type and amount of change

5. **Intervention**
   Manipulate stimuli
   "Doing" phase

6. **Evaluation**
   Determine direction and degree of change
   Reassess and revise plan as needed

---

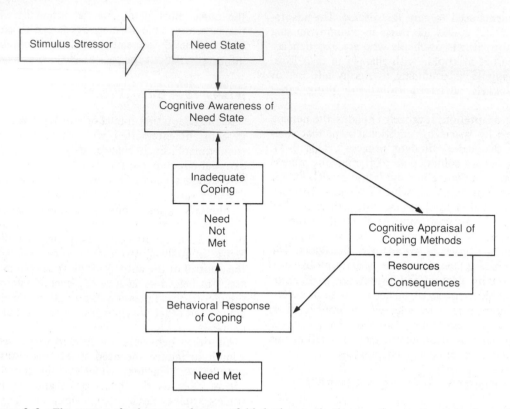

**Figure 2–2.**  The pattern of voluntary and purposeful behavior. A stimulus provokes an awareness of a need. The individual mentally reviews available coping mechanisms and initiates a response that satisfies the need. If ineffective, the stimulus continues to provoke an awareness of the need state.

The behavior should be described in specific terms because it pertains to the actions of a specific individual. By clearly describing the patient's actual behaviors, the nurse avoids making inferences and assumptions, which may or may not be true. Inferences are conclusions that are not derived from the observed behavior through the process of logic, although they are related, in some degree, to the behavior. Assumptions are the act of taking something for granted or supposing that it is factual without having supportive evidence. For example, when the diet tray was removed from John's bedside, the nurse noted that little or no food had been eaten. An inference is made if the nurse concludes that John did not eat because he had a poor appetite. An assumption is made by taking for granted that patients with poor appetites do not eat the foods on their trays. However, assessing his behavior, the nurse observes that John did not eat sufficient foods to meet his nutritional needs and that additional information is needed. There may be many different reasons why the food was not eaten: John may be weak and unable to feed himself, he may have been nauseated, the food may have been cold or unappetizing, or the diet may have consisted of culturally unfamiliar or disliked foods.

In summary, a behavior has meaning, is objective, factual, or specific and is a response of the body. Inferences and assumptions are general and subjective and impose a conclusion that may or may not be true. They often lack a specific meaning and therefore are open to many interpretations. See examples on page 21.

## GENERAL BEHAVIORAL PATTERNS

Although people respond in different ways to the same stimulus, the responses can be classified into four general behavioral patterns: (1) behaviors that move toward the stimuli, (2) behaviors that move away from the stimuli, (3) behaviors

Examples of the differences between behaviors and inferences are

| Behaviors | Inferences |
|---|---|
| — is 5 ft. 3 in. in height | — is tall |
| — drank 130 ml of juice | — taking fluids well |
| — grimaced when changing position | — having severe pain |
| — blood glucose of 125 mg/dl | — is diabetic |
| — has reddened area 1 in. in diameter over sacrum | — has decubitus ulcer |
| — states is feeling better | — no complaints |
| — temperature of 100°F. | — has fever |

that move against the stimuli (see Hagerman [1968]), and (4) no action. These patterns are normal and are used by everyone at various times. Although only one pattern is used at a time, one pattern may predominate and be selected most frequently to cope with stressors.

The moving-toward pattern of behavior is associated with individuals expressing dependency needs for affection, attention, and assistance. These individuals initiate interactions with others, seek to form relationships, and encourage incoming stimuli by making numerous demands on others and requests for care. Patients exhibiting moving-toward behaviors may want the nurse to stay with them and talk with them and may go to great lengths to be gracious, interesting, and pleasant in order to win the nurse's attention and favor. Such patients frequently leave decision-making to others—a spouse, the doctor, or the nurse—and show other forms of dependency.

Moving-away behaviors are used by individuals to avoid the stimuli and the resulting need states. They withdraw from interactions with others and tend to isolate themselves. They avoid responding to changes in their environment by ignoring or by denying stimuli. When troubled or ill, such individuals seldom initiate conversation spontaneously; they tend to keep communication to a minimum. These patients often reply to questions with short phrases, such as "I don't know" or "I don't care." Other behaviors they use to discourage people from interacting with them include keeping their eyes closed and sleeping. A less obvious moving-away behavior is exhibited by the patient who, in order to avoid the stress of illness, continues to conduct business from the hospital room. This behavior illustrates moving-away from one stressor and toward another.

Moving-against behaviors are normally used by individuals to overcome problems and to exercise control over their lives. This behavior pattern is important for meeting self-concept needs and those needs related to independence. Most productive work is accomplished through this

aggressive pattern of behavior, which seeks to subdue or control the stresses and disorganization in one's environment. Stressors and stimuli are met head-on, and the goal is to reduce their power and effect. In this behavior pattern, extremes of behavior are anger, hostility, distrust, fighting, and other aggressive forms. Patients who use moving-against behavior are critical of their care, make derogatory remarks about the hospital or other nurses, and show distrust and hostility (either overtly or covertly) toward those providing their care. Such behavior has often led frustrated nurses to label the patient as "difficult" or "a complainer," rather than trying to understand that this patient has unmet needs that are interfering with proper care.

Some individuals may make no response to a stressor. This nonaction can be assessed by the nurse as a behavior pattern. Nonaction can occur for many reasons: (1) The individual may have a neurological problem that affects sensory perception so the stimulus is not received or not perceived in the brain. (2) The strength of the stimulus may cause such a high level of anxiety that the individual is overwhelmed by panic and is unable to make any coping response. (3) The individual may deny the stressor as a defense mechanism.

## INFORMATION TO BE ASSESSED

The first level of assessment provides the nurse with information about the patient's current level of adaptation. Illness creates a major change in one's life by placing one closer to the illness end of the health-illness continuum. A change in the need state of one mode, such as illness in the physiological mode, is usually associated with changes in other need areas.

Several principles are used as guidelines for the first level assessment of behaviors.

1. The purpose of the initial assessment is to

determine the individual's location on the health-illness continuum. The patient's behaviors are assessed to ascertain the need state(s) in which the patient is having difficulty coping or in maintaining integrity.

2. The assessment of behaviors is concerned with the here and now. First level assessment is used to determine present status—the needs that exist at this time—and is not concerned with what happened yesterday or last week. (The past history of the patient is associated with the second level assessment of stimuli, which may influence the behaviors that exist now.)

3. The assessment information should be gathered in a systematic way to ensure that all areas are assessed. Complete information is needed for successful problem-solving because the whole individual has the problem and is affected by it; it is not just the digestive system experiencing nausea.

4. Assessment is a dynamic and ongoing process of collecting additional data and updating information that has already been gathered. Individuals are in constant interaction with their environment; thus their behaviors may change from moment to moment as they cope with changes in their environment. Ongoing assessment is necessary for the nurse to evaluate the effectiveness of the nursing care and any changes in the patient's ability to cope.

5. The nurse has a professional purpose for gathering information about the patient—to formulate an individualized care plan that focuses on the patient's problems in coping with changes.

In the adaptation model of nursing, more information is gathered about the patient than when one focuses primarily on a disease process and its treatment. In addition to gathering information about the illness or disease, the adaptation nurse examines how the patient is meeting needs in all four modes: self-concept, role function, and interdependence, as well as physiological. The assessment provides information about what the patient is able to do and the areas that are adaptive, as well as providing information about behaviors that do not promote integrity. For example, all nurses provide care of the diabetic patient by giving insulin as prescribed, testing the urine for glucose, monitoring the diet, recognizing the signs of insulin shock or diabetic coma, and teaching the patient about the disease. However, with the adaptation approach, the nurse assesses the patient's needs in each mode and is aware of the coping problems that frequently occur as one struggles with one's feelings about the disease and the effects it has on one's life. Teen-agers with diabetes may intellectually understand the

reasons for restrictions in their diet but refuse to observe these restrictions when they are with their peers. Assessment of the self-concept and interdependence needs of these teen-agers helps the nurse identify the problem of not staying on their diets as a problem related to their feelings about their friends considering them to be different.

The greatest value of the adaptation model is that it provides the nurse with a comprehensive framework for gathering information and it delineates what to assess. The nurse should develop and use a systematic approach to gathering the data so that every need area is assessed. Subsequent chapters in this book are devoted to exploring in greater detail the need areas associated with the modes. In each mode of functioning, there is a need for integrity that requires an adaptive response adequate to satisfy the need and to maintain wholeness. These responses are behaviors that the nurse observes or measures or are verbally reported by the patient. Areas that the nurse assesses in each mode include

> Physiological mode — *integrity related to*
> Oxygenation and circulation
> Fluid and electrolytes
> Nutrition
> Elimination
> Rest and activity
> Regulation — sensory and temperature
> Self-concept mode — *integrity related to*
> Physical self
> Somatic sensations
> Body image
> Personal self
> Self-consistency
> Self-ideal
> Moral-ethical self
> Role-function mode — *integrity related to*
> Primary and secondary roles
> Growth and developmental tasks
> Interdependence mode — *integrity related to*
> Dependent behaviors
> Help-seeking
> Attention-seeking
> Affection-seeking
> Independent behaviors
> Obstacle-mastery
> Initiative-taking

## SOURCES OF INFORMATION

Aiken and associates (1981) reported that the majority of nurses work in hospitals or in long-term care facilities. Therefore, it is important to review the sources that these nurses can use to gather information about patients and their need for nursing care. Nurses working in other settings or as nursing practitioners may use some sources more than others. In clinical practice, nurses obtain information from the patient, the patient's charts and other medical records, the Kardex, communication with others, and books and other reference materials.

**Patient.** Much of the information that the nurse needs to complete the first level assessment is obtained by observing and interviewing the patient. The adaptation approach is concerned with the present and the patient's current behaviors. Most patients are willing, even eager, to tell the nurse about themselves, their needs, how they feel, and their problems.

Assessment of the patient, including interview and examination, helps to establish the nurse-patient relationship and to promote trust. The nurse's attention to the patient's physiological need areas, to the behavioral responses that are observed, to the patient's verbal report of how he or she is managing to carry out the developmental tasks that are appropriate to age and sex, and to the history of the illness all reinforce the patient's feeling that the nurse is someone who sees the patient as a person and is able to and wants to help. The *process* of the assessment is often effec-

tive in helping to reduce the patient's anxiety about what is happening and thus has a therapeutic result.

The patient's condition determines how extensive the initial assessment should be. For example, if a person is admitted to the emergency room with a penetrating chest wound, the immediate areas for assessment are those of oxygenation: the degree of difficulty in breathing, the amount of hemorrhage, and signs of shock. These areas are quickly assessed, and treatment is initiated without delay; assessment of functioning in other need areas should be done only after the patient's cardiopulmonary status is stable. The nurse does a complete assessment of all need areas for patients who are alert and who have no acute discomfort and for other patients, gathers as much information as possible about the need areas and functioning.

**Chart and Medical Records.** The patient's hospital chart, or medical record, contains information that is useful to the nurse's assessment of the patient. The hospital chart is a record or history of everything that involves the patient's care during hospitalization. This chart documents the medical problem that placed the patient on the illness end of the health-illness continuum,

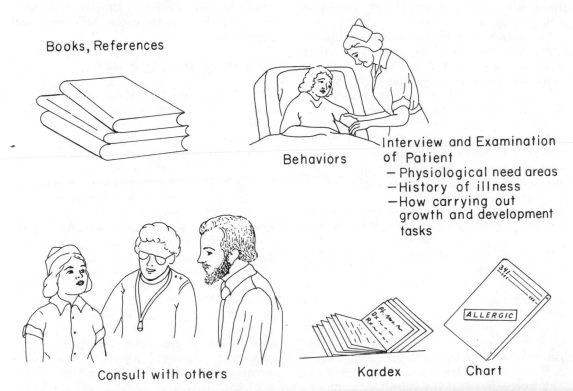

**Figure 2-3.** Sources of assessment data include the use of books and references, consulting the Kardex and the client's chart, interviewing and examining the client, and conferring with others, such as physicians, therapists, or family members.

the medical procedures and treatment that the patient received, and the nursing care that was given.

The standard hospital chart contains a number of routine forms that are used to document the patient's condition and care and other supplemental forms that may be needed for reporting special tests or procedures. Other health workers such as doctors, nursing assistants, medical receptionists, laboratory technicians, and so on, have gathered and recorded information about the patient that can be used by the nurse. The nurse refers to various forms of the chart to obtain the information needed in the assessment of the patient. This promotes more economical and efficient use of the nurse's time and helps to conserve the patient's energy by avoiding duplication.

**Kardex.** Most nursing units use an open-face file called a Kardex, containing a form for each patient that summarizes the doctor's current orders and the nursing care plan. The Kardex is kept up-to-date by the person who transcribes the doctor's orders, either the ward clerk (with supervision) or the licensed nurse. The typical Kardex card contains a list of the medication orders, the treatment orders, special tests or procedures that are scheduled to be done, and other therapies to be carried out. Nursing procedures such as enemas, intake and output, irrigations, and dressings are included in the treatment orders. Orders that have been discontinued are erased from the Kardex card. Whenever there is doubt about the accuracy of an order on the Kardex, the nurse must check with the original order in the chart and correct any discrepancy.

The nursing care plan should be complete for each patient and should be updated as changes occur in the patient's adaptation. Any problems, as well as specific goals and prescribed nursing interventions that will help the patient achieve these goals, are identified and recorded by the nurse. Nurses frequently use the information on the Kardex cards as a communication tool when giving reports at the change of shifts.

**Communication with Others.** Additional information about patients is often provided by those who know or who take care of them. The nurse gains this information through formal and informal communications, such as the change-of-shift report, consultations with the physician or other professionals, reports from the nursing assistants, or interviews with the patient's family or friends. Knowledge shared by the night nurse, such as the fact that the patient experienced a lot of pain during the night and didn't sleep well, may explain some of that patient's behavior the following day. Assessing the relationship between the patient and the patient's family or friends helps the nurse to identify the extent to which family and friends serve as a support system for the patient.

**Books and References.** Textbooks, manuals, and reference works are indirect sources where one can find information pertinent to patients and the changes that they are experiencing that alter the adaptive state and threaten body integrity. It is essential that nurses continue to expand their knowledge and understanding of human behavior and the technological advances being made in medicine so that they are aware of all aspects of changes in their patients. Nurses refer to books and references to learn the body's responses to the physiological changes associated with disease conditions, to learn specific details regarding certain types of cancer, or to learn the way people respond to various types of losses, such as a spouse's death or a job loss. With knowledge of the kinds of things people perceive as losses, the patterns of mourning, and the methods that can be used to assist them in resolving the loss, nurses are more likely to recognize these behaviors in their patients and to include interventions in the nursing care plan. The knowledge nurses acquire through education and experience becomes a memory bank from which they continually withdraw information to carry out the nursing process and to promote adaptation.

## METHODS OF ASSESSMENT

The nurse obtains information through observation and communication and by special equipment.

Observation refers to gaining information through the senses of vision, hearing, smell, touch, and taste, which is less commonly used. Through visual observations, the nurse gains on-going data about such things as change in the color of the skin or the nail beds, the physical appearance and size of the patient, the way the patient reacts to things in the environment, and the patient's relationships with others.

Through hearing or listening, the nurse notes the sounds of blood rushing through a vessel (for measuring blood pressure), the noisy rattles of an obstructed airway, the sound of peristaltic activity of the bowel, and the apical beat of the heart. Much of the nurses' assessments of the patients' psychological needs are obtained by listening to patients tell of their feelings, expectations, and values.

Sense of smell allows the nurse to detect unusual odors from a wound or drainage, from the breath, from foods, and from fumes that indicate pollution of the air. Nurses use the sense of touch to detect the temperature and characteristics of the skin, and the size and shape of body parts or tumors. Palpation is used to locate pulses in veins and to determine discomfort or pain in body tissue.

The most effective method of obtaining information through the communication process is the patient interview. An interview is a conversation with another person, usually face to face, that has a goal. In the interview, the nurse seeks information from others, usually the patient or someone representing the patient, such as the parent of a child or the spouse of a critically ill adult. The nurse should inform the patient of the purpose of interview—to learn more about the patient's needs so that the plan of nursing care will reflect these needs. Most patients are willing, even eager, to provide information that will, in turn, help them during their illness. As with all information concerning the patient and the patient's condition, the material obtained from the interview is confidential and is used only for professional purposes.

Effective interviewing skills are the result of experience and of observing principles of the communication process. One principle is for the nurse to identify the objective or goal of the interview. The nurse must keep in mind the purpose of the interview and the type of information that is needed to carry out the nursing process.

A second principle of interviewing is to make extensive use of open-ended questions and comments, as a way of encouraging continuation of conversation and additional input by the patient. Open-ended questions are questions that do not indicate an expected or a desired answer but that allow the patient to answer in any way. Probing questions or closed questions are used to follow up or clarify the meaning of the patient's statement. They can often be answered by "Yes" or "No" or by a simple statement of fact. Some open-ended questions and comments and some probing or closed questions are

### Open-ended

Good morning. How are you today?
Tell me about your family.
What kind of problems were you
    having when you became sick?
You seem to be tense and worried.

### Probing or closed

Are you having any pain?
Do you have any children?
Did you have a heart attack?
Are you anxious?

A third principle in effective interviewing is to validate the meaning of the responses. By actively listening, the nurse concentrates on the person who is responding and tries to understand the meaning of what has been said. Many patients provide clues to what they are thinking by what they say or by the symbolic use of language. For example, a patient who states "Well, I guess I'll be leaving soon" may not be referring to discharge from the hospital but to feelings and fear of dying. The nurse needs to validate what the patient means by the statement. In like manner, the nurse should validate the meaning of messages that seem to conflict with each other—for example, when the patient states that everything is fine but the nurse notices that the posture is tense and rigid and that the hands are clenched. There is an apparent discrepancy between the behavior observed by the nurse and what the patient reports, and this discrepancy should be explored to determine whether there is a problem.

Assessment data are also obtained through the use of various types of instruments. The stethoscope and sphygmomanometer are used to determine blood pressure, the thermometer is used to measure temperature, and the ophthalmoscope is used to examine the eye. Other instruments that are used to assess data include scales, urinometers, monitoring systems with electrocardiogram leads and oscilloscopes, and instruments that perform various laboratory tests on body fluids and tissues. Many medical procedures that provide the physician and the nurse with information about the body's internal function use instruments. Three such procedures are cardiac catheterization, radiographic studies, and computed tomography.

## PROCESSING THE INFORMATION

The first level assessment focuses on observing, measuring, and identifying behaviors that indicate the degree to which patients are able to meet their needs to maintain their integrity in all modes. To use the information in the nursing process, it is necessary to process the information by organizing the data, comparing the behaviors with criteria for judgment, and identifying the maladaptive behaviors that must be changed to promote adaptation.

**Organizing the Data.** The adaptation model provides a mechanism for identifying the information to be gathered and for organizing the data that are obtained. Behaviors of the first level assessment are assigned to one of the four adaptive modes. Some behaviors may not be specific to one particular mode. When this happens, the nurse decides where the behavior seems to fit best and places it in that mode. It is helpful for the beginning practitioner to assess, organize, and record the assessment data according to the need areas for each mode as listed on page 22.

**Comparing Behaviors with Criteria.** Each behavior that the nurse assesses is compared with a norm that serves as a criterion for judgment. The nurse does not decide subjectively that the patient's behavior is maladaptive and needs to be changed. Rather, a logical thought process and a more scientific approach are used by the nurse to identify problem areas in adaptation.

Behaviors related to the physiological mode are compared with the standards, or norms, for body temperature, pulse rate, blood pressure values, sodium level in the blood, and height and weight for different age groups that were learned from the study of human anatomy, physiology, and chemistry. Social and cultural norms are used to evaluate behaviors in the other modes as either adaptive or maladaptive by not contributing to the patient's integrity. The range of acceptable behaviors in the other modes is broader and often more variable than the range of acceptable behaviors in the physiological mode. There are norms for parents raising children, but a wide range of behaviors exists within what is considered acceptable by society. For example, some mothers breast-feed their babies; others feed their babies with bottles of formula. Some infants are kept on a strict feeding schedule; others are fed on demand. All these behaviors fall within the norms. Other norms for behaviors are those that are socially appropriate for the individual's age and sex. Crying and dependent behaviors observed in a 4-year-old child might fall within the acceptable norm, but the same behaviors in a 10-year-old child might be outside the norm and thus maladaptive.

Regardless of the social or cultural norms that influence the individual's behavior, the nurse's judgment should be based on whether or not the behavior is adaptive. For example, a young adult male may be a member of a neighborhood gang in which acceptable behavior includes frequent drunken brawls and daily smoking of marijuana. Although these behaviors are within the norms for this social group, they do not promote integrity in any of the modes and thus would be considered maladaptive.

**Identifying Maladaptive Behaviors.** Behaviors from the first level assessment that fall outside the norms or standards used as criteria for judgment are regarded as maladaptive behaviors. Many maladaptive behaviors may occur in a cluster or may be related to a specific need area. For these

behaviors, the nurse progresses to the second level of assessment.

## SECOND LEVEL ASSESSMENT

A second assessment is done to identify the causes of the behaviors. Although the second level assessment could be done for every observed behavior, it is usually done for maladaptive behaviors that indicate problems in coping with changes in life and in carrying out the activities of daily living.

### TYPES OF STIMULI

As previously stated, the adaptation model defines three types of stimuli that affect behavior: focal, contextual, and residual. An assessment of the factors that influence the behavior of an individual includes consideration of all three types of stimuli.

**Focal Stimulus.** The focal stimulus is the primary or causative stressor that initiated the need to respond, or change, in order to maintain integrity. As the degree of change from the comfortable adapted state of the individual becomes greater, so does the need to respond.

The focal stimulus for many of the patient's problems in coping with change stems from the diagnosed medical illness. The disease creates changes in the body's internal integrity and affects the need states not only in the physiological mode but also in all the other modes. To illustrate how the disease and the position on the continuum affect the need states, consider a male college student who develops acute bronchitis. Physiologically, the student has coughing spasms, tightness of the chest, temperature elevation, lack of appetite, decreased energy, and fatigue on exertion. In the self-concept mode, the student sees himself as ill and, because he's usually punctual and dependable also feels badly because he now will not be able to complete an assignment on time. In the role-function mode, he is unable to carry out the student role or to work at a part-time job; instead, he takes on the sick role and reports to the student health offices. In the interdependence mode, he seeks out medical help for his illness, relies on others to take notes in class for him, and asks his family for financial help to replace the lost wages.

When maladaptive behaviors occur in modes other than the physiological mode, the focal stimulus is often related to expectations that one has of or for oneself or to the expectations of others. When these expectations are not met, problems in coping occur. Some examples of ways in which expectations are a stimulus for maladaptive behavior are

- A female patient expected surgery to cure her low back pain, but weeks afterward, she continues to have pain and does not trust her doctor or the nursing staff to help her get better.
- The patient expects the call light to be answered immediately and becomes upset by the delay.
- A father expects his son to excel in basketball, as he did. The son tries but does not make the team and feels guilty for disappointing his dad.

**Contextual Stimuli.** Although the focal stimulus is the major cause of the change, many other stimuli modify the way the individual responds or influence the individual's behavior. Contextual stimuli may arise from internal sources or from external factors in the environment. When determining the contextual stimuli, the nurse considers all factors that may have contributed to the response that was assessed. The patient's age and sex are stimuli that influence how the patient responds to the focal stimulus. When the focal stimulus is the illness, the patient's response depends on contextual stimuli such as surgery, medical tests or procedures, drugs, and an order for bed rest. Drugs are important contextual stimuli that alter behaviors, as can be seen when the anxious patient is given tranquilizers and becomes calm and more relaxed.

**Residual Stimuli.** In addition to focal and contextual stimuli on behavior, a patient's responses are influenced by past experiences, values, beliefs, and attitudes (residual stimuli). The effects of these internal characteristics are difficult to detect and weigh. Therefore, nurses make assumptions or have "hunches" about these possible causes of patients' observed behavior.

Through exploration by nurses of patients' values, beliefs, and cultural patterns, residual stimuli become stimuli seen in context (contextual stimuli). In this way, nurses "hunches" and assumptions become validated.

## SOURCES OF INFORMATION

When obtaining information about stimuli, the nurse uses many of the same sources that were used when assessing the patient's behaviors. These sources include the patient, the hospital chart and medical records, the Kardex, consultation with others, and other references. However, the focus of the first level assessment is on behaviors "here and now"; the second level assessment of stimuli

uses information from the past as well as from the present. Factors that influence behavior can be found in past experiences, in the physical environment, and in the expectations of the self and of others.

**Past Experiences.** Feelings, events, and experiences from the past influence the way a person responds to stimuli. They are termed residual stimuli until they are explored and validated by the nurse. Assessing the patient's past history in the areas of previous health problems, such as illnesses, types of surgery (if any), and hospitalizations; unique experiences related to occupation and travel; and interests or hobbies is usually a very productive method of supplying information about other factors or stimuli that may have had an influence on current behavior. Information about the patient's daily activities provides insight into how the illness interferes with the patient's life and how the patient feels about this interference.

**Physical Environment.** Assessment of stimuli includes observations of the patient's environment or physical setting. The nurse looks for the adequacy of sensory stimulation for the patient, objects to aid in orientation, and resources for coping. The environment includes having a source of money, a job, insurance coverage, and family or friends. The environment also includes such things as television in the room, noise in the corridors, or a roommate who snores.

**Expectations of Self and Others.** Throughout their lives, people are guided by the rules of society or how they "ought to" and "should" behave. Every societal role includes expectations of how one should act and what one can expect in return. These expectations are stimuli for behavior. For example, mothers are expected to love their children and to provide for them; conversely, the children expect to be taken care of and to be loved. There are many expectations of nurses that guide their behavior. They are expected to know what to do, to be kind, to be accurate, and to not make mistakes or forget to do things. Such expectations represent the inner motivation or drive of a person to act as one does to meet one's needs.

## PROCESSING THE INFORMATION

When the second level assessment has been completed, the nurse has identified the stimuli associated with the maladaptive behaviors and proceeds to analyze them. When several behaviors have the same or similar stimuli, they are examined to see whether they are related or whether they represent a larger, more inclusive problem area.

Grouping related behaviors and stimuli into clusters is a preparatory step to identifying the patient's problems, the next step of the nursing process.

## SUMMARY

The first phase of the nursing process is assessment or the gathering of information. The adaptation model of nursing delineates the type of information to be obtained. The nurse completes a first level assessment, which focuses on the patient's current behaviors, and compares these observed behaviors with known standards or norms that are used for judging behaviors outside the range as maladaptive. The nurse then proceeds to a second level assessment to identify the stimuli causing the maladaptive behaviors. Now, the nurse is ready to proceed to the next step of the nursing process and to identify the problems that the patient has in adapting to changes.

(References for this chapter appear at the end of Chapter Three.)

# The Nursing Process: Identify the Problem, Plan Implement Care

**OBJECTIVES** Information in this chapter will help you to

1. Discuss two approaches to classifying the patients' problems:
   (1) integrated approach and (2) segregated approach.
2. Identify patients' problems from the assessed behaviors and the stimuli causing those problems.
3. Establish priorities, according to criteria, for identified problems.
4. Devise short-term and long-term goals in cooperation with the patient.
5. Plan interventions that manipulate the stimuli or factors that influence the problems.
6. Evaluate the effectiveness of the nursing interventions used and modify or reassess them, if necessary.

## THE PROBLEM-SOLVING PHASE OF THE NURSING PROCESS

The nursing process as a method of problem-solving represents a scientific avenue to nursing care—an avenue founded on a logical and relevant thought process. When people are ill, they are unable to do various things for themselves. They have difficulty coping with changes brought on by their illness. By assessing all the patient's need areas, the nurse focuses on both the adaptive behaviors that are to be encouraged and promoted and the maladaptive behaviors that must be changed to achieve adaptation. To promote adaptation, the nurse must identify the patient's coping problems. Unless these problems are identified accurately and explained clearly, resolving the problems will be difficult, and the patient will continue to expend energy on less effective behaviors. This energy could be channelled more productively toward the recovery of an adapted state, with improved physical health and greater ease in coping with environmental changes.

## PHILOSOPHICAL VIEWS OF PATIENT PROBLEMS

The greatest value of the adaptation model of nursing is that it provides an approach for nursing care and a guide for the type of information to be assessed. The model is flexible and can be used in more than one way to process information and arrive at a definition of patient and client coping problems that require nursing interventions. There are two major philosophical views of adaptive problems: (1) an integrated approach, which includes all behaviors and the effective level of coping, and (2) the segregated approach, which separates the medical disease and treatment as dependent functions of the nurse from behaviors that indicate problems the client has in coping with certain needs. Regardless of one's philosophical views, the comprehensive assessment of adaptation provides the nurse with the same information about the effectiveness of the client's coping behaviors. All coping problems should be included in the nursing care plan.

**Integrated Approach.** The integrated approach is based on the theoretical concept that ineffective behaviors indicate a disruption in clients' abilities to cope with changes in their internal or external environments. The focus of this approach is the specific behavior and the changing of this behavior to one that falls within the adapted range. Any behavior outside the normal range indicates a problem for the client and should be considered in the nurse's plan of care. For example, a patient has a reported hemoglobin of 6.5 gm. This is a behavior outside the normal range; the focal stimulus is assessed to be cancer of the colon; and the contextual stimuli are chemotherapy and a soft diet. The patient's coping problem is then stated in terms of a reduction of oxygen being delivered to body tissues. In the same way, a urinary output of 450 ml in a 24-hour period, a reddish-blue area of broken skin over the sacrum, and refusal to eat are ineffective behaviors that indicate problems a patient or a client has in

maintaining integrity and that concern the nurse who is planning the nursing care.

Characteristics of the integrated approach for solving problems of coping and maintaining adaptation are

1. It focuses on identifying all the ineffective behaviors that are assessed.
2. It is a cohesive and unified method of looking at behaviors that indicate problems in the internal need states.
3. It avoids the dichotomy between medical treatment and nursing care.
4. It advances the theory of a nursing science as an independently functioning profession.

**Segregated Approach.** The segregated approach is another philosophical view of client problems. It focuses on the needs that the client is unable to fulfill without help from others because of illness. The medical problem, with its characteristic signs and symptoms, is separated from other behaviors that indicate problems the client has in coping with some effects of the illness or its treatment or other changes that have occurred. The rationale for segregating the behaviors associated with the disease from other behaviors is that the disease is caused by changes affecting the internal structure or function on the cellular level, and this constitutes the area of medical practice. Problems of cellular function are diagnosed

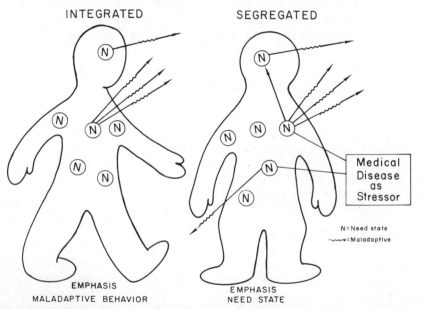

**Figure 3–1.** The integrated approach to identifying nursing problems focuses on all the ineffective behaviors outside the adaptive range. Each behavior or cluster of behaviors is handled as a problem, using the nursing process and nursing interventions.

In the segregated approach, behaviors arising from the medical problem and under treatment by the physician are separated from those that occur in other need areas as a result of the illness. The adaptation nurse carries out both nursing actions dictated by the medical treatment and the nursing process to identify problems in meeting needs or coping with changes.

as medical diseases; medical interventions are instituted on orders written by physicians; and these orders form the boundaries within which many functions of nursing take place. As nurses carry out medical orders and coordinate various types of therapy, they must function within the limitations imposed by the medical regime. In addition, nurses deal with other problems in coping that arise in patients and clients because of illness.

In the segregated approach to processing assessment information, the medical problem is seen as a potent stimulus for other problems that arise during an illness. The treatment or the effects of the disease pose additional difficulties for patients and clients in carrying out their normal activities of daily living (ADL), or in coping with their feelings about changes that have occurred in their lives. Using the same example that was described in the integrated approach, the nurse separates behaviors associated with the disease, cancer of the colon, and chemotherapy treatment. The assessed behavior of hemoglobin of 6.5 gm is a change on the cellular level, and this degree of anemia affects how the patient is able to carry out normal activities of daily living or to cope with feelings aroused by a changing environment. The anemia results in a greater amount of weakness, more time spent resting in bed, and other behaviors related to fatigue and decreased level of activity. In addition to the medical problem, the patient's need for nursing care is in meeting activity needs; the focal stimulus is the cancer that initially produced the illness; and contextual stimuli include the chemotherapy and the extremely low amount of hemoglobin.

Characteristics of the segregated approach, which separates the medical problem from the client's other problems in coping, are

1. It focuses on the clients' problems of meeting or satisfying the basic need states in order to carry out the usual activities of daily living, or to cope with feelings that interfere with adaptation.

2. It recognizes the area of medical practice and medical intervention as primarily affecting the cellular function and serving as a stimuli for other behavioral responses of clients.

3. It emphasizes that, in addition to illness, disturbances occur in other need areas and in other modes of function and that these problems must be incorporated in the nursing care plan to help the client regain an adapted state.

4. It considers the independent functions of the nurse in terms of actions taken beyond the dependent functions of carrying out the orders of the medical treatment regime. For example, The nurse carries out dependent functions for a medical order for a 500 mg sodium diet by ensuring that the correct diet is ordered from the diet kitchen, that it is delivered to the correct person, and that no additional salt is provided. In addition, the nurse initiates various independent functions, such as exploring the use of salt substitutes, checking food likes and dislikes, and health-teaching for clients and their families.

## IDENTIFYING THE PROBLEM

The most critical step of the nursing process is to identify correctly the patient problem.

Processing information regarding maladaptive behaviors and their causative stimuli generally shows clusters of behaviors that indicate a disruption in one of the need areas. It is important to remember that one maladaptive behavior does not necessarily cause a coping problem. To be considered problems, maladaptive behaviors should occur in a pattern, be persistent or recurrent, and be ineffective in meeting the patient's needs. In the individual who successfully cleared mucus from the respiratory passageway, several coughs would be judged as adaptive, not as a maladaptive indication of an infection or obstructed airway.

**Types of Patient Problems.** The assessment phase of the nursing process yields a mass of information about the patient, need areas, and stimuli that influence the maladaptive behaviors. The beginning nurse often feels overwhelmed by the sheer volume of the data and may experience difficulty stating the patient's problem. For this reason, it is helpful to have a classification system for problems. Although a number of systems may be devised, the following system has been useful for stating problems:

For physiological, role-function, or interdependence modes
   An excess of, or too much of, something
   A deficit of, or too little of, something
   The wrong kind of something
   None or the lack of something

For self-concept mode
   Presence of feelings or emotions with a negative effect
not contributing to integrity, such as fears, anxiety, worry,
anger, guilt, powerlessness, loneliness

When using the nursing process and identifying patients' problems, nurses should phrase the problems from the perspective of the patient, such as "patient has inadequate caloric intake" or "patient has fear of dying." The statement should specify the coping difficulty in meeting some need and should indicate the types of behaviors that are to be changed.

When the nurse defines the patient's problem, it is said that the nurse is making a nursing diagnosis. A nursing diagnosis is a statement or a conclusion about the patient's condition that carries common meaning for most nurses. Progress is being made in defining and classifying nursing diagnoses of the patient problems that are seen in professional practice. In 1973, a national conference of nurses made a notable beginning and produced a list of 100 nursing diagnoses (Gebbie and Lavin, 1975). Subsequent conferences have refined the concepts of unitary man as an open system with patterns of energy that have been categorized as wakefulness, activity, communication, relationships, knowing, material exchange (including such activities as eating, breathing, and eliminating), valuing, and making choices or goal setting (Kim and Mortiz, 1982).

It is possible that some system of nursing diagnoses will be in common use in the future; however, at the present time, our approach is to define problems in terms of patients' difficulties in carrying out some aspect of their daily routines or in coping with their feelings about something. The second level assessment of the causes of maladaptive behaviors and the problem itself focuses on a number of stimuli, such as anxiety, sensory deprivation, sensory overload, and pain.

**Priorities of Problems.** Up to this point, through the use of the nursing process, the nurse has assessed behaviors, compared them with standards or criteria to identify the maladaptive behaviors, and sought the stimuli causing or influencing these behaviors. Not every maladaptive behavior indicates a problem in meeting needs, as is the case with behaviors such as a papule ¼ inch in diameter located on the outer aspect of the knee. The maladaptive behaviors that indicate problems in a need area are grouped, and a statement about the coping problem is made. At each step of the assessment, the nurse condenses the mass of initial information until there are fewer problems with which to work. These problems are then ranked in the priority of their importance and urgency. By establishing priorities, the nurse arranges the order in which nursing services are to be provided.

Which problems are given the higher priorities and are most urgently in need of the nurse's at-tention? One basis for setting priorities is consideration of the hierarchy of needs, described by Maslow (1970). The highest (first) priorities are given to problems in the physiological need areas that must be met to ensure the individual's survival. As previously seen, even in this mode, some needs are more pressing and immediate than others. For example, how long can a person survive without eating? Hours? One or two days? A week? How long without drinking water or other fluids? Hours? One or two days? A week? How long can one survive without breathing oxygen? Hours? Days? In this case, if oxygen does not reach the brain within four to six minutes, permanent damage occurs, and death soon follows. However, there are unusual cases of individuals who nearly drowned in cold water and were resuscitated as much as 20 to 30 minutes after they stopped breathing.

Essential physiological needs have the highest priority, followed by those related to safety and comfort, love and belonging, self-esteem, and, finally, self-actualization. Bower (1972) describes another way of setting priorities by ranking them according to the following criteria:

Problems that threaten the individual's survival
Problems that threaten the body's integrity
Problems that interfere with the individual's normal growth and development

The nurse focuses the care plan on the highest priority problem. When that problem is resolved, problems with a lower priority assume a higher ranking. For example, a patient who is hemorrhaging is anxious about this condition and fearful of what is happening. The nurse gives the highest priority to the bleeding because the loss of blood threatens survival. Lower priority is given to the problem of anxiety that affects integrity or to problems of stressful living or smoking that may be problems in growth and development. Problems that threaten the body's integrity or cause destructive changes include illness, breakdown in communication, pain or discomfort, depression, and many of the other difficulties related to self-concept, role-function, and the interdependence modes. See Figure 8-1 on page 94.

Although the standards for assigning priorities are usually stated in terms of the individual, they can be used for families and for groups in the community. For example, higher priority is given to teen-agers who abuse drugs and alcohol, with their disruptive effects on families, and to the victims of rape or violence than to problems related to growth and developmental tasks, such as dealing with sexuality. On the community level, an epidemic of a disease such as cholera that threatens the survival or integrity of a segment of the population would be given a higher priority than a health education program on balanced nutrition for the elderly. As the more urgent problems are resolved, attention is directed to the remaining problems that had been given a lower priority.

When dealing with problems that do not pose an immediate threat to survival, other factors may influence the assignment of priorities. Whenever possible, consider the patient's view of what is most important and the problem that is causing immediate stress. Giving high priority to the problem that the patient perceives as the most urgent increases trust and receptivity to subsequent nursing care. Consider the severity of the problem or the degree of the unmet need. A more serious problem exists when the patient has a fluid intake that is only 10 per cent of normal than when the intake is 75 per cent of the normal amount, which is also a problem. Time is another factor in determining priorities. When a person is ill, some needs and their associated problems persist for days and weeks. Others may be solved or improved with immediate interventions and thus eliminated from further consideration.

## SETTING GOALS

Nurses usually set goals to specify the changes desired in the patient's behavior to promote adaptation. However, a preferable method is for the nurse and patient to work together in formulating goals and planning ways to achieve them. Goals serve as the targets for nursing actions. Effective goals have these characteristics: (1) They must be intimately related to the problem; (2) They must be reasonable and achievable; and (3) They must fall within the patient's value system or be acceptable to her or him.

Elements of the nursing process flow logically toward formulating the goal. Behaviors that manifest a problem are compared with a standard, or norm, in the first level assessment and judged to be maladaptive and in need of change. The standards help the nurse determine what the patient's response should be to fall within the adaptive range. Even stating the patient's problem as "patient has (too much, too little, the wrong kind, none, or feelings) of _____ " shows something that should be changed, and the goal then relates to the problem. When the problem specifies too much of something, the goal of action is to reduce the amount; if the condition were a deficiency of something, the goal would be stated to increase the amount. The goal indicates the change to be made and, whenever possible, the degree or amount of the change that can be measured. Some examples of statements of problems and their related goals are

### Problems

1. Patient has had no bowel movement for five days.
2. Patient has inadequate caloric intake.

3. Patient has decreased activity and exercise.

4. Patient has fears about losing health and dying.

### Goals

1. Patient will have a bowel movement regularly every one to two days.
2. Patient will increase caloric intake to 2000 calories daily.
3. Patient will increase activities and exercise to three hours per day.
4. Patient will have reduced fears about health and dying, as shown by increased periods of relaxation.

When setting goals, the nurse follows several principles. First, whenever possible, the patient should be involved in the process, as well as being involved in other phases of planning care. The patient is the person who has the coping problem, is not at ease, and will be changing to satisfy unmet needs. The nurse can use the nursing process to devise goals and a care plan that looks marvelous on paper, but such a plan is doomed to failure unless the patient accepts the goals as being reasonable and falling within his or her system of values or beliefs. This is illustrated by the case of Mrs. G.

Mrs. G., an active 68-year-old had a colostomy two weeks ago, and her postoperative course has been uneventful. The colostomy has been draining, and the nurse began teaching Mrs. G. how to take care of it herself. However, Mrs. G. has eaten only a few bites of food during the past week. The nurse identified the problem as inadequate caloric intake and, when setting the goal with Mrs. G.'s help, learned that Mrs. G. rejected the goal of increasing her caloric intake by eating more food. Further assessment revealed that the patient had hidden feelings of disgust about the odor and appearance of the colostomy drainage and attempted to reduce the drainage by cutting down on her food intake. This new information led to a revision of the care plan to include the newly discovered problem.

Another principle is to state the goal in terms of what the patient will do, not what the nurse will do. The focus is on the patient's coping problem or ineffective attempts to meet one or more needs, and the goal is what is required to meet these needs in an adaptive way—the patient is the one who acts or copes with the need state as independently as is appropriate to the position on the health-illness continuum. For the patient in the terminal stage of an illness, goals related to independence would be less appropriate than goals that meet the patient's needs with assistance from others.

To be relevant and effective for the patient, goals should have several characteristics. They should be specific and related to the particular problem, and they should indicate the direction and degree of the change that can be measured. The goal can also be seen as the patient's objective, which is stated in behavioral terms and contains conditions necessary for achieving it. Such a goal is stated as "patient will drink a total of 2000 ml per day." The nurse then has a better gauge for determining whether the patient has achieved the goal when the nursing care is evaluated because the patient's intake can be measured and the amount compared with 2000 ml per day.

Goals may be long-term or short-term. They should be reasonable, to enable the patient to reach or to achieve them. Long-term goals tend to be general and to specify such things as "will learn to walk again," or "will recover and return to own home." It is advisable to break down these general goals into specific short-term goals that can be achieved more readily. By reaching a short-term goal, both the patient and the nurse experience a feeling of success and are motivated to go on.

## PLANNING INTERVENTIONS

**Manipulating the Stimuli.** The next step of the nursing process is to plan the actions necessary to reach the goal and to resolve the problem. The interventions involve manipulating the stimuli that cause or influence the patient's coping problem.

In the case of Mrs. G., cited previously, the difficulty in satisfying one of her need areas produced maladaptive behaviors. The second level assessment identified the stimuli that caused or influenced that behavior. (The second level assessment should identify all the influencing factors that shape, or mold, the patient's response.)

A goal should indicate the change to be made by the patient and should state the plan of nursing care to be followed to help the patient to achieve the goal. (See Table.)

In the table, the focal stimulus causing the patient's problem is the metastatic cancer, the medical disease. This has placed her on the illness end of the health-illness continuum and led to hospitalization and the initiation of medical treatment by the physician. The treatments are listed as contextual stimuli, which can be manipulated by the nurse in planning how to help the patient meet her nutritional needs. Although the type of diet is specified by the physician, the nurse is able to manipulate or modify it by finding out the patient's food preferences, including those on the diet, and varying the size of the portions. Because the patient lived in the Orient for a number of years, she may like foods different from those generally available through the hospital kitchens. Additionally, the types of foods selected, the knowledge of which foods are high in calories, lack of exercise due to bed rest, the effects of radiation therapy, and her age influence other interventions that the nurse considers when planning this patient's care.

| Maladaptive Behaviors | Focal (F) and Contextual (C) Stimuli | Goal and Interventions |
|---|---|---|
| Patient has decreased caloric intake, manifested by behaviors of:<br>– refuses to eat breakfast<br>– ate only 3 tsp mashed potato, 1 tsp green beans, and tea for lunch<br>– weighed 122 lb on admission; has lost 4 lb in past week<br>– states that she feels nauseated and has no appetite since therapy began | (F) metastatic cancer of breast<br>(C) radiation therapy<br>(C) bed rest<br>(C) 75 yr of age<br>(C) regular, select diet<br>(C) back pain<br>(C) lived in Orient for 35 yr | Patient will increase her caloric intake to 2000 per day to maintain present weight<br>– assist in selecting high caloric foods<br>– give small, frequent feedings<br>– find out foods she likes and include on diet<br>– arrange radiation therapy for mid-morning or midafternoon, if possible |

Although age is a stimulus that cannot be changed by the nurse, it is a significant influencing factor in how one responds to one's various need states. Interventions that might be appropriate for someone two years of age may not as appropriate for someone 12 years of age; an appropriate action for someone 35 years of age may not be reasonable for an elderly person. The nurse may develop and use more than one approach for each stimuli to achieve the desired goal and change in behavior.

## IMPLEMENTING THE PLAN

Implementing the nursing care plan is the action or "doing" stage for the nurse. In carrying out the plan, the nurse and the patient are jointly involved—the nurse assists and helps the patient respond to need states in adaptive ways.

Some of the nursing approaches may meet goals in several need areas simultaneously. This is illustrated by the case of Mr. W.

Mr. W. has a draining wound, is at risk of developing pressure ulcers, and is lonely. When the nurse goes to his room to change his dressing, she also turns and positions him on his side and spends a few minutes talking with him so that she has intervened in all three of his problem areas. By doing a careful assessment of all Mr. W.'s need areas and identifying all his needs, the care plan has provided for deliberate interventions to meet the short-term goals that have been set.

## EVALUATING THE CARE PLAN

The final step in the nursing process is evaluation. It is a measurement of the effectiveness of the nursing interventions to meet the goals that have been set to change the patient's behaviors to those that are within the adaptive range. Adaptive behaviors are evidence that one is able to meet one's own needs again and that the problems have been resolved.

When the evaluation shows that the care plan has not solved the problems, it is necessary for the nurse to go back to the beginning of the process and reassess. Additional assessment of behaviors may yield other significant information, such as the negative feelings Mrs. G. had about her colostomy, or the second level assessment may provide other stimuli that can be manipulated. It is possible that the problem has not been correctly identified. A patient may have decreased intake of fluids and food, but the problem may not be inadequate caloric or fluid intake. Depression may be the main problem. The problem is then one that is generated in the self-concept mode rather than in the physiological mode.

**Measuring the Effectiveness of the Care Plan.** The nurse who is responsible for the patient and the patient's care continues to assess the behaviors in the problem areas and to compare them with the behaviors stated in the goals. The comparison shows that the current behaviors meet the goal and are adaptive or that they do not meet the goal and continue to be maladaptive.

*Behaviors meet the goal.* When the behaviors are within the adaptive range, the patient is able to meet the needs, and the problem no longer exists. Although the behaviors are no longer of immediate concern to the nurse, additional checking may be done periodically to assure that the behavior is stable. This is especially true of the vital signs. Even though the measurements of temperature, pulse, respirations, and blood pressure are within the normal range, readings are taken several times daily for hospitalized patients. Changes in vital signs may be an indication of problems in physiological or emotional need areas.

*Behaviors do not meet the goal.* Assessing the current behaviors may show that they are still in the maladaptive range. These behaviors are compared with the behaviors from the initial assessment or from some other period of time to determine the direction and degree of change. For example, the patient's hemoglobin was 6.5 gm/dl on admission; several days later, following transfusions, it was 9.6 gm/dl; and today it is 9.0 gm/dl. The assessment shows that there have been changes in the hemoglobin levels, although they are still outside the normal range.

Figure 3–2 illustrates how assessed behaviors are compared with the goal of adaptive behaviors. Using the following goals, try to describe behaviors for comparison and evaluation.

— Patient will have soft stool regularly, without straining.
— Patient will have adequate oxygenation of cells.
— Patient will increase fluid intake to 2000 ml daily.
— Patient will feed himself without assistance.
— Patient will have five or less outbursts of anger each day.

Two examples of behaviors for comparison and evaluation are (1) The constipated patient's goal is to have a soft stool regularly, without straining. The nursing interventions include activities such as adding roughage foods to the diet, increasing the fluid intake to a minimum of 2000 ml daily, and increasing the patient's physical activities.

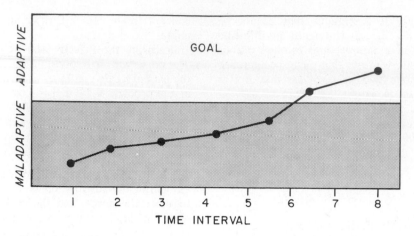

**Figure 3-2.** Evaluation of the effect in meeting the goal of an adaptive behavior.

Assessing bowel activity provides data about how the goal is being met. If the goal has not been met, assessment of behaviors related to the interventions may indicate how effectively the interventions have been carried out. (2) The patient who had a hemorrhage has a hemoglobin report of 7.5 gm on admission, which indicates a decreased amount of oxygen being delivered to cells throughout the body. For several days the hemoglobin is in the maladaptive range, and by the fifth or sixth day, it is in the adaptive area.

In summary, the nurse evaluates the effectiveness of the nursing care plan in an objective way by assessing how well the goals have been met. Present behaviors are compared with the goals, which is a statement of desired adaptive behavior to meet the problem in the need area. If the goal has been met, the behaviors are adaptive, and the need no longer exists or presents a coping problem. When the behaviors are still in the maladaptive range, the nurse checks to see the direction and degree of the changes. If the degree of change is too small or too slow or is a negative move away from adaptation, the nurse returns to the nursing process to find additional information or other stimuli to manipulate, validates the problem, and revises the care plan. Effective use of the nursing process produces more effective nursing care based on a logical, problem-solving approach to the patient's coping problems.

## SUMMARY

The complexities of modern life and the coping problems produced as people attempt to adapt to continuing changes require that the nurse use a problem-solving approach to plan high quality nursing care for the patient. This approach is called the nursing process and, when combined with the adaptation model of nursing, includes: (1) assessing which consists of two steps: (a) first level—information is collected about the behaviors that can be observed or measured and compared with standards, or norms, and (b) second level—to identify the stimuli that cause or influence the maladaptive behaviors; (2) analyzing the maladaptive behaviors and their stimuli which leads to identifying the problems and assigning priorities to them; (3) setting goals for the problems and planning interventions by manipulating the stimuli that cause the problems; (4) implementing the nursing care plan; and (5) evaluating the effectiveness of the actions by reassessing to determine the extent to which the goals have been met. When necessary, the care plan is revised by again using the nursing process as the problem-solving method.

## REFERENCES
### (Chapters Two and Three)

Aiken, Linda, Blendon, Robert, and Rogers, David: The shortage of hospital nurses: a new perspective. Am J of Nurs, *81*:1612–1618, (September) 1981.

Aspinall, Mary Jo: Nursing diagnosis – the weak link. Nurs Outlook, *24*:433–437, (July) 1976.

Blaney, Doris: An opinion on the scope of nursing practice. Am J Nurs, *79*:2000, (November) 1979.

Bower, Fay: The Process of Planning Nursing Care: A Theoretical Model. St. Louis, The C. V. Mosby Co., 1972.

Byrne, Marjorie L., and Thompson, Lida F.: Key Concepts for the Study and Practice of Nursing. St. Louis, The C. V. Mosby Co., 1972.

Carrierri, Virginia K., and Sitzman, Judith: Components of the nursing process. Nurs Clin North Am, *6*:115–124, (March) 1971.

Gebbie, Kristine, and Lavin, Mary, (Eds.): Classification of Nursing Diagnosis. St. Louis, The C. V. Mosby Co., 1975.

Gulbrandsen, Mary W.: Guide of health assessment. Am J Nurs, *76*:1276–1277, (August) 1976.

Hagerman, Zerita: Teaching beginners to cope with extreme behavior. Am J Nurs, *68*:1927–1929, (September) 1968.

Harris, Ruth B.: A strong vote for the nursing process. Am J Nurs, *79*:1999–2001, (November) 1979.

Kim, Mi Ja, and Moritz, Derry Ann (Eds.): Classification of Nursing Diagnosis. Proceedings of the Third and Fourth National Conference. New York, McGraw-Hill, Inc., 1982.

Levine, Myra: Adaptation and assessment: a rationale for nursing intervention. Am J Nurs, *66*:2450–2453, (November) 1966.

Little, Dolores E., and Carnevali, Doris L.: Nursing Care Planning, 2nd ed. Philadelphia, J. B. Lippincott Co., 1976.

Maslow, Abraham: Motivation and Personality, 2nd ed. New York, Harper & Row Publishers, Inc., 1970, pp. 32–40.

Murray, Ruth B., and Zentner, Judith P.: Nursing Concepts for Health Promotion, 2nd ed. Englewood Cliffs, NJ, Prentice-Hall, Inc., 1979.

Reynolds, Janis, and Logsdon, Jann: Assessing your patients' mental status. Nursing 79, *9*:26–33, (August) 1979.

Riehl, Joan, and Roy, Sister Callista (Eds.): Conceptual Models for Nursing Practice, 2nd ed. New York, Appleton-Century-Crofts, 1980.

Roy, Sister Callista: Adaptation: a conceptual framework for nursing. Nurs Outlook, *18*:42–45, (March) 1970.

Roy, Sister Callista: Introduction to Nursing: An Adaptation Model. Englewood Cliffs, NJ, Prentice-Hall, Inc., 1976.

Schaeffer, Jeannette: The interrelatedness of decision-making and the nursing process. Am J Nurs, *74*:1852–1855, (October) 1974.

Schoonover, Lois, et al: Assessment: a nursing model. Nurs Management, *13*:18–22, (April) 1982.

Smeltzer, Carolyn: Teaching the nursing process – practical method, JNE, *19*:31–37, (November) 1980.

Turnbull, Sister Joyce: Shifting the focus to health. Am J Nurs, *76*:1985–1987, (December) 1976.

Yura, Helen, and Walsh, Mary B.: The Nursing Process: Assessing, Planning, Implementing, Evaluating, 3rd ed. New York, Appleton-Century-Crofts, 1978.

# Guide for Nursing Care Plan: Adaptation Approach

| First Level Assessment<br>**Behaviors and Measures** | Patient's Problem | Second Level Assessment<br>Focal Stimuli | Contextual Stimuli |
|---|---|---|---|
| *Physiological Mode* | | | |
| Behaviors of body functions and structures that meet the human needs for<br>Oxygen<br>Fluids and electrolyte balance<br>Nutrition<br>Elimination<br>Rest and exercise<br>Regulation<br>  special senses<br>  temperature<br>  endocrine | Stated as<br><br>"Patient has _____ increased, excessive, or too much decreased, deficit, not enough inappropriate or wrong kind none<br>of _____" needed to satisfy the need area | Disruption of body structure or function (medical problem) | Other illness<br>Surgery<br>Bed rest<br>Pain<br>Fever<br>Diagnostic tests<br>Drainage tubes<br>Catheters<br>Effect of drugs<br><br>Environment:<br>  Heat, cold<br>  Isolation<br>  Chemicals<br>  Noise<br><br>Personal:<br>  Age and sex<br>  Anxiety<br>  Height and weight<br>  Others: specify |
| *Criteria for Judging Behaviors*<br>Comparison with normal range of function or normal measurements of biological function | | | |
| *Self-Concept Mode* | | | |
| **Physical Self**<br>*Somatic* — feelings that express response to change in health status; congruency of feelings or emotions about actual appearance or functions of the body | Stated as problem of loss, or loss of control<br><br>"Patient has feelings of _____ about _____" | Actual or perceived disruption of function (medical problem)<br><br>Expectations of self or others | Other recent losses<br>Anxiety<br>Bed rest<br>Cultural beliefs or values<br>Sensory deprivation<br>Cultural view of age, romance, productivity, sex, etc.<br>Medications<br>Required treatments<br>Surgery |
| *Body image* — feelings about perceived appearance or functions | | | |
| *Criteria for Judging Behaviors*<br>Positive coping with feelings or emotions about the physical self. Biological norms for body function and structure | | | |

| | Stated as | | Changes in: |
|---|---|---|---|
| **Personal Self** | | | |
| *Self-Consistency* — feelings about oneself as a person when performing or coping with daily situations or events. | Stated as problem of anxiety<br><br>"Patient has feelings of (anxiety, worry, fear, anger, depression) about _____." | Threat to sameness of the self | Family structure<br>Resources (income, time)<br>Attitudes<br>Expectations<br>Situation<br>Health<br>Support systems<br>Age |
| *Criteria for Judging Behaviors*<br>The expected or habitual patterns of acting or coping with daily life | | | |
| *Self-Ideal* — one's goals or ideals, what one strives for or would like to be | Stated as problem of powerlessness<br><br>"Patient has feelings of (powerlessness, helplessness, hopelessness, frustration, or anger) about _____." | Expectations of self | Expectations of others (actual or perceived):<br>Abilities<br>Talents<br>Resources (income, time)<br>Motivation |
| *Moral-Ethical Self* — the values, beliefs, ethics of "rightness" and "wrongness" | Stated as problem of guilt<br><br>"Patient has feelings of (guilt, shame) about _____." | Expectations of others | Expectations of self:<br>Strength of sanctions<br>Support systems<br>Circumstances<br>Cultural pattern of right or wrong, good or bad |
| *Criteria for Judging Behaviors*<br>The values of the social group: religious, legal, moral, or cultural | | | |
| *Interdependence Mode* | | | |
| **Dependency**<br>*Help-seeking* — need for assistance from others<br>*Affection-seeking* — being agreeable, wanting to please another to obtain love<br>*Attention-seeking* — desiring interactions with others<br>**Independency**<br>*Initiative-taking* — able to undertake and begin activities, projects<br>*Obstacle-mastery* — able to solve problems, cope with difficulties. | Stated as inappropriate dependence or independence<br><br>"Patient has (inappropriate, too much, too little) of (independent, dependent) behavior" | Internal need or drive of self for affiliation with others / achievement goals | Family relationships<br>Significant others<br>Other support systems<br>Age – maturation level<br>Child-rearing patterns<br>Level of learning<br>Rewards or sanctions<br>Illness<br>Economic resources<br>Environmental factors:<br>Time<br>Space<br>Location<br>Intrinsic factors:<br>Values<br>Feelings<br>Ideas or beliefs |
| *Criteria for Judging Behaviors*<br>Socially accepted patterns of control over internal drives and affectional integrity appropriate to the developmental stage in life | | | |

*Continued on next page.*

# Guide for Nursing Care Plan: Adaptation Approach (*Continued*)

| First Level Assessment<br>Behaviors and Measures | Patient's Problem | Second Level Assessment<br>Focal Stimuli | Contextual Stimuli |
|---|---|---|---|
| *Role-Function Mode* | | | |
| Behaviors used to carry out the primary, secondary, and tertiary roles of the individual to achieve instrumental goals or expressive goals | Stated as problems of role failure or as problem in other modes: Self-concept or Independence | Expectations of self or others | Resources available<br>Set of circumstances<br>Rewards<br>Sanctions<br>Consumer or beneficiary of interaction<br>Social or cultural values attitudes, beliefs |
| | "Patient has conflict between _____ and _____ roles" | | |
| *Criteria for Judging Behaviors* | "Patient fails to carry out requirements of _____ role" | | |
| Socially acceptable patterns of behavior for the growth and developmental tasks for stage in life | | | |

*Section TWO* _____

# THE NATURE OF BEHAVIOR

Nursing is defined as dealing with the way that people respond to illness and to disruptions in their state of health. But what makes people act the way that they do? Because people behave in so many different ways, how is it possible for the nurse to understand how they will respond in any given situation? Is it possible to organize and to classify the ways that people behave so nurses can anticipate and predict some of their responses? How does a nurse go about changing a patient's behavior when it interferes with therapy, delays progress in getting well, or has a negative effect on other people?

Nurses rely on observed behaviors, objective measurements of body functions, and the patient's statements to assess the level of adaptation and deviations from the norm that indicate various needs or problems. Through the use of the nursing process, the nurse formulates the goals and helps the patient change maladaptive behavior to behavior within the adaptive range. *The patient must change the behavior,* not the doctor, the nurse, or family members. The nurse intervenes to help the patient change the behavior by altering the stimulus, teaching new responses, or making other changes in the environment.

Behaviors are either voluntary or involuntary. Involuntary behaviors are under the control of the autonomic nervous system (ANS) and include measurements and observations made of body functions. The manufacture of red blood cells, blood pressure, pulse rate, formation of urine, and transmission of nerve impulses are functions too vital for survival to be left to discretionary control. They are regulated by an intricate system of automatic feedback mechanisms. Disturbances and diseases that affect these functions of the body or that occur on the cellular level become the concern of physicians and are treated with medications or by surgery.

Voluntary behaviors are learned ways of responding to various stimuli and situations. From birth, the infant is engaged in learning how to cope with a changing environment and throughout life, continues to learn how to act in social settings. People learn how to behave, or act, to meet their needs for oxygen, food, fluids, elimination, rest, and exercise and to communicate with others, to gain control of their emotions, to gain love and acceptance, and to get along with other people.

Behaviors are caused by the person as a response to a stimulus that has been perceived to have a certain meaning. Voluntary behavior tends to fall into patterns based on how the stimulus is approached—as something to be accepted or even welcomed, as something to be avoided, or as something to be attacked and overcome.

In this section, you will explore how the body perceives stimuli, ways to understand behaviors, how to categorize different patterns of behavior, and interventions that the nurse can use to help patients learn adaptive responses.

Changing one's behavior involves learning new ways to respond and being rewarded more often for the new behavior than for the previous behavior. Health-teaching by the nurse is one of the best methods of providing new information for patients. Behavior modification, insight therapy, and other specialized interpersonal therapies are also interventions that are used to promote learning. An analysis of the sick role provides standards for comparing assessed behaviors of patients with the expectations of patients, as well as with the expectations of the care-givers, families, and others. Stress and anxiety are strong and pervasive stimuli that pose difficult problems in coping with feelings, especially during illness. People behave differently at different stages of their illnesses, and the nurse needs to understand that what is normal and adaptive for the patient in one stage may not be desirable behavior for the patient in another stage. The standards and criteria for behavior change when the situation changes.

## Chapter FOUR

# Sensory Perception

## OBJECTIVES   Information in this chapter will help you to

1. Describe a theoretical framework for the perception of internal and external stimuli in terms of
   a. the components of the reticular activating system (RAS) and their functions.
   b. the purposes or advantages of a rich and varied sensory input.
   c. the disadvantages of reduced or repetitive sensory input.
2. Classify the alterations in sensory perception as a problem of
   a. sensory monotony.
   b. sensory distortion.
   c. sensory deprivation.
   d. sensory overload.
3. Assess alterations in sensory perception as possible stimuli for patients who have problems in coping with their environment.
4. State nursing interventions that manipulate the stimulus of altered sensory perception.

## THEORY OF SENSORY PERCEPTION

Everyone needs continuous stimulation for growth, development, and survival. At any given period of time, the normal individual is bombarded by innumerable stimuli. These include external stimuli from all that we see, hear, feel, smell, or taste as well as internal stimuli that arise from the body needs for food and oxygen, from tension in muscles, from invasion of the body by microorganisms, and so on. Although every stimulus is capable of evoking a response, if a person responded to all the stimuli that are received by receptors, his or her behavior would be disorganized and chaotic.

When individuals respond to stimuli, the highest priority is given to meeting those needs that are necessary to maintain integrity of the body and adaptation to the environment. Our human needs range from specific physiological needs for oxygen, fluids, nutrition, elimination, rest, exercise, and sensory regulation to needs related to our emotional, intellectual, and social growth and development. Maslow (1970) has described these human needs in the form of a hierarchy in which the urgency of the basic physiological needs must be met before attention is given to needs at another level. The highest priority is given to the physiological needs as they arise, and when these needs have been met, priority is placed in the order of our needs for safety, affection and belonging, self-esteem, and, ultimately, the need for self-actualization. (See Figure 1–3.)

Even among the physiological needs related to sustaining life, some needs have a higher priority than others. For example, oxygen is essential for life; we can survive only a few minutes without it. When a person has difficulty breathing, all other activity is stopped until an adequate supply of oxygen is obtained to meet bodily needs—the need for oxygen must be met within minutes. However, the need for fluids and urine elimination may extend for several hours without consequence, and the delay of a day or two in meeting the bodily need for food or sleep generally does not cause more than minor discomfort. Once the bodily needs of a high priority have been met, the lower priority needs emerge, such as studying for an exam, visiting with friends, or performing one's job.

## THE SENSORY PROCESS

The body is stimulated into action through the sensory process, which has two major components: (1) reception of stimuli through the sensory organs, and (2) perception, which is the conscious mental registration of sensory stimuli. Thus, sensory process is more than the simple stimulus-response formula; it involves a cognitive process of the brain.

### Reception of the Stimulus

The sensory process begins with the detection or the reception of the stimulus by the body. A stimulus is defined as any provoking condition that causes the body to respond. A stimulus may be external and found anywhere in the environment, or it may be an internal need state of the body that serves to motivate the body to some type of action.

The stimulus is detected by sensitive neural tissue called receptors. The sensory organ receptors of sight, sound, taste, smell, and touch help one to respond to the outside world, and various specialized receptors throughout the body monitor one's internal environment. From the receptor, the impulse, in response to a stimulus, is transmitted over the neural pathway to the spinal cord. From the spinal cord, impulses are either transmitted to the brain or synapse in reflex circuits of the spinal cord. Impulses that result

in reflex circuits of the spinal cord are not included in the sensory process. In the brain, the impulse passes through specific sensitive pathways in the reticular activating system (RAS) before it reaches the cortex where the response to the stimulus is initiated.

### Perception of the Stimulus

Some researchers have called perception "the dash in the S–R formula," which means that the stimulus acts upon the organism in some way before a response takes place. As stated previously, perception is the conscious mental registration of a sensory stimulus. Whether we acknowledge a certain stimulus will probably depend upon a number of factors, such as its intensity or power, its size, changes in it, its repetition, and its relevance.

The intensity of the stimulus refers to the power it has to cause a response. For example, a loud bang or a scream is an effective way to gain the attention of others, and bright, colorful displays are an effective means of advertising products in shopping centers. In general, the principle is that the more intense the stimulus, the greater the response that is evoked. However, people do respond to subliminal stimuli. Research has shown that visual images or messages that are projected on a screen for a fraction of a second during a movie may influence the viewer's actions even though the viewer was not consciously aware of seeing the image or message. A second principle is that the larger the stimulus, the greater the chance of a response. For example, a message on a billboard that is 30 feet in height attracts much more attention than a message on an index card.

A change in the stimulus alters its perception. If all sounds vibrated at the same frequency, there would be no different tones or music; all would sound alike. It is the change of the cycle that provides variety, and, thus, enjoyment of sounds. This applies to changes in many stimuli, such as seeing new sights when travelling, learning a new skill, or tasting different foods.

The repetition of a stimulus is a factor in sensory perception. The same stimulus may be repeated several times until it becomes familiar, predictable, and meaningful. Repeated stimuli lead to the organization of our lives, the formation of habits, and increased efficiency in responding. Student nurses learn new skills, such as donning sterile gloves or giving a bed bath, by repeating the stimuli and the responses that comprise the entire procedure.

People tend to perceive a stimulus more readily when it has relevance for them. Even though a stimulus is present and activates a receptor, it does not evoke a response unless the individual attaches some meaning to it. This is a common occurrence for people who travel in a foreign country and do not understand the language of that country. Although they hear words that are spoken all around them, they respond only to those words which have meaning for them. The situation is similar for nursing students. Even when signs and symptoms of the patient's condition are present, they do not perceive them until some meaning is given to them; then they are able to respond and to take action. For example, a nursing student has a patient with kidney disease. The student may notice that the patient's face looks different but attaches no significance to the extreme puffiness of the eyelids until this visual stimulus is related to fluid retention.

## THE RETICULAR ACTIVATING SYSTEM

An essential part of the sensory process is the reticular activating system (RAS), which controls the overall degree of central nervous system activity, including alertness and sleep. Reticular is a term that means "network." The RAS consists of reticular formation neurons that are located throughout the medulla, the pons, and the mesencephalon, which extends to the hypothalamus and into part of the thalamus. The reticular formation responds to impulses from the ascending sensory pathways and projects the transmission to the cortex, as shown in Figure 4–1.

The reticular formation is highly excitable, and when it is activated by stimuli, it alerts the brain and stimulates the cortex. The degree of stimulation determines the individual's degree of arousal and of being awake. Lack of stimulation reduces the activity in the RAS and leads to the state of sleep. However, the individual can be aroused by stimuli, such as noise, bright lights, or pain exciting the RAS again.

Although stimulation of the RAS produces arousal and wakefulness, questions remain concerning the cause of sleep. It still is not known what suppresses this system and decreases its response to impulses that continue to be transmitted from the receptors. One theory suggests that an intrinsic oscillator in the brainstem cycles between a wakeful center that activates the RAS, and a sleep center that inhibits it (Guyton, 1981).

Stimuli reach the RAS and activate the tissue in several different ways. One method consists of sensory stimuli picked up by receptors that transmit the impulse along the nerve fibers that enter the spinal cord to form ascending neural tracts. These fibers pass through the RAS and synapse with neuronal cells in the cortex. Another method of arousal is through motor activity. Nerve fibers from the motor regions of the brain pass through the RAS, and the increased muscular activity and proprioceptive impulses are potent stimuli promoting arousal and wakefulness. The activity of other parts of the cortex in the form of ideas, thoughts, memory, and feelings also function as internal stimuli that stimulate the RAS and form a feedback loop.

Finally, the RAS is stimulated by norepinephrine, a hormone secreted by the adrenal medulla when the autonomic nervous system is stimulated. The hormonal stimulation of the RAS and changes initiated immediately by the sympathetic

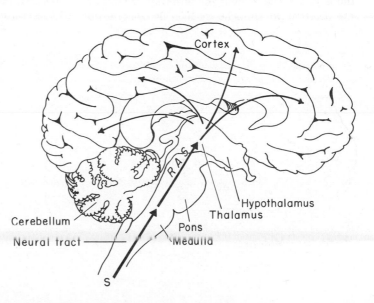

**Figure 4–1.** The neural pathway for stimuli through the reticular activating system (RAS). This system consists of excitable tissue in the medulla, the pons, the hypothalamus through which sensory stimuli pass before reaching the cortex of the brain.

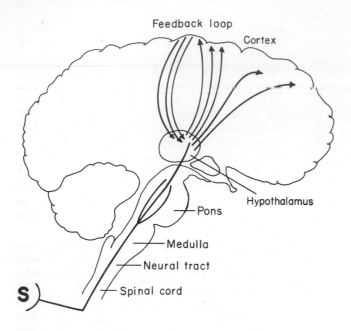

Figure 4–2. The internal feedback loop is formed when sensory stimuli ascend the spinal cord and pass through the reticular activating system (RAS) to the cortex. The cortex generates a stimulus to further excite the RAS and to send another message to the cortex. Thoughts and emotions are examples of the internal feedback loop.

nervous system prepare for the "fight or flight" response and cause the person to be more mentally alert to possible dangers.

From the reticular formation, the stimulus is transmitted to the cortex where the perception part of the sensory process occurs. It is in the cortex that meaning is attached to the stimulus. Different parts of the cortex have different functions as illustrated in Figure 4–3. The frontal lobe controls the formation of thought, the abstract type of reasoning, and judgment. The voluntary motor and body sensations are located on either side of the central fissure. Bilateral vision is associated with the posterior section of the cerebral cortex. The thalamic RAS activates specific portions of the cortex, which allows one to concentrate on certain mental activities. RAS stimulation of the hypothalamus activates many of the autonomic or involuntary control centers located in this area, such as cardiovascular regulation, body termperature control, eating, thirst, shivering, water conservation, excitement, and rage. The mesencephalon area of the RAS governs the arousal of the individual. When there are few or no input signals, the mesencephalon is dormant; however, an increase in stimuli causes arousal again. The stimulus can be in the form of a pain impulse from skin, proprioception from muscles, a visual signal from the eyes, or a physiological sensation, such as a cough.

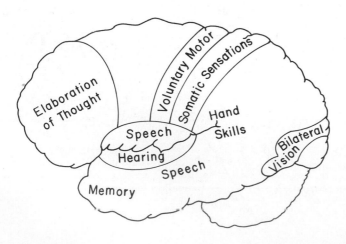

Figure 4–3. The functions of the cortex. Certain areas of the brain have been mapped according to their functions. (From: Penfield and Rasmussen: The Cerebral Cortex of Man: A Clinical Study of Localization of Function, New York, Macmillan Co; [Copyright 1950, renewal 1978 by Theodore Rasmussen.])

The function of the reticular formation can be summarized as follows:

- Reticular formation neurons exist physiologically.
- Reticular formation neurons are located at a strategic crossroad in the brain through which all incoming and outgoing messages must pass.
- The RAS is able to sample all neural activity.
- Activity in some portions of the RAS arouses the brain to a state of alertness and attention; the lack of activity in other portions of the RAS produces boredom, inactivity, and sleep.

## CONTROL OF STIMULI

At any one period of time, one is bombarded by stimuli in the form of light rays, visual images, sounds, muscle tension and proprioception of the body in space, internal and external temperature, the beat of the heart, and so on. There are literally millions of stimuli affecting the body from many sources and, if one were to respond to all of them, one would exhibit disorganized, chaotic, and ineffectual behavior. It is necessary to control the number of stimuli that reach the brain. One function of the RAS is to sample the sensory input messages and select those that will be given attention and meaning. The other 99 per cent or more of the incoming stimuli are blocked from reaching the cortex, and thus are not perceived. The RAS acts as a gate, allowing some impulses to pass through and preventing others from being perceived.

The precise mechanism that allows certain stimuli to pass through the RAS to the brain cortex and inhibits others is not known, but may be related to the concepts of adaptation, attention, and the "gate control theory." Adaptation is the process that involves the sensory receptors that respond rapidly to continued stimuli in the beginning, then progressively respond less rapidly and finally fade away. The rate at which adaptation occurs depends upon the type of sensory receptors, which range from those that adapt in a fraction of a second to those that probably never quite adapt to the stage of extinction. For example, olfactory receptors adapt rapidly; thus, odors quickly become extinct, whether from the fragrance of perfumes or from noxious odors. Hair cells in the cochlea of the ear also adapt rapidly. The familiar tick-tock of a clock is seldom noticed during the day when one is responding to larger, changing, or more intense stimuli. When first aboard, passengers on a plane hear the loud roar of the engines, but, soon after takeoff, the sound becomes monotonous and fades into the background. However, receptors in joints, muscles, and tendons adapt slowly and continue to transmit impulses to keep the brain aware of the position and status of the body.

An interesting theory that has gained some prominence in nursing in relation to the transmission of painful stimuli is the gate control

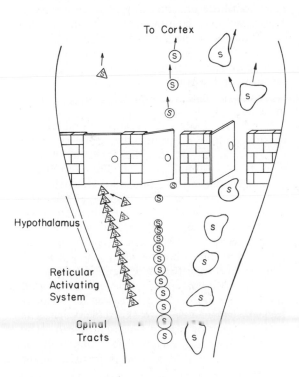

**Figure 4–4.** One way to illustrate selective "gating," or sampling, of stimuli in the RAS. The open gate, on the right, allows large and different types of stimuli to pass through to the cortex. The partially open gate, in the middle, allows some of the smaller or weaker stimuli to reach the cortex. The closed gate, on the left, blocks passage of all stimuli.

theory. According to the theory, pain sensations depend upon the activity of large and small nerve fibers carrying sensory messages from the skin to cells in the dorsal region of the spinal cord. The impulses of the large-diameter fibers excite the cells of the gating mechanism and inhibit the transmission of messages to the brain, while the small-diameter fibers keep the gate open even without stimulation.

This gating method of controlling stimuli can be demonstrated by pricking one's finger with a sharp object or by putting one's hand in hot water. Initially, one experiences a sharp, intense pain, followed, in a second or two by a duller, longer-lasting burning or aching pain. The gate control theory proposes that the intense stimulus activates many large fiber receptors and that their impulses rapidly go through the "gate" to produce the sensation of pain before shutting the gate behind them. Other slower impulses conducted over small fibers arrive at the spinal cord and open the gate to allow passage up the spinal cord, through the RAS, and to the cortex. Transcutaneous electrical nerve stimulation (TENS) is based on the gating theory and is used clinically to block pain sensations from peripheral nerves in selected patients. However, other factors may be involved, such as past experiences with pain, cultural attitudes, and other learned behaviors, which also modify the pain sensations.

Attention is the ability or power to concentrate mentally. It depends upon one's degree of wakefulness or arousal. One's degree of attention may vary from little or none, to general awareness of everything in the environment, to an intense concentration on a specific aspect of mental function. In other words, people have the ability to mentally focus on certain stimuli or on stored memories in the brain.

Control of incoming sensory stimuli may be influenced by a combination of any of these mechanisms. Different sensory impulses use specific pathways through the spinal cord and the reticular formation. When one tract is overloaded with stimuli, the impulses reverberate to parallel fibers and stimulate them. Attention and adaptation help to facilitate some incoming impulses and to inhibit others. Examples in everyday life that illustrate this process include being able to watch television and study at the same time and reading a book while listening to a rock concert. Christmas time at a busy shopping center can easily cause overload of the visual pathways and activate adjacent tracts as well, causing one to feel slight nausea or to experience changes in balance, resulting from the many movements and colors of the visual images. The inhibiting action occurs when one's attention is focused on the

many sights, flashing lights, and colorful displays, so that one does not realize that one has developed a blister on one's heel.

## PURPOSES OF SENSORY STIMULATION

For the greatest development of one's potential, one needs to be in contact with a rich and varied input of stimuli. Although everyone benefits from such variety, it is especially important for growing children. By responding to an abundance of stimuli of many kinds, they expand their ability to cope with a changing world.

**Benefits of Adequate Stimulation.**  Being exposed to and having experienced many stimuli provides the following advantages:

- *One learns to differentiate among many types of activities.* Some stimuli are like pebbles thrown into a pool and produce an expanding or ripple effect. Going to school involves more than walking into the classroom. It leads to a multitude of stimuli that are related to books, ideas and thoughts, relationships with teachers and other students, studying, examinations, and grades. Learning to be a nurse involves more than wearing a uniform and giving injections.

- *One learns to use many sensory modalities.* One's life is enriched by exposure to many experiences, such as taking ballet lessons, playing a musical instrument, playing tennis, eating foods from different cultures, or taking trips to museums. Even the simple act of swinging on a swing stimulates several senses: the feel of the rope and the seat of the swing, the proprioception of one's body as it swings out in a high arc and comes swiftly back, the view of the ground from the peak of the arc, and the exhilarating feeling of almost being free and flying.

- *One learns to use cues provided by the environment and to discern the relationship between cause and effect.* Dark clouds gathering in the sky are a clue that a storm is approaching. The evening news reports that cold weather has caused extensive damage to orange groves and lettuce crops. The result, or effect, will be fewer oranges and lettuce in the near future and prices will be higher owing to the short supply.

- *One learns to formulate more strategies to cope with events.* More options and ways of responding occur when one has multiple experiences with many varied circumstances. Nurses need continuous exposure to new patients to learn a variety of approaches in establishing the nurse-patient relationship. In much the same way, obtaining nourishment for the body's energy needs can be met in many ways other than growing the food oneself—food can be purchased from many stores in cans or frozen in packages; it can be prepared for meals at home or in a restaurant.

- *Varied sensory input provides opportunity for "trial and error" behavior.* A variety of stimuli and related responses enable one the freedom to pick and choose behavior(s) that works the best for him or her. Many situations exist in one's life in which there are no clear-cut responses. What might be the best way for the nurse to find out the fears of a patient or to respond to the patient who says "Get out. I don't want to be bothered now." The response to the latter situation is influenced by other stimuli, such as the time of day, the condition of the patient, the task to be done, the expectations of others that certain nursing care will be provided, and so on. One purpose of learning laboratory skills is to provide nursing students with an opportunity to use "trial and error" behavior as a method of learning.

**Disadvantages of Low Sensory Input.** Adequate sensory input is needed for the growth and development of the individual. Lack of adequate stimuli reduces a person's ability to function effectively; deprivation of sufficient stimuli results in death. Blockage of impulses travelling through over the conduction pathway in the heart leads to cardiac standstill. Even lack of affection in infants may lead to a progressive wasting condition called marasmus and to early death. Reduced amounts of sensory stimulation, although not resulting in death, cause the following disadvantages:

- *Reduced ability to discriminate.* Consider the child who receives only milk and cereal and does not learn to eat breads, meats, vegetables, and other combinations of foods. Unless one learns that these, too, are foods, one may spit them out and go hungry when not provided with one's usual milk and cereal. To one who lives in a warm climate where it never snows, the word "snow" refers to all cold, white material that falls on the ground in winter. However, the avid skier appreciates the differences among wet snow, powdery snow, icy snow, thick and heavy snow, and so on.
- *Lack of concentration and coherence.* Reduction of stimuli through the RAS produces a lack of attention and a state of lethargy. People who have reduced sensory input are less active and productive.
- *Tendency to use inferences to connect dis-*

*parate events.* Less learning occurs with reduced sensory stimulation, and more errors and misconceptions result from incomplete contact with the reality in the environment. For example, patients often assume that doctors and nurses are discussing them when talking in the corridor before entering their rooms and are not telling them everything. Children make many assumptions as they learn to respond to more input and to enlarge their knowledge of the world.

- *Decreased ability to manipulate one's environment to regain equilibrium or adaptation.* Decreased stimuli interfere with one's ability to think beyond the things that one can see or feel and to use ideas or thoughts to extend into the future. By developing responses to many stimuli, one can use these mental images and thoughts to change conditions when one is confronted with similar situations. The student who finds that his or her study load has become too much to handle may lack knowledge (previous related stimuli) of how to restructure the situation, such as by withdrawing from a course, reducing outside work commitments, changing family responsibilities, or rearranging study time. Poverty is a condition that reduces people's stimuli and alters their ability to change their environment. Child development centers and Head Start programs have been developed for children in low income neighborhoods in efforts to provide a wide variety of stimulating experiences to increase their ability to cope effectively with change.
- *Prevention of the development of attention, or selective "gating."* When only a limited number of stimuli are available, one pays attention to those that are available, and there is less opportunity to be selective. With reduced sensory stimulation, one becomes more aware of sensations that result from internal stimulation, such as the beating of the heart, the movement of the intestinal tract, or muscular twinges. Selective gating operates when two or more sensory tracts are stimulated, such as reading a book while the television or radio is on and not being distracted by the sound.

## ASSESSMENT OF SENSORY PERCEPTION

The sensory process involves the reception of a stimulus, the transmission of the impulse through the neural tract to the brain, activation of the RAS and the cortex, which then evokes a response.

The response is any action that occurs in the body—mental, emotional, verbal, or physical. In adaptation nursing, this response is known as a behavior.

## ASSESSMENT OF ADAPTATION

In the adaptation approach to nursing, nurses are concerned with the client's total response to changes in his or her internal or external environment. In an adaptive state, one exhibits behaviors that are within the normal, or accepted, range for adaptation. These are positive behaviors and contribute to one's integrity in all spheres of functioning and to one's comfort, welfare, and well-being. It is important that the nurse carry out a complete assessment of the client's behaviors to determine the adaptive state or the presence of a problem in coping in one or more of the modes (physiological, self-concept, role-function, or interdependence).

Illness or disease places the client somewhere on the illness end of the Health-Illness Continuum. (See Chapter One.) Behaviors that reduce the integrity or the functioning of the body are maladaptive and interfere with one's ability to cope with changes in the environment. Several maladaptive behaviors are closely associated with the disease process and are described in medical textbooks as signs or symptoms of the medical problem. As a result of the disease and one's location on the illness end of the Health-Illness Continuum, one may be unable to carry out normal activities or to cope with feelings effectively. Many ways of responding to changes in one's life exist, and probably, no two individuals would act the same way in similar situations.

Although the range of human behaviors is extensive and varies widely among individuals, it is possible to organize behaviors and, thus, reduce the complexity of their actions. External behavioral responses (those that can be seen, measured, or reported) can be broadly classified into the following categories:

1. *Attraction, or moving-toward behaviors.* Behaviors that are characterized by one who is approaching, seeking, or wanting more of the stimulus(i), being submissive, or by depending upon others for affection, assistance, or attention.

2. *Avoidance, or moving-away behaviors.* Flight, retreat, escape, and withdrawal behaviors used to avoid contact with further stimuli.

3. *Aggression, or moving-against behaviors.* To overcome, reduce or eliminate the stimulus(i), one uses anger, fighting, or competitive behavior.

4. *No overt action.* Although one perceives the meaning of the stimulus, one may elect not to respond to it.

In succeeding chapters, behavioral responses to sensory stimuli in the functions of the physiological, self-concept, and interdependence modes are described. Criteria for comparing behaviors, examples of coping problems, stimuli that cause or influence problems, and some nursing interventions are explained.

## ALTERATIONS IN SENSORY PERCEPTION

Several changes can occur in sensory perception, resulting in causes of or stimuli for behavioral problems in coping with one's environment. These alterations are described as sensory monotony, sensory distortion, sensory deprivation, and sensory overload. In some circumstances, nurses may state these alterations as the patient's problem rather than as the stimuli that cause the maladaptive behaviors. Although sensory deprivation may be used as a nursing diagnosis, it does not accurately illustrate how the patient is responding or behaving or how he or she is having difficulty in coping. Theoretically, alterations in sensory perception are changes in stimuli; thus, being the causes of behaviors, they are part of the second level assessment. Often the behaviors are similar but may be caused by different alterations in the stimuli. Therefore, it is important to assess the causes and the changes correctly in order to change the maladaptive behavior to adaptive behavior.

**Sensory Monotony.** Monotony is characterized by sameness and repetition of the patterning and the complexity of the stimuli. Everyone has experienced monotony at some time whether from the repeated ticking of a clock, to waiting in line for something, to the routine activities in one's daily life.

- *First Level Assessment:* Repeated and unchanged stimuli cause the behavioral responses of boredom, lack of interest, inactivity, lethargy, and sleepiness. They may be expressed verbally, through nonverbal expressions, by posture, and by reduced activity.
- *Second Level Assessment:* Causes include the sameness of the daily routine, lack of new stimuli, and stable, or nonchanging, conditions. Many jobs are of a routine nature and involve repeating the same steps over and over, often leading one to lose interest and to have feelings of boredom. This may happen to the mother who is at home caring for young children, to the electronic worker who is

soldering transistor terminals, and to long-term patients in hospitals.

- *Nursing Goal:* To change the behavioral responses to those related to increased interests and activities.
- *Nursing Interventions:* Manipulate the stimuli by introducing changes in the pattern, sequence, or routine. The client and nurse should plan together the changes that are to be made, based on the values, beliefs, and resources available to the client.

**Sensory Distortion.** An interference in the sensory process that occurs at the cortex leads to distortion of the incoming message. Thus, one interprets the message, from either internal or external sources, with a meaning that is distorted from the usual meaning. Sensory distortion is the result of disease or injury to the brain or to the sensory organs, such as the eyes or the ears.

- *First Level Assessment:* The client's behavior indicate that he has made errors in his observations of his surroundings or reality. He may have a shortened attention span and show fluctuations in his mental ability or functioning. Often, following a cerebral accident, patients have an inability to retain balance without assistance and neglect the affected side of the body. Some patients with hemiplegia also have defective vision, with half the visual field of each eye blocked out; thus, they are able to see only things on one side of the midline. Visual messages are also distorted in clients who have had cataracts removed. It is particularly difficult for them to judge distances accurately; thus, they often bump into objects.

  The statement of the problem will generally be related to one's inability to meet one's needs in one or more of the need areas or to cope effectively with one's feelings. The nurse might describe the problem as "Patient has decreased awareness of left side of body," "Client has difficulty judging distances accurately" or "Client has feelings of anxiety about loss of control of body."
- *Second Level Assessment:* Usually the direct result of a disease affecting the central nervous system, particularly the brain, or disruptions that involve the sensory organs of sight, sound, smell, taste, and touch. Diseases that are commonly associated with sensory distortion include cerebral vascular accidents, glaucoma, cataract extraction, Meniere's disease, and tumors of the brain. The nurse assesses for alterations in the structure or function of the organs that are involved.

- *Nursing Goal:* To increase the client's ability to interpret sensory messages and the reality of his world accurately.
- *Nursing Interventions:* Help the client to compensate for faulty perception or to increase the meaning of his or her sensory messages in a variety of ways. Manipulate the environment by simplifying the furnishings and by placing items in such a way as to encourage the use and awareness of the hemiplegic patient's neglected side. The client with visual distortion can be taught to scan objects in his or her surroundings. For other perceptual distortions, the use of cue cards may be helpful reminders of steps in a procedure or of a task that is to be performed. Colored markers or tags can be used to help designate things that go together or to indicate which is the right side, the "on" button, and so on.

**Sensory Deprivation.** The reception or perception of stimuli is lacking or blocked in sensory deprivation. There is repetition and decreased patterning and complexity of stimuli, leading to one of these three types of deprivation: (1) sensory underload, (2) relevance deprivation, or (3) altered reticular activating system.

As previously mentioned, sensory deprivation causes serious impairment of one's ability to cope with changes. The amount of stimulation that is required for optimum functioning varies from one individual to another; however, stimulation that is below one's level for optimum functioning leads to deterioration in behavior. Fortunately, when sensory stimulation is restored to adequate levels, people tend to recover from deprivation of stimuli within a short period of time.

- *First Level Assessment:* Behaviors include lowered or delayed response, reduced ability to concentrate and to think coherently, increased amount of time spent daydreaming, and occasional hallucinations. The client may experience moderate to high levels of anxiety and fail to recognize dangers to his safety. Withdrawal, or moving-away, type of behaviors may be seen, such as boredom and inactivity. Depression, confusion, and disorientation commonly occur.

  Patients who are deprived of visual input often show disturbed behavior, sometimes in just a matter of hours. They may have somatic complaints, feel like they are floating or being detached from their bodies, become disoriented, or lose their ability to comply with instructions, such as staying in bed or leaving their dressings in place. Patients who are deaf and even those who are hard of hearing have difficulty communicating their needs, which tends to isolate them from other people and to increase behavior that is related to confusion, agitation, and anxiety.

- *Second Level Assessment:* During the 1950s, preparations for space exploration and its effects on the astronauts stimulated research into sensory deprivation. Many conditions that reduced sensory stimulation and caused the behavioral changes just described were found. Weightlessness and immobility reduce tactile stimuli significantly. Isolation from other people and a nonchanging environment lead to monotony and deprivation. Institutions that restrict or control behavior, such as hospitals and prisons, and some aspects of military service, may reduce sensory input below one's adaptive level. Studies have been carried out that indicate that infants and small children show deprivation effects when isolated in incubators or in life-support systems but that they become more active and alert in that same environment when provided with added stimuli, such as cuddling, touching, talking, and providing colorful play objects, from their caretakers.

  Patients in hospitals are particularly prone to the effects of sensory deprivation. Many diseases occur in sensory organs or alter their function and reduce the number of incoming stimuli. This is prevalent in diseases of the eyes and ears. People who have difficulty seeing or hearing receive fewer cues from their surroundings and less information from others to help them cope with changes. In elderly patients, sensory perception and response is slower, and, when coupled with anxiety about their health, it is probably responsible for much of the disturbed behavior that occurs in this age group. Pain and the use of drugs that depress the central nervous system, such as narcotics, sedatives, tranquilizers, analgesics, and anesthetics, also reduce sensory stimulation. Intensive care units interfere with adequate sensory stimulation for both young and elderly people when there is constant use of artificial lights, constant noise from machines, and repetitive procedures that interrupt one's rest and sleep. Lack of sleep, particularly the REM or dreaming state of sleep, has an injurious effect on one's behavior.
- *Nursing Goal:* To change the behavior by increasing the amount and the variety of stimuli to an adequate level for adaptation.
- *Nursing Interventions:* Numerous methods that increase sensory stimulation are available and can be tailored to the needs of the indi-

vidual patient. Personal contact with the patient is very effective when the nurse uses goal-directed conversation as a focus for the patient's thoughts, validates reality, orients the patient to time and place, and gives information or reference points for measuring the progress toward recovery. Clocks, calendars, radios, television sets, and physical exercises are used to increase sensory input. Autostimulation is effective for some patients, who are encouraged to hum, sing, or whistle in order to set up a feedback loop between the RAS and the cortex. For the hard-of-hearing client, pictures of common articles, the use of large print to relieve the stress of visual overload, making eye contact when talking with him, and the use of simple words when speaking or writing messages are effective approaches.

**Sensory Overload.** The bombardment of one or more senses with stimuli causes excessive stimulation of the brain. It is thought that sensory overload overwhelms the gating process, by which the brain selectively responds to stimuli. As a result, there is a more intense response to impulses and a disorganizing effect on behavior. Less intense stimuli are ignored or crowded out, resulting in a type of sensory deprivation. Many behaviors associated with sensory overload are similar to those of sensory deprivation.

- *First Level Assessment:* Behaviors associated with confusion or decreased alertness, loss of direction, distractability, decreased understanding, changes in the thought process, inappropriate decisions and orientation to reality, and hallucinations. Frequently, the individual has somatic complaints of headache, nausea and vomiting, and dizziness.
- *Second Level Assessment:* Results from severe irritability of the sensory receptors in diseases such as Meniere's disease and acute labrynthitis. Excessive sensory stimulation is also associated with busy, noisy, bright, and active surroundings, such as a busy shopping center, a popular rock concert, or an amusement park. In the hospital setting, overload may occur in patients who are in the intensive care unit and who experience severe pain, frequent interruptions, and a change in their pattern, or routine, for sleep and activities of daily living.
- *Nursing Goal:* To reduce the number of stimuli being received by the client by manipulation of the causes, when possible.
- *Nursing Interventions:* The plan of care is based on methods that are used to decrease the number of stimuli or one's perception of

them, including removal or change of the noxious stimuli in the environment, such as noise, lights, movements, drafts, and odors. Interventions include measures for the relief of pain or discomfort, promoting rest or sleep, and providing for the safety of the disturbed patient. Reality orientation and the use of insight therapy to reduce anxiety are other effective measures that may help the patient understand what is happening.

## SUMMARY

Everyone needs adequate sensory perception to be able to grow and develop into an integrated person who is able to adapt and adjust to one's changing world. Adequate sensory input varies among individuals; what may be sufficient for one may not be enough for another. One's sensory perception depends upon an intact nervous system to receive the stimulation and a functioning reticular activating system to transmit the message to the brain cortex, where it is given meaning and a response is initiated. The response to the stimulus is a behavior that may be in the form of a body sensation, a motor activity, a verbal statement, or a mental thought or feeling.

The behaviors exhibited by the patient are the first focus of the nurse in the assessment of adaptation. Although one maladaptive behavior does not necessarily constitute a problem for the patient, it should alert the nurse to the possibility of a problem and suggest related areas of function to assess carefully. A spasm of coughing may be short and nonrecurring but should alert the nurse to the possibility of a respiratory infection or obstruction. Illness often causes a disturbance in the sensory process and in many behavioral responses seen in patients. Types of sensory changes associated with illness and hospitalization include sensory monotony, sensory distortion, sensory deprivation, and sensory overload. The overall result of these sensory changes is one's decreased awareness of what is real or meaningful and a state of confusion. Confusion causes behaviors that are in conflict with what others perceive or expect one to have.

Many causes or influencing factors for the incongruent behaviors assessed in patients exist. In the second level assessment, the nurse searches for the stimuli that produce or affect the behavior. In the hospital patient, the disease itself reduces the input of the sensory organs, or is accompanied by pain, which commands attention and "gates" out perception of other stimuli. Other factors that must be considered are medications that depress the brain and cloud perception, unfamiliar tests and procedures that threaten one's body images, such as catheters and nasogastric tubes, strangers sharing a room, disturbance of one's routine with the imposition of an unfamiliar routine, and repeated contact with strangers including doctors, nurses, and various technicians, who provide therapy or services.

In providing care for the patient with altered sensory perception, the nursing goal is to increase the patient's awareness of reality and to reduce confused or inappropriate responses. This is done by nursing interventions that manipulate the stimuli causing the problem. The nurse changes the amount, the type, or the complexity of the patient's sensory input through a variety of ways. Effective methods include making adjustments in the patient's surroundings, restoring or using familiar objects and routines when possible, and using available support systems, such as one's family, friends, clergy, and other health care providers. The effectiveness of the nursing interventions is measured by further assessment, which indicates that the patient is more alert, is interested in his or her surroundings, and is responding in an adaptive way.

## REFERENCES

Barnett, Dale, and Hair, Barbara: Use and effectiveness of transcutaneous electrical nerve stimulation in pain management. J Neurosurg Nurs, V13:6:323–325, (December) 1981.

Blancher, Gertrude: My trip through the semicircular canals. Am J Nurs, 74:1742–1743, (October) 1974.

Brown, Evan, and Deffenbacher, Kenneth: Perception and the Senses. New York, Oxford University Press, Inc., 1979, pp. 71–73.

Burt, Margaret M.: Perceptual deficits in hemiplegia. Am J Nurs, 70:1026–1029, (May) 1970.

Carlson, Neil R.: Physiology of Behavior, 2nd ed. Boston, Allyn and Bacon, Inc., 1981.

Chodil, Judith, and Williams, Barbara: The concept of sensory deprivation. Nurs Clin North Am, 5:453–465, (September) 1970.

Downs, Florence: Bedrest and sensory disturbances. Am J Nurs, 74:434–438, (March) 1974.

Ellis, Rosemary: Unusual sensory and thought disturbances after cardiac surgery. Am J Nurs, 72:2021–2025, (November) 1972.

Guyton, Arthur: The Textbook of Medical Physiology, 6th ed. Philadelphia, W. B. Saunders Company, 1981, pp. 671–683.

Herth, Kaye: Beyond the curtain of silence. Am J Nurs, 74:1060–1061, (June) 1974.

Knicely, Kathryn: The world of distorted perception. Am J Nurs, 67:999–1001, (May) 1967.

Kroner, Kristine: Dealing with the confused patient. Nursing 79, 9:71–78, (November) 1979.

Luckmann, Joan, and Sorensen, Karen: Medical-Surgical Nursing: A Psychosocial Approach. Philadelphia, W. B. Saunders Company, 1980.

Maslow, Abraham: Motivation and Personality, 2nd ed. New York, Harper & Row Publishers, Inc., 1970, pp. 34–40.

Meinhart, Noreen, and Aspinal, Mary Jo: Nursing interventions in hypovigilance. Am J Nurs, *69*:994–1000, (May) 1969.

Meyer, Theresa: TENS, relieving pain through electricity. Nursing 82, *12*:(9):57–59, (September) 1982.

Morris, M., and Rhodes, M.: Guidelines for the care of confused patients. Am J Nurs, *72*:1630, (September) 1972.

Murray, Ruth: Assessment of psychological status of surgical ICU patients. Nurs Clin North Am, *10*:69–81, (March) 1975.

Ohno, Mary: The eye-patched patient. Am J Nurs, *71*: 271–274, (February) 1971.

Perron, Denise: Deprived of sound. Am J Nurs, *74*: 1057–1059, (June) 1974.

Pontius, Sharon: Practical Piaget: helping children understand. Am J Nurs, *82*:114–117, (January) 1982.

Smith, Joan, and Nachazel, Delbert: Retinal detachment. Am J Nurs, *73*:1530–1535, (September) 1973.

Solomon, Philip, et al. (eds.): Sensory Deprivation. Cambridge, MA, Harvard University Press, 1965.

Thomson, Linda: Sensory deprivation: a personal experience. Am J Nurs, *73*:266–268, (February) 1973.

Wolff, Witzel, and Fuerst: Fundamentals of Nursing, 6th ed. Philadelphia, J. B. Lippincott Co., 1979.

Zubek, J. P. (ed.): Sensory Deprivation: Fifteen Years of Research. New York, Appleton-Century-Crofts, 1969.

# Chapter FIVE

# Understanding Behavior

---

BEHAVIOR PATTERNS
   *PRINCIPLES OF BEHAVIOR*
       *PATTERNS*
   *MOVING-TOWARD BEHAVIOR*
     *Interventions*
   *MOVING-AWAY BEHAVIOR*
     *Interventions*

   *MOVING-AGAINST BEHAVIOR*
     *Interventions*
TRANSACTIONAL ANALYSIS
APPLICATION TO CLINICAL PRACTICE

---

**OBJECTIVES** Information in this chapter will help you to

1. Identify behavior and classify it into one of the three basic patterns of behavior.
2. Describe the three basic patterns of behavior (moving-toward, moving-away, and moving-against) and the types of responses elicited by each.
3. Explain the approach used with each basic behavior pattern.
4. State the ways in which time is structured in the theory of transactional analysis.
5. Describe the three "ego states" individuals use as responses in interactions with others.

---

The adaptation approach to nursing is based on the assessment of the individual's behavior. An inexperienced nurse may feel overwhelmed when faced with the task of assessing behavior because every voluntary action, every statement, and every physiological function is considered a behavior. Many questions arise as the inexperienced nurse contemplates this task: "What do I do with all this information?" "Which of these behaviors are maladaptive?" "How do I tell what is adaptive and what is not, or is it a subjective judgment that one makes?" "What do I do if the patient doesn't like me or refuses to cooperate with the care I had planned to give?"

From observations and studies, we know that behavior is a universal response of all living beings and that behavior is dynamic or fluid and is capable of constantly changing or adjusting. Wide ranges of behavior are possible as people respond to situations in life and carry out the expectations of society. However, the nurse needs to classify and organize behavior in a way that will allow it to be better understood and to be dealt with in a more meaningful way. No two people respond in exactly the same way to the same illness, or share the same feelings about being ill. The nurse

must be able to adjust to these differences in people in order to provide effective nursing care that meets the needs of the individual. The approach used to provide nursing care to the quiet, withdrawn patient is different from the approach used to help the complaining patient who is irritated by everything and everybody. Nurses who have persisted in approaching all patients in the same way and who expect all patients to respond in the same way have had difficulties in the nurse-patient relationship with the patient who deviated from their expectations. These patients were labelled as being difficult, uncooperative, complainers or perhaps even worse.

Behaviors that fall in the normal, adaptive range and examples of maladaptive behaviors that are commonly associated with a particular problem or need area are described throughout this book. These behaviors form the standards, or norms, that the nurse uses as the criteria for the classification of behaviors as adaptive or maladaptive. In the physiological mode, the standard, or normal, range of various body functions such as temperature, pulse rate, blood sugar level, joint movements, and composition of urine form the criteria for the assessment of behavior as adaptive or maladaptive. In the role-function, self-concept, and interdependence modes, voluntary behavior (the way that people learn to respond to changes in their environment) forms the criteria for assessing behavior. The range of behaviors that are acceptable to society includes those behaviors that are appropriate to the circumstance. These behaviors constitute the adaptive range of behavior.

In this chapter, the three basic behavioral patterns are described. These behavioral patterns are used by everyone in response to changes in their environment. According to the theory of sensory perception, responses to stimuli are attraction to, avoidance of, or attacking the stimulus. These responses form the basic behavioral patterns. These behavior patterns combined with information about the emotional tone of the interaction in the ego states of transactional analysis help the nurse to understand behavior, to assess its meaning, and to structure and intervene appropriately to help patients meet their needs.

## BEHAVIOR PATTERNS

As previously discussed, man responds to stimuli from the environment; these responses are called behaviors. A behavior is any action of the body that can be observed, perceived, or measured. Purposeful voluntary behavior refers to a response that has been consciously made, and is regarded as a coping mechanism. Although one may see many types of behavior resulting from environmental stimuli, there are basically only three different patterns of behavior, or ways to respond. All assessed behaviors can be classified according to one of these three behavioral patterns:

1. Moving-toward behavior — attraction toward the stimuli
2. Moving-away behavior — avoidance of or being repelled by the stimuli
3. Moving-against behavior — aggression or attacking the stimuli to master or control them

(Lazarus [1966] includes a fourth category: denial, or no response to the stimuli.)

The following example illustrates these three behavior patterns. A psychology teacher assigns a theme on a certain topic and announces that the theme is due on Friday. Students respond to the assignment (stimulus) with many different behaviors, but each student exhibits only one of the three behavioral patterns. Bill goes to the library after class and begins to gather reference materials for the theme and discusses his ideas with his friend. Craig shows little interest in writing the theme because he doesn't like the class and

does not think that he would get a good grade on it anyway. Besides, he is on the football team and has to practice for the game this weekend. Linda wants to do well, so she talks with the teacher after class to find out exactly what information the teacher wants included in the theme. She phones her best friend to ask for her help in finding material to write about. Bill's behavior is an adaptive moving-against pattern of behavior, Craig's behavior is a moving-away pattern of behavior, and Linda's behavior is a moving-toward pattern of behavior.

During illness, when trying to cope with their feelings about what is happening to them, patients respond with the same three patterns of behavior. When they feel successful, the coping mechanism that they use and the pattern of behavior that they exhibit are positive and adaptive, but when patients do not feel successful, coping problems develop. Their behavior does not meet their needs and may interfere with medical or nursing care or impede recovery. Hagerman (1968) described ways in which nurses can deal effectively with behavior problems associated with each pattern.

## *PRINCIPLES OF BEHAVIOR PATTERNS*

When assessing patients' behaviors in order to identify particular behavior patterns, one should remember the following principles:

1. Everyone responds to stimuli in one of three ways: attraction toward the stimulus, avoidance of the stimulus, or attacking the stimulus.
2. No behavior pattern is better than another. All behavior patterns are valuable and are adaptive ways of coping with stimuli.
3. Only one behavior pattern is used at a time, but the pattern used may vary from one situation to another. For example, the worker who is quiet and downcast when criticized by the supervisor, and then goes home and kicks the dog uses two different behavioral patterns; but, only one at a time.
4. One behavior does not make a pattern or cause a problem. An isolated action has less meaning than repetitive or continuing behaviors that persist over a period of time.
5. An adaptive behavior pattern is one that is appropriate to the situation and leads to a positive response that enhances the integrity, or the wholeness, of the individual. For example, during the second stage of illness, it is appropriate for patients to be dependent upon others and to focus their attention on what is happening to

them, but these behaviors become less appropriate as patients progress into the third stage of illness.

6. One behavior pattern tends to become more dominant and, thus, is used more frequently than other behavior patterns. People tend to use the behavior pattern that is the most effective for them in achieving their aims. This behavior pattern becomes a part of their personality.

## MOVING-TOWARD BEHAVIOR

In terms of adaptation, the moving-toward pattern of behavior is used by individuals in their search for attention, affection, and assistance from various sources in the environment. As individuals explore their world and expand their experiences, they are attracted to stimuli that will help them to meet their dependency needs and that will promote their growth and development into mature and independently functioning adults. The role of the student or learner is an example of this type of behavior. The student ventures into the realm of the strange or the unknown and seeks assistance, guidance, or attention from others.

Patients often exhibit this behavior pattern when they are confronted with things they cannot do for themselves and need help from others to meet these dependency needs. The exhibited

behaviors are adaptive when they are appropriate to the situation and lead to a healthier state. The exhibited behavior is maladaptive when it is inappropriate for the circumstances or impedes the return to a healthier state. For example, Mrs. H. was hospitalized for treatment of varicose veins but now refuses to eat. Her problem is not one of being physically unable to eat or to feed herself but rather a problem of coping with her feelings that have arisen from the self-concept or the interdependence modes.

Typically, patients who use moving-toward behaviors make numerous requests, both verbal and nonverbal, of the nursing staff. The patient's dependency needs can be shown by a number of behaviors, including behaviors that are not immediately obvious, such as keeping the nurses engaged in interesting social conversations, as well as behaviors that are obvious, such as using the call light incessantly, calling to people as they walk past the door, and so on. Increased dependency needs are inevitable during the second stage of illness, in children who are ill, and in the aged population as their physical strength and resources decline. The behavior pattern is more appropriate in these circumstances and may be adaptive for meeting their needs.

**Interventions.** Nursing interventions suggested

**Figure 5–1.** "Moving-toward" behavior. Attracted to the stimuli.

for patients with maladaptive moving-toward behavior include these features:

1. *Support patients' dependency needs until they are able to move toward greater independence.* The need will continue to exist until the stimuli that are causing it are changes. Trying to force patients to be more independent cannot succeed while dependency needs are stronger, but may lead to additional coping problems. This leads to tension between the patient and the nurse and results in anger and further misunderstanding.

2. *Develop a trust relationship.* Patients need to feel that they can count on the nurse for help and to understand their point of view and their needs. The use of the nursing process and assessing behavior help to develop a relationship of trust. The nurse works cooperatively with the patient to identify potential and actual problem areas and to plan the care. To foster the trust relationship, the nurse follows through with any actions that are planned or with any commitment that is made.

3. *Help patients make decisions about their care.* When patients' dependency needs are greatest, as in the second stage of illness, the nurse provides total care, without any reservations, and transmits the message to patients that they are in good hands, that they are worthy of the care that they are receiving, and that the nurse is present to attend to their needs. As their self-esteem rises, patients are encouraged to begin to perform simple tasks and are praised for their efforts. Each independent behavior represents a decision made by the patient to actively do something rather than to passively depend upon others.

4. *Establish limits for dependency behaviors as may be appropriate.* As the nurse manipulates the stimuli that cause the behaviors, it may be necessary for the nurse and the patient to establish boundaries that indicate which behaviors are out-of-bounds, or are not tolerated. For example, an agreement is made that the teen-ager's crying and whining requests are outside the limits of acceptable dependent behavior, and that the nurse will ignore these requests, responding only to requests that are made in a calm tone of voice.

5. *Deal with the interventions and procedures one at a time, proceeding from the simple to the complex.* The goal of getting the patient to ambulate without assistance can be accomplished more effectively if the task is divided into several steps: (1) raise the head of the bed, (2) allow the patient to dangle the legs over the side of the bed for a few minutes, (3) allow the patient to stand to gain balance before walking to a chair, and (4) after a short rest, encourage the patient to take a longer walk.

## MOVING-AWAY BEHAVIOR

One can easily see how this pattern of behavior is used by people during illness. People would like to avoid, ignore, or run away from the stimuli that are associated with sickness and hospitalization. Notice how people turn their heads away when blood is drawn, emit little sighs or moans when told that the test result was abnormal, or show signs of resignation when the nurse gives another in a succession of injections.

This pattern of behavior may be maladaptive when patients are quiet and withdrawn, are reluctant to enter into conversations or even to respond to others, and avoid interacting with the nurse, visitors, or things in the environment. Avoidance behaviors indicate the reluctance, or even the fear, of the patient to accept help or attention from others when it is necessary or appropriate. Nurses and other people who are interested in helping the patient are discouraged by the patient's turning away and lack of conversation. Many then fail to offer the assistance and support that the patient needs.

This behavior pattern is used by some men who think that illness is incompatible with their perceptions of the male role and that being dependent on others is a sign of weakness. Their needs to be independent and strong override their need for help when ill. Other people may use moving-away behavior to mask feelings of anger and depression that they fear would result in uncontrolled rage or socially unacceptable consequences if expressed directly.

**Interventions.** Nursing approaches and interventions suggested for patients with moving-away behavior include the following:

1. *Identify ways to offer assistance without waiting to be asked.* Many patients are unwilling to ask for help, but if they have to do without assistance when it is need, this problem adds to the feelings of anger, unworthiness, or inadequacy they already have. The nursing plan of care should anticipate problems and need areas that have been identified through the use of the nursing process.

2. *Encourage patients' dependency needs before allowing them to move toward independence, if necessary.* It may be appropriate to give a patient a complete bath followed by application of lotion, or to spend more time with patients until they are able to enter into activities or interact with others. Some patients may benefit from having one staff member assigned to their care. It may be necessary to follow some patients' routines, or habitual ways of doing things, until they indicate that it is all right to vary or to deviate from their rigid routine. For example, 7-year-old Joey had burns over his chest and upper body.

Figure 3–2. "Moving-away" behavior. Withdrawal, or repelled by the stimuli.

He yelled and screamed whenever a new nurse came into the room to take care of him. He would cry and repeatedly say, "Go away, go away. No, don't touch me! I want Mary. Where is Mary?" The team leader looked beyond the crying and recognized Joey's dependency needs and his pattern of behavior as moving away from the stimuli, signifying changes in his environment. Mary was assigned to care for him until he could willingly accept contact and care by others.

3. *Use simple, concrete, and nonthreatening language when communicating with the patient.* Explain procedures simply. Avoid statements or making demands that could be perceived as threatening in any way. When the moving-away pattern of behavior is maladaptive, it indicates problems in the self-concept or interdependence modes that could be aggravated by aggressive or threatening actions by others.

4. *Show an interest in the patient as a person.* A complete assessment of adaptation, and the use of the nursing process to plan care is an excellent tool. It is often helpful to stay with these patients for a period of time, even if you only sit silently at the bedside. The nurse's physical presence conveys a message to withdrawn patients that they are not being avoided or abandoned.

5. *Plan activities to increase patients' involvement with the environment.* Diversions should be varied, colorful, and of a noncompetitive nature.

## MOVING-AGAINST BEHAVIORS

Responses to the aggressive drives inherent in people are classified as moving-against behaviors. Children are taught from infancy to curb and to control their aggressive behavior and to express themselves in socially acceptable ways. This type of behavior pattern is associated with growing independence and productivity and is characterized by meeting the challenge of the stimuli, conquering or surmounting obstacles, controlling or managing events, and being aggressive and assertive. Adaptive behaviors are socially acceptable and appropriate for the situation. Maladaptive behavior indicates a failure in coping with the stimuli and is expressed by feelings of anger or hostility.

Many patients who are labeled as "difficult" or "complainers" exhibit maladaptive aggressive behaviors. They make many complaints about their care or the lack of care, about the way a nurse on another shift treats them, that the food is cold and not fit to eat, that the other nurse does not know anything or care about people, and so on. These behaviors indicate that these patients have problems coping in one of the psychosocial modes.

**Interventions.** Nursing approaches and interventions for patients with moving-against behavior include the following guidelines:

1. *Remain objective when the patient expresses anger or hostility.* This is often difficult to do when patients make accusations and say things such as "You don't know anything," or "You aren't any better than the others; you don't care." Some things that can help the nurse to remain objective are to remember that: (1) the

patient probably would have said the same thing to anyone who came into the room, (2) the patient's statements often have no relationship to what the nurse has or has not done, and (3) the patient is expressing feelings that are real. The behavior represents efforts to cope with these feelings, and the nurse should seek to determine the cause or reason for the behavior.

2. *Listen for clues that explain the patient's feelings, if the patient has difficulty in expressing them directly.* On occasion, patients may become so angry that it is difficult for them to focus their attention on the stimulus that is causing the distress. One effective way to encourage communication is to acknowledge that they are feeling the emotion that they are expressing. In a calm manner, the nurse might say to the patient, "You seem very angry about something. Can you tell me about it?" or "Something seems to have upset you. What happened?"

3. *Do a second level assessment to find out the cause of the behavior and to help the patient recognize the cause of these feelings.* Allow the patient to express feelings and to talk about the situation; however, do not stop at this point. Use insight therapy and continue with the nursing process to take some positive actions with the patient to reduce the problem and to find more effective ways of coping.

4. *Reduce the frustrating elements in the environment.* When the stimuli and the influencing factors have been identified by the second level assessment, intervene to reduce or eliminate the stimuli and the factors that affect the coping problem. This may involve transferring the patient to a quieter room or changing roommates or even such a simple action as shielding the patient from glaring lights.

5. *Be dependable and reliable and keep any promises that you make.* It is important to foster and to promote trusting relationships with patients who use this type of behavior pattern.

It is important to remember the principles that no one uses one type of behavior pattern exclusively, nor is each pattern used equally, and that only one behavior pattern is used at a time. Most of the time, the behavior patterns are adaptive ways of coping with stimuli. They are maladaptive only when the coping mechanism is ineffective to maintain the positive responses that contribute to health and integrity, or adaptation.

**Figure 5–3.**   "Moving-against" behavior. Attacking or conquering the stimuli.

# TRANSACTIONAL ANALYSIS

In the adaptation approach to nursing, transactional analysis provides another tool for the nurse to use to analyze interpersonal relationships between the patient or client and others, to identify problem areas, and to intervene more effectively in order to help the patient or client reach a more adapted state.

Transactional analysis is the method used to examine the ongoing exchanges, both verbal and nonverbal, that take place between two or more persons. It was developed by Berne during the 1950s, based on the theory that the human organism has a stimulus-hunger as well as a food-hunger and that both must be satisfied in order to survive. The stimulus-hunger prompts the seeking of physical contact with others and recognition of the person as an individual. Berne (1964) views a "stroke" as any act implying recognition of another's presence and as the fundamental unit of social action. Berne states that everyone needs stroking. The learning that occurs in a person is behavior that has been reinforced by strokes or stroking.

Transactional analysis also includes how people structure their time in order to get recognition from others. People spend time in six different ways.

1. **Intimacy** — the open and honest exchange of feelings with another in the area of love and trust, without fears or exploitation.

2. **Game-playing** — a set of recurring transactions with a concealed motive or "payoff." Games are used as a means of getting recognition while avoiding intimacy or responsibility. They may be serious but are regulated by rules.

3. **Activities** — acts that result in work, productivity, recreation, hobbies, and so on.

4. **Rituals** — programmed and sterotyped transactions that avoid intimacy. The habits of getting up in the morning, getting dressed, and eating breakfast are ritualistic transactions. The ritual of greeting another person provides strokes through the exchange of "Hello" "How are you?" and "Fine, thanks," but it avoids being more intimate or disclosing true feelings.

5. **Pastimes** — transactions that are superficial social exchanges and represent nonthreatening behavior to get through the day. Pastimes are a form of game in which there is mutual stroking, as well as a basis for forming acquaintances. Pastime transactions include comparing cars, discussing sports, asking how much something costs or if someone has ever been to such and such a place, and so on.

6. **Withdrawal** — seeking solitude through daydreaming, fantasy, sleeping, use of alcohol or drugs, illness, or mental illness.

The varied ways in which people structure their time depend upon a number of psychological factors. These factors have been called "ego states" and represent behaviors associated with the Parent, the Adult, and the Child in each of us.

*The Parent* — reflects the ideas, feelings, and behavior of one's parents. This behavioral state is both nurturing and sympathetic, as well as critical and opinionated. The Parent uses words such as "should" and "ought to" and sets down rules.

*The Adult* — deals with facts and verifiable information and is the data processor, in an objective way. The Adult is the problem-solver; the vocabulary centers on the key words of "who," "what," "when," "where," "why," and "how."

*The Child* — involves the ego state of the natural child, which is one of curiosity, enjoyment, creativity, frustration, rejection, despair, and rage. The Child has adapted or learned to get along with the parents by being good and eager to please or by teasing, pouting, or using other types of behavior to get attention.

The Parent, the Adult, and the Child are present in each of us, and our behavior, at any given time, reflects one of them. We are also able to shift from one to the other with considerable ease. Typical interactions between doctors, nurses, and patients illustrate some of these ego states.

Nurse: "Well, I see you are ready to go to surgery. Good luck. We'll see you later." (Parent)
Patient: "Are you sure it will be allright? I don't know. Maybe I won't be coming back here." (Child)
Nurse: "Sure you will. Everything will be just fine. Don't you worry." (Parent)

Doctor: "What kind of night did Mr. J. have? We had to do some pretty extensive surgery on him yesterday." (Adult)
Nurse: "Well, he slept at intervals and had medication for pain twice. About 0230, he threw some PVCs, but he has had a normal sinus rhythm since then. His temperature is 37.4° C. this morning, and his blood pressure is 122 over 60." (Adult)

Nurse: "Mrs. K., what are you doing up? You know your doctor ordered you to be on bed rest." (Parent)
Patient: "I wanted to get my nail polish. I don't see why I have to stay in bed, anyway. I'm feeling good now." (Child)
Nurse: "I would have gotten your polish for you. It's important that you stay in bed for a few more days in order not to put more strain on your heart." (Parent)

Patient: "Well, I suppose I've got to do what you say. I just get so tired of lying here." (Child)

Nurse: "You haven't finished your charting yet." (Adult)

Nursing assistant (might respond in either of these ways):

"I was just about to get to it now that I've finished making the last bed." (Adult)

"Wouldn't it be great to have one of those new computers do the charting for us? Just push the button, and it's all done." (Child)

All three ego states are important in our interactions with others and are used by everyone at one time or another. Even though it would seem that the Child behaviors are childlike and unsure, Child to Child transactions are the most fun producing; Adult to Adult transactions are able to accomplish the most business; and the Parent to Child transactions are the most nurturing and tend to be the most critical. The Parent to Child transactions also allow for many automatic or routine responses, such as "That's the way it's done."

Communications break down when the transactions become crossed and no longer are complementary or follow the expected course or outcome, as is shown in the following example:

Nurse A: "You will be getting an admission to Room 306. Her name is Mrs. H. She has congestive heart failure and is receiving oxygen." (Adult)

Nurse B: "How come they admit all the patients to my team? I've got such a headache now; I'm going to go home." (Child)

Notice how Nurse B has effectively blocked communications with Nurse A. In order to continue the interaction, Nurse A is forced to try some other way. Her Child might respond in this way, "You might as well go home since you're not of much help around here." Her Parent response might be, "The other nurses have had some admissions today, too. Why don't you take something for your headache, and then I'll help you to admit her. Okay?"

The adaptation approach to nursing and the use of the nursing process to resolve the problems that patients have in meeting their needs and in coping foster the Adult to Adult transaction between nurse and patient. The nurse also recognizes the dependence needs of patients during illness and is able to effectively use the Parent ego state, with its nurturing and concern, for the patients' safety and welfare.

## APPLICATION TO CLINICAL PRACTICE

The behavior patterns discussed in this chapter provide a framework for organizing and provide understanding of the behavior of patients, coworkers, and others. The basic behavior patterns provide a general indication of how the individual is responding to stimuli, and approaches that the nurse can use effectively for each behavior pattern are described. Read the following case; then answer the questions.

Mrs. La D. was admitted a week ago with abdominal pain and distention. The diagnostic work-up indicated a mass in the splenic flexure of the colon, which was removed five days ago. Since surgery, she has been quiet, speaks only when necessary, uses monosyllables like 'yes' or 'no,' has a flat tone to her voice, and avoids making any eye contact with the nurses. She

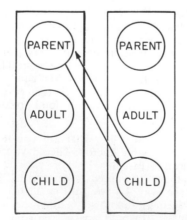
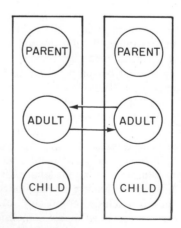

**Figure 5–4.** Complementary responses of ego states as used in transactional analysis. Parent to child and child to parent interactions accomplish many routine and expected responses. Adult to adult interactions result in more productivity and objectivity.

makes no complaints, takes most of her own baths, and sits in the chair while the nurse makes her bed. She is alone most of the time, except when it is necessary to provide her daily care or treatments.

What type of behavior is Mrs. La D. using? In what way is it interfering with her care or treatment? What kind of approach should the nurse use with patients like Mrs. La D.?

Your answers should indicate that she is exhibiting a moving-away pattern of behavior and that it is interfering with her care since it limits the relationship between the nurse and the patient. Nursing actions that may be effective include anticipating her needs or offering help to her without waiting to be asked, encouraging her to be dependent during this period of her illness, using simple concrete and nonthreatening language, showing an interest in her as a person, carrying out a complete assessment of all modes, spending time with her, and involving her in activities that stimulate her interest in her environment.

As you care for patients in the clinical setting, assess their patterns of behavior, state your plan of action or approach, and carry it out. Note the results.

We all know that behavior includes emotions and feelings. The way people respond in any given situation depends upon how they learned to respond as a child, how they saw their parents respond, and how they were influenced by them and their own adult ways of processing information objectively and factually. We all have the Parent, the Adult, and the Child in our psycho-logical make-up and use one or another of them in our interactions with others. When working with a patient in the clinical setting, select an interaction and analyze your responses and the patient's responses in terms of the ego states. What ego response did you make? What will happen if the patients response were that of the Parent? When you use your Adult and present objective information, does the patient respond with his or her Adult?

During much of their illness, patients are dependent upon nurses and others to assist them in meeting their needs. Which of the transactions would the nurse use most frequently during this time to help meet the patients' dependency needs? If there is a patient on the unit who is regarded as "difficult," try to assess the basic behavior pattern and the ego states that occur in the nurse-patient relationship. Using the information that you now have, how might you approach this patient more effectively?

## REFERENCES

Berne, Eric: Games People Play. New York, Grove Press, Inc., 1964.

Billings, Carolyn V.: Emotional first aid. Am J Nurs, *80*:2006–2009, (November) 1980.

Hagerman, Zorita: Teaching beginners to cope with extreme behaviors. Am J Nurs, *68*:1927–1929, (September) 1968.

Lazarus, Richard S.: Psychological Stress and the Coping Process. New York, McGraw-Hill, Inc., 1966.

Levin, Pamela, and Berne, Eric: Games nurses play. Am J Nurs, *72*:483–487, (March) 1972.

Wagner, Frank: T. A. for supervisors. Supervisor Nurse, *3*:53–56, (October) 1972.

# Chapter SIX
# Changing Behavior

**OBJECTIVES** Information in this chapter will help you to

1. Explain the concept of health teaching as an integral part of nursing and as an intervention used to change the patient's behavior.
2. Describe the conditions necessary for learning to take place.
3. State the principles related to motivation, efficient learning, and improved retention.
4. Discuss the teaching process and ways to evaluate it.
5. Describe the basic principles and process of interactional therapies to change behavior.
6. Identify the similarities between learning and behavior modification.
7. Identify reinforcers used to increase desired behaviors and to decrease undesired behaviors.

Through the use of the nursing process, nurses develop a rational thought process in which they gather and assess information about the patient, determine the maladaptive behaviors, identify the patient's problem in meeting certain needs or in coping, and take action to resolve the problem. Many kinds of nursing actions, or interventions, are used to change maladaptive behaviors and to move the patient into a more adapted state. These interventions include basic nursing skills and more complex interactional skills.

Early in their nursing education program, nursing students learn certain skills and procedures, such as giving a bed bath, making an occupied bed, giving an enema, and taking the vital signs. The complexity of the skills increases as the nursing students gain more knowledge and experience. They learn the skills that require the use of special equipment or machines and the administration of medications and injections and medical and surgical aseptic techniques. Nurses not only use motor skills to perform these interventions, but also must employ intellectual skills to make observations and judgments, to recognize possible hazards or complications, and to adapt the procedure to the specific needs of the patient. It is necessary that nursing students learn the theory and principles for interventions, as well as the procedures themselves. These interventions help to change behaviors. In this book, we mention some interventions that are appropriate for certain problems; however, for further details of how to perform these skills, consult a nursing skills or procedure manual.

This chapter focuses on interaction skills that are based on the communication process and the relationship between the nurse and the patient. Previously, nurses have been instructed to meet the needs of patients, to carry out health-teaching, and to give emotional support but have not been given the specific knowledge of "how" to proceed. Interactional skills are important interventions that the nurse can use to change behaviors that result from coping problems in the self-concept, role-function, and interdependence modes.

## HEALTH-TEACHING

One of the most important interventions used by nurses is health-teaching. This is especially true for those who use the adaptation model of nursing and the nursing process when the goal of the nursing care is to affect a change in the patient's maladaptive behavior. On a daily basis, nurses deal with patients or clients who have health problems related to meeting their basic needs or to coping with changes in their lives. Other patients or clients may have potential problems that nurses can anticipate and include in the plan of care.

Through the nursing process, the nurse identifies the ineffective behaviors that are associated with the health problem and carries out the second level assessment to determine the stimuli, or influencing factors. People cope in the best way that they can with the changes in their lives and in ways that will best meet their needs. When their old or usual ways of coping to not work, they need to learn new or more effective ways to modify their behavior. The nursing goal is a statement that defines effective coping, and states the planned interventions that are to be used to promote an adaptive state of behavior. This change from maladaptive to adaptive behavior involves learning by the patient. In order to help patients achieve this goal (adaptation), the nurse must know what constitutes the adapted state we call health and what changes must occur so that patients are able to meet their own needs independently. The nurse functions as a health expert who not only is a "doer," when performing tasks or procedures, but also is a "teacher," when providing information for the patient's learning needs.

## WHAT IS LEARNING?

Educators define learning in several ways. A simple definition of learning is the acquisition of information that causes a change in behavior. The change may be easily seen, as in some physical activity or in verbal statements, or less easily detected, as in its effect on attitudes, feelings, ideas, or ways of seeing relationships. The information may be obtained through any of the senses, in any type of setting, and by any method.

The five senses of sight, sound touch, smell, and taste provide us with an input of stimuli to which we respond. The resulting types of behavior to all sorts of stimuli have been examined and have been found to fall within one of three domains: (1) the cognitive domain, which deals with intellectual abilities and understanding; (2) the affective domain, which is related to the expression of feelings in attitudes, appreciations, interests, values, and beliefs; and (3) the psychomotor domain, which involves skills, responses, and motor activities ranging from very simple to complex actions.

Nurses teach patients in each of these domains, using particular skills and methods that promote effective learning in each domain. For example, teaching the diabetic patient about the effects and actions of insulin involves cognitive learning and is accomplished through the use of lectures, discussions, or audiovisual materials. The feelings that the patient has about the disease and about talking insulin injections fall within the affective domain. Skills that the nurse uses to promote adaptive changes in the attitudes or the feelings of the patient include insight therapy, behavior modification, and other interactional interventions (described later in this chapter). Teaching the patient to draw up an accurate dose of insulin in a syringe and giving the injection using aseptic technique is a complex psychomotor skill. Effective methods of teaching these skills include demonstration, step-by-step performance, discussion, and sufficient practice periods.

We are all familiar with formal settings for learning that are provided in organized classes, lectures, schools, workshops, and similar types of sessions. Perhaps even more learning occurs on an informal basis through people's experiences and their interactions with others. Nurses provide patients with health-teaching using both formal and informal settings. Through frequent contacts with patients, nurses have innumerable opportunities for informal teaching on a one-to-one basis. Health-teaching does not require a classroom or books, but the nurse should follow the principles for learning and formulate objectives when planning to use health-teaching as an intervention to promote adaptive behavior.

One's ability to learn is related to one's growth and development. During the first year of life, the maturation process determines the rate, the readiness, and the pattern of motor coordination and control. Children cannot learn to walk until they achieve some sensory-motor coordination and their muscles and bones have matured enough to support their weight. Piaget (1952) a child psychologist, describes four stages in the intellectual development of children as shown below.

The patient's age and level of development are important considerations in the nurse's second level assessment because they influence the

method and the content to be used in the planning of health-teaching. Adults as well as children vary in their ability to use intellectual skills of thinking. Some adults learn more rapidly from concrete situations; others learn more easily through actions and motor responses; and others more readily gain knowledge through reading, self-study, and methods that involve abstract concepts and skills. Additional factors that affect the rate of learning include anxiety (which reduces what can be learned), pain, immobility, malnourishment, fatigue, decreased mental awareness, and hypoxia—all of which are associated with illness and being unable to meet one's own basic needs.

## INFORMATIONAL NEEDS OF PATIENTS

Learning is a lifelong process. We live in a dynamic world that is constantly changing, and we also must grow, develop, and change with it. Illness produces additional changes that most of us have not previously experienced and places additional stress on our coping mechanisms. It increases our need for information in many spheres.

Consider the changes experienced by people who are admitted to a hospital. A hospital is a strange and unfamiliar environment for most people. Even doctors and nurses, who work in hospitals, find them different when experiencing them as patients. Patients are separated from family and loved ones and from their familiar environment. They often find themselves in an impersonal room with a stranger for a roommate. Members of the hospital staff are strangers who enter the room for many different reasons during a 24-hour period. Some of these strangers cause pain to the patients or increase their discomfort. It is often difficult for patients to understand the terminology that is used by these

| Stage | Age | Characteristics |
|---|---|---|
| 1 | birth to 2 years | Sensorimotor period. Learning about physical objects and performing skills of sitting up, reaching out, creeping, crawling, walking, and skipping. |
| 2 | 2 to 7 years | Preoperational thought period. Is egocentric, unable to take other's point of view. Preoccupied with language and use of symbols, such as pretending a tricycle is a fire engine. Progresses to intuitive thought and uses "because" to make simple associations between ideas. |
| 3 | 7 to 11 years | Concrete operations period. Increased ability to solve concrete problems, to understand relationships, to classify objects, to use arithmetic, and to learn deductive reasoning and logic. |
| 4 | 11 to 15 years | Formal operations period. Concerned with the real and the possible. Can use abstract thinking and concepts to build theories or systems. |

help-giving strangers. What does the nurse mean when he or she states, "You are to be NPO tonight for an IVP tomorrow"? When patients think that they understand instructions about being on bed rest, imagine their bewilderment when the nurse becomes upset when they go to the bathroom. "But", they explain, "I have been resting in bed all day. No one said that I could not go to the bathroom."

While nurses are providing care for their patients, they will find innumerable opportunities to use health-teaching to help the patients find effective coping mechanisms to meet their basic needs, to independently make decisions, and to manage their own lives. Areas in which additional information is often needed include

1. Patient's role and the expectations of that role.
2. Hospital routine and policies that affect patients.
3. Management and treatment of the disease. This is especially important for patients with a chronic illness. They need to understand the cause of the disease, the treatment, ways in which they can prevent complications, how to recognize problems associated with the disease, and the prognosis.
4. Instructions and any limitations that follow discharge from the hospital. Many patients receive inadequate information regarding special diets, activities, and drugs that they are to continue to take. They should know the actions of the medication and the side effects as well as the dosage and how often it is to be taken.
5. Coping with and reducing the sources of anxiety.

## CONDITIONS ESSENTIAL FOR HEALTH-TEACHING

One view of teaching is that it is any interpersonal influence used by an individual to change the way another individual can or will behave. It utilizes communication that is structured and intended to produce learning. There are several conditions associated with producing effective learning. These conditions make health-teaching more effective.

**Assess Needs and Problems.** The areas for concern should be determined by the first and second level assessments. The nursing process should be used to identify the problems, to set the goals, and to plan the interventions that are to be used, including health teaching. Only by the assessment of the patient or the nonhospitalized client in all of the adaptive modes is the nurse able to gather information about the patient's learning needs and to assess the many other factors that influence the conditions for learning.

**Readiness to Learn.** Readiness to learn indicates that the patient or client is receptive and is able to learn what is desired. People must have experiences that allow them to develop physical skills, intellectual abilities, and attitudes that serve

**Figure 6–1.** Effective health-teaching is based on the nurse's awareness and consideration of the patient's condition and readiness to learn, as well as principles of the learning process.

as a basis, or foundation, for learning additional information. Those people who have limited experiences in life, such as children, immature or irresponsible persons, and often, people from a low socioeconomic background, lack sufficient information to understand complex health or medical knowledge. A common error made by nurses is in thinking that patients have had the illness before or that those who have been in a hospital before have no further need for health-teaching about the disease.

Redman (1976) states that readiness to learn is more apparent when the person asks a direct question of the nurse or provides a clue to the need for additional information. "What does this medication do?" or "What does this mean on my menu — NAS?" or showing an interest in the stoma of a colostomy are signs of curiosity and a readiness to learn about these conditions. Readiness is also directly related to the individual's state of health and an intact, adequately functioning nervous system. During the acute phase of illness (the second stage), the ability to learn may be limited to those things that are essential in order to reduce physical danger or severe psychosocial distress. As the patient or client enters the convalescent stage, more energy is available to acquire the information needed for the management and prevention of health problems.

**Motivating the Learner.** Learning is more effective when the learner has a need to know something. Questions and statements about what caused the illness, whether the illness was the result of something the person did or did not do, or wondering how they will manage once they return home are indications of needs for more health-teaching. Learning is more effective when the learners are personally involved in the process. Their interest increases as they answer questions, discuss possibilities, explore meanings, explain the steps of the procedure, or demonstrate how to handle equipment.

Learning is motivated by success. To ensure success, the nurse structures the material to be learned so that it builds on what the patient already knows. The nurse proceeds from the known to the unknown, from the familiar to the unfamiliar, or new information, and from the simple to the complex. The nurse must determine the knowledge or skills that the patient needs in order to learn how to change maladaptive behaviors. For example, following a stroke, paralyzed clients must be able to sit upright, to balance their bodies, and to support their weight before they can be taught to walk again. Patients who are expected to learn about a low sodium diet and to adhere to it should have

basic information about the components of a balanced diet and an understanding of the relationship between salt and sodium (Na) and the sodium content of foods not commonly thought of as being salty, such as corn flakes, American cheese, or catsup.

The rewards for success are motivating factors, too. An external reward may be an extra treat, privilege or praise for learning. Gold stars on a chart or a graph are often the rewards children earn for learning a new behavior pattern, such as cleaning their room or brushing their teeth. The intrinsic reward that originates within the learning is the most effective reward. Learning to care for their own health needs is often the only incentive some patients need.

Health and adaptation form the basis for optimal learning. Poor nutrition has an adverse effect on learning. Many people are unable to meet their nutritional needs during illness. Research studies have shown that hungry, malnourished people in the lesser developed countries of the world are less able to learn or to be as productive as well-nourished people.

Universally, anxiety is a barrier to learning, although mild anxiety is associated with the need to learn. The "fight or flight" response of the autonomic nervous system makes it difficult to pay attention to new information until the threat or the danger has passed. The anxiety caused by illness or hospitalization may interfere with health-teaching and is the most common reason that patients forget what the nurse said yesterday or even an hour ago. Helping patients to acknowledge the anxiety state, to identify the cause of it, and to find more effective methods of coping may be necessary before beginning health-teaching.

**Health Beliefs and Values.** In planning for health-teaching, the nurse should gather information about the client's or patient's values and beliefs about health. These beliefs and values must be taken into consideration during health-teaching. If not, the patient or client may not accept what is being taught. Many people define illness in terms of not being able to work, and as long as these people are able to get out of bed or to walk, they do not believe they are ill. This influences the way they will respond to health-teaching in regard to such conditions as high blood pressure or chronic smoker's cough or the need to continue taking medications after symptoms disappear. Cultural groups that regard pregnancy as a normal event in life may reject the idea that prenatal care is necessary or even desirable. Other people may believe that illness is a form of punishment by God for their sins or that nature and time will provide for the healing of the body. Such beliefs will have a bearing on the way these people follow through with prescribed treatments or therapy.

Many studies have focused on socioeconomic status as an important factor in peoples' health beliefs and values. People who belong to socioeconomic lower classes have more differences in their values and beliefs about health and more barriers that interfere with gaining health care than people in higher socioeconomic classes. They are not as likely to understand functions of the body, to recognize symptoms, to seek out medical treatment, to keep appointments, or to be future-oriented in their thinking. These factors influence and may limit the amount of learning and the rate of learning of these people. For more information about the effects of socioeconomic status and poverty on health, see Chapter Twenty-Three, Poverty and Adaptation.

**Psychological Adaptation to Illness.** For effective learning to take place, patients not only need to be entering the convalescent stage of illness with physiological recovery from the illness but also must be adapting psychologically to their illness. Patients who have suffered a loss as a result of illness — the loss of a body part or the loss of some function — need time to cope with their feelings about the loss. During the denial stage of grieving over the loss, they are not ready to learn new ways of coping or managing their lives. Those who have suffered from traumatic stresses, such as extensive burns, crippling injuries, amputations, paralysis, or the crisis of cancer, often need more time before they are able to learn to cope with their conditions, or to manage their lives. However, use of the adaptation model of nursing to assess the total patient, including all of the modes, provides the nurse with information about the problems of coping and the effective interventions that can be incorporated into the nursing care plan to help the patient.

**Language the Patient Understands.** Two factors that influence patients' understanding are the difficulty of the words and the length of sentences used both in verbal and in written communication by doctors and nurses. Patients often complain that they do not understand what is being said when doctors or nurses use many medical terms. Although members of the health professions use medical terminology to convey a precise meaning, patients would have to learn nearly a thousand words to be able to understand treatment of diseases such as diabetes or cancer. Most people do not use such words as syringe, stoma, insulin, calories, or emesis in their everyday conversation.

Many ordinary words, such as bed rest, dirty, clean, large, small, good, or bad, are given new meanings when used by health professionals. Patients often have a difficult time understanding these terms and their meanings — for example, fresh linen taken into an isolation precautions room is then considered contaminated or "dirty," and must be removed as soiled linen even though it is not used and appears to be clean.

Written materials can be used effectively in health-teaching for people who have good reading skills. Good reading habits tend to be more characteristic of people who are in the middle class, have a higher level of education, and say that they like to read. However, the people who most often need health-teaching are people who have poor reading skills. They have a limited vocabulary, are less able to understand technical terms or concepts, and have difficulty in keeping written records. They are more confused by the use of abbreviations and tend to be misled by casual remarks that they may overhear. The use of medical terms leads to their misunderstanding of and misinterpretation of the material. These poeple benefit more from verbal discussions, a one-to-one basis for teaching, and information that is presented in a simplified and concrete way.

The degree of misunderstanding that may result when patients fail to understand health-teaching is illustrated by the following case histories:

Mrs. S. underwent a mastectomy one year ago for cancer of the breast. Since then, she had gained more than 80 pounds, and her weight was now over 220 pounds. While hospitalized for treatment of metastatic disease she worried about the low caloric diet the doctor prescribed for her and did not want to lose weight. She explained, "People who die from cancer lose a lot of weight and are just skin and bones. My doctor said that cancer robs the rest of the body of the food it needs so if I do not lose weight I will not die from cancer."

Bill H. is in his early 60s and was recently diagnosed as diabetic. Before being discharged from the hospital, he was taught how to test his urine, how to take care of his feet and skin, how to give himself insulin, and to note which foods are allowed on his diet. At a subsequent checkup, his blood glucose was very high, even though he reported that all of his urine tests were negative. When questioned about the method he used, he stated that he voided in the toilet, filled the medicine dropper from the toilet water, added plain water, and then added the Clinitest tablet. The test of the greatly diluted urine always produced negative results.

Diabetic patients have much to learn about managing their disease, and many are unable to learn everything in the short periods of time that they are given. Reeves (1979) reported the following case:

Mrs. D. and her 15-year-old daughter were diabetics but were still not under control, although taking up to 80 units of insulin daily. They had no understanding of the diabetic diet, and both had been eating only oatmeal for their meals. Even when hungry at night, they would get up and fix a bowl of oatmeal. They were amazed when the nurse informed them of the many different foods that were allowed on their diet.

Is it possible that during the health-teaching, Mrs. D. was given a written diet that she put aside because she did not understand it? Is it possible that the nurse may have said, "Well, oatmeal is allowed on your diet.... Now, you understand, you can only eat what is allowed on your diet."

Many patients are confused by directions given for taking their medications that seem complete and straightforward on the surface. For example, a patient may be instructed to take a drug "after each meal and at bedtime" in order to provide four doses daily. What if the patient eats only two meals a day? Should the medication be taken immediately after eating, or can it be taken two hours later, when the patient suddenly remembers it? If the instructions say to avoid taking the drug with dairy products does this refer to only milk, or does it include such foods as butter and cheeses?

We also communicate and learn through the use of written words and pictures. Booklets, pamphlets, and written handouts are useful teaching tools for patients with good reading abilities. To be most effective, these materials must be clear in their meaning and easily understood by the patients for whom they were prepared. Materials prepared for children differ from those written for adults. The use of familiar words and shorter sentences tends to make written text easier to read and understand. Charts, posters, video tapes, filmstrips and other audiovisual materials may be supplied by the hospital inservice education office or obtained from community organizations for use in health-teaching.

## PRINCIPLES OF LEARNING

Learning is a dynamic process that continues throughout life as we cope with changes and seek a sense of order and cohesion that we call adaptation, or health. Illness and injury produce many changes that limit or strain the ability to cope and expose people to many strange, unfamiliar, and, often, uncomfortable situations. Patients need to learn a great deal in order to cope effectively with their disease, its treatment, and the environment. To promote more effective health-teaching, the following principles have been compiled from previous material in this book and from other sources that deal with the learning process. These principles outline ways to increase the patient's readiness and motivation for learning and ways to improve retention.

### Principles for More Efficient Learning

1. Learning is more effective when it is in response to the expressed need. Patients express their readiness to learn when they ask questions and seek more information.
2. It is essential for the learners to take an active part in the process and they should be free to ask questions, to explore the content and its meaning, and to perform activities.
3. The information that is presented should be meaningful to the learner. It is extremely difficult for people to learn nonsense syllables or material that has no meaning to them. The information should relate to what the learner already knows, and proceed from the familiar to the new information, or the unfamiliar.
4. Repetition of mental or physical activities increases the amount of learning. For example, the learner may be encouraged to list, discuss, explain, recall or compare diet restrictions or asked to demonstrate physical ability by lifting a leg a certain number of times.
5. The sequence of material to be learned may be added one part at a time until all information is combined into the whole, or learning may begin with the entire general topic and proceed to examine each part. The step-by-step method is effective for learning concrete, factual information and psychomotor skills. Examining the whole topic and then proceeding to analyze each part may be used in the affective domain, when dealing with attitudes, feelings, and values.

### Principles to Improve Retention

1. To promote remembrance, material must be placed quickly within some existing structure. Isolated facts tend to be forgotten rapidly. Facts about carbohydrates are remembered when learners associate them with material that they already know about nutrition, types of foods, and so on.
2. Provide reinforcement of the information periodically. Some people believe that only seven new facts or ideas can be processed at

a time. It takes the learner time to integrate new information into an existing system or structure so that it has relevance and meaning. Teaching patients about diet, medications, and activities that they are allowed to undertake an hour before they are discharged from the hospital is probably less effective than when taught at a time that permits follow-up and reinforcement.

3. Space the review and reinforcement. Even though the nurse covered the material when health-teaching, the patient may not have learned it. The amount of information that is forgotten is greatest immediately following the health-teaching session but levels off after a day or two. Reviewing the material with the patient the day after it has been taught provides the nurse with feedback concerning what was understood and learned and what needs to be retaught.

4. Intervening events affect the amount of learning and its application. Material is retained better when it is put to immediate use and when few intervening events occur to upset learning, with subsequent change in behavior. Preoperative teaching is more effective when carried out a day or two before surgery than when done a week ahead of time. Events, such as the stress of surgery or a disagreement with a roommate, may interfere with what is learned.

## THE TEACHING PROCESS

Teaching as an intervention is dependent upon the use of the nursing process as the method of assessing the patient, identifying the problem, and planning the care. The first level assessment provides information about behaviors that need to be changed, as well as indicating potential problems or needs for additional information. Factors that influence the need for change are identified by the second level assessment. Goals are set and arranged in priority so that the immediate needs are handled first. Interventions are selected that manipulate the stimuli that are causing the problem. Many of these interventions will require some degree of health-teaching as a basis. After health-teaching has been completed, the nurse evaluates the effectiveness of the intervention in terms of the extent to which the goal has been achieved. Both formal and informal teaching by the nurse are based on a problem-solving approach in which there is assessment with identification of a problem and formation of a goal.

When providing information for health-teaching, the following format is suggested:

1. Assess the patient's level of knowledge.
2. Provide the information needed.
3. Obtain feedback from the patient.
4. Apply the knowledge by having the patient describe or demonstrate the information.
5. Correct errors or misinformation, and corrects gaps in knowledge.
6. Assess the patient's feelings and perceptions, using the five steps that are used for more efficient learning.
7. Arrange for follow-up or reinforcement.

When teaching specific information to the patient, the nurse should develop specific goals or learning objectives, similar to the objectives given at the beginning of each chapter of this book. Goals or objectives that use the terms "to know," "to understand," or "to appreciate" tend to be vague. It would be difficult to measure what is meant by these terms. Compare some of these general goals with goals that use more specific terms to state what the patient is expected to achieve.

### General Goals

1. Patient will force fluids.
2. Patient will increase activities as tolerated.

3. Patient will understand the diabetic diet.

4. Patient will know about cardiac medications and will take them accurately.

### Specific Goals

1. Patient will drink 2400 ml in a 24-hour period.
2. Patient will sit in chair t.i.d. for 15 minutes, and will increase the time by 5 minutes each day.
3. Patient will select a sample diabetic lunch from a menu, using exchange groups as necessary.
4. Patient will state the actions and side effects of cardiac medications and how to take them.

Specific goals make it easier for the nurse to evaluate the effectiveness of the health-teaching. They specify the behavior that is desired. The nurse reassesses the resulting behavior to see if the behavior has changed. If the behavior has changed, the nurse determines the direction and the degree of the change, and then may revise objectives or add new objectives to resolve the patient's actual or potential problem.

## BEHAVIOR MODIFICATION

When using the adaptation approach to nursing, nurses focus on supportive coping mechanisms that lead to adaptive behavior. Although the behavioral sciences are not a precise science, a basic law states that when behavior is rewarded it increases and recurs, while the response that is not rewarded decreases and fades (Reese, 1976; Yates, 1970). The coping mechanism is the behavioral response that people make in their efforts to meet or to satisfy the stimulus.

During this century, numerous studies by psychologists have focused on the process of learning as psychologists searched for answers to questions, such as "What is learning" and "How do people learn?" These studies led to advances in the behavioral sciences and to increased understanding of the learning process. Behavior modification is based on the theory of operant conditioning developed by B. F. Skinner. It was first used extensively in mental hospitals to change the maladapted or deviant behavior of patients to more socially acceptable responses. Although some people may regard operant conditioning as manipulative and as relying artificially on rewards to change behavior, the principles of behavior modification exist. The behavior that results from a stimulus is again selected as a response if it was reinforced the first time. A reciprocal relationship develops between two or more people when one's behavioral response becomes a stimulus for the other's behavior. In everyday life, these principles are observed during interactions between parent and child, teacher and pupil, peer and peer, and so on. Behavior modification is used for therapeutic purposes in clinics, hospitals, industry, schools, and community settings wherever people are trying to achieve effective coping behavior.

During their childrens' growth and development, parents use principles of behavior modification to reward acceptable actions, to ignore some behaviors, and to withhold rewards for undesirable behavior. They use reinforcers to encourage children to respond with desired behavior to a particular stimulus (Fig. 6–2). Read the following common occurrences, then identify the stimuli, the coping behavior or response, and the consequence or reinforcers.

Sally does not eat cooked carrots, but she ate a few during dinner because her mother had prepared them in a different way. Her mother then complimented Sally on her adventurous spirit.

From infancy, babies learn that crying gains attention and leads to pleasurable sensations. They are picked up, their wet diapers are changed, and they are fed. While crying leads to these physical

**Figure 6–2.** Rewarded behavior tends to be repeated. The adult throwing the ball is the stimulus, and the child's response of catching the ball is rewarded by the adult's praise.

rewards, babies soon perceive that smiling, cooing, and not crying are rewarded with the mother's kisses, smile, cuddling, and playing. Both the baby and the mother are responding to each other, and providing consequences that serve as rewards for the other.

Betty Lee helped her mother with the dishes after dinner. When they were finished, her mother hugged Betty Lee and said how lucky she was to have such an efficient dish drier.

Gary's bedtime is 7:30 p.m. every evening, but one night he begged to stay up later to watch a TV program. He was allowed to do so that evening, but the next night he again pestered his parents to stay up later. When they refused, he continued to think up excuses and reasons for not going to bed. Wearily, the parents gave in and let him stay up an hour longer. Within days, they found that they had a child who makes a fuss every night about going to bed.

The mother and aunt of three-year-old Gina were busily sewing and deep in conversation when they became aware that Gina was no longer there. After a short search, they found Gina in the bathroom, which she had reduced to a shambles. Globs of toothpaste were stuck on the walls, lipstick had been used like a crayon on the floor, the wash cloth was floating in the toilet bowl, hair curlers rolled over the floor, and toilet paper hung in streamers. The sight was so unexpected that the mother and aunt broke out in uncontrollable laughter. Gina joined in the laughter, too.

The stimuli, the behaviors or actions, and the consequences for these examples are shown in the table below.

The behavior that was rewarded increases and is chosen repeatedly as the response for the stimuli, regardless of whether the behavior is adaptive or maladaptive for the circumstances. Although most people tend to focus on the behavior of the baby in the second example, the reinforcer of the mother's behavior should not be overlooked. If the mother picked up the baby each time the baby cried, changed the diaper, and fed the baby, but the baby continued to cry, the mother's actions have not been rewarded.

The next time the baby cries, the mother will tend not to act in the same way, but may try something else, such as walking with the baby, turning the baby over, using a pacifier, or ignoring the crying. The behavior of the children in the other examples is likely to continue because each of these children received reinforcement from their families.

## THE PROCESS OF BEHAVIOR MODIFICATION

Because behavior modification focuses on the response to a stimulus, the emphasis is on the "here and now" rather than on exploring past events or anticipating the future. Behavior modification is concerned with the specific behavior and its causes. When nurses use principles of behavior modification as an intervention to help the patient change maladaptive behavior to desired behavior, the following steps are suggested.

*Determine the behaviors that are maladaptive and that need to be changed.* Use the nursing process to assess the behaviors in all modes and to identify problems and carry out the second level assessment to ascertain factors that cause or influence the behavior.

*State the goal, or the desired behavior.* If possible, involve the patient in setting a goal that seems reasonable and attainable, because it is the patient who is to make the change.

*Select appropriate reinforcers.* In order to be effective, reinforcers must influence the rate of behavior. A smile or other visual reward would not be effective with a person who is blind; nor is a smoking privilege a meaningful reward for a nonsmoker.

*Reward appropriate behaviors when they occur.* The reinforcement should be given only when the desired behavior has occurred, and it should be given promptly so that the patient closely associates it with the behavior. When toilet training a young child, parents give verbal encour-

| Stimulus | Behavior | Consequence |
|---|---|---|
| Sally — hungry at dinner | ate some carrots | mother complimented her |
| Baby — hungry, uncomfortable | crying | was picked up, changed diaper, fed |
| Mother — baby crying | picked up baby, changed diaper, fed | baby quiet, smiling, cooing |
| Betty — mother's presence | dried dishes | mother's hug and praise |
| Gary — 7:30 p.m. bedtime | fusses to stay up later to watch TV program | parents give in and let him stay up |
| Gina — free from supervision | played with things in bathroom, made a mess | mother and aunt laughed at mess she made |

agement, and after the child has eliminated, they give praise.

There are many situations when nurses can use behavior modification to help the patient use more adaptive behavior and avoid becoming a "difficult patient." How could you utilize behavior modification as an intervention in the following examples?

*Example 1.* Eleanor, a 43-year-old housewife, is now partially paralyzed following a serious automobile accident two months ago. Every 20 to 30 minutes during the day when she is awake, she asks to use the bedpan. She either voids a small amount or states that it was a false alarm and then apologizes for causing so much trouble. She is quite obese, and, after using the bedpan, asks the nurse to change her position, to prop her on her side with pillows, support her arm, or to rub her hands and fingers with lotion. She has no evidence of problems in the urinary tract; however, a short time later, she again calls for the bedpan and is pleasant as she converses with the nurse.

*Example 2.* Carlos is an elderly patient in an extended care facility. He has chronic brain syndrome characterized by poor memory but is active and walks about during the day. At meal times, he refuses to eat, gets up, and leaves the table when the nurses are busy helping the other patients. The nurses say, "Look, there goes Carlos again. Bring him back." Eventually, they tie him to the chair and feed him.

In applying the process of behavior modification one sees that, in the case of Eleanor, the behavior to be changed is her frequent request to use the bedpan and then voiding only small amounts. The goal set by the nurse and the patient would be to increase the amount of time between uses of the bedpan and to increase the amount of urine voided each time. Both the patient and the nurse should agree on the type of reinforcer to be used, and this reinforcer should be used to reward the modified behavior, when it occurs. In this case, they might agree that additional time spent with the patient in social conversation would be the reinforcer to be used when the patient was able to prolong the time between requests and to void more than a few ml at a time. In the second example, Carlos gains attention from the nursing staff only when he refuses to eat, gets up, and leaves the table. To change this behavior to an adaptive behavior in which Carlos would eat an adequate diet by himself, the nurse could bring Carlos to the table, stay with him, and give him verbal praise or smile each time he took a bite of food of his own accord.

## TYPES OF REINFORCERS

Many different kinds of incentives and rewards serve to reinforce behavior. Reinforcers are most effective when they are used consistently and immediately following the behavior that is desired. The reinforcer must be relevant and have meaning for the person whose behavior is to be modified. Common reinforcers include attention, verbal comments, praise, rest, food, trips and money.

Reinforcers are classified as being positive or negative in relation to the situation or to the environment in which they are used. Positive reinforcers refer to adding something desirable to the situation. Negative reinforcers refer to removing or subtracting something unpleasant or aversive from the environment.

**Positive Reinforcers**
*(add desirable)*

Smile, praise
Hug, stroke, pat
Social conversation
Special foods, candy
Use of TV, phone, car
VIP treatment

**Negative Reinforcers**
*(remove unpleasant)*

Turn down loud volume of TV, stereo
Change bed linen of incontinent patient
Give medication for complaints of pain
Stop child crying by giving in
Complete tasks not done by procrastinator

According to O'Neil (1975), positive reinforcers, and negative reinforcers are valuable in increasing the desired action, and in decreasing the undesired behavior. O'Neil states that negative reinforcers should not be regarded as punishment. Punishment is something unpleasant that is added to the situation or something pleasant that is removed from the situation. A motorist who goes through a red light and is seen by a police officer is punished for disobeying traffic rules. The ticket is something unpleasant that has been added to the situation. The teen-ager who stayed out late on a school night might be punished by not being allowed to go out at all. In this case, the removal of a pleasant privilege is the method of punishment.

## METHODS OF CHANGING BEHAVIOR

Reese (1976) described several ways in which behavior can be modified. Specific behaviors can be increased by avoidance, modelling and imitating or by negative reinforcement and escape. Techniques that decrease undesired behavior include punishment, restraint or confinement, satiation, and operant extinction.

**Avoidance.** Many desired behaviors are based on teaching the consequences that result from undesired responses. Desired actions occur in order to avoid unpleasant outcomes in the following situations: People pay income taxes to avoid penalties or imprisonment; people obey laws to avoid prosecution for committing crimes; students study in order to learn and to pass courses.

**Modelling and Imitating.** People learn how to behave in various situations by watching others and by imitating them. Children learn to speak by imitating the sounds made by their parents, to use eating utensils, and to respond to many situations by observing others. Nursing students learn the role of a nurse by following the actions of a role model. In health-teaching, the nurse uses this method when demonstrating the procedure of giving an injection of insulin and then having the diabetic patient carry out the same steps. Modelling and imitating help to increase desired behavior.

**Negative Reinforcement and Escape.** This method of behavior modification introduces an unpleasant factor into the situation in order to increase the response that is desired. The person who responds in the usual way to the situation is subjected to disagreeable consequences and, thus, changes this behavior to escape these consequences. Although introduction of an unpleasant factor is used as punishment to decrease an unwanted response, behavioral therapists use the term negative reinforcement and escape when the purpose is to increase the desired response. This is the basis for aversion therapy, which is used to help people stop smoking, stop drinking alcoholic beverages, stop stuttering, or stop overeating. An unpleasant factor, such as a mild electric shock or a disagreeable odor, accompanies the undesired behaviors of smoking or drinking. People then choose other ways to act in the situation in order to avoid the repulsive element.

**Punishment.** Punishment is the introduction of an unpleasant factor in order to decrease the undesired behavior. Since every interaction involves two or more people, punishment serves to suppress the behavioral response of one of the individuals and to strengthen the behavioral response of the other. The mother who yells at her children may find that this stops their unruly behavior temporarily but it also trains the mother to yell at them.

**Restraint or Confinement.** Restraint and confinement do not change behavior permanently, but they are effective ways to stop it from occurring when it may lead to undesirable side effects. The use of side rails on the patient's bed restricts movement on a temporary basis but helps to prevent the patient from falling while under sedation. Holding a small child's hand when crossing the street is a form of restraint that prevents the child from running into traffic and getting injured.

**Satiation.** Satiation is another method of reducing the strength of the behavior. A response occurs, is reinforced, and, eventually, decreases in strength. One becomes tired of the same old thing. The naming of children follows this pattern. For a period of time, baby girls are named Amy, Jennifer, or Susan. Then there is a period of time when baby girls are named April, Jessica, or Christie.

Satiation was used to change the behavior of a patient who collected and hoarded towels. She collected 20 to 30 towels a day and hid them in her room. Daily, the nurses searched her room for towels and removed them. To change her behavior, the towels were not removed from the room, and the nurse gave her towels without comment when she asked for them. When more than 600 towels were hidden in her room, she began to bring them out and no longer hoarded them.

**Operant Extinction.** Operant extinction is the term used to indicate changing the events that occur after the response. Operant conditioning is based on the principle that behavior is increased or decreased by events that occur after the person's response. Some reinforcers can be used to change this behavior. Consider Gary and other children who have bedtime temper tantrums for hours to put off going to bed. This behavior gains the parent's attention. The parent reads stories to the child, gets him drinks, and enters into emotional arguments with the child about going to bed. To change the child's behavior, it is necessary to change the events that follow the behavior. One method parents use is putting the child to bed, closing the door, and ignoring the yelling or crying. After one to two weeks, the unrewarded behavior diminishes and eventually, fades away.

## COMPARISON OF LEARNING THEORY AND BEHAVIOR MODIFICATION

Learning has been described as any acquisition of information that results in a change of behavior in any realm. The changes may affect the cognitive, the affective, or the psychomotor behavior.

Behavior modification is based on two laws: (1) all behavior is learned and has meaning to the one who is carrying out the behavior, and (2) because behavior is learned, it can be modified or changed.

Behavior is seen as a reciprocal reaction between two or more people. The behavioral response of one person is the stimulus for the behavioral response of the other.

Note the similarities and the differences between learning theory, as used in health-teaching, and behavior modification as stated below.

### Learning Theory

Change in behavior in any form: knowledge, feelings, beliefs, or skills.

Success leads to increased learning.

Internal need to learn provides strong motivation to change behavior.

Many factors affect readiness to learn.

Learning is improved when it is learner-centered and when the learner is involved in the process.

Information that is learned must be meaningful and placed into some existing structure of association.

### Behavior Modification

Behavior that occurs in response to a stimulus is rewarded.

Reinforcers may be positive and add something pleasant or may be negative and remove something unpleasant from the situation.

Behaviors are responses that can be seen, heard, or measured.

Is often regarded as "other" imposed in the goals or the behaviors to be changed.

Must be regarded as a reciprocal relationship between two or more people.

Events occurring after the person's response reinforce that behavioral response.

## OTHER INTERPERSONAL INTERVENTIONS

Behavior modification is only one way in which learning takes place and in which behavior is changed. Other interactions between the nurse and the patient help the patient change unwanted or maladaptive behavior to responses within the positive, adapted range. Therapeutic interactions, such as remotivation techniques, reality therapy, and transactional analysis, are useful interventions for people who have problems coping with their feelings or interacting socially with others.

## REMOTIVATION TECHNIQUES

About 1950, remotivation techniques were developed for use in psychiatric hospitals, and they produced significant changes in the maladaptive behavior of patients. Later, they were adapted for use with confused patients in geriatric settings. They have been successful in bringing older people who had been diagnosed as having chronic brain syndrome, senile brain disease, or cerebral arteriosclerosis back to reality.

Remotivation is a patient-group interaction program that is conducted by a member of the nursing staff. A group of up to six to eight patients usually meets with one leader. Each group meets twice a week for 45 minutes to one hour for a period of ten weeks. During each session, the group leader carries out steps that are designed to reawaken or renew the patient's interest in everyday live and in social surroundings. The first step is to establish a "climate of acceptance" by extending a personal welcome to each patient who attends the meeting. Then the leader begins to build "bridges to reality" through (1) reading poetry and showing pictures, (2) discussing the world in which we live, and (3) talking about the work that people do. Topics for discussion include animals, gardening, how to bake bread, and any subject in which the patients show an interest. The final step is thanking the patients for attending the session and inviting them to the next meeting.

Although remotivation techniques do not provide cures, the program leads to improvement in social behavior, and some patients improve to the extent that they can again function in their own homes and in the community setting. For others, it keeps the patients from regressing to the point where they are unable to care for their own physical needs.

At one hospital that uses remotivation techniques, nurses have developed subject packets of materials for use during the sessions in order to stimulate interest and motivation. One packet included an old coffee grinder, coffee beans, and pictures of people drinking coffee. Another packet contained swatches of different types of material, buttons, zippers, and knitted booties — all selected as possible ways to trigger memories and to initiate

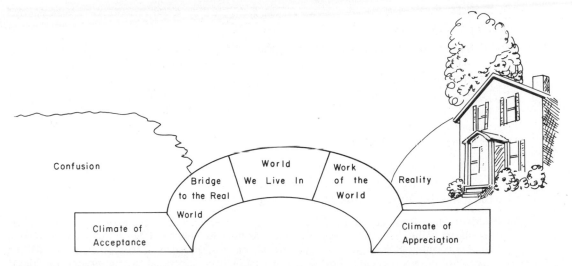

**Figure 6–3.** Remotivation therapy is one method to build bridges leading to a greater recognition of reality for persons who are confused or who have some degree of brain failure.

discussions and interactions among the patients. Creative and innovative ways can be used to reawaken patients' interest in the world around them.

## REALITY THERAPY

Unlike remotivation therapy, reality therapy is based on the premise that changes in behavior will cause changes in the way the person feels. The process was pioneered by Glasser and is used to change the way individuals see or feel about themselves. For example, reality therapy might be used with those who have a fear of flying, who will not ride elevators because of a fear of heights or a fear of falling, who ingratiate themselves with others in hopes of being liked by everyone, or overweight people who reward themselves with food each time that they feel slighted or at a disadvantage. It is a method of changing the person's response to a stimulus in order to establish a new emotion or feeling associated with the stimulus.

Reality therapy is based on the principles of patient involvement and dealing with the present. After talking about the behavior, the patient makes a value judgment as to whether the behavior is acceptable or not acceptable. Then, with either the nurse or the therapist, the patient helps to make a plan of action and makes a commitment to act in a specified way. The responsibility lies with the patient. Excuses are not accepted for the patient's failure to act as specified. However, the patient is asked to make another value

judgment of his or her behavior and a new plan of action. Reality therapy can be summarized as:

1. Deal with the present.
2. Examine the behavior associated with the problem.
3. Patient makes value judgment about the behavior.
4. Nurse and patient make plan of action.
5. Patient makes a commitment to the plan.
6. Patient is responsible for carrying out the plan.

Reality therapy is a useful method for clients in the community setting. The nurse may work with individual clients or with groups. The key to the success of this method of changing behavior is the client's commitment and responsibility for his or her actions, with the nurse involved in planning the action.

## OTHER TYPES OF THERAPIES

Several other types of interactional interventions have been developed that have specific goals. These include family therapy, conjoint therapy, and multiple impact therapy among others. They are based on the precept that the family evolves as a group over a period of time, as each member develops his or her own personality. Something that affects one member of the family group is felt by and affects all the other members. The goals of therapy are (1) to resolve the problem(s), (2) to improve communication and understanding among the members of the group, and (3) to strengthen the positive coping mechanisms of the group.

## APPLICATION TO CLINICAL PRACTICE

The only way that one can determine that learning has taken place is by a change in the behavior of the learner. A great deal of information about interpersonal interventions has been provided for nursing students in this chapter, but it has value only if it changes your behavior and is applied in your daily practice of nursing. As you provide nursing care to patients in the clinical setting, assess the type of behavior pattern that is used by the patient and the needs for health-teaching and then use various techniques as interventions to change to an adapted state.

### Health Teaching

Nurses are afforded many opportunities each day to teach the patient's family something about health or more effective coping.

Mr. G. had been well until about three weeks ago when he was hospitalized for congestive heart failure. He is 71 years old, and was born in Europe of Jewish parents, and came to this country at nine years of age. Mr. G. has responded well to treatment and will be going home in a few days. Both Mr. and Mrs. G. have expressed their apprehension about his care at home. During her visit with her husband today, Mrs. G. mentioned that Mr. G. is supposed to stay on a low salt diet at home, and asks the nurse what that means and what she will have to do.

In planning to teach Mr. and Mrs. G. about the low salt diet, you should follow the steps of the teaching process: (1) assess the level of Mr. and Mrs. G.'s knowledge about nutrition and the kinds of foods they usually eat, (2) provide the information that is needed, (3) obtain feedback from both of them showing their understanding of the information, (4) correct errors or fill in gaps in their knowledge to the situation.

As you care for patients in the clinical laboratory, identify two or three occasions when you were able to do health-teaching. Health-teaching can be done informally, such as when you provide information about the level of activity the patient should have, the nutritional needs, the amount of fluids that should be taken, or the preparation for some test or procedure. Identify some of the principles of learning that affect your patient's ability to learn and to retain the information that is presented.

### Behavior Modification

Frequently, some patients are labelled by the nursing staff as "difficult" or as "complainers." Often, it is because these patients have needs that are not met, or because they have maladaptive coping mechanisms. Ineffective coping can be changed through behavior modification techniques. Eddie is a patient with maladaptive coping mechanisms.

Eddie, 10 years of age, fell down some steps at school last week and broke his femur. Imagine that he is now a patient on your nursing unit and is skilled at noncompliance. If told to turn the TV volume down, as often as not, he will turn the volume up. He does not do what he is told or asked to do, such as washing his hands, taking his bath, brushing his teeth, turning out the light at bedtime, or putting his toys away. He ignores any request until it is repeated at least seven times, then he argues about it and counterattacks. He treats his parents the same way when they visit him and tell him to do something. He teases other patients, refuses to obey simple requests, and screams, upsetting other patients and the nursing staff.

What pattern of basic behavior is Eddie exhibiting? What nursing approaches could you use with this type of behavior? Describe what steps you might take to modify his aggressive behavior.

Eddie is using moving-against behavior as he tries to cope with the changes in his life. His independent and aggressive behavior is not socially acceptable to others, and it is in fact, alienating others because his behavior is regarded as extreme and inappropriate. The nursing approach planned for use with patients like Eddie includes remaining objective when they are hostile or angry, listening for clues to their feelings and the causes for these feelings, help patients to recognize the cause of these feelings, reducing frustrating elements in the environment, and being dependable in keeping your word. Behavior modification is used as an intervention to change maladaptive behaviors. Eddie and the nurse should talk about the undesired behaviors and agree on the desired behaviors, or the goal. Reinforcers are then selected that will serve to influence Eddie's behavior. These reinforcers should be used to reward the desired behavior when it occurs.

In the clinical setting, try to identify situations in which you could use the principles of behavior modification to promote the patient's learning of desired behavior. It may be helpful in influencing the patient to increase fluid intake, to do range-of-motion exercises for an affected joint, or to increase the amount of time spent out of bed.

## REFERENCES

**Health-Teaching**

Bullough, Bonnie, and Bullough, Vern: Poverty, Ethnic Identity and Health Care. New York, Appleton-Century-Crofts, 1972, p. 136.

Cohen, S.: Teaching a patient how to use crutches. Am J Nurs, 79:1111–1126, (June) 1979.

Falkiewicz, Juliana: Are group classes helpful in teaching cardiac patients? Am J Nurs, 80:444–445, (March) 1980.

Friedland, Geanne M.: Learning behaviors of a preadolescent with diabetes. Am J Nurs, 76:59–61, (January) 1976.

Hayter, Jean: Fine points in diabetic care. Am J Nurs, 76:594–599, (April) 1976.

Hilgard, Ernest R., and Bower, Gordon H.: Theories of Learning, 3rd ed. New York, Appleton-Century-Crofts, 1966.

Jones, Patricia, and Oertel, William: Developing patient teaching objectives and techniques: a self-instructional program. Nurse Educator, 2(5):3–18, (September-October) 1977.

Laird, Mona: Techniques for teaching pre- and postoperative patients. Am J Nurs, 77:1338–1340, (August) 1975.

Mayer, Gloria G., and Peterson, Carol W.: Theoretical framework for coronary care nursing education. Am J Nurs, 78:1208–1211, (July) 1978.

Meyer, Rita, and Latz, Paula: What open heart surgery patients want to know. Am J Nurs, 79:1558–1560, (September) 1979.

Mirhatz, Ruth, Smith, Dorsey, and Sietz, Pauline: Preoperative teaching for gynecologic patients. Am J Nurs, 74:1072–1074, (June) 1974.

Mitchell, Ellen S.: Protocol for teaching hypertensive patients. Am J Nurs, 77:808–809, (May) 1977.

Palm, Mary L.: Recognizing opportunities for informal patient teaching. Nurs Clin North Am, 6(4):669–678, (December) 1971.

Piaget, Jean: The Origins of Intelligence in Children. New York, International Universities Press, Inc., 1952.

Pontious, Sharon: Practical Piaget: helping children understand. Am J Nurs, 82:114–117, (January) 1982.

Rayder, Melinda: A new nurse asks why preoperative teaching isn't done. Am J Nurs, 79:1992–1995, (November) 1979.

Raymer, Mary C.: Improving patient teaching with an all-in-one program. Nursing 80, 10(8):18–19, (August) 1980.

Redman, Barbara K.: The Process of Patient Teaching in Nursing, 3rd ed. St. Louis, The C. V. Mosby Co., 1976.

Reeves, Ruth: Nurse, what are you all about? Am J Nurs, 79:2145–2147, (December) 1979.

Richter, Judith, and Sloan, Rebecca: The relaxation technique. Am J Nurs, 79:1960–1961, (November) 1979.

Small, Doreen: Adult diabetes. Am J Nurs, 78:889–890, (May) 1978.

Symposium on teaching patients. Nurs Clin North Am, 6:4, (December) 1971.

Walters, Jean: Four practical questions to ask when organizing preoperative classes. Am J Nurs, 79:1090–1091, (June) 1979.

Whitehouse, Rebecca: Forms that facilitate patient teaching. Am J Nurs, 79:1227–1229, (July) 1979.

Wolf, Zane: What patients awaiting kidney transplant want to know. Am J Nurs, 76:92–94, (January) 1976.

**Methods of Behavior Modification**

Berni, Rosemarian, and Fordyce, Wilbur: Behavior Modification and the Nursing Process. St. Louis, The C. V. Mosby Co., 1973.

Citrin, Richard, and Dixon, David: Reality orientation — a milieu therapy used in an institution for the aged. Gerontologist, 17(1):39–43, (February) 1977.

Deibert, Alvin, and Harmon, Alice: New Tools for Changing Behavior. Champaign, Illinois, Research Press, 1973.

Fisher, Mary Lou: Helping acutely ill patients put out the fire. Am J Nurs, 79:1104–1105, (June) 1979.

Glasser, William: Reality Therapy. New York, Harper & Row, Publishers, Inc., 1965.

Hahn, Karen: Using 24-hour reality orientation. J Gerontol Nurs, 6:130, (March) 1980.

Kahn, Alice Nelson: Group education for the overweight. Am J Nurs, 78:254, (February) 1978.

Kaluger, George, and Kaluger, Meriem: Human Development: The Span of Life. St. Louis, The C. V. Mosby Co., 1974.

Lyon, Glee: Stimulation through remotivation. Am J Nurs, 71:982–986, (May) 1971.

Minuchin, Salvador: Families and Family Therapy. Cambridge, Massachusetts, Harvard University Press, 1974.

O'Neil, Sally M.: Behavior modification: toward a human experience. Nurs Clin North Am, 10(2):373–379, (June) 1975.

Patterson, Gerald R.: Families: Application of Social Learning to Family Life. Champaign, Illinois, Research Press, 1971.

Reese, Ellen: The Analysis of Human Operant Behavior. Dubuque, Iowa, Wm. C. Brown Co., Publishers, 1976.

Shaw, Dale, et al.: Multiple impact therapy. Am J Nurs, 77:246–248, (February) 1977.

Steckel, Susan E.: Contracting with patient-selected reinforcers. Am J Nurs, 80:1596–1599, (September) 1980.

Whitman, Helen, and Lukes, Shelby: Behavior modification for terminally ill patients. Am J Nurs, 75:98–101, (January) 1975.

Yates, Aubrey: Behavior Therapy. New York, John Wiley & Sons, Inc., 1970.

# Chapter SEVEN

# Stress and Anxiety

## OBJECTIVES   Information in this chapter will help you to

1. Define terms related to stress and anxiety: stressor, threat, anxiety, stress, autonomic nervous system, coping mechanisms, and defense mechanisms.
2. State five causes of stress for a nursing student and five causes of stress for a person who is sick.
3. Describe the six steps of the anxiety process: the stressor, the perception of a threat, the anxiety response, the autonomic nervous system (ANS) response, the coping appraisal, and the coping behavior.
4. State five ways in which the ANS affects the body structure or function in response to anxiety and five ways in which the ANS works to restore adaptation.
5. Identify various coping mechanisms that are used to reduce anxiety and the behavior patterns that are commonly used as attack ("fight") or withdrawal ("flight").
6. State the steps of insight therapy that are used as interventions to reduce anxiety.

## DEFINITION OF TERMS

**anxiety** — the reaction to a real or imaginary danger or threat that leads to psychological tension, fear, dread, or apprehension and activates the autonomic nervous system.

**autonomic nervous system (ANS)** — the part of the nervous system of the body not under voluntary control that maintains body survival functions and a stable internal environment.

**coping mechanisms** — the behaviors used to respond to a stressor or to meet the need state.

**defense mechanisms** — behaviors used to block or mask the awareness of reality that is too painful or not acceptable to the person. They are used when coping mechanisms are unable to reduce the anxiety.

**homeostasis** — a uniformity or a return to the normal state of body systems and the internal environment. It is the adaptive state.

**parasympathetic nervous system (PNS)** — the portion of the autonomic nervous system that has an opposing or antagonistic effect to the sympathetic nervous system and restores adaptation.

**stress** — any physical or psychological stimulus that disturbs the homeostasis of the body or causes strain or tension.

**stressor** — a stimulus that calls for a response by the body and causes stress.

**sympathetic nervous system (SNS)** — the portion of the autonomic nervous system that mobilizes the body for "fight or flight" responses to stress.

**threat** — an actual or perceived danger or a possible cause of harm.

---

This period in time has been referred to as the "age of anxiety." In a modern, industrialized nation, the complexities of life and the geometric progression of changes that occur affect everyone. Stress and anxiety can result from changes that occur in our lives. Every change represents a new stimulus with which we must cope in order to regain and to maintain stability in our lives.

During this century, tremendous changes have occurred. A ripple effect has taken place as these changes initiate innumerable minor changes. The surge in the population growth has caused the doubling of the world population from two billion to four billion in a 35-year period, according to the New York Times (1981). This has led to greater competition for resources and to a great concentration of people in large urban areas. The explosion of knowledge has pushed man's horizons into the far galaxies, and through the marvels of electronics, the microcosmic world of the cell is being explored. Each year, governmental bodies pass thousands of new laws and regulations which mold, shape, and limit the activities of citizens or require more time and effort to comply with their imposed provisions. Through mass communications with satellite relay stations, television news takes us halfway around the world, enabling events in far-off places to influence our thoughts and actions. All these changes increase the complexity of our lives by subjecting us to greater burdens of stress and by threatening our self-concept and integrity as individuals.

The effect of change is a disturbance in the normal response to stimuli or in the usual pattern of one's life. The new, or unfamiliar, stimulus upsets the organization and cohesion of the accustomed way(s) to respond to familiar and recurring stimuli. Previously, health and adaptation were defined as having a sense of consistency and ease in life that enables one to maintain integrity. When a person's internal and external environment are predictable, life is more apt to proceed smoothly. Changes that disrupt and disorganize a person's life lead to maladaptation and physical illness. It is amazing however, that some people are so resilient that they are able to adapt or to cope with many changes and are able resist the damaging effects of stress and anxiety for extended periods of time.

When illness strikes, for whatever cause, it produces many additional changes with which people must cope, in addition to the associated stress and anxiety. Anxiety produces feelings of inadequacy, tension, and acute distress at the same time that people are worrying about the effects of their illness, the uncomfortable or painful treatment they they are undergoing, and whether or not they will survive. Anxiety can delay the recovery of those who are ill because it diverts energy that is needed for the healing process to the behaviors used in coping with the anxiety. Therefore, it is essential that nurses understand the process of anxiety, its effects, and ways to intervene to reduce the anxious state.

Anxiety is a universal experience. No one is immune to anxiety and stress, not even nurses. Situations that are frequently anxiety-provoking to the nurse include working with people who are terminally ill, emergency conditions of life and death that require swift action, and stressful working conditions.

In this chapter, you will study anxiety and stress and consider the following questions and some possible answers. What is the anxiety process? What is the difference between anxiety and stress? How does one cope with anxiety? Is anxiety only in one's mind or does it exist physiologically? What can be done about anxiety? While seeking answers to these questions, you will proceed to examine the anxiety process and to compare it with the process of purposeful behavior. The responses of the autonomic nervous system are identified, and behaviors show how body functions are affected by stress and anxiety. Coping mechanisms that are used to reduce discomforts, and ways to intervene with people who are experiencing anxious feelings are discussed. The nurse who has a better understanding of the anxiety process is better able to assess the anxiety and deal with it, as opposed to letting it persist and interfere with or prolong an individual's recovery.

## WHAT IS STRESS?

Stress has been described in many ways. It is any physical or psychological stimulus that disturbs the adaptive state or the homeostasis of the body. Stress involves all the body systems and upsets the delicate balance of the internal environment. It is a universal reaction that everyone has experienced many times, and it has the crucial purpose of activating the body to protect itself and to insure its survival. An exciting date for a party, the lack of a date, driving a car in traffic, or taking an examination can all be stress-producing stimuli. Many situations in everyday life can activate one's stress response. Selye (1956), a pioneer in the study of stress, described stress as the wear and tear that is caused to the body at one particular time.

Many factors cause stress. Some factors produce only biological changes in the body, while others produce both physiological and psychological responses. It is possible to have biological stress without anxiety, but it is not possible to have anxiety without stress. The causes of stress can be classified into five groups.

1. Biological factors — any pathogenic organism, infections.
2. Chemical factors — drugs, poisons, toxins, anesthetic agents, foreign proteins, blood reactions, electrolyte imbalances.
3. Emotional or social factors — anxiety, fear, pain, anger, powerlessness, depression.
4. Physical factors — heat, cold, drafts, sensory deprivation, monotony, or overload.
5. Physiological conditions — burns, immobilization, loss of sleep, surgery, trauma.

People who have a health problem in meeting one or more of their basic needs or in coping with changes in their lives are subject to additional stresses. Most people have some degree of anxiety because it is usually impossible to separate the biological being from the psychological being. The man suffering a heart attack is hospitalized in a coronary care unit in which bright lights are on continuously, is attached to monitors, is given medications that affect his cellular functions, is exposed to machines that make strange noises, and is separated from his family and familiar surroundings with sensory overload or monotony interrupted only by strangers coming in to perform tests or to carry out procedures. All these factors increase the stress and anxiety of the patient who has a damaged heart.

As a physician, Selye was interested in the effects of all types of stress on a cellular level. He was able to demonstrate the damage that resulted to tissues from excessive and prolonged stress responses of the body. He considered the stressors and the body responses as the general adaptation syndrome (GAS). He divided GAS into three stages.

1. *The alarm stage.* The defense mechanisms are activated, and the body is prepared for "fight or flight."
2. *The resistance stage.* The body attempts to cope with the stressor by limiting the response to that area and by using only the amount of activity necessary to control the stressor. Unaffected areas return to normal.
3. *The stage of exhaustion.* With a strong stressor or one that lasts for an extended period of time, the defense mechanisms wear down. The alarm stage is activated again. Unless the process is reversed, the stress causes damage to the body and can lead to death.

The effects of stress on the body are the result of the autonomic nervous system and hormonal activity. They produce predictable body responses of increased metabolism to provide immediate energy, increased blood supply to the brain, heart, and skeletal muscles, increased clotting factors in the blood, an increase in the amount of circulating blood, and an increase in the insensible loss of fluids through perspiration and breathing. Although these responses are protective in nature, they can be detrimental to some people. Patients with coronary occlusion, hypertension, thrombophlebitis, diabetes, liver disease, or poor nutrition or patients on steroid drug therapy are among the patients who are less able to cope with stress. The effect of stresses tends to be cumulative rather than diminishing.

The nursing actions used to combat physiological stresses are based on the use of the nursing process and the assessment of behaviors related to the stress response and involve manipulating the stimuli that cause the stress.

## THE STRESS OF ANXIETY

Anxiety is only one form of stress, but it is probably the most prevalent form. Anxiety is the reaction to a real or an imaginary danger or threat that leads to psychological tension, fear, dread, or apprehension. Anxiety is the major cause of problems of coping in the self-concept mode. Some people will deny that they are anxious about the complexities and the continual changes associated with modern life; yet, they will admit to being upset, worried, or concerned about something.

## CAUSES OF ANXIETY

Anxiety arises when a stressor is perceived to be a threat to the self-concept or to one's self-image. From early infancy, people grow and develop a sense of who they are. They see themselves in terms of being able to meet their own needs, being useful and productive in society, communicating with others, "belonging" and forming meaningful relationships, and being able to meet the goals and expectations that they have for themselves. Anxiety occurs when people are confronted with a situation that poses a threat to this self-image of being a competent person who is in control and is able to handle most changes in life.

No single stimulus provokes anxiety. What creates anxiety in one person does not necessarily cause the same response or the same amount of anxiety in another person. Whether or not a stimulus is perceived as threatening depends on the meaning that is attached to it. In order to experience anxiety, the individual must have mental faculties and sufficient intellectual development to form the concept of harm and the concept of self. Although infants and young children are subject to many types of stress, they probably do not experience anxiety until they are old enough to recognize something as a threat and to have developed a rudimentary self-concept.

## THE PROCESS OF ANXIETY

In Chapter Two, we discussed voluntary behavior of a purposeful nature. For this to occur, a stimulus must act upon the body, cause a mental recognition of a need state to be satisfied or the need to act, and be followed by a response. The anxiety process is based upon the same process but also includes a perceived threat and the activation of the autonomic nervous system (ANS). As with purposeful behavior, various coping mechanisms are appraised for their effectiveness and for their previous success in reducing the discomforts of anxiety. Then the most appropriate coping mechanism is selected and used. If it is successful, the anxiety is reduced; if it is not successful, there is a coping problem and the anxiety continues. This is shown in Figure 7–1.

The anxiety process is illustrated by the

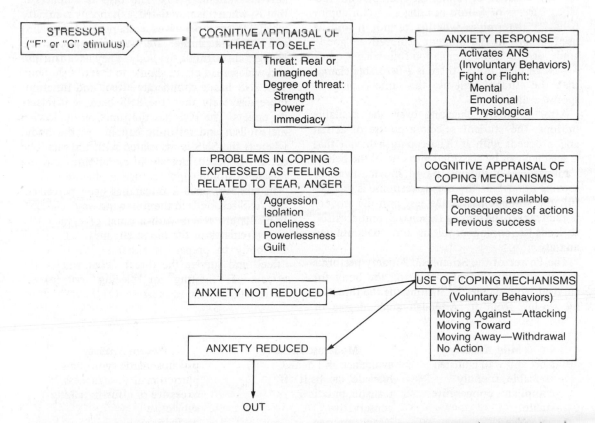

**Figure 7–1.** The framework for the anxiety process shows the changes that occur in purposeful behavior when the stimulus is perceived as a threat and activates the autonomic nervous system (ANS). Coping that does not reduce anxiety leads to the problems associated with fear and anger.

following example. Students are given examinations at intervals to assess their achievement in learning certain material. The examination is a stimulus that affects the students. It is perceived as a threat, in some degree, to the self. The strength of the examination as a stimulus depends on its importance. If it is a daily or a weekly quiz, it poses less of a threat than if it contributes to 50 per cent of the course grade. The stimulus causes less of a threat if it is to occur three weeks in the future than it does if it is to occur tomorrow. The thought of the threat activiates the autonomic nervous system (ANS), and the ANS prepares the body physiologically for "fight or flight."

Simultaneously, the student mentally looks over the possible coping mechanisms (in terms of the resources available), the consequences of these actions, and the previous degree of success that is associated with each action. The student then decides to study for the examination. The resources include class notes and books as well as a time to study and a place in which to study. The consequences of studying include passing the examination, getting a better grade than if one had not studied, or failing the examination. Previous success or failure in using a certain coping behavior determines whether or not it will be used again. If the student achieved a "good" grade on the last examination following a quick review of class notes, there is a favorable chance that the student will use the same coping response again.

After mentally checking over the available options, the student selects a course of action and proceeds with it. The coping behavior that is selected can be classified into one of the behavioral patterns of moving-toward, moving-away, or moving-against. If the coping response is successful, the student passes the test and the anxiety is reduced. If the coping response is unsuccessful, it leads to coping problems and to continued anxiety.

**The Power of the Stimulus.** Anxiety performs the useful function of mobilizing the body for survival from danger by fighting off the threat or by fleeing from it. Although some degree of anxiety may be helpful and motivates one for action, prolonged or high levels of anxiety can be destructive.

Although numerous scales have been devised to detect the presence of anxiety, it is difficult to measure. Nurses estimate the level of anxiety, however, by assessing a patient's behavior and associating it with behavior that is characteristic of the stages of mild, moderate, and severe anxiety.

Severe anxiety may progress to a panic state. In panic, the individual focuses on one detail or aspect to the exclusion of all others. Panic is accompanied by feelings of dread, of being adrift and being "out of control." The behaviors of panic are those of extreme discomfort, disorganization, and chaos.

**Autonomic Nervous System Response.** The internal environment of the body is governed primarily by the autonomic nervous system, which stimulates and regulates the functions of organs, the production of hormones, and the chemical reactions vital to life. The autonomic nervous system (ANS), is composed of the sympathetic nervous system (SNS) and the parasympathetic nervous system (PNS). The SNS is adrenergic; that is, when it is stimulated, as happens in anxiety when a threat is perceived, epinephrine (adrenalin) and norepinephrine are secreted and cause changes throughout the body. They have a diffuse and widespread effect similar to that of a shotgun. The PNS has a cholinergic effect and functions more discretely than the SNS because it selects its targets. The PNS has the function of slowing metabolism and restoring supplies to the body, whereas the SNS is associated with the catabolic actions of rapid increase in metabolism and the release of stored supplies, such as glucose.

In anxiety, once a threat has been perceived, the ANS responds in the following way. The SNS immediately reacts with a burst of epinephrine that circulates in the blood stream to all parts of the body to prepare it either to "fight" or to "flee" and survive the threat. What will be the effects of "fighting" or "fleeing" on: (a) the heart rate, (b) blood pressure, (c) the respiratory

| Mild Anxiety | Moderate Anxiety | Severe Anxiety |
|---|---|---|
| alert and well adjusted | avoidance and denial | psychosomatic symptoms |
| amicable, friendly | bravado, laughs it off | blurred reality, vagueness |
| compliant, cooperative | realistic, practical | excessive or effusive talking |
| stable | conservative | subjective |
| objective | intellectualizes | perfectionism |
| approaches directly | some guilt and hostility | rigid standards |
| avoids irritant or trauma | religious and moral expressions | emotional constriction |
| | | sense of foreboding |

rate, (d) the pupil of the eye, (e) the blood vessels of the skin and the mucous membranes, and (f) the clotting ability of the blood?

In stress and anxiety states, the blood pressure, pulse, and respirations increase to provide more oxygen to the brain and to the muscles. The pupil enlarges to let in more light, enabling vision to become more acute in order to see the threat or danger. To conserve the vital fluids of the body, the antidiuretic hormone is released to slow down the formation of urine, additional clotting factors are released into the blood stream, and vessels in the skin constrict, thereby shunting the blood to the skeletal muscles and to the vital organs. The activity of the digestive tract slows, with a marked decrease in the flow of all digestive juices.

The changes produced by SNS activity occur rapidly and last for a short period of time unless the SNS is stimulated again to release additional epinephrine and norepinephrine. The norepinephrine released at the SNS nerve endings exists for only a few seconds. However, the hormones secreted by the adrenal gland enter the blood stream where they remain active from 10 to 30 seconds. The hormonal secretion decreases in a period of one to several minutes. It is the effect one would feel when startled by a loud bang, and it lasts about as long as it takes for heart rate and breathing to return to normal. After the initial startle or anxiety response, the opposing action of the PNS takes over to restore the balance and to return the functions of the body to an adapted state. The PNS slows the heart and respiratory rates, lowers the blood pressure as peripheral blood vessels relax from their constricted state, causes the gastric functions to increase, and causes the kidneys to produce a greater quantity of urine.

Many people have developed a pronounced and specific response to the SNS actions that are produced by stress and anxiety. Sternback (1966) states that one body organ or system becomes the target for the SNS actions and responds with a stronger action than is seen in other body organs that experience the same amount of stress. This

Table 7–1. AUTONOMIC NERVOUS SYSTEM (ANS) RESPONSES

| Sympathetic Nervous System (SNS)<br>*The response to stress and anxiety*<br>*(diffuse, general, "shotgun")* | | Parasympathetic Nervous System (PNS)<br>*The steady state; recovery from the stress*<br>*response (discrete, selective, "rifle-shot")* |
|---|---|---|
| **SNS effect** | **Structure and Function** | **PNS effect** |
| − | Eyes − accommodation of lens | + |
| − | constriction of iris | + |
| − | Lacrimal gland − tears | + |
| − | Salivary glands − salivation | + |
| − | Gastrointestinal tract − peristalsis | + |
| − | Nasal mucosa − secretion, dilation | + |
| − | Stomach glands − secrete HCl, pepsin, mucus | + |
| − | Pancreas − secrete insulin | + |
| + | Heart − acceleration of the rate | − |
| + | Lungs − dilation of the bronchi | − |
| + | Adrenal medulla | 0 |
| + | Peripheral blood vessels − vasoconstriction | ? |
| + | Sweat glands − sweating | 0 |
| + | Pilomotor cells − piloerection | 0 |
| | Internal sphincters | |
| + | bladder − contraction, closed | − |
| + | intestine − contraction, closed | − |
| − | Bladder wall − contraction | + |
| − | Lower bowel − contraction | + |
| − | Genitalia − erection | + |
| + | Blood − coagulation | 0 |
| + | Blood − glucose | 0 |
| + | Basal metabolism − up 100% | 0 |
| + | Skeletal muscle strength | 0 |

**Key:** (+) increased response (facilitating effect)
(−) decreased response (inhibitory effect)
(o) no effect

(Adapted from Sternbach, Richard: The Principles of Psychophysiology. New York, Academic Press, Inc., 1966, and Guyton, Arthur: Textbook of Medical Physiology, 6th ed. Philadelphia, W. B. Saunders Company, 1981.)

has given rise to many phrases in our everyday language that are used to describe peoples' reactions, such as "I am so mad, I could blow my top," "He really gets under my skin," "Oh, my aching back," and "I've got butterflies in my stomach." Sternback also classified people who tend to have a greater response in one body system than in another when under stress as responders. Someone who becomes nauseated or has diarrhea when anxious or under stress has greater activity of the gastrointestinal (GI) tract than most other people and would be classified as a GI responder. Some behaviors that are associated with a particular response can be categorized.

*Skin responders.* People whose responses to stress include paleness, rashes, hives, itching, redness of skin areas, and excessive perspiration.

*GI responders.* People who have pronounced nausea, upset stomach, belching, heartburn, loose stools, or diarrhea when under stress.

*Circulatory responders.* People in whom anxiety and stress produce elevated blood pressure, palpitations of the heart, arrhythmias, tachycardia, and tension headaches.

*Musculoskeletal responders.* People who have muscular tension, rigidity, tremors, involuntary tics, backaches, and muscle strains associated with stress or anxiety.

*Respiratory responders.* People who exhibit rapid respiratory rates, sighing respirations, asthma attacks, wheezing, and hyperventilation.

Chronic anxiety with prolonged effects of SNS stimulation can produce cellular damage to the body, and often the target organ or system seems to break down. The GI responder who is bothered with heartburn and an upset stomach when anxious may develop a gastric ulcer. It is well known that ulcers are associated with and aggravated by emotional factors. Diseases that are frequently associated with anxiety are hypertension, asthma, colitis, backache, migraine headaches, hives, and rheumatoid arthritis.

**Voluntary Coping Mechanisms.** When the anxiety response is activated, a mental process assesses ways to reduce the threat and to cope with the anxiety. The method selected depends upon the resources that are available, the consequences of the action, and the previous success with that action. Resources that may limit one's choice of action are the amount of time that is needed, money, materials or supplies that are required, one's past experiences, the availability of services by other people, and one's physical abilities. The coping mechanism is selected and put into action as behavior that can be observed or assessed. The coping behaviors result in the direct reduction of the anxiety or in no reduction of the anxiety. If the anxiety continues, the stressor is reappraised as a threat, and the SNS is activated to prepare the body to meet the "emergency."

People cope with feelings of anxiety in a number of different ways. Most people use the following methods to cope successfully with perceived threats.

Oral satisfaction — eating food, chewing gum, smoking, drinking (soft drinks, alcoholic beverages)

Vigorous physical activity in work or play

Reassurance of touch, rhythm, sound, speech

Laughing; crying; swearing

Self-discipline, self-control

Creative activities — music, arts, crafts, building, sewing

Talking; thinking things out

Sleep; dreams

Coping behaviors that are used to deal with anxiety can be placed into one of the three behavioral patterns: moving-toward, moving-away, or moving-against. Adaptive coping mechanisms lead to behavior that is within the normal range, that meets the expectations of society, that is successful in reducing the anxiety, and that is more easily achieved through the use of problem-solving skills.

**Defense Mechanisms.** In addition to the common coping mechanisms previously mentioned, other coping mechanisms, including defense mechanisms, are used frequently by people in coping with changes in their lives. At some time, everyone uses defensive mechanisms to protect themselves from the discomfort or the pain of anxiety. Defense mechanisms are useful in defending ourselves from intolerable conditions, but they do not solve the problem or alter the cause of the anxiety. People who use defense mechanisms no longer feel the discomforts of stress or anxiety, but often they must use a great deal of energy to cover up and maintain a defensive attitude.

In many instances, the use of defense mechanisms is constructive and serves to maintain the person's stability and ability to function. For example, patients who have had a coronary occlusion and are soon to undergo open heart surgery or people who have just learned that they have cancer often use defense mechanisms. They frequently use forms of denial to protect themselves from the anxiety produced by the seriousness of their condition.

Coping and defense mechanisms associated with each of the three types of behavioral patterns are given on page 87.

*Moving-away behaviors*

1. Withdrawal; avoidance; denial.
2. Repression. The process of forgetting feelings, wishes, or impulses that lead to the awareness of a coping problem, its cause, and the resulting anxiety.
3. Daydreams; fantasy; temporary escape through movies, books, dramas, watching television, similar activities.
4. Rationalization and projection of "acceptable reasons" or excuses for one's behavior.
5. Regression. A return to a younger age level of functioning that was more satisfying or less stressful.
6. Sublimation and goal-substitution. Redirecting one's energies to other activities, objectives, or goals.
7. Identification. Participation in the strengths of others to escape one's own deficiencies.

*Moving-against behaviors*

1. "Taking it out on others," when anger or aggression is directed toward others or objects, hidden anger as seen in prejudice, in being accident prone, and in exploitation of innocent targets.
2. Negativism; uncooperativeness; criticism. Hurting or defeating others with a disguised form of aggression.
3. Use of superiority, bossiness, boastfulness, ostentation, and the aggressive use of power, wealth, or even poverty.
4. Overprotectiveness. Extreme protection or concern in the form of "smother love" expressed to repress feelings of hostility toward the person.

*Moving-toward behaviors*

1. Homesickness; inability to deviate from the known and familiar ways; overdeference to others; inability to make one's own decisions.
2. Illness. This allows a legitimate release from responsibilities or from the situation. Sickness insures being cared for by others and may be used as a means to manipulate or to punish others. The illness is real, but the cause is generally related to emotional problems.

Defense mechanisms that interfere with the person's ability to function effectively and that are used when coping mechanisms fail include

*Depression.* The attempt to deal with stress by anger turned inward. The person has feelings of self-punishment, unworthiness, depreciation, and hostility toward others or that events are beyond his or her control.

*Substances such as drugs and alcohol.* These substances are used to produce states of temporary oblivion

*Obsessions and compulsions.* The use of ritual and the avoidance of feared situations. The person with an unconscious fear of illness defends against the anxiety by constantly thinking about germs, seeing them everywhere, and acting to kill them by repeatedly washing hands, dishes, and wearing a mask and by carrying out other similar types of behavior.

*Hysteria.* The development of severe and crippling mental or physical disorders. The woman who is unable to accept the anxiety caused by her hostility toward her child may develop a paralysis of her arm so that she cannot use it at all, much less to carry out actions hurting the child.

Other more severe types of defense mechanisms may represent a "complete" break with reality and require psychiatric treatment.

## FIRST LEVEL ASSESSMENT OF BEHAVIORS

When stress and anxiety occur, people respond with a wide variety of behaviors, both physiological and psychosocial. The nurse must assess all modes of function in order to identify correctly the problem and its causes. The ANS response to stress and anxiety produces a definite pattern of physiological changes in the body. Most people have a more pronounced response in one system or organ than in another, such as being a skin responder and developing a rash or itching dermatitis, when anxious. In addition, people utilize a vast array of coping mechanisms and behaviors to deal with their feelings of helplessness, isolation, insecurity, or fear.

### PHYSIOLOGICAL MODE

When the stimulus is perceived to pose a danger or a threat to the person, the sympathetic branch of the ANS instantly increases its activity to mobilize the body defenses. The SNS acts to increase the metabolism, to increase the blood supply to skeletal muscles and vital organs, to increase the clotting of blood, and to conserve body fluids. Following the emergency, the effects of the PNS dominate to bring the body functions back into normal ranges. Therefore, the presence of SNS-related behaviors are seen in the early stages of anxiety and with ineffective coping mechanisms that keep the anxiety process going.

Behaviors that are associated with anxiety, particularly SNS responses, are given below and are listed according to the basic need areas to which they are related.

**Figure 7–2.** People may respond to the sympathetic nervous system effects of anxiety in one organ or system of the body more than in another organ or system. Some people show elevated systolic blood pressure, others develop itching of the skin, others retain fluid causing edema or show other types of disturbances.

*Oxygenation.*

Increase in blood pressure, especially systolic, such as 150 to 170/60.

Increase in pulse and respiratory rates

Possible palpitations, irregular beats, premature ventricular contractions (PVCs)

Pallor of skin

Mental alertness and awareness

Blushing, skin rash, itching

*Fluids and electrolyte balance.*

Retention of water, sodium, and chlorides

Decreased potassium with weakness, flaccid muscles

*Nutrition.*

Dry mouth, reduced secretions

Decreased peristalsis

Increased abdominal distention and flatus

Anorexia

Heartburn, nausea, vomiting (PNS action)

*Elimination.*

Decreased urinary output

Constipation

Increased tone of the anal and bladder spincters

Diarrhea (PNS action)

Polyuria (PNS action)

Increased perspiration of face, axilla, palms, and body

*Rest and activity.*

Muscles "set" for action or rigid

Unable to relax

Insomnia

Tremor or tic movement of muscles

*Sensory regulation and temperature control.*

Dilation of pupil

Decreased tactile sense of heat, cold, pressure, pain

More acute vision

## SELF-CONCEPT MODE

Psychosocial behaviors are assessed to determine the presence of anxiety. In the self-concept mode, anxiety is a stimulus that intervenes when one feels that there is a threat to one's self. Problems in coping with loss give rise to emotions that can be expressed in many different ways. One way to classify these behaviors is according to feelings of helplessness, isolation, and insecurity.

*Feelings of helplessness.*

A threat to the self arises from being powerless to direct or to control events or stimuli. There is an actual or a perceived loss or loss of control. Examples of behaviors:

"Hospitals aren't for human beings. People are always coming in and waking me up. I don't like it."

"I don't know how I'm going to live with that thing," stated the patient with a colostomy.

"The doctor said I was discharged, but I can't go home. I'm not any better than when I came to the hospital, and there's no one to take care of me."

*Feelings of isolation.*

Anxiety causes the person to feel alone abandoned by others who are too busy to care. There is a sense of alienation, of being set apart or different from others. Examples of behaviors:

A patient with an ileal bladder stated, "I'm not going out of my house where people can see that I have this bag hanging off my stomach."

"Nobody ever answers my light when I need something. It's hours before anyone comes."

"I don't have a say-so in my own affairs anymore. I guess I'm just a nothing now that my son has the power of attorney."

*Feelings of insecurity.*

Changes affect how people think of themselves and how they see themselves on a daily basis, upset the usual pattern of life, and cause questions to be raised about values or beliefs. These changes produce anxiety. Examples of behavior:

"I used to be very active. I helped other people all the time and enjoyed it. Now I can't even help myself."

"I had some very nice friends at the convalescent home where I lived before coming here, but they had to give my room to someone else. Now I don't even know where I live."

As shown by these examples, the assessment of the self-concept mode consists of expressions of emotions and verbal statements of how one feels or thinks of one's self. One statement or expression by itself does not necessarily indicate a problem but may provide a clue that indicates a need for further assessment. A group or cluster of behaviors provides more information regarding the presence and extent of a coping problem.

## SECOND LEVEL ASSESSMENT

A second level assessment is done to identify the causes of the maladaptive and ineffective behaviors that are found. When the stimulus poses a threat to the self, stress or anxiety is the cause of the behavior that is observed. Anxiety is a contextual stimulus, and whatever caused the anxiety is regarded as the focal stimulus (in terms of the Roy adaptation model of nursing).

Nurses continue to assess patients who have behaviors related to anxiety to identify the threat as it is perceived by the patient and to find other factors that influence or cause anxiety. Threats to the self result from changes in any of the following factors, and these threats lead to anxiety.

1. Expectations of the self
2. Expectations of others
3. Position on the health-illness continuum
4. Resources for meeting needs
5. Family structure and membership
6. Other support systems

What factors might cause anxiety in a nursing student? What factors might cause anxiety in a patient confined to the hospital? Some possible anxiety-provoking stressors are listed for the nursing student and the patient.

## TYPES OF PROBLEMS

Nurses who use the adaptation approach to nursing focus on patients' behaviors in meeting basic needs and in coping with changes in both the internal and external environment. When anxiety occurs as a result of a perceived threat to the self-concept, it is expressed through the coping mechanisms as behaviors. These behaviors include physical actions, expressions of emotions and statements that reveal the mental state, thoughts, and feelings of the patient. These reactions that result from a breakdown in the coping mechanism are the real problem and need to be changed.

Without a precise and accurate statement of

**Nursing Students**

Expect to be a good nurse
Want to get good grades
Fear of making mistakes
Pass tests with "C" or better
Demands of family
Money to continue studies
Home responsibilities
Heavy study load and reading assignments
Not knowing what to do if patient's condition becomes critical

**Patients Confined to Hospital**

Know they have a serious illness
Possible loss of sight, body organs
Fear of not getting well, of dying
Not getting medicines when needed
Being fed through tubes
Missing spouse, family
Not informed of test results, reasons for treatments
Lack of sufficient insurance or money to pay bill
Call light not answered promptly
Mistakes made in medicines, treatment, identification.

the patient's problem, the nurse is handicapped in resolving the problem. The statement of the problem in coping with anxiety focuses on the ineffective behavior that is being used and the feelings that are expressed. The following statements are examples of ways in which coping problems are expressed.

Patient has feelings of fear about dying.
Patient has feelings of anger due to illness and loss of control of muscles.
Patient has feelings of helplessness due to colostomy surgery
Patient is withdrawn due to change in body image.

When the nature of the threat is known, the stimuli that cause the problem are included in the statement of the problem. From the statement, the goal is formulated as a change in or a reduction of these feelings. Nursing interventions are then selected that enable manipulation of the stimuli that are causing the anxiety.

## NURSING INTERVENTIONS

Unresolved anxiety stimulates more anxiety. When the coping mechanism breaks down and is unable to reduce the threat, the threat becomes stronger and the anxiety grows. As anxiety grows and persists for a longer period of time, it is more difficult to handle; therefore, it is important that anxiety is recognized in its early stages and that interventions are used to help the patient cope more effectively with anxiety.

### INSIGHT THERAPY

The most important intervention used to reduce anxiety and to change the patient's behavior is insight therapy. Effective use of insight therapy makes it possible to actually see the patient's level of anxiety decrease. The patient may also make a statement to the effect that it really helped to talk about his or her feelings of anxiety.

To help the anxious patient, the nurse must be able to recognize anxiety and the many ways in which it is expressed. A patient's shouting or complaining behavior is likely to be an expression of anxiety rather than a reasonable and purposeful coping mechanism. Ordering the patient to "behave yourself" is apt to trigger additional angry behavior and not to solve the problem. The nurse should manipulate the second level stimulus of anxiety by using the steps of insight therapy:

1. Help the person to recognize the anxiety

2. Person gains insight into the cause of the anxiety or the threat
3. Person copes with the threat in a constructive way.

It is important for people who are anxious to examine their feelings at the time when they are anxious. People have the right to express their feelings, but they may not always be able to do so in an adaptive way. Often, it is helpful for the nurse to acknowledge the presence of peoples' feelings by making objective statements, such as, "You seem to be very upset by something. What happened?" or "I see that you are depressed. Can you tell me what is bothering you?" As they explore the patient's feelings, the nurse and the patient look at the perceived threat and at some of the factors that affect the threat. The threat of anxiety is due to change, and change means a disorganization of a segment of life and the learning of a new way of coping with that change.

When a patient's coping mechanisms have failed to reduce the anxiety state, the nurse can manipulate or alter parts of the anxiety process. Some ways to intervene are to

*Change the stressor.* It may be possible to reduce its power, to make it smaller, to change its character, or to alter its timing. Pain is a common stressor, and the nurse can do much to alter its effects. Medications can be given promptly to control pain, actions can be taken to reduce the pain by gentle handling or positioning for comfort, procedures or activities may be delayed until pain has been relieved, and emotional support and encouragement can be provided through touch and by one's presence.

*Change the person's perception of the stressor as a threat or danger.* A young boy, recovering from serious injuries and a tracheostomy, refused to eat as he became more alert. Days later, a nurse learned that he thought that the food had to travel down the same passageway as the tracheal tube and that the food would cause him to choke. Health-teaching and explanations given to patients help to dispel misconceptions and inadequate knowledge.

*Check available coping mechanisms.* The coping mechanism that is being used is ineffective in resolving the coping problem. What others might be used? The cardiac patient who is on strict bed rest is not able to use physical activities, sports, or jogging as coping mechanisms because of the consequences that they might have on the damaged heart. Perhaps reading a sports magazine or talking or some other method of coping would be effective.

Evaluate the person's behavior after insight therapy has been used. Did the behavior change? Were the threat and the anxiety reduced? Although it may not be possible to help *every* person who has a coping problem due to anxiety, it is possible to reduce the discomforts of this universal human experience in oneself and in others through the use of the nursing process and insight therapy.

## APPLICATION TO CLINICAL PRACTICE

In the clinical setting, assess your patient for anxiety, and, if anxiety is present, use the nursing process to plan and to carry out nursing interventions to reduce the anxiety state.

1. Name at least five stressors that cause patients to become anxious. What effect do they have on your patient?
2. Assess your patient for behaviors that are related to anxiety. Include physiological behaviors and statements of feelings that describe "Who I am," and "How I feel about myself."
3. In which body system is the anxiety response strongest or the most noticeable?
4. What is the stimulus that is causing the anxiety? What is perceived to be the threat?
5. What is the coping mechanism that is being used? What is the basic pattern of behavior?
6. State the nursing interventions you will take to reduce the anxiety.
7. What were the effects of the interventions that you used?

## REFERENCES

Cohn, Lucile: Coping with anxiety: a step-by-step guide, Nursing 79, 9(12):34–37, (December) 1979.

Dennis, Lorraine B.: Psychology of Human Behavior for Nurses, 3rd ed. Philadelphia, W. B. Saunders Company, 1967, pp. 188–221.

Ferguson, Ursuline: What Danny didn't know, Nursing 80, 10(11):136, (November) 1980.

Frain, Marita, and Valiga, Theresa: The multiple dimensions of stress, Top Clin Nurs, 1:1, (April) 1979.

Lazarus, Richard S.: Psychological Stress and the Coping Process. New York, McGraw-Hill, Inc., 1966.

Locke, S. E.: Stress, adaptation and immunity: studies in humans, Gen Hosp Psychiatry, 4:49–58, (April) 1982.

Marcinek, Margaret B.: Stress in the surgical patient, Am J Nurs, 77:1809–1811, (November) 1977.

Murray, Malinda: Fundamentals of Nursing, 2nd ed. Englewood Cliffs, NJ, Prentice-Hall Inc., 1980, pp. 335–348.

New York Times: The people boom. (October 6) 1981.

Programmed Instruction. Anxiety-recognition and intervention, Am J Nurs, 65:129–152, (September) 1965.

O'Flynn-Comisky, Alice I.: The type A individual, Am J Nurs, 79:1957, (November) 1979.

Selye, Hans: The Stress of Life. New York, McGraw-Hill, Inc., 1956.

Smith, Marcy J. T., and Selye, Hans: Reducing the negative effects of stress, Am J Nurs, 79:1953, (November) 1979.

Sparacino, Jack: Blood pressure, stress, and mental health, Nurs Res, 31:89–94, (March/April) 1982.

Stephenson, Carol A.: Stress in critically ill patients, Am J Nurs, 77:1806–1809, (November) 1977.

Sternback, Richard: The Principles of Psychophysiology. New York, Academic Press, Inc., 1966.

*Chapter EIGHT*

# Illness and the Sick Role

**OBJECTIVES**  **Information in this chapter will help you to**

1. Describe the stages of illness in terms of (a) the transition from health to illness, (b) the period of "accepted illness," and (c) the convalescent stage.
2. Identify the social requirements for taking on the sick role.
3. Describe the expectations of the sick role that are held by society and those that are held by the sick person.
4. State the tasks to be accomplished for each stage of illness, and give examples of patient behaviors for each stage.
5. Assess the effect of illness on the patient's integrity and functioning in all modes.
6. Assess patients' behaviors as either appropriate or maladaptive, using your understanding of the stages of illness and the sick role.

Illness is a universal experience; everyone has been ill at some time, if only with a cold, the flu, a cut on the hand, or a severe muscle strain. The illness shifted the person to a lower position on the health-illness continuum. To some degree, the illness changed the ordinary routine of the person affected as he or she sought to cope with the changes it made in meeting various needs. Think back to a time when you were ill. Remember how you felt more lethargic, weak, and tired and that it took more energy to do things than it usually does. Remember how you found it difficult to concentrate on what you were doing

or to show interest in others? Remember how you spent more time thinking about how you felt? The illness not only affected some local tissues or a part of the body but also affected your feelings and your mental activity, as well as social activities.

This chapter examines the condition of illness from the adaptation model approach and the stages of illness and tasks to be accomplished for each stage. The tasks and the typical behaviors for the stages of illness become the standard that we use to judge whether or not the assessed behaviors of the patient are appropriate. This chapter also focuses on the sick role, which gives guidelines for the way in which an individual should respond when sick. The characteristics of the sick role, the expectations that society has for the patient, and the expectations that the patient may have are defined.

Illness is a stimulus that causes many changes in the patients. The way(s) in which patients respond to these changes establishes how they will carry out their sick role. They may use any of the three basic behavior patterns to perform a wide variety of actions, and to express emotions and widely differing beliefs. However, the sick role involves some universal expectations concerning those who are ill, including how they feel about their treatment, or care. Such expectations are the standard, or norm, with which one compares the behaviors that one assesses in patients. The sick role is *not* a stimulus, it is *not* a behavior, it is *not* a problem, but it *is* a basis for judging whether the patient's behavior is adaptive or maladaptive for a particular stage of illness.

## THE CONDITION OF ILLNESS

What is illness? At what point does a person become ill?

- Rena is a 24-year-old secretary who is very thin, weighs only 87 pounds and becomes upset and angry easily. She has frequent spells of depression. During these spells she cannot work or stand to be with people.
- John S. is a successful insurance agent who is active in community projects and local politics, despite having diabetes and having had a serious heart attack three years ago.
- Dorothy is an active teenager, but each month she misses one or two days of school at the beginning of her menstrual period because of cramps and heavy flow.
- Mrs. B. G. has had frequent heartburn and eructations when eating certain types of foods. During the past few hours, she has been vomiting and has a severe pain in her right upper quadrant.

Which of these cases would you classify as being ill? If you indicated that each of the four people has behaviors that signify difficulty in coping with change or in meeting a need, you have a beginning level of understanding of adaptation concepts.

## *ILLNESS AND THE ADAPTATION MODEL OF NURSING*

In the adaptation model of nursing, man is

located somewhere on the health-illness continuum from optimum health (adaptation) on one end to serious illness and impending death (the complete failure of adaptation) on the other end (See Chapter One). A person's position is dynamic and changes from time to time as one experiences difficulty in meeting one's needs and in coping with changes in one's inner or outer world. Maladaptive behaviors result when one is unable to meet one's needs for integrity or the wholeness and efficiency of function. There is a breakdown in coping, and the unmet need causes a tension and discomfort that is a dis-ease.

Illness is any maladaptive behavior that leads to dis-ease. A person's coping mechanisms have become ineffective in maintaining adaptation in physical functioning and psychological comfort in social settings. Figure 8–1 shows the progression of coping difficulties to overt diseases that are associated with medical problems, to increasing failure of all adaptive mechanisms, and finally, death.

One of the great marvels of life is that people are able to adapt to a dynamic, everchanging world and to respond to most stimuli in an organized and meaningful way that meets their needs. In this way, people minimize surprises and the unpredictability of their surroundings and achieve a stability in internal functioning. When internal changes cause a breakdown in the body's ability to adapt or to compensate, behaviors become maladaptive, and the person moves toward the illness end of the health-illness continuum. By combining the health-illness continuum with Maslow's hierarchy of needs, one can see that the coping problems involve unmet needs associated with feelings, emotions, and interpersonal relationships, which have a lower priority for survival than do safety and physiological needs.

Depression or "the blues," drug or alcohol abuse, sexual impotence, and the inappropriate feelings of fear, anger, grief, or powerlessness are examples of coping breakdown. There is no distinct point where coping breakdown in self-concept, interdependence, or role-function modes produces physiological changes that lead to overt illness. However, because man is an integrated whole, and the physiological man cannot be separated from the psychosocial man, a problem in one of these modes often causes needs in another mode. As the person moves toward the incipient illness zone, some of the conditions that characterize it are acne vulgaris, dental caries, obesity, and headache.

When there is a breakdown in the ability of the body to cope with internal physiological changes, the individual moves into the overt illness zone

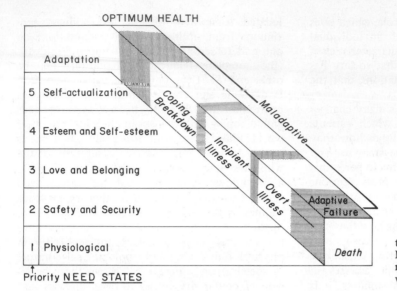

**Figure 8–1.** The relationship between the health-illness continuum and Maslow's hierarchy of needs assists the nurse in setting priorities for coping with problems.

of the continuum. Maladaptive coping represents a higher priority need to ensure the survival and the safety of the person. Internal changes affect the tissues or the cells, disrupt the functions of the cell, or interfere with the regulation of its function through chemical actions or by the responses of the endocrine or nervous systems.

The more complete the breakdown in the body's ability to cope with these changes, the more serious the illness. The complete failure of adaptation is death, whether of a local tissue or of the person. Overt illnesses are medically diagnosed conditions and diseases, such as pneumonia, diabetes, cataracts, electrolyte imbalance, cancer, and congestive heart failure.

Thus, the adaptation view of illness arises from within the person and involves the person's ability to adapt to changes. Illness is not an external condition or source that the person "came down with," or "caught." In the past two decades there has been widespread agreement about this theory of homeostasis or adaptation in nursing.

## CULTURE AND ILLNESS

A breakdown in a person's coping mechanisms places that person in the maladaptive range on the health-illness continuum. How the person behaves or acts as a result of being ill is determined culturally. One's behavior is shaped and influenced by the way health, illness, and health practices are defined by one's particular cultural

group. When the nurses care for patients from a social group or from a cultural background different from their own, it is important that they assess how the patient defines his or her (1) role in being ill, (2) attitudes toward health and illness, (3) values about health, and (4) health practices.

**Definitions of Being Sick.** Individuals vary in how they perceive illness. This variation affects how people assume the sick role. Many people do not admit to being ill as long as they can be active and go to work, attend school, or engage in some productive activity. The cultural values that are associated with work and productivity tend to be higher among these people than the health benefits to be gained by earlier recognition of illness. On the other hand, some people consider themselves to be ill if they have one or more symptoms. These people seek help and assume the sick role at the first sign of a cold, at the appearance of a headache, and so on. They place a high value on health and have sufficient information about health practices and possible consequences that may occur when health care is delayed.

How readily people acknowledge being ill varies, especially if the problem is one of coping and is psychological or social in nature. Cultural expectations dictate that individuals should be able to cope with events in their lives. Laws, regulations, rewards, penalties, and sanctions abound to guide behaviors and to affect emotions. Many people are reluctant to seek help for emotional or psychological problems unless the problem is of crisis proportion. Help in handling this type of illness is provided by clinical psychologists, psychiatrists, counselors, clergy, various types of "hot lines," and clinics.

Illness is also defined according to the duration of the condition and the severity of the symptoms. The person having a myocardial infarction (heart attack) experiences sudden chest pain and weakness and knows that something is wrong. When the pain is relieved and does not recur in succeeding days, the individual begins to wonder whether the pain was imagined or real. At this point, the individual no longer sees himself or herself as ill and is ready to resume regular activities. Conversely, people who live in a large urban area with frequent smoggy days may not consider themselves ill when their eyes smart and water because it is such a common occurrence. The semistarved native with an inadequate intake of calories and proteins considers his or her conditions as a normal state rather than a state of illness.

**Cultural Beliefs and Values.** When patients and those who care for them have the same background, the shared cultural beliefs and values are residual stimuli. In spite of minor differences, they have similar expectations and values in response to stress and illness. However, when patients are from a different cultural or social background than those who care for them, they may act in different and in unexpected ways. Cultural values and beliefs then emerge as contextual stimuli that influence their behavior.

Cultural factors should be considered as stimuli whenever the nurse observes noncompliant behavior(s) in the patient. Patients who get out of bed in spite of nurses' repeated explanations of why they should remain in bed, patients who refuse to take their medications or treatments, and patients who persist in doing the opposite of what has been prescribed for their care are frequently referred to as "difficult," "uncooperative," or "complaining" patients. In reality, these patients are not acting irrationally or capriciously. Their behavior has meaning to them and is used to cope with an unmet need. A second level assessment of their cultural beliefs often helps to show that their behavior is consistent with a basic belief or that it was previously used to achieve a goal that had great value to them.

When caring for patients from a background that is different from your own, it is important to remember that cultural patterns tend to persist and to resist change. This can be seen in immigrants who adapt to the culture of their adopted land, but when sick or under stress they revert back to many of their former values and beliefs, which are passed on to the next genera-

tion. Some patients may be from cultures that do not believe in the germ theory. Many people know about germs, yet they still believe that disease is caused primarily by an imbalance of the body humors of blood, phlegm, cholor (the yellowish bile of anger), and melancholia (the black bile of depression). Other people regard disease as part of nature and believe that nature is the best healer. In every culture, some people place their faith in the "magic men" who will cure them, such as doctors, faith healers, curanderos, medicine men, or shamans.

Cultural influences may not always be readily apparent. MacGregor described a patient of Swedish heritage who, following his operation, refused backrubs, extra nourishments, and offers of assistance from the nurses. The nurses were baffled by his behavior, especially when the patient's wife complained about the poor care that her husband was receiving. Only then did someone remember that in the Swedish culture it is good manners to refuse something the first time it is offered and that a sincere offer is urged upon one and is repeated several times. The patient was being polite by refusing the first offer. However, the nurses did not repeat the offer, so it appeared to him that they had not meant it. Other cultural beliefs and their effects on behavior are described in more detail in Chapter Twenty-two.

**Health Practices.** The health habits and practices of the individual provide information about his or her cultural beliefs and values. The nurse gains information about these practices through the first level assessment of behaviors. The assessment covers subjects such as smoking, types of medications taken on a regular or on an occasional basis, use of supplemental vitamins, use of health foods, use of drugs or alcohol, and type and amount of exercise. In some cultures, health practices include the use of magic, reliance on folk medicines, and following ceremonial rituals.

As each mode and need area is assessed, information is accumulated about the patient's beliefs and health practices. As the nurse develops interview skills, more of the general statements made by the patient are followed up to validate the meaning and to gain more specific data. For example, a patient may say, "I've always taken good care of myself," when describing how she sees herself in the self-concept mode. Rather than make assumptions, the nurse follows up her statement by trying to find out what she means by "good care." This kind of follow-up enables the nurse to validate some of the patient's cultural beliefs, which serve as contextual stimuli and can be manipulated to plan more effective care for the patient.

## THE SICK ROLE

The society in which we live has established sets of expectations of how a person should behave in certain circumstances, and what the person can expect in return. These obligations and expectations are designated as roles. Each of us performs a number of roles in our daily lives. Examples of roles include mother, father, son, daughter, student, voter, driver, engineer, doctor, and nurse. When one becomes ill, one takes on the sick role.

## COMPONENTS OF
## THE SICK ROLE

The social expectations regarding sickness and one's behavior when ill have existed for centuries, but it wasn't until the 1950s that it was described as the sick role, Parsons (1964), a sociologist, examined the interactions of the sick person and others in the social context and formulated four statements that became in essence, the components of the sick role.

1. *When assuming the sick role, the person is exempt from normal social role responsibilities.*

This component is relative to the nature and the severity of the illness. The person who thought he or she might be catching a cold because of sneezing several times would not be exempt from as many responsibilities, nor for as long, as would be the person who has a fever of 101°, chest congestion, and difficulty in breathing. Complaints of a headache are used often to escape social responsibilities; however, the person is then expected to assume the sick role and its obligations. The sick role provides legitimacy for not carrying out one's normal social role functions.

2. *The person assuming the sick role is obligated to accept help.*

People who are ill and unable to cope with internal physiological changes are not able to get well by making a decision to be better or by willing themselves to recover. There must be some change made in their condition to support the coping mechanisms that have broken down into maladaptive responses. They must become more dependent on others to help this change to occur.

3. *The person has an obligation to want to get well.*

Illness is a state of breakdown in adaptation that results in some needs not being met. These unmet needs create a discomfort or disease and the possibility of death from adaptive failure. The sick person is expected to place a higher value on self-preservation, survival, and hopes for the future than on other aspirations. This expectation includes the positive actions that are taken by the sick person in regaining independence in carrying out his or her own activities of daily living and giving up the dependencies of the sick role. However, some patients display maladaptive behaviors by remaining in the sick role to gain the advantages of help and attention from others and to avoid some of the responsibilities of being well.

4. *The sick person has an obligation to seek "technically competent" help.*

Because sick people cannot will themselves to recover but must accept help from others to get better, they should seek help from those who are qualified to give it. What constitutes "technically competent" help is defined according to the specific society or culture in which one is associated. In typical American society, this means seeking assistance from doctors, nurses, or other health professionals or technicans. In a rural Mexican community, it might mean seeking out the curandero, or on a remote Indian reservation, help is sought first from the medicine man.

In addition to seeking competent help, patients are expected to cooperate by doing what they are directed to do to get well. This requires that sick people have trust in those who are helping them. Often, patients are not able to tell who the "good doctor" or the "best nurse" is, but they are placed in the difficult position of having to accept help from strangers and to trust them to put their interests and welfare first.

## EXPECTATIONS OF THE
## SICK ROLE

A person's ability to take on the sick role and to carry out the related tasks is facilitated by certain factors. The sick person expends less energy in adapting to the sick role when the behaviors that are expected do not conflict with his or her personality needs. The sick role requires the person to seek help, to depend on others, and to give up other roles. The mother who feels that her family cannot get along without her, the person who is always in charge and gives the orders, and the independent individual who thrives in the out-of-doors are among those people who may have conflicts with the sick role. Adjustment to the sick role is easier when one's behaviors in other roles are compatible with behaviors of the sick role.

People who tend to be followers, who carry out directions and instructions of others, who ordinarily are thought of as having positions of less power, and women who follow traditional female roles tend to have behaviors that are compatible with the sick role. The sick role is assumed more readily when an individual's level of trust and confidence in the doctors and nurses is able to check his or her anxieties. Without trust, anxieties can cause severe coping problems that consume enormous amounts of energy and delay physical recovery. When patients have a relatively clear understanding of their illness and the plan of care, they are better able to carry out the sick role. Some knowledge of what is going to happen reduces any surprises and shocks, relieves some of the anxiety, and adds to the feelings of trust in those who are caring for them.

As you might expect, the sex of the person is an important factor in determining how one adapts to the sick role. This is particularly true for men. The type of behavior that is expected of the traditional male role differs a great deal from the behavior that is expected of a man when sick. The traditional adult male role emphasizes behaviors such as being independent, taking control, making decisions for oneself and one's family, standing up to adversity, and not crying or complaining about problems. In the sick role, this adult man is deprived of many of the elements, actions, and activities that he used to reach goals in his traditional role, and now has to depend on others to help him and to provide his care. Many decisions are made for him, and many of those decisions are made by nurses, who often are women. He may feel like crying, but a display of emotions is often regarded as a weakness.

On the other hand, behaviors of the traditional female role make it less traumatic for a woman to take on the sick role. The traditional female role sanctions more dependency on others than does the traditional male role, the use of expressive behaviors when showing emotional responses, and a more willing acceptance of decisions made by others.

**Societal Expectations.** The expectations of society for the people who assume the sick role define how sick people "ought to" act or behave. The components of the sick role include the expectations that the individual (a) is released from other social responsibilities, (b) accepts help from others, (c) cooperates to get well, and (d) seeks competent help.

Studies of hospitalized people show that patients stress the importance of their being cooperative, considerate of others, and not demanding. They believe that doctors and nurses expect this type of behavior and that deviation from this behavior leads to doctors' and nurses' disapproval. They believe that patients who conform to these expectations are considered "good patients" and are admired by those who care for them, "good

patients" do not make demands of the doctors or nurses unless there is ample justification. They believe that patients are often reluctant to ask for services or to express their dissatisfactions for fear that they will be regarded as being uncooperative. The extent of patients' efforts to meet their sick role obligations and the expectations of others is determined by several factors such as (a) fear that they will be abandoned or that they will receive less effective care, (b) seeking approval from those who care for them, or (c) feelings of responsibility for "sicker" patients, or for "overworked" staff.

**Personal Expectations.** People who assume the sick role have legitimate personal expectations. These expectations constitute what they perceive as their rights and what they can reasonably expect others to do for them. Personal expectations include

- that the sick person will be treated as a unique person with biopsychosocial needs and not merely as "the gallbladder in Room 325" or "the IV that has infiltrated."
- that the sick person will be given the needed care promptly and should not have to earn the care or to compete with others for it. One's illness is a unique experience that causes one anxiety and, frequently, physical suffering. Therefore, the most important expectations one has are the nurse's prompt response to one's needs and a "good" explanation by the physician of one's treatment and progress.
- that the health workers are skillful and competent. Because most patients lack evaluation tools to judge the skills and technical competence of doctors, nurses, and other professional and technical staff, they equate competence with "interest in the patient." The personalities of the nurses and the doctors are very important because a friendly or kind attitude is interpreted as a sign of dedication and a sign that mistakes and neglect are less likely to occur under their care.
- that those who give care to patients are serious about their work. Patients feel that their needs and care are more important than discussing plans for a vacation trip with a co-worker, worrying about make-up and not damaging long, tapering fingernails, or making flippant remarks or jokes about patients.
- that the care that patients need be given in an accurate and in a safe manner. Patients tend to be apprehensive about possible mistakes, confusion, indecision, and neglect. Signs of indecision, anxiety, and timidity by those

who give care arouse greater feelings of anxiety and decreases the trust in them.

- that patients are consulted and kept informed of their progress toward a healthier state. For patients, a "good explanation" of their progress is one that is given in terms that they can understand, that provides hope for their improvement, and takes their feelings into account.

These personal expectations are an expanded version of the factors discussed previously that help people to adjust to the sick role.

## STAGES OF ILLNESS

People behave in a wide variety of ways when they assume sick roles and must cope with the stresses of an illness. The condition of illness imposes certain tasks and obligations on people as they assume the sick role and pass through several phases of the illness. Different tasks need to be performed for each of the stages. A behavior that is appropriate for one stage may be inappropriate for another stage. Lederer (1965) stated that "The experience of illness is a complex psychological situation." He described three distinct yet overlapping stages of illness: (1) the transition from health to illness, (2) the "accepted illness" stage, and (3) the convalescent stage. By examining each of the stages in terms of the effects that it has on the patient, the tasks to be accomplished in that stage, and the appropriate types of behavior for that stage, the nurse has a standard by which to measure whether the patient's assessed behaviors fall within the accepted range.

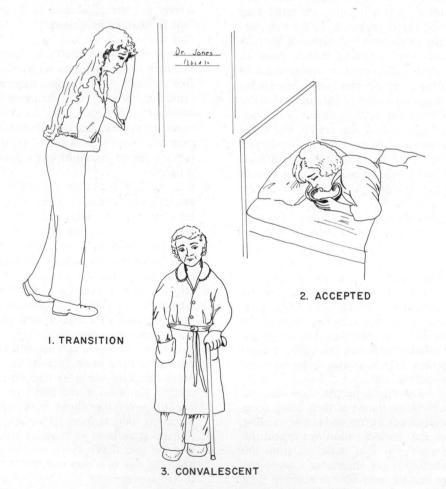

Figure 8-2. The stages of illness: (1) the transition from health to illness, (2) the "accepted illness" stage, and (3) the convalescent stage.

## THE TRANSITION FROM HEALTH TO ILLNESS

The first stage of illness is described as the transition period, when the individual has a growing awareness that something is wrong. One's efforts to cope with internal changes are not effective in maintaining an adaptive state. The resulting need states produce tension, discomfort, or pain or interfere with one's ability to carry on with usual activities. Physiologically, changes occur that affect the structure, function, or regulation of various cells, tissues, or organs of the body.

The change from health to illness can occur gradually and can extend over a period of time, or it may occur suddenly. When an individual suffers a stroke or a heart attack or is injured in an accident, there is rapid movement toward the illness end of the health-illness continuum. Other people may have to help the individual to carry out tasks that need to be performed when assuming the sick role and to obtain the necessary medical and nursing care.

**Tasks for the First Stage.** When an individual realizes that he or she is ill, there are certain tasks that have to be done to obtain help and to assume the sick role. The tasks for the first stage of illness are the same as the tasks for the sick role. They are

1. To be released from other social responsibilities.
2. To accept help when from others, presents oneself for diagnosis and initial treatment.
3. To cooperate to get well. One does this by recognizing the need for help, by keeping medical appointments, and by undergoing the prescribed treatment.
4. To seek competent help.

**First Level Assessment.** People in the first stage of illness are assessed according to behaviors that are related to the accomplishment of the four tasks just listed. Adaptive behaviors in the first stage of illness indicate that one has enough knowledge about health and illness to know that one is ill, is able to accept the discomforts or the restrictions that may be necessary in order to carry out diagnostic procedures needed to make the diagnosis, and keeps medical appointments. Keeping appointments involves arranging for the necessary time, or having transportation to get to the office or the clinic, and having resources to pay for the service. The person who is sick often is advised to cut back on activities and to get more rest and must place a higher priority on following medical advice than on carrying on other activities. Other adaptive behaviors include expressing trust in the doctor, in the nurses, and in other members of the health team, discussing what the illness means to the sick person, and being cognizant of how one's family and other people feel about one's illness.

When a sick person has difficulty in assuming the sick role or in carrying out any of the related tasks, the resulting behavior may be classified as maladaptive. Examples of ways in which people behave inappropriately include working long hours or doing heavy work to prove that they are not ill, minimizing potentially serious symptoms, and using trivial or insignificant symptoms to avoid social roles and responsibilities, lacking feelings about being ill, having inappropriate or exaggerated ideas about the effects of the disease or the illness, and using the illness to manipulate the actions of others for one's own benefit. Maladaptive behaviors tend to fall into categories that are related to being excessive — too much, too little, or the wrong kind of response to being ill.

## THE "ACCEPTED ILLNESS" STAGE

The second stage of illness begins when a person assumes the sick role and accepts the fact that he or she is ill. One no longer can deny that something is wrong and that one needs help. During this time, one has needs for integrity that extend beyond the physiological mode and that affect one's entire being. The disruption of physiological need areas causes stress and anxiety as one realizes the potential or real danger the illness poses to a person's integrity and survival. Because of this threat and the disturbance of one's life one's attention now centers on oneself — one's feelings and the services provided by others.

**Tasks for the Second Stage.** During the second stage of illness, the individual is ill and is expected to carry out the sick role. Patients in a hospital or in a similar health care setting should be in the second or third stage of illness, although some people who enter the hospital only for check-ups or for diagnostic testing may be in the first stage. Tasks for the second stage of illness are

1. To give up or to discontinue other social obligations.
2. To stop denying and to acknowledging one's illness.
3. To acknowledge and to accept help from others.
4. To concentrate one's energies and concerns on oneself and on one's response to therapy.

**First Level Assessment.** During the second

stage of illness, patients are concerned about their survival and the effect of the disease on their lives. As a result, their behaviors are very self-centered. These behaviors are considered adaptive for this stage of illness and are characterized by

1. *Egocentricity*. The patient becomes very subjective and judges everything in relation to himself or herself. If the nurse frowns when talking to the patient, the patient thinks that the nurse doesn't like him or her or knows some bad news about the patient's condition. When people are talking in the hall, the patient is sure that they are talking about him or her.

2. *Constriction of interests*. This occurs because the patient's main concern is oneself and what is happening to one's body or going on in one's room or in the immediate environment. During the second stage of illness, one's energies are diverted to trying to overcome the problems associated with the disease or medical condition and are not available for diversional activities. Some people may watch television, read a paper, or glance at a book but their span of attention is short, their interest is minimal, and the content is quickly forgotten.

3. *Emotional dependency*. This behavior is more apparent than the previous two behaviors. When ill, the patient is unable to meet some of his or her own needs and is physically dependent on others for help. This dependency creates feelings of ambivalence in which one likes and appreciates the assistance that one is getting and, at the same time, resents the condition and the need for the assistance. People who provide help are both liked and, often, resented. These feelings extend to the members of the health team, to families, and to others in the sick person's life.

4. *Hypochondriasis*. This behavior reflects the patient's intense anxiety about the usual and normal function of the body. When sick and anxious about recovering, the patient focuses attention on factors that he or she had not previously noticed – ordinary functions of the body, such as the beat of the heart, the breath sounds, and the movement of gas in the colon.

Figure 8–3 shows the relationship of these behaviors during the various stages of illness. The behaviors of egocentricity, constriction of interests, emotional dependency, and, to a lesser degree, hypochondria are common responses that can be observed in everyone at some time. However, these reponses increase during the first stage of illness and reach a peak during the accepted illness stage. As the patient's disrupted state and coping failure respond to therapy and he convalesces, these behaviors again decrease to their usual levels in the patient.

Maladaptive behaviors for this stage are behaviors that do not accomplish the tasks, such as giving up all hope of recovery, refusing to view oneself as ill or in need of help, using rituals to ward off danger, being suspicious of medications and treatment, lacking trust in the staff, avoiding discussing one's problems and feelings, and being uncooperative about one's care. The loss of health and the ability to carry on in a usual manner often lead to behaviors that involve the grieving process, such as making bargains as a means of getting well, seeking to manipulate and to keep control over everything that is happening to one, and feeling that one's illness is the "will of God" or punishment for one's sins.

## THE CONVALESCENT STAGE

Convalescence constitutes the third stage of illness, and it involves letting go of the sick role and resuming the normal roles that are associated with health. During the convalescent period, one is concerned with the re-establishment of one's

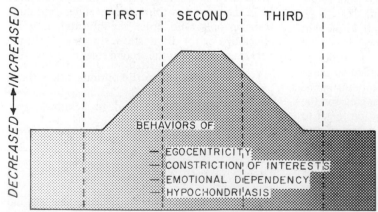

**Figure 8–3.** Self-centered behaviors normally increase in the second stage and decrease in the third stage.

self-confidence in coping independently and in exercising one's returning physical strength. In this stage, the patient must see his or her "healthy" world as more attractive and more satisfying than the regressive rewards of illness, when others were depended upon for attention and help.

**Tasks for the Third Stage.** During the third stage of illness, or the recuperative period, the patient disengages from the sick role and moves into the adaptive and healthy range again. Tasks for the third stage of illness are

1. To increase independence in correspondence with one's returning strength.
2. To broaden or to resume one's interests that go beyond oneself and one's immediate environment.
3. To increase objectivity in judging situations that are occurring in one's environment.
4. To succeed in taking on "healthy" behaviors, such as getting out of bed alone, walking in the hall, and being less reliant on medications or on the need for analgesics

**First Level Assessment.** During the third stage of illness, or the convalescent stage, adaptive behaviors are characterized by the patient's willingness to try to help himself or herself, to follow the rehabilitation program, and to make more decisions. There is decreased reliance on others. The patient makes statements about getting along, being glad to be feeling better, and hoping to be going home soon and shows increased interest in the activities of others. During this stage, the patient shows increased interest in resuming accustomed social roles and integrates feelings or perceptions of himself or herself as a person who is recovering from an illness.

Maladaptive behaviors for this stage are behaviors that prevent the achievement of the tasks, such as remaining in the second stage and clinging to the behaviors of egocentricity, constriction of interests, emotional dependency, and anxiety over bodily functions (hypochondria). Nurses should support behaviors that are considered adaptive to achieve the tasks for this stage of illness.

## EFFECTS OF ILLNESS IN ALL MODES

According to the adaptation model of nursing, man functions as a unified whole, and when a disruption occurs in one mode of function, the disruption will often involve or affect the function of other modes. Illness that results from the breakdown of physiological coping mechanisms affects the entire person. Not only the enlarged tonsils indicate illness but also the white blood count and the temperature rise; the person feels hot and lethargic, has pain in the throat, is unable to concentrate or to study, and sees himself or herself as sick. The illness affects many areas of one's being and the pattern of one's life.

## PHYSIOLOGICAL MODE

A major part of the nursing program is devoted to studying ways in which disease and illness affect the physiological functioning of the body. According to the adaptation viewpoint, the body is able to cope with changes in an adaptive way and to maintain integrity of the internal environment until a stimulus appears that causes a breakdown or overwhelms the coping mechanism. This stimulus produces changes in the structure of the tissue or organ or alters its function or regulation so that the need state is not met or satisfied.

The body responds to the causative stimulus in a limited number of ways. These responses are physiological methods of coping with internal changes and include the following:

- *increased cellular growth* — hypertrophy, the increased size of the cells; hyperplasia, the increase in the total number of cells, and neoplasia, the presence of new growth or tumors.
- *decreased cellular growth* — atrophy, and necrosis in the case of actual death of the tissue.
- *inflammation* — a complex vascular response to irritation or injury characterized by five primary symptoms: localized heat, pain, redness, swelling, and loss of function.
- *ischemia* — a reduction of circulation to the part of the body that decreases the oxygen and nutrients delivered to the tissues and a build-up of the waste products resulting from metabolism.
- *pain* — serves to notify the body of existing damage and the need to stop other activities and to rest.
- *immunity* — internal defense system against foreign bodies and microorganisms.
- *obstruction* — blockage of any passageway that results in dammed up secretions or fluids on one side and little or no fluids beyond the point of obstruction (probably more mechanical in nature than a physiological response).

Other methods of looking at the body and its defense mechanisms may classify coping mechanisms differently and may include other mechanisms. Regardless of the method used, knowledge of the physiological coping mechanisms simplifies learning the symptoms of each of the numerous diseases. For example, nurses can then apply their knowledge of the inflammatory process to any organ or structure in the body, and use it as a guide to assess for behaviors of localized heat, pain, redness, swelling, and loss of function.

## SELF-CONCEPT MODE

Most people perceive illness as a threat to their physical or personal self, and this threat arouses their anxiety. The degree of anxiety that accompanies illness is related to the strength, power, and immediacy of the stimuli that cause the maladaptive response. The *strength* of the stimuli refers to the seriousness of the threat as a cause of potentially grave consequences, such as the strength of the stimuli that cause the common cold as opposed to the stimuli that cause bilateral lobar pneumonia. The *power* of the stimuli to disrupt the person's life or to change his or her body image either temporarily or permanently is an influential factor in the anxiety that the sick person experiences. The *immediacy* of the stimuli that cause the illness is related to the time span in which the illness developed. When an illness develops gradually the person generally is able to adjust to it with less anxiety than when the illness appears abruptly. In the self-concept mode, problems arise when people are unable to cope effectively with their anxieties about how they feel about themselves and how they see themselves as people.

Many aspects of illness and assuming the sick role pose a real or a perceived threat to the self. Some of these concerns that the nurse should include in the assessment include the following:

* *concern about the disease, its progress, and its outcome*
    Patients frequently ask questions such as "Will I recover?" "Will I die?" "Will I be disfigured?" "Am I getting better?" "How long can this go on?" or "How long can I stand it?"
* *concern about the unknown, the strange, and the unfamiliar*
    Sick people seek answers to questions such as "What is going to happen to me?" "What did they find out?" "Will it hurt much?" "Are they telling me the truth?" "What do they want me to do?" or "Why are they doing that?"
* *concern about one's financial status*
    Illness produces additional stress in terms of the high cost of medical care, the loss of income because one is unable to work, the possible loss of the job itself, the benefits provided by any health insurance, and the effect of all of these factors on one's family.
* *concern about changes in one's environment*
    Illness that results in hospitalization poses additional sources of anxiety in the patient who is separated from family and familiar surroundings. People who are hospitalized are required to observe a different daily routine or pattern of living and are unable to participate in their usual activities. In addition, they often experience pain or loneliness.

## INTERDEPENDENCE MODE

During illness, one's relationships with other people become upset and disturbed because the sick role requires that other social roles and responsibilities be relinquished. The disabling effects of the illness upset the balance of dependence and independence so that there is greater dependency on others. Additionally, the sick person is less able to provide support or care to those who ordinarily depend upon him or her. During illness, one has an increased need for help-seeking behaviors and may need more attention and affection. Some patients in the sick role find it very difficult to give up behaviors that illustrate independence, such as obstacle mastery and initiative-taking.

The following example is based on an actual occurrence. Dr. John Smith is a hospital patient recovering from a myocardial infarction. Included in his current treatment regime are orders for a low sodium diet, bed rest, and use of a bedside commode. These orders have been explained to him, and, as a physician, he knows what they mean as well as knowing about his disease. However, he requested his son to bring him a pizza, and the nurses have observed him walking around the room and shaving in the bathroom several times. The behaviors show a disruption in Dr. Smith's performance of his sick role. What do these behaviors mean? Are they related to his interdependence needs? To his needs for integrity in the self-concept mode? After assessing the behaviors, it is important that the nurse do a second level assessment to find out the meaning of the behaviors and the stimuli that are causing them. With this information, the problem can be more accurately identified, a goal can be formulated, and interventions can be planned to change the inappropriate behaviors.

## ROLE-FUNCTION MODE

One of the social expectations of the sick role is that the individual is relieved of other social roles and obligations. This is an essential part of the individual's cooperation in accepting treatment and in his or her desire to get well. Sick people have only a limited amount of energy available, and this energy is needed in their attempts to meet their needs and to regain their ability to cope with internal changes. The person who has a chest cold uses more energy to breathe and has less energy available for engaging in strenuous work or sports.

Sick people are excused from their roles on a priority-type basis—the less essential roles are the first to be given up. Strenuous activities are delayed or canceled.

Everyone performs a number of roles that are transient, temporary, or diversional and that consist of more casual interactions with others.

Do you remember some of the first roles or activities you put off until a later time or did not carry out? Most people limit their role activities of shopping, participating in sports or games, attending the theater or movies, going to meetings or parties, and so on. When one assumes the sick role, one is relieved of even more responsibilities that are related to the roles one uses to accomplish the growth and developmental tasks for one's stage of life. These include the roles of parent, worker, student, landlord, housekeeper, civic committee member, church member, and so on. As one progresses into the third stage of illness, or the convalescent stage, one is expected by society to again begin to resume and, eventually, when well again, to accept one's role responsibilities and obligations.

## APPLICATION TO CLINCIAL PRACTICE

Match each of the statements of behavior with the stage of illness in which it would be the most appropriate and adaptive.

**Statements of Behavior**

1. Reduces daily activities.
2. Shaves oneself and brushes teeth.
3. Spends most of the day in bed.
4. Believes that the nurse does not like her.
5. "Tell me what you want me to do."
6. "Now I'll tell you what I want to do."
7. "I hope to go home in a day or two."
8. Phones the office, states that he feels awful and will not be in to work.
9. Shows no interest in newspaper or television programs.
10. "Nurse, could you help me turn on my side?"

**Stages of Illness**

A. First stage of illness
B. Second stage of illness
C. Third stage of illness

You would probably make the following matchings: 1.–A; 2.–C; 3.–B; 4.–B; 5.–B; 6.–C; 7.–C; 8.–A; 9.–B; 10.–B.

Read the following case history and answer the questions that follow.

Mr. M. is in his early fifties. He arrived on the nursing unit about one and a half hours ago. He is scheduled to have surgery tomorrow to repair bilateral inguinal hernias. He is assigned to a semi-private room, and the other bed is unoccupied at this time. There is a telephone in his room, but, since his arrival on the unit, Mr. M. has been in a telephone booth at the end of the hall, making one call after another.

The nursing assistant reported to the team leader that she had tried several times to get the admitting information from Mr. M. and that he refused to cooperate. The team leader then approached Mr. M. at the telephone booth, but he ignored her until she said, "I'm sorry to interrupt you, but we need to get some information from you." Mr. M. said, "Just a minute, Joe, the nurse is here. Okay, nurse, as soon as I finish up here," and he turned back to the phone, "Yeah, Joe, I can let you have four gross. Sure, the finest fabrics and the latest style..." The team leader waited a few minutes, interrupted one more time, and finally walked away.

In what stage of illness would you classify a patient such as Mr. M. who is scheduled to have elective surgery?

State some tasks for that stage of illness that the patient should carry out.

Assess Mr. M.'s sick role behaviors and the stimuli that seems to influence his interactions and try to identify his problem(s). What behavioral mode seems to be the most disrupted at this time?

Your answers to the questions should indicate that people who elect to have surgery to correct some condition are in the second stage of illness, or the accepted stage. Mr. M. has acknowledged that he has bilateral inguinal hernias, even though this condition is not causing him acute distress at this time. The tasks that Mr. M. has carried out include tasks from the first stage—he sought out a doctor, underwent the initial diagnosis and treatment, acknowledged that he had a physical illness, entered the hospital for treatment, and wants to recover. At this time, he seems to have some difficulty in carrying out the tasks of stage two but may find these tasks easier after surgery.

Compare your first and second level assessments of Mr. M.'s sick role behaviors with other nursing students' assessments of their patients.

Apply these concepts in your clinical practice. For each patient whose care you are assigned, determine the appropriate stage of illness, the tasks to be carried out, and the behaviors that indicate the extent to which these tasks are being accomplished. Illness is the stimuli, and the way in which the patient carries out the sick role is the response that is used to cope with the changes that have occurred. The behaviors that you assess are compared with behaviors that are in the adapted range for the specific stage of illness.

## REFERENCES

Lederer, Henry: How the sick view their world. *In* Skipper and Leonard, (Eds.): Social Interaction and Patient Care. Philadelphia, J. B. Lippincott Company, 1965.

Luckmann, Joan, and Sorensen, Karen: Medical-Surgical Nursing: A Psychophysiologic Approach. Philadelphia, W. B. Saunders Company, 1980.

MacGregor, Frances: Uncooperative patients: some cultural interpretations, Am J Nurs, 67:88–91, (January) 1967.

Mauksch, Hans, and Tagliacozza, Daisy: The patient's view of the patient role. Abstract. Chicago, Illinois Institute of Technology, 1962.

Parsons, Talcott: The Social System. New York, The Free Press, 1964, p. 436.

Peterson, Margaret: Understanding defense mechanisms (programmed instruction). Am J Nurs, 72:1651–1674, (September) 1972.

Porth, Carol: Physiological coping: a model for teaching pathophysiology, Nurs Outlook, 25:781–784, (December) 1977.

Rambo, Beverly: "Illness and the Sick Role." study guide. Los Angeles, Mount St. Mary's College, revised 1977.

Smith, Marcy, and Selye, Hans: Reducing the negative effects of stress, Am J Nurs, 79:1953–1955, (November) 1979.

Stephenson, Carol A.: Stress in critically ill patients, Am J Nurs, 77:1806–1809, (November) 1977.

Vincent, Pauline: The sick role in patient care, Am J Nurs, 75:1172–1173, (July) 1975.

Wolff, LuVerne, Weitzel, Marlene, and Fuerst, Elinor: Fundamentals of Nursing, 6th ed. Philadelphia, J. B. Lippincott Company, 1979, pp. 188–209.

# ASSESSMENT OF THE PHYSIOLOGICAL MODE

The assessment of the physiological mode focuses on behaviors related to six basic need areas that must be satisfied regardless of one's age or sex. These basic needs are oxygenation, fluid and electrolyte balance, adequate nutrition, elimination of liquid and solid wastes, rest and activity, and sensory regulation, including regulation of temperature. The function of reproduction is not considered a basic physiological need. It is considered a societal expectation to insure the perpetuation of the human race. The requirements that must be met to fulfill these expectations are part of the needs related to the self-concept and the interdependence modes.

The nursing assessment is carried out to determine whether or not the basic needs are being met regardless of the person's location on the health-illness continuum. Many of the basic needs are interrelated; thus, some behaviors appear in more than one need area. The pulse is an important factor in assessing the oxygenation need and in determining the fluid balance of the body, as well as in the area of temperature regulation. The amount of urine output is an important behavior to assess in the area of fluid balance and in the need for urine elimination. The nursing assessment is not the same as a physical examination that is made to diagnose a medical problem in terms of disruption in the structure, function, or regulation of an organ, system, or body tissue. A medical condition can, however, directly or indirectly affect the basic needs in one or more areas. For example, a fracture of the femur alters the structure of the bone and interferes with its function of weight-bearing. Following surgical repair of the femur, prolonged bedrest and pain may affect the patient's nutritional and elimination needs as well as his or her activity needs.

When assessing behaviors related to the basic needs, it is necessary to have an understanding of the physiological process underlying the need, the standards or ranges of behavior that are accepted as normal, and the kinds of behaviors that signify a maladapted state. When all the behaviors are within the normal limits, the basic needs are being satisfied by the individual. When behaviors are found to be outside the normal range, the basic needs are not being met, and the person has a problem that requires medical or nursing intervention.

The identification of a problem that is the result of an existing basic need that has not been satisfied utilizes many nursing actions and interventions that go beyond the medical approach. When a person becomes confused and exhibits irrational, unpredictable behavior, physicians focus their attention on trying to find changes in the cellular function of the brain and attempting to treat the cause of these changes. Nurses who use the adaptation approach to nursing look at the confused behavior as being outside the normal range, identify the patient's problem as one of "decreased awareness of reality," and seek to change the behavior by manipulating the stimuli that cause the confused behavior. Although they, too, consider the cellular changes and the medical problem, they also assess other stimuli that may influence or affect the confused, or maladaptive, behavior.

Behavior is assessed in the "here and now" to determine the patient's condition or location on the Health-Illness Continuum. A history of past events or behaviors is included in the second level assessment of factors that influence present behavior. The second level assessment also includes a standard for comparison of past and present behaviors. In some cases, it is easy to be misled by past behaviors. Suppose you are assessing the behavior of a patient who is hospitalized with abdominal pain. You learn from the chart that the patient has a history of alcoholism. The patient's present problems that require nursing interventions must relate to the patient's basic needs that are not satisfied and not to the fact that the patient is an alcoholic. The alcoholism is an influencing factor or a stimulus for his or her present problems but is not an actual behavior unless alcohol is presently being consumed. The alcoholism poses a potential problem when the patient is discharged or, more accurately, the alcoholism continues to be a stimulus for behavior outside the normal range.

The problems handled by the nurse in the physiological mode are those related only to meeting the physiological needs, such as oxygenation and fluid and electrolyte balance. They do not include problems of coping with feelings or interdependence needs. These problems are handled in one of the other modes. However, when describing a patient's physical problem such as inadequate intake of food that fails to meet nutritional needs, nurses use patients' statements to add greater dimension to the problem, such as "The food doesn't taste good. It tastes like garbage," or "I'm too weak to eat. What good would it do anyway?" These statements show the extent of the problem and convey feelings of anger and depression that lead the nurse to assess carefully the other modes to determine whether there is a problem in coping.

Problems that arise in the physiological mode are classified as disruptions in a need area due to a medical problem on a cellular level or to a behavioral problem that warrants the nurse's intervention to help the patient toward adaptation. The behavioral problems are further divided into those problems with "too much" of something, "too little" of something, "the wrong kind" of something, or "none" of whatever is required to meet the need. In principle, nurses take independent actions to handle unmet needs that occur in other need areas that are not affected by the medical diagnosis. However, if nursing actions are not successful in promoting adaptive behavior, the unmet needs then become a medical problem because the behavior resulting from the maladaptive state may endanger one's survival.

### Physiological Mode Problems

1. Medical diagnosis — changes on cellular level affecting structure, function, or regulation.
2. Behavioral problems — person's inability to meet own needs satisfactorily, without evidence of pathological change in tissues.
   A. "Too much of or increase" in something
   B. "Too little of or decrease" in something
   C. "Wrong kind" of something
   D. "None" of something

PHYSIOLOGIC MODE
Components

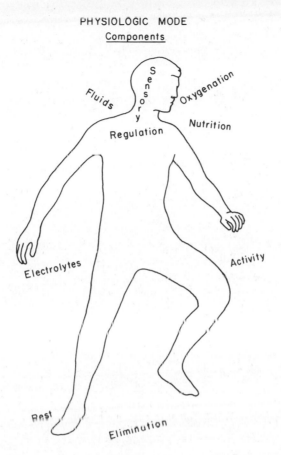

A person who is having physiological mode problems may be unable to eat sufficient food to meet the nutritional needs of the body. Gastritis, gastric ulcer, cancer of the stomach, and hiatus hernia are examples of cellular changes that are diagnosed as medical diseases and are treated as such. In the behavioral problem, individual does not have cellular disease but has a nutritional problem due to eating too many calories, eating too much food, taking in too little food, being deficient in an essential nutrient or vitamin, eating the wrong kind of food, or not eating anything. When the individual is physically able to eat but still does not eat, despite the nursing interventions, inadequate nutrition soon becomes a medical problem.

In Chapters Nine through Fourteen, the assessment of the physiological need areas is presented in more detail, including information about the normal function of systems and organs that are used to meet the need. Norms, or standards, for adaptive behavior are provided. The first level assessment lists the areas that the nurse assesses to gather information about how the need is being met. Maladaptive behaviors are identified, and the second level assessment is done to identify stimuli that cause or influence the behavior. The more common types of problems associated with the need area in addition to appropriate nursing actions and interventions are briefly described.

# Chapter NINE
# Oxygenation Needs

## OBJECTIVES  Information in this chapter will help you to

1. Differentiate between external ventilation and internal respiration.
2. Describe the body structures that are involved in supplying oxygen to the cells and in removing waste products.
3. Describe adaptive behaviors that indicate that oxygenation needs are being met adequately.
4. Describe the hypoxic state, maladaptive behaviors that are associated with it, and possible stimuli underlying this condition.
5. List the types of problems that the patient with an oxygen deficit may develop.
6. State nursing interventions that nurses use to meet oxygen needs and to maintain an open airway.

## DEFINITION OF TERMS

**alveolar** — pertaining to the air sacs in the lungs.

**ambient air** — air outside or in the atmosphere around us.

**anoxia** — complete lack of oxygen.

**apnea** — temporary stoppage of breathing.

**Biot's breathing** — an abnormality in breathing, with irregular periods of rapid breathing followed by an irregular period of not breathing; seen in brain injuries and in diseases.

**Cheyne-Stokes breathing** — a regular waxing and waning of respiration, with a period of deeper and more rapid breaths followed by decreasing and more shallow breaths or no breathing.

**diffusion** — the movement of molecules from a highly concentrated solution to a solution with lower concentrations.

dyspnea — difficult or painful breathing.

hemoglobin — a protein in the red blood cell that combines with gases to transport oxygen and carbon dioxide.

hemoptysis — coughing up blood in mucus or sputum.

hypoxia — a deficient supply of oxygen in the blood or in the tissues of the body.

Kussmaul's breathing — dyspnea, or air hunger, associated with the onset of diabetic acidosis.

orthopnea — the inability to breathe lying down in a supine position. The head and trunk must be elevated to breathe, as indicated in the terms "two-pillow" or "three-pillow" orthopnea.

rales — abnormal breath sounds, such as the popping or fizzing sound of a carbonated drink.

rhonchi — low-pitched, continuous sounds that originate in the larger air passages.

shock — circulatory system collapse with inadequate blood flow to the tissues.

stridor — a crowing, or whistling, sound from the partial obstruction of the air passages.

ventilation — the movement of air in and out of the lungs.

---

We will begin the assessment of the physiological mode by focusing on the extent to which people are able to meet their own needs and the extent to which nursing care is required to insure that peoples' basic needs are satisfied. All people have needs and are able to satisfy most of their own needs without assistance except when critically or terminally ill. However, difficulty in meeting the demands of the body in one need area creates disturbances in fulfilling other needs. Someone who is having dyspnea and is unable to breathe without a great deal of effort may refuse to carry out any exercise, including eating enough to meet nutritional needs.

Basic needs are most often classified in a hierarchy that proceeds from physiological needs to safety and comfort, to love and belonging, to respect or self-esteem, and, finally, to the pinnacle of self-actualization. In a hierarchy, some needs take precedence over others and must be at least partially satisfied before attention can be given to other needs. In general, the basic physiological needs that are related to survival have higher priority than needs of a psychological or a social nature. Even among the basic physiological needs, some needs are more important than others. One way to assess the importance of a need is to ask yourself how long you could survive if a body need is not met. How long could you live without breathing? without drinking liquids? without eliminating urine? Without having a bowel movement? It is no surprise that the need to breathe and to obtain oxygen takes priority over all other needs and that a total lack of oxygen causes death within a few minutes. Of all nursing responsibilities, perhaps the most important responsibility is more frequent assessments and

ongoing observations to insure that patients have an open airway and that they meet their oxygenation needs.

The assessment of the oxygenation needs begins with a brief review of the respiratory and the cardiovascular systems, including their roles in supplying and transporting oxygen, the ways in which they function, and how they are regulated. The first level assessment includes behaviors from a number of areas in order to indicate how much oxygen is needed to meet the particular demands of the body and the maladaptive behaviors that are associated with problems of oxygenation. The second level assessment includes focal and contextual stimuli that cause problems in meeting the oxygen needs. The problem of hypoxia, or oxygen deficit, is discussed in some detail because it is the most frequently found oxygenation problem among patients, although excesses of oxygen also produce harmful effects on tissues. Using the nursing process, the nurse assesses the behaviors, identifies the problem(s) in meeting the oxygen needs, makes a plan to manipulate the stimuli that are causing the problem, and carries out appropriate interventions.

## THE NEED FOR OXYGEN

All cells in the body must have a continuous supply of oxygen to live and to carry out their functions. Oxygen reacts with simple sugars to produce energy and carbon dioxide. This energy provided by the metabolic process is used to contract muscles, to move blood through vessels, to form new tissues, to transmit nerve impulses, and to carry on all the other work of the body. Without oxygen, the cells will die. Cells, however, vary greatly in their ability to tolerate low levels or total deprivation of oxygen. The tissues of the brain, heart, retina of the eye, and kidney are very sensitive to even small changes, whereas fat cells, bone cells, connective tissue, and nails are able to tolerate deficits and to survive longer.

Under ordinary circumstances, people obtain sufficient oxygen from the air around them. The air we breathe contains about 21 per cent oxygen and 79 per cent nitrogen and other gases. As one goes higher and higher above sea level, the amount of air in the atmosphere decreases; thus, one takes in less oxygen even though one is inhaling as deeply as at lower levels. Symptoms of oxygen deficit appear at an elevation of 5000 feet, where one of the earliest signs is loss of 23 per cent of one's night vision. Additional symptoms appear at an elevation of 9000 feet, and these symptoms progress to coma within a few minutes at 23,000 feet. People can adjust to decreased oxygen at higher altitudes by gradually becoming acclimatized over a period of time. Physiological changes that occur in response to low oxygen concentrations in the blood enable people in mountainous areas to live at higher altitudes without the symptoms of hypoxia. One group of people in the Andes lives at an elevation of 17,500 feet.

Whenever one considers oxygenation needs, one must examine the exchange of both oxygen and carbon dioxide, the by-product of the metabolic reaction. Carbon dioxide is an important part of the body's chemical buffering system and helps to keep the internal environment stable. Excess amounts of carbon dioxide are transported to the lungs, exchanged with the oxygen, and leave the body in the exhaled air.

## STRUCTURES USED FOR OXYGENATION

To recognize behaviors that are associated with oxygenation needs, one needs to review some of the basic structures and functions involved. Oxygenation is a complex process that includes the external form of respirations that are associated with moving air in and out of the lungs and the internal respirations that take place on a cellular level where metabolism of oxygen provides energy for the body. Oxygenation requires the synchronized actions of the pulmonary system, and various chemical and hormonal mechanisms that regulate oxygen supply.

### THE EXTERNAL FORM OF RESPIRATIONS

The external respiration process consists of ventilating the lungs. Through the behavior of breathing, oxygen enters the body and carbon dioxide is excreted from the body. Normal breathing is quiet and is carried out with minimal effort and on an almost automatic basis. Normal breathing requires the following components:

1. An intact chest cage with functioning muscles to expand and to contract it.
2. A patent and intact air passage.
3. Control of the respiratory rate by the nervous system.
4. Elastic properties of the lung tissue itself.

An adequate supply of oxygen requires a clear and unobstructed passage for air from the atmosphere to the alveolar cells of the lungs. The upper respiratory passages of the pulmonary system consist of the nose, the mouth, and the throat to approximately the level of the larynx. These airways are lined with mucous membranes that contain a generous blood supply that warms and humidifies the incoming air. The hair, mucous secretions, and cilia of the nasal epithelium filter particles and foreign matter from the air that moves into the lower air passages. These passages consist of the trachea, the bronchi, and the alveolar structures in the lung.

Various elements can obstruct the air passages and interfere with breathing a sufficient amount of oxygen. Cigarette smoke, smog, chemical fumes, mucus, aspirated foreign bodies, ingested irritants, and other air pollutants are known culprits. The body copes with these culprits by activating the cough reflex, an effective survival mechanism. People cough frequently to clear foreign matter from the lower air passages and sneeze to clear irritants from the nasal passages.

The ribs form the rigid, yet movable, chest cage by their attachment to the sternum in the front, to the spinal column, and to various muscles. The chest cage is moved up and outward during inspiration by contraction of the intercostal muscles and by contraction of the diaphragm that flattens and pulls the lungs downward. These contractions increase the negative pressure within the lungs and pull air in from the atmosphere. Expiration is ordinarily a passive action that combines the relaxation of the diaphragm and the intercostal muscles with the recoiling of the stretched lung tissues. However, the strong abdominal muscles can be brought into play when needed to force air from the chest. Even during expiration and relaxation of pulmonary structures, there is a slight negative pressure in the lungs due to the potential space between the two pleural linings. Breathing in a normal, quiet way requires 2 to 3 per cent of the

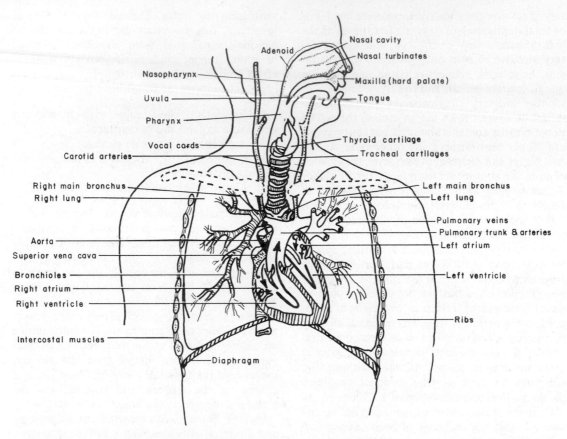

**Figure 9–1.** The external respiratory system includes the upper air passages of the nose, mouth, and throat; the chest cage; and the lower air passages consisting of the trachea, bronchi, and lungs.

total energy needs of the body, which increases only about 1 per cent during strenuous exercise because the total amount of energy released is also increased (Guyton, 1981).

The respiratory center consists of special neurons that are located in the medulla oblongata and the pons, which regulate the rate of breathing. The center responds directly to the concentration of carbon dioxide and the pH of the blood. When the levels rise, the breathing rate increases; when the levels fall, the respiratory rate slows. Other chemoreceptors that are located in the aortic arch and in the carotid arteries respond rapidly to changes in the oxygen concentrations in the blood. These receptors send messages to the respiratory center to increase ventilation when blood levels of oxygen fall even slightly. However, the basic factor that stimulates the respiratory center is the blood level of carbon dioxide.

Elasticity is the ability of the lung tissue to expand with the chest movement and to return to its original shape during relaxation. It is the ability of the alveoli to accommodate the volume of air when inflated during the inhaling phase.

The lung tissues lose much of their elasticity with increasing age; thus, elderly people must work harder and expend more energy to breathe. Other factors that contribute to the loss of elasticity include edema and fibrotic scarring, which is associated with smoking or with frequent respiratory infections.

## THE INTERNAL FORM OF RESPIRATION

Internal respiration takes place at the cellular level, where the gases diffuse across membranes and are transported by the blood stream. Structures of the cardiovascular system, including the heart, arteries, veins, and circulating blood, are essential for carrying oxygen to all the body tissues and for returning carbon dioxide to the lungs for removal from the body. To meet oxygenation needs, internal respirations rely on the following components.

1. Adequate external respiration or ventilation to deliver oxygen to the lungs.

2. A permeable alveolar membrane to the capillaries.

3. Effective pulmonary and systemic circulation.

4. Ability of the blood to transport the gases between the lungs and other body tissues.

5. Ability of the cells to metabolize oxygen and to eliminate carbon dioxide.

Inspired air must reach the alveoli, where most of the transfer of gases takes place. The walls of the alveoli are extremely thin and contain an interconnecting network of capillaries that form a "sheet" of flowing blood. There are more than 300 million alveoli in the lungs, and if this thin, filmy tissue were laid out flat, it would form a wall 7½ feet high and 100 feet long.

Under normal circumstances, the exchange of gases takes place in a fraction of a second. High concentrations of oxygen in the alveolar air diffuse across the membrane to the blood stream, which has been depleted of its oxygen. The high concentration of carbon dioxide in the blood passes into the alveolar air. The differences in the pressures or in the concentration of the gases allows diffusion to occur rapidly in the lung and at distal cellular sites.

Carbon dioxide, the by-product of the metabolic reaction, is important in the chemical buffering system of the body and keeps it within a narrow range that protects the tissues from damage by strong acids or alkalis. Carbon dioxide combines with water to form a weak carbonic acid, and this compound, in turn, forms bicarbonate and releases a hydrogen ion. The formula for this process is:

$$CO_2 + H_2O \rightarrow H_2CO_3 \rightarrow HCO_3 + H^+$$

The concentration of the hydrogen ion ($H^+$) in the blood, a measure of the acid-base balance of the body, is expressed as pH.

Gases are transported from the lungs to tissues and back by combining with the hemoglobin in the red blood cells. The amount of hemoglobin in the blood averages 15 gm per dl and carries 97 per cent of the oxygen when it is fully saturated. With high concentrations or pressures of

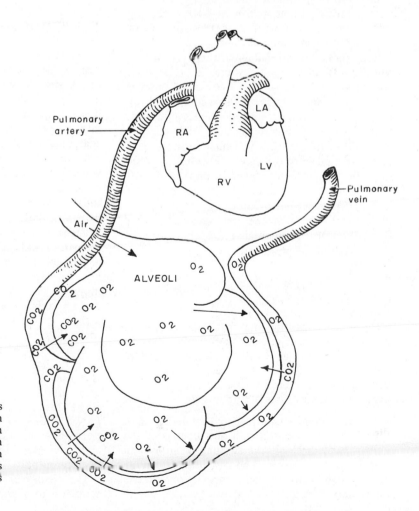

**Figure 9–2.** Diffusion of gases in the lungs occurs when oxygen in the inspired air passes through the alveolar wall to combine with hemoglobin in the blood stream and carbon dioxide ($CO_2$) passes in the opposite direction as it is exhaled from the lungs.

oxygen ($PO_2$), the oxygen combines with the hemoglobin, and, with lower $PO_2$ in the tissues, oxygen is released from the hemoglobin. Normally, about 25 per cent of the oxygen in the blood is released at the tissues but the release of oxygen can rise to as much as 75 to 85 per cent during strenuous exercise. When oxygen is released at the tissues, carbon dioxide is picked up by the hemoglobin of red blood cells, which can combine with tremendous amounts of carbon dioxide.

## HYPOXIA: AN OXYGEN DEFICIT

Meeting oxygenation needs is a far more complex process than just breathing air in and out of the lungs. Several factors can alter or disrupt the many components that are involved in external respiration and diffusion of gases and their transportation throughout the body. Whenever the oxygenation need is not met, hypoxia occurs. Hypoxia is a deficient supply of oxygen in the blood or in the tissues of the body. It poses a threat, regardless of to whom or when it occurs —the mountain climber, the deep-sea diver, the postoperative patient in the recovery room, the elderly sick person lying motionless in bed, or the child with pneumonia.

Hypoxia can occur suddenly whenever the person has difficulty in taking a breath, or the onset can be gradual and subtle. The gradual onset is misleading, and, unless it is accompanied by dyspnea, the hypoxic state is often overlooked. One of the most common causes of hypoxia is obstruction of the airway, which fortunately is easily treated in most cases. However, hypoxia must first be recognized and prompt treatment must then be instituted. Persistent states of hypoxia require the vigorous intervention and specialized efforts of the respiratory therapist, the laboratory technologist, the clinical nurse specialist, and the physician.

## CAUSES OF HYPOXIA

Respiratory insufficiency that leads to hypoxia has many different causes. As one might expect, diseases and injuries of the pulmonary system and the chest are common causes, but many other conditions can interfere with the body's oxygen needs. Frequent causes of hypoxia are

1. *Inadequate amount of oxygen delivered to the alveoli.* Associated with obstructions of the airway by secretions, the swelling of an inflammatory process, foreign bodies, near drowning, burns, high altitudes, and chronic obstructive pulmonary disease.

2. *Decreased neuromuscular function and movement of the chest.* Associated conditions include abdominal surgery, depressed central nervous system from drugs or trauma, any type of coma, multiple sclerosis, Guillain-Barré syndrome, chest injuries, extreme obesity, spinal arthritis, and pneumothorax.

3. *Decreased oxygen transport from the lungs to the tissues.* Associated conditions include anemia, carbon monoxide poisoning, congestive heart failure, myocardial infarction, valvular heart disease, and localized ischemic areas.

4. *Disturbance in the diffusion of gases.* Associated conditions include emphysema, shock lung, tumors of the lung, and pulmonary emboli.

The causes of hypoxia indicate that this is a serious condition and is often life-threatening. Every nurse should be able to assess a patient's or a client's behaviors and to recognize immediately the subtle, or less obvious signs of hypoxia, as well as the overt signs. Treatment consists of supplying oxygen and treating the cause of hypoxia.

## SYMPTOMS OF HYPOXIA

Regardless of the stimuli that cause the oxygen deficit, the results are the same. When the supply of oxygen does not meet the tissue demands, hypoxia occurs. However, the cells of different tissues respond to decreases in oxygen at different rates, depending on their ability to survive with anaerobic metabolism, that is, without oxygen. The cells of the retina of the eye are the most vulnerable cells, and without an adequate supply of oxygen, they show a decrease in function. The rods of the retina that provide the ability to see light and dark are particularly affected. Sudden changes in visual acuity are subtle, but they are the earliest indication of oxygen deficit.

The cells of the cerebral cortex cannot tolerate oxygen deprivation, and within three to four minutes, lack of oxygen produces irreversible damage to brain cells. Early symptoms of hypoxia include changes in mental processes, increased irritability or restlessness, a feeling of apprehension or that "something just isn't right," and a state of listlessness and apathy. When hypoxia is caused by difficulty in breathing, people become anxious, and all the effects of the "fight or flight" response of the autonomic nervous system (ANS) are seen. These effects include rapid pulse rate, increased respiration, pale and cool skin, increased blood pressure, and a decrease in urinary output.

The tissues of the heart and the kidney are sensitive to slight changes in oxygenation and

| Early signs | Later signs | Latest signs |
|---|---|---|
| "I can't breathe." | blood pressure down | cyanosis |
| sits upright | pulse rate down | retractions of chest or |
| change in visual acuity | use of accessory muscles | abdominal muscles |
| mental dullness | stridor, or crowing respirations | |
| blood pressure, pulse, and respiration rates up | | |
| memory lapse | | |

respond quickly to oxygen deficits. Impairment of coronary circulation to the cardiac muscle leads to chest pain, known as angina. Arrhythmias develop, and there is a loss of potassium from the cells.

Until recent years, hypoxic states were closely identified with cyanosis. Cyanosis is the bluish discoloration of the skin due to excessive concentration of reduced hemoglobin in the arterial blood. Severe states of hypoxia can occur without producing cyanosis, but, when cyanosis does appear, it is a late sign of respiratory failure. Cyanosis is rarely seen in hypoxia that is caused by anemia. Blue-tinged color of the skin also may be seen as a result of sluggish blood flow through the skin and a result of the thinness of the skin.

It is important to recognize these symptoms of oxygen deficits.

All body functions are depressed and impaired by a deficit of oxygen. In addition, the acid-base balance of the body is disturbed. Lack of oxygen in the bloodstream results in respiratory acidosis as inadequate ventilation fails to remove the build-up of carbonic acid from the extracellular fluid.

## FIRST LEVEL ASSESSMENT

The first level assessment is done to determine the extent to which one's oxygen needs are being met. The nurse gathers information from the following sources:

*The respiratory pattern*
*Early signs of oxygen deficit*
*The circulatory functions*
*Tolerance for exercise and activity*

When all the assessment data fall within the normal range for that function, regardless of the presence of a related medical diagnosis, it is assumed that the oxygenation needs are adequately being met and that the behavior is adaptive.

## THE RESPIRATORY PATTERN

The first observation that one makes when assessing oxygenation needs is whether or not the person is breathing. The nurse's primary responsibility, taking priority over all the other patient's needs for nursing care, is maintaining an open and patent airway. In the assessment of the respiratory function, the nurse gathers information about the character of the breathing cycle, the size and movement of the thoracic cage, the muscles used, the presence of chest sounds or secretions, and the protective mechanisms of coughing or sneezing. These behaviors are compared with the norms, or standards, and those behaviors within the normal range are supported. For maladaptive behaviors, the nursing process is carried out to identify the causative stimulus and influencing factors, the goal to be achieved, and the interventions to use to achieve the goal.

Dyspnea, or difficulty in breathing, is abnormal and is considered maladaptive, regardless of its rate or its depth. People with dyspnea have to work hard to obtain sufficient air with each breath. They have an anxious and drawn look on their faces from this exertion because they use abdominal, neck, and intercostal muscles in their fight to obtain oxygen. Orthopnea is the term used to describe the inability to breathe while lying down.

Several disrupted breathing patterns have been associated with various disease conditions, including Biot's breathing, Cheyne-Stokes breathing, and Kussmaul's breathing. Biot's breathing is associated with brain damage due to contusion or compression of the brain or to destructive diseases such as brain tumors. This pattern of breathing consists of periodic breathing with a series of two, three, or four regular respirations that are followed by a short period of apnea. Biot's breathing usually lasts only a short time before death occurs.

Cheyne-Stokes breathing is more common and is usually seen just prior to death in critically ill patients who have advanced cardiac failure. However with sluggish blood circulation to the brain, as occurs in many debilitating diseases, Cheyne-Stokes respirations may occur for months at a time. This pattern of breathing consists of alternating periods of rapid breathing, which eliminate much of the carbon dioxide from the

Table 9–1.   ASSESSMENT OF THE RESPIRATORY FUNCTION

| Factors to Assess | Normal Behaviors | Maladaptive Behaviors |
|---|---|---|
| Rate of breathing | Ratio of 1 respiration to 4 pulse beats | Hyperventilation — rapid rate |
|    Infants | 30 or more respirations/min | Hypoventilation — slow rate |
|    Children | 22 to 28 respirations/min | |
|    Adolescents | 18 to 22 respirations/min | |
|    Healthy adults | 14 to 20 respirations/min | |
| Depth of breathing | Normal, approximately 500 ml of tidal air (adult) | Shallow<br>Hyperpnea — very deep breaths |
| Pattern of breathing | Regular, even, effortless with short rest between breaths | Dyspnea; dilated nostrils |
|    Chest movement | | Use of neck and abdominal muscles; retractions |
|    Muscles used | | Orthopnea |
| | | Biot's breathing |
| | | Cheyne-Stokes breathing |
| | | Kussmaul's breathing |
| Breath sounds | Noiseless | Wheezing |
|    Upper passages | | Rales, rhonchi |
|    Chest | | |
| Secretions | Infrequent cough or swallowing of mucus | Obstructing air passages<br>Frequent paroxysms of coughing<br>Productive coughing |
| Subjective feelings | At ease; semiautomatic but can take voluntary control | "I can't breathe."<br>"I'm short of breath." |

blood. The respiratory center responds by halting respirations. The fall in the oxygen content in the circulation then triggers the respiratory center again. These changes are involuntary and under neurochemical regulation.

Kussmaul's breathing is also referred to as air hunger. It is associated with diabetes because it is most often seen with diabetic coma and with other forms of metabolic acidosis. Kussmaul's breathing is rapid and deeper than normal breath-

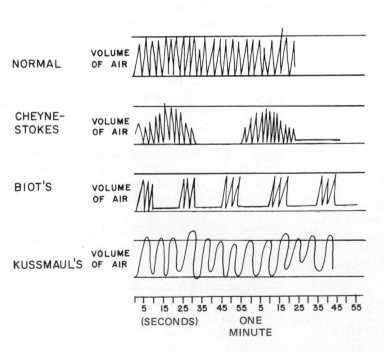

**Figure 9–3.** Breathing patterns vary, according to the volume of air exchanged and the rhythm or frequency of breaths. The pattern of breaths per minute is shown to illustrate normal, Cheyne-Stokes, Biot's, and Kussmaul's types of breathing.

ing, causing great amounts of carbon dioxide to be exhaled from the body. The presence of acetones produces a fruity odor in the breath.

## EARLY SIGNS OF OXYGEN DEFICIT

Once it has been determined that external ventilation is taking place, we can then focus our attention on how well the oxygen needs are being met in the various systems and organs of the body. Some tissues are more sensitive to lack of oxygen than others. The more sensitive tissues can be used as early warning indicators of oxygen deficit. The retina of the eye is the most suscep-

tible area to changes in the oxygen concentration, followed closely by the cells in the brain. It is essential to assess the level of consciousness because this indicates the ability of the brain to respond to incoming stimuli as they pass through the reticular activating system (RAS) and arouse the person. The cortex of the brain controls much of voluntary behavior. Sudden changes in the usual pattern of behavior, such as visual acuity, are related to the oxygenation status.

A decrease of oxygen in the blood level, particularly to the brain, produces deviations in one's behavior. Normally, people are aware of others and of their surroundings, and they respond to changes appropriately, according to their level of growth and development. People

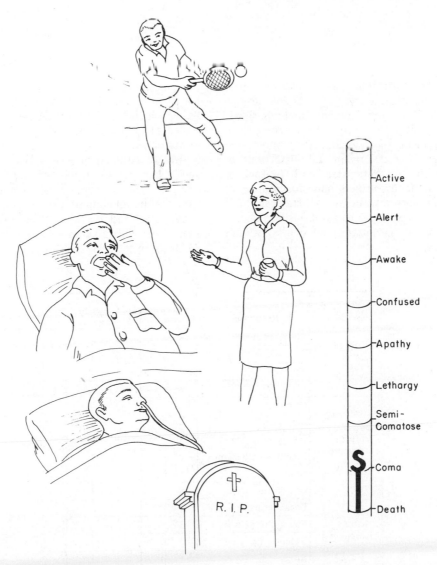

**Figure 9–4.** The levels of consciousness can be envisioned on a scale from active and alert functioning to the opposite extreme of unconsciousness, seen in coma.

**Table 9–2.   ASSESSMENT OF OXYGEN DEFICIT**

| Factors to Assess | Normal Behaviors | Maladaptive Behaviors |
|---|---|---|
| Level of consciousness | Wake and alert; able to respond to verbal and environmental stimuli appropriately | Lethargic<br>Semicomatose<br>Comatose; nonresponsive<br>Minimal use of language |
| Oriented to reality | Aware of reality<br>Oriented to person, time, and place | Confused; hallucinating<br>Irrational; irrelevant<br>Agitated; apprehensive<br>Memory loss; unusual irritability |
| Behavior patterns | Appropriate coping with moving toward, against, or away from stimuli | Unpredictable; unexpected behavior response |
| Visual acuity | Able to see things as well as usual | Loss of night vision; needs more light to distinguish between light and dark; blurring of print |

usually have a realistic view of the world and use language and other intellectual skills in their social relationships. They are awake and alert or are at the highest level of consciousness. A decrease in the oxygen supply to the brain slows, depresses, and dulls all functions. There is a progression from the normal, active state to the state of growing confusion and distortions of reality, to the apathetic state with its lack of feelings, to the drowsiness and sluggishness of lethargy. Patients in semicomatose states respond to some stimuli, such as change of position, movement, touch, some sounds, and painful stimuli (Table 9–2).

Often, it is difficult to distinguish the various levels of consciousness from one another—whether the patient is lethargic, semicomatose, or in a coma. One useful tool is the Glascow Coma Scale, which focuses on three neurological functions: (1) opening the eyes, (2) best verbal response, and (3) best motor response. Numerical values are assigned to several possible responses, and the patient's responses are totalled and assessed. The normal person scores 14 points, which is the maximum; a score of 7 or less indicates coma; and the lowest score of 3 signifies deep coma with no response to external stimuli. A sample of the scale is shown.

| Neurological Functions | Response | Score | 8 | 9 | 10 | 11 | 12 |
|---|---|---|---|---|---|---|---|
| | | | Hours | | | | |
| Opens Eyes | Spontaneously | 4 | | | | | |
| | To speech | 3 | | | | | |
| | To pain | 2 | | | | | |
| | None | 1 | | | | | |
| Best Verbal Response | Oriented | 5 | | | | | |
| | Confused | 4 | | | | | |
| | Inappropriate words | 3 | | | | | |
| | Inappropriate sounds | 2 | | | | | |
| | None | 1 | | | | | |
| Best Motor Response | Obeys commands | 5 | | | | | |
| | Localizes pain | 4 | | | | | |
| | Flexion to pain | 3 | | | | | |
| | Extension to pain | 2 | | | | | |
| | None | 1 | | | | | |

Source: Jones, Kathy: Glascow Coma Scale, Am J Nurs, 79:1551, (September) 1979.

For consistency, the arm is generally used for testing obeying commands. As a response to painful stimuli, the flexion or extension of the arm is not a purposeful behavior. Some preferred methods of providing painful stimuli include applying pressure on the upper orbital rim of the eye with the fingertips or pressing the nail bed of the patient's finger with a pencil or similar object.

The conditions of sick, hospitalized patients often change rapidly, sometimes in a matter of minutes. The patients' levels of consciousness and behaviors that indicate how basic needs are being met, even when the function is within normal limits, should be charted by the nurse at intervals. During a serious illness, the presence of adaptive behaviors can be as significant in the therapeutic regime as maladaptive behaviors, and adaptive behaviors help to provide a more complete picture of the patient's condition.

Assessments of visual disturbances due to oxygen deficits are often obtained from patients' statements that indicate that they cannot see as well as they could previously. However, in various studies of aviators, early changes in vision have been detected and documented. The rods in the retina of the eye are sensitive to hypoxia at an elevation of 5000 feet and the ability to see in the dark is greatly diminished.

Special care should be used when assessing behavior patterns of patients who are referred to as "good" or "quiet" because they never ask for anything, never complain, and just lie quietly in their bed, without even disturbing the covers. These patients tend to use moving-away behavior and are often candidates for hypoxia due to withdrawal and inactivity.

## THE CIRCULATORY FUNCTIONS

Assessment of the circulatory function of transporting gases involves information about the heart, the vascular network, particularly in the skin, and the blood components. The vital signs of the blood pressure and the pulse rate should be within the normal range. In the early stages of hypoxia and other conditions of stress, the blood pressure rises and the pulse rate increases as the cardiovascular system attempts to compensate and to meet the oxygen demands of the body. The blood vessels in the skin constrict, thereby increasing the vascular resistance and the volume of blood circulating with each heart beat. The heart must contract more forcibly to move the

**Table 9-3.** ASSESSMENT OF CIRCULATORY FUNCTIONS

| Factors to Assess | Normal Behaviors | Maladaptive Behaviors |
|---|---|---|
| Blood pressure – adults | | |
|   Systolic | 90 to 140 mm Hg | Hypotension – below usual systolic |
|   Diastolic | below 90 mm Hg |   pressure |
|   Pulse pressure | 30 to 40 mm Hg | Hypertension – systolic or diastolic |
| | |   pressure or both above normal |
| | | Shock |
| Pulse rate | | |
|   Newborn infant | 115 to 130 per minute | Bradycardia – slow pulse rate |
|   Child – age 5 | 95 per minute | Tachycardia – fast pulse rate |
|   Adult – normal range | 60 to 100 per minute | Arrhythmia – irregular pulse rate |
|   Some athletes | 45 to 60 per minute | |
| Blood values | | |
|   Erythrocytes – in men, | 4.8 to 5.5 million/mm$^3$ | |
|     in women | 4.5 to 5.0 million/mm$^3$ | |
|   Hemoglobin – in men, | 14.5 to 16.5 gm/dl | Anemias |
|     in women | 13.0 to 15.5 gm/dl | Carbon monoxide poisoning |
|   pH | 7.35 to 7.45 | Acidosis – 6.8 to 7.35 |
| | | Alkalosis – 7.45 to 7.8 |
|   $PaO_2$ | 80 to 100 mm Hg | Hypoxia – 70 mm Hg or below |
| | | Severe hypoxia – 50 mm Hg or below |
|   $PaCO_2$ | 35 to 45 mm Hg | Hypocapnia – below 35 mm Hg |
| | | Hypercapnia – above 45 mm Hg |
| Skin conditions | | |
|   Color | Pinkish tones to skin, | Paleness; grayness; blue-tinged |
| |   regardless of race | Cyanosis or redness – generalized or |
| | |   localized |
|   Temperature | Warm and dry to touch | Cool or cold and clammy |

additional volume of blood and to overcome the resistance of the contracted vessels. The interrelationships of the stroke volume (the amount of blood ejected from a ventricle at each beat of the heart), heart rate, and vascular resistance determine the blood pressure and any changes in the factors that alter the blood pressure. In later stages of hypoxia, both the blood pressure and the pulse fall as the circulatory system begins to fail, resulting from the increased workload and the deficit of oxygen that is needed to carry out the increased workload.

Laboratory tests provide important information about the ability of the blood components to transport oxygen from the lungs to the tissues. The number of erythrocytes and the amount of hemoglobin that they contain indicate the effectiveness of the circulatory system. Further evidence of internal respiration is obtained from arterial blood gases (ABG). A sample of arterial blood is obtained, and the pH, the arterial pressures of oxygen ($PaO_2$), and the arterial pressures of carbon dioxide ($PaCO_2$) levels in the blood are measured. Effective treatment of hypoxia and other respiratory problems is often based on changes in the ABG.

Skin color and temperature are other indicators of the amount of oxygen supplied to meet the body needs. In the normal person, the skin has a pinkish tone as a result of the red color of the oxygenated hemoglobin as it flows through the capillaries. People who have dark or black skin also have a pink hue to their skin pigments. Constriction of vessels in the skin decreases the available oxygen and causes paleness or a gray tinge to the skin. A continuous flow of deoxygenated hemoglobin produces the blue color of cyanosis. Normal skin is warm and dry to the touch whereas decreased circulation results in cool and, often, clammy skin.

In addition to the appearance of the skin, the assessment of the circulatory functions also includes local circulation to various body parts.

Signs of inadequate local circulation and resulting hypoxia of tissues can usually be seen, especially over bony prominences where pressure reduces the supply of blood. Initially, the pressure produces redness due to congestion in the circulation through the tissues, but continued deprivation of oxygen leads to death of cells and the formation of ulcers. Areas that are prone to and show the effects of pressure include the sacrum, the greater trochanter of the femur, the ankle, the heel, the scapula, and the elbow. Local circulation may also be impaired by obstruction of the vessel due to a thrombus (clot) or embolus, disease, or trauma, depriving tissues of an adequate amount of oxygen.

## TOLERANCE FOR ACTIVITIES AND EXERCISE

Assessment of the person's ability to perform physical activities involves determining how well he or she is able to work and exercise without causing undue stress. The amount of oxygen that is needed depends on the work or the exercise in terms of the forces, the distance, and the length of time involved (Table 9–4). For example, normal people are able to carry out many activities of everyday life, such as getting dressed, brushing the teeth, eating meals, and walking about the room, with only slight or minor changes in their cardiorespiratory systems in order to supply additional amounts of oxygen as required. Dressing at a leisurely pace increases the demand for additional oxygen only slightly, but rushing about and dressing in half the usual time requires more work in a shorter period of time and dramatically increases the need for more oxygen. The respiratory rate increases and the blood pressure and the pulse rate rise as the body adjusts to the greater demands that are being placed upon it.

Normally, increases in breathing and heart functions are sufficient to keep the blood gases within the normal ranges with all activities except

**Table 9–4.  ASSESSMENT OF TOLERANCE FOR ACTIVITIES AND EXERCISE**

| Factors to Assess | Normal Behaviors | Maladaptive Behaviors |
|---|---|---|
| Mild activities of daily living | Changes within the normal ranges of blood pressure, pulse, respiration, $PaO_2$, $PaCO_2$, pH | Shortness of breath<br>Dizziness<br>Fainting<br>Chest pain<br>Fatigue |
| Moderate to strenuous activities or exercise | Above values fall outside the normal range, but return to normal within short time after rest | |

strenuous exercise. With moderate activity, such as hopping 50 times on one foot, the pulse rate increases 20 to 30 beats above the resting rate but should return to normal within two minutes following the exercise.

## SECOND LEVEL ASSESSMENT

Assessed behaviors that do not fall within the normal range indicate possible problems in meeting oxygenation needs. The second level assessment is done to identify the stimuli underlying the maladaptive behaviors. Common stimuli that cause or influence the way oxygen needs are met include:

Diseases affecting the pulmonary and cardiovascular systems
Medical conditions or problems affecting other body need areas
  Altitude and climate
  Chemicals and medications
  Emotional states or anxiety
  Pain experience
  Metabolic changes
  Level of activity

### MEDICAL DISEASES AND CONDITIONS

Diseases that alter the structure, function, or regulation of the organs and the systems of the body associated with providing oxygen are a major source of stimuli that affect the body's oxygenation needs. These diseases include those that are stimuli for hypoxia and are described in the standard medical-surgical nursing textbook.

Diseases and medical conditions that affect other basic need areas may also influence oxygenation, such as fluid and electrolyte balance of the body with changes in the serum levels of $PaO_2$ and $PaCO_2$, the amount of hemoglobin or the presence of anemia, and extreme obesity, which restricts blood flow through the peripheral skin due to the accumulated pressure of the fatty tissues. Additional stimuli that may influence oxygenation include neurological conditions or injuries to the brain, severe edema, trauma to the chest cage, and paralysis of muscle(s) needed in breathing.

### ALTITUDE AND CLIMATE

Environmental factors influence the breathing rate and the body's demand for oxygen. In cold weather, blood vessels in the skin constrict to shunt the blood to the core of the body and to conserve body heat. Less blood in the skin makes it feel colder when one touches it, and the tissues freeze when exposed to freezing temperatures. The frozen tissues deprived of oxygen and die unless the skin is thawed and circulation is restored quickly. Initially, people become more active in the cold because they stamp their feet and swing their arms to generate more heat. Such increased physical activity causes more rapid breathing and an increase in heart rate and blood pressure. Prolonged exposure, with lowering of body temperature, leads to slowing of body functions.

Exposure to warm temperatures and heat causes vasodilation of vessels in the skin, with increased redness and perspiration. Heat speeds up the metabolic rate and increases the body's need for oxygen. A greater workload for the heart results because the blood pressure and the heart rate age increased to compensate for the decreased peripheral resistance in the dilated vessels.

The concentration of oxygen in the environmental air is an influencing factor in meeting oxygen needs. Air that contains great amounts of smoke, ashes, smog, and other foreign particles or noxious gases leads to irritation of air passages and impairs one's ability to obtain sufficient oxygen. Increases in elevation above sea level reduce the oxygen concentration in the air. Most people notice only a few effects or changes in their mental functioning at elevations below 9000 feet.

### CHEMICALS AND MEDICATIONS

Various chemicals interfere with the ability to obtain and utilize oxygen. These chemicals are poisons, and the major types are carbon monoxide, formaldehyde, and cyanide poisoning. Various drugs also affect oxygenation. Central nervous system depressants, such as narcotics or anesthesias, depress one's awareness of one's surroundings, and inhibit the respiratory center's response to changes in the $PaCO_2$ levels. A number of drugs, such as digitalis, enhance the action of the heart so that it is better able to circulate oxygenated blood. Vasodilator and vasoconstrictor drugs also have an influence on meeting oxygen needs.

### EMOTIONAL STATES AND ANXIETY

People with dyspnea have a definite emotional response to oxygen deficits. As they experience air hunger and fight to get enough air, they become anxious from the danger and the perception of the threat to their well-being. Stress or anxiety activates the autonomic nervous system (ANS), and the sympathetic nervous system (SNS) responds by readying the body for "flight or flight" as seen in the vasoconstriction of the vessels in the skin; the increase in the respiratory rate, heart rate, and blood pressure; and the release in antidiuretic horomone (ADH). Anxiety can be expressed through several different emotions, including fear, anger, aggression, frustration, helplessness, powerlessness, and alienation. Some people who have fears about not getting enough oxygen or who have a high level of anxiety may hyperventilate and exhale, or "blow off" so much carbon dioxide that tetanic spasms occur in their hands and feet.

When hypoxia has a more gradual and subtle onset, a slow dimming of brain functions occurs in judgment, concentration, memory, and the emotional states. People are often not even aware of the oxygen deficit; thus, they do not become anxious. Their emotional state, however, is depressed and resembles apathy or hopelessness.

## PAIN EXPERIENCE

Pain influences how the body's oxygen need is met. The discomfort caused by pain arouses emotional responses and anxiety. In addition, pain tends to limit the person's mobility and activity. For example, injury to the chest or surgery of the abdomen may restrict the muscular movement of the chest, enabling the person to take only shallow breaths. Medications given to control pain, such as narcotics, analgesics, and sedatives, tend to depress the central nervous system (CNS) and to produce drowsiness or sleep. Like general anesthesias, these drugs depress the respiratory center, reduce awareness of stimuli, and impair other intellectual functions.

## METABOLIC STATUS

The metabolic status of the body, is a stimulus for meeting the body's oxygen need. High metabolic rates require more oxygen; low metabolic rates require less oxygen. Infants and young children have a higher metabolism and greater requirements for oxygen than do normal adults. People who have hyperactive thyroid glands have high metabolic rates in addition to tachycardia and rapid respirations as they attempt to meet their greater need for oxygen. Oxygen need is increased when body temperature rises. Each degree of increase in body temperature above normal is accompanied by a 6 per cent increase

in the metabolic rate and a corresponding need for more oxygen. Therefore, an increase in temperature from 99° to 103° F. represents a four degree rise or a 24 per cent increase in metabolism.

Metabolism tends to slow down with increasing age and with the cooling of the body by vasoconstriction or lowering of the body temperature. The use of hypothermia during surgery is based on the principle that less oxygen is required to maintain the body at lower metabolic rates. Near-drowning victims, who survived having been submerged in near-freezing water for periods of 30 or more minutes, have proved that people can survive much longer than the four to six minutes that was thought to be the maximum time of survival without breathing.

## LEVEL OF ACTIVITY

Everyone has an upper limit of muscular activity, and it is not possible to go beyond that limit to work harder, to run faster, or to jump higher. One reaches one's limit when the cells consume all the available oxygen, and the circulation is not able to increase the amount of oxygen being delivered to the muscles. Exhaustion follows extreme activity.

Hypoxia is more often associated with inactivity than with too much activity, especially with people who are confined to bed and have their activities limited because of injury, surgery, or treatment. Lack of mobility reduces the expansion of the chest cage, leads to the collapse of alveolar air spaces in the lungs, and slows the blood circulation throughout the body. All these factors reduce the available oxygen and contribute to the deficit.

## PROBLEMS OF OXYGENATION

Patient problems in the physiological mode essentially are due to changes in the structure, function, or regulation of a part of the body or a need area. When assessing the oxygenation needs of the body, one must remember that many factors are involved in the ventilation of the lungs, the diffusion of gases, and the transport of gases to and from the cells and that alterations in any of these factors can cause problems. Changes can produce conditions, such as "too much," or an excess, "too little," or a deficit, the "wrong kind" or "none" of whatever may be necessary. These conditions are frequently used to state problems in the physiological mode.

A disturbance in one physiological need area, such as oxygenation, can cause problems in other physiological need areas and in other modes. For example, a reduction in oxygen decreases one's ability to work or to perform activities, reduces the circulation to the kidney and the formation of urine, causes emotions such as fear or feelings of anxiety in the self-concept mode and increases one's dependency needs for help or attention in the interdependence mode.

Patients' problems consist of one or more related maladaptive behaviors that describe the extent of the disruption. Many nurses find it helpful to state the problem and then add the phrase "due to" and state the focal stimuli causing the maladapted state. The statement of the problem differs according to the philosophical views of those who are using the integrated approach or the segregated method, separating the medical problem and treatment from the patient's problem in meeting basic needs or in coping with one's feelings and with others.

## THE INTEGRATED VIEW OF PROBLEMS

In the integrated approach to nursing care, all maladaptive behaviors are considered amenable to change by the nurse. Impaired functioning on a cellular level as well as maladaptive voluntary behaviors are defined as problems, and the nursing process is used to plan the nursing care for both kinds of problems. This requires that the nurse utilize a wide range of knowledge about the sciences and social behavior.

Problems in which the integrated approach is used include:

"Patient has hypoxia due to hypoventilation."
"Patient is confused, or disoriented, due to cerebral arteriosclerosis."
"Patient has poor local circulation in sacral area."
"Patient has decreased hemoglobin due to recent hemorrhage."

## THE SEGREGATED VIEW OF PROBLEMS

The medical diagnosis, in addition to the behaviors that constitute the signs and symptoms of the condition, the current orders for treatment as prescribed by the physician, and the nursing actions that are used to carry out the medical regime, form one part of the care plan. Relevant behaviors, both adaptive and maladaptive, are used to evaluate the effectiveness of the medical treatment and the patient's progress. Because of the illness, the patient may have other problems that require nursing care, such as not being able to perform activities of daily living in order to meet basic needs or not being able to cope with feelings or to form relationships with others.

Many oxygenation need problems occur on a cellular level, and the resulting maladaptive behaviors form well-defined medical conditions. Diagnosis is necessary because the treatment of hypoxic states is not uniform but varies because of infections or a depressed respiratory center or other cellular changes. The effect of the unmet need, however, affects how the patient performs activities of daily living (ADL) or copes with changes. These variants constitute nursing problems, such as

"Patient has decreased awareness of reality due to congestive heart failure (CHF)."
"Patient is unable to communicate own needs to others due to confusion."
"Patient is unable to carry out own ADLs due to lobar pneumonia."
"Patient is fearful of dying from cancer of the lung."
"Patient has no respirations due to respiratory or cardiac failure."

## NURSING INTERVENTIONS

The nursing process consists of gathering information by the first and second level assessments, identifying problems, formulating appropriate goals, and planning interventions to promote adaptation. When dealing with oxygen deficit, the nurse recognizes that brain function is depressed and cognitive skills, such as awareness, concentration, decision-making, and memory, are impaired. Although the patient may be wholly ignorant of any problem or need, the nurse assumes responsibility for (1) providing for the patient's safety and welfare and (2) nursing actions and health-teaching to prevent complications. Complications that are commonly associated with the cardiovascular and respiratory systems are shock, thrombus formation, embolism, and infection.

Several interventions that are used by nurses to maintain an open airway and to help meet the body's need for oxygen will be described. For additional information or for instructions of how to carry out specific procedures, consult a procedures manual or a reference book on nursing skills.

1. *Encourage patient to turn, cough, and deep breathe at least five times every hour.* Even though one's activity is limited during illness, patients are to turn from side to side, to remove secretions from the air passages by coughing, and to breathe deeply at least five times every hour to ventilate

the alveolar sacs of the lungs. Weak or debilitated patients confined to bed need much encouragement and assistance from the nurse to increase their ventilating efforts.

2. *Provide proper positioning.* Keep the segments of the body in good alignment when patients are lying in bed, sitting up, or ambulating. Patients who have dyspnea find relief and relaxation when placed in a cardiac position with the arms supported by pillows and the head and trunk in an upright position in bed or supported by a cardiac chair. Patients can also obtain relief by sitting on the side of the bed and resting the arms on pillows placed on a bedside table or stand. Patients with emphysema and other obstructive diseases of the lungs can relax the neck, shoulder, and arm muscles (thereby reducing the body's demand for oxygen) by sitting in a chair, leaning forward, and resting their forearms on their thighs.

3. *Increase the oxygen supply.* Oxygen therapy increases the concentration of oxygen in the air that enters the lungs utilizing nasal prongs, an oxygen mask, a Venturi mask, a catheter, or intubation. The concentration of oxygen in room air is approximately 20 per cent; a concentration of 40 per cent provides twice as much oxygen; and pure oxygen, at 100 per cent, is five times the normal amount. Because oxygen is very drying to tissues, it is essential to provide humidity. Oxygen is also toxic when high concentrations are continued for a prolonged period of time. Oxygen is measured either in per cent of concentration or in terms of volume of gas flowing per minute. The small flow of 2 to 3 liters per minute may be beneficial, while high flows of 6 to 8 liters per minute may be detrimental to some patients and decrease their drive to breathe; so, oxygen is not used indiscriminately. When oxygen is used, safety precautions are followed to prevent sparks, fires, or explosions. Open flames and smoking should not be allowed in any area where oxygen therapy is being used.

4. *Remove obstructions of the air passages.* The most common obstructions of the air passages are (a) accumulation of secretions and (b) the tongue occluding the back of the throat, especially in the debilitated or the unconscious patient or during recovery from a general anes-

thesia. The use of an airway device keeps the tongue in place and the airway open in unconscious patients. Turning the patient's head to one side also prevents the airway from being obstructed by the tongue. Suctioning is used to remove secretions that gather in the respiratory passages when patients are unable to clear the obstructing materials by coughing or by postural drainage. Suctioning deep in the tracheal and bronchial passages is done in the briefest period of time possible and by using sterile technique. The patient must be well-oxygenated before suctioning because oxygenated air is removed as well as the secretions, and vigorous suctioning leads to severe hypoxia and cardiac arrhythmia.

Intubation is the treatment of choice for patients who have serious obstruction or impairment of the respiratory system. Those with an endotracheal or a tracheostomy tube are unable to speak and express their needs; thus, they may also become very anxious. The nursing care of these patients includes carrying out procedures that are related to the care of the tube, suctioning effectively, humidifying the air, and preventing complications such as infections.

The general public, as well as nurses, should know and be able to use the emergency measures to rescue victims who choke on food or who have a sudden complete blockage of the air passages. The series of back blows and abdominal thrusts as recommended by the American Heart Association and the Heimlich maneuver have been successful in dislodging the obstructing object.

5. *Promote drainage of secretions.* Secretions are drained by using postural drainage, clapping and vibrating, medications such as expectorants and bronchodilators, and steam humidifiers in addition to other methods. In many agencies, breathing exercises and postural drainage are carried out by respiratory therapists.

6. *Provide mouth-to-mouth and cardiopulmonary resuscitation.* In the event of respiratory or cardiac failure, immediate action is required to provide basic life support to the victim. In hospitals, cardiopulmonary resuscitation is started by the first person on the scene and continues until the CPR team arrives.

## APPLICATION TO CLINICAL PRACTICE

For each patient that you care for in the clinical setting, carry out a complete assessment of the oxygenation mode. To be consistent, you may want to develop a method for organizing the information needed. The nursing goal is to find all of the patient's behaviors in the adapted range, indicating that the oxygenation needs are being met.

The initial assessment of the patient's oxygenation needs is done at the time of your first contact of the day and is continually up-dated or revised by on-going assessments during subsequent visits.

Nurses who are learning to assess the various physiological need areas have found the following chart to be useful. Each need area is covered either in the column that lists common adaptive behaviors or in the column that lists maladaptive behaviors. Circle the behaviors that you have assessed in your patient or write in any behaviors that have not been given. Using the maladaptive behaviors that you have assessed, complete the second level assessment and use the nursing process to identify the problem, to set goals, and to plan interventions.

### OXYGENATION NEED AREA

| Normal or Expected Behaviors | Unusual or Maladaptive Behaviors |
|---|---|
| Awake; alert; asleep | Lethargic; nonresponsive; comatose<br>Minimal response to talk, touch, or movement |
| Oriented to reality — time, person, and place | Confused; hallucinating<br>Irrational; irrelevant; memory loss<br>Unusual irritability; headache<br>Apprehension; agitation; restlessness |
| Usual degree of visual acuity | Sudden visual blurring, or dimming, or seeing spots |
| Vital signs within normal range<br>B/P (lying) _____<br>B/P (sitting) _____<br>Pulse _____<br>Respirations _____ | Vital signs outside normal range<br>B/P ↑ in early acute hypoxia<br>B/P ↓ in progressive or severe hypoxia |
| Pulse — regular and full<br>No pulse deficit | Pulse — rapid, weak, thready<br>Arrhythmia — pulse deficit of _____ |
| Respirations — rhythmic and effortless; normal chest movement; no complaints of shortness of breath | R — rapid, labored, shallow; intercostal or substernal retractions<br>Excessive use of scalenus or abdominal muscles; barrel-shaped chest<br>Complains of shortness of breath; chest pain; dilated nostrils<br>$O_2$ at _____ L per minute |
| Unobstructed airway | Wheezing — audible rales or rhonchi<br>Excessive mucous or secretions<br>Worried — apprehensive facial expression |
| Skin — cool to warm<br>Pink, healthy color of mucous membrane and skin | Clammy, perspiring skin<br>Pale, gray, or blue-tinged skin<br>Reddened areas over bony prominences |

**Laboratory Findings**

| | | | |
|---|---|---|---|
| RBC | M = 4.8 to 5.5 million/mm³<br>F = 4.5 to 5.0 million/mm³ | RBC | _____ |
| Hgb | M = 14.5 to 16.5 gm/dl<br>F = 13.0 to 15.5 gm/dl | Hgb | _____ |
| $PaO_2$ | 80 to 100 mm Hg | $PaO_2$ | _____ |
| $PaCO_2$ | 35 to 45 mm Hg | $PaCO_2$ | _____ |

# REFERENCES

Adult respiratory distress syndrome: a true test of nursing skills. Nursing 80, *10*(5):51–57, (May) 1980.

Affonso, Dyanne, and Harris, Thomas: Continuous positive airway pressure. Am J Nurs, *76*:570–573, (April) 1976.

Brandeburg, Janice: Inhalation injury: carbon monoxide poisoning. Am J Nurs, *80*:98–100, (January) 1980.

Brannin, Patricia: Oxygen therapy and measures of bronchial hygiene. Nurs Clin North Am, *9*(1):110–121, (March) 1974.

Cho, Joan: Assessment of physiological mode. Unpublished study guide. Los Angeles, Mount St. Mary's College, 1977.

Dingle, Rebecca, et al: Continuous transcutaneous $O_2$ monitoring in the neonate. Am J Nurs, *80*:890–893, (May) 1980.

Felton, Cynthia: Hypoxemia and oral temperatures. Am J Nurs, *78*:56–57, (January) 1978.

French, Ruth: Guide to Diagnostic Procedures. New York, McGraw-Hill, Inc., 1975.

Fuchs, Patricia: Getting the best out of oxygen delivery systems. Nursing 80, *10*(12):34–43, (December) 1980.

Gaston, Susan, and Schuman, Lorna: Inhalation injury: smoke inhalation. Am J Nurs, *80*:94–97, (January) 1980.

Guyton, Arthur: Textbook of Medical Physiology, 6th ed. Philadelphia, W. B. Saunders Company, 1981.

Jones, Cathy: Glascow coma scale. Am J Nurs, *79*:1551–1553, (September) 1979.

Kroner, Kristine: Dealing with the confused patient. Nursing 79, *9*(11):71–78, (November) 1979.

Luckmann, Joan, and Sorensen, Karen: Medical Surgical Nursing: A Psychophysiologic Approach. Philadelphia, W. B. Saunders Company, 1974.

Numbrecht, Barbara, and Van Parys, Eileen: From assessment to intervention: how to use heart and breath sounds as part of your nursing care plan. Nursing 82, *12*(4):34–41, (April) 1982.

Programmed Instruction. Blood-gas and acid-base concepts in respiratory care. Am J Nurs, *76*:1–30, (June) 1976.

Programmed Instruction. Mechanical ventilation: patient assessment and nursing care. Am J Nurs, *80*:2191–2217, (December) 1980.

Rifas, Ellene: How you ... and your patient ... can manage dyspnea. Nursing 80, *10*(6):34–41, (June) 1980.

Segal, Sydney: Oxygen: too much, too little. Nurs Clin North Am, *6*(1):39–54, (March) 1971.

Shrake, Kevin: The ABCs of ABGs or how to interpret a blood gas value. Nursing 79, *9*(9):26–33, (September) 1979.

Sumner, Sara, and Grau, Pamela Eaton: Emergency! first aid for choking. Nursing 82, *12*(7):40–49, (July) 1982.

Sweetwood, Hannelore: Acute respiratory insufficiency: how to recognize it ... how to treat it. Nursing 77, *7*(12):24–31, (December) 1977.

Teasdale, G., and Jennett, B.: Assessment of coma and impaired consciousness, a practical scale. Lancet, *2*:81–84, (July 13) 1974.

Waldron, Mary: Oxygen transport. Am J Nurs, *79*:272–275, (February) 1979.

When, why, and how to administer oxygen safely, Consultation with Robert A Promisloff. Nursing 80, *10*(10):54–56, (October) 1980.

Wood, Lucile, and Rambo, Beverly: Nursing Skills for Allied Health Services, Vol 3, 2nd ed. Philadelphia, W. B. Saunders Company, 1980.

# Chapter TEN
# Fluid and Electrolyte Balance

## OBJECTIVES   Information in this chapter will help you to

1. Describe the body's fluid and electrolyte needs in terms of their purposes, how they are usually met, and how they are distributed to various compartments of the body.
2. Describe fluid balance in maintaining a stable internal environment in terms of supplying the water and electrolytes needed daily to replace those lost.
3. List groups of people who are at risk of having a fluid or electrolyte imbalance.
4. Describe the structures involved in regulating the fluid and electrolyte balance.
5. Assess behaviors associated with the fluid and electrolyte need area and compare these behaviors with norms, or standards.
6. State the kinds of stimuli that cause or influence maladaptive behaviors and lead to problems of imbalance in terms of fluid volume loss, fluid volume gain, and electrolytes.
7. Describe nursing interventions that are frequently used to meet this basic need.

## DEFINITION OF TERMS

**acidosis** — the degree of acidity, or concentration of hydrogen ions; in the body, a pH of less than 7.35.

**aldosterone** — hormone secreted by the adrenal gland that acts on the kidney to regulate the levels of sodium and potassium.

**alkalosis** — a decrease in the concentration of hydrogen ions, leading to an increase in base; in the body, a pH above 7.45.

**antidiuretic hormone (ADH)** — suppresses the secretion of urine by stimulating the reabsorption of water, resulting in concentration of the urine.

**anuria** — failure of the kidney to produce urine.

**ascites** — a collection of fluid in the abdominal or peritoneal cavity causing distention and a loss of circulating fluids.

**dehydration** — undue loss of water from the body or tissue; the imbalance caused by more water being lost than is taken in.

**diaphoresis** — excessive or profuse perspiration, or water loss through the skin.

**diffusion** — molecules of a substance move from a high concentration to solutions with a lower concentration of the same substance.

**diuretic** — a drug or medication that increases the formation and secretion of urine.

**edema** — an accumulation of fluid in the spaces surrounding the cells resulting in a loss of circulating fluids.

**electrolyte** — any charged particle, or ion, capable of conducting an electric current.

**extracellular fluid** — fluids located outside the cells and comprised of blood, plasma, interstitial fluid, cerebrospinal fluid, intraocular fluid, and gastrointestinal fluids.

**interstitial fluid** — the portion of body fluids located outside the cells and excluding the plasma.

**intracellular fluid** — fluids lying within the cell.

**ion** — a charged particle that conducts an electrical charge.

**oliguria** — decreased amount and frequency of urination.

**polyuria** — excessive amount and frequency of urination.

**potassium (K)** — important ion of intracellular fluid; an electrolyte that is essential for cell function and muscle action. Hyperkalemia is excess potassium; hypokalemia is a deficit of potassium.

**sodium (Na)** — important ion of extracellular fluid; an electrolyte that determines the water balance of the body. Hypernatremia is excess sodium, hyponatremia is a deficit of sodium. Sodium is one of the elements of salt (NaCl).

**turgor** — the tension or elasticity of the skin that enables a pinched fold to return to its original shape.

---

Why are fluids important to the body? How are they distributed and in what volumes? What happens when fluids are out of balance? How does one detect an imbalance of the fluids or the electrolytes? What are electrolytes?

The role of fluid and electrolyte balance in body function can become very involved and complex; however, we will attempt to describe it as simply as possible in relation to understanding behavior.

After oxygen needs have been met, water is the most important basic physiological need. The body is continually losing some of its fluids through a variety of different routes. These fluids must be replenished to maintain a balance. This is accomplished by ingesting fluids at periodic intervals during the day. Fluid balance occurs when the amount taken in equals the amount that is lost. Imbalance occurs when there is too much, or an overload of fluid, and, more commonly, when there is a deficit in the amount

needed to replace the losses. Many conditions and diseases affect fluid balance and pose a serious hazard to the individual. The need for water is readily seen in cases in which people have been lost in the desert or on a raft at sea without fresh water to drink. Although they can survive without food for quite a long period of time, they will die without water within a few days.

In this chapter, fluid and electrolyte needs are described, including how to meet the fluid and electrolyte needs, how the balance is achieved between the fluid losses and the amount of fluids taken in, and how this balance is regulated by various organs and systems of the body. Adaptive behaviors associated with fluid balance, maladaptive behaviors that result from imbalances, and a normal, or standard, range of behaviors are described and listed. When fluid and electrolyte needs are not met, serious imbalances threaten one's survival. Some people are more at risk of having imbalances than other people. Nurses must recognize peoples' susceptibilities and try to prevent these conditions when possible or to intervene when appropriate. Types of stimuli that contribute to fluid imbalances are described in this chapter, in addition to nursing interventions that are frequently used to meet fluid needs and to restore adaptation.

## THE NEED FOR FLUIDS AND ELECTROLYTES

The human body has been likened to an internal sea that is confined inside the layers of skin. Like the sea, the body fluids consist of water and substances that are dissolved in it that are essential for life. Although fluids are continually being lost from the internal sea and additional fluids are continually being added, the composition and distribution of fluids within the body remain remarkably stable.

### PURPOSES OF FLUIDS

Body fluids consist of all the water located within the cells and outside the cells. Body water performs the following functions that are essential to life:

1. Provides a stable internal environment for chemical changes to occur.
2. Stabilizes and regulates the body temperature.
3. Gives shape and form to the body tissues.
4. Cushions delicate organs from jarring injuries.

A stable internal environment and temperature require continual, fine adjustments of the body to fluid losses and to fluid gains. These adjustments protect the cells from being flooded with excess amounts of liquid or from becoming dried up and wrinkled when more fluid has been lost than has been supplied. The water in the body is distributed into one of two compartments:

the intracellular fluid (ICF) located within the cells where the greatest metabolic activity takes place and the extracellular fluid (ECF) located outside the cells and in the vascular system. The extracellular fluid consists of the blood, bile, saliva, gastric juices, tears, cerebrospinal fluid, and other secretions as well as the fluid in the interstitial spaces that bathes the cells. The intracellular fluid accounts for 40 per cent of the body weight, extracellular fluid accounts for 20 per cent; 15 per cent is found in the interstitial spaces, and 5 per cent is found within the circulatory system (Fig. 10–1).

When an imbalance occurs with a decrease in the amount of body water, the fluid needed to cover the loss comes first from the extracellular fluid and is followed by shifts from the intracellular fluid to the plasma of the extracellular fluid. When there is an excess of water in the body, the shift is from the plasma to the intracellular fluid, where the cells are expanded by the fluid overload.

### COMPOSITION OF BODY FLUIDS

Body fluids and secretions vary in their compositions in order to maintain a stable internal environment and yet to provide the conditions necessary for many different chemical reactions to take place. The water contains various dissolved substances that are known as electrolytes and nonelectrolytes. Electrolytes are particles that are electrically charged when placed in solution. They enable the body, composed fluid, to conduct an electrical current. Although the amount of electrical current generated is extremely small, it is the stimulus for muscular contraction, the conduction of nerve impulses, the transmission of impulses through the cardiac tissue, and other equally vital functions.

The minerals that are usually present in the diet provide the source for the electrolytes. Sodium chloride, (NaCl), or common table salt, is an important substance that forms the electro-

**Figure 10–1.** Amount of fluids in the different compartments of the body.

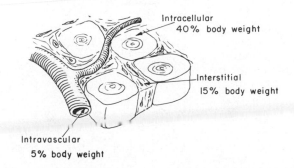

Intracellular
40% body weight

Interstitial
15% body weight

Intravascular
5% body weight

lytes of sodium and chloride when in solution. The amount of sodium present in body fluids determines, to a great extent, the water balance. Other important electrolytes are potassium, calcium, magnesium, and bicarbonate. The extracellular fluid contains a high concentration of sodium and chlorides, while the intracellular fluid has a high concentration of potassium. Other body fluids have various concentrations of these electrolytes, and an abnormal loss of these fluids causes imbalance of the specific electrolyte, disturbs the acid-base balance of the body, and can lead to death. Laboratory tests measure the concentration of electrolytes in the blood.

Nonelectrolyte substances in the body fluids include plasma proteins and other organic compounds. Albumin and globulin are the main plasma proteins, and, because of their large size, they help to exert an osmotic pressure that influences the shift of water from one compartment to another. Other nonelectrolyes include glucose, amino acids, fatty acids, and urea.

In addition to electrolytes in body fluids, the pH of the blood measures the acid-base balance of the body, which is essential for optimal functioning of the cells. The term pH refers to the concentration of hydrogen ions in the body fluids. In the blood, the pH is maintained within the very narrow range of 7.35 to 7.45, but other fluids may be much more acidic or may vary to a greater degree. The lower the pH number, the greater the concentration of hydrogen ions. A pH of less than 7.35 is known as the clinical state of acidosis, and a pH greater than 7.45 is known as alkalosis. Acidosis and alkalosis may result from metabolic causes related to a deficit or an excess of bicarbonate or from

respiratory causes related to a deficit or an excess of carbon dioxide. Acid-base imbalances are not easy to diagnose because they almost always occur as a complication of the underlying cause, such as diabetes or obstructive lung disease. The body uses other mechanisms to compensate for the imbalances.

## VOLUME OF BODY FLUIDS

The average adult has about 40 liters of water in the body, but the volume of fluids varies according to one's age. The highest volume of fluids is in the newborn infant. One's volume of fluids decreases with age. The normal adult man averages about 60 per cent of his body weight in the form of water. Adult women have about 55 per cent of their weight in the form of water because they tend to have a higher proportion of body fat than men. Obese people have less body fluid in relation to their weight because fat cells contain no water. Their volume of fluids may fall to 45 per cent, leaving them with virtually no water reserves to use for maintaining a fluid balance.

Infants have the highest level of body fluids, with about 75 to 80 per cent of their body weight in the form of water. They have a rapid turnover of water, and use three times as much water for their size as do adults. This is due to their high metabolic rate, which provides for rapid growth in the first two years, to the larger amount of water in their extracellular spaces that make babies seem so soft, and to the inability of their kidneys to concentrate urine. They void frequently and have moist, perspiring faces when they cry or eat. Because of these factors, the very young are

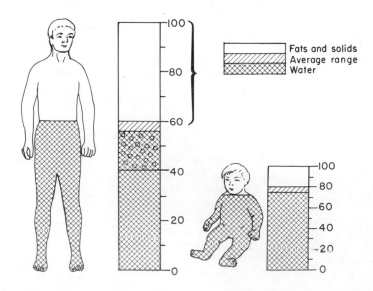

**Figure 10–2.** Percentage of water to total body weight for an adult male (55–60 per cent) and for an infant (75–80 per cent).

WATER LOSSES (in ml)

| | Obligatory | Normal | Strenuous, prolonged exercise |
|---|---|---|---|
| Urine | 500 | 1400 | 500 |
| Feces | 200 | 200 | 200 |
| Sweat | 100 | 100 | 5000 |
| Insensible loss | | | |
| Skin | 350 | 350 | 350 |
| Lungs | 350 | 350 | 650 |
| Totals | 1500 ml | 2400 ml | 6700 ml |

extremely susceptible to fluid deficits and develop signs of severe imbalances within a few hours. Losses in any of their extracellular fluids, such as with vomiting or diarrhea, lead to water being drawn out of the cells and to rapid dehydration.

## MEETING FLUID NEEDS

Each day, the body loses some of its water as a result of various body functions. This water must be replaced to maintain adaptation. There is only a limited amount of fluid reserves; thus, additional supplies must be obtained every few hours. The daily fluid loss amounts to approximately 1500 ml, even when there has been no intake of fluids. This is called the "obligatory loss." The body is committed to lose this amount of water in order to remove waste products from the blood and, through vaporization, to control body temperature. For adults, a minimum of 500 ml of urine is required to remove dissolved waste products, and, in cases of diseased kidneys, a much larger quantity of urine is needed to remove the impurities. Water lost through the skin and the lungs totals 800 ml, and 200 ml of water is lost in the feces, for a total of 1500 ml of obligatory loss. Normal fluid losses average close to 2500 ml, while strenuous work or exercise produces substantially larger losses, as shown in the table above.

The fluids and electrolytes needed each day to replace those lost are supplied through the foods in our diet and the liquids that we drink. Most adults drink between one and two liters of water and other liquids, and foods in the diet with a high content of water in their makeup provide about another 800 ml. A small amount of water is provided as a result of metabolism within the cell; this amounts to about 10 ml for every 100 calories burned. These three sources provide a fluid intake of 2500 ml and, under normal circumstances, balance the fluid loss.

More fluids are needed when the fluid losses are higher than normal. The need for additional fluids triggers thirst, which is the conscious desire for water. In hot weather, as much as 1000 to 2000 ml of fluids are lost by visible perspiration on the skin. Profuse diaphoresis that necessitates changing the patient's gown and other linens represents this amount of fluid loss. When electrolytes are dissolved in the fluids that have been lost to the body, the intake of electrolytes must also be increased.

## REGULATION OF FLUID BALANCE

Based on the information that you have learned up to this point, one can say that fluids and electrolytes are in balance when the total amount of fluids is 60 per cent of the body weight—about 40 liters in an average adult man. One third of the fluids is distributed in the extracellular fluid and two thirds of the fluids are distributed in the intracellular fluid, with a normal concentration of serum sodium, as shown by laboratory tests. Finally, the 24-hour intake of 2500 ml of fluids balances the 24-hour output of 2500 ml of fluids.

The amount of fluids taken into the body can vary widely, and, on occasion, large amounts of fluids are ingested in a short period of time. Body systems and hormones act quickly to make adjustments to maintain the fairly constant blood volume and distribution of body fluids. When one drinks two or three large glassfuls of a beverage, the liquid passes quickly from the digestive system either into the blood stream or into the interstitial spaces, where it is held in temporary reserve. As water is used to meet the "obligatory losses," reserve fluids are drawn out of the extracellular fluid.

The regulation and maintenance of the fluid and electrolyte balance is complicated and involves the entire body. Several structures play particularly important roles. These include (1) the kidneys, (2) the thirst center in the hypothalamus, (3) the hormones of the pituitary and the adrenal glands, and (4) the digestive system.

**The Kidneys.** More than any other organ, the kidney is important in the regulation of the body fluids. The kidneys function in the following ways: to maintain a relatively stable blood volume, to regulate the volume of extracellular fluids, and to control the concentration of electrolytes, the ratio of water to other solutes, and the acidity of the body fluids.

Each kidney is composed of more than one million working units called nephrons, which consist of a glomerulus that filters fluids and dissolved substances from the blood, and the long tubule where urine is formed. Approximately 21 per cent, or one fifth, of the blood volume of the body is filtered through the kidneys each minute. The purpose of this filtering is to clean, or "clear," the blood plasma of wastes and unneeded materials, which are then excreted from the body in the form of urine. The filtrate fluid diffuses into the glomerulus and contains nearly the same constituents as blood itself except for the large molecules such as proteins and bacterias or the red and white blood cells.

As the filtrate fluid moves along the tubule of the nephron, water and essential substances needed by the body are reabsorbed. The entire 1200 ml of filtrate fluid that moves through the nephron each minute does not terminate in the bladder as urine. About 99 per cent of the filtrate fluid is reabsorbed into the blood stream, including albumin, glucose, electrolytes, and fluid, leaving only the amount that is in excess of the body's needs to be excreted.

These mechanisms of renal filtration and reabsorption serve to regulate the body's fluid volume and its electrolytes. Any condition that interferes with the blood flow to the kidney or the failure of the nephrons to function causes an imbalance of the body's fluid and electrolyte needs.

**The Thirst Receptors.** Thirst is the conscious desire for water and the primary regulator of fluid intake. The thirst center consists of specialized cells located in the hypothalamus that respond to a reduction of water. Cells such as those in the mucous membranes of the mouth become dry, usually as the result of a shift of fluids out of the cell or the loss of potassium from the intracellular fluid, which leads to the shrinking of cell size and the loss of water. Everyone has experienced great thirst on hot summer days when large amounts of body water are lost through the skin. Large quantities of fluids are consumed to obtain temporary relief from thirst.

**The Regulating Hormones.** Hormones secreted by the pituitary and the adrenal glands help to regulate fluid balance. The antidiuretic hormone (ADH) is secreted by the posterior pituitary gland, and it regulates the amount of water reabsorbed in the kidney tubule. When the cells of the nearby thirst center are stimulated by the sodium concentration in the blood or by stress,

the pituitary gland releases ADH and increases the ability of the tubule to absorb more water and concentrates the urine and other solutes. ADH acts to conserve body water while sodium is excreted. The retained water dilutes the sodium concentration in the blood, bringing it back to normal levels. When less ADH is produced, the amount of urine increases as less water is reabsorbed.

The adrenal glands produce aldosterone, a hormone responsible for the regulation and concentration of sodium and potassium (K) in the extracellular fluid. A certain amount of aldosterone, a mineralocorticoid, is present at all times in the circulation so that some potassium is secreted from the kidneys daily. This potassium must be replaced either by foods in the diet or by direct supplements of potassium. Small variations in the concentration of potassium in the extracellular fluid controls the rate of aldosterone secretion. An increase in the potassium level raises the level of aldosterone in the blood and leads to greater excretion of potassium in the urine. Conversely, a decrease in the potassium level in the extracellular fluid causes a lower rate of hormone secretion and greater reabsorption of the electrolyte.*

Both hormones, ADH and aldosterone, play an important part in the body's response to stress. One of the immediate responses of the autonomic nervous system is the release of increased amounts of ADH to prepare the body for "fight or flight," because ADH helps to conserve body fluids. Aldosterone is also released. The initial effects of stress include:

1. Reduction in the amount of urine produced.
2. Retention of sodium and fluid.
3. Increased loss of potassium from the body.

It is important that nurses recognize the effects that stress and anxiety have on the regulation of fluid balance when assessing this need area in patients. When ill, people are subjected to many stresses and anxieties that may easily lead to fluid or electrolyte imbalances.

**The Role of the Digestive System.** Under normal circumstances, people satisfy their fluid needs by eating foods and by drinking liquids. Food and liquids are mixed with the digestive juices and move through the stomach into the small intestine. Throughout the intestinal tract, water diffuses out of the gut into the rich capillary bed surrounding it and into the interstitial fluid. However, most of the absorption of water, electrolytes, and nutrients occurs in the ileum of the

*Guyton, Arthur: Textbook of Medical Physiology, 6th ed. Philadelphia, W. B. Saunders Company, 1981, p. 444

small intestine and in the proximal portion of the large intestine.

Enormous amounts of gastric secretions enter the digestive system daily, and all but a small fraction of these fluids are reabsorbed into the blood stream. Gastric juices, bile, pancreatic secretions, and intestinal juices are rich in sodium and chlorides. They are classified as extracellular fluids, which have sodium as the predominant electrolyte. The digestive juices and electrolytes are reabsorbed by the time they reach the transverse colon; thus, only 100 to 200 ml of liquid remains in the fecal material. When severe vomiting or an obstruction of the small bowel prevents the chyme from reaching the absorbing structures, not only is there an imbalance of fluids, but also there is decreased sodium, or hyponatremia.

The digestion of food provides the nutrients, potassium, sodium, calcium, magnesium, chlorides, iron, and other trace metals that are absorbed from the small intestine. As the chyme passes into the large intestine, juices are secreted that contain large amounts of bicarbonate, which helps to neutralize acids such as those resulting from the increased bacterial action that occurs in the colon. The loss of any body secretions by abnormal routes leads to imbalances of fluid volume and electrolytes (Table 10-1). The reason that diarrhea is a serious condition in small children is because the intestine secretes huge amounts of water to flush out the irritated organ, and with the rapid loss of the sodium, signs of shock appear and progress to coma and death unless treated.

## PEOPLE AT RISK OF IMBALANCE

Although anyone can develop an imbalance of fluids and electrolytes, certain groups of people are more prone to do so than are others, and special attention must be given to the fluid needs of these people. Illness greatly affects people's ability both to obtain and to retain sufficient fluids. An imbalance may be caused by the disease or condition, but some types of treatment also contribute to problems, especially for people who have fewer fluid reserves. Patients who are placed on NPO (nothing by mouth) or who have a restricted fluid intake as well as those with abnormal fluid losses must have careful monitoring of fluids.

People with an imbalance in fluid volume or electrolytes usually belong to one of these groups or are victims of one of these diseases:

| | |
|---|---|
| infants | congestive heart disease |
| elderly people | ulcerative colitis |
| obese people | cirrhosis of the liver |
| surgery | diuretic medications |
| kidney disease | low sodium diets |
| diabetes | intravenous fluids |

## FIRST LEVEL ASSESSMENT

The balance of fluid and electrolytes provides a stable internal environment to enable the chemical reactions of the body to take place, to regulate the temperature and keep it within the normal range, and to provide the shape of cellular structures. Fluids are continually being lost through the skin, lungs, and feces and as urine from the kidney. Electrolytes and nonelectrolyte substances in the blood exert physical pressures that are needed for osmotic movement through cellular membranes. The concentrations of these elements are measured by various laboratory tests.

The assessment of fluid needs focuses on behaviors related to (1) fluid gains or losses, (2) the vital signs, (3) the circulatory status, (4) hydration of structures such as the skin, (5) the laboratory values for the various components of the ECF, and (6) the electrolyte status.

**Table 10-1.** ELECTROLYTE COMPOSITION OF BODY SECRETIONS OR FLUIDS

| Type | Sodium (Na) mEq/L | Potassium (K) mEq/L | Chlorides (Cl) mEq/L | Bicarbonate (HCO₃) mEq/L |
|---|---|---|---|---|
| Extracellular fluid (ECF) | 142 | 5 | 104 | 27 |
| Intracellular fluid (ICF) | 35 | 123 | 5 | 10 |
| Saliva | 10 | 25 | 10 | 15 |
| Gastric juice – fasting | 60 | 10 | 85 | 0–15 |
| Biliary tract fistula | 148 | 5 | 101 | 40 |
| Jejunal suctioning | 111 | 4.6 | 104 | 31 |
| Ileal suctioning | 117 | 5 | 105 | – |
| Ileostomy (recent) | 129 | 11 | 116 | – |
| Diarrheal stools – children | 116 | 17.5 | 8 | – |

Source: Bland, John: Clinical Metabolism of Body Water and Electrolytes. Philadelphia, W. B. Saunders Company, 1963.

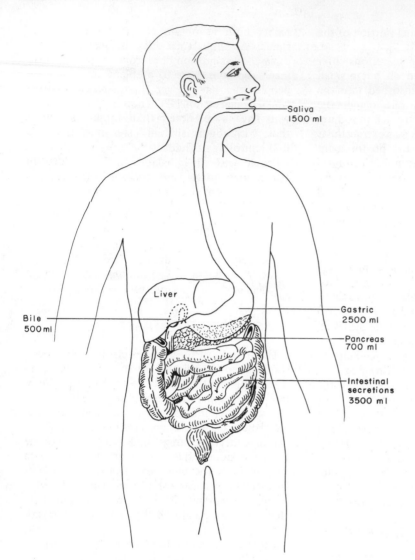

**Figure 10–3.** Volume of digestive secretions produced in a 24-hour period.

## FLUID GAINS OR LOSSES

Assessment begins with determining the current intake and output of fluids for a period of several hours or a 24-hour period. The record of the intake and output of fluids for previous days often provides information about the trend toward balance or imbalance. Special attention is given to the urinary output because this is a critical indicator of the body's need to conserve or to excrete fluids and electrolytes. Most records of output include urine and abnormal losses from various body secretions but exclude the "obligatory losses" from the skin, lungs, and feces that average about 1000 ml daily. The intake of fluids should be sufficient to cover the recorded losses of liquids plus the unrecorded basic losses.

The maladaptive behaviors include the excessive loss of water through profuse perspiration and through the lungs as well as through the loss of significant amounts of other body secretions that are normally reabsorbed into the system. During periods of stress and anxiety, urinary output is decreased initially as ADH and aldosterone cause the retention of fluids and sodium. Later, increased frequency of urination occurs as greater amounts of fluids are excreted through the domination of the parasympathetic nervous system (PNS).

Fluid gains and losses also occur through altered means as a result of medical treatment. Various tubes are used to instill or to drain fluids from various parts of the body. Whenever these tubes are present, nurses should be aware of an

**Table 10–2.** ASSESSMENT OF THE FLUID NEEDS

| Factors to Assess | Normal Behaviors | Maladaptive Behaviors |
|---|---|---|
| Fluid intake | 2500 ml/24 hr or sufficient to cover losses | Increased intake <br> Decreased intake |
| Fluid output | 2500 ml/24 hr or to balance intake | Decreased urinary output <br> Excessive urinary output |
| Urine | Straw to amber color; normal constituents | Concentrated; contains sugar, blood, or proteins; ammonia odor |
| Abnormal loss of body fluid | No abnormal loss of body fluid through nasogastric suctioning, vomiting, hemorrhage, profuse perspiration, wound drainage, diarrhea, serious fluid loss in burns, polyuria | Loss of fluids. Specify type and amount _____ <br> _____ |
| Tubes to instill or to drain fluids | No use of tubes | Use of IV, hyperalimentation, catheters, suction, and drainage tubes |

actual or a potential problem in meeting fluid needs. For example, chest tubes are placed in the thoracic cavity to remove serosanguineous drainage after surgery, and additional fluids are given by intravenous infusion. Table 10–2 can be used as a guide to begin the assessment of the fluid needs.

## VITAL SIGNS

Changes in the vital signs are not specific to the fluid need area, but they are affected by changes in the fluid volume. A decrease in volume as seen in dehydration results in a rise in temperature because there are less circulating fluids to dissipate the heat. In fevers, the elevated temperature leads to additional loss of fluids through sweating. Changes in blood pressure also occur. In the normal individual, the blood pressure taken while sitting is equal to or slightly lower than the blood pressure taken while lying down. However, the "sitting" blood pressure is much lower in people who have decreased fluid volume. The difference of more than 15 mm Hg systolic and 10 mm Hg diastolic between lying and sitting blood pressures indicate a fluid volume deficit.

Changes also occur in the pulse and respiratory rates. Excess fluid volume is associated with a full, bounding pulse. A weak, thready pulse that is easily obliterated accompanies fluid deficits. Decreased fluid volume results in acceleration of both pulse and respiratory rates as the body attempts to compensate for the smaller amount of circulating blood. These changes are the same as those one would see in meeting the body's demands for oxygen. Arrhythmias in the heart rate

occur with imbalances of potassium, the major intracellular electrolyte. Both deficits and excesses of potassium cause arrhythmias. In cases of metabolic acidosis, the breath usually has a characteristic fruity odor.

## THE CIRCULATORY STATUS

An accurate way to detect changes in fluid status is the daily measurement of body weight. Weight gains result from the actual body tissue build-up as excessive calories are stored as fat cells or by the retention of water. Rapid changes in weight from one day to the next are more likely to reflect the gain or loss of fluids. One liter (1000 ml, or 1 quart) of fluids is equal to the gain or loss of one kilogram, or 2.2 pounds, of body weight. Weight is closely monitored in patients who are receiving diuretic therapy in order to evaluate the effectiveness of the drug that is being used to reduce the water retention. Increased weight indicates retention of sodium and water in the body.

Not only are fluids lost through various exits of the body but also the circulating volume is reduced when fluids become trapped and accumulate in a body space not usually used for this purpose. This becomes a fluid loss because the fluid is no longer available for use. These losses include accumulation of fluids between the pleura of the lungs (pleural effusion), in the peritoneal cavity (ascites), in the pericardial sac, and in the tissues (edema). When these behaviors are not assessed directly as problems, the losses may influence other behaviors and function as stimuli for maladaptive behaviors.

The filling of veins is another method used to assess fluid balance. Normally, the veins of the neck fill when one is in a supine position and are not filled or distended when one is in a sitting position. They become distended when intrathoracic pressure is increased such as when people hold their breath, shout, or exhale forcefully. The small, superficial veins of the hand can easily be assessed without greatly disturbing the patient. When the hand is elevated, the veins quickly empty; however, when the hand is dropped below the level of the heart, the veins promptly (within a few seconds) fill again. The same effect is achieved by blocking the distal part of the vein with one finger, "milking" the vein empty with another finger, and observing the time it takes for the vein to fill when the pressure is released. With fluid volume deficits, more time is needed to fill the vein, and, with excessive fluids, it takes longer for the vein to empty.

## HYDRATION AND THE SKIN

Observations of the skin and the mucous membranes provide the nurse with an immediate and economical measure of the fluid status of the body (Table 10–3). Normally, the skin is warm and dry, with good turgor. Turgor is the tension within the cells that provides the shape of the structure. When a fold of skin is pinched up between the fingers, skin with good turgor immediately returns to its usual shape when released. When indented by finger pressure, it springs back to its original position within a few seconds. Skin with poor turgor takes much longer to resume its previous shape.

In fluid volume gains, the tissues are distended with fluid in the characteristic firmness of swelling or edema. Edema initially occurs in the ankles, fingers, around the eyes, and in the sacral area. When the tissue is depressed by finger-tip pres-

sure, a pitting indentation remains. This indentation is classified as 1+, 2+, or 3+ pitting edema, depending on the length of time it takes the skin to regain its former shape. The following periods of time serve as a guide: 30 to 60 seconds = 1+, 1 to 2 minutes = 2+, and more than 2 minutes = 3+.

The mucous membranes and the tongue are normally pink in color and moist. With fluid deficits, they become dry, sticky, red, and cracked, and the tongue becomes furrowed. The eyes appear sunken because the fluid that normally supports the tissues is lost. The intraocular tension of the eye is reduced when the fluid volume is reduced; thus the eye feels soft when the finger is pressed gently over the lid.

## LABORATORY VALUES

Laboratory tests offer the most accurate measure of electrolytes and other components of the extracellular fluid. When imbalances occur, repeated tests serve as the best method of evaluating the effectiveness of the treatment. Because fluid and electrolyte imbalances occur with numerous clinical conditions, laboratory tests are often taken of many patients' sodium, potassium, chloride, phosphate, calcium, and magnesium levels. Nonelectrolyte tests include the proteins of albumin and globulin, blood glucose, and blood urea nitrogen (BUN) levels.

The hematocrit is used widely to determine blood loss and fluid status. It is the measure of the volume of blood occupied by the red blood cells. Both the hemoglobin and the hematocrit are decreased when there has been a blood loss of red blood cells or an excess of fluid that dilutes the concentration of red blood cells. An increase of the normal values indicates the presence of more cells in less fluid (Table 10–4).

These values and the values for nonelectrolytes

Table 10–3.   ASSESSMENT OF HYDRATION AND THE SKIN

| Factors to Assess | Normal Behaviors | Maladaptive Behaviors |
|---|---|---|
| Fluid volume | No unusual retention of fluids | Edema of feet, ankles, hands, eyelids, or sacrum<br>Ascites; gurgling rales |
| | Maintains body weight | Gain or loss of more than ½ pound per day |
| Vein filling | Neck veins fill in supine position, not in sitting | Neck veins fill in sitting position, or neck veins flat when lying down |
| Mucous membranes | Moist; pink | Dry; complains of thirst |
| Skin | Warm; dry | Cool; cold; clammy; hot |
| | Good turgor, rapid return to previous shape | Poor turgor, slow or poor return to previous state |

Table 10-4. ASSESSMENT OF LABORATORY VALUES

| Factors to Assess | Normal Behaviors* | Maladaptive Behaviors |
|---|---|---|
| Hematocrit — % RBC/dl | Men — 44–52<br>Women — 39–47 | Elevated in hypovolemia<br>Decreased in fluid volume gain |
| Hemoglobin — gm/dl | Men — 15–18<br>Women — 13–16 | Elevated in hypovolemia<br>Decreased in fluid volume gain |
| Serum pH | 7.35 to 7.45 | Over 7.45 = alkalosis<br>Under 7.35 = acidosis |
| Sodium — $Na^+$ | 137–147 mEq/L | Above 147 mEq in hypernatremia<br>Below 137 mEq in hyponatremia |
| Potassium — $K^+$ | 3.5 – 5.0 mEq/L | Above 5.0 mEq in hyperkalemia<br>Below 3.5 mEq in hypokalemia |
| Calcium — $Ca^{++}$ | 4.5 – 5.8 mEq/L | Above 5.8 mEq in hypercalcemia<br>Below 4.5 mEq in hypocalcemia |
| Chlorides — $Cl^-$ | 98–106 mEq/L | Above or below the range |

*Laboratories may report other normal ranges because of differences in procedures.

may vary slightly as laboratories establish their normal values because differences in procedures may affect the actual test result. Most laboratory reports now include the normal ranges for each test.

## ELECTROLYTE BALANCE

Electrolytes are particles that break down in water and carry a positive or a negative charge. Positive ions are called cations and consist of sodium, potassium, calcium, and magnesium. Negative ions, or anions, consist of chlorides, bicarbonate, phosphate, sulfate, proteins, and organic acids. Electrolyte balance is maintained when there are 154 cations and 154 anions in one liter of body fluid in terms of milliequivalents (mEq) or when the same number of electrolytes are chemically active and able to combine with others. Electrolyte balance enables the cells of the body to carry out their functions, whereas an imbalance interferes with the electrochemical activity.

The electrochemical activity is especially important to certain cells of the body that are capable of transmitting the resulting impulse along the membrane. These cells include muscle, nerve, and, possibly, glandular cells. Imbalances cause changes in the conduction of nerve impulses, the function of the brain, and the muscular activity of the body. In some cases, an imbalance in an electrolyte, such as potassium, produces effects on the cell that lead to maladaptive behaviors, such as muscular weakness beginning in the lower extremities and progressing upward, a flattening of the muscles, flaccid paralysis that leaves the person with the strength of a "limp noodle," and

development of cardiac arrhythmias. In a similar manner, sodium excesses or deficits may lead to mental changes characterized by behaviors of confusion and lethargy that progress to convulsions and coma if untreated. Although these behaviors are suggestive of electrolyte imbalances, laboratory tests must be used for confirmation.

## SECOND LEVEL ASSESSMENT

Maladaptive behaviors in the fluid and electrolyte need area are caused by a wide variety of stimuli. These behaviors have been classified, and examples of stimuli for each group have been given.

1. *Disease affecting the kidney, gastrointestinal system, pituitary, or adrenal gland functions.*
Peptic ulcer, intestinal obstruction, renal insufficiency, glomerulonephritis, Addison's disease, Cushing's syndrome, diabetes insipidus, diabetes mellitus, colitis.

2. *Diseases or injury of other body systems or structures.*
Congestive heart failure, cirrhosis of the liver, stroke, burns, massive crushing injuries, brain injury or infection, pleural effusion.

3. *Excessive loss of fluid and electrolytes by normal routes.*
Profuse sweating, vomiting, diarrhea, hyperventilation, pulmonary emphysema, increased urinary output.

4. *Excessive loss of fluids and electrolytes by abnormal routes.*
Hemorrhage, nasogastric suctioning, colostomy, ileostomy, paracentesis, thoracentesis.

5. *Factors in the external environment or treatment.*

Availability of food, fluids, and electrolytes, no access to water, inability to swallow, inhaling water by near-drowning, use of distilled water to irrigate a nasogastric tube, excessive number of tap water enemas, too rapid infusion of IV fluids, abuse of antacids and laxatives, prolonged immobilization, hot weather, medications, including diuretics and antidiuretics, supplemental electrolytes.

6. *Other influencing factors.*

Age, fear, anxiety, pain, anesthesia, other stresses.

## PROBLEMS OF FLUID AND ELECTROLYTE IMBALANCE

In the segregated approach to nursing care, the nurse is confronted with the problems of imbalance expressed in terms of fluid volume gain or fluid volume loss. Because the concentration of electrolytes is directly related to the volume of fluids, the electrolytes become part of the medical and nursing treatment to restore the adapted state of balance. The problems of fluid and electrolyte imbalance are very important and will be described, including behaviors that are associated with them.

### *FLUID VOLUME GAIN*

With fluid volume gain, the patient's problem is inadequate kidney function to rid the body of extra sodium and fluid. An adequate amount of fluid may be taken in, but the body is unable to excrete enough sodium or fluid to maintain a balance. In other cases, fluid retention occurs because of a high salt intake or because fluids enter the body faster than the circulation and the kidneys can handle them, such as in the case of a "runaway" IV. A statement of such a problem is "Patient has excessive fluid retention due to uremia."

The maladaptive behaviors characteristic of fluid gains are associated with the interstitial spaces being swollen with water and the cells literally swimming in fluids. Think what this means to the functioning of the heart, the lungs, and the brain; to the volume of fluids in the superficial veins; and to the appearance of the skin.

There is edema of the eyelids, the face, and the extremities. There may be abdominal distention and a feeling of heaviness. Dyspnea may be present in addition to gurgling rales, a full and pounding pulse, and an increase in blood pressure as the extra fluid load increases the peripheral resistance. There is increased mental irritability and in increase in weight because the intake of fluids exceeds the loss of fluids.

### *FLUID VOLUME DEFICIT*

A deficit of body fluids occurs when the total output exceeds the amount of fluids taken into the body. Fluid volume deficit may occur as a result of inadequate intake of fluids or abnormal loss of fluids. When the volume of fluids in the body is reduced, water shifts from the cells to the blood stream, causing the cells to shrink in size, the mucous membranes to become dry and sticky, skin turgor to be poor, and the person to have thirst. The skin becomes dry, warm, and flushed because of the rise in body temperature,

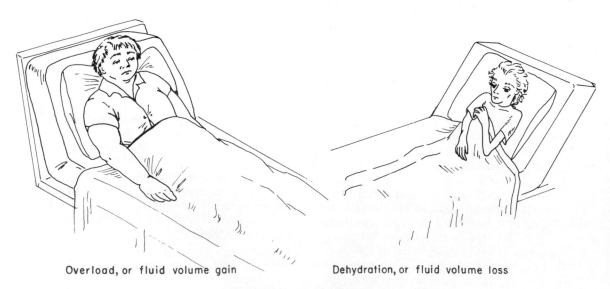

Overload, or fluid volume gain          Dehydration, or fluid volume loss

Figure 10–4.  Fluid imbalance.

as the decreased blood is shunted from vessels in the skin to the internal vital structures. A loss of body weight and reduction in urinary output occur. When the loss of fluids occurs rapidly, as in hemorrhage, diarrhea, or bowel obstruction, the symptoms are those of shock. The decrease in the volume of circulating blood leads to a reduction in the oxygen delivered to the cells and an increase in waste products, resulting in metabolic acidosis. In rapid loss of fluids, the skin is cold and clammy, the blood pressure falls, the pulse rate is rapid, urinary output drops almost to zero, and the person becomes restless and apprehensive. The laboratory reports show an increased hematocrit count. With slow fluid losses over a period of time, the hemoglobin increases, as there are more red blood cells concentrated in a smaller volume of fluid.

An imbalance of electrolytes will also occur when the fluids are lost through any of the abnormal routes or when excessive amounts of fluids are lost through normal routes, such as sweating, diarrhea, or potent diuretics. Statements of such problems include "Patient has inadequate intake of fluids because of weakness and limited activity" and "Patient has excessive fluid loss due to frequent vomiting."

## ELECTROLYTE IMBALANCES

In the integrated approach to nursing care, the nurse focuses on each change in electrolyte imbalance as an individual problem. In the segregated approach, electrolyte imbalances are generally part of the medical condition that is being treated. The more common problems encountered in the care of patients clinically are imbalances of sodium, potassium, calcium, and the hydrogen ion, leading either to a state of acidosis or to a state of alkalosis. These problems will be described briefly.

**Sodium Imbalance.** Sodium controls the distribution of water in the body and is the major electrolyte in the extracellular fluid.

*Hyponatremia* — less than 130 mEq/L. Brain cells swell, causing malaise, headache, nausea and vomiting, confusion, lethargy, coma, and death if not treated.

*Hypernatremia* — more than 145 mEq/L. Brain cells shrink, leading to behaviors of thirst, oliguria, confusion, lethargy, muscle weakness, twitching, convulsions, and coma.

**Potassium Imbalance.** Potassium regulates the electrolyte balance of intracellular fluid and the transmission of electrical impulses in nerve and muscle cells.

*Hypokalemia* — less than 3.5 mEq/L. Muscle cells are less sensitive to stimuli, resulting in abdominal distention, muscle weakness, flaccid paralysis, polyuria, and cardiac arrhythmias.

*Hyperkalemia* — more than 5.0 mEq/L. Muscle cells act and cannot be restimulated, resulting in colic and diarrhea, muscle weakness, flaccid paralysis, irritability, and cardiac arrhythmias.

**Calcium Imbalance.** Calcium is the most abundant electrolyte, 99 per cent of which is found in bones and teeth; the rest is in solution. Calcium promotes nerve impulse transmission, blood clotting, muscle contraction, and chemical activities within the cell.

*Hypocalcemia* — less than 4.5 mEq/L. Increased neuromuscular excitability, leading to muscle cramps, twitching, carpopedal spasm, tetany, convulsions, and cardiac arrhythmias.

*Hypercalcemia* — more than 5.8 mEq/L. Decreased neuromuscular response, resulting in nausea, vomiting, constipation, headache, muscle weakness, depression of the central nervous system, renal calculi, pathological fractures, and cardiac arrest.

**Hydrogen Ion Imbalance.** Changes in the delicate balance of acids and bases in the body lead to conditions of acidosis or alkalosis (Fig. 10–5). Imbalance disturbs the central nervous system; thus, the acidotic state produces depression of the central nervous system, whereas alkalotic conditions stimulate the central nervous system. Severe forms of either type of imbalance may lead to death if not reversed.

*Metabolic acidosis* — the serum pH is less than 7.35 and base bicarbonate is reduced, leading to Kussmaul's breathing, delirium, weakness, stupor, acidic urine, coma, and cardiac arrhythmias from the often associated imbalance of hyperkalemia.

*Metabolic alkalosis* — the serum pH is over 7.45 and base bicarbonate is increased, leading to irritability, disorientation, depressed respirations, tetany, convulsions, and cardiac arrest.

*Respiratory acidosis* — an excess of carbon dioxide produces a serum pH less than 7.35 and above normal bicarbonate and $PaCO_2$, leading to hypoxia, dyspnea on exertion, rapid pulse, weakness, urine pH less than 6.0, disorientation, and coma.

*Respiratory alkalosis* — a deficit of carbon dioxide produces a serum pH over 7.45 and a low $PaCO_2$. Alkalosis seldom occurs except when overbreathing, usually from psychogenic causes or when ascending to high altitudes. Behaviors include overbreathing and neuromuscular irritability with twitching, tetany, and convulsions.

## NURSING INTERVENTIONS

Nurses use several interventions to control the fluid intake and the electrolytes in order to pro-

| Imbalance | pH | Bicarbonate | pCO2 |
|---|---|---|---|
| Respiratory acidosis | ↓ | ↑ | ⬆ |
| Respiratory alkalosis | ↑ | ↓ | ⬇ |
| Metabolic acidosis | ↓ | ⬇ | ↓ |
| Metabolic alkalosis | ↑ | ⬆ | ↑ |

**Figure 10–5.** Acid-base imbalances result from changes in pH, bicarbonate, and carbon dioxide levels. Large arrows indicate the primary disturbance.

Source: Brunner, Lillian, and Suddarth, Doris S.: Textbook of Medical-Surgical Nursing, 4th ed. Philadelphia, J. B. Lippincott Co., 1980.

mote adaptation. The problems of fluid need include either too much or too little water; thus, stimuli are manipulated to regain balance. This process includes the treatment of the disease or condition that is causing the imbalance, provisions for ongoing assessment, means of supplying oral fluids and electrolytes, usage of intravenous and other routes for fluids, and manipulation of other influencing factors, when possible.

## TREATMENT OF THE CAUSE

Because so many illnesses disturb the fluid and electrolyte balance of the body, nurses need to know the medical and nursing treatment for restoring balance to the body. Edema of the extremities that is the result of congestive heart failure represents a loss of fluids as well as a circulatory problem. Treatment involves strengthening the heart action with digoxin, diuretics to stimulate greater output of urine, a low sodium diet to reduce the retention of water, supplemental oxygen if needed, bed rest, and replacement of potassium if needed.

One must be cautious when performing various procedures that instill or irrigate cavities of the body where fluids can easily cross a membrane. Solutions that are hypotonic to body fluids cause movement of water into the intracellular spaces. The sudden shift of fluids into the cells may lead to shock and to cerebral edema. This type of fluid shift follows procedures such as using tap water to give enemas or to irrigate a nasogastric tube. Ice cubes or chips made from tap water also may cause water to move into the intracellular fluid when given to quench the thirst of patients who are ordered to have nothing by mouth (NPO). Large amounts of water may be ingested in this way, increasing the patient's fluid intake. The nurse may not be aware of such an increase unless the liquid content of the ice cubes is measured. A normal-sized ice cube contains as much as 40 ml of liquid.

Hypertonic solutions cause water to move out of the cell and into the solution. Hypertonic solutions given rectally draw water out of the body, resulting in a larger volume of water being expelled, such as when a saturated salt solution is used as a saline enema. Hypertonic solution, such as 50 per cent glucose, 10 per cent glucose in water, and 5 per cent dextrose in lactated Ringer's solution, pull water out of the intracellular fluid when given intravenously to reduce cerebral edema and fluid retention. However, patients should be observed for possible fluid overload, resulting from rapid shifts of water to the vascular system. The use of isotonic solutions, such as normal saline, Ringer's solution, and Darrow's solution, does not lead to a shift of water but helps to restore the balance between the inside and the outside of the cell.

## ASSESSMENT SKILLS

The recording of intake and output of fluids is essential for most patients during the acute phase of an illness because many conditions lead to an imbalance of fluids or electrolytes. Unfortunately, keeping track of the intake and output of fluids is often viewed by nurses as a chore and is done haphazardly. They may not recognize its importance in determining the fluid balance of the body. In most hospitals and agencies, the intake and output records do not reflect fluid balance because the records do not include the obligatory amount of approximately 1000 ml that is normally lost through the lungs, skin, and feces. The intake should replace previous losses, the current recorded output, and the obligatory amount lost. Whenever possible, fluids lost through abnormal routes as well as the urine output should be measured. Measured amounts are more specific and meaningful than amounts that are described in terms of "small," "moderate," or "large."

Weighing patients daily provides the nurse with an early indicator of fluid retention when weight varies more than ½ lb per day. Patients are weighed on the same scale, at the same time (usually before breakfast), and wearing the same amount of clothing. Bed scales are used for patients who are unable to stand on an upright scale long enough to be weighed. However, bed scales have the disadvantage of being big and hard to handle.

## PROVIDING ORAL FLUIDS AND ELECTROLYTES

The fluid needs of most patients are supplied by the liquids they drink and the foods on their diets. They can be encouraged to increase their fluid intake through a variety of juices, milk shakes, and other beverages. Many foods have a high water content. Cooked cereals, soups, peaches, oranges, berries, watermelon, ice cream, and puddings add to one's fluid intake.

Patients who are unable to swallow, resistive to eating, or unconscious may be given fluids and nourishment by tube feedings. They need more water, in addition to the amount of the formula, when these conditions exist: mouth dryness, thirst, and diarrhea. Fluid imbalances are apt to occur, especially fluid deficit and hyponatremia, unless fluid needs are assessed accurately (Kubo, 1976).

Within the dietary restrictions imposed by medical treatment, the nurse is able to intervene to control the supply of electrolytes. Patients who have a deficit of an electrolyte are encouraged to eat foods that are rich sources of that substance. Patients who have an excess of an electrolyte should avoid foods that are rich in that substance. Examples of foods that are rich in electrolytes:

*Sodium* — salt, bacon, bologna, ham, olives, crackers, pretzels, catsup, pickles, mustard, sardines, cheese, potato chips, and foods containing salt.
*Potassium* — whole grains, meats, legumes, fruits (especially bananas), vegetables, dates, dried figs, beans, peas, potatoes, oranges, prunes, and peanuts.
*Calcium* — milk, cheese, egg yolk, legumes, nuts, whole grains, and leafy green vegetables.

Fluid intake is limited in patients with fluid gain or fluid retention. In patients whose fluid intakes are limited to 800, 1000, or 1500 ml per day, the nurse should develop a plan to distribute the intake throughout the day, providing for intake at meals and when taking oral medications. One such plan provides the major portion of intake during the day shift hours to cover the two meals normally served within that time and the remainder of the intake for the evening and night.

| Shift | Total Fluids | Amount for 1000 ml |
|---|---|---|
| 7 — 3 | 50% | 500 ml |
| 3 — 11 | 33% | 330 ml |
| 11 — 7 | 17% | 170 ml |

Whenever possible, involve patients in planning the distribution of fluids and in taking responsibility for measuring or staying within the limits. The amount of fluids provided on the diet tray should be within the amount allowed for that meal period. A plastic medicine cup may be used for measuring. Excess amounts of fluids found on the diet tray should be removed before delivery of the meal to the patient.

## PROVIDING PARENTERAL FLUIDS

Parenteral fluids are given to patients who are unable to take sufficient fluids orally, such as those who must be NPO following surgery, as part of the treatment of the disease, or as an immediate life-saving measure. The two main parenteral routes are the intravenous (IV) approach and hypodermoclysis which infuses fluids under the skin. The intravenous route is the more widely used route because it delivers the solution directly into the bloodstream, where the solution begins to produce immediate effects as it circulates throughout the vascular system.

The type of fluid given intravenously depends upon the need and the purpose. Solutions are available that contain electrolytes, vitamins, glucose, amino acids, fat emulsions, alcohol, blood, plasma, serum albumin, and plasma expanders. Isotonic, hypotonic, and hypertonic solutions can be given intravenously; however, only isotonic fluids are infused under the skin by clysis.

When patients are receiving parenteral fluids, the nursing care plan includes the following nursing actions:

1. Checking the needle site frequently for signs of infiltration or malfunction.
2. Running the fluid at the prescribed rate to prevent fluid overload or a speed shock reaction from solutions that contain other drugs.
3. Maintaining sterility of the solution, the administration set, and the needle site to prevent infection.
4. Recording an accurate intake and output of fluids.

The intravenous route is also used to measure the central venous pressure (CVP) of critically ill patients. A catheter is inserted into one of the central veins, usually the vena cava close to where it empties into the right atrium, and the venous pressure is measured at intervals. Low central venous pressure is associated with fluid volume losses; high central venous pressure is associated with fluid overload. Catheters are also placed in large veins for hyperalimentation, or to supply a nutritionally rich solution into the circulation. The fluids that are provided by these methods are included in the record of the patient's total fluid intake.

## MANIPULATING OTHER INFLUENCING FACTORS

As previously mentioned, age is a factor in the amount of fluids that one requires and increases the risk of imbalance for the very young and the old. People who are obese are also at risk of fluid imbalance. Imbalances occur particularly when patients are unable to respond to the thirst stimulus or to communicate their need for fluids to others.

Electrolyte and acid-base imbalances cause changes in one's mental status; thus, the nursing plan must contain provisions for this interference in brain function. The nurse may raise the side-rails on the patient's bed and use other available resources to provide safety and comfort for the patient. Precautions are taken to prevent complications from occurring. Edema from fluid retention increases the risk of tissue damage as circulation slows through the area. Air mattresses, egg-crate pads, and other protective devices are utilized to prevent pressure damage to tissues.

Extensive health-teaching can be done by the nurse, regardless of the age of the patient. Both young and old people need to know the importance of meeting their fluid needs during illness, especially people with chronic conditions. Most people need additional information about the kinds of fluids to take, the amount to drink, signs of problems, things they can do to manage their problems, and what effects the drugs they take may have on their fluid and electrolyte balance.

## APPLICATION TO CLINICAL PRACTICE

As a nurse, you will encounter many common situations that involve a disturbance in fluid and electrolyte balance. Keeping in mind the areas that are assessed to determine fluid balance, determine the type of imbalance described in the following statements. For statements 1 to 4, select an answer from A through D.

A. Fluid volume loss       C. Sodium imbalance
B. Fluid volume gain       D. Potassium imbalance

1. On a hot summer day, Joe played tennis for several hours. Sweating profusely, he went to the water fountain and drank a large amount of water. He soon complained of nausea, weakness, and abdominal cramps.
2. Mr. Newtown is a 52-year-old construction worker. Lately, he has been gaining weight, in spite of efforts to lose weight because of a heart attack three years ago. He complains of swelling of the ankles and some difficulty in breathing.
3. Mrs. Jones worried about her operation that took place two days ago. Today, she seems limp in bed and states that she is so weak that she cannot wash her face or lift her coffee cup. Her pulse is weak and irregular.
4. You phoned your grandmother, aged 68, to find out how she is. She said she had the flu for several days and still has a slight temperature. She said she has no appetite and is so weak that she stays in bed except for going to the bathroom three times yesterday.

For the following hydrogen ion imbalances, you may use your medical-surgical nursing textbook as a reference. For statements 5 to 8, select an answer from E through H.

E. Metabolic acidosis       G. Respiratory acidosis
F. Metabolic alkalosis      H. Respiratory alkalosis

5. Mr. Rubin has been hospitalized for an intestinal obstruction and has been vomiting at least every hour or so since 0300 until the nasogastric tube was passed at 0830.

6. Leah, a 21-year-old college student, now weighs 98 pounds and complains of extreme weakness. She has lost 11 pounds in the last three weeks on a special weight reduction diet.
7. Mrs. Ikol, a secretary, has been home ill with a cold that has settled in her chest. She has a "tight" feeling in her chest and cannot catch her breath, even though she has 28 to 30 respirations per minute.
8. When told that her husband had been seriously injured in an automobile accident on the freeway, the wife cried out hysterically and briefly lost consciousness.

The correct answers are 1 – C, 2 – B, 3 – D, 4 – A, 5 – F, 6 – E, 7 – G, 8 – H.

When caring for assigned patients in the clinical setting, the following list of adaptive and maladaptive behaviors can be used as a guide in the assessment of the fluid and electrolyte need area. After identifying the maladaptive behaviors, use the nursing process to state the problem, the stimuli that are influencing the problem, and your plan of care.

## FLUID AND ELECTROLYTE BALANCE

| Normal or Expected Behaviors | Unusual or Maladaptive Behaviors |
| --- | --- |
| Daily ranges of<br>Intake _____ ml<br>Output _____ ml | Increased intake; decreased intake<br>Increased output; decreased output |
| Urine – normal color and constituents | Concentrated; contains sugar, blood, proteins, or has ammonia odor |
| No abnormal fluid loss through<br>Nasogastric suctioning<br>Vomiting<br>Profuse perspiration<br>Wound drainage<br>Hemorrhage<br>Diarrhea<br>Serious fluid loss in burns | Loss of body fluids.<br>Type _____<br>Amount _____ |
| No use of tubes | Use IV, hyperalimentation, catheters, suction, or drainage tubes |
| No unusual retention of fluid | Edema of feet, ankles, hands, eyelids, or sacrum<br>Ascites; gurgling rales |
| Maintains usual weight | Gain or loss of more than ½ lb/day |
| Neck veins fill in supine position | Neck veins fill in sitting position; flat when lying down |
| Pink, moist mucous membranes | Dry mouth and mucous membranes<br>Thirsty |
| Skin – warm, dry, good turgor | Skin – cool, cold, clammy, hot, poor turgor |
| No unusual impairment of muscles, brain function | Examples of imbalances:<br>**Loss of K:** large muscles soft and flaccid; extreme weakness; abdomen distended<br>**Loss of Na:** Dizziness; abdominal cramps; weakness; loss of fluid<br>**Loss of Ca:** Muscle twitching; muscle and abdominal cramps |

**Laboratory Findings**
Hct _____
K _____
Na _____
Ca _____

# REFERENCES

Brunner, Lillian, and Suddarth, Doris S.: Textbook of Medical-Surgical Nursing, 4th ed. Philadelphia, J. B. Lippincott Co., 1980.

Burgess, Audrey: The Nurse's Guide to Fluid and Electrolyte Balance. New York, McGraw-Hill, Inc., 1970.

Felver, Linda: Understanding the electrolyte maze. Am J Nurs, *80*:1591–1595, (September) 1980.

Grant, Marcia, and Kubo, Winifred: Assessing a client's hydration status. Am J Nurs, *75*:1306–1311, (August) 1975.

Guyton, Arthur: Textbook of Medical Physiology, 6th ed. Philadelphia, W. B. Saunders Company, 1981.

Heath, Joleen K.: A conceptual basis for assessing body water status. Nurs Clin North Am, *6*(1):189–198, (March) 1971.

Intravenous therapy: a special feature. Am J Nurs, *79*: 1268–1296, (July) 1979.

Kubo, Winifred, et al: Fluid and electrolyte problems of tube-fed patients. Am J Nurs, *76*:912–916, (June) 1976.

Luckmann, Joan, and Sorensen, Karen: Medical Surgical Nursing: A Psychophysiologic Approach. Philadelphia, W. B. Saunders Company, 1974.

Metheny, Norma A.: Water and electrolyte balance in the postoperative patient. Nurs Clin North Am, *10*(1): 49–57, (March) 1975.

Metheny, Norma A., and Snively, W. D., Jr.: Nurses Handbook of Fluid Balance, 2nd ed. Philadelphia, J. B. Lippincott Co., 1974.

Murray, Malinda: Fundamentals of Nursing, 2nd ed. Englewood Cliffs, New Jersey, Prentice-Hall, Inc., 1980.

Programmed Instruction. Fundamentals of i.v. maintenance. Am J Nurs, *79*:1274–1287, (July) 1979.

Programmed Instruction. Metabolic acid-base disorders. part 1. chemistry and physiology. Am J Nurs, *77*: 1619–1649, (October) 1977.

Programmed Instruction. Metabolic acid-base disorders. part 2. physiological abnormalities and nursing actions. Am J Nurs, *78*:1–20, (January) 1978.

Programmed Instruction. Metabolic acid-base disorders. part 3. clinical and laboratory findings. Am J Nurs, *78*:443, (March) 1978.

Snively, W. D., Jr. and Roberts, Kay: The clinical picture as an aid to understanding body fluid disturbances, Nurs Forum, Vol. XII, No. 2, 1973, pp. 133–159.

Taylor, Sister Virginia: Meeting the challenge of fistulas and draining wounds. Nursing 80, *10*(6):45–51, (June) 1980.

# Nutritional Needs

## OBJECTIVES  Information in this chapter will help you to

1. Describe the basic concepts involved in meeting the nutritional needs of the body, the structures involved, and the components of an adequate diet.
2. State how the nutritional needs of the body are met in terms of the foods consumed and the calories required by the body functions and activities.
3. Assess the client's behaviors that are associated with meeting the nutritional needs and compare these behaviors with the norms, or standards, of adaptive behaviors.
4. List stimuli that cause maladaptive behavior or influence the individual's ability to meet nutritional needs independently.
5. State the problems of nutrition in the physiological mode as being related to the consumption of too much food, too little food, or no intake of food, which requires altered means of nourishment to insure survival. If you are using the integrated approach, state all problems manifested by maladaptive behaviors.
6. Describe nursing interventions that are commonly used to meet nutritional needs.

## DEFINITION OF TERMS

**adipose tissue** — fatty tissue.
**amino acids** — organic compounds containing nitrogen that make up the structure of protein.
**anorexia** — loss of appetite for food.

**calorie** — unit of measuring heat needed to raise the temperature of 1 gram of water 1° C. The amount of energy produced by the metabolism of foods is stated in terms of calories.

**carbohydrates** — organic compounds of carbon, hydrogen, and oxygen that are major sources of energy in the body. Carbohydrates are found in most foods—chief sources include sugars and starches.

**malnutrition** — poor nutrition due to an inadequate or unbalanced diet or to the inability of the body to use nutrients properly.

**minerals** — inorganic substances usually supplied by vegetables and animal sources, thirteen of which are essential to health.

**negative nitrogen balance** — condition that occurs when the nitrogen losses in all protein sources exceed the nitrogen gains. Associated with catabolism, or breaking down into simpler forms.

**nutrient** — a food or substance that provides nourishment and is essential to life.

**postprandial** — after eating or ingesting food.

**protein** — an amino acid containing nitrogen necessary for building and repairing tissues. Major sources of protein include meats, fish, poultry, and eggs.

**vitamins** — complex, organic substances that are vital to health and are not manufactured by the body but are supplied in foods.

---

Human life is sustained by oxygen, fluids, and essential nutrients. These nutrients must be provided from the time of one's birth and must continue to be provided throughout one's lifetime so that one can grow and engage in active and purposeful activities. Nutrients provide the energy that is needed for all body needs.

Nutrients are substances that provide nourishment and are essential to life. They are not manufactured in the body but must be obtained from the external environment. All necessary nutrients are supplied by the foods that we eat as they are assimilated and used by the body. Not every food contains a sufficient supply of each essential nutrient; thus, a variety of foods must be eaten to supply the required nutrients.

Food provides the materials that are needed for the growth and development of the body as well as the maintenance and repair of tissues and is the source of energy for carrying out body functions. Without an adequate source of energy, one would be unable to work, play, or carry out normal activities of daily living. Food is the fuel that provides the energy necessary for the life processes that are involved in breathing, digesting food, circulating the blood, forming urine, and the many other intricate actions that regulate the body's internal environment.

Food not only is a physical necessity, but also has a variety of meanings and uses. Food is used by many people as a reward or as gratification for a need. From infancy, the satisfaction of the hunger drive and the pleasant lassitude of a full stomach are associated with a sense of well-being. Feasts are held universally to celebrate a special occasion, and inviting others to share a meal is regarded as a sign of friendliness and hospitality. Certain foods are used as "treats" on a special occasion or to "make up for" a disappointment. The psychological and social meanings that are attached to food greatly influence how people meet their nutritional needs.

Meeting one's nutritional needs plays an important part in one's life. For many people, their life's work is to till the soil and to raise crops, to hunt or to raise animals that will be used as meat, or to cast their nets for fish. Other people must use part of their earnings from other labors to buy the food they need. In each family, one or more members assumes responsibility for obtaining and preparing the supply of food. These people spend hours going to markets, buying supplies, storing the food, and planning and preparing the meals. When markets are a distance from one's home, public or private transportation is necessary to get one's supply of food home.

Malnutrition occurs when a person's food intake lacks one or more of the approximately 35 different nutrients needed daily. The inadequate diet fails to provide the nourishment needed by all cells for optimal development and leads to deficiencies that cause anemia, rickets, scurvy, or other pathological conditions. The lack of sufficient calories in one's diet results in weight loss, and, in extreme cases, leads to starvation and death. In spite of the astounding technological advances that have allowed men to land on the moon and to explore outer space, malnutrition is a major problem of the modern world. Millions of people suffer from lack of adequate food, and untold thousands starve to death annually, mostly in the lesser-developed nations. People who do live despite lack of adequate food have stunted physical growth, decreased physical strength, retardation of intellectual and mental abilities, and increased susceptibility to infectious diseases and illness.

People anywhere can suffer the effects of malnutrition when they are unable to meet all of their nutritional needs. Malnutrition does not occur only in far-off countries where people are starving. When illness strikes, many people are unable to meet their needs for nutrients or to assimilate their food because diseases disturb the digestive system. People are often required to abstain from food or fluids when undergoing laboratory tests, x-ray studies, and other diagnostic tests or procedures that require a fasting state. Patients are NPO during and following surgery until they are able to tolerate fluids and foods taken orally. The anesthesias and many of the medications that are administered to patients depress the appetite and the functions of the digestive system. Illness places additional demands on one's body. More energy is needed for the process of healing and repairing tissues. People are at risk of being malnourished during illness; thus, it is essential that nurses assess each patient's nutritional status and be sure that each patient consumes the nutrients that are needed to promote adaptation.

In this chapter, basic concepts related to the nutritional needs are described, including an overview of the essential nutrients, a review of the structures of the digestive system, and the nutritional needs during one's lifetime. Different amounts of nutrients are required at different ages. The adequate diet, composed of the four food groups, is discussed, and the caloric values for some common foods are listed. The first level assessment focuses on adaptive and maladaptive behaviors that may be used to meet the nutritional needs. The second level assessment examines stimuli that cause problems or influence food intake. Common problems of nutrition are given, and nursing interventions that help to satisfy the patient's nutritional needs are summarized.

## THE ESSENTIAL NUTRIENTS

All nutrients needed by the body can be obtained through food. Although no single food provides all nutrients, many kinds and combinations of foods can be used to meet body requirements. Each nutrient has a specific function in the body. All nutrients are necessary, although some nutrients are present in minute quantities, and others are found in greater abundance.

The essential nutrients have been divided into categories: carbohydrates, proteins, fats, minerals, vitamins, and water. The energy needs of the body are supplied by the calories contained in the carbohydrates, proteins, and fats. Wide variations can be made in the amounts of these nutrients in one's diet. Excess amounts that are not needed for immediate energy needs are stored or converted to fat and deposited as adipose tissue.

## CARBOHYDRATES

Foods that are high in carbohydrates provide the body with its best source of readily available energy. They are easily metabolized, and each gram yields 4 calories of energy. The body must be continuously supplied with carbohydrates. If not, the available stores of glucose in the liver and muscles will be depleted within a 48-hour period. When the blood sugar drops or when the body is unable to utilize sugar, as with diabetes, the body tissues of fats and proteins are broken down to provide the energy that is needed. This breakdown of tissues is called metabolic acidosis (see Chapter Ten).

Sources of carbohydrates are the sugars and starches in the diet, such as breads, potatoes, rice, macaroni, spaghetti, honey, jellies, and all of the prepared pastries that have a high sugar content. Carbohydrates account for approximately 45 to 50 per cent of the calories in the typical American diet. However, in other countries, carbohydrate content may be as high as 75 to 80 per cent. People with low incomes tend to eat more carbohydrates because they are more economical than meats and other proteins.

## PROTEINS

Proteins consist of several amino acids that are used by the body as construction material for tissues and cells. Proteins are used as the basis for lean body mass in muscles, as structural tissue or collagen tissue, as antibodies in the form of gamma globulin, as hormones and enzymes, and, in the blood, in the form of albumin, globulin, and hemoglobin. Albumin and globulin contribute to the osmotic pressure of the extracellular fluid.

Eight different proteins are essential for growth and development. The best sources of protein are meat, fish, milk, cheese, eggs, and, to a lesser degree, grains and legumes, such as lima beans and peas. Metabolism of proteins produces 4 calories per gram, and the average adult requires about 60 to 65 grams per day. The protein tissues of the body are the last tissues that are used or broken down to meet the body's caloric needs. Lean tissue has an energy potential of 1850 calories per pound. When it is used to supply body needs, weight is lost very rapidly (1 kg × 4 cal/gm = 4000 cal ÷ 2.2 lb/kilo = 1850 cal).

## FATS

Fats are organic substances that feel waxy, oily, or greasy to the touch and that do not dissolve in water, but do dissolve in alcohol or in ether. The basic structure of fats is an actual or potential ester of a fatty acid, which is a compound formed from an alcohol and an acid. The fatty acids may be saturated with hydrogen, or unsaturated and able to combine. The saturated fats are the harder and more solid fats, generally obtained from animal sources of suet, tallow, and lard. Unsaturated fats are obtained from plant sources and are the free-flowing oils. These plant oils include oils from olives, peanuts, corn, soybeans, and safflower.

The purpose of fats in the diet is to supply a concentrated source of energy. Fats produce 9 calories for every gram metabolized. The deposits of fatty tissues protect and cushion vital organs. The essential fatty acids also serve to strengthen capillary and cell membranes, to lower the serum cholesterol, and to prolong blood-clotting time. Most American diets are extremely high in fats, with as much as 40 per cent of one's total calories supplied by fats. A low fat intake of 15 to 20 per cent is found in the diets of people from some Oriental countries, whereas the Eskimo diet has a much higher fat content.

## MINERALS

Minerals are inorganic elements that are essential to the body and are provided in the foods that one eats. They constitute 60 to 80 per cent of the nonfluid material of the body. Like electrolytes, minerals perform a wide variety of functions. Minerals are the builders of bones, the regulators of chemical processes, and the controllers of processes such as shifts in body water distribution.

The major minerals in the body are calcium, sodium, chlorides, potassium, phosphorus, magnesium, and sulfur. Trace minerals, or those found in very minute amounts, include iron, copper, iodine, cobalt, zinc, manganese, and molybdenum. All minerals are obtained through foods. It is seldom necessary to take supplemental forms of minerals when one's diet is adequate and includes a variety of foods.

The recommended dietary requirements for all essential nutrients, including minerals and vitamins, have been set by the National Research Council. The average diet is rich in calcium. Any excess amounts of calcium are excreted from the body. Most people have an average intake of 4 grams of sodium or salt per day, although half that amount is sufficient for adults. A potassium intake of 2 to 4 grams per day is adequate. Both potassium and magnesium are widely distributed in foods, so they are readily available in one's diet.

## VITAMINS

Vitamins are organic compounds that are vital to life and cannot be manufactured by the body itself. They are needed in very small quantities. Their lack in one's diet results in the so-called deficiency diseases. No one is sure how many vitamins there are because all vitamins have not been discovered yet. The National Research Council has made recommendations for the daily requirements for the known vitamins. Vitamin requirements increase for people who have a large body and during periods of rapid growth, exercise, disease and fevers, pregnancy and lactation, and when larger amounts of carbohydrates are metabolized.

Vitamins are classified as either fat-soluble or water-soluble. The fat-soluble vitamins do not dissolve in water; thus, they remain fairly stable during normal cooking of foods. Vitamins are stored in cells and in the liver. People can go without an intake of fat soluble vitamins for about one month before signs of deficiency occur. Contrarily, water-soluble vitamins do not store well, and the amounts in the cells are used in a short period of time. Symptoms of vitamin B deficiency can be recognized in a few days, and the absence of vitamin C causes symptoms within a few weeks. A list of vitamins, their functions, and food sources of vitamins can be found in Table 11-1.

## WATER

Water is an essential element in one's diet. It is provided in the liquids that are included with foods, and approximately 10 ml of water are provided by the metabolism of every 100 calories of carbohydrates, proteins, and fats. The body's water needs were discussed in detail in Chapter Ten.

Table 11-1.  VITAMINS, THEIR FUNCTIONS AND FOOD SOURCES

| Vitamin | Functions | Food Sources |
|---|---|---|
| **Fat-Soluble** | | |
| Vitamin A | Aids visual adaptation to light and dark and health of skin | Liver, green and yellow vegetables, cream, milk, yolk |
| Vitamin D | Calcium absorption and deposition in bone<br>Deficiency causes rickets | Fish oils, fortified milk |
| Vitamin E | Protects RBCs and unsaturated fatty acids in body<br>Commercially used to retard spoilage | Vegetable oils |
| Vitamin K | Promotes blood clotting by synthesis of prothrombin in the liver | Liver, cheese, yolk, green leafy vegetables |
| **Water-Soluble** | | |
| Thiamine (B₁) | Necessary for carbohydrate metabolism<br>Deficiency causes beriberi and symptoms due to less energy from glucose for cells to do their work | Lean meats, whole grains, legumes, eggs, fish |
| Riboflavin (B₂) | Essential for protein metabolism<br>Deficiency causes tissue inflammation and breakdown, poor healing | Milk, glandular organs of liver, kidney, heart |
| Nicotinic acid (niacin) | Aids in converting proteins and fats to glucose and oxidizing glucose to release energy | Meat, peanuts, beans, peas, enriched grains |
| Pyridoxine (B₆) | Metabolizes amino acids and to lesser degree carbohydrates and fats<br>Deficiency causes anemia, convulsions, neuritis | Liver, meat, corn, wheat |
| Folic acid (folacin) | Aids in regeneration of RBCs<br>Vital to cell growth and reproduction<br>Deficiency leads to anemias | Liver, kidney, green leafy vegetables, asparagus |
| Cobalamin (B₁₂) | Aids in metabolism of proteins, the nucleic acid and proteins of the cells, including blood cells<br>Deficiency results in pernicious anemia | Liver, kidney, lean meats, milk, eggs, cheese |
| Ascorbic acid (vitamin C) | Provides cement for connecting tissue, bone matrix, cartilage, and dentine<br>Deficiency causes pinpoint bleeding, bruising, bleeding gums, capillary fragility of scurvy | Tomatoes, citrus fruits, berries, green and yellow vegetables |

Water and the essential nutrients of food might be distributed in the body of a healthy male adult weighing 160 pounds in the following amounts:*

| Water | 100 lb |
|---|---|
| Protein | 29 lb |
| Fat | 25 lb |
| Minerals | 5 lb |
| Carbohydrate | 1 lb |
| Vitamins | ¼ oz |
| Total | 160 lbs |

*Source: U.S. Department of Agriculture: Food for us all. Yearbook of Agriculture 1969. Washington, D.C., U.S. Government Printing Office, 1969.

## THE ADEQUATE DIET

Among the great varieties of foods and the countless ways to prepare them, how does one determine what foods constitute a balanced diet? Most foods can be classified into one of the four basic food groups: milk and dairy products, meats and poultry, fruits and vegetables, and breads and cereals.

Healthy people are able to eat and to assimilate all foods without any restriction, other than the food's availability and cost and the person's likes or dislikes. The average adult obtains the required nutrients by consuming a daily diet that consists of two or more milk products, two servings of meats, four servings of fruits and vegetables, including citrus fruits, four or more servings of breads and cereals, and sufficient fluids. Addi-

**Figure 11–1.**   Foods in the milk and dairy group.

tional calories are gained from eating more of these foods or from adding sugars and fats in the form of sweets, butter, margarine, and oils.

## MILK AND DAIRY PRODUCTS

Foods in this group include all kinds of milk, cream, ice cream, and cheeses, as well as other foods made of milk. Milk is served as a beverage, poured on cereals or fruit, and used to prepare cream soups, puddings, or white sauce. It is a rich source of calcium, protein, vitamin A, and riboflavin.

### Servings Daily

| | |
|---|---|
| Child (1–9 years) | 2–3 cups |
| Child (9–12 years) | 3 or more cups |
| Teenager | 4 or more cups |
| Adult | 2 or more cups |

## MEATS AND POULTRY

Foods in the meat group include beef, lamb, pork, veal, fish, poultry, eggs, cheeses, and plant foods, such as peas, beans, nuts, and peanut butter. These foods are rich sources of protein, iron, and B vitamins.

### Servings Daily

2 or more
  meat — 3 oz
  cheese — 1 oz
  beans, peas — ½ cup

## FRUITS AND VEGETABLES

Most foods in this group contain insignificant amounts of fats and proteins but are a source of calories, vitamins, and minerals. Fruits and vegetables add taste, variety, and bulk to one's diet. One serving per day should include a citrus fruit or a tomato, which are excellent sources of vitamin C. Some vegetables are very low in calories and are used extensively on diets that restrict caloric intake. Examples are cabbage, cauliflower, celery, lettuce, greens, mushrooms, string beans, and tomatoes.

### Servings Daily

4 or more: 1 citrus fruit and 1 green vegetable
  fruit — 1 unit or ½ cup
  juice — 1 cup (8 oz)
  vegetable — ½ cup or more

## BREADS AND CEREALS

Foods in this group include breads of all kinds, crackers, tortillas, grits, cooked and dry cereals, macaroni, noodles, rice, spaghetti, and baked goods made with enriched flour or whole grains. These foods supply protein, minerals, and vitamins, especially valuable amounts of several B vitamins.

### Servings Daily

4 or more
  bread — 1 slice
  cereal — ½ to ¾ cup

**Figure 11–2.**   Foods in the meat group.

**Figure 11–3.** Foods in the fruits and vegetables group.

## CALORIC VALUE OF FOODS

In addition to knowing the number of servings from each of the four food groups that will provide essential nutrients to the body, it is also helpful to know the amount of energy that these foods supply to the body. The energy that is released by foods when they are metabolized in the body is measured in terms of the calories that are produced. A calorie is the amount of heat needed to raise the temperature of 1 gram of water 1° C. Scientific methods have determined the caloric value of foods as well as the amount of other nutrients that they contain. The caloric value and protein content of some common foods are shown in Table 11–2.

**Weight Control.** The caloric intake of foods should be sufficient for necessary growth, metabolic and physical activities, tissue repair, and maintenance of one's usual weight. When helping people to meet their nutritional needs, nurses should focus on weight control. The weight of one's body should be evaluated in terms of total body size, proportion of body fat to the lean masses, and amount of body water throughout one's life cycle. To control weight, one's expenditure of energy must balance one's intake of energy. Gain or loss of weight reflects an imbalance of energy levels.

**Weight Gain**
Decrease expenditure
Increase intake

**Weight Loss**
Increase expenditure
Decrease intake

Weight loss is often associated with illness. Many patients are served an adequate diet that consists of the recommended number of servings from the four food groups, yet they have a poor appetite or push the meal tray away after taking only a few bites. People's caloric needs may be greatly increased by the stress of illness. Surgery and extensive burns require tremendous amounts of fuel and at times when patients are least able to meet the increased demands of the body. Patients fail to eat an adequate diet to supply the body's energy demands resulting in loss of weight. Nutritional balance is best measured by computing the calories needed and the calories consumed.

Foods provide the energy to meet the needs of the body in the following amounts:

carbohydrates – 4 calories per gram
proteins – 4 calories per gram
fats – 9 calories per gram

Carbohydrates are the most immediate source of energy for the body and are utilized first to

**Figure 11–4.** Foods in the breads and cereals group.

**Table 11–2.  CALORIC VALUES AND PROTEIN CONTENT OF SELECTED FOODS**

| Food | Portion | Protein (gm) | Calories | Food | Portion | Protein (gm) | Calories |
|------|---------|--------------|----------|------|---------|--------------|----------|
| *Milk and Dairy Foods* | | | | *Fruits and Vegetables* | | | |
| Milk, whole | 1 cup | 9 | 150 | Apple juice | 1 cup | trace | 120 |
| Milk, nonfat | 1 cup | 9 | 90 | Grapefruit juice* | 1 cup | 1 | 100 |
| Cocoa | 1 cup | 9 | 235 | Orange juice* | 1 cup | 1 | 110 |
| Cheese–American | 1 oz | 7 | 105 | Tomato juice | 1 cup | 2 | 45 |
| Cottage cheese | 1 cup | 38 | 195 | Applesauce–sweet | 1 cup | 1 | 230 |
| Ice cream | ⅛ qt | 3 | 145 | Banana | 1 | 1 | 85 |
| Pudding–plain | 1 cup | 9 | 275 | Cantaloupe | ½ | 1 | 60 |
| | | | | Grapes, seedless | 1 cup | 1 | 95 |
| *Protein Foods* | | | | Peaches–canned | 1 cup | 1 | 200 |
| Eggs, whole | 1 | 6 | 80 | Pear halves–canned | 1 cup | 1 | 195 |
| Bacon | 2 slices | 7 | 110 | Prunes–cooked | 17–18/cup | 2 | 295 |
| Beef–hamburger, reg. | 3 oz | 21 | 245 | Strawberries–raw | 1 cup | 1 | 55 |
| Beef–sirloin steak | 3 oz | 20 | 330 | Asparagus spears | 1 cup | 4 | 35 |
| Chicken breast–fried | 3 oz | 25 | 155 | Beans–green, snap | 1 cup | 2 | 30 |
| Ham | 3 oz | 18 | 245 | Cabbage–coleslaw | 1 cup | 1 | 120 |
| Lamb chop | 1 | 25 | 400 | Carrots–cooked | 1 cup | 1 | 45 |
| Pork chop | 1 | 16 | 260 | Cauliflower | 1 cup | 3 | 25 |
| Ocean perch | 3 oz | 16 | 195 | Corn–sweet, canned | 1 cup | 5 | 170 |
| Fish sticks–breaded | 4 oz | 19 | 200 | Lettuce–Iceberg | 1 head | 4 | 60 |
| Tuna–oil packed | 3 oz | 24 | 170 | Peas | 1 cup | 9 | 115 |
| Beans with pork | 1 cup | 16 | 320 | Potato–baked | 1 medium | 3 | 90 |
| Peanuts | 1 cup | 37 | 840 | Potato–french-fried | 10 pieces | 2 | 155 |
| Peanut butter | 1 tbsp | 4 | 95 | | | | |
| | | | | *Fats and Oils* | | | |
| *Breads and Cereals* | | | | Butter or margarine | 1 pat | trace | 50 |
| Bread–cracked wheat | 1 slice | 2 | 60 | Oil–cooking | 1 tbsp | 0 | 125 |
| Bread–rye | 1 slice | 2 | 55 | Salad dressing | | | |
| Bread–white | 1 slice | 2 | 60 | Bleu cheese | 1 tbsp | 0 | 80 |
| Corn flakes–plain | 1 oz | 2 | 110 | French | 1 tbsp | trace | 60 |
| Crackers–saltine | 2 | 1 | 55 | Mayonnaise | 1 tbsp | trace | 110 |
| Cookies–plain | 1 3-in | 1 | 120 | Thousand Island | 1 tbsp | trace | 75 |
| Cake–chocolate with | | | | | | | |
|   icing | 2-in | 5 | 445 | *Sugars and Sweets* | | | |
| Macaroni | 1 cup | 6 | 190 | Candy–milk chocolate | 1 oz | 2 | 150 |
| Oatmeal | 1 cup | 5 | 130 | Candy–hard | 1 oz | 0 | 110 |
| Pie–apple | 4-in | 3 | 345 | Chocolate syrup | 1 tbsp | trace | 50 |
| Rice | 1 cup | 3 | 185 | Honey | 1 tbsp | trace | 65 |
| Spaghetti and meatballs | 1 cup | 19 | 335 | Jams and jellies | 1 tbsp | trace | 55 |
| Wheat–puffed | 1 oz | 4 | 105 | Sugar–granulated | 1 tbsp | 0 | 45 |

*frozen and diluted with three parts water

Selected data from U.S. Department of Agriculture: Nutritive value of foods. Home and Garden Bulletin No. 72. Revised 1978.

provide fuel for body needs. They are easily digested and are reduced to glucose, which enters the blood stream for circulation to the cells. Fats and proteins in the diet provide additional calories. Excess amounts of all calories are stored in fat cells. Each pound of body fat has the potential energy of 3500 calories. The body must consume 3500 excess calories to gain one pound and must expend 3500 calories either to metabolize or to lose one pound.

When the body receives fewer nutrients than it needs, fatty tissues are broken down and metabolized to supply nutrients, and when these nutrients are depleted, proteins are utilized. Lean tissue, such as is found in muscles, consists primarily of protein, which yields only 4 calories

per gram when metabolized, or approximately 1850 calories per pound. Metabolism of fatty tissue provides nearly twice as many calories per pound. This comparison of fatty tissue and lean tissue helps to explain why people who are of normal or above normal weight lose weight less rapidly than do lean and underweight people.

People with inadequate food intake, for whatever cause, are at risk of metabolic acidosis when metabolism of fats is incomplete and results in the accumulation of ketone bodies. Metabolic acidosis occurs as a result of insufficient carbohydrates in the diet, starvation, or diabetes mellitus, which results when the body is unable to utilize glucose. Metabolic acidosis is a serious complication that can be prevented in part by accurate assessment of nutritional needs and intervention to provide for these needs.

**Convenience Foods and Snacks.** The appeal of convenience foods for the American family has been a significant development in recent times. Convenience foods fall into two major categories: ready-to-heat and ready-to-eat. The ready-to-heat foods are the commercially prepared foods or meals that are packaged and refrigerated or frozen and are available in the supermarket. They tend to be more expensive than the same foods prepared in the home but are timesaving because they require only heating before they can be eaten. Packaged foods must list the enclosed ingredients and any added chemicals to comply with labelling regulations. Many packaged foods include the calories per serving in addition to information about nutrients that are contained in the foods.

Ready-to-eat foods refer to hot dogs, tacos, pizza, hamburgers, and other foods provided by fast-food stores. Most people of all ages like a meal that consists of a hamburger, french fries, and a beverage, often a malted milk or a Coke. Some critics, however, have pointed out that fast foods are quite high in fats, carbohydrates, sodium, and calories in relation to other nutrients that they contain. A summary of typical fast foods shows some of the nutritional values.

Snacks are often referred to as "empty calories" because they supply extra calories to the diet, but often very few essential nutrients. Popular snack foods include all types of potato or corn chips, Coca-Cola and other carbonated drinks, candies, cakes, cookies and other types of desserts, and nuts. Fruits and raw vegetables are excellent between-meals snacks that do not add unnecessary calories.

## STRUCTURES RELATED TO NUTRITION

Foods that we eat supply nutrients that are vital to all the cells of the body; thus, the effects of an adequate diet as well as the effects of malnutrition can be seen in all body tissues. An adequate diet leads to an overall appearance of being alert and responsive. An adequate diet also results in hair that has body and is springy and shiny; lips, tongue, and gums that are firm, pink in color, and moist; teeth that are firm and well-shaped; a skeleton that is well-formed with straight, long bones and smooth contours to the rib cage; an abdomen that is flat; and muscles that are firm and well-developed. People who have an adequate diet have a good appetite and regular bowel movements.

Processing the food in the body requires a functioning gastrointestinal system. The gastrointestinal system includes the mouth, pharynx, esophagus, stomach, small intestine, large intestine, and accessory organs, which include the liver, gallbladder, and pancreas. All structures from the mouth to the anus carry out special functions that are related to the digestion of foods and the absorption of nutrients into the blood stream and the lymph. Any condition or disease that interferes with these functions is a deterrent in meeting the nutritional needs of the body.

Digestion begins with the mixing of food with saliva in the mouth while the food is being chewed. Between 7000 and 8000 ml of gastric secretions are mixed with the food during the digestive process each day, and most of the fluid portion is reabsorbed in the ileum of the small intestine and the ascending portion of the large intestine. If these secretions are prevented from reaching the absorption section of the bowel, large quantities of fluids and electrolytes are lost to the body. After the nutrients, fluids, and electrolytes have been absorbed, waste material is excreted as feces.

Other systems of the body are also required to function to meet the nutritional needs. Eating is a conscious effort that requires some degree of

| Fast Foods | Protein | Calories |
|---|---|---|
| Cheese pizza, $1/8$ of a 12-inch pie. Provides nutrients from milk and bread groups. | 6 gm | 145 |
| Hamburger on a bun, french fries, milk shake. Provides nutrients from bread, meat, vegetable, and milk groups. | 34 gm | 1100 |
| Fried chicken dinner: 3 pieces of chicken with roll, mashed potatoes, gravy, and cole slaw. Provides nutrients from bread, meat, vegetable, and milk groups. | 42 gm | 800 |

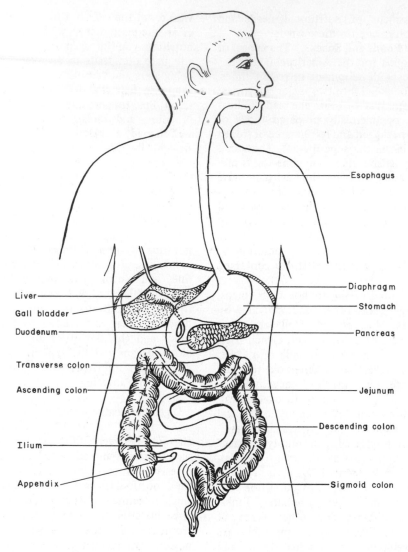

**Figure 11–5.** Components of the gastrointestinal tract.

mental alertness and the ability to chew and to swallow food. Finally, the motor activity involved in feeding oneself requires sufficient energy and the ability to use one's upper extremities. Without these physical abilities, alternative ways may be necessary to provide the body with nutrition.

## FIRST LEVEL ASSESSMENT

The nutritional status of each patient or client should be determined during the nurse's initial comprehensive assessment. Nutritional needs are then assessed frequently, or daily for patients who are acutely ill or who are in the early stages of the convalescent period and for anyone who has a problem related to nutrition.

When providing care for sick people, the nurse's attention should be focused on the present time and on finding out to what extent their nutritional needs are being met in the HERE and NOW. What are the patient's caloric needs? How much food has he or she eaten? It is necessary to know what the patient's usual eating pattern is and what it has been previously in order to balance the intake of calories with needed calories. Further assessment is concerned with body weight in comparison with age and height, general body appearance, and level of vitality.

**Table 11–3.** RECOMMENDED DAILY REQUIREMENTS
OF PROTEIN AND CALORIES ACCORDING TO
AGE GROUPS AND AVERAGE WEIGHT

|  | Age (yr) | Weight (lb) | Protein (gm) | Calories |
|---|---|---|---|---|
| Infants | 1–1/6 | 9 | 9 | 480 |
|  | 1/6–1/2 | 15 | 14 | 770 |
|  | 1/2–1 | 20 | 16 | 900 |
| Children | 1–2 | 26 | 25 | 1100 |
|  | 2–3 | 28 | 25 | 1250 |
|  | 3–4 | 35 | 30 | 1400 |
|  | 4–6 | 42 | 30 | 1600 |
|  | 6–8 | 51 | 35 | 2000 |
|  | 8–10 | 62 | 40 | 2200 |
| Boys | 10–12 | 77 | 45 | 2500 |
|  | 12–14 | 95 | 50 | 2700 |
|  | 14–18 | 130 | 60 | 3000 |
| Girls | 10–12 | 77 | 50 | 2200 |
|  | 12–14 | 97 | 50 | 2500 |
|  | 14–16 | 114 | 55 | 2400 |
|  | 16–18 | 119 | 55 | 2300 |
| Men | 18–35 | 154  69 in | 60 | 2800 |
|  | 35–55 | 154  68 in | 55 | 2600 |
|  | 55–75+ | 154  67 in | 65 | 2400 |
| Women | 18–35 | 128  64 in | 55 | 2000 |
|  | 35–55 | 128  63 in | 55 | 1850 |
|  | 55–75+ | 128  62 in | 55 | 1700 |
|  | (Pregnant) |  | 65 | (+ 200) |
|  | (Lactating) |  | 75 | (+ 1000) |

Source: Food and Nutrition Board. Recommended dietary allowances. Washington, D.C., National Academy of Sciences, National Research Council, 1968 Review.

## BODY WEIGHT

When caring for sick patients, the nurse's goal is to balance their intake of nutrients to meet body needs, rather than to emphasize weight gain or weight loss. Information about the patient's nutritional status can be obtained from the nurse's first contact with the patient by observing body height and size. As the nurse proceeds with the assessment, these observations are validated by weighing and measuring the patient, asking the patient for information, or obtaining it from hospital records. Most conscious patients know their height and weight, although children often do not.

The amount of calories and proteins in one's diet varies during one's lifetime. Growth rates are very rapid during early childhood and continue at decreasing rates for the first 18 to 20 years of life, then slowly taper off. The amount of protein in one's diet must be sufficient to build the new tissues that are responsible for growth. Table 11–3 lists the recommended daily requirements of protein and calories according to age

group and average weight. One average weight is given for all adult men of average height, 69 inches. Table 11–3 shows that caloric needs vary at different ages and that aging causes one to shrink in height. Statistics are also shown for the average woman. However, adults vary a great deal in height and in desirable weights for different size body frames. A guide for recommended weight ranges for adults is shown in Table 11–4.

When a weight table is not available, nurses estimate the ideal weight and use it as a guideline in assessing the patient's nutritional status. For women, allow 100 pounds for the first 5 feet of height, then add 5 pounds for each inch over 5 feet. For men, allow 110 pounds for the first 5 feet of height, then 5 pounds for every additional inch of height (See Table 11–5).

## TOTAL CALORIC NEEDS

The daily caloric need is the sum of the calories that it takes to fulfill one's basal needs, plus the allowance of calories for one's activity needs in a 24-hour period. Special conditions that change

Table 11–4.  DESIRABLE WEIGHT RANGES
FOR ADULTS

|  | Height (in)<br>(without shoes) | Weight (lb)<br>(without clothes) |
|---|---|---|
| Men | 64 | 122–144 |
|  | 66 | 130–154 |
|  | 68 | 137–165 |
|  | 70 | 145–173 |
|  | 72 | 152–182 |
|  | 74 | 160–190 |
| Women | 60 | 100–118 |
|  | 62 | 106–124 |
|  | 64 | 112–132 |
|  | 66 | 119–139 |
|  | 68 | 126–146 |
|  | 70 | 133–155 |

Source: U.S. Department of Agriculture: Calories and Weight: USDA Pocket Guide, No. 364, Washington, D.C., U.S. Government Printing Office, 1974, p. 5.

the basal metabolic rate also change the daily caloric need.

**Basal Needs.** The basal caloric needs are the energy requirements that one needs to sustain one's life processes. Even when people are asleep or at rest in bed, energy is needed for the expansion of the chest for breathing, the pumping action of the heart, the circulation of the blood through the vessels, the secretions of glands, and the digestive process and all the other internal body functions.

The energy need requires one calorie every hour for each kilogram of body weight. One calorie per hour equals 24 calories per day; thus, the body weight in kilos is multiplied by 24 calories to obtain the number of calories needed per day—for example, for a woman who weighs 120 pounds, or 54.5 kilograms, multiply 54.5 kilograms by the 24 calories per day, which gives a basal caloric need of 1308 calories per day. A man weighing 185 pounds, or 84 kilograms, has a basal need of 2018 calories per day. The basal requirement depends upon body mass, or weight, and varies as the weight varies.

**Activity Needs.** The activity caloric needs are the energy requirements that one needs to carry out one's daily activities. Feeding oneself in bed, turning over, sitting up, and reaching for items

Table 11–5.  ASSESSMENT OF BODY WEIGHT

| Factors to Assess | Adaptive Behaviors | Maladaptive Behaviors |
|---|---|---|
| Height _____ |  |  |
| Body weight |  |  |
|    Current weight _____ | Within normal range | Overweight _____ lb |
|    Ideal weight _____ | for age and height | Underweight _____ lb |
| Weight trend |  |  |
|    Previous weight | Varies less than ½ lb | Loss of _____ lb |
|  |  | Gain of _____ lb |

| Activity | Calories Needed |
|---|---|
| Complete bed rest | 10% of basal need |
| Sedentary work: desk work, typing, sewing, driving | 30% of basal need |
| Moderate work: making beds, cleaning house, washing windows | 50% of basal need |
| Strenuous work: swimming, running, bicycling, lumbering | 100% of basal need |

increases one's caloric needs. Walking around a room, bathing, dressing, making a bed, or sitting in a classroom requires additional energy. Activity needs are classified according to the amount of work that the body must do to carry out various actions. The guide above is used to calculate the approximate number of calories needed for daily activities.

Table 11-6 lists caloric needs for each hour of performing an activity, such as sitting, standing, walking, and swimming. This information is helpful when it is necessary to increase one's activity level for weight control.

**Additional Metabolic Needs.** Several factors can increase the basal metabolic rate, thus increasing one's caloric needs. Hypothermia, or lowered body temperature, lowers one's caloric needs. Metabolic activity is increased by fever in the following amounts (Guyton, 1981):

each 1° F above 98.6° F =    6% increase in rate
each 1° F above 110° F = 100% increase in rate
each 1° C above 37° C   =  10% increase in rate

On the basis of an increase in the metabolic rate, a fever of 104° F represents a 30 per cent increase in the amount of calories that are needed to satisfy one's basal needs.

Hyperthyroidism and pregnancy increase one's basal metabolic activity and caloric needs. Excess thyroid hormones can increase the metabolic rate by 60 to 100 per cent. During the last half of one's pregnancy, when the most rapid growth of the fetus occurs, one's metabolism increases about 15 per cent. Pregnant women require additional amounts of protein and other essential nutrients during this period. Although lactation does not significantly affect metabolic rate, the nutrients contained in the milk are drained from the mother and need to be replaced in the diet.

**Table 11-6.** AMOUNT OF ENERGY USED FOR EACH HOUR OF SPECIFIC ACTIVITIES

| Activity | Calories/hour |
|---|---|
| Sleeping | 65 |
| Awake—lying still | 77 |
| Sitting—at rest | 100 |
| Standing—relaxed | 105 |
| Dressing and undressing | 118 |
| Sewing (tailoring) | 135 |
| Typewriting—rapidly | 140 |
| Light exercise | 170 |
| Walking—slowly (2.6 mph) | 200 |
| Active exercise | 290 |
| Severe exercise | 450 |
| Swimming | 500 |
| Running (5.3 mph) | 570 |
| Very severe exercise | 600 |
| Walking—very fast (5.3 mph) | 650 |
| Walking upstairs | 1110 |

Source: Guyton, Arthur: Textbook of Medical Physiology, 6th ed. Philadelphia, W. B. Saunders Company, 1981, p. 883.

## DAILY CONSUMPTION OF FOOD

Healthy people have few or no restrictions in the types of foods that they eat. They can easily digest and tolerate most foods. They are able to eat heartily, chew and swallow foods, and retain the foods that they eat.

Illness interferes with peoples' abilities to meet their nutritional needs. Some sick people suffer from nausea and vomiting or have an intolerance for certain types of foods. Those who are ill often have a decreased appetite or may dislike the foods that they are served. Others may be too weak to eat without assistance, may have difficulty chewing, or may choke when trying to

swallow. Some patients depend upon altered means for meeting their nutritional needs, such as parenteral hyperalimentation or various types of feeding tubes. The nutritional requirements of the patient are being satisfied as a result of treatment for a health problem rather than as a result of adaptive behaviors.

The medical treatment of patients often requires placing some restrictions on their diet. In hospitals, for the acutely ill special diets are commonly used. People who have certain chronic illnesses may need to follow a special diet in-indefinitely. Commonly used special diets are listed in Table 11–7. Special care is taken to provide most or all essential nutrients on special

Table 11–7.   COMMONLY USED SPECIAL DIETS, THEIR RESTRICTIONS AND THEIR PURPOSE

| Diet | Restrictions | Purpose |
| --- | --- | --- |
| Soft | Raw, fried or spicy foods | Easy to chew and to digest foods for those with trouble chewing, swallowing, or GI malfunction |
| Clear liquids | Allowed only clear broth, apple juice, gelatin, ginger ale, coffee, tea, water, ice, etc. | Provide fluids and few calories for decreased tolerance of foods or impaired function of GI tract due to disease or surgery |
| Full liquids | Allowed milk and milk products and all fruit juices in addition to clear liquids | Increase tolerance for fluids |
| *Special Therapeutic Diets*<br>Bland | Foods with high bulk, fiber, or that are raw, fried, or spicy | Avoid irritation of GI tract and provide easily digested foods |
| Low Sodium<br>500 mg<br>1000 mg | Salty foods and those high in sodium used in processing, preserving, or seasoning | Control water balance and reduce fluid retention |
| Diabetic<br>1200 cal ADA*<br>1500 cal ADA<br>1800 cal ADA | Provides balance of carbohydrates, proteins, and fats, such as 2:1:1 basis<br>Limits refined sugar, pastries, and starches | Limit calories and carbohydrates to meet the needs of the diabetic person |
| Restricted calorie<br>800<br>1000<br>1200 | Same as diabetic diet | Limit calories for weight control |
| High calorie, high protein, high vitamin | Allows increased sugars, starches, as well as the four basic food groups | Provide for deficiencies and increase intake for weight control |
| Low fat | Limits butter, oils, and other fatty or fried foods | Intolerance to fats in diseases of gallbladder and liver |
| Low purine | Limits purines, a nucleoprotein found in lean and glandular meats, some grains and legumes | Reduce uric acid by-products and formation of kidney stones |
| Low residue | Foods free from fiber, seeds, skins, or other residue<br>No milk, fruits, or vegetables except strained juices | Avoid trauma or irritation of GI tract or following GI surgery |
| Tube feedings | Commercially prepared or blended liquid foods | Provide fluid and nutrients to people unable to take foods orally due to illness, coma, or surgery |

*American Diabetes Association

diets within the restrictions that are imposed. However, some special diets are not able to provide *all* essential nutrients.

In the daily assessment of the foods that the patient consumed, the nurse should focus on the foods that are actually eaten. The food delivered to the patient on the diet tray has no value to the patient unless it is eaten. The nurse may want to calculate the caloric values of foods that are eaten by patients who have an inadequate diet. The nurse evaluates the meals that the patients choose from the selective menu to see that each meal consists of the recommended servings from the basic four food groups. There are significant nutritional differences between patients who eat all their breakfast if one patient has only a cup of coffee and one slice of toast while the other patient has milk, corn flakes, a dish of apple sauce, a poached egg, two slices of bacon, a sweet roll, and a cup of coffee.

## GENERAL APPEARANCE AND VITALITY

Adequate nutrition promotes feelings of vitality and vigor and a healthy, well-developed body that is capable of productive work and pleasurable activities. Malnourishment and the lack of essential nutrients affects cellular functions. External signs of both can be seen in the skin, mucous membranes, skeleton, abdomen, hair, teeth, and other structures.

## LABORATORY VALUES

Among the laboratory tests that measure some aspect of nutritional status, the concentration of glucose in the blood is the most commonly performed. When one is fasting, the body maintains a glucose level of between 80 to 90 mg/dl. This glucose level provides for proper osmotic pressure in the body fluids and direct utilization by the cells of the brain and the retina. After consuming a meal, one's glucose level rises abruptly as carbohydrates and other foods are absorbed but falls to its former level within approximately two hours. The accepted range for normal glucose concentrations is between 65 and 120 mg/dl. In diabetes and the lack of insulin, glucose accumulates in the blood where it reaches levels of 300 to 500 mg/dl or higher. After reaching a certain level, excess amounts of glucose are excreted in the urine, in addition to larger amounts of water that are needed to dilute the glucose.

Other laboratory tests, including serum albumin, urine creatinine, and urine urea nitrogen findings, may yield valuable information.

## SECOND LEVEL ASSESSMENT

Maladaptive behaviors that are associated with the nutritional need area are examined for the stimuli that produced or influenced the response(s). The most common types of stimuli are:

1. *Medical problem or disease to the digestive system or to organs related to the digestive system.* The following list reveals the wide diversity of diseases and conditions that interfere with nutritional needs or that have a direct influence on how nutritional needs are met: tonsillitis, tooth extraction, gastritis, peptic ulcer, hepatitis, diabetes mellitus, bowel obstruction, cholecystitis, and surgery performed anywhere on the gastrointestinal tract. Generalized infections, brain injury, anemias, severe trauma, and debilitating diseases of other parts of the body also affect one's appetite and the intake, digestion, movement, or absorption of food. Many diseases cause nausea and vomiting; therefore, the emesis of gastric contents not only is an observable behavior but also is a stimulus for some of the resulting nutritional problems.

2. *Medications and treatments.* Anesthetics, narcotics, analgesics, and tranquilizers are among the drugs that depress the central nervous system and cell functions elsewhere in the body. Examinations and procedures may require patients to fast, missing one or more meals per day. The use of nasogastric or intestinal suctioning requires that the body draw on its own reserves for energy until the gastrointestinal tract resumes its functions.

3. *Physical activity levels.* Bed rest and inactivity reduce both hunger and energy demands. People who live in urban areas, work in sedentary jobs, and get little exercise require few calories beyond the body's basal caloric needs.

4. *Emotional and physical sources of stress.* Anxiety, worry, crisis events, and stresses such as surgery influence nutritional needs. Eating may be used as a coping mechanism and food may serve as a form of reward or compensation for disappointments.

5. *Sociocultural background.* Members of various social and cultural groups differ in the types of foods that they include in their diet, the manner in which they prepare their foods, the significance that certain foods have for them, and their eating patterns. Some foods are prohibited by religious beliefs. One's level of educa-

**Table 11–8.** ASSESSMENT OF NUTRITIONAL NEEDS

| Factors to Assess | Adaptive Behaviors | Maladaptive Behaviors |
|---|---|---|
| Total caloric needs | Basal needs _____ cal<br>Activity _____ cal<br>Metabolic _____ cal<br>Total _____ cal | Fever _____° ↑ or ↓ metabolic rate |
| | Consumes sufficient foods to meet caloric needs | Food intake lacks _____ cal |
| Daily intake of food | No restriction of foods | Special diet. Specify (e.g., NPO):<br>_____<br>_____ |
| | Eats normally and retains foods | Nausea, vomiting |
| | Chews and swallows food easily | Lacks teeth to chew<br>Difficulty swallowing, chokes easily |
| | Eats balanced diet from four food groups | Food dislikes<br>_____ |
| | | Nutrients    Excess    Lack<br>Proteins<br>Fats<br>Carbohydrates<br>Minerals<br>Vitamins |
| General vitality | Energetic, vigorous | Feels "tired," "nervous," "weak" |
| | Blood glucose<br>  fasting – 65–120 mg/dl<br>  2 h postprandial – 80–90 mg/dl | Outside normal range |
| Motivation | Hunger before eating<br>Good appetite | No hunger or appetite |
| Body appearance | Skin – pink, firm, moist | Dry, pale, flaky |
| | Skeleton – well-formed | Bowed legs, deformed rib cage |
| | Abdomen – flat | Protruding, swollen |
| | Hair – shiny, springy | Dry, brittle, lifeless |
| | Teeth and gums – strong and smooth | Dental caries, swollen gums |

tion and knowledge influences meal-planning and following an adequate diet. Financial resources or the ability to grow foods has a direct bearing on the availability of an adequate diet.

6. *Age and metabolic rate.* Energy needs are highest for infants and remain high during the rapid growth in childhood, then gradually decline with aging. Fevers, abnormal lowering of body temperature, changes in thyroid hormones, and pregnancy are stimuli that affect metabolic rate.

7. *Availability and palatability of foods.* The supply, storage, distribution, and preparation of foods influence what foods are available and how they taste. The location where food is served, the surroundings, odors, and other environmental factors affect one's appetite and intake of food.

## PROBLEMS OF NUTRITION

As with problems in the previously discussed need areas, problems of nutrition are classified in slightly different ways, depending on the approach that is used. With either the integrated or segregated approach, the nurse assesses the same behaviors and identifies the maladaptive behaviors and the stimuli that are causing these behaviors. All problems that result from maladaptive behaviors are handled by the nurse at some time in planning the nursing care, depending upon the approach that is used.

In the integrated approach, the patient or client is viewed as a whole entity with a number of maladaptive behaviors that are identified as problems individually or in related clusters. The patient's medical problems and treatment are not viewed separately but are included in the problems and the nursing interventions that are used to promote adaptation. In addition to problems of too much of "something," too little of "something," or no intake, the patient may have one of the following problems:

"Patient has a nasogastric feeding tube due to organic brain disease."

"Patient has elevated blood sugar due to diabetes."

"Patient has difficulty swallowing due to a cerebrovascular accident."

"Patient has persistent vomiting due to drug reaction."

In the segregated approach, maladaptive behaviors that are symptoms of the medical problem are considered individually. The nurse seeks to change these behaviors to adaptive behaviors by carrying out the necessary medical orders and nursing actions. Maladaptive behaviors and problems that are not part of the medical problem are viewed as the nurse's primary responsibility. In the nutritional need area, the patient's problem is an excessive intake of "something," a decreased intake of "something," or no nutritional intake. Examples of statements of such problems are

"Patient has excessive intake of carbohydrates due to craving for sweets."

"Patient has decreased caloric and food intake due to chemotherapy."

"Patient has had no caloric intake for two days due to semicomatose state."

## NURSING INTERVENTIONS

Nursing interventions for nutritional needs include methods that manipulate the stimuli that are causing the maladaptive behaviors and problems. Treatment of the disease condition is directed primarily by the physician, and nursing actions must fall within the boundaries set by medical orders. Medications and treatments are prescribed by the medical staff, and the results and responses are assessed by the nurse. Changes in the treatment can be made following the nurse's consultation with the doctor. Age as a stimulus cannot be manipulated but must be considered as an influencing factor. The nurse can change some of the factors that affect the metabolic rate, such as giving cool sponge baths for an elevated temperature or using hypothermia pads.

The other stimuli that affect nutrition are more easily manipulated. These stimuli include one's level of activity, emotional and physical stress, environmental factors, and sociocultural habits and attitudes. Interventions that nurses use include assisting with nutrition, providing a pleasant atmosphere for meals, performing procedures to supply nutrients via an alternate route, and health-teaching.

## ASSISTANCE WITH NUTRITION

The goal of nursing care is the adaptation of patients to meet their own needs. Often, however, during periods of illness, patients are unable to meet their own needs without assistance. When sick, people are unable to obtain or to prepare food to eat, and, if hospitalized, they may need assistance to fill out their menus or to select balanced meals and may even require someone to feed them. Some patients can manage by themselves if the nurse opens milk cartons for them or cuts their meat into small pieces. Patients who have an impaired use of the upper extremities may benefit from specially designed forks and spoons that are used in rehabilitation. Patients who are fed by someone else should be allowed sufficient time to chew and swallow.

## PROVIDING A PLEASANT ATMOSPHERE

People have a better appetite and eat more in pleasant surroundings. Even in hospitals, it is possible to arrange the setting to resemble a normal mealtime. Patients who are physically able may be allowed to sit in a chair for their meals. Foods on the diet trays can be arranged attractively and the trays served promptly so that hot foods are hot when patients get them. Some agencies have dining areas so that patients may eat with others in a social setting.

Preparation of bed patients for meals includes providing facilities for using the bedpan, if needed, and washing the patient's hands. Odors in rooms can be controlled, and procedures such as enemas or dressing changes can be done at other times.

## ALTERNATIVE METHODS FOR NOURISHMENT

Nurses carry out various procedures to furnish nourishment through feeding tubes or intravenously. Nasogastric tubes, including the familiar

Levin's tube, the newer, small gauge feeding tubes (7-12-French sizes), and the gastrostomy tube, are commonly used for feeding. Hyperalimentation is used more extensively to provide nutrition to patients with serious emaciation. Sterile solutions of nutrients are infused by means of a central venous catheter. Extreme care must be taken to prevent infections. Nutrients given by small-gauge tube or by hyperalimentation are controlled by infusion pumps. Nurses must be familiar with the procedures involved, the equipment that is used, the hazards and possible complications that might occur, and the amount of nutrients that is provided.

## HEALTH-TEACHING

Changes in patients' behavior are based on learning; thus, health-teaching is one of the most valuable interventions. Many of the sociocultural and psychological factors involve habits, attitudes, and feelings. Health-teaching helps patients to find new ways to respond to these stimuli.

Health-teaching should begin early in the convalescent period for patients who will be on a special diet indefinitely, such as diabetics and patients with certain heart and renal diseases. These patients need to know the purpose of their diet, the foods that they are allowed, the foods to avoid, how long the diet should be followed, and how they can adjust the diet to their eating pattern and lifestyle.

Learning to adjust to new eating habits is difficult for anyone. Diabetics, as a group, are often overwhelmed by the changes that they must make and are confused by the food exchanges. Health-teaching requires reinforcement and should include a follow-up to correct misinterpretations. (The principles of learning and the process of health-teaching were discussed in Chapter Six.)

## APPLICATION TO CLINICAL PRACTICE

In preparation for assessment of the nutritional needs of patients, calculate your own caloric needs and analyze your dietary intake of essential nutrients.

1.  Calculate your total caloric needs.

    Weight _____ kilograms
    Basal caloric need _____ (kilos × 1 cal × 24 hr)
    Activity needs    _____ (allow 50% for 1 day of clinical nursing, 40% for ½ day of clinical nursing, 30% for 1 day of sitting in classes.)
    Metabolic needs   _____
    Total calories    _____

2.  Analyze your food intake. List the foods you ate in the last 24-hour period.

    **Breakfast**          **Lunch**          **Dinner**          **Snacks**

3.  How many servings did you eat from each of the four basic food groups?

    Milk and dairy products _____
    Meats and poultry     _____
    Fruits and vegetables   _____
    Breads and cereals     _____

4.  To what extent does your diet meet your nutritional needs?

When taking care of patients in the clinical setting, add the assessment of the nutritional needs to the assessments of the oxygen and fluid and electrolyte balance needs.

Table 11–5 in combination with Table 11–8 may be a useful guide for assessing nutritional needs.

## REFERENCES

Brody, Jane E.: How good are fast foods? Readers' Digest, p. 127–129, (February) 1980.

Caly, Joan C.: Assessing adults' nutrition. Am J Nurs, 77:1605, (October) 1977.

Cho, Joan: Assessment of physiological mode. Unpublished study guide. Los Angeles, Mount St. Mary's College, 1977.

Cook, Kathleen: Diabetics can be vegetarians. Nursing 79, 9(10):70–73, (October) 1979.

Dansky, Kathryn: Assessing children's nutrition. Am J Nurs, 77:1610, (October) 1977.

Fleshman, Ruth: Eating rituals and realities. Nurs Clin North Am, 8(1):91–104, (March) 1973.

Food and Nutrition Board: Recommended Dietary Allowances, 8th ed. Washington, D.C., National Academy of Science, National Research Council, 1976.

Fulmer, Teresa T.: If elderly patients can't chew. Am J Nurs, 77:1615, (October) 1977.

Griggs, Barbara, and Hoppe, Mary: Update: nasogastric tube feeding. Am J Nurs, 79:481–485, (March) 1979.

Guyton, Arthur: Textbook of Medical Physiology, 6th ed. Philadelphia, W. B. Saunders Company, 1981.

Luke, Barbara: Nutrition in renal disease: the adult on dialysis. Am J Nurs, 79:2155–2157, (December) 1979.

Oakes, Gary K., Chez, Ronald A., and Morelli, Irene C.: Diet in pregnancy: meddling with the normal or preventing toxemia? Am J Nurs, 75:1134–1136, (July) 1975.

Parker, Cherry: Food Allergies. Am J Nurs, 80:262–265, (February) 1980.

Price, Mary: Nursing diagnosis: the patient is starving... RN, 42(11):49–56, (November) 1979.

Rose, James C.: Nutritional problems in radiotherapy patients. Am J Nurs, 78:1194–1196, (July) 1978.

Salmond, Susan W.: How to assess the nutritional status of acutely ill patients. Am J Nurs, 80:922–924, (May) 1980.

US Department of Agriculture: Desirable weight ranges for adults. Calories and Weight: USDA Pocket Guide, No. 364. Washington, D.C., US Government Printing Office, 1974.

US Department of Agriculture: Food for us all. Yearbook of Agriculture. 1969. Washington, D.C., US Government Printing Office, 1969.

US Department of Agriculture: Nutritive value of foods. Home and Garden Bulletin, No. 72. Washington, D.C., US Government Printing Office, Science and Education Administration, Revised 1978.

Williams, Emily: Food for thought: meeting the nutritional needs of the elderly. Nursing 80, 10(9):60–63, (September) 1980.

Williams, Sue Rodwell: Nutrition and Diet Therapy, 2nd ed. St. Louis, The C. V. Mosby Co., 1973.

Wilson, Jeanne, and Colley, Rita: Meeting patients' nutritional needs with hyperalimentation. Nursing 79, 9(9):62–69, (September) 1979.

# Elimination Needs

## OBJECTIVES   Information in this chapter will help you to

1. Explain the basic concepts and structures related to the elimination of fluid and solid wastes from the body and the normal characteristics of the waste products and structures involved in the process of elimination.
2. Assess client's behaviors that are associated with meeting elimination needs and compare these behaviors with the norms, or standards, of adaptive behaviors.
3. List stimuli that cause maladaptive behavior, or influence one's ability to rid the body of wastes without assistance.
4. State the problems related to fluid elimination by the kidneys and the skin and elimination of solid materials.
5. Describe nursing interventions that are commonly used to promote elimination of wastes.

## DEFINITION OF TERMS

**acholic** — absence of bile, lack of color in the stool.
**anuria** — secretion of less than 100 ml of urine in a 24-hour period.

**cathartic** — medication that releases irritants in the colon to stimulate movement of the bowels.

**chyme** — partially digested food and digestive secretions that form the liquid mass in the intestines.

**constipation** — sluggish action of the bowel leading to infrequent or incomplete bowel movements.

**Credé's maneuver** — placing manual pressure over the bladder to promote emptying.

**diaphoresis** — excessive perspiration.

**diarrhea** — frequent passage of loose, watery stools.

**diuresis** — increased urinary output; polyuria.

**dysuria** — painful urination.

**flatus** — gas in the stomach and intestines.

**Foley catheter** — indwelling or retention catheter in the bladder.

**Harris flush** — irrigation of the colon used to relieve distention.

**hematuria** — blood in the urine.

**impaction** — accumulation of hard fecal masses in the rectum and sigmoid colon.

**incontinence** — loss of voluntary control over the bowel and/or bladder.

**micturition** — the act of voiding, or urination.

**nocturia** — urination during the night, either by going to the bathroom or bed-wetting.

**oliguria** — decrease in urinary excretion to 100 to 400 ml in a 24-hour period.

**peristalsis** — wavelike movement that propels gastric contents through the alimentary canal.

**polyuria** — increased urinary secretion.

**retention** — inability of the bladder to empty itself of urine.

**sphincter** — a circular muscle that constricts to close a passageway or opening of various tracts or structures in the body.

**stoma** — mouth or opening, either natural or artificially created.

**tenesmus** — painful straining at stool.

---

To maintain health and adaptation, there is a need to rid the body of extra materials and waste products. As long as people are able to expel wastes periodically, they pay little attention to this need area until problems arise. Unless waste materials are eliminated from the body, they can pose a threat to life itself.

Waste products and excess materials are excreted by the lungs, skin, and kidneys and from the rectum. Once the body has obtained supplies of oxygen, fluids, and foods to meet its metabolic needs, it is faced with the need to get rid of unwanted materials. Excess amounts of carbon dioxide are exhaled from the lungs every few seconds, or at about the same rate that oxygen is taken in. There is a daily need for additional fluids to replace those that are lost. Some fluids are lost continually through breathing and urine formation. Thirst signals the need for fluids every few hours. As the bladder fills with urine, there is a need to empty it several times a day to relieve pressure and to provide room for further collection of urine. One's daily consumption of foods provides essential nutrients, and the waste materials are stored in the rectum, which empties every day or so. Elimination needs are closely related to the intake of vital materials and the demands of the body.

In our culture, as in most other cultures around the world, children are taught at an early age to control their bowel and bladder function. Usually by the age of three years, they have learned to inhibit the urge to void or defecate until they reach the toilet. Elimination is accomplished in private, and people seldom talk about it in public. When sick, many people, both young and old, are ill at ease or embarrassed talking about or asking for help with their elimination needs. For example, an elderly woman refused to eat or drink while in the hospital to avoid her embarrassment about using the bedpan. The nurse's investigation into her nutritional needs and the lengthening period of time since her last voiding led to the discovery of the problem that was caused by her feelings of embarrassment.

The assessment of the elimination needs provides the nurse with valuable information regarding the internal conditions and functions of the body. The appearance and concentration of the urine indicate the fluid balance. Substances that are not normally found in the urine or that are present in greater amounts indicate medical problems within the body. The appearance and other characteristics of the bowel movement are significant indicators of the conditions of the digestive tract, the motility of the intestines, and the absorption of nutrients, fluids, and electrolytes.

In this chapter, the normal functions of eliminating fluids and solids are described, including the characteristics of the waste products and the body structures that are involved. The first level assessment focuses on the factors to assess and provides examples of normal and maladaptive behaviors associated with each need area. The second level assessment identifies the stimuli that cause or influence the maladaptive behaviors. Various problems of elimination are described, and interventions that are used to manipulate the stimuli are explained briefly. Through the use of these interventions the nurse assists the patient in achieving and maintaining regular elimination from the bowel and the bladder.

## MEETING ELIMINATION NEEDS

People vary to some degree in the manner in which they meet their elimination needs. Some people may void 10 to 15 times per day, and others may void only 4 to 5 times per day. Babies may have 5 or 6 bowel movements, often after each feeding. Some adults normally have one bowel movement every three days. As long as the bowel and bladder are operating efficiently to remove wastes from the body, such variations are not significant. Some people find that changes in their lives or stress causes irregularity in their normal patterns of elimination. Some irregularities respond to minor adjustments and can be tolerated, whereas others cause problems in elimination that require medical or nursing interventions.

## *ELIMINATION OF URINE*

The elimination of fluids is the function of the urinary bladder. The kidney's function is to regulate the body's fluid volume and to "clear" the blood of wastes. However, it is essential for the kidney to form the urine that carries the dissolved organic and inorganic materials in it for excretion from the body.

**The Urinary System.** The structures of the urinary system include the kidney with its blood supply, the ureters, the bladder, and the urethra.

Normally, there are two kidneys, each of which contains more than 1 million nephrons that selectively separate out the unwanted substances from the blood. The renal arteries supply blood to the kidney. Approximately 21 per cent of one's blood volume flows through the kidneys each minute so that the waste products of metabolism are removed and proper concentrations of substances are maintained in the body fluids. Unnecessary organic and inorganic materials are dissolved in water and form urine.

Although the kidneys are continually forming urine, they are able to concentrate it by reabsorbing more water into the body or to dilute it by reabsorbing less water. More water is retained in the body following the release of the antidiuretic hormone (ADH) and at night when the body is at rest and the basal metabolism is lower. A large intake of fluids and certain drugs, such as diuretics, are common stimuli for increased urinary output, or diuresis. Urine from the nephron collects in the pelvis of the kidney, which has a capacity of about 5 ml, and then passes down the ureters.

The ureter connects the kidney to the bladder and serves as the passageway for the urine. A slight peristaltic movement keeps the urine moving toward the bladder. There, a fold of tissue obstructs the opening and prevents urine from flowing back into the ureter, even under the pressure of a full bladder. The ureters are richly supplied with pain receptors, and any foreign object, such as kidney stones, causes severe spasms and excruciating pain.

The urinary bladder is a hollow muscular organ that serves as a reservoir for urine. It is largely under the control of the autonomic nervous system (ANS). The sympathetic branch of the autonomic nervous system inhibits the action of the bladder wall and constricts the sphincters so that urine is retained. The parasympathetic nerves carry the motor impulses that cause the contraction of the bladder muscle and the relaxation of the sphincters so that micturition occurs. Urine collects in the bladder until the volume causes sufficient pressure to stimulate the sphincter to relax and to open. With bladder control, the sphincters can be voluntarily contracted or relaxed. The capacity of the bladder varies, depending upon many factors, including age, disease, fluid intake, action of drugs, intactness of nervous control, and even the weather. The bladder is considered a sterile organ, although it is often the site of infections.

The urine from the bladder drains through the urethra to the outside of the body. In women, the urethra is 1½ to 2½ inches, or 3.7 to 6.2 cm in length and is located just above the vaginal opening. The male urethra is located in the penis and is part of the urinary system and the repro-

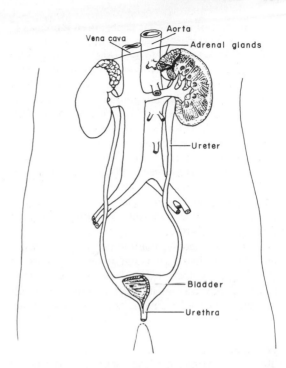

Aorta
Vena cava
Adrenal glands
Ureter
Bladder
Urethra

**Figure 12–1.** Urinary system of the kidneys, ureters, bladder, and urethra with blood supplied by renal arteries branching off the descending aorta.

ductive system. It is 5½ to 6½ inches, or 13.7 to 16.2 cm, long. At the juncture of the bladder and the urethra, the prostatic gland surrounds the urethra. In older men, enlargement of the prostate is a common cause for the obstruction of the urine flow through the urethra and for the retention of urine in the bladder. In both the male and female urethras, the external sphincter is under voluntary control.

**Characteristics of Urine.** Urine provides a wealth of information about the kidney and other biological functions of the body; thus, analysis of a urine specimen is routinely done as part of a physical examination. Urine is composed of water (95 per cent), organic wastes (3.7 per cent), and other materials (1.3 per cent). The organic wastes are nitrogen-containing compounds—namely, urea, uric acid, creatinine, and ammonia. Urea is formed from the metabolism of proteins and amino acids supplied through the diet or by the breakdown of body tissues. Electrolytes in excess of the body's needs are also secreted; thus, the urine contains sodium chloride and small amounts of calcium, potassium, magnesium, and phosphorus. Various other substances are also eliminated in the urine, including hormones.

Urine normally does not contain red blood cells, although occasionally one "leaks" through. Nor does it contain glucose, ketone bodies, bilirubin, casts, epithelial cells, pus cells, bacteria, or calculi, and if these occur, they indicate maladaptation elsewhere in the body. Urine produced by the kidney is sterile and contains no bacteria unless it has been contaminated while passing through the urethra or by an infection somewhere in the urinary tract.

Normal urine is clear and straw-colored due to the presence of a pigment called urochrome. Dilute urine is lighter in color, and, when concentrated, it is a much deeper yellow or an amber color. Other changes in color are associated with eating certain foods and the presence of blood, drugs, or bilirubin. Beets cause a pinkish hue to urine, and blood produces a range of colors from a pinkish tinge to red, to deep wine red, and to a rusty brown, depending upon the amount and the time it entered the urinary system. Because urine mainly consists of water, the specific gravity varies according to the amount of dissolved substances that it contains. The specific gravity of water is 1.000, and the range for urine averages between 1.010 and 1.025 but may be lower for very dilute urine or higher for concentrated urine. The pH is usually acidic due to the proteins and fats in the American diet and averages between 6.0 and 7.0. An alkaline pH occurs when the diet consists of many citrus fruits and vegetables and fewer proteins.

**Voiding Frequency and Volume.** People drink between one and two liters of fluids per day and void between 1000 and 1500 ml of urine per day.

The amount of urine that is produced increases if the fluid intake increases and decreases if large amounts of water are lost through the lungs, the skin, or from the intestines. A minimum of 500 ml of urine is needed to clear waste products from the blood. Larger amounts are needed for this purpose when the kidneys are diseased. Most nurses regard 600 ml for a 24-hour period, or 25 ml per hour, as a minimum standard for acceptable kidney function. Oliguria is reduced urinary output that falls between 100 ml and 400 ml per day. Anuria refers to an output of less than 100 ml of urine per day, or renal shutdown. The production of large amounts of urine is called diuresis, or polyuria.

In healthy people, voiding occurs easily, without pain or discomfort and leads to a sense of relief. The bladder is stimulated to empty when it contains a certain amount of urine, and this amount varies according to age, sex, muscle tone, habit, and other factors. Women tend to void when the bladder holds between 250 and 300 ml of urine, and men are more likely to void between 300 and 500 ml of urine. Smaller amounts are voided when the bladder is emptied more frequently.

People differ in the number of times they void during a 24-hour period; however, everyone tends to establish a personal pattern of voiding. Most people void after arising in the morning, before going to bed at night, and several times during the day, depending upon their fluid intake and personal habits. Some people go without voiding for periods of 8 to 12 hours, and infants void as often as once or twice an hour. In general, most people should void about once every 3 to 4 hours during the day, and they do not void during the night unless they have had a large intake of fluids.

People who void infrequently have been found to have a higher incidence of bladder infections than those who void more often. This is probably due to the stagnation of urine in the bladder and to the growth of bacteria ascending the urethra. Cystitis is more common in women than in men, and the inflammation of the bladder wall gives rise to the symptom of increase frequency and urgency to void that is almost as continual as the urine flowing into it. Urinary frequency is increased in people during times of stress and anxiety, as well as following the administration of diuretic medications.

## ELIMINATION THROUGH THE SKIN

There are approximately 2 million sweat glands in the body. The largest sweat glands are located under the arms and in the groin. The chief function of the sweat glands is the regulation of the body temperature. They play only a minor role in the excretion of wastes from the body. Perspiration consists mainly of water and sodium chloride, with small amounts of urea, lactic acid, and potassium. Underarm perspiration is not tolerated by most Americans, who control the wetness and odor through the use of deodorants and antiperspirants.

The amount of water that is lost through the skin varies greatly. Under normal conditions, about 100 ml of water is excreted as perspiration and 350 ml is excreted as moisture that is not visible but evaporates from the skin. Hot weather, increased muscular activity, and fevers increase the amount of fluid eliminated through the skin in the effort to lower body temperature. Every degree of increased body temperature causes vaporization of approximately 1000 ml of water, and visible sweat on the skin in a 24-hour period increases the loss of fluids by 1000 to 2000 ml. Excessive perspiration leads to loss of sodium chloride and water; thus, replacement of only the fluid leads to water intoxication unless the salt is also replaced. Fluids lost through the skin increase one's thirst and reduce urine output until the losses are made up. The greatest problems resulting from diaphoresis are hyponatremia, or loss of sodium, and fluid volume deficit.

With renal failure, the skin increases its secretions of waste products but is not nearly as efficient as the kidney, and dialysis must be used to clear the blood of unnecessary materials. With uremia, waste products accumulate in the blood and the skin appears to be "frosted" by the salts that are left when the water evaporates. This condition is called uremic frost, and it has a slightly aromatic odor, similar to that of urine.

## ELIMINATION OF SOLID WASTES

To sustain life, solid wastes must be eliminated from the body at regular intervals. Any condition that interferes with this need poses a threat to one's survival. The foods we eat are digested in the gastrointestinal tract after being mixed with digestive secretions, and, as the liquid chyme travels through the intestines, the body absorbs the essential and usable substances. The amount of waste that remains is influenced by the quantity of residue in the diet, the motility or speed at which it travels, and the presence of certain chemicals and bacteria. All waste materials form the feces, which are expelled from the body by the act of defecation, commonly called the bowel movement.

**Structures Involved.** Primarily, the elimination of solids is the function of the lower intestinal tract. The large intestine consists of the ascending colon on the right side of the body, the transverse colon lying above the umbilicus, and the descending colon on the left side of the body, which form a frame for the abdomen. The sigmoid colon ends in the rectum and the anus opening. The entire colon is approximately 5½ feet in length. The flow of chyme from the small intestine is controlled by the ileocecal valve at the point where the ileum joins the cecum, or ascending colon.

The absorption of nutrients and fluids takes place in the small intestine; however, the proximal half of the large intestine absorbs more water and electrolytes. Each day, approximately 500 to 1000 ml of chyme passes through the ileocecal valve to the colon, where water and ions are absorbed while mucus is secreted. Among the various bacteria that are normally present in the colon is *Escherichia coli*. Bacterial action is important in many ways: it helps digest small amounts of cellulose in the foods, produces the various gases that make up flatus, which inflates the bowels, and most importantly, forms vitamin K, vitamin $B_{12}$, thiamine, and riboflavin.

**Peristaltic Movement.** Peristalsis is the rhythmic contraction wave that progresses down the digestive tract and propels the bowel contents toward the anus. Peristaltic waves occur in smooth muscles in the esophagus, stomach, and intestines, as well as in the bile duct and in the ureters. The peristaltic waves occur at the rate of 10 to 12 times per minute in the small intestine, and they slow to 6 to 7 times per minute at the terminal end of the ileum. The waves produce the bowel sound of gurgles, crackles, and tinkles as the chyme is pushed forward. It moves about 1 cm per minute through the small intestine; thus, it takes from 3 to 10 hours to pass from the pylorus to the ileocecal valve. This provides time for complex digestive processes to occur and for the absorption of nutrients, water, and electrolytes.

Movement of the bowel contents in the large intestine is sluggish because contractions similar to peristalsis mix the fecal matter and extract most of the water. Mass movement then propels fecal material toward the anal end as a segment of about 20 cm contracts. When the mass has been forced into the rectum, it stimulates the urge to defecate. This mass movement occurs a few times each day, more frequently in the hour following breakfast. This accounts for the fact that many people have a bowel movement at this time.

**The Defecation Urge.** Three reflexes are commonly identified in relation to the urge to defecate: the gastrocolic reflex, the duodenal colic reflex, and the defecation reflex. The first two reflexes occur when the stomach or the duodenum is distended with food, giving rise to the desire to defecate. This is commonly observed in young children. The defecation reflex is triggered by the distention of the sigmoid colon and movement of the fecal mass into the rectum. However, if people do not respond to the urge immediately, it will disappear within a few minutes. Habitually inhibiting the urge to defecate may result in constipation.

The voluntary control of the urge to defecate

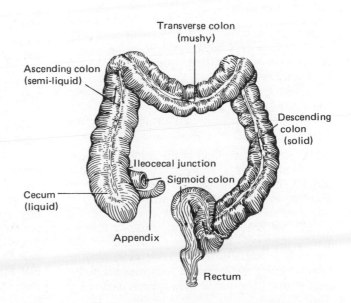

**Figure 12–2.** Parts of the large intestine and the consistency of bowel contents at various points.

allows one to suppress the urge until a more convenient time or until toilet facilities are available. The defecation reflex can sometimes be initiated by taking a deep breath and contracting the abdominal muscles to increase pressure on the colon; however, this is seldom as effective as the natural urge.

**Characteristics of Feces.** When the defecation urge occurs, most people normally move their bowels without pain or discomfort. The stool consists of soft feces that are round in shape like the sigmoid colon and are brown in color. The odor of the stool varies according to the bacterial action of the colon and the foods that have been eaten.

Contrary to common opinion, the stool is not composed entirely of residue from foods, but contains other materials; thus, defecation may occur even though the intake of food has been minimal. More than ¾ of the stool is water and ¼ is solid matter. Of the solids, the stool is composed of dead bacteria (30 per cent), inorganic material (10 to 20 per cent), and undigested food, fats, protein, bile pigment, and epithelial cells. Mucus that is secreted by cells in the large intestine binds these materials together. When the bowel is inflamed or greatly stimulated by severe emotional distress, these cells can produce thick, ropy mucus that results in frequent bowel movements, as often as once every 30 minutes. Patients with a functioning colostomy may still pass a mushy, grayish bowel movement through the rectum because of the mucus that is secreted in the remaining distal colon.

Although the normal bowel movement is brown in color due to the presence of bile, the diet may produce feces of a different color. Examples of different-colored stools and the conditions that cause them include:

*Dark greenish black, or meconium* — infant's stool for first few days of life
*Yellowish orange with a strong smell* — breast-fed babies
*Yellow; brownish yellow* — bottle-fed babies whose formulas contain malt sugars
*Soft, yellowish stool* — anyone receiving a tube feeding

The presence of blood in the stool is abnormal and should always be regarded as potentially serious until the cause has been determined. Bleeding in the lower part of the intestinal tract produces fresh red blood that coats part of the outside surface of the stool, clots, or forms a pool of blood. Blood from bleeding in the stomach or small intestine takes more time to travel through the intestinal tract where it undergoes partial digestion. It then appears dark red or

almost black in color and has a tarry consistency, and it is mixed throughout the entire fecal mass. Black, tarry stools commonly result from a bleeding gastric ulcer. Other abnormal stools have the following changes of color:

*Pale white, or clay-colored* — absence of bile, or obstruction to the passage of bile into the intestine
*Chalky white* — presence of barium used for x-ray examinations
*Light tan color* — undigested fats in the stool
*Green, watery* — infants who get too much sugar in their feedings
*Green, normal consistency* — products containing chlorophyll
*Coal black, normal consistency* — ingestion of medications containing iron
*Ova and parasites* — presence of pinworm, roundworm, hookworm, or tapeworms or their eggs

# FIRST LEVEL ASSESSMENT

## BLADDER FUNCTION AND URINARY OUTPUT

The assessment of the elimination of urine focuses on the characteristics of the urine and the amount of the output, the sensations associated with micturition, the effective emptying of the bladder, and the use of any altered means of urinary elimination.

**Characteristics of Urinary Output.** The nurse is interested in the complete voiding pattern, which includes the amount of urine voided in a 24-hour period, the number of voidings, and the amount that is voided each time. The kidney output of urine should average between 25 ml and 100 ml per hour, for a total of 600 to 2400 ml of urine voided per day. The urine should be normal in appearance, with a straw to slightly amber color and be clear and have a slightly aromatic odor when freshly voided. The laboratory report of the urinalysis should be within the normal ranges.

Frequency of urination varies with different age groups and depends upon the bladder capacity. An infant may void between 5 and 40 times per day. The average healthy adult voids between 5 and 10 times per day. The bladder should be able to hold urine for 3 to 8 hours, and the normal adult does not have frequent voidings of less than 100 ml per voiding. Unusual frequency may

**Table 12-1.** VALUES OF COMPONENTS
FOUND IN NORMAL URINE
OF A HEALTHY PERSON

| Routine Urinalysis | Normal Value |
| --- | --- |
| Appearance | Clear, straw color |
| Specific gravity | 1.010 to 1.025 |
| pH | 4.5 to 7.5 |
| Erythrocytes—RBCs | Occasional cell |
| Leukocytes—WBCs | Less than 4 per high power field |
| Casts | 0 |
| Crystals | Most are not significant |
| Acetone—ketone bodies | 0 |
| Glucose | 0 |
| Protein—albumin | 0 |

result from the overflow of urine from an over-distended bladder that cannot hold any more or, when accompanied by feelings of urgency or burning, may be a sign of bladder irritation or infection.

**General Sensations Related to Urination.** Urination should be accomplished with ease and free from pain or the continued feeling of urgency. With voluntary control, one can stop and start the urinary stream at will. Between the ages of two and three years, children gain control during daytime hours. Night control is achieved by most children by the age of four or five years. For some, bed-wetting, or enuresis, may persist longer because of poor neuromuscular function and anxiety.

Patients are expected to void within eight hours following surgery or the delivery of a baby as evidence that the kidneys and bladder continue to function normally. When the bladder becomes distended with urine, its dome rises above the pubic symphysis and can be palpated through the abdominal wall in all but obese people. Steps are then taken to promote the emptying of the bladder.

**Altered Means of Elimination.** As a result of various diseases or physical conditions, the physician may change the structures or functions involved in meeting the excretion of urine. Catheters are often used to provide free drainage of urine from the bladder in patients who have diseases that affect the kidney, neurological conditions that include spinal and head injuries, decreased levels of consciousness, or the inability to move about easily.

Common methods used to alter the urination process include the indwelling catheter, of which the Foley catheter is the most widely used, and cystostomy catheters, which are inserted through the abdominal wall into the bladder. Less common are the ureteral catheters and nephrotomy tubes and any of the methods used for urinary diversion following the removal of the diseased bladder. Although these altered means are necessary to meet the need for eliminating fluid wastes, they do not fall within the normal range of adaptive behaviors and their presence indicates a medical treatment for a temporary or a permanent problem with which the patient must cope. (See Table 12-2.)

**Table 12-2.** ASSESSMENT OF BLADDER FUNCTION AND URINARY OUTPUT

| Factors to Assess | Normal Behaviors | Maladaptive Behaviors |
| --- | --- | --- |
| Characteristics of urinary output | _____ ml/24 hr | Less than 25–30 ml/hr<br>Oliguria, anuria<br>Less than 100 ml/voiding |
| Components | Clear, yellow to amber<br>Normal urinalysis | Contains glucose, blood, protein, acetone, sediment<br>Other:_____ |
| Control | Continent, controls sphincter<br>Can stop and start stream | Loss of control, dribbling<br>Retention of urine |
| Sensation | Voids easily<br>No discomfort | Pain on voiding, bladder spasms, urgency, burning, frequency, or bladder distention |
| Altered means | Voids normally | Use of catheter, cystostomy catheter, ureterostomy tube, or urinary diversion |

## FLUID ELIMINATION BY THE SKIN

Under normal conditions, most people are unaware of any loss of fluids through the skin. This is called the insensible fluid loss, and it consists of approximately 100 ml of perspiration and 350 ml of fluid through evaporation from the skin surface. Visible amounts of perspiration and each degree of elevated body temperature increase the amount of fluids lost. (See Table 12–3.)

## BOWEL ELIMINATION

The assessment of the elimination of solid wastes from the body includes the characteristics of the bowel habit, presence of bowel sounds, other general behaviors that are related to inadequate bowel function, and altered means of eliminating feces.

**Characteristics of the Bowel Habit.** A wide range of normal behaviors exist for eliminating solid wastes; thus, it is important to learn each patient's bowel pattern. This includes the regularity of the bowel movement, the frequency, the usual time of the day that it occurs, and the appearance of the stool. Some people believe that drinking a cup of hot coffee or a glass of orange juice promotes the urge to defecate.

The normal stool is brown in color, semiformed or formed in consistency, and the number of stools ranges from two or three per day to one every two or three days. Passing two or three formed stools per day should not be confused with diarrhea, which is an abnormally frequent evacuation of liquid stools. Mass movement of the large intestine may occur several times per day and move feces from the sigmoid into the rectum, creating the urge to defecate. Any stool that contains blood is considered maladaptive, as are other changes in the bowel habit and in the characteristics of the stool.

**Examination of the Abdomen.** Peristaltic movements propel liquid chyme through the intestinal tract and facilitate the excretion of waste materials. Peristalsis occurs mainly in the small intestine, where peristaltic waves occur approximately every 5 to 10 seconds, or at a rate of 6 to 11 or 12 waves per minute. As the chyme moves through the intestines, various sounds are produced as gurgles, rumbles, or tinkles. These sounds can be heard by placing a stethoscope at various points over the upper and mid abdomen.

No peristaltic movement results in an accumulation of flatus and fluid in the bowel. The abdomen becomes distended and often tympanitic so that even soft finger-tapping produces a hollow, drumlike sound and no bowel sounds can be heard. Various diseases and conditions as well as medications like atropine are able to depress or to completely block the peristaltic movements. Patients who have been NPO or been given only liquid diets must have some bowel sound before they are allowed a diet of solid foods. Bowel sounds are assumed to be present and normal in people who eat foods and pass flatus through the rectum daily.

Hypoactivity refers to sluggish action in the intestine with slow or ineffectual peristalsis. If one's food intake continues, this results in feelings of "fullness" and infrequent bowel sounds, and, often a mass of feces can be felt in the descending colon on the left side of the abdomen. This can lead to the problem of infrequent bowel movements, constipation, and impaction of the feces.

Hyperactivity occurs when the intestinal contents are swept rapidly through the alimentary canal by strong peristaltic movement. This swift, cramping movement allows inadequate time for the absorption of nutrients and water, resulting in bowel movements of a liquid or semiliquid nature, as seen in diarrhea.

**General Behaviors of Inadequate Elimination.** Some behaviors, such as headache, malaise, anorexia, furred tongue, and lethargy, are not specific indicators of inadequate elimination or bowel irregularity. When these behaviors are accompanied by a lack of a bowel movement for several days, the patient should be checked for an im-

**Table 12–3.** ASSESSMENT OF FLUID ELIMINATION BY THE SKIN

| Factors to Assess | Normal Behaviors | Maladaptive Behaviors |
|---|---|---|
| Insensible loss | Dry skin, no visible perspiration | Visible sweating, profuse diaphoresis (loss of 1–2 L water/24 hr) |
| Body temperature | Normal or below 37° C or 98.6° F | Elevated temperature (loss of 1 L water/1° fever) |

paction. Lack of appetite, or anorexia, reduces one's food intake, and furred tongue indicates a decreased fluid intake. Headache, malaise, and lethargy are also related to decreased activity of the digestive system.

Frequent soiling of the body or bed linens with small amounts of liquid brown stool is sometimes mistaken for adequate bowel movements. However, this is often the sign of a fecal impaction in which the bacterial action has liquefied the outer surfaces of the hardened mass. It represents the body's attempt to rid itself of the retained stool and is a maladaptive way of meeting the elimination needs.

**Altered Means of Elimination.** When the defecation reflex does not lead to regular elimination of feces, other means must be found to expel these wastes. Laxatives, cathartics, stool softeners, enemas, and Harris flush or colonic irrigations are some of the alternative methods that are used. Obstructions, tumors, and other diseases of the intestines may require surgery to create an artificial stoma, or opening, for the elimination of feces, rather than eliminating them through the anus. A colostomy is a stoma in the large intestine, and an ileostomy is a stoma in the ileum of the small intestine.

The degree of control of fecal drainage through the stoma depends upon its location and the consistency of the fecal matter. A continual leakage exists from the ileostomy because most of the water in the chyme is absorbed in the large intestine. The drainage of a colostomy located in the ascending colon is liquid. In the transverse colon it is mushy and soft because more water has been absorbed. In a colostomy of the descending colon, the stool is soft and more of a solid nature and is more easily controlled, enabling bowel

movements to occur every one to two days. See Figure 12–2.

## SECOND LEVEL ASSESSMENT

The second level assessment identifies the underlying stimuli that cause the maladaptive behaviors. Common stimuli for elimination needs include:

1. *Medical diseases or conditions in related structures and organs.* Urinary problems result from conditions that disrupt the urinary system, such as stones, infections, tumors, spinal injuries that interfere with neurological control of the bladder, obstruction of the ureters or urethra, and injury or trauma. Problems with bowel elimination are caused by diseases of the gastrointestinal system, infections, inflammation, or surgery of related organs.

2. *Amount of food and fluid intake.* Both bowel and bladder elimination depend upon good hydration, and the fluid intake should average 2500 ml. Total body fluid level is governed by the kidney, and output is reduced when the total volume has been reduced through dehydration, diaphoresis, or bleeding. Bowel elimination is influenced by the type of diet and amount of food, orders for NPO, or restricted residue in the food.

3. *Medications.* Bowel elimination is affected by laxatives, cathartics, suppositories, and stool softeners that stimulate evacuation as well as by narcotics, anesthesias, atropine, and other drugs that depress or stop peristalsis and bowel motility.

4. *External factors.* The location of toilet facilities, their suitability, the amount of privacy,

**Table 12–4.** ASSESSMENT OF BOWEL ELIMINATION

| Factors to Assess | Normal Behaviors | Maladaptive Behaviors |
| --- | --- | --- |
| Characteristics of bowel elimination | Has stool on regular schedule q 1–3 days | Irregular elimination |
| Color | Brown | Black, tarry appearance; bloody, clay-colored, mucoid |
| Amount | Moderate | Small, hard particles |
| Consistency | Semiformed to formed | Liquid stool |
| Control | Voluntary control, able to inhibit or to initiate urge | Incontinent, loss of control; leaking of liquid brown stool |
| Examination of abdomen | Abdomen soft Passes flatus Active bowel sounds | Distended, tympanitic Gas pains, cramping No bowel sounds |
| Altered means | Normal defecation | Use of laxatives, cathartics, stool softener, enema, suppositories; colostomy or ileostomy |

the availability of assistance, if needed, the amount of time allowed, and the limitations imposed by a busy schedule affect one's elimination behaviors.

5. *Age and developmental stage.* Control of bowel and bladder are established at different ages. Some diseases that affect elimination are commonly associated with certain periods of life. For example, cancer of the colon is a leading cause of death for both men and women between the ages of 50 and 70, prostate enlargement occurs in older men, hydrocele occurs in young males, and cystitis afflicts more women than men.

6. *Level of activity.* Bed rest and immobility reduce muscle tone of the bladder and bowel. Sitting up or ambulating helps movement of the waste materials to prevent stagnation of urine in the kidney pelvis and the bladder and constipation of the bowel.

7. *General mental and emotional condition.* Stress and anxiety reduce the functions of the digestive system and elimination of both liquid and solid wastes. Stress produces strong sympathetic stimulation that constricts blood flow to the kidney; thus, urine output falls to near zero. Antidiuretic hormone (ADH) also influences the kidney to retain fluids in the body. However, the gastrointestinal tract is under the control of the parasympathetic nervous system (PNS). Sympathetic stimulation has slight effect on increasing secretions, but the constriction of the blood vessels results in an overall decrease in the amount of secretions. Parasympathetic stimulation produces copious amounts of mucous secretions in the lower colon and motility; thus, some people have frequent diarrhea during times of stress. Sympathetic stimulation during stress and anxiety inhibits some secretions, such as those in the duodenum, leaving the intestinal wall unprotected from the acid chyme from the stomach, which, in some people, then forms ulcers.

8. *Social or cultural customs, attitudes, and habits.* Values, beliefs, and attitudes are greatly influenced by child-rearing practices, social class, and customs that are learned and shared from generation to generation. Culture may be a dominant factor in peoples' attitudes of present-oriented or future-oriented lifestyle—the view of illness as being out of balance with nature, the will of God, or a matter of bad luck; polite conversation or direct expression of what one means, "saving face"; suppressing or expressing one's feelings. Cultural attitudes about touching and other feelings concerning personal space should be observed.

Identify a sufficient number of stimuli, or causes, for the maladaptive behaviors so that they can be manipulated to promote adaptation.

## PROBLEMS OF ELIMINATION

The assessment of the elimination need area and the information provided by the maladaptive behaviors help the nurse to determine the kind and extent of the disturbance to the patient's daily living habits.

### FLUID ELIMINATION PROBLEMS

A decrease in urinary output is a potentially dangerous sign that indicates that waste materials are accumulating in the body and causing it to become toxic. Whenever patients are unable to void voluntarily for a period of hours, it is necessary to determine whether it is due to failure of the kidney to produce urine or to failure of the bladder to expel urine. Other diseases of the urinary tract produce symptoms of oliguria, anuria, pain, burning and urgency, abnormal contents in the urine, and tumors. Treatment of these conditions involves the use of catheters, surgical procedures, and alterations in the structures of the system, which occurs in suprapubic cystotomies and urinary diversions. The nursing assessment of this need area provides behavioral information that helps in the evaluation of the patient's response to treatment or progress toward recovery. Integrated problems of fluid elimination might be stated as:

Patient has sugar in urine due to diabetes.
Patient has frequency, pain, and urgency when voiding due to bladder infection.
Patient has blood in urine on the second day after prostate surgery.

In addition to diseases of the urinary system, maladaptive behaviors in this need area are generally related to urinary retention and to incontinence or to the loss of voluntary control of voiding. These problems are frequently stated as:

Patient has not voided for _____ hours due to surgery this AM.
Patient has urinary incontinence due to decreased mental awareness.

**Urinary Retention.** Retention refers to an interference with the function of the bladder. The kidney continues to form urine, which collects in the bladder, but the bladder does not empty. Retention becomes a problem when the person has not voided for several hours, has distention of the bladder, and suffers some discomfort because of the inability to void. The time period varies, depending upon the amount of fluid intake and the ability to palpate the bladder. Usually, if the person is unable to void after 8 to 10 hours, the nurse may need to obtain medical orders to catheterize and to drain the bladder.

Gross distention of the bladder is frequently seen in men who have enlarged prostate glands. Some people have accumulated more than two liters of urine in the bladder by the time they seek medical help. Minute tears occur in the inner wall of the overdistended bladder, giving the urine a blood-tinged appearance and cause the organ to lose its muscle tone. Large amounts of urine should not be drained off rapidly because this would change the intra-abdominal pressure and might lead to shock. After removing approximately one liter of urine, the catheter preferably should be clamped and additional urine should be drained from the bladder over a period of time.

**Loss of Bladder Control.** The loss of urinary control may be the intermittent emptying of the bladder or the continuous leakage of urine. Stress incontinence results in the dribbling of urine when coughing, sneezing, or straining. Many older people have this type of incontinence because of the relaxation of sphincters and muscles. It may also occur in some women following childbirth.

Illness often interferes with voluntary control of urination. Some people may void involuntarily each time that the bladder fills with a certain volume of urine, wetting the bedding or clothing. Others may have control when awake but may be incontinent following medications for pain or sleep. Wet linen and urine on the skin can be irritating to the skin and cause a breakdown with a secondary infection unless the skin is kept clean and dry.

## PROBLEMS OF PERSPIRATION

Other than being a sign of a medical condition such as fever or uremia, excessive perspiration is seldom a physiological mode problem. When it affects one's self-concept and causes problems in coping with feelings the excessive wetness, especially in the axillary area, and odor can be controlled by cleanliness of the skin and the use of deodorants and antiperspirants.

## PROBLEMS OF SOLID ELIMINATION

The problems of bowel elimination include too many, too few, or the wrong kind of bowel movements or no stool at all. Serious problems that interfere with the body's ability to rid itself of solid wastes require medical interventions to treat the causes, because problems such as those that follow can jeopardize one's life: an acute bowel obstruction, a hyperactive bowel with diarrhea, abnormal contents in the feces, and tumors or inflammatory conditions that necessitate altering the structures by creating artificial stomas. Obstructions of the small bowel are associated with vomiting fluid that contains fecal particles and odor, while bowel movements may occur containing feces already stored in the colon. The abdomen becomes distended with flatus and bowel sounds disappear. Obstruction of the large bowel leads to severe constipation and less vomiting. Goals of treatment are to relieve the obstruction by the use of intestinal tubes, suctioning, enemas, and colonic irrigations or by surgery.

The hyperactive bowel rapidly flushes the liquid chyme through the intestines with insufficient time for absorption of essential nutrients and results in frequent, strong expulsions of liquid stools. Other complications of dehydration and electrolyte imbalance can occur within a short period of time. Infants with diarrhea can die from dehydration in less than 24 hours if treatment is not begun in time to correct the condition. In addition to frequent stools, other maladaptive behaviors may include skin irritation around the anal area, accidental spillage that embarrasses the patient, and the loss of body fluids. A nursing responsibility is the prevention of cross contamination and the spread of pathogenic organisms that cause the diarrhea. Solid elimination problems may be stated as:

Patient has frequent, liquid stools (_____ in _____ hours) due to _____.
Patient has acute abdominal distention due to possible bowel obstruction.
Patient has had black tarry stools for two days due to upper gastrointestinal bleeding.
Patient has colostomy due to diverticulitis.

Some elimination problems are primarily the responsibility of the nurse. These problems occur when diseases in other organs or systems of the body interfere with bowel function and consist of inadequate bowel movements or no bowel movement for several days or incontinence of the bowel, or loss of control. These problems may be stated as:

Patient has constipation with no bowel movement for _____ days due to _____.
Patient has possible impaction due to prolonged bed rest.

Patient has incontinence of feces due to recent cerebrovascular accident (CVA).

**Inadequate Bowel Movements.** Illness often results in hypoactivity and sluggishness of the bowel, which leads to irregularity, constipation, impaction, and abdominal distention. The slow movement of fecal material permits greater absorption of water, which leaves the feces more compact and harder to pass rectally. More straining and discomfort occurs with constipation. The flatus expands the intestines and may lead to gas pains as a result of the slow peristaltic movement. Continued retention of feces in the colon for several days with more material entering the storage area from the upper tract leads to impaction. Although medications, suppositories, or enemas facilitate removal of constipated stools the impacted feces may need to be removed manually. Constipation and impaction are both uncomfortable and can be prevented by attending to elimination needs, adequate fluid intake, a diet with roughage or fiber, and exercise.

**Loss of Bowel Control.** Lack of control of the bowels is very stressful for adults. When it occurs among older patients, they feel that they are entering their second childhood and that no one will continue to like them or to respect them if they cannot control their bowels. It leads to feelings of low self-esteem and self-worth. It occurs more often among those who have reduced mental awareness, resulting from disease or medications that depress cell functions or from impaired neurological or muscular control.

Bowel incontinence responds to treatment more readily than does urinary incontinence. Different methods of bowel retraining can be used, including the use of suppositories, stool softeners, laxatives, and a regular time for evacuation. Sufficient intake of fluids helps to keep the feces soft. One's diet should provide some roughage. Privacy aids in gaining regular evacuation of the bowels.

## PROBLEMS IN OTHER MODES

Elimination difficulties that involve the functions of the physiological need areas often become stimuli for problems in the other modes. The altered means of elimination and the loss of bowel or bladder control may create serious coping problems in the self-concept mode. Patients who have problems are faced with changes that affect their own body image, and these changes create different body sensations. The loss of regular function or the loss of control cause anxiety and grieving. People attempt to cope using their feelings of fear, anger, depression, and powerless-

ness. The physiological problems of elimination serve as stimuli for the coping problems.

Problems of interdependence arise when patients fail to meet the expectations of others as to what is appropriate behavior for the circumstances. Some patients use their concern about drainage from a stoma, the appearance of the urinary flow in the catheter, or their constipation as a means of gaining attention. Others refuse to help themselves reach self-care and independence by continuing to rely on nurses or on family members for assistance. Problems in the other modes might be stated as:

### Self-Concept

Patient has feelings of _____ due to loss of bowel control.

Patient has feelings of _____ due to loss of control of bladder.

Patient has feelings of _____ due to colostomy.

### Interdependence

Patient has dysfunctional dependence due to refusal to care for stoma.

## NURSING INTERVENTIONS

There are many interventions that nurses can use to manipulate the stimuli and to achieve the goals of the nursing care plan for promoting and maintaining bowel and bladder elimination.

## PROMOTING URINARY FUNCTION

**Autostimulation.** Various methods are used to stimulate the patient's urge to void, including running water in the sink, having the patient place his or her hands in water, and stroking the lower abdomen lightly with a feather or an ice cube to stimulate the contraction of the bladder. Pouring water over the perineal area often relaxes the sphincter muscle for voiding and assuming the accustomed position of sitting or, for some male patients, standing at the bedside is effective.

Patients can be taught to palpate the bladder and then to use Credé's maneuver to increase pressure on the bladder, stimulating the urge to void. Continued manual pressure helps to empty the bladder.

**Provide Assistance.** The patient may need the nurse's assistance to use the bedpan or the urinal, to ambulate to the bathroom, or to use a bedside commode. Help should be provided promptly to allow the appropriate responses for the urges to void and to defecate rather than incontinence or the suppression of these reflexes.

**Catheters.** Catheters are widely used among the acutely ill to drain urine from the bladder and to monitor the kidney functions. Nurses insert catheters into the urinary bladder on a one-time basis or use the indwelling or Foley catheter for continual drainage. Sterile technique must be used to insert catheters, to irrigate them, and to obtain urine specimens from them. Special three-way catheters allow for continual irrigation of the bladder as well as drainage of the urine. Other types of catheters include ureteral, nephrostomy, suprapubic, and cysto-catheters, which are generally inserted by the physician.

**Reduce Risk of Urinary Infection.** The use of a catheter introduces some organisms into the bladder. The presence of the tube in the urethra provides an avenue for ascending organisms to reach the bladder. Because bladder infections commonly occur with catheterization, many physicians routinely prescribe sulfisoxazole (Gantrisin) as a preventative measure. The application of skin disinfectants such as povidone-iodine on the skin that surrounds the urethral opening twice a day has been found effective in reducing infections. The catheter must remain open, and the gravity drainage system should remain intact. It should not be disconnected for any reason without taking appropriate steps to prevent contamination. Other principles involved in catheter usage include positioning the drainage tubing to allow the free flow of urine and avoiding loops in the tubing that force the urine to run uphill to the collection bag and increase the pressure in the bladder. A record is kept of the intake and output of urine, and fluids should be increased to 3000 ml per day unless contraindicated by medical reasons.

In early childhood, females should be taught to wipe the perineal area from the front to the back after voiding or having a bowel movement. This simple action avoids the transference of organisms normally found on the skin back to the urethral opening and causing an ascending infection of the bladder.

**Bladder Retraining.** The nursing assessment should provide information about the voiding habits of the incontinent patient, from which a schedule can be made to toilet about half an hour before voiding usually occurs. The goal is to toilet the patient before his or her bladder empties involuntarily. If the patient is already wet, the skin should be washed and kept as dry as possible to prevent irritation and possible breakdown. For the incontinent patient, the fluid intake should be increased to between two and three liters per day unless contraindicated.

## PROMOTING BOWEL ELIMINATION

**Medications and Suppositories.** Nurses administer various types of medications that stimulate the bowel and promote the evacuation of feces. The time that medications are given depends upon their purpose and how long it takes for the drug to act. Many laxatives are given in the evening and produce results the next morning. Cathartics may produce results in a matter of a few hours. Suppositories are inserted rectally and produce results from about 20 minutes to a few hours from insertion. Stool softeners have become popular as a means of promoting bowel movements in hospitalized patients. These drugs have a wetting quality that binds more water in the feces, thereby increasing bulk. The chronic use of laxatives and cathartics should be avoided if possible because their use further reduces the tone of the colon and leads to a vicious circle of dependence upon them.

**Enemas and Harris Flush.** Enemas may be ordered occasionally to stimulate the defecation urge and to flush feces from the bowel. Approximately 200 ml of solution is sufficient to promote the bowel movement. This is the usual amount of solution that is supplied in the commercial disposable types of enema. The Harris flush, or colonic irrigation, is an effective method for removing flatus from the large bowel. In this procedure, about 200 ml of fluid is instilled into the rectum, then the fluid container is lowered below the level of the anus and the solution drains back into the container and flatus is released. These steps are repeated until no more gas is released. Rectal tubes may also be used to reduce flatus but should be removed after 30 minutes to prevent anal irritation and reinserted later, if needed.

**Care of Stomas.** Thousands of people in this country have an artificial stoma for urine or bowel elimination. To provide for their elimination needs, the nurses need to become familiar with the various types of appliances and drainage bags that are worn. People who have a regulated colostomy use disposable plastic bags that are emptied and discarded when filled with fecal material. The bags should not be thrown into the toilet because they will block the plumbing. People who have stomas of the ileum and the ascending and transverse colon wear permanent bags. These bags remain in place, and the lower end of the bag opens to allow removal of the contents. Because the bowel is not a sterile organ, tap water can be used to rinse the inside of the bag.

It is extremely important to take care of the skin of the stoma patient. The fecal drainage contains enzymes and acids, especially at sites located above the sigmoid colon, that are extremely irritating to the skin. Keeping the skin dry and free of drainage can be a challenge with edematous and protruding stomas. A sticky, brown substance called karaya is effective in protecting the skin. It may be cut to fit around the stoma. Some stoma bags are manufactured with a karaya ring around the opening to prevent the drainage from reaching the skin. Other medications may also be prescribed to apply to the skin.

The control of colostomies located lower in the descending colon is often achieved by irrigating the stoma. Essentially, the colostomy irrigation is an enema given through the stoma. Care must be taken not to instill the fluid under high pressure, which could cause damage to the fragile bowel tissues, and sufficient time (up to an hour) must be allowed to expel the solution.

**Health-Teaching.** Other effective nursing interventions involve the use of health-teaching, or providing the patient with additional information in order to change the behavioral responses that have previously been used. For example, patients need health-teaching when their fluid intake is to be increased because they need to know the reasons for the increase, the amount of fluids to drink, the type of foods or fluids to take, and so on. Patients with constipation benefit from learning about the influence of one's diet, adequate fluids, and regular exercise in promoting bowel regularity. Patients with altered means of elimination need to learn how to manage their lives, whether the change involves a catheter for a short period of time or a permanent stoma.

## APPLICATION TO CLINICAL PRACTICE

When caring for patients clinically, add the assessment of the patient's elimination needs to the assessment of their other need areas. The assessment now includes the oxygen, fluid and electrolyte, nutrition, and elimination need areas. The following outline can be used as a guide for your assessment.

| Normal, or Expected Behaviors | Unusual, or Maladaptive Behaviors |
|---|---|
| *Urine Elimination* | |
| _____ ml/24 hr | Less than 25–30 ml/hr<br>Oliguria, anuria<br>Less than 100 ml/voiding |
| Normal characteristics:<br>   clear, aromatic, yellow to amber in color | Contains glucose, blood, protein, acetone, sediment<br>Other:_____ |
| Continent, control of sphincter<br>Can stop and start urine stream | Loss of control, dribbling<br>Incontinence<br>Retention of urine |
| Voids easily<br>No pain or discomfort | Pain on voiding, bladder spasms, urgency, burning, frequency, or bladder distention |
| Voids normally | Use of catheter, cystostomy catheter, ureterostomy tube, or urinary diversion |
| *Elimination by Skin* | |
| Dry skin, no visible perspiration | Visible sweating, profuse diaphoresis |
| Normal body temperature | Elevated temperature of _____ degrees |
| *Bowel Elimination* | |
| Has regular bowel movement every 1 to 3 days | Irregular elimination, no bowel movement for _____ days |
| Brown color, moderate amount, and formed stool | Black, tarry appearance; bloody, clay-colored, mucoid<br>Small, hard particles<br>Liquid stool<br>Other:_____ |

| Voluntary control, able to initiate or suppress urge | Incontinent, loss of control |
| | Leaking of liquid brown stool |
| Abdomen soft | Abdomen distended, tympanitic |
| Passes flatus | Gas pains, cramping |
| Active bowel sounds | No bowel sounds |
| Normal defecation | Use of laxatives, cathartics, stool softener, enema, suppositories; colostomy or ileostomy |

# REFERENCES

Aman, Rose Anne: Treating the patient, not the constipation. Am J Nurs, *80*:1634–1635, (September) 1980.

American Cancer Society: Care of Your Colostomy. A Source Book of Information. New York, The American Cancer Society, 1974.

Bass, Linda: More fiber – less constipation. Am J Nurs, 77:254–255, (February) 1977.

Beber, Charles: Freedom for the incontinent. Am J Nurs, *80*:482–484, (March) 1980.

Blackwell, Ardith, and Blackwell, William: Relieving gas pains. Am J Nurs, *75*:66–67, (January) 1975.

Broadwell, Debra, and Sorrells, Suzanne: Loop transverse colostomy. Am J Nurs, *78*:1029–1031, (June) 1978.

Brunner, Lillian and Suddarth, Doris S.: Textbook of Medical-Surgical Nursing, 4th ed. Philadelphia, J. B. Lippincott Co., 1980.

Cho, Joan: Assessment of physiological mode. Unpublished study guide. Los Angeles, Mount St. Mary's College, 1977.

DeGroot, Jane: Catheter-induced urinary tract infections. How can we prevent them? Nursing 76, *6*:35, (June) 1976.

Delehanty, Lorraine, and Stravino, Vincent: Achieving bladder control. Am J Nurs, *70*:312–316, (February) 1970.

Gibbs, Gertrude, and White, Marilyn: Stomal care. Am J Nurs, *72*:268–271, (February) 1972.

Guyton, Arthur: Textbook of Medical Physiology, 6th ed. Philadelphia, W. B. Saunders Company, 1981.

Habeeb, Marjorie C., and Kallstrom, Mina D.: Bowel program for institutionalized adults, Am J Nurs, *77*:816–817, (May) 1977.

Hollister Ostomy Guide. Chicago, Hollister, Inc., 1972.

Northridge, Judith Schramm: Helpful hints for assessing the ostomate. Nursing 82, *12*(4):72–77, (April) 1982.

Reed, Sharon: Giving more than dialysis. Nursing 82, *12*:58–63, (April) 1982.

Shafer, Kathleen N., et al.: Medical-Surgical Nursing, 6th ed. St. Louis, The C. V. Mosby Company, 1975.

Stark, June: BUN/creatinine: your keys to kidney function. Nursing 80, *10*(5):33–38, (May) 1980.

Tudor, Lea L.: Bladder and bowel training. Am J Nurs, *70*:2391–2393, (November) 1970.

Watt, Rosemary C.: Colostomy irrigation – yes or no? Am J Nurs, *77*:442–444, (March) 1977.

# Chapter THIRTEEN
# Need for Motor Activities and Sleep

**OBJECTIVES**  Information in this chapter will help you to

1. Discuss the basic concepts involved in meeting physical activity and sleep needs of the body and the systems that are involved.
2. Assess the behaviors associated with meeting the needs for activity and sleep and compare these behaviors with the standards of the adaptive range of behaviors.
3. Explain the effects of immobility on the various body systems and the hazards or complications that can result from insufficient activity.
4. Assess the stimuli that cause or influence one's ability to carry out voluntary activities and to regularly obtain sufficient sleep for physical and mental restoration.
5. State the problems that result from maladaptive behaviors in meeting sleep and activity needs.
6. Describe nursing interventions, including the use of bed rest, that are frequently employed by the nurse to meet activity and sleep needs.

**DEFINITION OF TERMS**

**atrophy** — a decrease in size, or wasting, of a tissue or organ.
**calculi** — stones, or small hard masses, formed in hollow organs or passages.
**circadian rhythm** — repetition of events in a 24-hour period, especially biological occurrences that occur at about the same time each day.
**contracture** — a permanent shortening of muscle tissue due to immobility of a joint.
**electroencephalogram (EEG)** — a record of the electrical activity of the brain.

**enuresis** — involuntary voiding, especially at night; bed-wetting.

**exercise** — physical movement used to improve health or to correct a deformity.

**immobilization** — the causing of any part of the body to be incapable of movement.

**insomnia** — sleeplessness during the normal sleeping period.

**isometric exercise** — contracting the muscle with both ends fixed and with no change in the muscle length.

**isotonic exercise** — contracting the muscle with movement of the ends and with change in the muscle length.

**myclonic spasm** — a sudden, forceful contraction of muscles and jerking of the body that frequently occurs as a person is about to fall asleep.

**narcolepsy** — the uncontrolled desire for sleep; falling asleep instantly at inappropriate times.

**osteopororis** — a failure to form bony matrix, causing decreased deposits of calcium salts and thinning of the bone.

**rapid eye movements (REM)** — a stage of sleep characterized by rapid movement of the eyes, dreaming, and an increase in body functions.

**somnambulism** — walking in one's sleep.

**thrombosis** — the formation of a clot within a blood vessel.

**Valsalva's maneuver** — a series of actions of setting the chest muscles, holding one's breath, and straining against the closed glottis that affects the functioning of the heart.

---

The quality of our lives depends upon the ability of our body to grow and to develop in a manner that permits us to perform a wide variety of voluntary actions. For our health and well-being, we must be able to move about as well as be able to meet our other survival needs, including obtaining oxygen and food, maintaining an adequate fluid balance, and eliminating waste products on a regular basis. We spend more than two thirds of each day actively moving about and exercising, and the remaining one third of the time is devoted to sleeping and to restoring body tissues for the next period of activity. Even during sleep, most normal people are not entirely at rest but move about and change position frequently.

Motor activity in the form of muscular activity and exercise is essential in carrying out the tasks of daily living. All activities require some degree of mobility—for example, blinking the eye, changing one's facial expression, getting up in the morning, dressing, brushing one's teeth, eating breakfast, working, watching television, or reading a book. Additional programs of regular exercise contribute to the physiological maintenance of the body. People who exercise the large muscle groups are healthier, have better heart efficiency and circulation, and have improved muscular tone of vital organs than people who do not exercise. Motor activity stresses the cells, increasing their metabolic activity.

Although motor activity stimulates growth,

periods of sleep are essential to restore and to repair the body from the wear and tear of daily living. It is easier for people to go without food for 48 hours than to go without sleep for the same period of time. In addition, food deprivation will result in fewer adverse effects than deprivation of sleep. People need various types of sleep, and lack of particular types of sleep can affect their physical and mental functioning. Sleep is the recharging of the "physiological batteries."

In this chapter, the need for motor activity and the need for sleep will be discussed. Basic concepts underlying motor activity and exercise include principles of body alignment and positioning, the types of movement involved in all activities, and the types of activities in which people engage. The structures and systems used for activities are described briefly. The stages of sleep and the characteristics of each stage are described. Understanding the sleep cycle enables the nurse to assess the sleep needs of the patient who complains. "I didn't sleep at all last night," even though the patient's chart indicates that he or she had a good night.

The first level assessment focuses on the kinds of information needed and the types of behavior often observed. Examples of normal behaviors serve as a guideline for judging observed behaviors as adaptive or maladaptive in meeting the needs for sleep. The second level assessment describes common stimuli that affect exercise and sleep.

Statements of the problems related to activity and rest needs include a discussion of the effects of immobility on the various body systems. Several nursing interventions, including bed rest, are described briefly. These are methods that the nurse uses to help move the patient toward a more adapted state.

## BASIC CONCEPT OF EXERCISE AND SLEEP

### THE NEED FOR ACTIVITY

Have you ever thought what it would be like not to be able to walk, to use your arms, or to move about as you desired? What if you were unable to feed yourself, to scratch your nose when it tickles, to pick up a book, or to do any of the thousand other activities that are part of your daily life? Without the ability to move about, you would find that your life was greatly restricted and you would become dependent on others for many necessary services. The ability to move is essential for the optimal growth of the body, for the development of skills related to being independent, and for mastering obstacles. Without motor activity, one's quality of life is greatly reduced and one becomes a prisoner of an immobile body.

The ability to move about is so important that a large part of childhood is spent learning the physical skills and coordinating movements. Infants first learn to focus their eyes and to grasp an object, such as someone's finger. As they grow, they learn to sit up, begin to crawl, and progress to the more complex skills of walking, feeding themselves using a cup and spoon, buttoning clothes, and tying shoe laces. During the toddler stage of life, they refine the motor skills of running, jumping, climbing steps, and riding a tricycle and all the other activities that are part of their life. Throughout our lifetime, we are able to carry out the work that has to be done and to engage in the many art, sports, and other recreational activities that enrich our daily lives.

Motor activity is essential for the proper growth and development of the physical body as well as for the social and cultural activities of life. The muscles that move the skeletal frame enable all parts of the body to function more efficiently. Bones become harder and stronger from the stress of use and from bearing the body weight. Muscles gain shape and tone so that the position of the body can be maintained for periods of time without undue fatigue. One's heart becomes stronger and the stroke volume is increased, one's appetite is enhanced, and one's breathing becomes fuller and deeper as all parts of the lung are aerated. Activity stimulates the gastrointestinal tract and increases the peristaltic movement, which is necessary for proper absorption and elimination of solid wastes. Sitting up and walking about promotes the flow of urine by gravity, and prevents stagnation in the kidney pelvis or in the bladder itself.

### STRUCTURES INVOLVED IN MOTOR ACTIVITY

All voluntary movement results from the action of muscles on the skeletal system in response to the sensory and motor messages transmitted over the nerve pathways. Other systems of the body supply the oxygen and nutrients needed by the muscle and bone cells, remove waste products, and regulate the surrounding fluids and various chemical reactions. If these need areas are not fulfilled, one either lacks energy for vigorous or prolonged physical activity or the build-up of toxic wastes interferes with the ability of muscles to contract.

Motor activity primarily depends upon the functioning of the skeletal, muscular, and nervous systems.

**The Skeletal System.** Bones form the framework of the body and provide protection for various organs of the body. Bones are connected by means of tendons, ligaments, or fascia. Skeletal movement occurs at the joint where two or more bones meet. Joints are classified as fixed or movable, depending upon the amount of movement that they allow. Fixed joints are found in the sacrum and in the pubic symphysis where little or no movement occurs. The jaw, shoulder, elbow, and wrist and joints of the lower extremities are examples of movable joints.

**The Muscular System.** Muscles cause movement by contracting, which shortens them, or by relaxing and becoming longer. Muscles work in groups; thus, one set of muscles contracts to cause flexion at the joint and the opposing set of muscles when contracted straightens the joint or produces the movement of extension. Large, strong muscle groups are found in the shoulders and upper arms, the diaphragm, the abdomen, where they are essential in breathing, and the lower extremities, for ambulating. Shorter muscles, such as those connected to the spine, are less powerful.

Muscle tone is the tension in the muscle produced by the contraction of a few muscle fibers in relays, which provides periods of activity and rest for any given fiber. Most fibers run the entire length of the muscle and are stimulated by a nerve fiber that is attached at the middle. When stimulated, the contraction begins at the center and spreads toward both ends of the muscle simultaneously. This results in a strong and coordinated contraction of the muscle fibers.

**The Nervous System.** Muscles are stimulated by impulses transmitted by the nervous system. Stimuli are picked up by sensory nerve fibers that transmit the impulse up the spinal cord, through the reticular activating system (RAS) to the cortex of the brain where the motor nerve fibers are activated. One motor fiber may excite as many as 1000 muscle fibers, although the typical motor unit stimulates about 180 muscle fibers.

Other structures in the central nervous system (CNS) are important for motor activity. The sense of vision provides us with depth perception and a knowledge of the environment where activities occur. The equilibrium of the body is maintained through vision and the vestibules of the inner ear. The brain also provides us with the sense of proprioception, or knowing where your body is in space, and the relationship of the different parts of the body to each other.

## TYPES OF ACTIVITY

All voluntary movements consist of some combination of the various types of movement allowed at a given joint. Because most muscles are paired with muscles that have an opposing action, the following types of movements are produced:

*flexion* — the act of bending; reduces the angle formed by the bones being moved.

*extension* — the act of straightening; increases the angle formed by the bones being moved.

*abduction* — moving away from the midline of the body.

*adduction* — moving toward the midline of the body.

*supination* — turning the body or the palm upward and toward the front.

*pronation* — turning the body or the palm downward or toward the back.

*rotation* — turning around on an axis.

*circumduction* — a circular movement of a limb that forms an imaginary cone.

*hyperextension* — moving beyond the straight line, or more than a 180° angle.

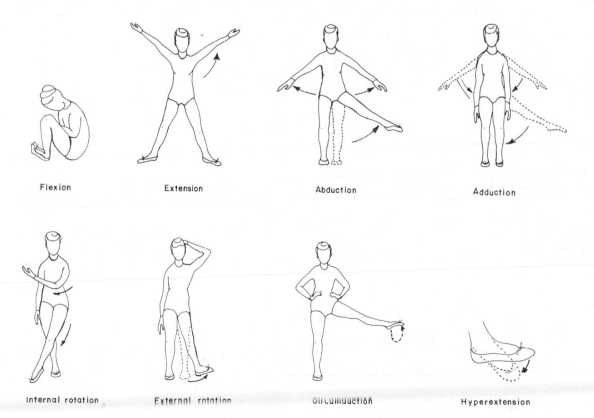

| Flexion | Extension | Abduction | Adduction |

| Internal rotation | External rotation | Circumduction | Hyperextension |

**Figure 13–1.** Types of movements that occur at joints.

All our activities, whether work or play, consist of various combinations of these movements. Consider the skill of walking. It is one of the first skills we learned when young, but, on examination, it is a complex combination of movements of many muscles and joints as well as involving several perceptions by the brain. Before taking a step, one must be able to balance, to know where the various parts of the body are in space, and to perceive sensations such as the soles of the feet on the ground or the wind blowing against one's body. When beginning to walk, the gluteal muscles are contracted to extend one hip joint, other muscles are flexed to bend the other hip while the hamstrings contract to bend the knee,

and the gastrocnemius muscle is flexed to raise the foot to take a step forward. Other muscles are brought into play as the body is propelled forward, the weight is shifted to the lead foot, and the arms swing back and forth with each succeeding step to keep the balance of the body. Other motor activities are equally as complex, as anyone who is learning to ride a bicycle, to drive a car, or to catheterize a patient can tell you.

Balance and equilibrium of the body are also achieved by motor activity. Proper positioning of the various segments of the body provides stability and requires the minimal amount of energy to overcome the forces of gravity. Without balance, body weight is distributed unevenly, muscles are

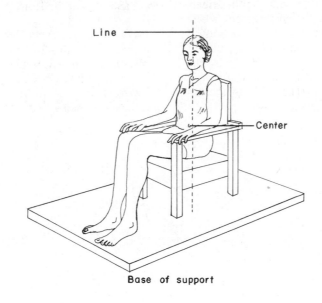

Base of support

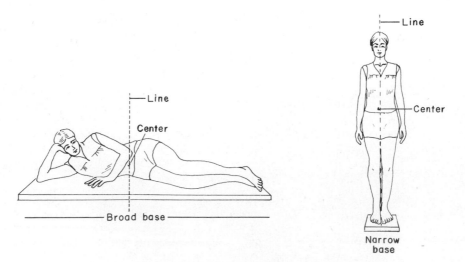

**Figure 13–2.**   Stability of the body when standing, sitting, or lying down.

unable to work together, and gravitational pull is increased. Balance is essential to keep the body erect and upright without assistance. The basic positions of the body are lying down in the supine, prone, or lateral position, sitting up, or ambulating. Segments of the body are placed in alignment with each other so that they are balanced and stable. Stability of the body is provided by a wide base of support, a low center of gravity, and the line of gravity that is within the base of support. The standing position is less stable than sitting or lying down.

Good alignment for activities begins with a broad base of support, with the feet about 8 to 12 inches apart, one slightly ahead of the other. The knees are flexed slightly to prevent locking, the buttocks are tucked under the body, and the pelvis is tilted forward. The abdomen is pulled in and the chest is elevated to permit full expansion of the lungs. Finally, the head is held erect over the neck, and the arms are allowed to fall naturally at the sides.

The alignment of patients on bed rest follows the principles of keeping the segments of the body in good relationship to each other to reduce the strain on muscles, ligaments, and tendons. The spine and torso are kept straight, the head and neck are aligned, and the extremities are supported as necessary. The arms and legs may be flexed for comfort but must be extended periodically to prevent stiffness and contractures. Most people are fairly active even when resting in bed and move about frequently to change their position and to relieve pressure on various parts of their bodies. Studies have shown that people make between 25 and 225 spontaneous movements during an eight-hour period of sleep and that crying, hungry infants make as many as 50 movements per minute. When one is unable to move about independently, it is necessary that assistance be provided to change one's position at least once every two hours.

## PRINCIPLES OF MOTOR ACTIVITY

When assessing a patient's need for activity and exercise and when planning the care to meet these needs, nurses rely on principles, such as

1. *Active exercise of muscles is the most beneficial, but passive exercise is better than no exercise.* In passive exercise, the nurse or therapist moves the body part without help from the patient.

2. *"Use it or lose it."* Unless muscles are exercised regularly, they lose their tonicity and strength. They become smaller in size as the

fibers atrophy, and the effects of immobility can be seen throughout the entire body.

3. *The motion allowed at any joint is its range-of-motion, and any movement beyond the range that produces pain should be avoided.* The range-of-motion of each joint should be performed at least twice a day unless medically contraindicated.

4. *Flexor muscles are more powerful than extensor muscles.* Positions of flexion should be alternated with positions of extension to avoid contractures or permanent shortening of the muscles.

5. *Muscles must have a sufficient amount of oxygen and nutrients to supply the energy needed for the activity.* During very strenuous exercise, additional energy is supplied by anaerobic (without oxygen) chemical reactions but only for short periods of time.

6. *Larger muscles are stronger and capable of more work than smaller muscles.* When lifting, pushing, or pulling heavy objects, the larger gluteal and thigh muscles are more effective than the smaller muscles of the back.

7. *The weight of any body part on another surface produces pressure, and frequent moving reduces the effects of pressure.* Pressure on skin structures reduces the blood circulation and leads to cellular breakdown and decubitus ulcers within a matter of hours. Pressure on body organs as a result of remaining in one position produces many other ill effects, including pneumonia, formation of blood clots, hypoxia, and renal calculi.

## SKILLS FOR DAILY LIVING

Only through the ability to perform motor activities do people learn to become independent, overcome obstacles, and gain the ability to carry out the developmental tasks appropriate to their stage of life. Infants are the most helpless people, being dependent on others for their basic needs and comfort. As children grow and learn motor skills, they are able to meet more of their own needs and to gain increasing control of their environment. The skills that people need to live independently, to take care of their own needs, and to carry out the pattern of their daily lives are called the activities of daily living (ADL). These skills include:

*Balance and equilibrium* — individuals must learn to balance their head, to sit up, and to stand erect without support, and to maintain their position in spite of some degree of resistance.
*Ambulation* — people must be able to stand erect, stand on one foot, move both legs in ex-

tension and flexion, and stabilize the knee to bear weight on the feet. Unrestricted ambulation means that people can walk up and down steps, around objects, and run when indicated.

*Skills for hygiene and basic physiological needs* — individuals are able to perform activities such as bathing, oral hygiene, nail care, toileting, care of the hair, and shaving without assistance. They are able to obtain food and to feed themselves. In dressing, they are able to button clothing, use zippers, tie shoelaces, put on pullover and cardigan types of garments as well as pants, and manipulate fasteners in front or in back.

When people become ill, they are unable to carry out all their activities of daily living. Assuming the sick role allows them to become dependent upon others for their care and excuses them from their other social roles. The nursing plan of care provides assistance and support in carrying out the essential activities of daily living until the patient is able to do so without help.

## THE NEED FOR REST AND SLEEP

In the same way that motor activity is necessary to stimulate growth, rest and sleep are the means for restoring and repairing bodily structures and functions. During rest and sleep, most physiological processes slow down, allowing restoration to take place. When engaging in physical activities over an extended period of time, it is necessary to rest periodically to give the muscles time to recover from their fatigue. This period of rest provides time for replenishing the supply of glycogen and oxygen needed by muscles for additional activity. As these fuels provide the energy for movement, the build-up of metabolic byproducts serves to slow down the muscular activity and diminish the strength; this is the cause of fatigue.

Rest is more than just a state of physical inactivity. It consists of physical and psychological serenity and peacefulness. Rest contributes to the restoration process as one relaxes, and emotional tension and stress diminish. People are more apt to rest when there is a predictable pattern or an organized routine of everyday events in their lives rather than when unexpected and chaotic happenings occur over which they have little control. For most people, and especially those who are ill, rest means periods of peace and quiet during the day, freedom from numerous interruptions, provisions for privacy as desired, and the completion of purposeful or meaningful activities as well as being accepted by others and being treated with respect.

One's need for sleep is dependent upon one's physiological and psychological make-up, accustomed pattern of sleep, and desire to defer sleep to carry out other activities. Sleep is one of the circadian rhythms that occurs on a predictable cycle each day. One's rhythmic nature of sleep emerges in about the third month of life. Although people vary in the amount of sleep that they need, they tend to require a definite quantity of sleep each day, ranging between six and nine hours for most adults. More sleeping time is required by children.

## CYCLES OF REST AND SLEEP

People carry out their activities of daily living, including eating, working, and sleeping, according to their 24-hour "clock" that establishes their regular cycle. These cycles are called circadian rhythms (*circa* — a Latin word meaning about and *dies* meaning a day) and include other biological functions, such as the sleep cycle, fluctuations of body temperature, and the release of hormones, that occur on a daily cycle. Circadian rhythms tend to persist and to adjust slowly to changes that result from deprivation of sleep, working a night shift, or rapid travel through several time zones that causes "jet lag." In addition to the 24-hour "clock," a basic rest and activity cycle of 90 minutes has been identified. During periods of sleep, as well as when awake, there are periods of activity and alertness followed by periods of slowness and inaction that occur on a 90-minute cycle for most adults. It has been found that children have 45- and 60-minute cycles for rest and activity.

## STAGES OF SLEEP

Sleep is not just a quiet and passive state that resembles unconsciousness but is, in fact, an established pattern of repeated cycles, or stages, each with definite characteristics. There are two distinct cycles of sleep: the nonrapid eye movement (NREM) cycle, often referred to as slow wave sleep, and the rapid eye movement (REM) cycle. These cycles cover a 90-minute period, and there are four or five cycles each night.

**NREM Cycle of Sleep.** The type of sleep that occurs during NREM, or the nonrapid eye movement, cycle of sleep is the obligatory type of sleep. When the sleep need arises, obligatory sleep must be met first because one's physical well-being seems to depend upon obtaining an adequate amount of NREM sleep. NREM sleep is thought to be responsible for physiological restoration. It consists of four stages, each with slightly different types of brain wave activity identified on electroencephalograms (EEGs).

| Stage | Characteristics | EEG Waves |
|-------|-----------------|-----------|
| Stage I | Dreamy, relaxed, somewhat aware of surroundings, has fleeting thoughts, and is easily aroused; may have myoclonic jerking movements | Alpha rhythm |
| Stage II | Unaware of surroundings, but easily awakened; has fleeting thoughts or dreams | Some spindles appear |
| Stage III | Progressively deeper sleep; vital signs decrease and oxygen consumption falls below normal; difficult to awaken | More sleep spindles and delta waves begin to appear |
| Stage IV | Deep sleep of oblivion; very relaxed, little movement occurs; physiological functions slow, or below normal; difficult to awaken; may have enuresis or sleep-walking; high levels of growth hormone | Delta waves predominate |

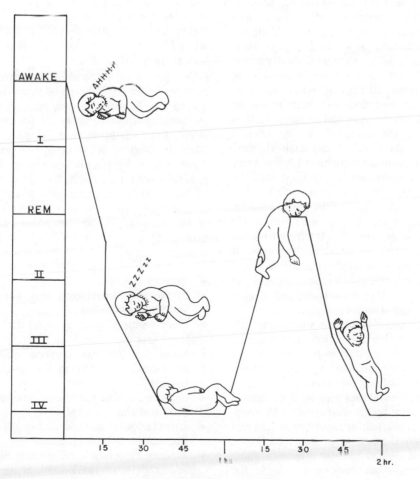

**Figure 13–3.** Stages of sleep.

The sleeping person progresses, in an orderly fashion, through Stages I, II, and III in about 40 minutes and reaches Stage IV of the cycle. Most Stage IV sleep occurs in the first three sleep cycles, validating the old saying that "the best sleep comes before midnight." Young children have more Stage IV sleep than other people, and the amount diminishes with age until it is no longer observed on the EEG of older people. In the normal sleep pattern, the amount of Stage IV sleep decreases and the amount of REM sleep increases; thus, most deep sleep occurs in the first hours of sleep, and dreaming of REM sleep occurs in the last few hours before awakening.

From the deep sleep of Stages III and IV, people gradually go back through the stages. However, instead of entering Stage I or awakening, they enter the REM stage. The entire cycle lasts from 90 to 100 minutes and is repeated four or five times during the night. When people are awakened during one of the stages, they have to begin with Stage I and proceed through the stages of sleep again. People who are awakened frequently may get little deep sleep and be deprived of REM sleep. Hospitalized patients often suffer from deprivation of essential sleep because of interruptions for nursing interventions.

During part of the night, body temperature falls as much as 1° to 2°, then, in the early morning hours, it begins to rise again as the adrenal hormones secreted during the REM stages increase the metabolism. Body temperature reaches its peak during the morning and remains stable at that level during the day until evening when it begins to fall again in its circadian rhythm. People who are good sleepers have a fall in body temperature that corresponds with their bedtime. Their body temperature continues to fall during the night and then rises before they awaken. They feel energetic and alert in the morning. On the other hand, people who tend to be poor sleepers have less of a temperature decline at bedtime. Their body temperature is still falling in the morning; thus, when they arise, they still feel tired and would prefer to stay in bed longer. People who are good sleepers and early risers are often called the larks, and those who reach their peak later in the day are called the owls. The differences between these two groups lie in the relationship of their circadian rhythms and the effects of them on biological functions.

Studies have shown that the level of human growth hormone is higher during Stage IV sleep. This hormone is needed for regulating height and weight, speeding the healing of fractured bones, and stimulating tissue growth. Through these functions, it plays an important role in the physical restoration of the body. It is no coinci-

dence that during the years when growth is most rapid, in young children, more hours are spent in Stage IV sleep when the growth hormone level is highest.

Research studies indicate that reduction of the incidence of heart attacks, asthma attacks, and bleeding ulcers can be achieved by prolonging the NREM, or Stage IV sleep. The amount of Stage IV sleep can be increased by additional physical activity during the day, the use of barbiturate drugs, and the ingestion of alcohol.

**REM Stage of Sleep.** The REM, or rapid eye movement, cycle of sleep occurs between Stages I and II and is important for psychological restoration. During this stage, dreaming takes place and the eyes move rapidly. The need for REM sleep is related to the amount of stress and anxiety that one is experiencing. Luce (1971) stated that "sleep scientists have concluded that REM sleep is a time when we adapt emotionally. In the stillness of slumber, the busy mind may be pulling out the file drawers of memory, placing the images and feelings of our most recent experiences into the proper slots for future memory." During periods of great stress, people may spend considerably more time in REM sleep, which makes them feel that they "didn't sleep a wink all night," and do not feel well because less time was spent in NREM sleep.

The period of REM sleep lasts from 7 to 15 minutes in the early hours of sleep, increasing to 10 to 20 minutes in the later cycles before awakening. Approximately 25 per cent of one's sleeping time is spent in REM sleep. If one has been deprived of REM sleep, one goes into the REM cycle more quickly and remains in it longer, as if to make up for the lack of sleep. In the early cycles of REM, dreams consist of daily events of an ordinary nature; however, in the later cycles, in the morning, dreams are more symbolic and bizarre. Other characteristics of the REM cycle include

- Hard to arouse
- Rapid eye movements that are observable under closed eyelids
- Flaccid muscle tone and total slackness of the lower jaw
- Males of all ages have penile erections
- Increased oxygen metabolism and rise in body temperature
- Increased gastric secretions that peak between 1:00 AM and 3:00 AM
- Irregular pulse and respiratory rate with wide fluctuation in blood pressure
- Increased secretion of adrenal hormones in spurts. (The adrenal hormones are secreted an average of eight times per day, five times dur-

ing the REM cycles in the early morning and three other times during the day. They prepare the person mentally and physically to meet the new day.)

**Nursing Implications Regarding REM Sleep.** Based on knowledge about the effects of REM sleep on the body, certain implications emerge that are important for nurses to know. Patients with epilepsy have more convulsions during the early morning hours before arising for the day than at any other time. Brain activity and temperature rise during REM sleep; more REM sleep occurs in the early hours of the morning. Nurses should closely observe patients for any signs of convulsions.

Studies have shown that many medical emergencies, such as heart attacks, asthma, and bleeding ulcers, take place during REM sleep. Patients who have heart problems are more apt to have myocardial infarction and cardiac arrhythmias during the early morning hours when more time is spent in REM sleep than at any other time. Those with angina tend to awaken at this time with chest pain and shortness of breath because both pulse and respiratory rates are irregular during REM sleep. People who have gastric ulcers are more apt to awaken with pain at about the time of the second REM sleep cycle, which occurs between 1:00 AM and 3:00 AM, when

gastric secretions are greatest. In addition to these emergencies, people who are aroused directly from REM sleep may initially be unable to move until their muscle tone returns, usually in a matter of a few seconds.

REM sleep is decreased by frequent interruptions of the sleep cycle so that this stage may not be reached or insufficient time is available for this cycle. Sedatives, tranquilizers, and alcohol also reduce the amount of REM sleep.

## FIRST LEVEL ASSESSMENT

The pattern of our daily lives consists of the many motor activities in which we engage and the periods of rest and sleep following any physical exertion. Both activity and rest are essential for our health and well-being, and the beneficial effects of both can be seen throughout the body.

In the adaptation method of nursing, the nurse focuses on the patient's ability to meet activity and rest needs by assessing the following areas: functions of the musculoskeletal system, maintenance of body posture and position, ability to perform all activities of daily living, and sleep habits, including the quality and amount of sleep usually obtained. (See Table 13–1.)

**Table 13–1.** ASSESSMENT OF MOTOR ACTIVITY AND REST NEEDS

| Factors to Assess | Normal Behaviors | Maladaptive Behaviors |
|---|---|---|
| *Musculoskeletal functions* | | |
| Body parts and appearance | All body parts present and in proper proportion<br>Symmetry of body | Amputation of _____<br>Curvature of spine; hump back<br>Asymmetry: Body part _____<br>_____ |
| Muscle mass and size | Moderate in size; good definition and tone | Atrophy; hypertrophy |
| Movements | Smooth and coordinated<br>Deliberate and purposeful | Jerky; uncoordinated; tremors; constant motion; very fast; very slow |
| Range-of-motion | No limitation of motion or pain in a given joint | Flexion contracture of _____<br>Pain on movement<br>Foot–drop |
| Strength | Grip in both hands equal<br>Moves independently and overcomes some resistance | Weak grip – right, left, both<br>Requires support; needs assistance; easily fatigued |
| *Posture* | | |
| Balance and equilibrium | Holds head up and balanced over body<br>Bears weight on both feet | Unstable; wobbly; sways<br>Unstable; unable to bear weight |
| Change of position | Able to turn over and to sit up without assistance | Requires help to turn, to change position, to sit up |

## ACTIVITIES OF DAILY LIVING

One hallmark of health and adaptation is the ability to carry out all activities of daily living independently. With maturity, individuals are able to meet their own basic needs and to carry out the developmental tasks of selecting a mate, establishing a home of their own, raising a family, providing for financial needs, preparing and engaging in their life work, relating to others, developing leisure time activities, and meeting their civic responsibilities. However, when illness strikes, they are unable to carry on all the activities that constitute the usual pattern of their lives. They are obliged to take on the sick role, give up their social roles and responsibilities, and accept help.

During the second, or acute, stage of illness, people not only are unable to work, maintain their home, or engage in other social activities, but also have difficulty in meeting their own basic needs. The disease, the treatments, and their age as well as other factors that prevent them from carrying out these universal actions are considered stimuli, or influencing factors. The degree to which infants, children, the sick, and the aged are unable to perform these activities indicates the degree of their dependence upon others for their care. To meet basic physical needs, people are assessed according to their ability to perform the following activities:

1. *Need for nourishment* — open cartons and containers; cut meat and vegetables; chew and swallow food; feed self by getting food to mouth
2. *Dressing and undressing* — obtain, put on, and take off clothes; use zippers and buckles; fasten buttons; tie shoelaces
3. *Bathing* — turn on and run water; adjust water termperature; get into or out of tub or shower; dry body with towel
4. *Grooming* — comb or brush hair; brush teeth; shave; apply deodorant and make-up; shampoo hair; wash clothes
5. *Elimination* — control of bowel and bladder; get on and off toilet alone; use toilet paper
6. *Ambulation* — balance and stand; walk without assistance; go up and down stairs or curbs; good walking gait; stable when erect

As patients progress into the convalescent stage of illness and begin to take more interest in returning home and resuming their usual pattern of life, additional activities of daily living assume importance. By assessing these areas, the nurse often discovers that patients are worried about their ability to get along without help. The nurse may be able to help resolve some potential problems. The additional activities of daily living focus on the following areas:

1. *Housekeeping and maintenance of the home* — ability to wash and dry dishes; shop for food; make the bed; wash clothes; use the stove and refrigerator to prepare meals; dust and keep the home orderly; perform seasonal tasks such as gardening, washing windows, putting on storm windows, doing minor repairs, mowing the lawn, shoveling snow
2. *Management of finances* — have access to some financial resources; make daily purchases; write checks to do banking; pay bills on time

**Table 13–2.   ASSESSMENT OF ABILITY TO PERFORM ACTIVITIES OF DAILY LIVING**

| Factor to Assess | Normal Behaviors | Maladaptive Behaviors |
|---|---|---|
| Nourishment | Feeds self | Unable to open cartons, cut food, feed self |
| Dressing | Dresses and undresses self<br>Selects own clothing | Unable to dress and undress self, use zipper, buttons, buckles, ties |
| Bathing | Washes and bathes self | Bed bath<br>Partial bath<br>Unable to use tub or shower without help |
| Grooming | Performs own grooming needs | Needs assistance for oral hygiene, shaving, combing hair, care of nails, use of make-up |
| Elimination | Voluntary control of elimination | Unable to go to bathroom, get on or off toilet without help |
| Ambulation | Ambulates without assistance<br>Stable when standing erect<br>Normal gait when walking | Unable to balance on feet—unstable, wobbly<br>Shuffles feet—short or tottering steps<br>Has difficulty climbing steps |

## REST AND SLEEP

People vary widely in the amount of sleep that they need to leave them feeling rested and restored. Research in the nature of sleep has shown that the quality and quantity of sleep in addition to the number of awakenings during the night vary with different age groups.

Sleep habits are formed early in one's life and are synchronized with various biological circadian rhythms. The amount of sleep that an individual needs remains fairly constant throughout his lifetime. Children spend more hours in sleep and receive more sleep in Stage IV, with its increased amounts of growth hormone that provides for their spurts of rapid growth. Older people have far less deep sleep and less REM sleep, with decrease in dreaming. As a result, older people are far more vulnerable to the effects of sleep deprivation than are younger people.

Table 13–3 provides some norms, or standards, that nurses can use to assess behaviors related to sleep and rest for different age groups.

Newborn infants spend about half their sleeping time in REM sleep and the other half in NREM sleep, in cycles that occur about every 55 to 60 minutes. By eight months of age, they do more of their sleeping during the night hours, in cycles that are the same as the 90 minute average seen throughout the rest of one's lifetime. The amount of REM sleep has declined at the same time that the amount of NREM has increased, although the amount of sleep in Stage IV declines over the years, until it is no longer seen on the EEG records of older adults.

Elderly people need the same amount of sleep, but it now takes them longer to fall asleep, they awaken earlier in the day, and they may be off schedule with release of hormones or other biological cycles. They awaken more often, as many as six times per night by 60 years of age, or about once for every cycle of sleep. They awaken to void, or empty the bladder, more often during the night. Because more time is spent awake during the night, many older people take naps during the day and distribute their sleeping time on the 90 minute rest and activity cycle. Adult males take more naps than do females; however, this may be due to changes in lifestyle and retirement.

The quality of sleep obtained through naps varies — for example, naps taken in the morning hours continue to replenish REM sleep and naps taken in the late afternoon hours provide the deep sleep of NREM, with no REM sleep. People who nap in the afternoon are often more difficult to arouse and feel logey when awakened. Hospitalized patients who have slept at night with the aid of sleeping medications may benefit from morning naps that provide an opportunity for REM sleep. Those who dreamed or who had light sleep may benefit more from a nap later in the day that leads to deep sleep.

Table 13–4 provides the areas to assess for rest and sleep needs.

## SECOND LEVEL ASSESSMENT

Various factors influence peoples' abilities to meet their needs for motor activity and rest or sleep. The assessed maladaptive or ineffectual behaviors are most often caused or influenced by the following stimuli:

1. *Disease of the musculoskeletal or nervous system.* Orthopedic conditions that interfere with ambulation and physical activities include fractures of bones, sprains and strains of structures surrounding the joint, osteomyelitis, rheumatoid and osteoarthritis, herniated intervertebral disc, low back strain, amputation, and so on. Injury and disease of the central nervous system affects both mobility and rest. Common conditions in-

Table 13–3. SLEEP AND REST NEEDS

| Age Group | Total (hr) | NREM Sleep | REM Sleep | Cycles (min) | Awakenings |
|---|---|---|---|---|---|
| Infants | | | | | |
|   Newborn | 19–20 | 50% | 50% | 55–60 | q 3 hr |
|   4 wk | 16½ | 50% | 50% | 55–60 | q 4 hr |
|   8 mo | 13 | 66% | 33% | 85–90 | 0 |
| Child–8 yr | 10–12 | 3 hr IV | 25% | 85–90 | 0 |
| Teen-ager | 7–8½ | 2½ hr IV | 25% | 85–90 | 0 |
| Adult–under 35 yr | 7–8½ | 1½ hr IV | 25% | 85–90 | 1 |
| Adult–over 60 yr | 7–8½ | no IV | 18% | 85–90 | 1–6 |

Table 13–4.  ASSESSMENT OF SLEEP AND REST NEEDS

| Factors to Assess | Normal Behaviors | Maladaptive Behaviors |
|---|---|---|
| Amount of sleep | Usual bedtime _____<br>Usual rising time _____ | Too few, too many hours of sleep |
| Amount of rest | 7–8½ hr of bed rest or as appropriate for age | Bed rest _____ hr<br>Less than 7 hr, more than 8½ hr<br>Naps—morning; afternoon |
| Interruptions of sleep | No interruptions<br>Awakens at end of sleep cycles as appropriate for age | Interruptions for treatments _____ times<br>Unable to go back to sleep easily<br>Voids _____ times during night |
| Quality of sleep | Awakens well rested, refreshed<br><br>Falls asleep easily | Tired, yawning<br>Inability to concentrate<br>Dark circles around eyes<br>Use of sedatives, other drugs, alcohol to initiate sleep |

clude dizziness, Meniere's disease, strokes, paralysis, coma, and encephalitis.

2. *Diseases of other parts of the body.* Any disease or condition that reduces the amount of oxygen or nutrients available for energy needed to move about reduces activity, including anemia, congestive heart failure, myocardial infarction, asthma, pneumonia, emphysema, vomiting, hepatitis, intestinal obstruction, ulcerative colitis, and widespread cancer. Infections that cause fevers and toxic reactions also limit activity and cause changes in the rest and sleep needs.

3. *General medical treatment and restriction of activity level.* Physicians most often order some restriction in the level of activities permitted by the patient. These restrictions include bed rest, bathroom privileges only, the use of a commode, or sitting up in chair several times a day. Other limitations result from surgical incisions, bulky dressings on wounds, use of traction, presence of Foley catheter and drainage tube, use of intravenous infusion, or use of monitoring equipment or other machines.

4. *Use of drugs or alcohol.* Drugs can only increase or decrease the normal functions of the tissues or organ. Alcohol, sedatives, narcotics, tranquilizers, and other drugs that act as depressants reduce the performance or endurance of motor activities and promote more rest and sleep. Drugs that stimulate, or increase, functions, especially those of the central nervous system, also interfere with rest and activities.

5. *Age.* As stated previously, physical activities are learned at different stages in childhood and adolescence as one matures toward greater independence. Older people slow down and are less active than they were when younger. The sleep pattern also varies for different age groups, in

amount of sleep, type of sleep, and number of awakenings during the night.

6. *Pain and psychological stress.* Physical activity and sleep are inhibited by pain, stress, anxiety, fears, or worries.

7. *External factors and physical environment.* The fulfillment of one's rest and sleep needs is often related to external factors, such as a familiar bed or surroundings, light during the day and darkness at night, decrease in the amount of noise, and freedom from noxious odors or other distractions. Physical movement requires space for the activity and may be influenced by weather and temperature and factors such as air pollution.

8. *Internal factors, drives, or interests.* Activity and sleep are affected by one's circadian rhythms, or cycles, for many biological functions, one's sleep and activity patterns that have been learned, one's level of knowledge and understanding about health needs, and one's social and cultural values or beliefs.

## PROBLEMS RELATED TO ACTIVITY AND REST NEEDS

Problems that arise in this need area are primarily those of activity, especially the lack of activity or immobility. Although the amount of rest or sleep is occasionally a problem, lack of sleep often serves as an influencing factor, or stimulus, for the amount of activities performed. People often say, "I'm too tired to do that now, I didn't sleep well last night," or "Just leave me alone, I want to take a nap now," as a result of lack of sleep. The problems that nurses encounter as a result of assessing the physical need for activity are those of too much activity, too little activity, the wrong kind of activity, or no activity. Too little, or decreased, activity is by far the most common problem. Statements of such problems may include:

Patient is excessively active due to high level of anxiety.

Patient is unable to turn over or carry out his or her other activities of daily living due to extreme weakness.

Specific activities could be specified in the definition of the problem or described by the list of behaviors pertaining to what the patient can or cannot do without assistance.

Patient has continual purposeless tremor of arms due to _____.

Patient has no voluntary motor activity due to comatose state.

Patient has difficulty sleeping due to postoperative pain.

Patient has insufficient amount of sleep due to _____.

Inactivity not only is the most common problem of the need area but also is a major stimulus for problems that affect other needs and other systems of the body. The effects of immobility are widespread throughout the body and also alter one's emotional and intellectual functioning. Close examination of immobility reveals the extent of these related problems.

## EFFECTS OF IMMOBILITY

During illness, most people are unable to carry out their usual activities of daily living because of the distress caused by the symptoms, pain, or the effects of medication or other treatments. They are instructed to rest in bed because rest is usually necessary to reduce the demands on the body and allows for the repairs needed for tissues to recover. People who are ill also have less energy available for moving about actively because more

**Table 13-5.** EFFECTS OF IMMOBILITY ON THE VARIOUS SYSTEMS OR PARTS OF THE BODY AND THE RESULTING HEALTH PROBLEMS OR COMPLICATIONS ASSOCIATED WITH THESE CHANGES

| Body Part or System | Effect of Immobility | Problem, or Complication |
|---|---|---|
| Cardiovascular system | Venous stasis<br>Venous obstruction or injury<br>Edema, mottling of skin | Thrombosis<br>Pulmonary embolism |
| Skin and integument | Redness of skin<br>Ischemia and necrosis of tissues | Decubitus ulcer |
| Respiratory system | Decreased pulmonary ventilation<br>Slower respiration<br>Stasis of secretions | Hypoxia<br>Hypostatic pneumonia<br>Atelectasis |
| Heart | Use of Valsalva's maneuver 10–20 times/hr by those on bed rest<br>Increased workload | Tachycardia<br>Cardiac arrest<br>Increased pulse rate |
| Muscles | Decreased tension and size of muscle mass with disuse for 48 hr<br>Fibrosis of connecting tissues and shortening of fibers | Atrophy, weakness<br><br>Contractures |
| Skeletal system | Loss of calcium from bone matrix<br>Decrease in bone size | Osteoporosis<br>Bone pain |
| Urinary system | Precipitation of calcium salts<br>Stasis of urine | Renal calculi<br>Infection, backache |
| Gastrointestinal system | Anorexia<br>Metabolic change to catabolism and negative nitrogen balance<br>Decreased peristalsis | Malnutrition<br>Metabolic acidosis<br><br>Constipation, impaction |
| Brain | Decreased sensory input<br>Altered sensory perception<br>Decreased mental functioning<br>Feelings of insecurity, anxiety | Sensory deprivation<br>Confusion, disorientation<br>Boredom<br>Depression or regression |

energy is needed to cope with the changes brought about by the illness and for healing damaged tissues.

Although rest is beneficial, confinement to bed must be moderated by some degree of exercise or movement. Lack of activity produces effects on many systems and organs of the body. Immobility is a very important stimulus for problems and complications, such as decubitus ulcers, constipation, lack of appetite, contractures, formation of blood clots, and mental disturbances. These ill effects are summarized in Table 13–5.

Early signs of immobilization are less dramatic than the complications listed in Table 13–5; however, early signs are equally important. Early signs occur within a day or two and include the rapid loss of strength in muscles, weakness, becoming easily fatigued, poor coordination, stiffness in the joints, abdominal distention, and metabolic changes seen in the laboratory chemistries of blood and urine samples. Disability occurs rapidly, and recovery takes a long time — for example, it may take six weeks for blood chemistries to return to normal, decubitus ulcers often take months to heal, and contractures of muscles lead to permanent damage to muscles, tendons, and ligaments.

## DECUBITUS ULCERS

Decreased voluntary movement by patients often leads to decubitus ulcers, also known as pressure sores, or bed sores. They are the result of pressure on the skin over a bony prominence caused by lying in one position for a period of time. The usual location of decubitus ulcers is over the sacrum, but they also occur over the head of the femur on each hip, the heel, the bony prominence of the ankle, the elbows, and the scapula. The first sign of pressure is redness of the skin from impaired circulation through the skin lying over the bone. The cells turn darker red or bluish in color as a result of lack of oxygen and nutrients, and they begin to die, causing the skin to break down.

Decubitus ulcers can occur in just a few hours from lying in one position. Some patients have been known to develop them while lying on a firm operating room table during a lengthy operation. People are at risk of having pressure sores if they are unable to change their position at least every hour, or about 25 times in a 24-hour period. Other people who are at risk of having their skin break down are those immobilized for any reason, elderly people, those with poor nutrition, those with circulatory diseases, and the very weak. Decubitus often become infected and take weeks and months of treatment to heal,

especially when structures under the skin are involved.

## CONTRACTURES

Contractures are "frozen joints" that have little or no movement as a result of fibrotic changes in the tendons, ligaments, and the muscles themselves. This prevents the muscle from contracting or stretching and further limits motor activity. Contractures are generally of the flexion type because the flexor muscles are stronger than extensors; thus, a contracture of the elbow, hip, or wrist prevents the person from straightening out or extending that body part.

Contractures can occur in an immobilized joint in less than three weeks. The damage is permanent and difficult to treat, even with the use of surgery to excise the fibrotic tissue or to transplant tendons. Contractures that develop in hospitalized patients are considered to be the result of ineffective nursing care because they can be prevented through proper positioning, range-of-motion exercises, and early ambulation of the patient.

## DEPRIVATION OF SLEEP

Disturbances of rest and sleep cause fatigue and tend to decrease the amount of activity that is undertaken. Patients who have been deprived of their normal amount of sleep show behavioral changes, including withdrawal, lack of concentration, apathy and depression that alternate with periods of anxiety, irritability, feelings of detachment, or increased aggression. Even though people go to bed and awaken at the usual time, they may not have gotten their usual amount of sleep, as a result of numerous interruptions of the sleep cycle.

Interruptions and awakenings interfere with the deep sleep associated with Stage IV and REM sleep. Lack of Stage IV sleep makes people feel physically uncomfortable, depressed, and concerned about vague complaints or changes in normal physical functions. When deprived of sleep for more than 48 hours, many people exhibit serious mental changes, including confusion and hallucinations and other signs of psychotic behaviors.

Deprivation of REM sleep disturbs the circadian rhythm of the body, and, although some adrenal hormones are secreted, they are out of tune with the biological rhythms. Instead of giving the boost and vitality that one needs to meet the new day, the decreased amounts of hormones lead to feelings of fatigue, depression, and loss of concentration, even to the extent of forgetting what one was saying in conversation. Other mental symptoms related to lack of REM sleep include irritability, apathy, the display of poor judgment, and increased sensitivity to pain or discomfort.

Many people suffer from insomnia, which refers to the difficulty one has in falling asleep and remaining asleep throughout the night. All stimuli that interfere with sleep are causes of insomnia, such as sensitivity to slight noises, light, sharing a bed with another person, a heavy meal eaten before retiring, drinking beverages containing caffeine, weight of blankets, the degree of firmness of a mattress or pillow, and personal problems or worries. In the hospital, patients are frequently given sedatives that help them to fall asleep more easily.

## NURSING INTERVENTIONS

Nursing interventions that are used to solve problems related to rest and mobility needs include turning the patient every hour, as needed, positioning and maintaining proper body alignment for lying down, sitting, and standing, using mechanical aids for mobility, and having the patient do various exercises to increase activity.

## PROVIDING BED REST

Whenever someone complains of a pain or not feeling well, the usual advice is to take it easy and to get more rest. People who take on the sick role generally have some limitation of activity prescribed by the physician, often in the form of bed rest.

The term bed rest means different things to people, and it is necessary for the nurse to determine what is meant when bed rest is ordered. Complete or strict bed rest generally means that the person is to be in bed for the entire 24-hour period. He or she is not to get out of bed for any reason, to sit on the side of the bed, to dangle the feet over the edge, or to be overly active in bed. Some people may even interpret complete bed rest to mean that the nurse feeds the patient, gives him or her a bed bath, and assists with all activities.

Bed rest, as it is generally used, means that patients are confined to bed but they are allowed to carry out the activities of eating meals, caring for their personal hygiene, taking a bath, and using the bed pan in bed with assistance, as needed, from the nursing staff. Limited exercise is permitted and encouraged. Bed rest with bathroom privileges allows the patient more activity by permitting him or her to go to the bathroom several times a day.

**Beneficial Effects of Bed Rest.** Rest in bed is more than mere physical inactivity. It should be a state of tranquility and peacefulness for the person who is resting. However, it is difficult to achieve the rest when anxiety, worry, or fear stir one's emotions and churn one's mind. To promote rest, nurses can plan nursing interventions that provide

1. Privacy when it is needed.
2. A satisfying order to each day's events, a predictable schedule that shows that things are under control and in capable hands.
3. Freedom from unnecessary interruption, minor irritations, such as noise or chatter, and pain or physical discomfort.
4. Acceptance of patients as being important and concern for their personal problems that hinder rest or treatment.

Bed rest is beneficial as a method of alleviating pain by decreasing any movement that irritates injured tissues, by reducing the oxygen demands of the body, and by reducing the workload of an injured heart muscle. Rest promotes healing and repair of tissues, helps the return of venous circulation through the elevation of the feet, and supports the entire body of weak and debilitated patients.

## POSITIONING

Nurses need to pay particular attention to positioning the patient and maintaining the alignment whether the patient is lying in bed, sitting in a chair, or ambulating. Cradles and footboards are used to remove the pressure of bedding from the toes and to keep the feet in a neutral position to prevent foot drop. Pillows are used to support other parts of the body. One of the greatest tragedies is having a patient walk into the hospital with a treatable disease and then develop permanent contractures and foot drop that prevents him from standing and walking again. These complications of immobility can be largely prevented by nursing care that is devoted to correct positioning, range-of-motion exercise of joints, nutritional status, and early ambulation or exercise.

## MECHANICAL AIDS

Some people must rely on the use of mechanical devices to increase their level of activity. These devices include casts and braces applied to support parts of the body, and wheelchairs, walkers, crutches, and canes. Nurses teach patients the proper use and precautions to be observed with these aids.

## EXERCISES TO INCREASE ACTIVITY

Many people in this country perform less physical work than did people in previous generations. They lead sedentary lives, do less manual labor, and spend more hours sitting down. They tend to be spectators rather than participants in sports and in other forms of exercise. People can improve their health and the functioning of their bodies through increased exercise. This should be done gradually, allowing for a warm-up time to stretch and to ready the muscles, and after a medical examination to rule out any contraindications for an exercise program. Motor activities that produce dynamic effects on the body systems include walking, running, jogging, and swimming and particularly exercises that involve arm movements, such as gardening, washing windows, or playing ball.

Exercise may be incorporated into the nursing care plan for patients to increase their activity levels. Breathing exercises are often taught to the preoperative patient, and bed exercises are used to strengthen the upper torso in preparation for using crutches or braces. Other exercises are ordered to strengthen specific muscle groups following surgery.

**Classifications of Exercises.** Several different types of exercises are used by the nurse in providing for increased activity of the patient. All motor activities of a voluntary nature can be divided into two groups: active movement and passive movement. Active exercise is movement by the individual without personal or mechanical help of any kind. Passive exercise is when the movement is done by another person.

Movement is also classified according to its effect on the muscle: isometric or isotonic. Isometric exercise is tensing or contracting the muscle without moving the part, such as performing "quad sets," or tensing the quadriceps muscles in the thigh. In isotonic exercises, the muscle is tensed and the part is moved. This type of movement occurs whenever people "set" and contract their muscles. Body builders use isotonic exercises when they flex their arm and torso muscles and pose in various positions.

Another form of exercise is the resistive type in which the movement is performed against additional weights. It is similar to isotonic exercises in which little or no change of the length of the muscle occurs after the initial contraction. Weightlifting, carrying, pulling, or pushing fall into this category.

**Scheduling or Pacing Activities.** When planning to increase the patient's activities, the nurse should be specific about the type of exercise, the amount, and the times to be set aside for it. Frequent rest periods may need to be provided in a program that schedules, or paces, the activities according to the patient's tolerance. Postoperative patients may need to be given an injection for relief of pain before the bath is given or befor the patients are gotten out of bed to sit in a chair. Patients receiving oxygen on a prn basis should not have it discontinued at one moment and be expected to get out of bed to walk to the bathroom the next moment. Patients need time to adjust to the lower oxygen content in the room air before additional oxygen demands for activity can be placed on the body.

## APPLICATION TO CLINICAL PRACTICE

The assessment of the activity and sleep need areas should be added to the assessment of the other need areas. The following outline of adaptive and maladaptive behaviors can be used as a guide for your assessment. After identifying maladaptive behaviors, use the nursing process to state the problem, list the stimuli that are influencing the problem, and plan your interventions.

| Normal, or Expected Behaviors | Unusual, or Maladaptive Behaviors |
| --- | --- |
| Body parts present and in good proportion | Amputation of _____<br>Curvature of spine; hump back |
| Good muscle size, definition, and tone | Atrophy of muscles; hypertrophy |
| Smooth, coordinated movement; deliberate and purposeful | Jerky; uncoordinated; tremors; constant motion; very fast; very slow |

| | |
|---|---|
| Unrestricted movement of joints | Limited movement: flexion contracture of _____; pain on movement; foot drop |
| Good strength; moves independently, overcomes some resistance | Weak grip of right, left, or both hands<br>Requires support; needs assistance; tires easily |
| Good balance; holds head up; bears weight on both feet | Unstable; unable to bear weight; unsteady; wobbles; sways |
| Turns over, changes position, and sits up without assistance | Requires help to turn, change position, or sit up |
| Carries out activities of daily living – dresses self, feeds self, washes or bathes self, grooms self, controls elimination functions | Requires assistance to dress, undress, cut food, feed self, for partial bath, or complete bath; unable to shave, comb hair, go to bathroom, use toilet or bedpan without help |
| Ambulates without assistance; is steady; has normal gait | Unstable; shuffles feet; short or tottering steps; difficulty climbing steps |
| Usual bedtime _____<br>Usual rising time _____ | Too few or too many hours of sleep |
| 7–8½ hours of bed rest or as appropriate for age | Bed rest _____ hr. Less than 7 hr, more than 8½ hr<br>Naps – morning, afternoon |
| No interruptions of sleep, but may awaken at end of sleep cycles as appropriate for age | Interrupted sleep for treatments – _____ times<br>Unable to fall back to sleep easily<br>Voids _____ times per night |
| Awakens well rested, refreshed | Awakens tired, yawning; difficult to concentrate |
| Falls asleep easily | Use of sedatives, other drugs, or alcohol to promote sleep |

## REFERENCES

Campbell, Emily: Nursing problems associated with prolonged recovery following trauma. Nurs Clin North Am, *5*:551–562, (September) 1970.

Cho, Joan: Assessment of physiological mode. Unpublished study guide. Los Angeles, Mount St. Mary's College, 1977.

Frankel, Lawrence, and Richard, Betty: Exercises help the elderly live longer, stay healthier, and be happier. Nursing 77, *7*(12):58–63, (December) 1977.

Grant, Donna A., and Klell, Cynthia: For goodness sake – let your patients sleep. Nursing 74, *4*:54–56, (November) 1974.

Hartmann, E.: The Functions of Sleep. New Haven, Yale University Press, 1973.

Hayter, Jean: The rhythm of sleep. Am J Nurs, *80*:457–461, (March) 1980.

Luce, Gay Gaer: Body Time. New York, Pantheon Books, Inc., 1971.

Meissner, Judith: Which patient on your unit might get a pressure sore? Nursing 80, *10*(6):64–65, (June) (1980).

Meissner, Judith: Evaluating your patient's level of independence. Nursing 80, *10*(9):72–73, (September) 1980.

Murray, Ruth B., and Zentner, Judith P.: Nursing Assessment and Health Promotion Through the Lifespan, 2nd ed. Englewood Cliffs, New Jersey, Prentice-Hall, Inc., 1979.

Narrow, Barbara: Rest is.... Am J Nurs, *67*:1646–1649, (August) 1967.

Olson, Emily V., et al.: The hazards of immobility. Am J Nurs, *67*:779–795, (April) 1967.

Rambo, Beverly, and Wood, Lucile: Nursing Skills for Clinical Practice, 3rd ed. Philadelphia, W. B. Saunders Company, 1982.

Reinisch, Elizabeth: Quick assessment of hemiplegics' functioning. Am J Nurs, *81*:102–104, (January) 1981.

Snyder, Mariah and Baum, Rebecca: Assessing station and gait. Am J Nurs, *74*:1256–1257, (July) 1974.

Thompson, June M., and Bowers, Arden G.: Clinical Manual of Health Assessment. St. Louis, The C. V. Mosby Company, 1980.

Yurick, Ann Gera, et al.: The Aged Person and the Nursing Process. New York, Appleton-Century-Crofts, 1980, p. 418–430.

# Need for Sensory, Temperature, and Endocrine Regulation

**OBJECTIVES  Information in this chapter will help you to**

1. Discuss the regulation of body functions in terms of the sensory organs through which we perceive the world around us, maintaining the internal environment by controlling body temperature, and the hormonal secretions of the endocrine system.
2. Assess the behaviors associated with meeting these regulatory needs and compare them with the normal range of behaviors.
3. Describe the second level stimuli that cause or influence the maladaptive or ineffectual behaviors and recognize that impaired function of the regulatory systems is a stimulus for problems in other need areas.
4. Describe the problems related to maladaptive regulation in terms of the medical problems that involve the specific organ or system, altered sensory function, pain, and inability to communicate effectively with others.
5. Explain nursing interventions that are used to manipulate the stimuli that are causing the problems.

## DEFINITION OF TERMS

**accommodation** — change in pupil size for near and distant vision.

**acuity** — sharpness, keenness, or clearness of perception.

**aphasia** — loss of use of spoken or written language, speechlessness.

**conduction** — transfer of heat away from an object by direct contact.

**consonants** — all of the nonvowel letters of the alphabet.

**convection** — transfer of heat away from an object by currents of air or fluid.

**evaporation** — giving off moisture by turning a liquid into a vapor.

**febrile** — having fever, i.e., body temperature above normal.

**gustatory** — referring to the sense of taste.

**hypothermia** — cooling, body temperature below normal.

**nystagmus** — involuntary, rhythmic movement of the eyes.

**olfactory** — referring to the sense of smell.

**ophthalmoscope** — instrument used to examine the interior of the eye.

**otoscope** — instrument used to examine the ear.

**presbycusis** — loss of the ability to discriminate or hear high-pitched sounds, occurring with age.

**pyrexia** — fever, elevated body temperature.

**radiation** — transfer of heat by electromagnetic rays.

**Snellen's chart** — commonly used to screen for visual acuity.

**tactile** — pertaining to the sense of touch.

**tonometer** — instrument for measuring pressure or tension of the eyeball.

---

The growth and development of human beings depends upon the adequacy of sensory stimulation and the regulation of body functions. By these means, the infant who is totally dependent on others for most basic physiological needs grows and emerges as a mature adult who is capable of dealing with a dynamic, changing world. Without sensory input and the ability to maintain a stable internal environment of our bodies, our lives would be chaotic, disorganized, and unpredictable. Both are essential for adaptation and the ability to voluntarily participate in activities that form the pattern of our daily lives.

Sensory perception was discussed in Chapter Four. The focus of this chapter is the assessment of the regulatory functions of the body, which include three major components: (1) the sensory apparatus that consists of the special organs of sight, hearing, smell, taste, and touch, (2) the temperature regulating mechanisms, and (3) the hormonal output of the endocrine glands.

Through the sensory organs, we are able to perceive and to react to events in the world in which we live, as well as being able to respond to internal sensations and thoughts. Any deviation from the normal sensory input of stimuli will affect what is perceived as reality and how one relates to oneself. Internal stimuli are associated with visceral sensations, such as the beating of the heart, hunger pangs, movement of intestinal contents, pain, or pressure from staying in one position for a period of time. These sensations motivate actions to seek food, to obtain relief from the pain, or to change position. Other internal stimuli make it possible for us to know the location of various parts of the body in relation to each other in space and the movement of muscles. The senses of proprioception and balance are basic to most motor activities and skills, from sitting up or walking to piloting a space craft to the moon, where lack of gravity poses other types of problems.

People gain knowledge of the external world by stimulation in one of the five senses and a functioning central nervous system, where meaning is given to it by the brain cortex. The senses include sight, hearing, taste, smell, and touch. To respond to these externally generated stimuli, language is used for communication. Language is a pattern of sounds or words that have a certain meaning for a particular group of people and can be used to communicate thoughts and ideas to others. Skin serves as an insulating cover that protects the inner structures of the body and is the boundary between the internal and external environment. One major contact with one's environment is through the tactile sensory receptors located in the skin.

The control of body temperature within a relatively narrow range is essential to promote or to control the vital chemical reactions that take place in the body fluids or on the cellular level. Metabolic processes rely on a stable temperature that is relatively free from external influences, such as the weather.

Finally, growth and development of the physical body are intimately tied to the hormonal secretions of the endocrine glands. Sexual development and other metabolic processes are also dependent upon the endocrine glands. The regulation of hormones affects size, height, weight, symmetry of the body, metabolic rate, and the utilization of calcium, glucose, or other essential elements. Signs of impaired functions are not unique to this need area; however, they are usually assessed in one or more of the other need areas.

Maladaptation or impairment of sensory organs, temperature regulation, and hormonal secretions indicate medical diseases or conditions. Nurses intervene to carry out prescribed treatments. These medical conditions are stimuli for additional problems that the patient may have in relation to carrying out his or her activities of daily living or coping with feelings or changes as a result of the disruption. Patients who are hard of hearing are unable to hear clearly what has been said; thus, they respond inappropriately, if at all, and give the appearance of being confused. People with decreased vision have great problems in mobility and safety, difficulty in orienting themselves, and less ability to act independently, or to care for their own needs. Elevated temperatures to the fever range increase the metabolic rate of the body and the demand for additional calories to supply the energy that is needed. Information that is obtained concerning sensory functioning may be used in the second level assessment for these problems as well as for related problems in other need areas.

## REGULATION OF THE SENSORY ORGANS

Can you imagine what it would be like not to be able to see or to hear? The inability to see or hear greatly limits one's world and confines one's social as well as mental skills. People who are without vision *and* hearing are shut off from communicating with others. When loss of vision *and* hearing occurs in young children before they have learned to speak a language, it is almost an insurmountable handicap. The life of Helen Keller has served as an inspiration to many people. Although she became deaf and blind in early childhood, she learned to speak and communicate with others. With aging, there is a gradual loss of function of the sensory organs; however, these losses pose less severe problems because older people have learned communication and social skills earlier in life and can compensate for some of the effects that these losses have on their accustomed way of life.

Through their senses, people are in constant contact with the environment, and, in health, all the senses work in a coordinated way to give greater meaning to stimuli. One's appetite is due, in part, to the taste of the food, to the smell or aroma, as well as to its appearance and texture. The beauty of a sunset on the water is heightened by the gentle lapping sounds of the waves and the sound of the breeze through the trees. An impairment of one of the senses reduces the meaning provided by the other senses.

Alterations or changes in sensory perception lead to behavioral changes in individuals and in the way that other people respond to them. For example, if a person fails to answer when spoken to, most people will repeat the statement in a louder voice.

The changes that occur in sensory organs are primarily decreases in function that lead to deficits or to impaired acuity. People vary in how well they can adjust to these changes. In many instances they are able to compensate; thus, they act normally, as though no impairment existed. Although all the senses are important, vision permits us to be in direct contact with our environment and hearing is essential for communicating with others and maintaining social contact.

## THE EYE AND VISUAL FUNCTIONS

The ability to see the wonders of nature, human accomplishments, and all the sights that make up the world around us is possible through the structures of the eye and the nerve pathways that carry the impulse to the cortex of the brain, where it is given meaning. The eye and its major structures are shown in Figure 14–1. Light rays enter the eye through the pupil and pass through the lens where the rays are bent or refracted and the image is projected onto the retina. The retina is a thin, filmy tissue that lines the inner surface of the eye globe and is sensitive to light. It contains two major types of receptors: the rods, which are responsible for vision in the dark, and the cones, which react to the color of the light waves. Nerve fibers pick up the impulses from the retinal cells and collect to form the optic nerve that carries the impulse to the visual center in the occipital lobe of the brain.

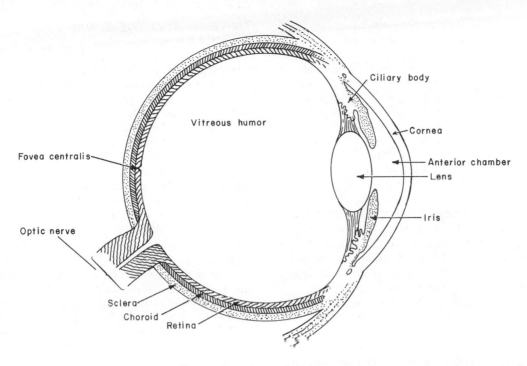

**Figure 14–1.** Structures of the eye.

The globe of the eye has three coats: the sclera, which is seen anteriorly as the white of the eye, the choroid lining, which contains the blood vessels, and the retina. The color of the eye is contained in the pigment of the iris. Several sets of muscles control the movements of the eyes in the side-to-side, the upper and lower temporal, and the upper and lower nasal fields of vision. The eyelids and eyelashes help to protect the sensitive cornea. The conjunctiva is the membrane that covers the front of the eyeball and the lining of the eyelids. The lacrimal system provides tears that wash over the tissues, removing foreign material that irritates the eye.

**Sensitivity to Light.** The ability to see depends upon light rays reaching the retina and the image being transmitted to the brain. The amount of light that enters the eye is controlled by the size of the pupil. The ciliary muscles and the muscles of the iris dilate to let in more light during darkness and constrict the pupil, thereby decreasing the stimulation from bright light.

When entering a dark room, the eyes become more sensitive to the darkness, and, after a period of time, the outline and shape of objects can be seen. Even in minimal light, the rods of the retina have been stimulated by the low intensity but remain insensitive to details of the images. Too much light and glare also interfere with vision because the light-sensitive chemicals decompose in the retinal cells and do not have time to reform. Focus, visual acuity, and details of the visual image are then lost.

**Visual Acuity.** Visual acuity is how well one is able to see. The usual manner of determining acuity is measuring what should be seen at a distance of 20 feet and what actually is seen at that distance and comparing the findings. Standardized shapes or letters are used to test acuity, and results are expressed as 20/20, 20/30, and so on. The numerator is the distance from the chart, and the denominator represents the figure that can be recognized at distances of 30, 70, or 100 feet by those with normal visual acuity.

The area seen by the eye at any given time is the visual field, and the size of the visual field determines how much can be seen. Visual acuity is much greater in the central portion of the field because more cones are located there, and these cones are the first to respond to brightness, color, and contour. The image becomes less sharp or distinct in the outer portions of the field, where the rods predominate and discern mainly between light and darkness. The optic disc produces a blind spot in the field where the optic nerve and blood vessels enter and leave the retina.

**Accommodation.** Near and far vision is achieved by accommodation. This is the process of adjustment, of keeping a distant object continually in focus as it approaches the eye. The major change involved in accommodation is in the shape of the lens of the eye. In normal vision, both eyes move simultaneously, and the lenses continually adjust to keep objects that are at different distances in focus. Other structures of the eye help to bend or refract the light rays to project the image clearly on the retina. These structures include the cornea, the anterior chamber, the size of the pupil, and the vitreous humor. With age, the lens loses its ability to change its shape and to produce a sharp focus of the image, a condition called presbyopia.

The best focus and sharpness of detail in the image is provided by a small pupil opening. The smaller pupil reduces the number of light rays that enter the eye. Pinhole goggles are often used for patients following eye surgery because they further restrict the amount of light that enters the eye. The pinhole brings any image into focus, regardless of its distance from the eye.

## THE EAR AND THE SENSE OF HEARING

Hearing plays a major part in our growth and development as social beings who are able to communicate with others. Hearing requires the ability to receive sound waves, to relay the impulse to the brain, and to attach meaning to the sound. The meanings attached to sounds lead to the use of language and allow us to make accurate judgments about the world based on recognition of sound stimuli and their proper sequence. Serious errors occur when the sounds "ABC" (A = "stove," B = "burns," C = "hand") are heard as "AC" or "CBA."

The ear is the organ for hearing and equilibrium. It consists of three parts: the external or outer ear, the middle ear, and the inner ear. The pinna, the portion of the external ear not contained within the head, gathers the sound waves and directs them into the auditory canal. The sound waves strike the tympanic membrane, or eardrum, which separates the external ear from the middle ear. Vibrations of the eardrum are transmitted by the three bones located in the middle ear that bridge the space from the tympanic membrane to the cochlea of the inner ear.

**Table 14–1.   ASSESSMENT FACTORS FOR VISION AND HEARING**

| Factors to Assess | Normal Behaviors | Maladaptive Behaviors |
|---|---|---|
| *Vision* | | |
| Appearance of eyes | Appropriate size, color and shape Sclera—white, clear | Skin discolored; lids swollen Sclera—red, tearing, drainage |
| Visual acuity | Able to see near and far objects | Wears glasses or lenses Unable to see near or far objects; blurring of images; distortion of images; blind |
| Accommodation | Pupils react promptly and are equal in size Eye movements parallel and in unison | Cataracts; removal of lens; pupils unequal in size Squint; "crossed eyes"; irregular movements; nystagmus |
| Color perception | Identifies different colors | Unable to see certain colors; sees only grays and light and dark |
| *Hearing* | | |
| Sound intensity | Hears voices within normal range | Uses hearing aid Ringing in ears; sounds merge as noise |
| Sound frequencies | Hears sounds ranging from high to low tones | Loss of high frequency sounds Makes errors distinguishing words beginning with b, d, p, etc. |
| *Speech Formation and Perception* | Speaks clearly; initiates and understands language | Mumbles; slurs words; stutters; talks irrelevantly; rambles; uses non-sensical words |
| | Speaks dominant language | Speaks _____ language |

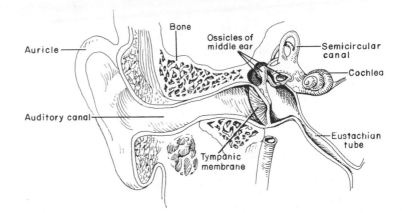

**Figure 14-2.** Structures of the ear.

Sound waves are transmitted by the basilar membranes, the hair cells of the organ of Corti, and by the lymphatic fluid within the inner ear. The vibrations are changed to neutral messages as the fibers of the auditory nerve are stimulated. The nerve fibers collect to form the auditory nerve that serves as the pathway to the brain, where the sound impulses are perceived and given meaning. This complex process involves the use of language for the intellectual activities of interpreting sounds and giving meaning to other sensory input.

**Intensity of Sound.** The intensity, or loudness, of sound refers to the highest point of deflection of the sound wave. It is the pressure that is exerted by the sound wave and is measured in decibels (dB). The louder the sound, the stronger the vibration.

**Noise.** Noise is a sound of any kind. Most noise is unpleasant, sharp, shrill, disorganized, or loud or has some other disagreeable characteristic. Loudness or a great intensity of noise can produce damage to the hearing receptors. The louder the sound, the stronger the vibration, the more hair cells that are activated, and the less time there is for the cells to recover their ability to fully vibrate again. Continued intense noise produces hearing loss for the higher frequencies. Hearing loss is so common at 4000 cycles that it is called the "4000 cycle dip" when seen on an audiogram. People with this type of sensory loss of hearing acuity tend to speak somewhat louder than is appropriate for the occasion. People with conduction loss speak more softly than is appropriate.

**Vibration Frequencies.** Sound waves must vibrate at a certain speed, or number of cycles per second, to be heard. Each frequency produces a slightly different tone or sound. The usual range of sound frequencies is between 500 and 8000 cycles per second, although it is possible to hear low bass sounds of 40 cycles per second if they are loud enough or very high shrill tones of 15,000 to 20,000 cycles per second. Most speech sounds occur in the relatively low frequencies, although some of the consonants have a higher vibratory speed.

The vibratory wave that results from a low frequency travels for a longer distance along the length of the receptor in the inner ear and stimulates fewer of the nerve fibers than vibratory waves from high frequencies. (See Figure 14-3.) Sounds in the middle range, such as those with 4000 cycles per second, have a shorter wave and activate more fibers because there are more cycles stimulating the receptor. Very high frequencies activate so many nerve fibers and receptors that the sound may produce pain and cause damage to the cochlea itself.

Hearing acuity diminishes with age as a result of loss or damage to the hair cells and to other cochlear structures. This sensory loss of hearing is called presbycusis, and it begins in men at about the age of 32 and in women at about the age of 36. The hearing loss is first evident for sounds in the higher frequencies and in discriminating between sounds that are similar. Little or no changes occur in middle-pitched or low-pitched sounds. People who have presbycusis often state, "Don't shout, I can hear what you're saying." On the other hand, people who have conduction deafness have a hearing loss that is about equal for all frequencies of sound.

**Speech Formation.** Language is learned from infancy by hearing people speak and by associating certain meanings to the sounds. Babies learn to speak the language of their parents because

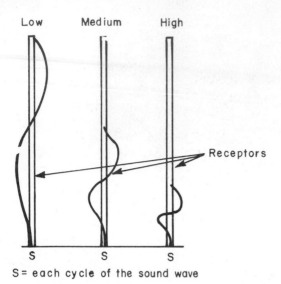

Low    Medium    High

Receptors

S       S        S

S = each cycle of the sound wave

**Figure 14–3.** Duration of sound waves at different frequencies.

these are the sounds that they hear, and they receive positive reinforcement whenever they imitate these sounds.

Speech consists of making words through a combination of different sounds. The letters in the English alphabet are composed on one or more sounds that have different cycles or frequencies. The vowels *a, e, i, o, u,* and the letter *y* are characterized by sounds that are in the middle range of frequencies and that are louder and more lasting than consonant sounds because they are formed with a column of air being pushed out of the mouth. Consonants are more apt to be misunderstood and are more difficult to distinguish from each other. Many consonants begin with a higher frequency sound that is short-lived and change to a vowel sound. Consider the following letters: *b, c, d, g, p, t, v,* and *z.* Each letter begins with a short higher cycle and ends with the "eee" sound. Other similar sounding letters that lead to confusion when words are not heard clearly are *s* and *f* and *m* and *n.*

Sensory hearing loss associated with aging affects one's ability to hear the higher frequencies of the consonants and to distinguish one from another. The phrase "It is time to eat" may sound like gibberish to the older person who heard only the vowels "Is I ya ee" and fails to respond appropriately. Because hearing loss occurs gradually, many people are able to adjust to the changes and to continue their social interactions. Severe hearing loss is a disadvantage to the person in both personal and general conversations and may lead to social withdrawal.

**Conduction Pathways.** Sound waves travel readily through air or water but less easily through denser materials such as bone. *Air conduction* is the most effective means of transmitting sound waves; the air around us is filled with sound waves. These sound waves are picked up by the pinna of the ear and compressed in the auditory canal to amplify the sound waves that are transmitted through the middle ear to the inner ear, which is filled with fluid. *Bone conduction* is less effective, but under certain circumstances, sound waves can be transmitted through the bones of the skull. Conduction loss of hearing occurs when something interferes with the transmission of the sound wave through the structures of the ear.

## SKIN, SENSE OF TOUCH, AND TEMPERATURE REGULATION

The skin provides the boundary between our inner body and the external surroundings. It is the largest organ of the body, and through the free nerve endings that are located in it, we are kept in touch with the reality of the outside world. Through the skin, we are able to distinguish light from firm touch, to perceive shapes and textures, and to experience heat, cold, pressure, and pain stimuli.

The skin consists of the epidermis, with its layers of cornified cells that are continually being sloughed off, and the layers that constitute the dermis, or the true skin. The dermis contains the nerve endings or receptors, sweat glands, hair follicles, and blood vessels. The epidermis is very thin; it is thickest over the palms of the hand and soles of the feet.

**Functions of the Skin.** The skin is the largest and most visible organ of the body. Therefore, one's physical appearance is affected by the texture of the epidermis, evenness of the surfaces, color, and unbroken continuity of the skin. This influences how one feels about oneself and how others respond to one. In the physiological mode, the skin performs the following functions:

1. Skin contains sensory receptors that enable us to feel heat, cold, pain, and pressure.

2. Skin regulates body temperature by layers of subcutaneous fat and sweat glands.

3. Pigments of the skin guard against damage from the sun's ultraviolet rays.

4. Skin provides a protective barrier that prevents invasion of the internal body by microorganisms and other harmful substances.

5. Skin covers the internal structures of the body and cushions delicate organs and tissues from mechanical and physical harm. It allows the body to be active and to engage in motor activities without upsetting the internal environment.

6. Skin aids in the elimination of waste products through the sweat glands.

Of special interest to nurses when assessing sensory regulation and perception are the functions of the tactile senses, temperature regulation, and the intactness of the skin as a protection from infection.

**The Sense of Touch.** The sense of touch is provided by nerve receptors in the skin that are sensitive to pressure and pain and are able to discriminate between the temperature changes of heat and cold. The dermal layer of the skin is richly supplied with nerve endings, although some parts of the body are less sensitive than others. Physiologists believe that sensory receptors are specific and respond only to certain types of stimuli. Chemoreceptors in the tongue respond to the tastes produced by chemicals such as salts, and certain receptors in the skin, deep tissues, and cochlea respond to the mechanical changes of pressures and stretching. Pain receptors respond only to stimuli that harm the cell, not to pressure or to touch.

Various types of nerve fibers have been identified that conduct the sensory impulses at different speeds from the receptor to the cerebral cortex. The "A" fibers are large in diameter, have a myelin sheath, and conduct impulses rapidly at the rate of 5 to more than 100 meters per second. The small "B" fibers are associated with the sympathetic nervous system, and the

**Table 14–2.** ASSESSMENT FACTORS FOR TOUCH
AND TEMPERATURE REGULATION

| Factors to Assess | Normal Behaviors | Maladaptive Behaviors |
|---|---|---|
| *Sense of Touch* | | |
| Pressure sensations | Distinguishes size, shape, or texture of objects | Makes errors in identifying objects by touch |
| Pain sensations | At ease, comfortable | Pain<br>  Location_____<br>  Pattern_____<br>  Type — itching; numbness; tingling; sharp; stabbing; burning; aching; dull; severe; etc. |
| Integrity of skin | Intact, healthy skin | Reddened; damaged; bruised; discolored; ecchymosis; rash<br>Broken area; surgical incision; decubitus ulcer; wound |
| *Temperature Regulation* | Temperature in normal range — 37° C, 98.6° F (± 1°) | Elevated temperature _____<br>Increased pulse; respirations; skin warm; malaise; headache; delirium; convulsions<br>Hypothermia_____<br>Skin cold, numbness and loss of feeling, shivering, lethargy |

"C" fibers are smaller and unmyelinated and conduct neural impulses at the slower rate of 0.2 to 2.0 meters per second. Stimuli that produce sharp pain are thought to travel rapidly to the brain, and the aching, throbbing type of pain that follows is the result of the stimulation of the slower transmitting "C" fibers.

*Pressure and Pain.* Stimuli that activate the touch and pressure receptors allow one to feel the size, shape, and texture of objects and to respond to vibrations and to feelings of sharpness and dullness and provide a means of communicating with others. The sense of touch is important in nursing because it can provide a positive message of caring about another person. The internal organs of the body have few pain receptors, but they have many receptors that respond to pressures and stretching stimuli; however, the skin contains receptors for both pressure and pain stimuli.

Wide variations exist of how individuals experience and perceive pain. Studies have shown that the pain threshold, the point at which people first identify the sensation as pain, is about the same intensity for all people when they are tested with a gradually increasing electrical stimulus. In contrast to visual, hearing, taste, and olfactory receptors, pain receptors do not adapt or lose their ability to respond to painful stimuli. This serves as a protective mechanism for the body; pain receptors continue to send impulses to the brain until the stimulus is removed. The body begins to pull away from a harmful stimulus by reflex action even before the person is aware of the pain. If the hand touches a hot object, it is immediately withdrawn from contact before there is a mental awareness that it was burned. This reflex action occurs even in people who are asleep or who are in a comatose state.

*Temperature Receptors.* The nerve endings that respond to cold stimuli are located in the dermis of the skin; the heat receptors are found in the deeper structures of the skin. Temperature receptors adapt readily to changes in the temperature of the skin or the temperature of one's surroundings as the mechanisms of vasodilation and vasoconstriction are utilized to keep the body temperature stable. The body's adaptation to temperature changes is apparent when a bather plunges into a pool or body of water and perceives the water to be cold, but, within a few minutes, feels exhilarated and is no longer chilled. Temperature receptors and the skin itself are damaged by extremes of temperatures below freezing and by temperatures above 45° C or 113° F.

*Temperature Regulation.* Human beings are warm-blooded and are capable of maintaining a consistent body temperature, even though external environmental temperatures vary from extremely cold to extremely hot. Body temperature is essentially the temperature of the circulating blood and the internal tissues and fluids. It is representative of the internal part, or "core," of the body, where the temperature must be maintained with a narrow normal range so that critical metabolic and chemical reactions can continue to take place. Excessive body heat is very harmful to nerve cells and causes damage to the central nervous system. High fevers are associated with behaviors of convulsions, delirium, and disorientation, resulting from heat on the nerve cells in the brain. Hypothermia, or a low body temperature, has a depressant effect on all metabolism and body cells; thus, conditions that lead to excessive body heat or to excessive loss of body heat are life-threatening.

*Heat Production and Loss.* Body heat is produced by cellular metabolism as nutrients are converted to energy. A thermal regulatory center in the brain functions as the internal thermostat, and temperature receptors in the skin respond to changes in the external surroundings. The thermostat is set at the critical temperature of 37° C (98.6° F), which varies less than one degree in the healthy person during a 24-hour period. When body temperature falls below this setting, the heat-producing mechanisms of vasoconstriction and shivering intervene. Temperatures above the thermostat setting initiate vasodilation and sweating to increase heat loss.

The production of heat is increased by muscular activity, the sympathetic nervous system, the effects of thyroxine hormone, and the effect of heat itself on the cell. The energy needed for motor activities, work, and exercise is obtained from stores of glucose that are then metabolized by the muscle cells. Even muscular tensing and shivering increase the amount of heat produced. The stimulation of the sympathetic nervous system and the release of norepinephrine readies the body for "fight or flight." This causes vasoconstriction of vessels in the skin, thereby diverting blood to the inner structures and preventing heat loss. The hormone thyroxine speeds up metabolism, and the increase in body temperature itself increases the metabolism in the cells. In fevers, the metabolic rate rises about 6 per cent for each degree Fahrenheit, and about 10 per cent for each degree Celsius. The added heat further increases the rate of the chemical reactions that are involved in the metabolic process.

Body temperature is increased with heat produced by physical exercise, the tensing of muscles, the inflammatory process, and infections. Body heat is conserved by voluntary behavior, such as

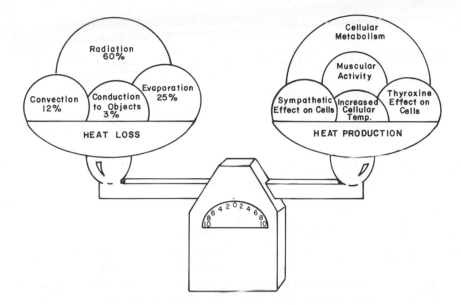

**Figure 14–4.** Body temperature is a balance of heat production and heat loss.

moving toward heaters or sources of external warmth, putting on warm clothing or blankets, and reducing heat losses.

Heat loss is largely dependent upon the voluntary actions that people take to control their environment and their own body temperature. When people feel hot as a result of increased internal temperature, they remove heavy clothing or blankets, open doors or windows, reduce the heat from stoves or heaters, and move to cooler locations.

Methods of lowering body temperature and losing heat include radiation, evaporation of water from the lungs and skin, conduction, and convection. Radiation is, by far, the most effective method. Vasodilation brings vast amounts of blood to the skin surfaces, and heat is given off in the form of rays. Radiation is effective as long as the surrounding temperature is less than that of the body. Otherwise, heat rays from external sources are absorbed and the body heat is retained. On hot, humid summer days, the inability to lose heat elevates the body temperature, resulting in heat stroke, with temperatures as high as 106 to 110° F (41 to 43° C).

## THE SENSE OF TASTE

The taste of foods and other substances is the result of stimulation of the taste buds, which are located on the tongue, and is greatly enhanced by the odors of the foods. Four types of taste buds detect chemicals that we perceive to be sweet, sour, bitter, and salty. These chemicals are activated in various combinations and intensities to provide us with a wide range of taste sensations.

The location of the different taste buds on the tongue helps to protect the body from ingesting noxious or harmful substances. The sweet taste buds are located at the front of the tongue and promote the intake and enjoyment of foods that are high in carbohydrate and supply a ready source of energy to the body. The salt and sour taste buds are located more on the lateral aspects and monitor the amounts of these substances that enter the body. If bitter or harmful tasting materials pass the isolated bitter taste buds when taken into the mouth, a concentration of these taste buds at the posterior of the tongue helps to prevent extremely bitter foods or materials from being swallowed.

With advancing age, the sense of taste is altered by the loss of many sweet taste buds; thus, candy and pastries and other sweet foods no longer taste as sweet. Adding additional sugar to a cup of coffee fails to make it taste much sweeter because the loss of taste is due to fewer taste buds. Some salt taste buds are lost in time, with the least amount of loss in sour and bitter taste buds.

Table 14–3. ASSESSMENT FACTORS FOR TASTE,
SMELL, AND ENDOCRINE REGULATION

| Factors to Assess | Normal Behaviors | Maladaptive Behaviors |
|---|---|---|
| *Gustatory Sense* | Identifies sweet, sour, salty, or bitter tastes, and combinations of tastes | Loss of taste for sweets or salt. Metallic or abnormal taste sensations |
| *Olfactory Sense* | Identifies different odors | Unable to discriminate odors; abnormal odor sensations |
| *Endocrine Regulation* | Normal body growth and development | Stunted growth; excessive size |

## THE SENSE OF SMELL

Olfactory receptors are located in the nose, and they are activated by contact with vapors that are given off when solid materials change to a gaseous state. Odors of perfumes and cooking foods result from these volatile molecules. The receptors adapt readily; thus, with continued exposure to the vaporized molecules, the smell diminishes and is less noticeable.

One's degree of pleasure and preference for certain odors is probably the result of maturation. Women seem to have a more acute sense of smell than men until after menopause; thus, sense of smell is believed to be related to the level of estrogen. Unpleasant odors lead to warnings of danger from smoke, fire, scorched food, noxious fumes of gases, or offensive body or breath odors. Many disagreeable odors are suppressed by the use of deodorants, sprays, and good hygiene.

## ENDOCRINE REGULATION

The hormonal output of the endocrine glands is largely a result of the autonomic nervous system and various feedback mechanisms and is not generally considered to be under voluntary control. Deviations in the usual hormonal levels of the body cause cellular changes that constitute readily diagnosed medical problems. These conditions tend to serve as stimuli for the other problems that individuals have in meeting their basic physiological needs or affect the way they cope with their feelings or get along with others.

## FIRST LEVEL ASSESSMENT

Nurses assess the sensory regulation of the body to determine the individual's ability to carry out activities of daily living or to cope with feelings or relationships with others. Cellular changes in the sensory organs generally indicate the presence of a medical problem. Medical problems then serve as stimuli or influencing factors for behaviors in the basic need areas. Alterations in the sensory input affect the person's ability to understand what is happening. People with cataracts are unable to see clearly; thus, they are unable to drive a car safely, to read street signs when riding on a bus, to read the instructions on a label of a prescribed medication, or to see any of the thousands of things that other sighted people take for granted. People who have difficulty hearing have problems understanding other people when they speak, fail to hear warning horns, sirens, or whistles, or cannot use the telephone without special sound-amplifying attachments. The impairment of any of the senses constricts one's world and alters one's perceptions of reality.

## DEVELOPMENT OF VISUAL ACUITY

Humans are born with the ability to see; however, visual acuity for near and far objects takes time to develop. The newborn baby sees only objects and faces that are within the central field of vision and at a distance of about two to three feet. With the passage of time and maturation, the baby learns to control eye muscles and eye movements and to focus on more distant objects. Normal vision, 20/20, occurs at about six years of age, as shown in Table 14–4.

Visual acuity declines with aging. The lens of the eye loses its ability to change size and to accommodate both near and far vision. By the age of 45 or 50 years, the eyes can no longer adjust their focus, and, in order to see clearly, most older persons must wear bifocal glasses or corrective lenses.

Table 14–4. DEVELOPMENT OF VISUAL FUNCTIONS ACCORDING TO AGE

| Age | Visual Acuity | Other Visual Functions |
|---|---|---|
| Birth | Very limited; approx 20/300 | Pupils react to light<br>Some photophobia; keeps eyes closed most of time<br>May have some nystagmus |
| About 4 weeks | | Stares at source of light<br>Follows examiner's finger to midline<br>Tear glands and ducts begin to function |
| About 3 months | | Uses both eyes<br>Follows moving object from side to side, moving head and eyes<br>Fascinated with bright lights and colors |
| About 6 months | | Able to blink<br>Has some accommodation for near and far vision<br>Ultimate color of iris can now be determined |
| 1–1½ years | Approx 20/100 | Can associate objects with their verbal meaning<br>Gazes intently at shapes, forms, and facial expressions<br>Keen interest in pictures<br>Has crude depth perception |
| 2–3 years | 20/30 | Smooth convergence of eyes<br>Good accommodation |
| 5 years | | Distant vision between 20/20 and 20/40 for those over age 3 years<br>Recognizes colors<br>May have reading readiness |
| 6 years | Approaches 20/20 | Discriminates shades of color<br>Depth perception fully developed |

NOTE: Based on Chinn, Peggy, and Leitch, Cynthia: Child Health Maintenance: A Guide to Clinical Assessment, 2nd ed. St. Louis, The C. V. Mosby Co., 1979

## SENSORY CHANGES IN OLDER PEOPLE

As people grow older, certain changes occur in their sensory organs. There is a decrease in the number of cells that respond to stimuli; however, these losses do not happen at the same age, at the same rate, or to the same degree among individuals. Most people *do* suffer losses, and sensory functions are further affected by (1) an increase in the time required for an impulse to reach the brain, (2) a slower response time, (3) a stronger stimulus being needed to produce a response, and (4) decreased ability to perform complex sensory and motor skills, such as threading a needle.

Some of the sensory changes that occur are:

*Vision*

At age 45 years, about 10 per cent of the people have visual acuity of 20/70 or less.

At age 65 years, about 50 per cent of the people have visual acuity of 20/70 or less.

The size of the pupil decreases, enabling less light to reach the retina; brighter light is needed to see the same things that younger people see normally.

After age 60 years, glasses are worn by 88 per cent of the people.

More women have significant visual deficits than do men.

*Hearing*

Presbycusis (characterized by the loss of ability to hear high frequency sounds) occurs in males at about the age of 32 years, and in females at about the age of 36 years.

After age 65 years, 30 per cent of the people have a significant hearing loss.

More men have serious hearing losses than do women.

*Taste*

Sense of taste declines after the age of 50 years.

By age 60 years, most persons have lost about 50 per cent of their taste buds, mainly the sweet and salt taste buds.

*Olfactory*

Little change occurs until very old age.

Over the age of 80 years, about 40 per cent of the people have difficulty identifying common substances by smell.

*Tactile*

After age 45 years, there is a decrease in the number of receptors for light touch and pain; thus, people have fewer responses to indicate the presence of harmful stimuli.

Decreased response of temperature receptors and greater sensitivity to colder temperatures occurs with aging.

## SECOND LEVEL ASSESSMENT

Further information is gathered to identify the underlying stimuli that are causing maladaptive behaviors associated with sensory regulation. The following types of stimuli commonly cause or influence changes in sensory functions. These stimuli are similar to the stimuli that have previously been discussed for other basic needs.

1. *Diseases affecting the sensory organs.* Frequently encountered diseases include glaucoma, cataracts, conjunctivitis, iritis, detached retina, ruptured tympanic membrane, otitis media, otosclerosis, labrynthitis, sinusitis, and colds.

2. *Diseases of related structures.* Frequently encountered conditions that interfere with the reception of the stimulus or the transmission of the impulse to the brain or its perception at the cortex include cerebral vascular accidents, brain tumors, infections, and injury to the spinal cord or to other nerve fibers.

3. *Age or developmental stage.* Age is one of the more important influencing factors when determining the type of intervention or approach to utilize. Interventions that are used for a 6-month-old child may be inappropriate for a person 20 years old. People are expected to behave in different ways as they grow older and have more life experiences from which to draw. For example, providing a clock or a calendar for a child who is unable to read or to tell time would not increase his or her sensory input or orientation to reality.

4. *Adequacy of the sensory environment.* One's physical environment should contain sufficient, varied stimuli to give an image of the people, events, and things that make up the real world. The stimuli include things such as the climate, humidity, and noise.

5. *Medical treatment.* Changes in sensory regulation may be the result of bed rest, treatment in an intensive care unit, isolation or confinement to a hospital room, subjection to frequent interruptions, undergoing stressful or painful tests and procedures, and the effects of medications that depress or stimulate the central nervous system.

6. *General mental, emotional, or physical condition.* Intense emotions, anxiety, and even apathy or boredom reduce or block out other stimuli. Anxiety heightens attention and alertness; however, high levels of anxiety constrict one's awareness and attention to anything else but the threat that has been perceived.

Although changes in sensory regulation are caused by these various factors, the alterations themselves serve as stimuli for many of the other behavioral problems that individuals experience with sensory perception. Any change in the number of incoming stimuli or the manner in which they are perceived leads to the general states of sensory deprivation, sensory overload, monotony, and distortion (see Chapter Four). Because of altered sensory input, individuals are less aware of their surroundings and the world around them. They are restricted in their ability to be independent, to pay attention to their own needs and goals, and to avoid dangers of every kind.

Changes in the function of a specific sensory receptor are also stimuli for the general conditions previously given and for other problems that the person has in meeting basic needs and in coping with these changes. The following sensory alterations have frequently been found to cause problems or to influence how people behave:

1. *Decreased visual acuity; blindness.* Decreased ability to see clearly interferes with the way people carry out their usual activities. Changes in vision affect people's ability to see near or far objects, to read printed material, to discern colors, to see people and objects nearby, and to move about freely. Visual losses may be in one or in both eyes and may be corrected by glasses or lenses. However, the person has to rely on using the corrective glasses in order to see well.

2. *Decreased hearing; deafness.* People who have decreased hearing ability are probably more disadvantaged than people who have visual handicaps, because their disability is not visible. Loss of the ability to hear clearly reduces one's communication with others, lessens one's responses to conversations when the words have not been heard, and greatly reduces one's social contact with others. People with hearing loss have difficulty discriminating words spoken by others when there are competing sounds in the background, such as a radio, television, or even general conversation by others. People who have presbycusis hearing losses can hear normal voices, and they resent having others speak loudly or shout at them, which is necessary for people who have otosclerosis and conduction types of hearing losses. Hearing aids are essential to amplify

sounds and to provide some degree of hearing for those afflicted by these hearing losses.

3. *Decreased sense of taste.* Although not of the same magnitude as the loss of visual or hearing acuity, the loss of many taste buds in aging may influence one's eating habits and nutrition. Older people have about one sixth as many taste buds as a 20-year-old person, and the greatest number of taste buds that are lost are the sweet taste buds, followed by reduction in the salt receptors. Some older people may eat large amounts of sugar, candy, and other sweets to recapture the sweet taste of foods and to satisfy their "sweet tooth." Increased use of salt may occur for the same reason.

4. *Fever.* Fever occurs when the body's temperature is set at a higher level by the body's temperature control center, usually as a means of combatting an infection or inflammatory process somewhere in the body. Febrile states are a common symptom of medical diseases and become a stimulus for other problems affecting the patient. The following example illustrates how these sensory regulation changes operate as stimuli that affect other need areas in our daily lives. Jane called her supervisor and said, "I won't be able to come to work today because I'm running a temperature of 101°." The use of the word "because" indicates that the reason or the stimulus for her inability to carry out her usual activities will follow. In this case, the stimulus is the elevated temperature.

5. *Pain.* Pain, like fever, is a common symptom of a medical problem. Complaints of pain can be included in the nursing care plan in a variety of ways: as part of the patient's medical problem or as a stimulus for other problems such as reluctance to get up and walk around because of pain in the back, or it can be stated as the presenting problem itself in the integrated approach.

## PROBLEMS ASSOCIATED WITH SENSORY REGULATION

Alterations in sensory stimulation and perception greatly change the way in which the world and reality are perceived. It is largely through the senses of sight, hearing, and touch that we communicate with others and carry out the social functions of our lives. When sensory regulation is altered, the most common change is in the decrease in function that occurs with vision and hearing and the areas most greatly affected are social interactions and communications with others. Such problems are caused by stimuli that represent actual changes in sensory functions and can be stated as:

Patient has decreased awareness of reality or is confused.
Patient has difficulty communicating with others.
Patient has postoperative pain in abdominal incision area.

## DECREASED AWARENESS OF REALITY

With a change or decrease in the sensory messages being received, more errors are apt to be made in the meanings attached to them. This leads to disorganized behavior that fails to correspond to the behavior that is normally expected; this state is called confusion. Confused behavior is not congruent with reality. Reality is the quality or state of being actual or true. Most people would agree that a chair is an object with legs that support a ledge, which is located about the level of one's knees, on which

**Table 14–5. RANGE OF BODY TEMPERATURES FOR CERTAIN CONDITIONS AND EFFECT OF THE THERMAL REGULATING CENTER**

| Body Temperature °F | °C | Condition | Regulation |
|---|---|---|---|
| 114 | 45 | Upper limit of survival | Seriously impaired |
| 106–111 | 41–44 | Heat stroke; brain lesions | Seriously impaired |
| 105–106 | 40–42 | Fever therapy | Efficient |
| 97–106 | 36–41 | Febrile disease; hard exercise | Efficient |
| 97–100 | 36–38 | Normal range | Efficient |
| 94–97 | 34–36 | Low range | Efficient |
| 84–94 | 29–34 | Hypothermic | Impaired |
| 71–84 | 23–29 | Severe hypothermia | None |
| 74 | 23 | Lower limit of survival | None |

one sits and with a vertical extension that is used to support the back. A sign of confused behavior would be if one interpreted the chair to be a perch for birds or an electric motor.

Disorientation is another term that is used to refer to confusion and to the state of having decreased awareness of reality. Sensory deprivation, sensory overload, and sensory distortion may all lead to confusion or to disorientation. The affected person is unclear about relationships of time, space, and person. Confused persons may not know who they are, where they are, who others are, or what day or year it is. Some confused people become quite skilled at covering up their areas of misunderstanding and deficits; confusion need not be total or involve all functions of the brain. Some confused people may know who they are and be oriented to time yet not understand where they are or what is happening to them.

Individuals may be located anywhere on the health-illness continuum, ranging from a mild to severe decreased awareness of reality. Minimal impairment involves making minor errors in interpreting conversations and in other sensory stimuli or in forgetting some details. Severe disorientation involves a major disability and total dependence on others for many of one's basic needs. Patients in profound confusional states require total care, including being bathed and dressed, fed at meal times, given fluids to drink, toileted at intervals, provided with periods of exercise and rest, protected from dangers, and continually oriented to reality. Additional sensory stimulation should be provided to reinforce their contact with reality.

The stimuli that cause confusion and decreased awareness of reality are those that cause altered sensory input. Confusion is frequently associated with illness, injury, infections, tumors of the brain, cerebral vascular accidents (strokes), abuse of drugs and alcohol, anxiety, and psychiatric conditions. Anxiety is a common cause of confusion because it restricts the attention that is paid to other incoming stimuli while the greatest attention is being focused on the threatening situation. Many older people are at risk of confusion that is caused by anxiety when they are faced with a crisis, such as death of a spouse, serious illness, or admission to a nursing home. In addition, they often have memory loss of recent events, which further reduces their knowledge and understanding of the real world. Older people tend to forget things that happened when they felt powerless to control what was happening to them or that failed to result in desired outcomes.

## DECREASED ABILITY TO COMMUNICATE

A wide range of conditions exist that affect one's ability to communicate. From birth, infants hear sounds and begin to learn to discriminate the sounds, but months pass before they learn to focus their eyes to see. It is not until years later that they learn to read, long after they have learned to speak. Problems that occur as people attempt to communicate with others generally involve language because it is through language that we are able to experience all sensations and stimuli. The stimuli are given meaning through language and can then be remembered or recalled at a later time. Problems that may occur include stuttering, remembering, selecting words, pronouncing words, forming words, understanding verbal sounds, and using language for other intellectual skills such as decision-making, analyzing, and mathematical computation. Mutism generally does not involve the loss of the ability to speak but involves a psychological barrier that prevents the use of language to communicate.

Aphasia occurs frequently among persons who have some form of brain damage. It includes the inability to name objects and to find the correct words to use and difficulty in learning. Recent studies have shown that speech is most likely to be a function of the left hemisphere of the brain and that lesions of the left brain cause different types of responses than do lesions of the right brain. The left hemisphere puts together the sensory input and interprets it in terms of language. The right hemisphere qualifies and processes the information and is also the center for artistic and musical abilities.

A frequent barrier in communicating with others is different languages. The language that one learned as a child is considered one's primary language. Languages that are learned later in life are more difficult to master. People who emigrated to the United States and learned English as an adult often revert back to using their primary language when they are ill or under a great deal of stress.

## PAIN PERCEPTIONS

Pain is one of the greatest teachers that one has. It commands our attention as few other teachers are able to do. It is a warning of injury to the body and serves indirectly as a defense mechanism that indicates the need to repair damaged tissues or to replace an exhausted supply of energy. Pain forces one to rest. People who suffer from pain find it difficult to do anything except collapse on their beds and rest.

**What Is Pain?** Pain is an elusive and complex sensation that is experienced by most people at some time during their lives. It is a private and personal feeling that cannot be seen, measured, felt, or experienced by others. It is considered to be as great, as mild, as important, or as severe as the person who is experiencing the pain says that it is. Pain is the physiological response to tissue damage and the psychological reaction to the stimuli that are causing the pain. The psychological perceptions of pain are learned behaviors that are based on one's early experiences in childhood, the attention that one received by others, the cultural values attached to pain, and the emotional responses.

**Sensitivity to Pain.** Physical pain is the result of tissue damage which releases a chemical that stimulates the pain receptors. The amount of cellular damage that is needed to trigger the pain receptors is about the same for all people and is called the threshold of pain. However, one's sensitivity to pain varies in different parts of one's body, and some tissues are more sensitive with more receptors than are others. Sensitive tissues are located extensively in the skin, muscles, and connective tissues. Few pain receptors are located in the internal organs because these organs are protected from the types of injuries that are sustained by the skin surfaces.

Pain tends to be more severe in the denser tissues, resulting from increased pressure of the inflammatory response to the damaged area. Muscles, tendons, ligaments, fascia, and the periosteum of bone vary in density, with the periosteum being the most sensitive to painful stimuli. The pleura and diaphragm are also highly sensitive to pain as are the hollow viscera, such as the ureters and common bile duct, which are also very sensitive to spasms and stretching. Disturbances in these structures can cause severe pain. Fairly pliable tissues, such as the peritoneum, mesentery, and blood vessels are very sensitive to stretching, handling, and cutting. Blood vessels also respond to cold temperatures with the sensation of pain.

The physiological responses of pain result from the activation of the sympathetic nervous system with an increase in blood pressure, pulse, and respiratory rate; vasoconstriction of superficial blood vessels; and so on. People who suffer pain are increasingly restless, become apprehensive, display some irritability, and verbally complain of their discomfort.

**Responses to Pain.** Because physical pain is caused by damage to one's body, from an early age people perceive pain as a threat and fear it; thus, anxiety is an integral part of the pain response. From one's earliest experiences, the cry of pain brought comfort from a loved adult, and the pain was relieved. Later, when the loved adult became angry, pain resulted from the displeasure and punishment. For any pain that continues, the child thinks that the older loved one has chosen not to take away the pain and that the pain is a punishment or a signal that he or she is not loved. These feelings produce fear and anxiety in addition to the pain.

Continuous or recurrent pain with no evidence of tissue damage is a pain response to the psychological discomfort of anxiety and the interpersonal needs for dependency, attention, and atonement for guilt, revenge, and other similar conditions.

The question has been raised as to whether anxiety causes the perceptions of pain. Cases have been cited that show that extreme tissue damage itself does not inevitably lead to pain. Soldiers who were wounded in combat often felt no pain or anxiety when they knew that the injury was the reason that they would be sent home and that the war was over for them. In some primitive cultures, rituals of initiation are often painful procedures, but the participants are euphoric rather than in pain. Yogis and people who believe in a super being (God, Allah, doctor) also do not perceive painful stimuli as pain in the same way that others would. It may be that, in the absence of anxiety, people develop their own supply of endorphins (a group of endogenous brain substances that bind to opiate receptors in various areas of the brain and thereby raise the pain threshold), sufficient to control the pain stimuli and perceptions.

**Types of Pain.** Pain is classified in several different ways. It can be acute or chronic. Acute

| Anxiety (fear, guilt) | + | Tissue Damage | = | Pain |
|---|---|---|---|---|
| 0% | | 100% | | possibly no pain |
| 20% | | 80% | | 100% acute pain |
| 50–80% | | 20–50% | | 100% chronic pain |
| 100% | | 0% | | 100% pain |

types of pain are temporary, have a sudden onset, and eventually subside, often without any treatment, as the cellular damage is repaired. The sudden pain from a sprained ankle, headache, or inflamed appendix is useful when it prompts the person to seek the cause of the pain and to remedy it. Chronic pain persists for a long period of time, may be continuous or intermittent, and is resistant to efforts to treat and eliminate it. Diseases such as rheumatoid arthritis, osteoarthritis, advanced stages of cancer, and tic douloureux are characterized by chronic pain. This type of pain is frustrating to the sufferer because it is constant, exhausting, and debilitating. It is seldom severe or high intensity pain but is more in the moderate range of discomfort. High intensity pain usually indicates damage to the nerve receptor itself, and, once damaged, it no longer responds as it did previously.

Pain is also regarded as superficial pain, central pain, or deep pain. Superficial pain results from stimulation of receptors in the skin. It may be slow in onset with a burning sensation, or it may be abrupt with more of a prickly feeling. This pain produces no nausea and is described as mild to moderate, itching, burning, cutting, and sharp. Deep pain is associated with deep organs in the body, referred pain, and spasms or contractions of skeletal muscles. It may be slow or abrupt in onset and is accompanied by nausea and sweating. This pain is usually described as dull, aching, cramping, boring, throbbing, sore, or burning. It is common following abdominal surgery and in diseases of the stomach, gallbladder, and colon.

Referred pain is felt in a part of the body other than where it originated. The pain from ischemia of the heart muscle is referred to the left arm or to the neck and jaw or is felt between the shoulders in the back. Central pain refers to an injury to peripheral nerves, to lesions of the central nervous system, and to the pain of a "phantom limb" after the actual limb has been amputated.

**Assessing the Pain.** When obtaining information about a pain experience, the nurse assesses the following areas:

1. Origin and history of occurrence of the pain.
2. Location of the pain, including the depth, extension, or radiation to other areas.
3. Quality or intensity of the pain; terms used to describe the pain.
4. Pattern of onset—predominantly day or night pain. Pains that occur during the day are made worse by physical or mental activity. These pains include rheumatism, sinusitis, or sciatica.

Night pains are typical of diseases that involve organs, such as gastric ulcers and colic.
5. What it is that relieves the pain.

A complete pain assessment enables the nurse to plan interventions that are effective in reducing and in controlling the pain.

## NURSING INTERVENTIONS

When planning the interventions to use to achieve the goal of adaptive behaviors, the nurse manipulates the causative stimuli or influencing factors that were identified by the second level assessment. Goals that specify the direction of the change of behavior should also include some indication of how the changes would be measured. For example, goals for the problems of sensory regulation may be: "Patient will have increased awareness of reality as shown by orientation to time, person, and place" or "Patient will have decreased pain as shown by taking pain medication two or fewer times per day." After using the interventions, the nurse compares the present behaviors with the goal to evaluate the effectiveness of the nursing care.

Because changes in the sensory organs serve as stimuli for other problems that the person may have, several interventions are suggested that may be used to help to change the problem behavior to more adaptive behavior.

1. *Visual Deficits:* Provide glasses or lens as needed; keep clean and available for use. Provide more light. Use light colors on floors and paint edges of steps to provide better depth perception. Eliminate clutter of furniture; keep traffic lane clear of obstacles. Use large print for books, magazines, and reading material. Provide verbal instructions instead of written instructions.
2. *Hearing Deficits:* Use of hearing aid. Hearing aid is often removed at night; thus patients are unable to hear. Use pad and pencil or magic slates for written messages. Use gestures, picture cards, or an alphabet list to spell out words.
3. *Speech Formation and Communication:* Use common language. Give person sufficient time to respond. Use touch. Give verbal stimuli. Make lists of common words and their meaning. If patient uses a different language, provide pictures of common items or words that the person can point to if unable to say the word. For nonverbal patients, use verbal stimuli and speak in simple sentences about concrete things. Devise a code of signals for "yes" and "no," such as nodding the head or hand movements and ask direct questions that can be answered by "yes" or "no."

Observe closely for nonverbal responses and behaviors related to basic needs.

4. *Decreased Tactile and Touch Sensation:* Encourage use of loose clothing and shoes. Schedule frequent change of position to prevent pressure sores. Encourage regular exercise. Devise ways to protect the person from injury. Caution person to avoid using applications of extreme heat or cold (hot water bottles, hot pads, ice packs) to skin surfaces, especially the extremities in older patients, and to use a bath thermometer to measure the temperature of hot water to insure that it is 105° F (40.5° C) or less.

5. *Control of Temperature:* Devise methods to increase body temperature and reduce feelings of being cold, such as adding more warm clothing or blankets, increasing physical activity or exercise, eating warm foods and drinking warm liquids, moving closer to a source of heat, and applying warm objects to the skin (warm water bottles, hot pads, or warm baths). Manipulate the environment by increasing the heat or temperature of the room. Decrease heat loss by closing doors or windows. Eliminate drafts or air currents.

Use intervention methods to decrease body temperature and reduce feelings of being too hot, such as removing warm clothing, increasing the amount of skin exposed to the air to aid vaporization of sweat, decreasing physical activity, increasing fluid intake, and applying cold objects or substances to the skin (alcohol sponge, cool bath, hypothermia blanket, or ice packs). Manipulate the environment by lowering the room temperature (air conditioning or fans) and increasing the movement of air or air currents. Give antipyretic medications as ordered to lower the temperature and antibiotics to fight the infection.

6. *Control of Pain Sensations:* Reduce anxiety through anticipatory guidance and insight therapy. Use analgesics and narcotics to control the pain. Immobilize the injured part. Promote rest periods. Position for comfort. Apply hot or cold packs. Use diversional activities, such as stimulating the large muscle fibers by massage or use of electronic skin stimulators.

Additional interventions for increasing the individual's awareness of reality include the use of clocks, calendars, radio, television, newspapers, and various reorienting techniques.

---

## APPLICATION TO CLINICAL PRACTICE

The sensory regulation need area provides you with a more complete view of the physiological functions of the body and the way in which the individual meets basic needs and carries out the activities of daily living.

Use Table 14–6 on page 216 as a guide for assessing sensory regulation. Other information may be added as necessary, or the assessment tool may be expanded to meet the needs of particular patients.

Following your assessment of all the physiological need areas, use the nursing process and formulate a plan of care with the objective of returning the person to an adaptive state. List the maladaptive behaviors and group related behaviors together to identify the overall problem affecting the need area rather than dealing with each ineffective behavior. After examining the problem, determine the direction of the change that is needed to return the behaviors to the adaptive range and state this as your goal. Include your method of measuring the amount of change needed, whenever possible. From the list of stimuli that cause or influence behaviors, select those that can be manipulated and state the interventions you would use to change these behaviors. Use the format for writing your nursing care plan that is required in your nursing program, or use the Guide for Nursing Care Plan at the end of Section One. Sample nursing care plans are provided in Appendix B.

Table 14–6.   ASSESSMENT OF SENSORY REGULATIONS

| Normal Behaviors | Maladaptive Behaviors |
| --- | --- |
| *Vision* | |
| Able to see near and far objects | Wears glasses or lenses<br>Unable to see near or far objects; blurring of images; distortion; blind |
| Appropriate size, color, and shape of eyes<br>Sclera white | Skin discolored; lids swollen<br>Sclera—red, tearing, drainage |
| Pupils react promptly and are equal in size<br>Eye movements parallel and in unison | Pupils unequal in size<br>Squint; "crossed eyes"; irregular movements; nystagmus<br>Cataracts; removal of lens |
| Identifies different colors | Unable to see certain colors; sees only grays and light and dark |
| *Hearing* | |
| Hears voices within normal range | Uses hearing aid<br>Ringing in ears; sounds merge as noise |
| Hears sounds ranging from high to low tones | Loss of high frequency sounds<br>Makes errors distinguishing between words beginning with b, d, p, etc. |
| *Speech Formation and Perception* | |
| Speaks clearly; initiates and understands language | Mumbles; slurs words; stutters; talks irrelevantly; rambles; uses nonsensical words |
| Speaks dominant language | Speaks _____ language |
| *Sense of Touch* | |
| Distinguishes size, shape, or texture of objects | Makes errors in identifying objects by touch |
| At ease, comfortable | Pain<br>   Location _____<br>   Pattern _____<br>   Type—itching; numbness; tingling; sharp; stabbing; burning; dull; aching; severe; etc. |
| Temperature in normal range—37° C, 98.6° F (± 1°) | Elevated temperature _____<br>Increased pulse; respirations; skin warm; malaise; headache; delerium; convulsions<br>Hypothermia _____<br>Skin cold, numbness and loss of feeling, shivering, lethargy |
| Intact, healthy skin | Reddened; damaged; bruised; discolored; ecchymosis; rash<br>Broken area; surgical incision; decubitus ulcer; wound |
| *Gustatory* | |
| Identifies sweet, sour, salt, or bitter tastes, and combinations of tastes | Loss of taste for sweets or salt<br>Metallic or abnormal taste sensations |
| *Olfactory* | |
| Identifies different odors | Unable to discriminate odors; abnormal odor sensations |
| *Endocrine Regulation* | |
| Normal body growth and development | Stunted growth; excessive size |

# REFERENCES

Boyd-Monk, Heather: Examining the external eye, part I. Nursing 80, *10*(5):58–63, (May) 1980.

Boyd-Monk, Heather: Examining the external eye, part II. Nursing 80, *10*(6):58–63, (June) 1980.

Bozian, Marguerite, and Clark, Helen: Counteracting sensory changes in the aging. Am J Nurs, *80*:473–476, (March) 1980.

Capobianco, Julia A.: Keeping the newborn warm: how to safeguard the infant against life-threatening heat loss. Nursing 80, *10*(5):64–67, (May) 1980.

Cho, Joan: Assessment of physiological mode. Unpublished study guide. Los Angeles, Mount St. Mary's College, 1977.

Common problems in managing adult diabetes mellitus. Special section. Am J Nurs, *78*:871–889, (May) 1980.

Cummings, Dana: Stopping chronic pain before it starts. Nursing 81, *11*:60–63, (January) 1981.

David-Sharts, Jean: Mechanisms and manifestations of fever. Am J Nurs, *78*:1874–1877, (November) 1978.

DeLapp, Tina Davis: Taking the bite out of frostbite and other cold weather injuries. Am J Nurs, *80*:56–60, (January) 1980.

DiBlasi, Marie, and Washburn, Carolyn: Using analgesics effectively. Am J Nurs, *79*:74–78, (January) 1979.

Fagerhaugh, Shizuko, and Strauss, Anselm: How to manage your patient's pain... how not to. Nursing 80, *10*:44–47, (February) 1980.

Fultz, John M., Jr., et al.: When a narcotic addict is hospitalized. Am J Nurs, *80*:478–481, (March) 1980.

Gedrose, Judith: Prevention and treatment of hypothermia and frostbite. Nursing 80, *10*(2):34–36, (February) 1980.

Gever, Larry N.: Brompton's mixture: how it relieves the pain of terminal cancer. Nursing 80, *10*:57, (May) 1980.

Gramse, Carol Anne: Dorsal column stimulation. Am J Nurs, *78*:1022–1025, (June) 1978.

Guyton, Arthur C.: Textbook of Medical Physiology, 6th ed. Philadelphia, W. B. Saunders Company, 1981.

Holm, Carol: Deafness: common misunderstandings. Am J Nurs, *78*:1910–1912, (November) 1978.

How to test your patient's hearing acuity. Nursing 80, *10*(7):60–61, (July) 1980.

Jacox, Ada: Assessing a patient's pain. Am J Nurs, *79*:895–900, (May) 1979.

Johnson, Joyce, and Cryan, Maura: Homonymous hemianopsia: assessment and nursing management. Am J Nurs, *79*:2131–2134, (December) 1979.

Maxwell, Mary B.: How to use methadone for the cancer patient's pain. Am J Nurs, *80*:1606–1609, (September) 1980.

McCaffery, Margo: Understanding your patient's pain. Nursing 80, *10*:26–31, (September) 1980.

McCaffery, Margo: Patients shouldn't have to suffer — relieve their pain with injectable narcotics. Nursing 80, *10*:34–39, (October) 1980.

McCaffery, Margo: Relieving pain with noninvasive techniques. Nursing 80, *10*:55–57, (December) 1980.

McGuire, Lora, and Shayne, Dizard: Managing pain... in the young patient... in the elderly patient. Nursing 82, *12*(8):52–57, (August) 1982.

McMahon, Margaret, and Miller, Sister Patricia: Pain responses: the influence of psychosocial cultural factors. Nurs Forum, *17*:58–71, (November) 1978.

Meissner, Judith: McGill-Melzack pain questionnaire. Nursing 80, *10*:50–51, (January) 1980.

Meyer, Theresa: TENS — relieving pain through electricity. Nursing 82, *12*(9):57–59, (September) 1982.

Norman, Susan, and Baratz, Robin: Understanding aphasia. Am J Nurs, *79*:2135–2138, (December) 1979.

Ozuna, Judith, and Foster, Charlene: Hypothermia and the surgical patient. Am J Nurs, *79*:646–648, (April) 1979.

Pace, J. Blair: Helping patients overcome the disabling effects of chronic pain. Nursing 77, 7:30–43, (July) 1977.

Pain and suffering. Special supplement. Am J Nurs, *74*:489–519, (March) 1974.

Sacksteder, Sarah, et al.: Deep hypothermia. Am J Nurs, *78*:271, (February) 1978.

Shore, Herbert: Designing a training program for understanding sensory losses in aging. Gerontologist, *16*(2):157–165, (April) 1976.

Silman, Judith: Reference guide to analgesics. Am J Nurs, *79*:74, (January) 1979.

Steele, Bonnie: Test your knowledge of postoperative pain management. Nursing 80, *10*:76–78, (March) 1980.

Stern, Elisabeth: Helping the person with low vision. Am J Nurs, *80*:1788–1790, (October) 1980.

Valentine, Amy, Steckel, Steven, and Weintraub, Michael: Pain relief for cancer patients. Am J Nurs, *78*:2054–2056, (December) 1978.

Yurick, Ann Gera, et al.: The Aged Person and the Nursing Process. New York, Appleton-Century-Crofts, 1980.

# ASSESSMENT OF THE PSYCHOSOCIAL MODES

Virtually every nursing philosophy in this country contains a statement to the effect that people are biopsychosocial beings and that the nursing care considers the whole person. However, many nurses raise questions similar to the following when making an assessment of psychosocial functioning.

"Why should I, as a nurse, be concerned with the psychosocial part of my patients' lives?"

"What do my patients' social lives have to do with their illnesses?"

"Isn't it intruding into my patients' lives in an area in which I have no right to be?"

"My patients are sick, so shouldn't I focus on the physical problems of their bodies?"

Perhaps these questions are based on a hopeful belief that when people are sick only the biological body is involved, that the psychological and social parts are "put on hold" until the biological body has recovered. A more likely reason for the questions may be the nurse's feelings of inadequacy and lack of knowledge or skills with which to routinely assess these areas of functioning. As a result, nursing care is restricted to the more familiar areas of following medical therapy and taking care of physical needs.

Yet, as we all know, when people become ill, the illness affects many, if not all, areas of their lives. People who suffer from the flu have tearing eyes, runny noses, slight temperatures, aching in the joints, and malaise. Mentally, they are restless and unable to concentrate for any period of time. They lack the energy to go to work and feel so badly that they cancel social engagements. The illness has influenced how they feel and think, as well as altering their social activities.

People respond to the changes that are caused by their illness, and these changes affect not only their bodies but also their minds, making them more dependent on others as they take on the sick role. The illness is most often the focal stimulus for maladaptive behaviors and for problems that patients have while in the hospital setting. Following colostomies, mastectomies, heart attacks, or strokes, patients not only have to cope with the effect of the disease on their bodies but also their feelings about their loss of control over what has happened, the changes in their body image, and the alterations in their relationships with others. Their spouse, family, or friends may either encourage or resent their increased dependency in areas of their daily lives as the disease interferes with what they can and cannot do for themselves.

Patients often suppress their negative emotions about their illness as they attempt to be "good patients," and to meet all the expectations held by the doctors and nurses. However, if patients do have these hidden feelings, a lot of energy must be used to keep them disguised, and this energy is diverted from the healing process. Tense, worried, and depressed patients take longer to recover from their illnesses than patients who are relaxed. When the nurse is able to help patients reveal these coping problems and work on resolving them, patients begin to feel better as their coping becomes more adaptive.

Other patients express their negative feelings of fear or of being mad or sad in many overt ways. They may complain about the food or the noise at night, use the nurse call light continually, shout, cry a lot, become angry and throw things, or seek reassurance about everything that they do. Patients who have been labelled by their caregivers as complainers, "difficult patients" or "crocks" or any other derogatory names are patients who probably have a psychosocial problem in coping. They may have needs that have not been met, and their efforts in coping have failed. By the time these patients have been described in these terms by exasperated members of the nursing staff, the situation has become even worse, with lines of communication no longer open. What is needed is a psychosocial assessment with accurate identification of the coping problems and a plan of care to strengthen effective coping mechanisms or to reduce the stimuli that are causing the response.

The goal of a psychosocial assessment is to promote adaptation of patients or clients in dealing with feelings or the image of one's self and in dealing with their relationships with the other important people in their lives.

# Role Function and Assessment

## OBJECTIVES  Information in this chapter will help you to

1. Define the terms that are used to refer to the conditions, the components, and the classification of roles in the adaptation approach to nursing.
2. Classify roles as primary, secondary, and tertiary and be able to define and give examples of each type of role.
3. State the purposes of role function as (1) a method of assessing and organizing data about the self-concept and interdependence modes, (2) providing criteria for the judgment of behavior as being within the normal range, and (3) a framework for second level assessment of possible stimuli or factors influencing the person's psychosocial behaviors.
4. State examples of expectations, norms, values, and sanctions associated with different roles, such as the role of the nurse.

## DEFINITION OF TERMS

**achieved roles** — roles that are attained through special effort, experiences, or other personal qualifications.

**alter** — the other person; a person related to the ego or to the person who is being discussed.

**ascribed roles** — roles that are present from birth onward and are not related to one's abilities or differences.

**ego** — the self; the person under discussion or the person who is experiencing something.

**expressive goals** — interactions that have an emotional or gratifying outcome.

**instrumental goals** — interactions that have an achievement or action outcome.

**norms** — shared frames of reference; standards of behavior that are learned and considered as fixed standards by members of a social group.

**position** — the name for the place that an individual occupies, or one's status, in the social system. It is the "unit of society."

**primary role** — the perception of one's self in one of the developmental stages of life; essentially one's age and sex.

**role** — a pattern of behavior that is expected of a person in a certain position. It is a regular way of acting that is expected of all persons who occupy a given position in the social order and who confront others. It is the "unit of culture."

**sanctions** — behaviors that serve to support actions and that produce greater compliance with current expectations.

**secondary roles** — roles that are assumed to carry out the tasks associated with the developmental stage of life.

**self** — the individual; a sense of personal identity. It is the "unit of personality."

**society** — a complex collection of organized relationships that form a social system. It lasts long enough to span the life of normal individuals and to recruit new members through biological reproduction and then socializes the new generation.

**tertiary roles** — freely chosen roles that have little influence or a temporary influence on other roles.

**transient roles** — roles that are fleeting and change from moment to moment.

Why would nurses who utilize the adaptation approach to nursing concern themselves with role function? What does role function have to do with the nursing care provided for patients? Isn't role function outside the scope of nursing, and doesn't it involve prying into the patient's personal affairs?

Assessment of roles and role function is essential for determining the psychosocial adaptation of the individual. Roy describes role function as one of the four modes by which people respond to maintain their integrity as integrated and whole beings. Further development and application of the concepts was done by Randall (1976). By means of role function, people are able to know who they are in relationship to others and the expectations of society, so that they can act appropriately.

The reason for assessing role function lies in the belief that man is an integrated biopsychosocial being. This belief acknowledges the complex interrelationships between the biological self, the psychological self, and the social self. People strive to keep all these selves whole and in harmony with each other. When a disturbance affects one part of the self, all the other parts are also affected. People who have appendicitis not only have an inflamed appendix and an elevated leukocyte count, but also have certain feelings or anxieties about being ill, are unable to carry out some of their usual activities, and have a greater need for assistance from the doctor and others. Therefore, nurses are concerned about patients' feelings that are related to their psychological perceptions and the behaviors that express their social interactions with others.

In this chapter, the concept of roles, the social and cultural components of roles, and present methods of classifying roles will be discussed. Although role functioning is seen by many people as a separate mode of behavior, in this chapter, the focus is on the assessment of roles as the method of obtaining information regarding psychosocial integrity. Roles are the ways in which people carry out their work, and other activities. How people feel about their role(s) provides information for the self-concept mode. How people relate to other people provides information for the interdependence mode.

## WHAT ARE ROLES?

In every society, from the most primitive to the most technically advanced, members of the society are needed to carry out the work that keeps the social system functioning. Members of a society are given a place in society, or status, in relation to the tasks that they perform and the work that they do. This place in society is called position, and the title of the position indicates the type of work that is done. The action, or behavior, that is required to carry out the work or to complete the task is called role performance. The work of society includes raising children, providing food and shelter for the people, regulating, or governing the behavior of the members, and passing the culture on to others. Some titles of positions include mother, son, farmer, hunter, fisher, builder, roofer, engineer, senator, king, police, judge, singer, reporter, and teacher.

As Shakespeare wrote in *As You Like It* "All the world's a stage, And all the men and women merely players." As in the theater, people in everyday life perform roles that fortell how they are to act and what they are to feel and say. The individual, or the self, has the starring role and carries out the pattern of behavior that is expected of any person who is in that position. Because social interactions involve other people, roles exist only in relationship to other roles; they are reciprocal in nature. The individual, or self, interacts with others, or alters, who also regard themselves as principal role performers. For example, for there to be the role of a mother, there must be the role of a child or of someone to be mothered; the role of a teacher requires that others take on the role of learners. Other members of society, although not engaged directly in the action, serve as the audience, who applaud pleasing role performances and show disapproval in various ways for poor or inadequate performances.

## SOCIAL DETERMINANTS OF ROLES

The social behavior of people is a result of their role performance. Through the roles that we carry out, we are able to know who we are in relationship to other people. Whenever we meet strangers, one of the first things that we do is to find out some of their roles. This is accomplished, in part, by social dialogue: "Hello. How are you?" "Are you from around here? Where do you live?" "Are you married?" "Do you have children?" or "What kind of business are you in? Where do you work?" As we learn more about peoples' roles, we gain an understanding of how they feel about themselves, how they relate to others, and how they cope with changes in their lives.

## POSITIONS AND ROLES

The social roles that one performs depend upon the position that one occupies in society. Position refers to the place that an individual occupies in the social system. Through positions and performance of roles, the social system seeks to achieve certain goals, which include maintaining itself as a system, protecting the welfare of its members, passing its culture on to others, and providing the most satisfying life for its members.

Types of positions and their titles and roles that are found in a society and are needed to carry out the goals of a society as shown below.

People in any of these positions are expected to relate to other people in prescribed ways and to carry out appropriate actions associated with their position. As previously stated, positions are often interrelated and are significant only in relationship to other positions; thus the roles are reciprocal. The position of mother requires that there be positions of son, daughter, or father; the position of nurse requires that there be positions of patients.

## CONDITIONS FOR ASSUMING POSITIONS

How does one obtain one's position in the social system? What determines the positions that a person occupies in society? What determines how many positions a person occupies at one time? How does one keep one's positions and associated roles? Under what conditions might these positions and associated roles be

| Types of Positions | Titles of Positions and Roles |
|---|---|
| 1. Sex | Male; female |
| 2. Specific age | |
| 3. Age relationship to other | Generations; grades; peers |
| 4. Race | White; black; Oriental; Indian |
| 5. Birth order | Oldest; youngest |
| 6. One of plural birth | Twin; triplet |
| 7. Genetic heritage | Handicapped; intelligence; small; tall |
| 8. Kinship ties | Son; daughter; brother; sister; grandchild |
| 9. Citizenship | American; Canadian; Mexican; Californian; New Yorker |
| 10. Social class | Upper; middle; lower; blue collar |
| 11. Occupation | There are about 40,000 different job titles in the United States; retired |
| 12. Educational level | First grader; junior in high school; college degrees |
| 13. Economic status | High, medium, or low income; unemployed |
| 14. Member of organizations | Policital; cultural; charitable; fraternal |
| 15. Religious affiliation | Baptist; Catholic; Jewish; Moslem |
| 16. Personal attributes | Consumer; athlete; collector; friend; leader; helper |

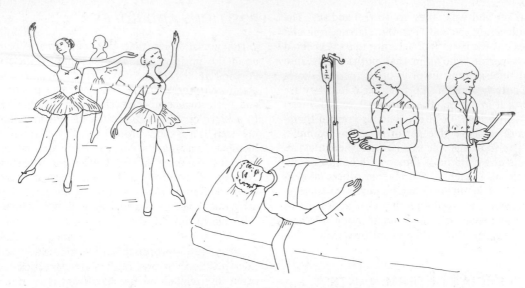

**Figure 15-1.** "All the world's a stage."

given up? The answers to these questions aid in the understanding of role function, or in how people carry out the social actions of their lives.

Basically, one gains positions by three different methods: (1) being born into positions, (2) earning positions, or (3) selecting the positions that one wants. The positions that are accrued as a result of our genetic inheritance are referred to as *ascribed positions.* They are positions over which we have little or no influence. Some examples of ascribed positions are sex, age, race, single or plural birth, place in family structure, and inherited family background and genetic make-up.

*Earned positions* are those based on having the qualifications or the abilities to carry out the duties or responsibilities that are associated with the position. Many roles that are used in carrying out the activities of our daily lives fit into this category. They are based on having or developing special abilities, experiences, or qualities or through special efforts. Level of education, use of artistic or athletic abilities, and preparation for a career are examples of earned positions. *Selected positions* are those that people choose based on their special interests, values, beliefs, and desires. Examples of selected positions include football or baseball fans, theater-goers, voters, tennis players, and members of various clubs or organizations.

Although one is eligible for and can occupy several positions in society, carrying out role functions depends upon certain conditions. A primary condition is being in good health to insure performance of the tasks or work involved

in the positions. The positions must also be appropriate for one's age and stage in life, as judged by the members of the society. For example, a child ten years of age is not expected to go to work and to support other members of his or her family. Other conditions that are related to position include:

1. *Conditions of membership.* Ascribed positions are assigned without regard to differences or to abilities and can be predicted from birth. Whether one is of the male sex or the female sex determines many of the roles of the child and adult. The type of one's genes and one's inherited background determine other roles. The positions and subsequent roles of a child born into a royal family differ from those of a child born to a farmer. The achieved and selected positions and roles require the possession of special abilities or qualifications.

2. *Symbols of identification.* Many symbols are associated with the various positions. In the position of nurse, they include dress and accessories, such as uniforms, nurse's cap and pin, rings, or badges. Speech, manners, or gestures such as military salutes, grammar, the southern drawl, or special acts of courtesy, may also identify positions.

3. *Conditions of maintenance of membership.* To continue in a particular position as a member of the group, one is expected to participate in certain activities, to pay dues, to continue observing the standards of the group, and to avoid violating the ethics and expectations of the group. When applied to a student in a nursing

program, these conditions mean that to remain a member of the group one must register, pay tuition fees, buy books and uniforms, attend classes, study assignments, pass the examinations, practice safe nursing care, use good judgment, and meet many other expectations associated with the role of the nurse.

4. *Conditions of departure.* Being released from a position and its accompanying role may involve or be due to resigning, losing an election, stopping payment of the dues, flunking out of the course or job, losing one's skills, growing old, or becoming ill and being unable to perform one's expected role. As a rule, ascribed positions and their roles are the least likely to be lost or given up. As people reach old age, more of the achieved and selected positions are given up because their physical strength and abilities wane. Other less active roles may be assumed.

## COMPONENTS OF ROLE PERFORMANCE

Every person born into a social group has to accomplish certain tasks to grow and to develop as a human being. Behavioral scientists have defined developmental tasks that are associated with each distinct stage of life from infancy to old age. These tasks indicate the positions that a person occupies and the roles that a person assumes during his or her life. The society or culture has set up expectations and standards for the way these tasks "should" be done. These expectations describe the way that a person "should" behave or act while carrying out his or her roles.

Although social groups permit wide variation in the behaviors associated with each role, the performance of a role by the self depends upon:

- *The role performance of others.* There is a social expectation that each of us will play a part in the same drama; not that each will play a part in a different drama. Peoples' roles are interrelated and are reciprocal. Unless consistency exists in the following of the script and predictability exists in peoples' actions confusion occurs. This is demonstrated when the nurse asks the patient "How are you today?" and the patient does not respond in the expected way but says something such as "They are getting away! Quick, call the police!"
- *The individual role performer's capabilities and personality.* No two people perform the same role in exactly the same way. Each person brings to the role individual attitudes, values, ideas, concerns, expectations, and feelings. Different facets of one's personality may be revealed in some roles but not in others. Consider the adult who carries out several different roles, each emphasizing different ranges of his or her capabilities and personality characteristics: the parent of school-age children who require guidance and care, a full-time employee with job responsibilities and expertise, and a student who displays motivation and other learning skills in a continuing education program.
- *The resources necessary for performing the role.* The role performer must have access to the supplies, services, facilities, and time needed to perform the tasks of the role. Consider the resources required when someone takes on the simple role of preparing a meal for one's family. To carry out this task, the person needs money to buy the necessary food, ability to go to the market and to transport the food home, access to supplies of basic foods that are stored in cabinets or in a refrigerator, pots or pans in which to cook the material, a stove, a cookbook for consulting recipies, dishes on which to serve the food, a table, and so on. The lack of any one of these resources can jeopardize the successful outcome of preparing the meal and, thus, the person's role performance. Performance of most roles requires the use of resources and materials.
- *The availability of role models and role cues.* People become socialized and learn expected responses and actions of their roles more readily when they can see how others perform the roles. Cues to role behavior are also provided by verbal statements, instructions, written directions, and patterns. From early childhood, parents serve as role models for their children. The child learns to identify with the parent when given role cues such as "Brush your hair, just like Mommy does" or "Eat your meat and vegetables so you will grow strong like Daddy." Nursing instructors serve as role models and give role cues to nursing students in the classroom and in clinical settings. Stable, well-established roles provide adequate role models and role cues that reduce one's chances of making errors or of failing to carry out one's role satisfactorily.
- *Those who observe and react to the performance of the role.* Various groups in society observe how well one's role is performed and serve as an audience. Their responses provide feedback to the role performer as to whether or not his or her actions and responses meet society's expectations for that role.

## ROLE EXPECTATIONS, NORMS, AND SANCTIONS

Every role carries with it three distinct components, (1) other peoples' expectations of how the role should be performed and what each performer "should" do, (2) the role performer's expectation of behavior according to the norms, and (3) the consequences that might occur when the role performer fails to meet these expectations. Norms refers to the range of behaviors that are learned and considered as fixed standards by members of society in meeting the expectations of role performance. For example, the role of the mother consists of many expectations that society holds about the way a woman should act toward her child. The mother is expected to behave in ways that show care for the child, such as feeding, sheltering, protecting, and showing affection in any of a wide range of ways that society finds satisfactory. The norms allow the mother to punish the child but sets limits to prevent her from abusing or inflicting severe injury to the child.

Roles are dynamic, and no two people perform the same type of role in exactly the same manner or under the exact set of circumstances. Differences in the performance of the mother role, for example, are due, in part, to lack of complete agreement about the expectations of the role and to a wide range of norms for the role. This allows the role performer some latitude to act according to personal values, experiences, and perceptions. Most mothers cuddle their child, kiss away tears from a bump, feed, and clothe their child. Some expectations of the mother role allow a mother more freedom to provide a flexible schedule of rest and play or to encourage her child's interests in music, art, nature studies, or sports.

Sanctions are those expectations of role performance that lead the person toward more conforming behavior or toward observing the norms that are associated with the expectations. Sanctions are both positive and negative. In positive terms, the sanction is the reward obtained by meeting the expectation of the role. It results in approval and praise and in gaining the desired outcome. Sanctions also specify the consequences that may follow if the behavioral responses are outside the normal range, such as the threat "You should do it this way or else this ill fortune will befall you."

## CLASSIFICATION OF ROLES

Individuals learn to function in society or in subcultures by assuming new and different roles and learning the skills required for these roles.

Through role performances, they carry out the social interactions that give meaning and structure to their lives. The resulting roles can be classified in several ways.

Sociologists classify roles that result from corresponding positions as "ascribed" and "achieved." Ascribed roles are those that relate to positions over which we have little or no control, such as sex, age, genetic heritage, and kinship. Achieved roles refer to those attained by special efforts or qualifications, such as nurse, lawyer, Rotarian, student, ambassador, or Girl Scout leader. Other methods of classifying roles and positions consider one's biological attributes, one's social characteristics, and one's personal characteristics. They add other dimensions to the way in which one looks at roles. There is not only a "biological self" with various roles but also a "personal self" with additional roles that arise from both the biological attributes and the social or environmental influences.

**Positional Importance.** The method of classifying roles in the adaptation model of nursing considers the positional importance of the role in the social structure and refers to it as a primary, secondary, tertiary, and transitional role. The roles resemble a tree with all roles branching off from the primary role of the individual.

The role-tree method of classification is based on several assumptions about people. The first assumption is that people must exist to occupy positions and to have roles to perform. These people grow and develop, occupying progressive positions on the age continuum. The newborn infant continues to grow and moves along the age continuum to 1 year, 2 years, 10 years, 30 years, and so on. Finally, people must be able to perceive in order to meet the expectations of others and to perform the role behaviors for that position that they occupy. Role performance by very young children is limited to beginning skills until they develop perceptions of themselves as individuals, separate and apart from the mother or care-giver.

*Primary Role.* At any specified time in life, one occupies a sex position and an age position within one's developmental stage. Age and sex constitute the primary role that influences much of the one's way of life. Developmental stages of life have been described by Erikson and Havighurst, among others, and consist of general statements of what individuals should be able to do. Developmental stages serve as the norm, or standard, of what is expected of a person at a particular age. Primary roles are stated as "ten-year-old girl," "man, age 22," or "67-year-old man."

*Secondary Roles.* Secondary roles are those

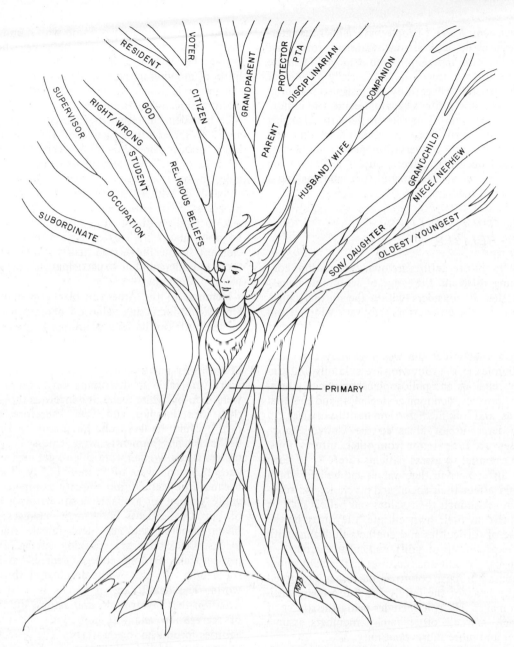

**Figure 15–2.** Role tree of positional importance.

that one person assumes to complete the tasks associated with the primary role and the developmental stage. These roles influence one's life and behavior in a variety of social settings. Although people have only one primary role, they have numerous secondary roles in the general areas of occupation, education, and kinship. A 20-year-old woman may have the following secondary roles: daughter, sister, girlfriend, student nurse, choir singer, part-time waitress, and tennis player.

***Tertiary Roles.*** Tertiary roles are freely chosen and have a temporary or lesser influence on one's life than do secondary roles. When a tertiary role becomes an important factor in one's life, it moves into the category of a secondary role. Examples of tertiary roles for the previously mentioned 20-year-old woman may include committee member for Careers Day, piano player, collector of a rock star's records, and roller-skater.

*Transient Roles.* People have numerous interactions daily and assume transient roles that change from moment to moment yet facilitate the way that they interact socially. Transient roles generally have only an insignificant influence on one's life and are fleeting in nature. Examples of transient roles include the changing back and forth between that of speaker and listener during a conversation, being a member of an audience at a concert, buying an item from the clerk in a department store, and making a deposit at the bank.

## CULTURAL VALUES AND BELIEFS

Each culture defines its own expectations concerning roles and the range of acceptable behaviors that it considers within the normal range. However, these behaviors may vary widely from one culture to another. People from different cultures may have very different values and beliefs that affect the way that they carry out their roles in the following areas: family and kinship, religious and philosophical practices, education, politics, economics, technical and material goods, and folk medicine and health practices.

In large urban areas in the United States, nurses care for patients from other cultures; thus, it is essential to assess patients carefully to learn any differences in their values and beliefs, which would affect their social and psychological adaptation. Although their values and beliefs may be adaptive in their own culture, they may be the cause of difficulties and conflicts in dealing with the expectations of a different cultural group.

In many traditional cultures, particularly those of some European countries, the father is regarded as the head of the family and the primary decision-maker. His role includes being the source of power, and all other family members assume lesser and more subservient roles.

In some cultures, a man's virility and his wealth are measured by the number of children he has sired, and the role of the woman is to produce the children.

According to Madsen, the male role of the Mexican-American centers around the concept of "machismo." Machismo is based on the belief that men are stronger, more reliable, and more intelligent than are women. Machismo influences his feelings of honor and requires him to avoid being proved wrong in any decisions that he has made. Any sign of weakness may cause him to feel humiliated. Whereas women are regarded as sexually desirable, men assume the role of conquerer. In the traditional Latin family, the father is an authoritarian figure who commands respect and obedience from his children, whereas the mother is seen as the one who cushions the hurts of growing up and who is able to influence the father in subtle ways. In the area of health, many Mexican-Americans are caught in the conflict between the scientific theory of medicine and the supernatural beliefs of folk medicine. Most Mexican-Americans gained their knowledge of diseases and their treatment from folk medicine, Indian folk medicine, and scientific medicine, all of which may be used to solve health problems. Most Latins believe that illness is subject to God's will and, therefore, that little can be done about it. This imparts a supernatural element to the illness and makes it difficult for them to understand or to participate in preventive medical programs.

Members of the American black communities are placing increasing value on being black and on their African heritage. Through long years of racial discrimination, black families tended to be matriarchal, with the mother as the central figure of authority and stability. Black men were much more vulnerable to discrimination because they were seen by white males as dangerous threats to their jobs, families, and lives. Therefore, black men became the last to be hired and the first to be fired and frequently were harassed by the police. Black women were able to get jobs and to keep them and were often more highly educated because they could more easily compete with white women for available positions. As a result of the Civil Rights movement, changes have taken place in the male and female roles of blacks. Black men are speaking out against injustices, are earning college degrees, and are succeeding in the white-dominated business world. The health-care of blacks is a complex situation that involves cultural values, the forces of segregation and discrimination, and the inequities produced by poverty. The effects of poverty are perhaps the most significant factor that restricts nonwhites from receiving medical care; thus, they make fewer doctor appointments per year, seek help only when acutely ill, lack early diagnosis and treatment of serious illnesses, and rely heavily on folk medicine.

In the past decade, an increasing number of Filipinos immigrated to the United States, many of whom are professionals, seeking to improve their professional competence and socioeconomic status. Even among the younger generation, traditional values are observed, such as a strong feeling of love of one's family, respect for elders, and self-esteem. Filipinos are deeply religious, with a strong sense of destiny that is expressed as leaving things in the hands of God. They tend to be submissive to authority and reluctant to ask questions or to express their opinions. Doctors and nurses are regarded as authorities to be accepted without hesitation. When ill, Filipinos regard the illness as God's will, but they hope and pray that it will result in the best for them.

Changes in cultures often have profound effects on the roles of both young and old people. Cultural attitudes regarding the value of youth, romance, and productivity have enhanced the roles of the young but have had adverse effects on the roles of the aging and the elderly people in this country. Cultural influences on role performance cannot be minimized, and it would be advantageous for the adaptation nurse to assess these values and beliefs carefully when planning to meet the psychosocial needs of patients from a culture different from that of the nurse.

## ASSESSING ROLES

Nurses who use the adaptation model of nursing, assess the patient's psychosocial behaviors to obtain information about how he or she relates to the world. The information that is gathered includes how one sees oneself as a person and how one relates to other people for supportive, affectional, and fulfilling needs. In other words, data are assessed about the self-concept and interdependence modes.

When making an assessment of the self-concept and interdependence modes, nurses seek answers to questions such as "What kind of information should I obtain?" "What behaviors are significant?" and "How do I decide which behaviors indicate a problem in coping?"

One method of arriving at satisfactory answers to these questions is assessing the patient's or client's roles and comparing the behaviors with the norms, or standards, for that role. The primary role places one in some stage of life with growth and developmental tasks to fulfill. Secondary and tertiary roles accomplish these tasks (described in further detail in Chapter Sixteen). Nurses are guided in the type of information to obtain by knowing the tasks that people are expected to carry out at certain stages of their lives. They identify the roles that are used by the person to achieve these tasks, and they assess the behaviors or the ways in which the tasks are carried out. Behaviors that are not within the norms for the role or indicate that the person has a problem in coping with feelings are maladaptive. The plan of nursing care will attempt to bring these maladaptive behaviors within the normal, or adaptive, range.

When making a psychosocial assessment of the self-concept and interdependence modes, use the following steps:

1. Identify the primary role of the patient or client.
2. Determine the person's appropriate growth and developmental stage of life, according to his or her primary role.
3. Determine the developmental tasks that the person needs to achieve and the secondary roles that are used to accomplish these tasks.
4. Gather additional information about the primary and secondary role performance of adults in terms of their self-concept (how the person sees or feels about oneself) and the interdependence (how the person relates to others) modes.
5. Compare the behaviors of the person with the expectations of society and the individual's specific role, keeping in mind the norms, or range, of behaviors that are acceptable for that role in society.
6. Assess maladaptive behaviors (those outside the norms for the role) to define problems of coping in the self-concept or interdependence modes.
7. State the primary and secondary roles as stimuli or influencing factors for the problems that have been identified.

The assessment of psychosocial functioning is an essential part of the nursing care plan for the patient and should be carried out as part of the initial assessment interview unless contraindicated by the patient's physical condition. The initial assessment interview provides several positive results when carried out preoperatively and prior to complex medical and diagnostic treatments. It helps to promote a trust relationship between the patient and the nurse, helps to identify potential coping problems which the patient and nurse can plan ways to avoid or reduce, helps to decrease the patient's anxiety level because of the nurse's consideration for the patient as a whole person, and, through all the above, promotes a more rapid recovery to an adapted state.

Some patients in the second stage of illness may be too ill or may lack the energy to provide information for the psychosocial assessment until a later time. Priority is given to meeting the basic physiological needs and to stabilizing the physical condition; nursing attention is then directed to the psychosocial needs. Conscious patients who are seriously ill generally are anxious about their condition and have problems coping with their feelings of fear, anger, and depression. When patients are unable to provide information directly, the nurse gathers information from other sources. The patient's age and sex provide the primary role and place the person in a stage of life that is characterized by certain growth and developmental tasks that are to be carried out during that stage. Admission records and other hospital records provide information about the patient's marital status, place of residence, and occupation and other personal data, such as next of kin, religious preference, and place of birth. When a patient enters the convalescent stage of illness and the condition improves, the nurse assesses the roles to determine either adaptation or the presence of coping problems in the self-concept and interdependence modes.

## APPLICATION TO CLINICAL PRACTICE

In preparation for assessing roles, answer the following questions about role theory:

1. The unit of culture is _____.
2. The unit of personality is _____.
3. The unit of society is _____.
4. A definition of role is _____.
5. List the roles that you have as you carry out your daily life.
   Primary role _____
   Secondary roles _____
   Tertiary roles _____
6. Interview your assigned patient and list the primary and secondary roles that he or she has now or had prior to becoming ill.

| Primary | Secondary |
| --- | --- |
| | |
| | |
| | |

## REFERENCES

Baca, Josephine: Some health beliefs of the Spanish speaking. Am J Nurs, *69*:2172–2176, (October) 1969.

Banton, Michael: Roles: An Introduction to the Study of Social Relations. New York, Basic Books, Inc., Publishers, 1965.

Biddle, Bruce, and Thomas, Edwin: Role Theory: Concepts and Research. New York, John Wiley & Sons, Inc., 1966, p 10.

DeGracia, Rosario: Filipino cultural influences. Am J Nurs, *79*:1412–1414, (August) 1979.

Erikson, E. H.: Childhood and Society, 2nd ed. New York, W. W. Norton and Co., Inc. 1963.

Grier, William, and Cobb, Price: Black Rage. New York, Basic Books, Inc., Publishers, 1968.

Havighurst, Robert J.: Human Development and Education. New York, Longman, Inc., 1953.

Linton, Ralph: The Study of Man. New York, Appleton-Century-Crofts, 1936.

Love, Lucile: The process of role change. *In* Carlson, Caroline (ed.): Behavioral Concepts and Nursing Intervention. Philadelphia, J. B. Lippincott Co., 1970.

Madsen, William: The Mexican-American of South Texas. New York, Holt, Rinehart and Winston, 1973, pp 70–107.

Pontius, Sharon L.: Practical Piaget: helping children understand. Am J Nurs, *82*:114–117, (January) 1982.

Rambo, Beverly: Role function mode. Mimeographed study guide, revised. Los Angeles, Mount St. Mary's College, Associate Degree Nursing Program, 1977.

Randall, Brooke: Development of role function. *In* Roy, Sister Callista (ed.): Introduction to Nursing: An Adaptation Model. Englewood Cliffs, NJ, Prentice-Hall, Inc., 1976, pp 256–264.

Wilson, Everett: Sociology: Rules, Roles, and Relationships. Homewood, Illinois, The Dorsey Press, 1966, p. 232.

# Growth and Developmental Tasks of Children

## OBJECTIVES  Information in this chapter will help you to

1. State the stages and the psychosocial conflicts associated with each stage in the lives of children.
2. List the growth and developmental tasks that children must learn in each stage.
3. Assess the behaviors that children use to carry out growth and development tasks to gather information regarding the functioning of the self-concept and interdependence modes.
4. Compare childrens' behaviors with norms, or standards, set by society, and identify those behaviors that indicate ineffective coping with feelings or relationships with others.
5. Describe health care needs and leading causes of death for each childhood stage of life.

## DEFINITION OF TERMS

**ambivalent** — having both positive and negative feelings about something or someone—like and dislike, love and hate.

**cognition** — the ability to become aware of or gain knowledge of an object; includes the processes of perceiving, sensing, conceiving, recognizing, reasoning, and judging.

**development** — refers to functional or psychological changes in a person that are qualitative and occur as a lifelong process of personality.

**developmental tasks** — the skills, attitudes, habits, and behaviors that must be learned for personal and social adjustment at various stages of life.

growth — an orderly and continuous process that is organic and quantitative in nature until a certain point of maturity is reached at which no further growth occurs.

maturation — the process of attaining maximum physiological growth; programmed for certain levels of growth to occur before learning can take place.

puberty    the maturing of the reproductive organs; the earliest age at which one is capable of sexual reproduction.

From the hour of one's birth, one is continually moving along the age continuum, growing older with each passing day. Tremendous spurts of growth occur during the first year of life. Growth slows during childhood but accelerates again at puberty before leveling off and stabilizing as one reaches adulthood. Maturation is a stable and predictable pattern of growth that enables the newborn infant who weighs an average of 7.5 pounds and is 20.5 inches in length to grow to an adult stature of appropriate height and weight and to have the necessary motor skills. In addition to growth, certain nonorganic or developmental changes must occur at each stage of life. These changes, like growth changes, occur in an orderly manner so that new experiences are built on previous experiences. They emerge as coping mechanisms or responses that the individual learns to use to control emotions and form the basis for attitudes, values, and beliefs that make up what is commonly referred to as the personality. Whereas physiological growth is achieved by the time one enters adulthood, the task of coping with psychological and social changes is dynamic and continues throughout one's life.

In the assessment of the physiological mode, the focus was the function of body parts in the maintenance of life and health. Data containing information about how one met one's basic needs of oxygen, fluids and electrolytes, nutrition, elimination of wastes, rest and exercise, temperature control, and sensory regulation were collected. Assessment of growth and developmental tasks provides additional information about body stature and learning of psychomotor skills, as well as psychological and social functioning. An extremely wide range of behaviors that may be observed exists because no two people react to the same change in exactly the same way and because no individual reacts exactly in the same way from one day to the next. Nurses need a method of assessing behavior that is dynamic and changing and standards for comparing the patient's behaviors with what "should be" or "ought to be." Without some criteria for judging whether the patient's behavior is within the adaptive range, nurses might make judgments based on personal and subjective feelings, which might differ radically from the decisions made by other nurses.

Information about the growth and developmental tasks through the life span provides the nurse with a framework for gathering assessment data about the patient's biopsychosocial functioning. The culture and the society in which one lives provides standards for comparing behaviors that have been observed. The culture provides the roles that one performs to maintain one's place, or position in society, and society defines expectations for these roles, sets boundaries for the range of acceptable behaviors, and defines the sanctions that encourage people to conform to the requirements of the roles. By assessing the roles that patients carry out, nurses gather information about how patients see themselves, feel about their lives, and interact with others, which are the functions of the self-concept and interdependence modes.

According to Erikson, one progresses through eight states during one's lifetime. The first five stages, which encompass the growth and development from infancy through adolescence, will be discussed in this chapter. The three stages of adulthood will be discussed in Chapter Seventeen. Information is included about the population, health problems frequently encountered, and major causes of death in each stage. Thus, nurses gain knowledge about the health care needs of patients in different stages.

## PRINCIPLES OF GROWTH AND DEVELOPMENT

As nurses prepare to assess areas of growth and development in their patients and clients, they should keep several principles in mind.

Primarily, all growth and development occurs as a continuing process that is orderly, occurs in definite sequences, and forms a predictable pattern.

Secondly, all individuals follow this definite pattern of growth; however, slight variations occur because individuals grow at different rates, at different times, and in different manners.

Stimuli causing these individual differences include sex, heredity, nutritional level, hormone activity, position in family, state of health, rate of intellectual growth, and attitudes of parents and family.

Thirdly, biopsychosocial development results from both maturation and learning. Even doting mothers are unable to toilet train their children until certain levels of growth have occurred in the maturation process. The levels of growth include the eruption of teeth, being able to eat solid foods, stabilization of the digestive process and functions of the intestinal tract, ability to sit upright, and the ability and motivation to learn bowel and bladder control. Children must reach the "readiness" state of maturation for learning to occur. In order to catch a football, a child must have visual acuity with which to see the approaching ball, some depth perception, control and coordination of the upper extremities to grasp the moving object, and the ability to understand that the action is play, which is enjoyable. In a similar manner, the readiness to read, ride a bicycle, and learn other skills depends upon reaching a certain level of maturation and learning the new pattern of behavior.

The orderly and predictable pattern of growth incorporates these three principles: (1) growth occurs in sequence from the head to the foot, (2) growth occurs from the central body parts to those more distant, and (3) growth proceeds from the general to the specific. At birth, the infant's head is 60 per cent of the size of an adult's head due to more growth being concentrated in the head and upper trunk. If the size of the rest of the body was equal in percentage to the head, at birth, the infant would be more than 40 inches in length rather than the average 20 to 21 inches in length. Continued growth and maturation occur first with the head and neck; thus, infants learn to raise their heads and look around before they are able to reach for things with their hands or to control their legs and feet. Later growth occurs in the neck and trunk of the body, and, during the teen-age years, rapid growth is found in the long bones of the extremities—teen-agers seem to grow inches practically overnight.

Growth also occurs first proximally, or in those body parts that are nearest the center of the body. The infant gains control of the shoulder before being able to control movements of the elbow, and control of the elbow is gained before learning to perform coordinated movements of the hand and fingers.

Growth follows the principle of differentiation—it progresses from the general to the specific and from the simple to the complex. The first movements of the infant are massive—when the infant cries, the entire body is involved, with arms and legs waving, the trunk heaving, and the face being contorted. As differentiation progresses, the crying becomes more specific with movement confined to the arms and upper body, and, finally, only the eyes cry. Socially, the infant responds to people in general before learning that it is the mother figure who is preferred. In other areas of psychological and social functioning, the same pattern of general to specific and simple to complex occurs.

One's basic personality is formed during infancy and early childhood. Physiological and psychological traits and the preferred coping pattern of behavior (moving-toward, moving-away, or moving-against) are established by age five years, and these behaviors, attitudes, and coping determine how one will respond later in life, whether as an optimist or a pessimist, a leader or a follower.

Each stage of life has its own typical characteristics that set it apart from the other stages. These are the traits, features, and developmental tasks that must be accomplished or learned to meet the requirements and expectations of society.

## THE CHILDHOOD STAGES OF LIFE

As one progresses through life, one passes from infancy to childhood to adulthood. Each stage of life is associated with growth and psychosocial changes and the need to develop new patterns of behavior, or to carry out different roles. Erikson described eight distinct stages of life, each with its psychosocial conflict that confronts the individual and must be worked through so that the individual can relate satisfactorily to the social world. Although the conflict is characteristic of one stage, it continues to be modified, expanded, or refined in other stages and serves as a building block for more complex conflicts.

Erikson's stages of life have been modified and labelled as follows: infancy, toddler, preschool, school-age, adolescent, young adult, generative adult, and mature adult. (See Table 16–1.) For purposes of assessment, each stage has been assigned an approximate age range, although the boundaries for these periods of life are somewhat ambiguous. For example, some people between the ages of 60 and 64 may have more in common with people in the mature adult group, coping with developmental tasks associated with that group, than with people in the generative adult group. However, the age of 65 is a common dividing point between the two groups and is the usual age of retirement and Social Security benefits.

**Table 16–1.    THE STAGES OF LIFE, SHOWING DEVELOPMENTAL TASKS, RELATIONSHIPS WITH OTHERS, SOCIAL SKILLS TO BE LEARNED, AND THE ADAPTIVE OUTCOME TO BE ACHIEVED IN EACH STAGE**

| Stages (approximate ages in yrs) | Psychosocial Developmental Conflict | Relationship (with) | Social Skills (to be learned) | Adaptive Outcomes |
|---|---|---|---|---|
| Infancy (birth–1) | Trust versus mistrust | Maternal person | To get, to give back | Drive, hope |
| Toddler (1–2) | Autonomy versus shame and doubt | Parents | To hold on, to let go | Self-control, willpower |
| Preschool (3–5) | Initiative versus guilt | Family | To make, to make believe | Direction, purpose |
| School-age (6–12) | Industry versus inferiority | School, neighborhood | To compete, to cooperate | Method, competence |
| Adolescent (13–18) | Identity versus role confusion | Peers, ingroups, outgroups | To be oneself, to share being oneself | Devotion, fidelity |
| Young adult (19–34) | Intimacy versus isolation | Partner in sex, friendship, competition | To find oneself, lose oneself in another | Affiliation, love |
| Generative adult (35–64) | Generativity versus stagnation (self-centered) | Community, next generation | To be needed, to take care of | Productivity, caring |
| Mature adult (Over 65) | Integrity versus despair | Mankind, one's own kind | To be oneself, to face one's death | Renunciation, wisdom |

Adapted from: Erikson, Erik H.: Childhood and Society, 2nd ed. New York, W. W. Norton and Co., Inc., 1963.

**Figure 16–1.**    Stages of life: mother and son change as they age together over a period of years.

**Table 16–2. BIRTH TRENDS**

|  | 1950 | 1960 | 1970 | 1975 | 1978 |
|---|---|---|---|---|---|
| Live births (in 1000s) | 3632 | 4258 | 3731 | 3144 | 3333 |
| Birth rate (per 1000 women, ages 14 – 44) | 106.2 | 118.0 | 87.9 | 66.7 | 66.6 |
| White | 102.3 | 113.2 | 84.1 | 63.0 | 52.7 |
| Black; other | 137.3 | 153.6 | 113.0 | 89.3 | 89.3 |

Source: Bureau of Census: Statistical Abstract of the United States 1980, 101st ed. Washington, DC, 1980, p. 62.

Each stage will be described in detail, including a summary of the characteristics, health problems, growth and developmental tasks, typical roles, and examples of behaviors of each stage.

## THE INFANCY STAGE

Between 3 and 4 million babies are born in the United States each year. In recent decades, the birth rate has been decreasing steadily, although some years have shown a slight increase in the number of babies born. The number of children per both white and nonwhite family is decreasing although nonwhite families continue to consist of more children. (See Table 16-2.)

At birth, the newborn baby is not really new but is about 280 days old, carrying the genetic traits that will influence its future growth and response patterns. A newborn baby weighs about 7.5 pounds and is about 20.5 inches in length when born. It seems tiny, its skin is often wrinkled, its facial features include fat cheeks, a short flat nose, and a receding chin that facilitates sucking; its neck is just a fold in the skin, and its head is wobbly and large in comparison with the rest of the body.

**Growth and Maturation.** A baby's first year of life is a period of immense motor activity. Two complex tasks that are learned in infancy are control of the body in an upright position and in locomotion and reaching, grasping, and manipulating objects with the hands. The mouth is the first organ used for gratification and exploration. Only later are the hands used, when maturation progresses from head to foot and from proximal to more distal parts of the body. In learning to walk, the infant progresses through stages that include holding the head up (by about the fourth week), crawling around without lifting the body from the floor (by the fifth month), sitting alone without support (by about the seventh month), creeping with the body off the floor and propelling one-self by all fours, and finally, walking alone (by about 14 months). By the end of the first year, an infant has nearly tripled its birth weight, grown half again as much in length, and cut about nine teeth.

From birth, babies can see, and vision is so important that it has been said that infants understand their world through seeing it before they can "grasp it" with their hands. The eyes are the first body parts one uses to learn patterns of

Figure 16–2. Infancy: learning to relate to mother and sitting up alone.

behavior. By four weeks of age, the infant sees objects that are dangled in front of him and can follow objects with its eyes; however, not until about four months of age can the infant hold a rattle and look at it at the same time. Through rapid growth of the visual apparatus, other senses, and motor neurons, the infant begins to form perceptions of the vague, fluctuating "blobs" that form the visual world; thus, these "blobs" become the faces of people and objects.

**Developmental Tasks.** During the first year of life, the infant experiences rapid growth and tremendous changes. In addition to physical growth, certain developmental tasks must be learned that are basic to those associated with later stages of life. These tasks help to prepare the infant to grow into a competent person who is capable of independent living. The developmental tasks of infancy include

*Distinguishing between pleasant and unpleasant experiences.* The mouth is the primary organ of gratification and exploration, and sucking provides the greatest sense of satisfaction. The infant is an egocentric person whose desires and needs mostly originate from within. When a strong need such as for food arises, the infant responds by crying and with quite intense movements of the entire body. From birth, infants show an excitement type of emotion. After four weeks, the excitement is followed by distress. At about eight weeks, the infant shows delight, followed at six months by anger, disgust, and fear. Because the mother is the first person to expose the infant to an emotional climate, how the mother feels about the infant is very important.

*"Getting" what is needed for survival and comfort.* At birth, the baby is completely dependent upon others but has no interest in others or in companionship as long as his or her needs are met. By the end of the second month, the infant is beginning to respond to those who provide care, and, soon after, follows the mother's movements and smiles. The mother and infant develop reciprocal responses; each reinforces the other to form behavioral patterns. In addition to meeting the basic physiological needs, the infant has the psychological needs for contact with others, protection, and security. These needs are met by the mother as the infant snuggles, nurses, and cuddles.

*Developing trust.* The most significant person in the infant's life is the mother or the caregiver. At first, the newborn baby does not differentiate between the mother and self. By four to six months, the infant responds to faces, and, by eight months, recognizes the mother's face. The quality of the maternal-child relationship is very important for the development of trust, which affects one's coping and behavioral responses throughout life. The mother should be consistent in providing soft, warm, and gentle contact with the infant and should provide comfort and security while meeting the infant's physical needs. Loss of security and lack of trust lead to crying and rocking back and forth and, later, to the behaviors of withdrawal and depression and, in extreme cases, death.

*Seeing the mother or care-giver as distinct from all others.* By nine months of age, the infant is aware of the loss of the mother and, if picked up by others, will cry and look around for the mother. The infant is able to distinguish between familiar persons and strangers and between smiling and frowning faces and is able to recognize the mother's voice.

*Responding to language and imitating sounds.* By three months of age, the infant smiles when socially stimulated and makes preverbal sounds in the mouth and throat. By the end of the first year, the infant responds to various sounds, begins to imitate sounds, and imitates the sounds made by the parents. The infant pays attention to a few familiar words and recognizes his or her name and the names of other family members and family pets.

**Self-Concept and Interdependence Modes.** At birth, the baby is completely egocentric and lacks any concept of the self beyond the primitive impulses and reflexes intended to assist in survival. These impulses and reflexes influence most of the infant's behavior during the first two years of life, until the self-identity begins to emerge.

Infancy is the period of immaturity and dependence upon others for survival. Help-seeking behaviors include excitement, sucking, rooting, crying, and gross motor activity. By the age of five or six months, attention- and affection-seeking behaviors can be observed in the infant when it smiles, shows interest, and begins to play simple "give and take" games.

**Health Needs and Problems.** The first year of life is one of the most hazardous years. The death rate is higher for this stage than for any of the other stages until one reaches old age. Table 16–3 lists the common causes of death among infants in the United States in 1977.

As shown in Table 16–3, many deaths are associated with birth. Immaturity caused by premature birth accounts for the largest number of infant deaths and is followed by deaths that occur at about the time of birth. Causes for these deaths include difficult births, long labor, birth injuries, and disease of or injury to the mother.

**Table 16–3.** COMMON CAUSES OF DEATHS AMONG
INFANTS IN THE UNITED STATES

| Causes | Rate per 100,000 Live Births | Total Number in 1977 |
|---|---|---|
| Immaturity | 407.7 | 13,564 |
| Birth-associated | 294.4 | 9,794 |
| Congenital birth defects | 253.1 | 8,421 |
| Sudden infant deaths | 142.8 | 4,751 |
| Influenza and pneumonia | 50.6 | 1,683 |
| Septicemia | 32.7 | 1,088 |
| Accidents | 27.7 | 922 |
| Total—from all causes | 1412.1 | 46,981 |

Source: Revolution in health care urged in new surgeon general's
report. Am J Nurs, *79*:1672, (October) 1979.

Following deaths caused by congenital birth
defects are sudden infant deaths, commonly
referred to as "crib deaths" and deaths caused by
respiratory failure and other infections and
accidents.

Infants are totally dependent upon others for
their survival, health, and security. Social conditions such as poverty, hunger, and ignorance
can destroy health, especially the health of
infants and children. In some poorer countries
of the world, as many as four of five children
die before reaching their fifth birthday. The high
death rate is due to poor nutrition, poor sanitation, lack of knowledge by the parents, and
infectious diseases. Infants need adequate nourishment, which includes an adequate number of
calories and sufficient protein, vitamins, and
minerals to provide for growth and development
of their bodies and minds. Breast-fed babies
receive additional immunity to some infectious
diseases by the substances contained in the
mother's milk. Immunization against other
childhood diseases, such as diphtheria, whooping
cough, smallpox, scarlet fever, measles, and
poliomyelitis, should be accomplished in the first
year of life.

## THE TODDLER STAGE

The second year of one's life is dominated by
motor skills, such as walking, examining objects
with one's hands, beginning to use language, and
beginning to control bowel and bladder functions.
The child is engaged in taking control of walking,
eating, bending, climbing on things, and removing objects from cabinets and putting them back.
As the child explores and investigates his or her
surroundings, he or she experiments with two
important social approaches: (1) holding on, and
(2) letting go. Through the expectations and
attitudes of others, the child learns that holding
on may be a pattern of caring or that it can be a
restrictive and cruel restraining. Letting go involves turning loose destructive or uncontrolled
forces, or it can be an easy "let it be." Through
the processes of "to hold on" and "to let be
(go)," the child learns the basis for self-control
and will power.

**Growth and Maturation.** Growth continues in
an orderly manner during the second year as the
infant becomes a toddler and continues the process of becoming a unique individual. Although
all children follow the same patterns of growth,
they do so at their own rate, which can differ
greatly from one child to another. The physiological tasks for the toddler include

*Learning to walk and use the finer muscle
groups.*
*Learning to control the bowel and bladder.*
*Learning to eat solid foods.*
*Learning to communicate.*

During this stage, the child's motor skills are
still awkward and inconsistent, but the child is
very active and learning to control its body. The
toddler develops the ability to control half the
body at a time and to transfer movement to the
other half as he or she marches, hops, or skips or
uses scissors to cut paper. The child's preference
for using the right or left hand begins to emerge.
By three years of age, the child has better coordination and is able to stand on one foot, climb
stairs by alternating the feet, and swing the arms
when walking rather than holding them outward.

With the emergence of the baby teeth, the
child is equipped to eat solid food. During the
second and third years, the child gains an average
of three to five pounds and the two-year-old is
now approximately 32 to 36 inches tall.

When the child has gained some understanding

**Figure 16–3.** The toddler stage: mastering the skills of walking and control of other muscle groups for locomotion.

of language, bowel training can begin. Some children gain voluntary control by 18 months, others take much longer. Some children achieve control of the bladder during the day by the end of the second year, but nighttime control may not occur until the third year.

Vision continues to develop during the toddler stage. The child's visual acuity increases from 20/100 at one year of age to 20/40 by two years of age. The toddler shows an intense interest in pictures and is able to scribble on paper. However, depth perception is poorly developed, often causing him or her to overreach or to underestimate the location of objects.

Use of language accelerates during this stage. At one year of age the child recognizes approximately 10 words and uses about three words. However, by two years of age, the toddler recognizes approximately 1200 words and has a vocabulary of about 270 words. Speech and language are acquired by hearing the sounds, discriminating among them, and imitating them. Any disturbance to hearing or verbal stimulation produces a severe handicap for the child in learning to use language to communicate. Language also provides the symbols that one uses for thought processes and the mental skills that are essential in adapting to changes and in leading satisfying lives.

**Developmental Tasks.** Like the infant, toddlers are egocentric, they feel that the universe revolves around them. They experience reality in a vague, universal way—in the "here and now," having no past or future. They are unable to see how their actions affect others or things with which they come in contact.

The major developmental task of toddlers is resolving the conflict of autonomy versus shame and doubt by developing self-control without the loss of self-esteem. After having developed trust in the mother when they were infants, toddlers now realize that they are separate from the mother and that they can function on their own. They are able to use their body as a tool and can do many things by themselves, such as feeding themselves, walking and running, climbing stairs and walking back down, and reaching for the toys or books that they want. As toddlers assert themselves, they feel a sense of autonomy in directing their actions as they desire. However, parents must set boundaries in a way that will encourage toddlers to make choices and to "stand on their own feet," and, at the same time, will protect them from shame and doubt, resulting from the disapproval of their behavior by others. This is the stage in which parents restrict children by saying "That is a no-no" and children reply to requests by saying "No, no." Self-control is learned by holding on or holding in a caring way and by letting things be or letting go without feeling a loss of control or a fear of being attacked. After resolving the conflict, the toddler emerges with the feeling "I am a person" or "I am what I desire."

**Self-Concept and Interdependence Modes.** The self-concept of the toddler is in the early formative stage. Seeing oneself as a person is a slow developmental process. Children may recognize themselves in a mirror as early as one year of age. However, their speech indicates the slowness of the process. As they call themselves by their own name as if they were an object and only gradually make the transition to using personal pronouns. They use personal pronouns in this sequence: "Mary down," "me get down," and "I want it" or "I do it." The child's growing sense of freedom and autonomy in this stage of life leads to the development of "I," and to a feeling of being in charge of parts of his or her personal world. From infancy, parents begin shaping the child's gender role, through which the child is encouraged to imitate and to identify with the parent. Little girls are handled more gently than are boys, are told to do things "just like Mommy" and are given toys such as dolls and doll carriages so that they can imitate the mother. Little boys are subjected to more rough and tumble play than are girls and are given toys to manipulate, pound, and hit.

Toddlers continue to have many dependent needs; however, the significant others in their lives now extend from the mother to include the father. Although they can now take care of basic needs, such as eating solid food, communicating with others, understanding responses of others, moving about with more ease, and controlling elimination to some degree, they continue to look to others for attention and affection. Children of this age seek attention as they explore their surroundings and enjoy being the center of attention by jabbering, waving bye-bye, and playing peekaboo and patty-cake. The self-assertive behavior of the child's second year leads to the "terrible twos" and temper tantrums, resulting from the parents decision that the child must learn that he cannot have whatever he wants and that crying will not get it for him. Toddlers show initiative behaviors by actively exploring things such as pots and pans in the kitchen cabinets and by obstacle mastery, working very hard to achieve or to reach a goal, such as turning on a faucet or turning a doorknob.

**Health Needs and Problems.** On the average, children in this stage of life enjoy better health and have a lower death rate than those in the infancy stage. Toddlers' health problems primarily consist of disturbances of the gastrointestinal tract and respiratory infections and other diseases similar to those of the preschooler.

Toddlers have less experience than older children in coping with new stressful situations. Parents provide the most security for them, and the fear of being separated from the parents causes the greatest anxiety. They lack the vocabulary to express their fears and anxieties; thus, behavioral responses that are most often observed include crying, intense motor activity, and withdrawal behaviors. When caring for sick toddlers, effective nursing interventions employed to reduce their anxieties include having the parent present during procedures and to hold them afterwards, using simple words and explaining one thing at a time, and encouraging the children to play "nurse" and to touch or handle the stethoscope, syringe, or other pieces of equipment.

## THE PRESCHOOL STAGE

Children from three to five (or six) years of age continue to be egocentric and to think that they are the center of the universe. They are evolving from the infant stage of becoming aware of the concrete world about them to becoming an individual who is ready to be a part of the world of books, reading, and abstract ideas and expand their cognitive skills. Their vocabulary expands at a tremendous rate. In the first half of this stage, they ask "What?" continuously as they seek to learn the names of things. In the latter half of the stage, they gather additional information about things by asking "Why?" Preschool children have no sense of time, although they use basic time words and make a pretense of telling time. They live in the "here and now" but can be persuaded to wait for things. The mother is still the most important person to them; however, most preschoolers have a pleasant relationship with the father and enjoy special occasions or outings with him. The preschooler is active and refining motor skills by running up and down stairs, throwing a ball, galloping, jumping, racing on a tricycle, and climbing. More time is spent in play, and they have developed a vivid imagination that enriches their periods of play.

The major task of the preschool stage of life is determining the answer to the question "What kind of person will I be?" This question follows the task of autonomy, resulting in the child feeling "I am a person." By learning to make things and by manipulating symbols in make-believe, young children add initiative to their sense of autonomy as they undertake a task, plan it, and carry it out. Their active curiosity and interest cause their behavior to be intrusive in the following ways: (1) physically, onto other people's bodies as they climb, pull, and tug, (2) into other people's minds and ears, by their aggressive talking, (3) into space, by their vigorous movements and activities, and (4) into the unknown, by their curiosity.

**Growth and Maturation.** Children in the preschool age continue to refine their gross motor activities, which began in previous stages, and begin to use and control the finer and more specific motor groups. Instead of scribbling on paper in a haphazard fashion, they now begin to draw circles, progressing to squares and triangles. They are better able to stay within the lines when coloring and, by five years of age, can cut on the lines with scissors. The preschool areas of growth and maturation include

*Achieving an integrated control of motor and perceptual activities.*
*Gaining complete voluntary control over the elimination of wastes.*
*Achieving physiological stability.*
*Improving the ability to communicate and to understand others.*

During the first five (or six) years of life, children pick up stimuli from the environment through the sensory organs, and, at first, they attend to only the most prominent of the millions of stimuli that "bombard" them. As they integrate these stimuli, they become more aware of complex and intricate stimuli and develop a perceptual process of attaching meaning to them. This provides the structure, or organization, for future learning. By three years of age, the effects of previous growth and development result in greater self-control of motor abilities. Preschool children are conforming to and agreeable with others. They display a "threeish" scope to their attention and insight; they count to three, name three objects in a picture, build a tower of nine blocks, and compare two things, which requires a three-step thought process. They have almost complete control of bowel and bladder functions. Finer control of muscles is shown by their ability to copy circles, squares, and other figures. Three-year-olds are able to distinguish different sounds in speech and to speak sentences that average three or four words. They understand up to 3600 words and have a vocabulary of up to 900 words. They can identify some colors and tell stories that are understandable.

Four-year-old children are characterized as having lively minds and as being assertive in their relationships with others. They have entered the world of play and have vivid imaginations, which allows them to experiment with words, symbols, ideas, and thoughts. They jump from one thought to another in rapid succession as they engage in dramatic play and socialize with others, where they are bossy, dogmatic, boastful, and praise themselves by bragging. Four-year-olds use sentences of five or six words, have a vocabulary of 1500 words, can recite jingles, and sing songs. They want to know why things happen and may ask as many as 500 questions per day. Their motor skills have become more refined; thus, they can throw a ball with more accuracy and do two activities at a time, such as talking while eating or washing their face and hands.

By the time they reach five years of age, children make the focus of their activities clearer and perform their work and play more completely than when they were four years of age. At five, they have an idea in mind before they begin to draw and are able to criticize themselves by saying "I want to draw a lion, but I don't know how." Their motor coordination is better defined, and they are nearly independent in taking care of their personal duties and in performing simple household tasks. They have a sense of their own identity and take pride in their possessions and clothes. Their language skills continue to expand rapidly; they now understand more than 9000 words and have a vocabulary of about 2000 words. They can print simple words, read by identifying pictures, and are able to single out a word to ask its meaning.

**Developmental Tasks.** During the preschool stage of life, children are gaining control of their bodies, learning to control primitive drives and their emotions, and developing social skills that they will use when they enter the world beyond the protection of their family and home. The developmental tasks of the preschool stage include

*Achieving independence in self-care activities.*
*Learning sex differences and sexual modesty.*
*Forming simple concepts of reality and of how to behave toward persons and things.*
*Learning to relate emotionally to one's parents, brothers and sisters, and others.*
*Learning to distinguish right from wrong and developing a conscience.*

The way that children learn these developmental tasks largely depends upon the way that others, as role models, act in their surroundings. The social environment of preschool children is extremely important as they initiate actions to expand their horizons and establish the personality characteristics of the type of person that they want to be. They want to be like their parents, whom they view as being omnipotent, big, beautiful, and very powerful. When two-year-olds were learning autonomy, their behavior was limited by their parents when their actions were not approved. In the preschool stage, children are ready to learn more. They copy the way that the parents act and respond to gain approval. They pass through a phase of suggestibility as they reflect the moods, attitudes, and outlooks of the parents and then identify with people whom they love or who have traits or abilities that they admire. It is their way of reaching out for the personal characteristics that they would like to have.

**Self-Concept and Interdependence Modes.** At the preschool stage in life, one's self-concept is beginning to emerge. By the age of five, one's basic personality is established. Children have gained control of motor muscle groups and are able to use their body as a tool to carry out many activities. They have an image of their body and know sensations associated with it.

Although sex roles are less clear today than they were in the past, children generally have worked through basic attitudes of sexuality by the end of this stage. They know the difference between men and women by exploration of the genitals and they know which sex they are. Little boys tend to identify with their fathers and little girls with their mothers.

During this time, the concepts of right and wrong are being formed; however, they are limited to the things that the parents permit or forbid. They begin to learn right from wrong when the parents set boundaries for the troublesome two-year-olds, learning to assert themselves. By three years of age, children want to conform to the parents' expectations so they ask "Do it this way?" Four-year-olds may begin to understand about "rules" and five-year-olds often believe that God is responsible for everything.

During this stage, children make giant strides toward independence as they learn to take care of their own personal needs. They are able to feed, dress, and wash themselves, as well as help their parents with simple household tasks. They have enlarged the space in which they live to beyond a room in the house, and they spend more time outside and playing. With wider social horizons, they are less dependent upon the parents for help and attention while still very dependent upon them for emotional support and affection.

**Health Needs and Problems.** The major developmental conflict of this stage is between developing initiative and resolving feelings of guilt when this task is not achieved. During the preschool stage, children are faced with the need to develop new ways of coping with changes that are occurring in their lives. Through the development of skills in movement and in language, a greater self-awareness emerges. Children are able to use imagination and to control anxiety by play-acting and making believe. They learn that successful ways of coping lead to feeling good about oneself as a real person and that failure to achieve the feeling of "I who can become whatever I image me to be" and forming an identity, or self-concept, of "I have ability to try to be (the parent role) even though I am little" leads to overwhelming guilt. Too much guilt results in confusion in the psychosexual role, rigidity in relationships with others, and lose of initiative in exploring and learning new skills.

Although preschool children are subject to gastrointestinal disturbances and upper respiratory infections, they and children to 14 years of age have, by far, the lowest death rate of any stage of life. Motor accidents and all other types of accidents are the leading causes of death, with cancer as the distant third cause.

## THE SCHOOL-AGE STAGE

The school-age stage of life extends from about six years of age to the onset of puberty, which occurs at about the age of 12 or 13. Experiences in the school-age stage help children to answer the question "What can I do now that I am a person?" School-age children are preparing for entrance into life as an adult in a specific culture and preparing to win recognition by what they produce. In every culture, school-age children are given instruction in a systematic way in how to be a worker and how to provide for oneself and one's future family. They learn the fundamentals of the technology used in their specific culture, or society, and handle the tools, weapons, and objects used by the adults in that culture. Performing tasks and activities satisfactorily and learning the basic knowledge and technology of one's culture leads to a sense of adequacy. One's self-esteem is enhanced by a feeling of being "someone who can master" what needs to be accomplished. The failure to initiate, plan, and achieve the task or to gain control of one's body and objects in the environment leads to feelings of inferiority.

**Growth and Maturation.** Physiological growth is slow and steady during the school-age years. The average child grows two to three inches in height and gains three to six pounds in weight each year. However, growth rate varies greatly among children. Boys tend to be taller and heavier than girls until 10 years of age when the girls tend to be taller. Early in the school-age stage, children begin to lose their baby teeth. Permanent teeth begin to appear at about eight years of age. At age six, children are able to hop, skip, tie a bow, and ride a tricycle but lack small muscle control needed for precise writing or drawing. They are more physically active and become restless in a short period of time while sitting still. Seven- and eight-year-old children spend more time in imitative and explorative types of play and delight in activities, such as walking on ledges, playing with balls that they can now aim, and kicking cans, rocks or balls. In the latter half of this stage, children have an excessive amount of energy that they devote to games and playing. Favorite activities include riding a bicycle, jumping rope, skating, swimming, and playing hopscotch. Team sports are popular, and "I dare you" types of activities help them to develop strength and speed.

Socially, children in this stage are venturing beyond the home and family as they attend school and make friends with their peers. They develop relationships with members of the same sex, and acceptance by many friends is important. They often form "gangs" of friends. Whereas girls like to play with boys at any age, by nine years of age, boys have adopted the attitude of "no girls allowed" in their "gang" or peer group. At this stage, boys are engaged in activities that express their masculinity, toughness, and adventurous spirit and girls form their own tight-knit groups. Only in later childhood do boys and girls associate with the opposite sex, when they tend to choose friends who are very much like themselves.

Thinking is concrete and based on a simple "cause and effect" approach among younger school-age children. Most older school-age children use simple deductive reasoning and have a fairly realistic view of the ways of the world. They are "learning the rules" that are needed for getting along in the adult world. They are able to tell time, imitate ideas, make up rhymes, write, and understand concepts such as grief and pity.

**Developmental Tasks.**   From infancy, the child has grown through distinct stages of life that required learning specific skills to cope with an expanding awareness of oneself and the world. It has been a logical sequence from learning to cope with "I am a person" to "What kind of a person will I be?" and now to "What can I do?" Whereas the rate of physical growth of the body has slowed during these years, the central nervous system has continued to mature, especially the functions of the brain. Developmental tasks associated with the school-age stage include

*Using tools and acquiring game skills.*
*Relating positively with peers.*
*Developing a sense of conscience.*
*Refining communication skills.*
*Building a wholesome self-concept.*
*Identifying with one's sex role.*
*Learning basic technology through reading, writing, arithmetic, and reasoning skills.*

Many of these developmental tasks are an extension of those begun in a previous stage, but continue to be important factors in this stage. Children learn to move from the simple to the complex and from the concrete to the abstract while continuing to refine behaviors and coping skills that were used previously. During the school-age years, children begin to carry out behaviors associated with the additional secondary

roles of student, friend, family member, team member, and so on. Both boys and girls carry out their primary role by preferring friends of the same sex, dressing in the latest styles as prescribed for their own sex, admiring certain individuals of the opposite sex, and engaging in showing off types of behaviors. They are also learning how to master feelings of rivalry with other children in the give-and-take relationships of their peer groups.

**Self-Concept and Interdependence Modes.**   As children gain control of their body functions and activities, they develop a knowledge of their physical self and acquire a unique image of their body. They take pride in their motor skills and abilities when these approach the quality of adults' or when they do a task as well as Mom or Dad. At this stage, children have a fear of bodily harm and injury. Minor injuries may produce reactions of distress and fear that are out of proportion to the actual damage to tissues. Yet after the initial tears, the scratches, bruises, and bandages are worn as badges of honor and courage.

The everyday behavior of the personal self becomes more consistent as children become increasingly sure of their identity and sexual role. They send out the message "I am what I do" as they mimic their friends in behavior and manner of dress and use all the current "in" expressions of their peer group. The self that they hope to be is based on an adult who is admired and imitated. They identify with this person, whether it be a parent, sports star, entertainer, or Superman. They are able to tell what they would like to be when they grow up and give reasons for selecting that occupation. Morally, children in this stage are able to follow most rules, although some may protest vigorously. By 11 years of age, they are able to understand the pain and hurt feelings that others experience by putting themselves in another's place. They have also learned that adults are not omnipotent, that they do not always follow the rules that they teach, and that they sometimes tell lies or break their promises.

There is a growing shift toward more balance between dependent and independent behavior. School-age children still rely on the family for emotional support, even though the peer group is assuming more importance in their lives. They use the family to try out their new ideas and language. This frequently leads to questioning the parents' authority. They continue to exhibit many behaviors to seek attention and arouse the curiosity of others through showing off, bragging about skills, adopting secret passwords and hideouts, or displaying trophies or awards. Younger school-age children often seek affection from parents by snuggling or asking for help when it is not really needed, whereas older school-age children are ambivalent in displaying affection toward parents but will ask for verbal expression of affection.

Greater independence is seen in the increase of obstacle mastery behaviors when children report on their accomplishments in school, such as printing their name, counting by threes, jumping rope a certain number of times without missing, or getting an "A" on a school paper. They also accept and carry out responsibilities in school and at home by doing things, such as cleaning the chalkboards, picking up their toys, cleaning up their rooms, and emptying the waste baskets.

**Health Needs and Problems.** The coping problem that occurs during this stage is inferiority, or feeling inadequate to control their bodies and situations. When one has failed to master some task, has not measured up to an expectation of the parent, or been denied entry into a peer group, one feels that one is not good enough, and this leads to feelings of inferiority. School-age children are very vulnerable to those feelings as they learn to get along with their peers and with other people in social settings outside the home.

The healthiest age for children is between the ages of 9 and 12. By then, they have endured the childhood diseases and built up immunities to other diseases and have more lymphoid tissue in their bodies than at any other stage, as added protection. Physically, they sleep regularly, are tremendously active, and have excellent appetites.

As mentioned previously, the mortality rate for this stage and the preschool stage is lower than for any other stage of life. In 1976, the mortality rate was 31 deaths for every 100,000 children. As with the preschool stage, the major causes of death are accidents; motor vehicles and all other types of accidents cause about half the deaths and diseases cause the other half. More boys die from accidents because they often dart between cars, climb higher in trees, swing from ropes, and are more daring and take more risks than do girls.

## THE ADOLESCENT STAGE

Adolescence is the stage of life that bridges the gap between the dependency of childhood and the self-sufficiency of adulthood. It covers the teen-age years from 13 or 14 through the age of 18, although some authorities believe that it extends to the age of 21. Most young people between the ages of 19 and 21 probably resemble young adults more closely than do younger teen-agers and would resent being called adolescents. They have a higher degree of sophistication than did previous generations, although they may not show physical, moral, or emotional differences.

The extent of adolescence is determined by one's culture. In some societies, adolescence ends with puberty. In these cultures, youths are regarded as adults after they have reached sexual maturity. In more advanced cultures, such as our own, a longer period of dependence for teen-agers exists, during which they learn the economic, social, and intellectual complexities of adult life. Yet in every culture, teen-agers rework the questions "Who am I?" and "What am I?" as they leave the familiarity of childhood and venture into the unknowns of adult life. The coping mechanisms that were learned as children must now be extended and applied to a wider variety of situations. The sense of trust that they established with parents is now extended to peers, to partners in working and recreational endeavors, and to the social world, including institutions, such as business and government. The sense of autonomy and control that they had over their bodies as children is shaken by a sudden spurt of growth as they acquire the secondary sexual changes of puberty. The childhood response "I am me" is no longer sufficient, and new responses must be learned to carry out the appropriate masculine or feminine role. The initiative and industry of an earlier age is now directed toward examining the issues of "What do I wish to be as an adult?" "In what ways will I carry out my life as an adult?" and "What will be my various roles in life?" The goal of the adolescent's developmental tasks is to attain an identity that permits the pursuit of educational, occupational, and marital relationships as a responsible adult.

**Growth and Developmental Tasks.** When children enter their teen-age years, they must alter their relationships with their parents and the past to achieve an adult identity that allows them to make decisions and to cope with the stresses of adult life. The following growth and developmental tasks that one must carry out to gain this identity include

*Adapting to changes in one's body and physical appearance.*
*Responding to an appropriate sexual role.*
*Establishing emotional independence from adults and, especially, parents.*
*Refining relationships with peers of both sexes.*
*Developing language, intellectual, motor, and social skills necessary for participation in individual and community activities.*
*Achieving a sense of economic independence.*
*Acquiring moral values, attitudes, and beliefs about one's social world.*

During the year or two that precedes puberty, rapid changes occur in the rate of growth in the areas of height, body weight, contours of the body, and hormonal activity. Girls tend to develop more rapidly than do boys and hold their lead until they reach adult maturity. During puberty, the skeletal system often grows faster than the supporting muscles, causing the teenager to be clumsy, lack coordination, and have poor posture. Sebaceous glands in the skin become more active and often cause pimples and acne, to the great distress of the teenager.

The secondary sexual changes that occur in boys, in the order of their appearance, include increase in the size of the genitalia; swelling of the breasts; growth of pubic, axillary, facial, and chest hair; change in voice to a lower range; production of spermatozoa; increase in the width of the shoulders, beginning at about 13 years of age. Changes that occur in girls from 12 years of age are the development of breasts; change in vaginal secretions; growth of pubic and axillary hair; the onset of menstruation; and broadening of the hips. During the first year of menstruation, the periods may be irregular. By age 15 or 16 years, both boys and girls have matured and are capable of reproduction. After puberty, which occurs within a range of 11 to 15 years of age in girls and a year or two later in boys, the growth process slows and changes in body shape occur more gradually.

During this developmental stage, teen-agers are torn in two directions: on the one hand, they are striving to integrate their inner emotions and urges with outside stimuli and expectations in order to establish their own identity and role while, on the other hand, many confusing inner and outer demands lead to a sense of instability. During adolescence, they make a commitment to specific roles, which are selected from many alternatives and to learning the appropriate behavior for the masculine or feminine role for this age group, including a peer group member role, a family member role (sibling to sibling, child to parent), a student intellectual role, an interest group role, an occupational role, and a society member role. They experiment with interests, extremes, and opposites as they seek their role identity and their prospective place within society. Teen-agers' need to experiment and to try a wide range of alternatives often places them in conflict with parents or with other adults and may lead to obstinate types of behavior. Teen-agers talk things over endlessly with a friend of the same sex and age group in their search for their role identity. During mid-adolescence, they must solve the conflict of feeling love and anger toward the same person, usually a parent, sibling, or peer.

Teenagers increase their general knowledge and mental skills during the junior and senior high school years. Mentally, they understand abstract ideas and can retain what they have learned and evaluate the adequacy of their reasoning. They are able to use reason or logic to arrive at the best answer, and they show concern for the real world, which is inferior to their ideal view of what life and the world should be. They are able to think beyond the present to the future and back to the past and are able to build concepts, or theories, for their use.

**Self-Concept and Interdependence Modes.** An important aspect of the self-concept of teen-agers is their appearance, or body image. In our culture, desirable characteristics of appearance include being sexually attractive to others and having easy access to and being accepted by one's peer group. Boys are concerned with being tall, having good muscular development, including a broad chest and broad shoulders, and having an adequate amount of facial and body hair. They look forward to shaving. Girls are concerned with their hair, figures, and facial features and with having clear, unblemished skin. Research studies indicate that boys who mature later than their peers tend to be less popular and more talkative and bossy than those who matured earlier and tend not to be leaders. Few late maturers felt matter-of-fact about their late growth and maturing or were able to laugh about it. The physical changes of their bodies caused teen-age girls to be concerned about menstruation, cramps, irritability, and tension, whereas teen-age boys worried about masturbation, nocturnal emissions, and embarrassment.

One's ideal self-concept undergoes some modification as most adolescents contrast themselves with their ideal person. Most teen-agers state they are not entirely satisfied with themselves and would like to change some things. Their ideals reflect the stereotypical ideal, in which masculinity is associated with largeness and femininity is identified with smallness. Tall girls want to be shorter, and short boys want to be taller; however, both boys and girls complain of blemishes, acne, and other skin eruptions.

Personal consistency in one's self-concept increases as teen-agers behave in ways that they believe that their ideal would behave in similar circumstances. Standards of morality evolve as they define certain behaviors as good or bad. They select a basic philosophy or religion that serves as a stabilizing factor in their lives.

Teen-agers tend to be extremely loyal to those who think and believe as they do and are inflexible in their prejudices. To stabilize their own sense of self, they seem to need to be against and to oppose something or someone. They continue to search for internal consistency because the values that they have about one aspect of life may be inconsistent with their other values. Teen-agers move from the self-centeredness of childhood to a broader view of life as they contemplate social injustices and problems, such as pollution, nuclear power, abortion, endangered animal species, and drug abuse. By the end of the adolescent stage, most youths hold values that are similar to those of the parents and family who are now seen in a new way and with less tension and stress than in earlier years.

During this stage, teen-agers are seriously trying to be like adults, and their major goal is to establish independence from their parents. Conflict is bound to arise because society imposes certain obstacles that prevent complete independence from the family. However, beyond the age of 18, many youths remain financially dependent upon their parents, especially during college or vocational training. Some people live at home until they are married, with their food and shelter provided by the family. Many older adolescents experience great anxiety if they are required suddenly to assume real independence, after having been rewarded for their dependent behaviors.

As teen-agers expand their social world, they share their dependent needs for help, attention, and affection with others — their friends, roommates, and coworkers, with whom they form supportive relationships. Their relationships with family members may be turbulent, with periods of pleasantness and cooperation followed by periods of negativism and rebellion.

With growing independence, adolescents learn to have affection and respect for their parents while relying on others outside the home for additional emotional support. Teen-agers are increasingly able to work at tasks and to persevere until the task is completed, and they have learned to cooperate with others and to coordinate their work. By the end of adolescence, they are able to choose an occupation for which they have some ability and to prepare for it, have acquired a positive attitude about family life and children, and have gained knowledge about home management and child rearing. Adolescents now join the adult world with the ability and desire to deal with it, even though their values may differ from those of preceding generations.

**Health Needs and Problems.** Teen-agers are faced with the task of establishing their identity as an emerging adult by carrying out their primary role with the appropriate behavior for a male or female person of a specific age, as well as gaining the knowledge and skills necessary to carry out the secondary roles that they will use in adult life. Failure to succeed in these develop-

mental tasks leads to feelings of inferiority. Some problem areas in which feelings of inferiority arise are

*Poor body image.*
*Delayed puberty with later maturation than peers.*
*Continued dependency upon parents for emotional, economic, and physical needs.*

Feelings of inferiority are associated with anxiety and stress and may be expressed through any of the behavior patterns of moving-against, moving-toward, or moving-away. Some adolescents may attempt to cope with these feelings by deviant or ineffective behavior, such as that seen in street gangs and juvenile delinquents. Others may revert to childhood behaviors or withdraw from social groups because of their feelings of rejection or loneliness.

The physical health of the adolescent group is usually good, and their death and illness rates are lower than those for infants and adults. Prominent among their health problems are those with a behavioral component and arising from social interactions. Important medical problems of teenagers include

Malignancies (cancer)
Influenza, pneumonia, and respiratory infections
Mental and emotional problems
Pregnancy
Venereal disease
Dental disease
Injuries from accidents and violence
Hepatitis

The main causes of teen-age deaths are external rather than disease conditions of the body; therefore, they are largely preventable. Accidents, especially those involving motor vehicles, account for 70 per cent of all teen-age deaths; diseases cause 30 per cent. Murder is the second leading cause of death among nonwhite teen-agers, particularly males 15 to 19 years of age; however, among white teen-agers, suicide is more prevalent.

## SUMMARY

Children are not miniature adults. They begin life being totally dependent upon others and possessing only primitive reflexes and responses. As they pass through the various stages of childhood, they grow and mature in a distinct pattern, although the rate of growth often varies from one child to another. Specific levels of growth must be reached before other learning can take place and mental concepts can be developed about the self, one's own identity, time, space, language and thought, truth, and the moral sense of right and wrong.

The younger the child, the fewer roles he or she has. The emergence of one's awareness as a person separate from the mother occurs gradually during the toddler stage as one wrestles with the conflict of autonomy versus shame. Children continue to be self-centered until about the age of six years. During these years, they are confronted with learning about the self and their primary role, but socialization into various roles continues at a more rapid pace during the school-age years. By the middle teens, they are more adept at carrying out the roles of son, daughter, brother or sister, friend, student, team or club member, ball player, and so on.

## APPLICATION TO CLINICAL PRACTICE

As you provide nursing care to children, focus your assessment of their growth and developmental tasks on the following areas:

1. Gross motor skills.
2. Fine muscle coordination.
3. Language development.
4. Personal and social skills.

After completing the assessment of the physiological mode, list the growth and developmental tasks of the particular stage of life as well as any information that has been gathered about the child's behaviors and psychosocial adaptation. Use the following assessment form.

Primary role _____   Stage of life _____
Growth and developmental tasks              Roles
1. _____                1. _____
2. _____                2. _____
3. _____                3. _____
4. _____                4. _____
5. _____                5. _____
6. _____                6. _____
7. _____                7. _____

## REFERENCES

Barber, Janet, Stokes, Lillian, and Billings, Diane: Adult and Child Care. A Client Approach to Nursing. St. Louis, The C. V. Mosby Co., 1973.

Bernard, Harold W.: Human Development in Western Culture, 2nd ed. Boston, Allyn & Bacon, Inc., 1966.

Bureau of Census. Statistical Abstract of the United States 1980, 101st ed., Washington, DC, 1980.

Chin, Peggy, and Leitch, Cynthia: Child Health Maintenance: A Guide to Clinical Assessment, 2nd ed. St. Louis, The C. V. Mosby Co., 1979, p 75.

Erikson, E. H.: Childhood and Society, 2nd ed. New York, W. W. Norton and Co., Inc., 1963.

Gesell, Arnold, and Ilg, Frances: Infant and Child in the Culture of Today. New York, Harper and Row, Publishers, Inc., 1943.

Hamburg, David A.: Healthy People. Surgeon General's Report on Health Promotion and Disease Prevention. Pub. #79–55071, Washington, DC, 1979, pp. 340–343, 377–379.

Kaluger, George, and Kaluger, Meriem: Human Development, The Span of Life. St. Louis, The C. V. Mosby Co., 1973.

Revolution in health care urged in new surgeon general's report. Am J Nurs, 79:1671–1672, (October) 1979.

US Department of Health, Education, and Welfare. Monocular Visual Acuity of Persons 4 – 74 Years, United States 1971–1972. Rockville, MD, National Center for Health Statistics, (March) 1977.

US Department of Health, Education, and Welfare. Current Estimates from the National Health Survey, United States 1978. Rockville, MD, National Center for Health Statistics, (November) 1979.

# Chapter SEVENTEEN

# Growth and Developmental Tasks of Adults

OBJECTIVES Information in this chapter will help you to

1. State the growth and developmental tasks for each of the adult stages of life.
2. State some of the roles that people use to carry out the developmental tasks of certain stages of life.
3. Assess the behaviors that the adult uses to carry out the developmental tasks to gather information regarding the functioning of the self-concept and the interdependence modes.
4. Compare the adult's behaviors with norms, or standards, for those roles and identify those behaviors that indicate ineffective coping with feelings or relationships with others.
5. Describe the roles that are used to carry out developmental tasks as stimuli or influencing factors for problems in coping.
6. Describe health care needs, common illnesses, and the most prevalent causes of death for each adult stage of life.

## THE ADULT STAGES OF LIFE

The growth and developmental stages of childhood and adolescence prepare individuals to assume the social and family responsibilities of the adult world. Human beings are the only creatures that have such a long period of childhood and dependency, extending nearly one fourth of their total lifetime. Most people spend 50 years or more of their lives as adults. As they progress through these years, adults must cope with continual changes, both in their environment and within themselves. Their experiences in living create major differences among them; thus, adults in their 20s differ from those in their 40s, and those over the age of 65 differ from both younger adult groups. These differences result in developmental tasks with which the adults must work and cope successfully to maintain their adaptation. Based on these developmental tasks, three distinct adult stages of life emerge: (1) the young adult stage, from the ages of about 18 to 34 years, (2) the generative adult stage, from the ages of 35 to 64 years, and (3) the mature adult stage, over the age of 65 years.

The population of the United States is growing older as the number of births has been declining during the last few decades. In 1900, half the population was under the age of 22 years, but, by 1979, the median age was 30 years. The population of the United States from 1960 to 1979, by age groups and percentage, is shown in Table

**Table 17–1.** POPULATION OF THE UNITED STATES
FROM 1960, BY AGE GROUPS AND PERCENTAGE,
SHOWING DECREASE IN NUMBER OF CHILDREN
AND INCREASE IN PEOPLE OVER AGE 65

| Age group (yr) | 1960 (%) | 1970 (%) | 1979 (%) | Population 1979 |
|---|---|---|---|---|
| birth to 17 | 35.7 | 34.2 | 28.4 | 62,571 |
| 18 to 34 | 21 | 24.1 | 29 | 63,892 |
| 35 to 64 | 33.5 | 31.9 | 31 | 68,978 |
| over 65 | 9.2 | 9.9 | 11.2 | 24,658 |
| Total Population (in 1,000s) | 179,323 | 203,235 | – | 220,099 |

Source: Bureau of the Census. Statistical Abstract of the United States 1980, 101st ed. Washington, DC, 1980, p 29.

17–1. Adults now constitute more than 70 per cent of the total population of the United States. The implication for nursing is that more of those who will be requiring nursing care will be adults, especially older adults.

The ease with which young people move into adulthood depends upon how well they have resolved the developmental tasks at each stage of childhood. One's overall goal is to attain psychological and social integrity. This requires a sense of identity, including knowledge of one's motivations, use of intellectual processes, and control of one's emotions. Socially, young people have learned satisfying ways of coping with both internal and external changes. As adults, they will continue to strive for adaptation to psychological stresses and social changes. The ways in which people cope and respond to changes are an indication of the state of their mental health.

Good mental health is based on successfully reaching the goals for each stage of life. Erikson described these goals as trust, autonomy, initiative, industry, identity, and intimacy. During adulthood, individuals continuously revise these goals as they cope with more complex changes and relationships in carrying out their generativity. They are then able to advance to old age with ego integrity based on having lived satisfactory lives and having made the right decisions. Good mental health can be described as

1. *Understanding and accepting one's self.* Possessing insight and understanding one's motives, strengths, and weaknesses.

2. *Using reason to solve problems.* Having the ability to make decisions based on facts and on analysis of the situation and taking responsibility for these decisions.

3. *Possessing worthwhile values.* Having moral values based on a knowledge of right and wrong or a code of ethics. One's values and beliefs may

be based on a religious code of ethics, nursing ethics, scientific ethics, legal ethics, or any other standard for behavior.

4. *Being able to control one's emotions.* By controlling one's primitive urges and emotions, one avoids being a slave to passions and to the extremes of emotions.

5. *Having a social conscience.* Having some degree of unselfishness and showing concern for others.

6. *Having the ability to be happy.* Enjoying life and obtaining pleasure from such things as a child's laugh, a beautiful sunset, or the smile of a loved one.

7. *Continuing to search for truth and wisdom.* Understanding the real world in which truth and facts are relative and become obsolete as new knowledge and relationships are discovered.

## THE YOUNG ADULT STAGE

In the young adult stage, one is at one's peak of physical and mental strength. This stage of life includes people between the ages of 18 and 34 years. It may be broken down into two parts: (1) the transitional period, which provides the bridge between adolescence and full maturity and (2) the period for establishing the family. Although those in the transitional stage are still establishing their identity, all young adults are faced with resolving the crisis of intimacy. They must learn how to use the confidence that they have in their own identity and how to extend their feelings of trust and initiative to enable them to establish an intimate relationship with a special person. Intimacy requires that one places the wishes and welfare of the other person before one's own or, literally, that one abandon one's own self by committing it to the other person. Intimacy means sharing oneself in sexual union and in close relationships that are characterized by devotion and loyalty. The inability to share oneself with others leads to a sense of isolation and self-centeredness.

**The Transitional Period.** The transitional period is the growth and developmental period between adolescence and full maturity. For some people, it may last from ages 18 to 20 years, whereas for others, it may continue through age 23 or 24 years. During this period, young people still have many adolescent traits, even though they physically resemble mature adults. They are busy consolidating their independence and achieving emotional stability and social integrity.

Throughout the centuries, a characteristic of this transitional period is the way young adults assert themselves, showing themselves as a force to be reckoned with in society. They do not fully realize that their ability to make good decisions is restricted by their limited experience, their lack of depth or breadth in knowledge, and even by their idealism which may produce a narrow or simplistic view of reality. It is a case of "those who have seen little are amazed by much." When people fail to live up to the ideals and perceptions of young adults, the young adults become disillusioned and engage in negative forms of behavior, such as riots, violence, withdrawal from society, joining deviant groups, or relying on drugs.

The culture of young adults is essentially a liberal culture, seeking freedom from the restraints, authority, and pressures for conformity imposed by the older generations. They want the world to know that they have come of age, that they know things, and that they have a voice that must be heard and respected. They want freedom to "do their own thing," to decide the morality of issues, to change what is unjust, and to dissent from the majority opinion. Another feature of their culture is an intense involvement in music, especially the kinds of music that are particularly associated with their age group.

*Developmental Tasks.* For each developmental task described for young adults in the transitional period, examples are given of the types of roles that might be used and behaviors that illustrate the integrity of the self-concept and interdependence modes.

1. *Selects and prepares for an occupation or a vocation*
**Roles:** student; apprentice; employee; homemaker.
**Self-Concept:** *Physical self* — sees self as strong, healthy, and capable, and as having the physical and mental abilities required for one's selected field of work or endeavor. *Personal self* — ideals not firmly set; sees self as a worthy being and as

**Figure 17–1.** Young couple forming bonds of intimacy and love prior to establishing a family unit.

productive and knowledgeable; may have unrealistic perception of achievable goals.

**Interdependence:** *Dependence* — accepts help or financial support from family; seeks advice and opinions of others; patterns self after role model. *Independence* — earns most of own money; decides how to spend money and takes care of own living expenses; moves away from family and sets up own home; completes each segment of education needed.

2. *Prepares for the selection of a mate and marriage.*

**Roles:** friend; date; roommate; fiancé; lover; confidante.

**Self-Concept:** *Physical self* — believes that body image, appearance, and stature may influence acceptance by friends and potential mate; control of sexual urges; confirmation that one has the ability to be a sexual partner. *Personal self* — preference for heterosexual relationships; chooses individuals with tastes and interests similar to one's own; selects those who fall within the range of what is acceptable in a friend or mate; develops an intimate relationship with another person.

**Interdependence:** *Dependence* — seeks companionships; relies on others to supply food and shelter; seeks approval from family or friends; includes friends in family functions; responds to pressures from others regarding marriage and type of mate; gives attention to appearance and to performing acts for approval by other person; is loving, tender, or seductive in relationship to potential mate. *Independence* — plans dates and activities with others; makes own decisions; gets things done; pays own bills; maintains a controlled, or social, contact with own family.

3. *Refines a value system or code of ethics and develops socially responsible behavior.*

**Roles:** may be related to any of the secondary roles. Member of interest group, church or religious affiliation, political party, or community action group; voter; neighbor; citizen.

**Self-Concept:** *Personal self* — compares reality with ideal in relation to own perceptions; may question or rebel against controls and restrictions imposed by parents, government, or others; feedback from others influences values and behaviors; most values resemble those of family.

**Interdependence:** *Dependence* — follows instructions; conforms to the expectations of others; puts others before self; considers feelings and wishes of others; is comfortable with others who share same values and beliefs; obeys laws, rules, and regulations. *Independence* — dares to be different; does not impose ideas or values on others; eccentric; can disregard social pressures to conform to set pattern of behavior or expectations; follows own sense of right and wrong.

4. *Develops a civic consciousness.*

**Roles:** member of interest group, church or religious affiliation, political party, or community action group; member of the military service; voter; art patron; consumer advocate; demonstrator.

**Self-Concept:** *Physical self* — sees self as fully mature adult capable of taking on duties and responsibilities of social group. *Personal self* — sees self as able to influence others and to convert them to one's own values and beliefs; able to cause changes; sense of power and control rather than powerlessness and apathy.

**Interdependence:** *Dependence* — carries out instruction; functions as a team member; is a follower; seeks help from other community agencies. *Independence* — assumes leadership roles; acts to provide for others who are less fortunate; acts as "his brother's keeper"; organizes groups of people toward a common goal; works to improve quality of life for self and others.

**The Family-Establishment Period.** For most young adults, the ages from 25 to 34 years are devoted to the family-establishment phase of life, when their energies are directed to their homes, families, and careers. It is the most stable time of life. However, their freedom is very restricted because of their increased responsibilities. The primary task of this period is to nurture, support, and provide for one's mate and children by carrying out the following tasks in a satisfactory way.

1. Adapting housing arrangements to provide space and facilities for the expanded family.
2. Maintaining a satisfactory marriage relationship.
3. Working out patterns of responsibility and accountability for the home and children.
4. Meeting the added costs of supplying the needs of the family.
5. Creating effective communications between members of the family.
6. Cultivating relationships with relatives.
7. Establishing ties with life in the community and with resources outside the family.
8. Working out a suitable philosophy of life.

**Roles:** husband; wife; mother; father; parent; homemaker; head of household.

**Self-Concept:** *Physical self* — sees oneself as potential producer of children; capable of being pregnant and accepting changes in form of body; capable of fathering a child. *Personal self* — sees self as parent and meeting expectations of others in care of the family; identity of self influences child-rearing practices and discipline; family-planning and birth control practices conform to moral-ethical beliefs; self-ideal influences whether wife and mother works outside the home.

**Interdependence:** *Dependence* — seeks advice from experienced persons, such as parents, teachers, other friends, nurse, or doctor on how to handle problems of child-rearing; seeks praise and recognition for work and efforts; displays pictures and objects to gain affection; shows pride in spouse's and children's accomplishments; expects affection and attention from spouse and children. *Independence* — personal freedom is restricted by needs of dependent children during most of the family-establishment phase. Parents must initiate plans or actions to discipline children, establish schedules of activities, and share responsibilities of providing an income and of maintaining the home.

**Health Problems.** As a group, young adults are among the healthiest people physically, although they often have problems coping with the many changes in their lives. Adjusting to the demands of a job, working out the challenges of marriage, and adapting to the responsibilities of parenthood all create stresses and tensions for young people.

Physical health problems related to this stage include injuries such as fractures, sprains, lacerations, and burns that result from accidents; upper respiratory infections; gastrointestinal disturbances; and conditions related to sexual activity and reproduction. The majority of all babies are born to mothers under the age of 35 years. Although venereal diseases can affect people in any age group, they are more prevalent among the young adult group, who tend to be more active sexually. The most commonly performed operations among this age group are hernia repair in men and dilatation and curettage (D & C) in

women. Appendectomies are the second most common.

The death rate among young adults continues to be low but is beginning to increase above that of the childhood groups. From Table 17–2, one can see that accidents remain the leading cause of death for 18- to 24-year-olds, with suicides and homicide following close behind. For 25- to 34-year-olds, cancer and heart disease are the leading causes of death.

## THE GENERATIVE ADULT STAGE

The middle years of life represent a long plateau in one's lifetime. This stage is known as the generative adult stage and includes ages 35 through 64. There is much overlapping at both ends of this stage because some young adults enter this stage at an earlier age and those at the older end of the stage may move into the mature adult stage before the age of 65 years. In 1979, there were 68,978,000 people in the generative age group, or 31.3 per cent of the total population of this country.

The hopes and dreams that one wishes to achieve during one's lifetime are generally accomplished during one's thirties, forties, and fifties. This period of life is characterized by stability, productivity, and self-actualization. Educated persons may take longer to enter the generative stage of life because they spent more years acquiring an education and may have delayed marriage and having children until they were older. In middle-aged years, adults have more freedom because their children are in school or have left home to begin their own lives. Middle-aged adults often have succeeded at their jobs and achieved more financial security, and often

**Table 17–2.** LEADING CAUSES OF DEATH OF YOUNG ADULTS, WITH REPRESENTATIVE NUMBERS OF DEATHS BASED ON THE 1977 DISEASE RATE APPLIED TO THE 1979 POPULATION OF THE UNITED STATES

| Cause of Death — 18- to 24-yr-olds | Number | Cause of Death — 25- to 34-yr-olds | Number |
|---|---|---|---|
| 1. Accidents—motor | 12,801 | 1. Cancer | 10,354 |
| 2. Accidents—all other | 5,341 | 2. Heart disease | 8,890 |
| 3. Suicide | 3,948 | 3. Accidents—motor | 8,053 |
| 4. Homicide | 3,687 | 4. Accidents—all other | 6,450 |
| 5. Cancer | 1,887 | 5. Suicide | 6,031 |
| 6. Heart disease | 726 | 6. Homicide | 5,439 |
| 7. Congenital birth defects | 464 | 7. Cirrhosis | 2,998 |
| Total population in age group | 29,029,000 | | 34,863,000 |
| Total deaths—all causes | 33,992 | | 63,625 |

Sources: Bureau of the Census. Statistical Abstract of the United States 1980, 101st ed. Washington, DC, 1980, p 29, and Revolution in health care urged in new surgeon general's report. Am J Nurs, 79: 1671–1672, (October) 1979.

have more money to spend and more leisure time in which to pursue new interests and activities. Women who have spent much of their time caring for children now find that they have free time in which to expand their social activities or interests without the pressures that they had when their children were younger.

Erikson has described the life task of this stage of life as generativity versus stagnation. Between the ages of 35 and 64 years, it is important that adults interact with others, with the "next generation." Only through this interaction with the young are the characters and personalities of children molded and shaped to prepare them for entering the adult society. Young adults need to be oriented to their work and to the tasks that they are to carry out as they establish families and produce new members of society. Middle-aged adults who do not marry and have children still serve as role models to the next generation as they provide stability and carry out their family, work, and civic roles.

The generative adult is involved in the following tasks:

1.  Guiding and teaching the next generation as it matures and takes its place in society.
2.  Implementing and maintaining society through personal industry, productivity, research, and creativity.
3.  Providing for those in society who are dependent and must be cared for or helped by others — the ill, the poor, and the orphaned.

Failure to carry out these tasks leads to a self-centeredness and a self-absorbed attitude about life. People often become nonproductive and regress to former childhood stages of dependency when they fail to help guide and support others.

Physical strength and functioning of the body continues at a high level well into the generative stage. Scientists working with the American space program considered the age of 38 years to be the peak year of adult development. At this age, people have greater mental alertness, are physically sound, and have stable personalities and emotional control. However, gradual changes do occur during this period of life. A slowing of one's metabolism, causing one to use energy more carefully because it takes longer for it to be replenished and a decline in sensory acuity occur. Women undergo menopausal changes at the age of 50 years, with a decline in hormonal activity. When compared with men 30 years of age and at 100 per cent capacity, men at 60 years of age show these physical changes:

61 per cent of maximum breathing capacity.
82 per cent of filtration rate of kidney.
78 per cent of cardiac output at rest.

**Developmental Tasks.** The stability and the freedom of the generative adult stage of life are more apparent in the developmental tasks that relate to interpersonal relationships and to their own interests, and, for the first time, also stress the comforts of life. Parents have time to renew their relationship as husband and wife and to resume activities as a couple, while reassuring each other of their identity as individuals. Developmental tasks of the generative adult include

1.  *Maintaining an established economic standard of living.*
**Roles:** head of household; homemaker; taxpayer; homeowner; renter; employee; businessman; administrator; plumber; teacher; nurse; engineer.
**Self-Concept:** *Physical self* — healthy enough to continue working; strong; coordinated to carry out job; skillful and energetic enough to care for home. *Personal self* — has obtained most material things desired; concerned with quality of life; more emphasis on intangible things, such as happiness and integrity; adopting ways to maintain or to improve health.
**Interdependence:** *Dependence* — shares decisions about major expenditures with spouse; establishes working relationships with boss, supervisors, and coworkers; tries to "keep up with the Joneses"; follows rules and regulations in business; requires assistance from other sources or welfare to meet living expenses. *Independence* — can make choices about where to live and type of home; can hire others to carry out work or delegate work to children; has gained status or prestige in community; plans for "rainy day" or retirement.
2.  *Assisting children in their growth and development.*
**Roles:** parent; teacher; grandparent; role model; minister; counselor; worker.
**Self-Concept:** *Physical self* — has health and energy to involve self with children; aware of aging changes in self. *Personal self* — imparts values and beliefs to next generation; stresses moral values of social group (the Golden Rule, Ten Commandments, "everybody does it," "the end justifies the means"); shows tolerance and understanding of others rather than stressing differences and prejudices; may use compensatory means if has no children, such as Big Brother or Big Sister organizations, scouting, or planning outings with groups of children.
**Interdependence:** *Dependence* — seeks opinions, ideas and suggestions from others; consults experts for information; advertises or solicits support for causes in which involved; expects growing children to "report in" to parents; practices doing "good" for special group as a way of seeking recognition. *Independence* — reworks relationships with maturing children to allow their

independence; accepts new generation's ways of doing things; sense of satisfaction from own accomplishments and from those of the new generation; achieves improvement in conditions in the environment or in existing situations.

3. *Developing satisfactory leisure time activities.*
**Roles:** various secondary and tertiary roles related to sports, arts, music, hobbies, collections, and other interest group activities.
**Self-Concept:** *Physical self* — perceives body as capable and of having energy level for the activity. *Personal self* — interests, values, and beliefs influence types of activities chosen; gains feelings of self-satisfaction from activities; likes challenge and participation; may model ideal self after a sports star.
**Interdependence:** *Dependence* — spectator at various sports, music, theater, and other events; receives attention and recognition as result of hobby or activity; needs others to engage in group activities, such as partner for tennis, member of musical group, competitor for races, or team for games. *Independence* — initiates and plans outings for groups and others; tries innovative ways to express oneself in activities; carries out hobbies or activities that can be done alone; makes up or follows own rules in group activities.

4. *Assuming civic and social responsibilities.*
An extension of the developmental task of young adults. As generative adults become more active in the community and society they carry out the task of integrating the younger generations into society.

5. *Relating to one's mate as an individual rather than as a role.*
**Roles:** husband or wife; companion; confidante; lover.
**Self-Concept:** *Personal self* — awareness of personal needs to be more than just "Mom" or "Dad"; has interests other than mate, children, and home; understands and discusses national or world affairs; takes a broad view of one's place in the world; sees spouse as multidimensioned person with many roles rather than only the parent role.
**Interdependence:** *Dependence* — looks to mate for recognition, affection, and attention in roles of companion, lover, sharer of interests and hobbies; needs to be regarded as an individual with a unique personality, or self. *Independence* — husband and wife can develop separate interests as well as shared interests; growing independence of children allows more freedom and time for parents to become involved in other interests and to carry out other roles; mother is able to develop interests outside the home and to expand circle of friends to include new groups.

6. *Accepting and adjusting to physiological changes of the middle years.*
**Roles:** primary role of stated age and sex.
**Self-Concept:** *Physical self* — feelings about wrinkles, "middle-aged spread," gray hair or becoming bald; decrease in amount of strength and stamina; being "out of condition"; hormonal changes and menopause in women; perception of growing old that adults deal with in more realistic terms at about the age of 48; emergence of some chronic health condition; may seek to deny aging by acting and dressing as a young adult or by having cosmetic surgery, such as a face-lift. *Personal self* — has a stable self-identity and behaves in consistent ways; more free to express oneself and to be true to oneself than in previous stages; can stand up for and defend beliefs or positions to others; adjusts to and accepts differences between ideal self and reality; in spite of aging, examines life goals and philosophy of life; may need to "prove" oneself in areas most important to self-concept, such as virility, flirting, extramarital affairs, competitiveness, social prestige, or cooking for or dictating activities of family.
**Interdependence:** *Dependence* — seeks help or assistance for strenuous work; assigns household chores and errands to growing children. *Independence* — most generative adults continue active and productive lives while providing guidance and support to the young, poor, and aged.

7. *Continuing relationship with aging parents or with parents-in-law and assisting them as necessary.*
**Roles:** son; daughter; son-in-law; daughter-in-law.
**Self-Concept:** *Personal self* — development of mature self-identity so one can treat parents as one wants to be treated if in the same situation; morally, can see one's responsibility to give attention and assistance to aging parents; may begin to identify with one's parents when own children are grown and leave home.
**Interdependence:** *Dependence* — asks parent for advice and opinion; seeks attention and affection from parent; invites parents for visits; makes phone calls to, sends cards to, and expresses affection for parents; shares memories and experiences, and tells about activities. *Independence* — initiates obtaining services and resources for parents; helps them plan or obtain medical care, arranges for upkeep of their home or apartment or assists with financial support; places parent with declining health in a nursing, boarding, or retirement home.

**Health Problems.** As years pass, generative adults begin to experience a significant number of losses. Parents, relatives, and friends die, while illness and disability claim others as their victims.

Children grow up and leave home, going off to college, taking jobs, and establishing lives and homes of their own. The "empty nest syndrome" is the cause of varying degrees of separation anxiety and feelings of loss for parents, particularly for the nonworking mother whose life centers on her children and home.

Many middle-aged people face an identity crisis as they are confronted with the realization that life is short and that more than half their life is over. They take stock of their lives in terms of the dreams and hopes that they have been able to fulfill and the goals that have not been reached and, now, may never be achieved. Resolving this challenge to one's self-concept is probably as difficult for the generative adult as the task of establishing a personal identity is for the adolescent. Some middle-aged adults change jobs or occupations in their attempt to cope with the questions "Who am I?" and "Is this what I want for the rest of my life?" Others may pursue the feelings of romance of their bygone youth and escape feelings of being trapped by engaging in extramarital affairs. Women generally experience these feelings in their midforties and men during their late forties.

In the area of physical health, more than 77 per cent of the men and 82 per cent of the women have no limitation of activities, although they may take a little longer to perform tasks and may need more time to recover from strenuous work or play. Physical changes related to aging occur gradually in this stage of life. More than 88 per cent of the adults over the age of 45 years wear eyeglasses to correct some visual defect. One's hearing acuity decreases. More men are hard of hearing than are women. One's ability to learn new things and one's use of intellectual skills continue at very high levels of functioning.

Beyond the age of 45, there is a dramatic increase in the incidences of illness due to chronic and degenerative diseases, as well as a sharp increase in the death rate for these diseases. Conditions commonly found in people in this age group include diabetes, arteriosclerotic heart disease (including coronary occlusion), gastric ulcers, gallbladder disease, inguinal hernias, pneumonia, and gastroenteritis. Surgical procedures frequently performed on people in this age group include cholecystectomy, gastrectomy, hemorrhoidectomy, hernia repair, hysterectomy, mastectomy, and varicose vein ligation.

The leading causes of death for generative adults between 35 and 44 years old are the same as for the latter stage of the young adult group. An upsurge in deaths occurs for adults between the ages of 45 and 64, when heart disease and cancer each claim more than 100,000 lives per year. (See Table 17–3.) As one becomes older, motor vehicle accidents are responsible for fewer deaths. In the adolescent and young adult stages, motor vehicle accidents account for 44 deaths per 100,000 population; in the generative adult stage, 18.3 deaths per 100,000 population are caused by motor vehicle accidents.

## THE MATURE ADULT STAGE

The last stage in the life cycle is called the mature adult stage. It covers the period from retirement until death and is considered to begin at age 65 years, although some adults enter this stage at age 60 or, perhaps even before age 60 years. However, it is convenient to use 65 years as the dividing age because the government uses that age for statistical purposes. It is the age at which one becomes eligible for social security

Table 17–3.  LEADING CAUSES OF DEATH OF GENERATIVE ADULTS, WITH REPRESENTATIVE NUMBERS OF DEATHS BASED ON THE 1977 DISEASE RATE APPLIED TO THE 1979 POPULATION OF THE UNITED STATES

| Cause of Death – 35- to 44-yr-olds | Number | Cause of Death – 45- to 64-yr-olds | Number |
|---|---|---|---|
| 1. Cancer | 7,447 | 1. Heart disease | 154,099 |
| 2. Heart disease | 6,394 | 2. Cancer | 132,894 |
| 3. Accidents–motor | 5,792 | 3. Stroke | 23,005 |
| 4. Accidents–all other | 4,639 | 4. Cirrhosis | 17,210 |
| 5. Suicide | 4,338 | 5. Accidents–all other | 11,195 |
| 6. Homicide | 3,912 | 6. Suicide | 8,385 |
| 7. Cirrhosis | 2,156 | 7. Accidents–motor | 8,034 |
| Total population in age group | 25,075,000 | | 43,903,000 |
| Total deaths–all causes | 45,762 | | 439,030 |

Sources: Bureau of the Census. Statistical Abstract of the United States 1980, 101st ed. Washington, DC, 1980, p. 29, and Revolution in health care urged in new surgeon general's report. Am J Nurs, 79: 1671–1672, (October) 1979.

retirement benefits, and it is used extensively by researchers in their studies.

The mature adult group is the most rapidly growing segment of our population because people are living longer. Every day, more than 4000 Americans are celebrating their 65th birthday. People beyond the age of 65 years now constitute 11 per cent of the population—up from 9.2 per cent in 1960 and a significant increase from 3.5 per cent in 1900. Many older adults are still vigorous and have a great vitality for life. Never before has any society had so many of its people in retirement. This implies the need for tremendous changes in social, political, economic, and medical areas associated with aging.

This stage of adult life can encompass from 25 to 35 or more years of one's life, as more people live into their 80s and 90s and more than 10,000 people are over 100 years of age Although the elderly have many characteristics in common, people age at different times and at different rates. Individual differences are probably more pronounced in this stage than in any other stage. People in their 80s may be very active in volunteer work and in arts or crafts, and people much younger may be senile. At any given period of time, people in this age group are relatively healthy and active and are living their lives in an independent and satisfying way.

Mature adults are content to maintain their position and status in life and are relieved of the struggle for further gain. Their way of life is a compensation for their earlier struggles and striving to get along. Earlier stages of life centered on gaining status and the symbols of material success, such as a home, two cars, a good job, a good education, beautiful children, and frequent vacation trips. Many of these status symbols can be lost in middle and old age, whereas developing good mental health habits and building kind and generous interpersonal relationships will endure through old age.

The retirement years can be a time of enjoyment and contentment, with a freedom to select activities that was previously unknown. Good adaptation to aging is achieved by adults who have good physical and mental health, who have provided for their financial security, and who have a meaningful purpose in life. For many mature adults, this is a stage of life with more leisure time — time that they can devote to their interests and to contemplation and time to be themselves more truly than ever before. Unfortunately, for others, old age means poor health, poverty, loneliness, and dependence upon others.

Although people age at different rates, three stages of old age have been described: (1) the "free wheeling" stage, (2) the "sitting down" stage, and (3) the "lying down" stage. These stages are not limited by age or by specific times, and people may advance through them gradually or rapidly or may even omit one or more of them. Mature adults in the "free wheeling" stage are those who enjoy their leisure time and engage in activities that are of interest to them, such as traveling, raising prize roses, converting a hobby in collecting antiques into a small business, or being creative in various forms of art. They are also able to live their lives in an independent manner by maintaining a home and are not restricted in how they carry out their daily pattern of life. The "sitting down" stage is a period of slowing down, when less vitality and energy dictate taking the more passive role of sitting on the sidelines and watching others. Although these people remain relatively healthy, they have a decrease in endurance, an inability to ambulate for more than short distances, or need some assistance in carrying out the more strenuous tasks of daily living. The "lying down" stage is characterized by a marked decrease in vitality, activity, and ability to provide for one's own needs. The advancing aging process produces impairment of sensory perceptions and increased weakness that cause the person to spend more time lying down, to be more dependent upon others, and usually signal the terminal phase of life.

People adapt to old age with either high morale or low morale. Those with high morale make a good adjustment to aging, like themselves and what they are doing, and are satisfied and contented with their lives. They are more apt to be better at solving life's problems, better educated, and more healthy and to feel financially secure than those with low morale. On the other hand, adults with low morale tend to have health problems, emphasize material possessions and values rather than good mental health values, have a lower economic and social status, and suffer from deprivation of some of their needs. They are apt to be self-centered, unhappy, anxious, and fearful.

The following six ways of coping are compiled from the high and low morale states in each of the three stages of aging:

1. *"Free wheeling" adults with high morale.* Delightful, active, and interesting people who take part in a wide variety of activities and show concern for others. They are usually healthy and require only periodic checkups or care.

2. *"Free wheeling" adults with low morale.* Active people, but spend more of their energies complaining. They are more dissatisfied with

**Figure 17–2.**  High morale seen in the joy of an elderly woman holding her great-grandson. The sickly woman confined to a wheelchair displays low morale.

their lives, the condition of the world, the lack of attention from their children, and the state of their health.

3. *"Sitting down" adults with high morale.* These individuals have some chronic ailment or weakness but are cheerful and seem to rise above it by being interested and involved in activities that they can do sitting down.

4. *"Sitting down" adults with low morale.* These people have one or more chronic disabilities and are depressed and quite dependent upon others. They often resent and find fault with what others do for them.

5. *"Lying down" adults with high morale.* These people are "good troopers" in the face of serious illness; they are cooperative with others who provide their care. Their effective coping causes others to regard them with admiration and empathy.

6. *"Lying down" adults with low morale.* These people are very depressed and are unable to cope with threats to their health or life and may be resistive to care. They are often labeled as problem, uncooperative, or confused patients. Their coping abilities are overwhelmed by the stresses of life, especially during illness, and they are often seen in general hospitals, convalescent hospitals, and nursing homes.

**Developmental Tasks.**  The major life task for mature adults is to achieve ego integrity and satisfaction with their lives — to reach old age with

high morale rather than with the feelings of despair and depression of low morale. Many studies of aging have been conducted that indicate that successful aging is characterized by having relatively good physical health, adequate coping mechanisms for psychological health, and adequate economic resources. Although adequate coping and high morale are complex factors to measure, research indicates that through the life stages of adulthood, men tend to emphasize activities that are directed toward work goals and productivity, whereas women are more interested in the feelings that they have and that others have for them.

People who reach the mature stage of life with ego integrity and high morale tend to be those who have had a less complex life and who have developed self-protective and stress-avoiding patterns of coping with changes in their lives. In a comparison study of adults in four stages of adult life (leaving home, establishing a family, middle age, and preretirement), Lowenthal found more differences between men and women than between age groups. Women of all age groups reported more stressful experiences than men, whereas men had a stronger and more positive self-image, which showed mellowness and social ease by preretirement years. Men who were exposed to higher stress were those with more social roles, who had a higher educational status, and who were in occupations that required more use of mental faculties than physical skills. The highly stressed people were more involved in the social and political world around them, and their higher socioeconomic status permitted more varied life experiences, which, by nature of change, are stressful. Lowenthal also found that the older women who had less stress tended to have a lower level of education, a flatness, or sameness, about their lives, and a restricted family-centered lifestyle.

Developmental tasks of the mature adult include

1. *Adjusting to decreasing physical strength and declining health.*
**Roles:** primary role of stated age and sex.
**Self-Concept:** *Physical self* — feelings and perceptions about changes in the body or its function due to aging and health problems. Feelings regarding the loss of memory about recent events. *Personal self* — those with "high morale" like themselves, are satisfied with their lives, are contented, make good decisions, see themselves as healthy and as having enough security to meet their needs. Those with low morale" feel deprived, are unhappy, feel isolated from others and left out, lack sufficient resources, or are threatened by health problems or illness.
**Interdependence:** *Dependence* — makes adjustment in daily living habits to provide for additional rest periods and to avoid more strenuous activities; seeks help for health problems from family members, doctors, or others; looks forward to contact with and visits from children, grandchildren, and friends. *Independence* — carries out own habits of healthy living; tries to increase one's physical attractiveness (uses cosmetics, hair tints, etc.); adjusts activities to abilities and interests, such as gardening, travel, playing cards; is able to live alone and take care of self and most of own needs; makes own decisions.

2. *Coping with retirement and changes in financial status.*
**Roles:** retired worker.
**Self-Concept:** *Personal self* — seeks new ways to structure time and keep occupied during the days; seeks new purpose to life or new values through activities chosen; tends to develop more conservative attitudes about life and politics and is less adaptable to sudden changes; is more free to say and do what one wants because no longer needs to please a boss.
**Interdependence:** *Dependence* — fixed income with pension or social security may not be enough to keep up with inflation or with unexpected expenses; may need to accept help from family or government; spends more time with spouse in shared activities around the home. *Independence* — continues to be active and participates in activ-

ities; uses resources of time and money as desired in pursuits of own choosing; travels, plays golf, and engages in hobbies or interests if financially able.

3. *Maintaining satisfactory living arrangements.*
**Roles:** homemaker; head of house; homeowner; renter; resident.
**Self-Concept:** *Physical self* — sees self as capable of taking care of own home or apartment; able to do own shopping and cleaning and care for personal hygiene. *Personal self* — feelings of loss if forced to give up home; feels more secure having personal possessions and familiar objects around; has feelings regarding alternative living arrangements in a retirement or nursing home or living in home of grown child.
**Interdependence:** *Dependence* — needs children or grandchildren to assist in some living arrangements or tasks; has a friend or spouse as a confidante; asks for help in transportation or for companionship; depends upon children or others the same as children used to depend upon parents. *Independence* — continues to maintain home; initiates appropriate changes in living arrangements; does own cooking and cleaning; drives own car or makes own travel plans; handles own financial affairs and pays own bills.

4. *Adjusting to loss of significant others and to death of one's spouse.*
**Roles:** widow; widower; relative; friend.
**Self-Concept:** *Physical self* — death of spouse brings intense awareness of one's own mortality; finds emotional strength to survive the grief and mourning period. *Personal self* — previous experiences with loss determine how one copes with loss of spouse, a child, friends, or other important people or objects in one's life; additional losses in a short period of time increase stress; may obtain great comfort from religious beliefs; friendships take on new importance after the loss of a spouse; one's ideal self and moral values determine behaviors regarding dating, remarriage, and choice of friends or activities; depression is common.
**Interdependence:** *Dependence* — seeks advice from others about changing life style, financial matters, or moving from home after death of spouse; attends church and seeks company of others; talks of past life and accomplishments; displays pictures; phones or visits family and friends; invites friends and relatives for dinner or visits; does thoughtful things for others. *Independence* — works through own grief and mourning; re-establishes a pattern of living without loved one; becomes involved in own interests and activities, selects new confidante and friends; may resume dating and select a new mate.

5. *Reworking relationships with grown children, relatives, and others of one's age group.*
**Roles:** parent; grandparent; aunt; uncle; friend.
**Self-Concept:** *Personal self* — accepting own self with strengths and weaknesses; feels that one did a good job of raising children; able to see oneself as parent of children who are now generative adults; maintains responsibility for self and for own decisions.
**Interdependence:** *Dependence* — looks to children and grandchildren for attention and affection; depends upon family to help out when ill; participates with children and grandchildren in various activities; spends time with grandchildren; holds old friends in high regard; may find it difficult to go out and make new friends; phones or visits with family and relatives. *Independence* — overcomes obstacles by occasionally "babysitting" with grandchildren or helping out children within limits of one's strength or ability; considers oneself a worthwhile member of society and making a good contribution; seeks out and re-establishes closer ties with brothers, sisters, and cousins who are near one's own age; initiates actions to please others, such as cooking son's favorite foods and making cookies for grandchildren.

6. *Assuming a new pattern of social and civic responsibilities.*
**Roles:** member of church or religious group, political party, fraternal organizations, social clubs, charitable groups, retirement centers, senior citizen's groups.
**Self-Concept:** *Physical self* — must physically be able to get around and participate; sees self as healthy and in control of body and mind; changes in health or body image may restrict these activities; may begin giving up roles or participation as energy declines or from reluctance to "put up with the 'hassle.'" *Personal self* — chooses activities and interacts with people who have value system similar to one's own; continues activities that brought pleasure in previous years; may decline taking an active part because of feeling that one has done one's share and that it is time for others to take over; has a reluctance to join new groups and to be the newcomer.
**Interdependence:** *Dependence* — depends upon neighbors or friends for help; uses "Meals on Wheels," visiting nurses, and others to be able to continue living in the community; seeks social groups according to own likes, values, interests, and physical abilities; talks to others about achievements of self and family. *Independence* — joins various classes and social groups; develops new skills or improves previous skills; begins painting, square dancing, or other hobby; votes

in elections; volunteers to work for charitable causes; gains satisfaction from helping others.

**Health Problems.** The majority of people in this age group are relatively healthy, and most of them are able to live their lives in an independent manner, in their own homes in the community. Only 5 per cent of those over the age of 65 years are patients in hospitals, convalescent hospitals, nursing homes, or other related health care facilities. However, health problems and chronic illnesses are much more prominent during the mature adult stage, as one approaches the end of life.

For many people, this stage of life represents the "golden years," with greater freedom to enjoy the things that they like to do and a period of great contentment. However, others see it as a time for despair as they struggle to cope with the stresses caused by illness, loneliness, and living on a fixed income that, for many, is in the poverty range. Adults in this age group continue to face losses of loved ones and friends. Because women live longer than men, there are more widows in old age than widowers. More than 52 per cent of the women who are older than 65 years of age are widowed compared with only 14 per cent of the men of the same age. Widows who live on low incomes suffer the effects of poverty in terms of housing, medical care, essential services, and transportation.

Common characteristics of old age are a decrease in the number of roles that one performs and a gradual disengagement from the mainstream of society as one's physical strength and stamina decrease. Physically, about 38 per cent of mature adults have some limitation of an activity that lasts for more than one day, compared with a rate of 10 per cent for the total population. Among mature adults, two out of three have some impairment of their hearing by age 70 years, a marked loss of pain sensitivity that occurs sometime after the age of 50 years, a disturbance of the proprioceptive sense, and an increase in the length of reaction time required, especially in deciding how to respond. Visual acuity and accommodation to light decrease, and more than 88 per cent of older adults wear glasses.

More illnesses and deaths in this stage are caused by the chronic diseases than in previous stages. People are hospitalized for treatment of cardiovascular diseases, general arteriosclerosis, cancer, arthritis, strokes, fractures, and other degenerative conditions. When hospitalized, their length of stay tends to be about twice as long as for patients under the age of 65 years. The types of surgery that are most often performed on adults in this age group include prostatectomy in males, cataract extraction, colostomy, and fixation of a fractured femur. The most frequent causes of death and representative numbers of deaths that occur from each cause are shown in Table 17–4.

**Table 17–4.** LEADING CAUSES OF DEATH OF ADULTS OVER THE AGE OF 65, WITH REPRESENTATIVE NUMBERS OF DEATHS BASED ON THE 1977 DISEASE RATE APPLIED TO THE 1979 POPULATION OF THE UNITED STATES

| Cause of Death — Over Age 65 | Number |
|---|---|
| 1. Heart disease | 575,542 |
| 2. Cancer | 243,744 |
| 3. Stroke | 162,299 |
| 4. Influenza and pneumonia | 41,844 |
| 5. Arteriosclerosis | 28,727 |
| 6. Diabetes | 24,781 |
| 7. Accidents—all others | 19,258 |
| Total population in age group | 24,658,000 |
| Total deaths—all causes | 1,303,940 |

Sources: Bureau of the Census. Statistical Abstract of the United States 1980, 101st ed. Washington, DC, 1980, p. 29 and Revolution in health care urged in new surgeon general's report. Am J Nurs, *79*:1671–1672, (October) 1979.

## APPLICATION TO CLINICAL PRACTICE

A significant advantage of the adaptation approach to nursing is that it extends the assessment of patients or clients to include the psychosocial aspect as well as the physiological functioning. With this additional information, nurses are able to evaluate the way patients cope with feelings about internal and external changes in their lives and their ability to manage interactions with other people. The plan of care that the nurse prepares is more complete when the patient is regarded as a whole and unique individual.

All those who must depend upon another person, such as a parent, doctor, or nurse, for care want that person to be someone whom they trust. People develop trust in those who show interest in them in a caring way rather than in someone who treats them impersonally. Although you may feel hesitant about carrying out a psychosocial assessment, most patients welcome the chance to talk about themselves and are pleased that the nurse takes the time for them and shows an interest in them. The nurse's assessment of patients' growth and developmental tasks leads to three distinct advantages: (1) it fosters the trust relationship between the nurse and the patient or client, (2) the trust in the nurse leads to a decrease in the patient's anxiety, and (3) early identification and intervention in problems of coping with feelings leads to greater patient comfort and ease.

When caring for patients in the clinical setting, it is important to practice assessment of psychosocial functioning and interview skills. However, the first priority is completing the assessment of the physiological mode for patients in the second stage of illness and gathering information about their feelings about their illness, hospitalization, and treatment. Then, as their condition permits, continue to assess the way they carry out the roles that they use to achieve the growth and developmental tasks for their stage of life. The following steps (see Chapter Fifteen) can be used as a guide for your assessment.

1. Identify the primary role of the patient or client.
2. Place the patient in the appropriate stage of life.
3. State the growth and developmental tasks to be accomplished for that stage.

4. Gather information about the way the patient carries out the roles necessary to achieve these tasks.
5. Compare the behaviors with the standards, or norms, for that role.
6. Assess maladaptive behaviors to indicate problems of coping in the self-concept or interdependence modes.
7. State the roles that may be stimuli or influencing factors for the problems that have been identified.

| Primary role _____ | Stage of life _____ |
|---|---|
| **Growth and developmental tasks** | **Roles** |
| 1._____ | 1._____ |
| 2._____ | 2._____ |
| 3._____ | 3._____ |
| 4._____ | 4._____ |
| 5._____ | 5._____ |
| 6._____ | 6._____ |
| 7._____ | 7._____ |

It is necessary to process the information that you obtain about how people perform their roles. Information and behaviors involving feelings, emotions, values, beliefs, or concerns that one has about oneself are functions of the self-concept and describe the physical or personal self. Information and behaviors that involve relationships with other people and achieving goals or being productive are classified as dependent or independent behaviors in the interdependence mode. The behaviors that you assess are compared with the expectations of that role and with its range of socially acceptable behaviors. Adaptive behaviors lead to a positive and healthy response, whereas ineffective coping behaviors cause discomfort, are disruptive, or produce negative effects. The framework of the self-concept and interdependence modes helps nurses to classify behaviors and to more accurately identify problems in coping that occur in specific parts of each mode.

## REFERENCES

Barber, Janet, Stokes, Lillian, and Billings, Diane: Adult and Child Care. A Client Approach to Nursing. St. Louis, The C. V. Mosby Co., 1973.

Bureau of the Census. Statistical Abstract of the United States 1980, 101st ed., Washington, DC, 1980.

Erikson, E. H.: Childhood and Society, 2nd ed., New York, W. W. Norton and Co., Inc., 1963.

Estes, E. Harvey Jr.: Health experiences in the elderly. *In* Hendricks, Jon, and Hendricks, C. Davis (eds.): Dimensions of Aging Readings, Cambridge, Mass., Winthrop Publishers, Inc., 1979.

Hamburg, David A.: Healthy People. Surgeon General's Report of Health Promotion and Disease Prevention. Pub. #79-55071, Washington, DC, 1979, pp. 340–343, 377–379.

Havighurst, Robert: Human Development and Education. New York, David McKay Co., Inc., 1953, pp. 269–276.

Kaluger, George, and Kaluger, Meriem: Human Development, The Span of Life. St. Louis, The C. V. Mosby Co., Inc., 1973.

Lowenthal, Marjorie, et al.. Four Stages of Life. San Francisco, Jossey–Bass Inc., Publishers, 1975.

Rambo, Beverly: Role Function Mode. Unpublished study guide. Los Angeles, Mount St. Mary's College, 1975.

Revolution in health care urged in new surgeon general's report. Am J Nurs, 79:1671–1672, (October) 1979.

US Department of Health, Education, and Welfare. Vital and Health Statistics: Inpatient Utilization of Short Stay Hospitals by Diagnosis, United States 1968, Rockville, MD, National Center for Health Statistics, Series 13, No 12, (March) 1973.

US Department of Health, Education, and Welfare. Vital and Health Statistics: Surgical Operations in Short Stay Hospitals, United States 1968. Rockville, MD, National Center for Health Statistics, Series 13, No 11, (March) 1973.

US Department of Health, Education, and Welfare. Monocular Visual Acuity of Persons 4 – 74 Years, United States 1971–1972. Rockville, MD, National Center for Health Statistics, (March) 1977.

US Department of Health, Education, and Welfare. Current Estimates from the National Health Survey, United States 1978. Rockville, MD, National Center for Health Statistics, (November) 1979.

Yurick, Ann, et al.: The Aged Person and the Nursing Process. New York, Appleton-Century-Crofts, 1980.

## Chapter EIGHTEEN

# The Self-Concept Mode

## OBJECTIVES   Information in this chapter will help you to

1. Describe the theory of how the self-concept is developed and continues to change during one's lifetime.
2. State the framework of the self-concept, including the physical self and the personal self with their component parts.
3. Assess the individual's psychological adaptation by gathering information about how he or she carries out the growth and developmental tasks associated with his or her primary role.
4. Compare the individual's behaviors with the social expectations for the role, or the adapted range of responses, and identify those that indicate a problem of coping with feelings.
5. Define problems of the self-concept mode as the emotional, or feeling, responses to anxiety and to losses.

## DEFINITION OF TERMS

**body image** — the mental picture that one has of one's own body, or "How I feel about my body and self."

**mind** — the mechanism by which one is conscious of the continuous, complex process of the body as a unit in action and of "doing something."

**moral-ethical self** — the part of the self concerned with the formation of a conscience, the knowledge of right and wrong, the setting of standards, and evaluating the degree to which "I am who and what I say I am."

**personal self** — the part of the self that answers the questions "Who am I?" and "What do I want to become?" Behaviors express one's personality.

**personality** — the behavioral patterns and coping mechanisms that are characteristic of an individual in meeting the various situations of life.

**physical self** — the sensations and feelings about one's body functioning, appearance, size, and wholeness, or "How my body feels or looks to me."

**self-concept** — the combined feelings and beliefs that one holds about oneself at any given time which result from perceptions formed by social contact and direct one's behavior.

**self-consistency** — the part of the self that strives to maintain uniformity and organization in daily life for adaptation.

**self-esteem** — one's perception of one's worth.

**self-ideal** — the part of the self that is concerned with what one can be or expects to be and do.

**significant others** — the people who provide the rewards and sanctions in one's life.

The self-concept mode is concerned with psychological integrity, and psychological integrity involves the psyche, or the mind. Through the mechanism of the mind, one gains consciousness that the body acts as a unit and that one is "doing something." The mind is not only the brain but a complex functioning of the organs and systems of the body as a whole, with the psychomotor skills, perceptions, emotions, and intellectual processes by which individuals are able to meet all their basic needs in an independent manner. This mind is called the self-concept, and it provides the method by which one adapts to or negotiates between the changes in internal environment of our bodies and the changes in the external world, populated with others.

It is through the self-concept that one is able to gain a picture of oneself as an individual and to answer the universal questions "Who am I?" and "What am I?" The picture of who one is is formed by mental images, beliefs, and attitudes that one has selected, as well as the reflection of how one thinks that others see one. Although the mental image of oneself is not a concrete thing that one can feel or see, nevertheless, the self-concept is real and is a powerful influence on one's behavior.

No one was born with a self-concept or with the ability to see oneself as a separate and unique person; the self-concept develops gradually during childhood. It is the product of the socialization process of human beings and the composite of all the social experiences that occur within one's lifetime.

In this chapter, the self-concept mode and each of its components are described. These components are used as a framework for classifying the information obtained by the nursing assessment. In this chapter, the development of the self-concept during childhood and adolescence will be summarized, and a guide will be provided for assessing the behaviors that are used to carry out the roles for the developmental tasks of adult life.

## WHAT IS THE SELF-CONCEPT?

Have you ever watched people at a concert, a ball game, an airport, or a shopping center? People watching is an interesting pastime because people are so different in their physical appearance and in the way they act. They vary physiologically, according to the genes they inherited from their parents. Genes influence height, size of bones, racial characteristics, cellular function of organs, and hormonal and chemical responses in the body. Yet, despite the differences that make each person unique, common characteristics about the physical body can be observed, measured, and defined. The adaptation nurse gathers information about the functioning of the body through the assessment of the physiological mode.

People function as an integrated whole being, including the body and the mind. The mind makes it possible for one to think that this is my body and this is what I can do with it. This process of learning how to reflect on one's self and to see it as one thinks that other people do forms one's self-concept. Because other people influence how one sees oneself, the self-concept is part of psychosocial adaptation. Nurses who care for people who are ill or having health problems are concerned not only with physiological changes, but also with providing care for the entire person. The mind is involved when the body is affected because the person must attempt to cope with the condition of being ill, with altering one's view of oneself, and with the changes in one's daily life.

## DEFINITION OF THE SELF-CONCEPT

Social scientists have had difficulty defining the self-concept because of its dynamic, fluid, and abstract qualities. As used in the adaptation

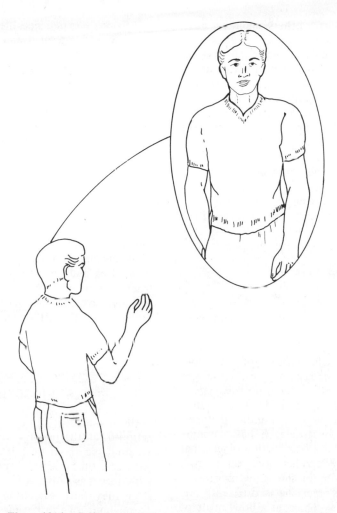

**Figure 18–1.** Self-concept is the mental picture one has of oneself.

approach to nursing, the self-concept consists of feelings and beliefs that permit the individual to know who he or she is and to feel that this self is adequate in meeting needs and desires. Self-concept is the total appraisal of one's appearance, abilities, resources, attitudes, feelings, and background, acting as a dynamic force in directing behavior.

The self-concept is formed, or shaped, by all one's social contacts, beginning with the mother and extending to significant others, as well as all one's experiences in life. The feelings and beliefs that any person has about one's self are exhibited through behaviors. Individuals use coping behaviors that conform to the way they see themselves and the way they think others perceive them. For example, the young boy who thinks of himself as brave and daring and is eager to show what he can do is the first to propose games and activities. Thus, he is regarded by the other boys and their parents as a leader. The young girl who sees

herself as pretty makes it a point to smile frequently and to use nice manners that favorably impress other people. Thus, even strangers remark how pretty she is. The self-concept is influenced by feedback obtained from the social setting and from the individual's own reactions to him- or herself in this environment.

The way that people see themselves and cope with their feelings in the self-concept mode is molded by the way they go about living their daily lives and carrying out their work as members of society. Thus, the behaviors of the self-concept are related to how people carry out the roles they assume and the manner in which they meet the requirements and expectations society has for each role. The kinds of work, or tasks, that one performs in the social world provide one with feedback as to what type of person one is. Feedback reflects how effective one is and the kind of skills that one possesses as a member of one's social group.

To live peaceably with others, one must learn to trust others and to be trusted in return, to act in predictable ways, and to avoid harming others. Social living also requires that individuals be responsible and dependable by controlling their bodies and strong emotions so that rage is not expressed whenever their desires are thwarted. Members of a social group must see themselves as cooperating with others as well as competing to achieve goals and being independent in meeting their own needs. They must be able to think ahead while living in the present. Social feedback provides the view as to whether one is being productive in work and providing the children of the next generation.

## UNIQUENESS OF THE SELF-CONCEPT

No two people have exactly the same view of themselves, and no person's concept of the self remains unchanged over a period of time. Throughout life, one's self-concept undergoes revisions and modifications as one attempts to cope with the stresses produced by the changes of an increasingly complex world. Even though two people may see the same stimulus, they perceive it differently because each has a unique self-concept. Consider a bright shiny object that is seen by the mother and her three-year-old son. Both translate the stimulus into something meaningful; however, the meaning is different. The mother sees the shiny object as a bowl made of sterling silver, fashioned in an antique style with scrolls, having a monetary value and an even greater sentimental value because it is a family heirloom. Her three-year-old son sees the shiny object, recognizes it as a bowl, sees that it holds some fruit, and decides to eat some of the fruit as he runs out to play. The feelings, beliefs, and experiences that each of them has accumulated during their lifetime account for the differences in meaning.

Even children in the same family develop self-concepts that differ from those of their brothers and sisters. Parents are inexperienced with their first child; they are learning how to raise a child. By the time the second child is born, the parents have gained experience and see themselves as more capable of caring for the newcomer. The first child, who had been the center of attention, must now share the parents with someone he or she regards as an intruder to the family circle. The second child's self-concept develops differently because his or her world contains a sibling as well as the parents, who divide their love and attention between two children.

Individuals experience life and changes in the world in very personal and unique ways, based on the thoughts, feelings, and perceptions that they have accumulated. In spite of the variations in the way people see themselves and express their self-concept, some observable patterns of behavior can be identified. Stress and anxiety generate emotions and feelings that influence behavioral responses. Emotions of anger, rage, depression, sadness, and fear are upsetting and, generally, indicate problems that people have in coping with perceived threats to the self. These emotions are expressed in voluntary behaviors that are classified as either moving-toward, moving-away, or moving-against patterns of behavior. Individuals exhibit behaviors of one of these patterns depending upon the way that they see themselves and the feedback that they receive from others. (Stress, anxiety, and behavioral patterns have been covered in previous chapters. Problems of the self-concept caused by strong emotions are examined in more detail in Chapter Nineteen.)

## COMPONENTS OF THE SELF-CONCEPT

The self-concept can be regarded as the organization of all the feelings and beliefs that one has accumulated about oneself and that continues to serve as a fundamental frame of reference. One's self-concept is resistant to change in most adults after they have established their self-identity. Throughout one's lifetime, the self-concept is continuously being reworked, expanded, and clarified so that, hopefully, in old age, each person can look back in his or her life and say "I am satisfied with what I am" and "I am the kind of person I want to be."

The uniqueness of the self-concept permits one to exhibit many different "faces" in various circumstances, as one adjusts to the role expectations of others. One's attitudes about the self are influenced by one's physical appearance and ability. These characteristics also influence others. Specific personality traits are often attributed to people with a certain physical appearance. These traits are then reinforced by social contacts, forming a powerful influence on the self-concept. The self-concept, which serves as the unifying whole of our identity, has these two major components:* the physical self and the

---

*The original literature review, including the development of this classification and the theory underlying the self-concept mode, was done by Marie J. Driever at Mount St. Mary's College under USPHS Grant No. 5T02MH06442 1969–1970.

personal self. The physical self is defined in terms of the somatic self, or body sensations, and the body image. The personal self is partitioned into self-consistency (how the self is viewed day after day), the moral-ethical self, and the self-ideal.

## THE PHYSICAL SELF

The physical self is concerned with how one feels about one's body, its various parts, one's control over its functions, and one's mental image of it. The mental view and feelings about the body are different from the physiological mode, which focuses on the actual body and its functioning. Getting out of bed and walking is a function of the musculoskeletal system, whereas wanting to stay in bed and being afraid that one is too weak to walk are behaviors related to the physical self. The development of a positive and healthy physical self permits one to accept one's body with less preoccupation of its functions and leaves one free to engage in other experiences of living.

The physical self is divided into two parts for analyzing behaviors: the somatic self and body image represent different views of the physical

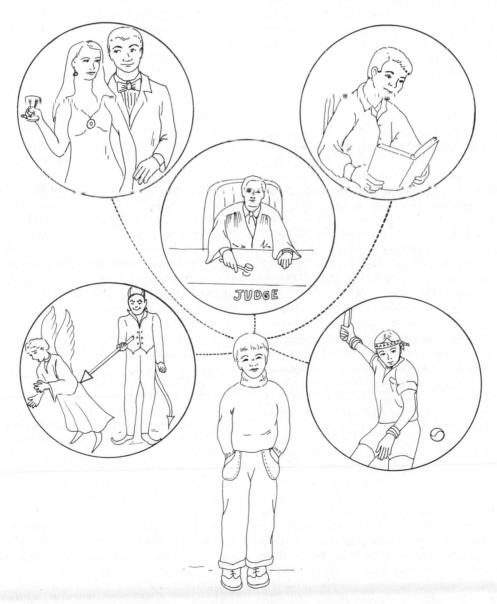

**Figure 18–2.** Individuals develop many mental images of themselves that form the various dimensions of the self-concept — the physical self, the moral-ethical self, the ideal self, and self-consistency.

self, although resulting problems of coping with feelings are similar.

**The Somatic Self.** The feelings and sensations that one has about one's body constitute the somatic self. It is concerned with "What I can do" and how one feels about doing it. One of the first indications of the self-concept is when a baby becomes aware of his or her body. The baby waves his fist in front of his face and sucks on his thumb for a long period of time before becoming aware that the fist and thumb belong to him and that he can control them. One's awareness of the body expands during childhood, as the child learns to control body movements, to correlate body sensations with body actions, and to perfect psychomotor skills. Essential for the child's psychological integrity is a body that functions as it should and at the appropriate time and place.

The somatic self includes feelings that people have about their bodies, in terms of the size and shape, height, weight, ease of movement, control of elimination and other body functions, and feelings of health or illness. When illness strikes, people are faced with coping with changes in their view of the body, their control over it, and its functions. The loss of control, damage to or loss of a body part, and loss of function alter how people view their body; some people have difficulty in coping with their feelings about these changes. The more that a particular part of the body is valued and central to a person's overall being, the more vulnerable the person is when that particular body part is affected by illness, even on a temporary basis.

**Body Image.** The mental picture that one has of what one's body looks like is called the body image. It includes all the feelings that one has about one's appearance, such as fat, thin, tall, short, plain, attractive, strong, coordinated, clumsy, and flat-chested. Studies have shown that most teen-agers are dissatisfied with the way they look and would like to change some feature —most frequently mentioned is the nose.

In our culture, great emphasis is placed on the ideal adult figure, and this exerts a powerful influence on how young people view their physical appearance and body image. During early adulthood, the sexual nature of human development is strongest and presents young people with the need to achieve acceptance by the opposite sex in a variety of interpersonal relationships. To a great extent, their self-concept is formed by their perception of their own bodies and their acceptance by others. Some young people develop a distorted view when comparing their body with the ideal appearance and may believe that their

body is overly important or more perfect than it is. The young man with broad shoulders may concentrate on exercises to enhance his upper torso and engage in other activities in which his shoulders would be noticed and admired. However, the tendency among young people is to overemphasize what they perceive to be a defect, and to feel that it makes them less worthy or less acceptable. Young women are very susceptible to feelings of insecurity because most of them do not attain the perfect figure or great beauty and have doubts about their attractiveness to men.

Different parts of the body are regarded in terms of good or bad, adequate or inadequate, and clean or dirty and are valued accordingly. Women place a high value on the face and devote more attention to the body than do most men. Men place a high value on having a larger body stature, muscular strength, wide shoulders, and hair on their heads and body. They are more distressed by impairment to their legs than are women because many of their activities involve the use of the legs in locomotion, agility, and strength. For both sexes, any circumstance that alters or endangers the sexual organs or one's sexual identity can have a profound effect on the self-concept.

**Effect of Illness on the Physical Self.** Illness is a focal stimulus for many coping problems that affect the physical self-concept. Diseases and injuries that may seem to be of a minor nature to some people may be a serious threat to the body image of others when they affect highly valued parts of the body. Diseases and injuries related to sexual identity and occupational roles affect one's body image: An injury to the fingers is a crisis for the concert pianist; a bursitis of the shoulder is a major impediment for the tennis pro or the window washer.

Although obesity is more a health problem than an illness, obese people who have lost considerable weight find that they must change their body image and their personality. The enlarged body size often represents a defense against a hostile world, a symbol of independence and importance, and, after losing weight, the body image of the fat person no longer fits. People who have suffered a myocardial infarction (heart attack) must deal with their feelings about the damage to the heart that occurred with little or no warning. From that time, they are less able to rely on the heart to sustain life in the same casual and unconcerned way that they did previously. After they have recovered, some people become more dependent upon others and greatly restrict their activities because they fear another heart attack. Others who recover with no visible evidence of heart damage may resist any change in their lifestyle and maintain their preinfarction body image.

Cancer is one of the most dreaded diseases, and its assault on the body causes a threat to its victim's life. The feelings aroused by anxiety for one's survival create numerous problems in coping that can recur and persist. The cancerous growth produces symptoms that interfere with some function of the body, and the loss of function alters the way that one views the physical self. Further losses occur when surgery that may be mutilating is performed in the attempt to prolong life. Chemotherapy and radiation produce uncomfortable side effects, and changes such as loss of hair further batter one's body image. Mastectomy (removal of the breast) is particularly traumatic for a woman's body image. During the postoperative period, a woman is coping with the effects of surgery, the threat of the disease, and feelings of relief that she is alive. Changes in body image and problems with the way she sees herself and how others see her arise at a later time, when she attempts to re-establish her life. Husbands, as well as wives, must cope with changes, and a number of marriages have failed within a year or two of the surgery. People who have colostomies, amputations, and other radical body mutilations tend to resist accepting the reality of surgery; they view it as a bad dream that will go away. Although they may seem to accept and adjust to the change in their body, they tend to see their bodies in terms of their previous image of an intact body.

## THE PERSONAL SELF

The personal self consists of all the feelings and experiences in life that shape the kind of person one is. It is the response to the questions "Who am I?" "What are my beliefs?" "What do I think I should be?" and "How well do I measure up to what I ought to be?" The way that people act, or behave, letting others know what they are really like, is called personality. Elements of the personal self are usually formed by the age of 5 years, but, like the physical self, the personal self is continuously undergoing adjustment and change as a result of what people think of themselves and the feedback that they get from others.

Development of the personal self leads to feelings of self-esteem, or the overall perception of one's worth. An inverse relationship exists between self-esteem and anxiety. When anxiety is high, one perceives numerous threats or persistent danger to the self. Danger to the self leads to doubts, ineffective coping, and problems associated with low self-esteem, or low morale. On the other hand, people with high self-esteem have low levels of anxiety. They are characterized by being mentally healthy, having a positive attitude toward life, and being in control of their bodies as well as events in their lives through good decision-making. Some feelings and responses that are associated with high and low levels of self-esteem include

### High Self-esteem
Self-assured; poised
Effective in solving problems
Trusting; friendly
Unselfish
Happy; sincere
Productive; active
Independent
Realistic view of the world
Optimistic
Hopeful

### Low Self-esteem
Poor view of self; unsure
Lack of control; gives way to impulses
Distrusting; demanding
Self-centered; egotistic
Frustrated; angry
Depression; despair
Withdrawn; isolated from others
Negative outlook; pessimistic
Helpless; dependent upon others
Rebellious; acting-out behavior

During childhood, the personal self develops along three different dimensions: self-consistency, self-ideal, and the moral-ethical self. These elements do not develop at the same rate or at the same time. One's mental view of "Who am I?" must be shaped before one is able to evaluate whether something is right or wrong or the ideal. Problems that arise in the personal self are those resulting from trying to cope with feelings of anxiety.

**Self-Consistency.** People express their feelings and act in fairly stable patterns as they carry out their activities of daily living. They have learned to organize their lives and to cope with the usual changes in a predictable way, which is called self-consistency. It is the way in which they express their identity, or answer the questions of "Who am I?" and "What am I?" This aspect of the self-concept consists of the actual performance and the responses that one has to everyday events and situations. It includes the feelings, attitudes, and beliefs that make up one's personality. The personality is the behavioral patterns and coping mechanisms that are characteristic of an individual in meeting the various situations in life.

People express their personality and view of who they are through the feelings, attitudes, and beliefs that accompany the growth and developmental tasks they carry out for each stage of life. Some personality traits are described by the following terms: (I am . . .) ambitious, athletic, active, confident, dependable, organized, happy, friendly, responsible, trusting, prompt, and hard-working. Part of one's body image, such as being fat or thin or tall or short, may be part of self-consistency when it has become a dominant feature or has been overemphasized.

**Self-Ideal.** The mental image of what one would like to be or do forms an aspect of the self-concept called the self-ideal. One's self-ideal is achieved by incorporating the traits and actions that one admires in others into the image of what one would like to be. It includes one's expectations, desires, and wishes about what one would like to be or to achieve. The self-ideal serves to guide behavior toward achieving these goals. One's actual self-image as expressed through the personality of self-consistency may differ from that of the self-ideal. Some people may never be able to achieve their self-ideal image, for a variety of reasons, and difficulties in coping with this inability leads to problems of powerlessness.

**Moral-Ethical Self.** After a consistent image of one's self begins to emerge, one needs to develop the ability to judge the resulting perceptions and behaviors as desirable or undesirable. The moral-ethical self takes over the function of evaluating to what degree one is what one says one is. This part of the self-concept learns to distinguish right from wrong and to set standards for behavior based on values gained from the family, peer groups, and others in one's culture. It consists of all one's beliefs about what is good or bad, right or wrong, and fair or unjust. When one's behavior fails to measure up to the standards of the moral-ethical self, feelings of guilt occur.

## DEVELOPMENT OF THE SELF-CONCEPT

One's self-concept is formed by accumulated social experiences and contact with significant others. The skills, attitudes, habits, and behaviors that must be learned for personal and social adjustment at each stage of life are called developmental tasks, and these are the foundation of the self-concept. The developmental tasks for each stage of life are described in more detail in Chapters Sixteen and Seventeen. For each stage, the individual must accomplish three things:

1.  Learn to live with tools that aid in physical control or mastery of the *physical self*.
2.  Learn to live with the self by dealing with the realization, acceptance, and handling of impulses, urges, and feelings, or the *personal self*.
3.  Learn to live with others by gaining skills and the ability to relate to others, or *interdependence*.

The first two tasks involve the formation of the self-concept. The third task involves the interdependence mode. Developmental tasks are related to the formation of perceptions or the attachment of meaning to stimuli, the control of emotions, the appropriate responses in interpersonal relationships, the use of language, and intellectual skills, such as reasoning and problem-solving.

Babies have no concept of self. Newborn infants are bombarded with stimuli from both internal and external sources, and they can handle these stimuli only on a physiological basis. In this chaotic, disorganized world, stimuli are interpreted by babies as sensations of either pleasure or pain. As their experiences increase, they begin to differentiate one stimulus from another. Among the first perceptions to emerge are the relief of hunger and the pleasure of being held and cuddled by the mother. Soon the baby is able to distinguish between the stimuli and realizes that being held is gratifying even when not hungry. The stress and anxiety of having unmet needs is felt by the infant as a physiological response that gives rise to a painful or an unpleasant sensation. The child's self-concept enlarges and extends as he learns to master and control his own body and objects in his environment.

The development of the self-concept is shown in Table 18–1. The developmental psychosocial tasks, degree of emotional control, description of emergence of the self-concept, and some consequences resulting from failure to achieve these tasks are described for each stage of life during childhood and adolescence.

## FIRST LEVEL ASSESSMENT

Nursing is concerned with how the individual copes physically and psychologically with the condition of being sick or having a health problem. Psychological coping involves the self-concept as the person struggles to cope with the threat that illness poses to the body and, often, to life itself, as well as with the disruption it causes in one's daily life. How one is coping involves the present, or the "here and now." The nursing assessment also focuses on the patient's current feelings and behaviors and includes verbal statements, expressions of feelings, thoughts, or

**Table 18-1.** THE DEVELOPMENT OF THE SELF-CONCEPT DURING THE CHILDHOOD AND ADOLESCENT STAGES OF LIFE, INCLUDING THE PSYCHOSOCIAL TASKS TO BE ACCOMPLISHED AT EACH STAGE AND THE TYPES OF PROBLEMS THAT OCCUR AS A RESULT OF FAILURE TO RESOLVE THE TASK

| Stage of Life | Psychosocial Tasks | Physical Self | Self-Consistency | Emotional Control | Moral-Ethical Self | Self-Ideal | Failure to Achieve Psychosocial Tasks |
|---|---|---|---|---|---|---|---|
| Infancy: birth to 1 year | **Security vs mistrust.** Overwhelmed by stimuli at birth—unable to focus on one, attach a meaning, or make an adaptive muscular response. Nursing provides relief of hunger and pleasure—begins to differentiate and respond to mother in reciprocal way. | By 4 wk—holds up head; by 8 wk—smiles; by 4–6 mo—responds to faces; by 8 mo—recognizes mother; explores world using mass movements of muscles and body. | Complete dependence upon others for all needs. Unmet needs create tension—met needs give pleasure. Mouth is major source of pleasure—nipple is the organ, mother is the significant person. Dependence and rage lead to power or omnipotence. | Ruled by pleasure principle. Satisfaction of needs is pleasurable, tension and discomfort lead to rage. Expressed by massive body movements. By 8–10 mo—develops fears. Can smile, laugh, and coo when happy. | By 1 yr—may be inhibited by saying "no-no." | Aware of mother as important care-giver. | Tension and anxiety lead to crying, depression, and withdrawal. In adult life, leads to chronic mistrust of self and others and to dependency. |
| Toddler | **Autonomy vs shame and doubt.** Child must alter behavior and natural desires to conform to parents' wishes. Language and locomotion skills lead to more freedom; some antagonism with mother who sets limits, but love for mother wins out. | Period of learning muscular control, including walking, climbing, sphincter control, table manners, and so on. | By 2 yr—calls self by name, calls other children "baby," more responsive to mother and more dependent upon her, although father may be a favorite when child is not tired, hungry, or wet. | At 1 yr—gives up object on request. At 1½ yr—shows affection to doll or toy (teddy bear); has many fears of noises; hits, kicks, and cries when angry. At 2½ yr—has temper tantrums. | Imitates others by calling self "good" or "bad." At 1½ yr—blames others. At 2½ yr—wants own way, shows little desire for gaining adult approval. | Responsive, demanding, and dependent upon mother. | Anxiety leads to self doubt, shame, fear of exposure, and use of ritualistic actions to ward off harm. |
| Preschool | **Initiative vs guilt.** The play age develops self-awareness, conscience, and fantasy of "I can become —" and "I have worth or ability," to try to act like (father or mother) even though I'm small and inexperienced. | Spurt in intellectual growth and acquisition of language. From 4½–5 yr—rapid shift from baby to child body build. | At 3 yr—expresses and affirms own sex by "I am a _____" (boy–girl); shows interest in marriage and no distinction between sexes in play. At 4 yr—very interested in genital organs, where babies come from, and own navel. Mother is still favored person. | Has more visual fears, such as the dark, the bogeyman, of mother leaving. Has more self-control over anger. Uses more verbal aggression such as "I'll kill you." | At 3 yr—tries to conform and please. At 4 yr—begins to understand rules, good and bad, and is interested in God. At 5 yr—"good," obeys, and conforms. | Beginning of a value system. Identifies and takes on attributes of admired person—often parent of same sex; acts as though he were the other person. | Anxiety leads to guilt and rigidity in interpersonal relationships, confusion of psychosexual role, or lack of initiative in learning new skills. |

**Table 18–1.** *(Continued)*

| Stage of Life | Psychosocial Tasks | Physical Self | Self-Consistency | Emotional Control | Moral-Ethical Self | Self-Ideal | Failure to Achieve Psychosocial Tasks |
|---|---|---|---|---|---|---|---|
| School-age | **Industry vs Inferiority.** Period for developing a sense of adequacy as one who performs tasks, as "one who can master"; learns work identity and basic technology of the culture. | Steady rate of growth; thinking in concrete terms. Learning the rules, manipulating objects and simple concepts. More motor control. By 10–12 yr–interested in appearance. Boys become fatter by 11 yr, girls taller and heavier by 12 yr. | At 6 yr–realizes one has a past, some sex play and exploration. At 8 yr–interest in sex is high, peeping, how babies are made; plays with those of same sex but very aware of opposite sex. More friction with parents. Peers gain importance. | At 6 yr–physically and verbally aggressive; says he is mad. At 8 yr–less aggression, more curiosity, responds with hurt feelings. By 10–12 yr–less open in expressing love, often talks back, rebels, is discourteous; has more fears and suspicions about adults. | Relates good and bad to specific things allowed by parents. Often claims, "That's not fair." At 8 yr–interested in religion, knows good and bad, and wants to be good. By 10–12 yr–believes in justice and fair play. Conflict over adult authority and pressures of peers. | In early school years, parent, family member, teacher, or other admired person is ideal, but no longer acts as if he were the other person. In later years, has crush on teacher or sports or music star. "Hero worship." | Failure or anxiety leads to feelings of inferiority, a sense of being one who is unable to master the task or skill. |
| Adolescent | **Identity vs identity diffusion.** Focuses on seeking identity as individual, gains emotional independence from parents, and establishes self as independent from adults. Gains skills needed for individual and group relationships with opposite sex. | Accepts changes in body due to puberty, increased hormonal output, changes in body contour. Concern about appearance as basis for acceptance by peers and opposite sex. Secondary sex characteristics by age 13–14 yr–maturity by 18 yr for girls, by 19 yr for boys. | Learns to accept adults in life in way that reflects how one was treated as a child by parents. Growing independence causes conflicts with parents. Seeks opportunities to play out sex role in social activities, dating, friendships, and love relationships. | Anger is a major emotion and expressed verbally with name-calling, jealousy in dating relationships, and envy. Finds happiness in comic situations when at ease with self and when feeling superior. Has less fear and worry. | Tends to be idealistic, recognizes right and wrong and what is the truth. Takes a stand on what he believes in. Follows values and behaviors of peers and will participate in activities such as smoking, drinking, or drug use. Questions authority. | Beginning to emerge based on a melding of attributes in an admired person plus own values and beliefs. | Failure or anxiety leads to sense of inadequacy in controlling strong feelings or gaining confidence to compete and master new social relationships. Inability to synthesize own personal goals, values, and identity. |

beliefs, that give a mental image of the person. The problems that patients have in coping with their feelings often interfere with their nursing or medical treatment. Those who hide their feelings of worry or anxiety are tense, uncomfortable, and distressed, and, often, have delayed healing or complications that are due in part by the activity of the autonomic nervous system. When nurses get to know patients as individuals, it fosters trust in the nurse, allows early identification of actual and potential problems, and lets patients know that it is okay to discuss fears and anxieties. The following case histories illustrate how problems in coping with feelings obstruct the patient's care.

Maria B. is a 65-year-old woman who appears to be much younger than her age. She is depressed and refuses all types of medical and nursing care. She was scheduled for a bronchoscopy this morning but stated that she was too cold to have the procedure and refused it even though the doctor came in to talk with her. She stated that it was "useless" now that she has cancer, and she does not want to have anything else done because her condition is hopeless. She refused to have a bath and to let the nurse change the linen on her bed but stated several times that she wanted to be left alone so she could sleep.

RG is a 50-year-old man who questions everything about his medical and nursing care. He tells nurses that he does not need their help and that his wife will take care of him when she comes, give him his bath, shave him, and so forth. He is getting oxygen per cannula and becomes angry when it is necessary to have an enema or sterile catheter care or when there is a delay in receiving medications for severe pain in the spine.

Further assessment revealed that Maria was born in Costa Rica, came to this country as a young girl, married a citizen, but had no children. She was admitted to the hospital one month ago with pneumonia of the upper lobe and was diagnosed as having an oat cell carcinoma of the bronchus. She was started on radiation therapy, which was discontinued when she developed severe gastritis and anemia. Her sister flew here from her home in Costa Rica and is staying at Maria's home. However, there is tension because the sister does not speak English and Maria's husband does not speak Spanish. Maria wants to return to her birthplace in Costa Rica. She believes that everything that the doctors have done to treat her cancer have only made her feel worse. Because so much has happened to her in such a short period of time, she is afraid that she will die before she can make her trip.

RG was born in New York City to immigrant parents and now operates a thriving business in California. He has always worked hard and long hours, and, in recent years, his wife also has worked for the firm, now that their two children are grown. Their daughter is married and lives about 40 miles away, and their son is a student at the university. RG and his wife believe in being active, and, when they can spare the time, they like swimming and going to Las Vegas to see the shows at the casinos. RG was in an automobile accident and received spinal and chest injuries. He worries about how his business will continue during his long convalescence because his assistant is not a "go-getter," and it is too much for his wife to handle. When assessing RG's developmental tasks, the nurse focused on the "here and now," enabling RG to see that he was expressing much of his frustration and anger in demanding care from his wife and rejecting care from the nurses. With help, he was able to change these behaviors.

The assessment of the individual's growth and developmental tasks provides a less threatening approach and yields more information than is usually obtained by direct questions or by requests such as "Describe yourself physically" or "Tell me what kind of person you think you are." People use roles to carry out the developmental tasks or the work of their lives; thus, the assessment seeks information about one's feelings related to the areas of occupation, family, housing, finances, and activities. The recommended procedure for this assessment is explained in more detail in Chapter Fifteen on Role-Function and specific developmental tasks for each stage of life are contained in Chapters Sixteen and Seventeen. The recommended method consists of the following steps:

1. Determine the primary role of the individual.
2. Classify the person in the appropriate stage of life.
3. List the developmental tasks to be carried out for that stage.
4. Assess the roles used to carry out the tasks. (Roles also serve as stimuli for the second level assessment.)
5. Gather information about the performance of roles and process it with feelings and beliefs related to the self-concept and process relationships with other people as belonging to the interdependence mode.
6. Compare behaviors with the norms for the roles in that social group and identify coping problems manifested by the maladaptive behaviors.

Developmental tasks for adults involve their occupation, housing, families, finances, activities, and interests that are appropriate for their stage of life. When assessing the roles used to carry out the tasks, look for expressions of feelings about these areas.

*Occupation* — present; past; if retired, retired from what?

*Family* — number of children, ages, other members of family, their location; confidant; significant others, including pets.

*Housing* — own or rent; location; size and adequacy; distance from other family members; inconveniences; shopping; cleaning; errands.

*Activities* — use of leisure time; hobbies; how one passes the time of day.

*Finances* — cost of health care; affordable leisure time activities; standard of living.

If all these are within the adaptive range, the person is coping effectively. When coping problems exist, anxiety is expressed by feelings of anger, sadness, depression, fear, or some aspect of these because the self-concept is threatened.

## SECOND LEVEL ASSESSMENT

The self-concept is formed by the beliefs and feelings that people have about themselves from experiences in their lives and from the reactions of other people. Problems in coping with one's feelings occur whenever one perceives a threat or danger to the self-concept, or a lessening of one's self-esteem, and whenever the coping mechanism that is used is ineffective in reducing the anxiety. Almost all types of stimuli can produce maladaptive feelings and lead to coping problems. However, focal and contextual stimuli vary for the physical self and the personal self, as shown on the Guide for Nursing Care Plan (at end of Section One) and in Table 18–2. The roles that are used by people to carry out their developmental tasks and their expectations about how the roles should be performed are important stimuli.

Table 18–2 shows the components of the self-concept mode, the types of problems associated with each component, and the stimuli most frequently found to be causing the problems.

## PROBLEMS AND NURSING INTERVENTIONS

Although anxiety is referred to as the major problem of the self-concept, it is more accurately a major stimulus that causes coping problems.

Table 18–2.   THE SELF-CONCEPT COMPONENTS, PROBLEMS ASSOCIATED WITH EACH COMPONENT, AND THE STIMULI MOST FREQUENTLY FOUND TO BE CAUSING THE PROBLEMS

| Components | Description | Problems | Stimuli |
|---|---|---|---|
| **Physical Self** | | | |
| Somatic Self | How one's body feels and how one feels about one's body | Feelings of loss of body function or part of **loss of control** | Physical illness (F)<br>Medical treatment<br>Past losses |
| Body Image | Feelings about how one's body looks | | Medicines<br>Pain<br>Reactions of others<br>Health habits<br>Health beliefs |
| **Personal Self** | | | |
| Self-Consistency | Personality traits: how one sees oneself in relation to actual performance or response | Feelings that express **anxiety** (anger, sadness, fear, or some form of these) | Any threat to the self (F)<br>Changes in family structure, support systems, resources or situation, attitudes or expectations, health |
| Self-Ideal | What one would like to be; related to what one is capable of being or achieving | Feelings that express **powerlessness** (or anxiety) | Expectations of self (F)<br>Expectations of others<br>One's abilities, resources, time, money, motivation |
| Moral-Ethical Self | One's spiritual or ethical view of self; related to value system, beliefs of "right and wrong" | Feelings that express **guilt** (or anxiety) | Expectations of others (F)<br>Expectations of self<br>Strength of consequences or sanctions<br>Support systems<br>Circumstances<br>Resources |

NOTE: F indicates the usual focal stimulus; the others are more often the contextual stimuli or influencing factors.

Any perception of a threat to the self activates the autonomic nervous system that readies the body for "fight or flight." Common coping mechanisms that are selected to reduce the discomfort caused by the anxiety include eating, sleeping, physical exercise, chewing gum, or talking it out. If the anxiety is not reduced, the responses are accompanied by expressions of various emotions, such as anger, sadness, or fear. The individual might state his problem as having feelings of fear about declining health, fears about dying, feelings of anger about being ill, feelings of frustration because of helplessness, or feelings of depression because of leg amputation.

Other problems of the self-concept include loss and grief, feelings of guilt and shame, and feelings of powerlessness. These problems occur frequently and are discussed in greater detail in Chapter Nineteen.

## APPLICATION TO CLINICAL PRACTICE

When caring for patients in the clinical setting, after assessing the physiological need areas, continue by assessing psychosocial functioning in order to identify problems that patients may have in coping with their illness. Identify the primary role and the stage of life, then list the developmental tasks for that stage and the roles used by the patient to carry out those tasks. Gather information about each patient's performance of the roles and any feelings or beliefs that he or she has.

Process the information that you obtained according to the framework of the self-concept mode. This should make it easier to develop skill in classifying behaviors and accuracy in defining problems that result from maladaptive or ineffective coping. For the physical self, the somatic self and body image can be combined because they are closely related and both cause problems of loss and grieving. Write a short paper describing the patient's image of himself or herself using these components as headings to organize your findings.

| Component | Manifested Behaviors/Statements |
|---|---|
| Physical Self | |
|   Somatic self and body image | _____ |
| Personal Self | _____ |
|   Self-Consistency | _____ |
|   Self-Ideal | _____ |
|   Moral-Ethical Self | _____ |

As you can see, the assessment includes many adaptive behaviors that help us to evaluate who the patient is, what kind of person he is, and some of the things that are important or of value to him.

### CASE STUDY

The following case study is a narrative form of how one nurse conducted a complete assessment of a patient and obtained information not only of physiological functioning but also of psychosocial adaptation.

Mr. James Peters, age 51 years, was admitted to the Medical Center for treatment of a detached retina of his right eye. The admission note on the hospital chart was as follows:
1345 – Admitted to Rm. 418–1 by wheelchair. States he has a tear of the retina (OD) and is scheduled for OR in the AM. Lab work done prior to adm. Wearing glasses and contact lens on OS. No dentures. No complaints of pain but has funny vision and flashes of light in affected eye. BP–180/90, T–98°, P–76, R–16.
1430 – To treatment room for exam by Dr. Healer.
Additional information from the hospital admission form revealed that Mr. Peters is

married but that his mother-in-law is listed as the person to be notified in case of an emergency. His occupation is teacher, and he has Blue Cross insurance coverage.

Mona was assigned as Mr. Peters' primary care nurse. She went to his room to begin her assessment of his needs for care. Mr. Peters was wearing his own pajamas, lying on the bed, and reading a magazine. He looked up as Mona entered the room and put down his magazine as she greeted him. "Hello Mr. Peters, I am Mona, and I will be your nurse. I would like to find out more about you in order to plan your care while you are in the hospital."

The assessment of his physiological need areas revealed the following behaviors:

*Oxygenation:* Awake, alert, converses readily, skin warm to touch, BP–180/90, P–76, R–16. Has decreased vision and blurring in OD. CBC report not available.

*Fluids and Electrolytes:* Averages 8 to 9 cups of coffee per day with 2 to 3 glasses of water, juice for breakfast, and usually 1 beer after work–approximately 2560 ml/day. Output qs. No abnormal loss of fluids. Lab results not back yet.

*Nutrition:* Weighs 162 lb, which is his usual weight. Height is 5' 10". Basal caloric need is 1750 plus light activity (20 per cent) of 350 for a total of 2100 calories. Regular diet ordered. States he is not fussy about his food and eats just about everything.

*Elimination:* Voids qs. Usually has bowel movement every day just after breakfast.

*Rest and Activity:* Goes to bed about 10:30 PM and gets up about 6:30 AM. Wakes up 1 to 2 times per night. Performs all activities of daily living; no limitation of movement in joints. Tries to exercise several times per week doing yardwork and playing softball with son.

*Integument:* Skin clear–no rash, ecchymosis, or noticeable scars.

*Sensory Regulation:* T–98° F. Vision–wears glasses; unable to see far objects; has blurring and distortion of objects in OD. No decrease in hearing, olfactory, taste, tactile, or speech formation. Resting comfortably.

Mona asked about his present illness and the circumstances when he first noticed a problem with his vision. He stated that he has always had lots of trouble with his eyes. Four years ago, he had surgery to remove a cataract from his left eye. He now has a cataract of his right eye, as well as the detached retina. In addition, he is being treated for glaucoma. "Whatever goes wrong with eyes seems to be what I get," he said with a sigh.

As he talked, Mona noticed that his hands were clenched into fists and that his speech was alternately halting and rushed. As he paused, Mona placed her hand on his clenched fist and said, "You seem very tense. It seems as though this business with your sight is upsetting you." At Mona's touch and words, the tears welled up in Mr. Peters' eyes, and he turned his face toward the wall. Sobs escaped as he sought to regain control. He replied, "Oh God! I'm so afraid that the surgery won't work and that I'll lose my sight. Then I don't know what I would do!"

At this point, Mr. Peters has expressed some very strong emotions, and the interaction between Mr. Peters and Mona is at a crucial point. The direction it takes is often up to the nurse's ability to use the nursing process to identify the patient's problems and to carry out the appropriate interventions. Nurses who want to reassure the patient that he is in good hands and repeat "You are going to be okay. We'll take good care of you, and the surgery isn't that serious" probably have not helped the patient to overcome his feelings. The nurse also does not know why he is feeling this way unless further assessment is carried out.

Make a list of the developmental tasks Mr. Peters has to carry out and the roles that he uses for these tasks, based on the information that has been presented up to this time.

Primary role _____          Stage of life _____
Tasks _____                  Roles _____
_____                         _____
_____                         _____
_____                         _____
_____                         _____

The nurse continued to assess Mr. Peters' psychosocial functioning. She encouraged communication by using open-ended statements, and the patient expressed many of his concerns. Rather than probing questions, Mona used reflective phrases, restated a few words, or used a follow-up question to obtain the following information.

As Mr. Peters sought to control his emotions, Mona asked softly, "You're afraid that you might lose your sight?" Mr. Peters replied, "The doctor said he was going to use the laser beam in surgery. He didn't know if it would work on my eye. If it did, I could go home in a few days. If it didn't, then I would have to stay longer for more surgery. And I can't afford to be in the hospital now. I should be home. My wife needs me." Again he paused to take several deep, gasping breaths.

Mona sat down in a chair at the bedside and asked, "Would you like to tell me more about this?" The words seemed to come tumbling out as Mr. Peters explained. He felt that his place was at home because his wife was terminally ill with cancer. Although she was still able to be at home, she had difficulty sleeping at night. He was afraid that she wouldn't get much sleep even though his mother-in-law would give her the pain medication. When she had pain at night, Mr. Peters would rub her back, and that helped her to relax. He resented being hospitalized now with this eye problem when there was so little time left for them to be together. Yet he had to take care of his eyesight because he had to see. He needed to be able to see because he was a math teacher in a junior high school, and he would have to raise Jimmy alone when his wife died. Jimmy is their seven-year-old son.

Mr. and Mrs. Peters have been married for 10 years. This is the second marriage for each of them. Both had children from their former marriages, but these children are grown and no longer live at home. Mr. Peters was greatly concerned that he might go blind and lose his job. He needed to be able to care for Jimmy, to take him hiking and fishing as other fathers do with their sons, and to send him to college when the time came. He said that he was not young anymore, but he had to keep working because he had a young son.

When he finished talking, Mona said to him, "I can understand why you are so concerned. Now let us think of some ways in which we can help you with your eye problem and prepare for your surgery tomorrow." Mr. Peters agreed and replied, "You know, I feel a whole lot better just telling you about all this. I don't know what got into me — I've always kept my problems to myself before!" After planning his care, Mona rechecked his blood pressure and noted that it was now 144 over 84.

Using the nursing process, begin a plan of care for Mr. Peters. Identify behaviors related to his physical self and to his personal self. How would you identify the problem that he is having in coping with his feelings at the present time?

| Patient Problem (Manifested by Behaviors) | Stimuli (Focal and Contextual) | Goal and Interventions |
|---|---|---|
|  |  |  |

*Evaluation:* Mona and Mr. Peters followed the nursing plan of care that they had devised. Mr. Peters knew what was expected of him after surgery and ways in which Mona could help him. The operation with the laser was successful, and Mr. Peters was able to go home within three days. As he prepared to leave, Mr. Peters thanked Mona for all she had done and said, "I really think the way you handled my anxiety was the main reason the operation was so successful and why I've recovered so well."

# REFERENCES

Coelho, George, Hamburg, David, and Adams, John (Eds.): Coping and Adaptation. New York, Basic Books, Inc. Publishers, 1974.

Craft, Carol: Body Image and obesity. Nurs Clin North Am, 7(4):677–686, (December) 1972.

Dempsey, Mary O.: The development of body image in the adolescent. Nurs Clin North Am, 7(4):609–616, (December) 1972.

Gallagher, Ann: Body image change in the patient with a colostomy. Nurs Clin North Am, 7(4): 669–676, (December) 1972.

Gesell, Arnold, and Ilg, Frances: Child Development. New York, Harper and Brothers, 1943.

Kaluger, George, and Kaluger, Meriem: Human Development: The Span of Life. St. Louis, The C. V. Mosby Co., 1974.

Knowles, Ruth: Dealing with feelings: positive self-talk. Am J Nurs, 81:535, (March) 1981.

Murray, Ruth: Body image development in adulthood. Nurs Clin North Am, 7(4):617–630, (December) 1972.

Pescatore, Edward: Personal reaction to weight loss. Am J Nurs, 74:2227–2229, (December) 1974.

Rambo, Beverly: Case study – Mr. Peters. Unpublished study guide. Mount St. Mary's College, revised 1979

Rubin, Neva: Body image and self esteem. Nursing Outlook, pp. 10–23, (June) 1968.

Smith, Catherine: Body image changes after myocardial infarction. Nurs Clin North Am, 7(4):663–668, (December) 1972.

Sullivan, Harry Stack: The Interpersonal Theory of Psychiatry. New York, W. W. Norton and Co. Inc., 1953.

Walter, Jean: Coping with a leg amputation. Am J Nurs, 81:1349–1352, (July) 1981.

# Coping Problems of the Self-Concept

## OBJECTIVES  Information in this chapter will help you to

1. Define loss as a disruption of the individual's adaptation and integrity.
2. State examples of the types of losses that occur in the physiological, role-function, and interdependence modes and how these losses serve as stimuli for disruptions of the self-concept mode.
3. Name the stages of grieving according to Engel and compare these stages with the stages of dying described by Kubler-Ross.
4. State the differences between grieving and depression.
5. Assess behaviors that are manifested by feelings of depression, powerlessness, guilt, or shame.
6. Describe interventions that the nurse can use to strengthen coping mechanisms and to change the client's ineffective coping mechanisms.
7. Examine your own feelings about losses and death individually, in group discussions, or in a seminar setting.

## DEFINITION OF TERMS

**alienation** — a form of self-estrangement; being out of touch with one's self as well as being out of touch with other people.

**depression** — a reaction to the loss of a valued person or object that results in feelings of dejection and melancholia.

**grief** — the normal emotional reaction that follows the realization or anticipation of the loss of a loved one or valued object; it is a necessary process to heal the sorrow and psychological pain.

**guilt** — painful feelings that result from violating moral demands or prohibitions to act in specific ways, committing wrongs, or sins.

**loss** — the deprivation, giving up, or absence of a valued source of psychological gratification. The valued source may be a person, an object, or an abstract idea.

**mourning** — the total psychological process that follows the actual or anticipated loss of a valued person or object, including the grieving process.

**power** — the ability to achieve goals; the inherent characteristic of a tendency to dominate, to compete for influence.

**powerlessness** — the lack of control over events in a certain situation.

**shame** — uncomfortable feeling that part(s) of the self have been exposed at a disadvantage, that one's view of "What I am" has been lessened by some act.

---

Problems of the self-concept occur when coping mechanisms that one uses do not reduce one's anxiety level and the feelings that it has engendered. The way one sees one's physical self leads to the knowledge of "What I can do," and one's perceptions of the personal self form the image of "This is what I am." The self-concept as a whole is based on one's experiences in life in relation to physical appearance and abilities, resources available for personal use, relationships with other people, and the feelings and beliefs that one has. Any thought or event that reflects negatively on one's self-concept represents a threat that lowers the self-esteem and generates anxiety.

By their very nature, physical stress and anxiety are almost universally present during illness and influence behavior as people attempt to cope with them. Any stimulus that is perceived as a threat to the self activates the autonomic nervous system; thus, not only is anxiety a mental picture of possible harm, but also it causes physical changes. It leads to a tense or uneasy state or to an uptight feeling and arouses emotions of some form of anger, sadness, or fear. When methods of coping fail to reduce the anxiety, the person has problems in coping with these feelings. The resulting behavior may interfere with the patient's or client's medical treatment or nursing care. This presents a challenge to nurses. They must now help the patient achieve psychological adaptation as well as recover from the physical illness.

The types of coping problems most commonly found with disturbance of various parts of the self-concept are given in Chapter Eighteen. In summary, the physical self consists of one's feelings about one's body, how one's body feels, and the mental image one has of it. Disease and injury change the body in distinct ways by interfering with its normal functions or by causing a change in its parts or appearance. A coronary occlusion causes damage to the heart muscle, which is regarded as the core of life; cancer of the breast leads to mastectomy, or removal of the breast; and a sprained ankle prevents one from walking without discomfort. All these conditions affect a person's self-concept and may lead to problems in coping with feelings.

In this chapter, anxiety will be discussed as the underlying stimulus for the problems of the self-concept, especially for those who take on the sick role. Illness or injury causes several losses for individuals and constitutes problems of coping with feelings resulting from these perceived changes in the physical self. The losses from chronic illness and the resulting changes in one's daily life have a profound effect on the personal self. These losses, the grieving process, and the psychological stages that people pass through in dealing with death and dying are discussed, in addition to other problems of coping with changes in the personal self that lead to feelings of depression, powerlessness, and guilt or shame. Nursing interventions that may be used to help resolve coping problems are outlined.

## COPING WITH ANXIETY

The original purpose of the anxiety response in primitive man was to protect the individual from physical harm and to insure a better chance of survival. However, in our complex and ever-changing world, anxiety is more the result of mental thoughts of harm to the image that one has of oneself. The same physiological changes occur whether the danger is a real physical one or an imagined one originating in the brain cortex.

Illness is a common focal stimulus for the anxiety response because it represents a threat to the functioning of the body and arouses fears about whether the body will recover its former ability or whether one will indeed survive any of the things that could go wrong with one's body. In addition to the physical discomfort and pain of an illness, many aspects of the treatment of the disease create anxieties.

The unknown produces further anxiety, and the sick person requiring medical care or hospitalization is subjected to many strangers and unfamiliar procedures in an alien environment. Sources of fear and anxiety include undergoing uncomfortable diagnostic tests and invasive procedures, such as catheterization and intravenous infusions, taking potent or disagreeable tasing medicines, sharing a room with a stranger, being separated from one's family or friends, staying on bed rest, and being told what to do by a total stranger who just walked into the room without knocking. Coping with the illness itself may strain the person's resources to the limit, and trying to cope with these added threats to the self-concept is more than the person can handle. These conditions become contextual stimuli or influencing factors for the ineffective behaviors and coping problems that arise.

The following case history illustrates how one patient was overwhelmed by many aspects of her illness, the hospitalization, and the change in her body image as a result of surgery.

Mrs. C. is a 51-year-old woman who entered the hospital with a history of bladder infections during the past 12 years and polyps that were found to be malignant. She underwent surgery 4 days ago to remove the cancerous bladder and to create an ileal bladder. Today, the following behaviors were observed: She looks away whenever the nurse checks the incision and drainage from the stoma on her abdomen. She states, "I don't know how I'm going to live with this thing" and jerks away from any movement of the nasogastric tube, saying, "that thing makes ne nervous." She has uncontrolled muscular tremors of her arms and legs while lying in bed in a tense and rigid posture. Shortly after this, her speech was mumbled and incoherent as she pleaded, "Please put me back in my right room; I don't belong here." She cried that she was afraid of nightmares and stated that her husband and daughter were called to the hospital at 2:00 AM that morning because of her cancer. In an agitated voice, she said that her husband had informed her that she

had cancer cells in her urine and cancer spots on her lungs.

Although one nurse had assessed Mrs. C.'s responses to feelings about her health at the time of the biopsy, other nurses were assigned to care for her in the period before surgery and in the intensive care unit. At this time, Mrs. C. has anxiety at the panic level that is being expressed in hallucinations about the family's visit during the night, her inability to cope with her feelings of fear about cancer, and the disgust she felt about the urinary stoma. Although the coping problems that other patients have may be less obvious than those of Mrs. C., they do cause the individual discomfort and may delay recovery.

## EMOTIONS EXPRESSING ANXIETY

The problems of the self-concept mode consist of difficulties in coping with feelings. Feelings are subjective moods that people have that may be uncomfortable or painful, leading to a negative state. The major feelings have been described by some as feelings of being glad, sad, mad, or fearful. However, there are many forms and shades of these emotions.

**Positive feelings**
belonging
contentment
delight
gladness
happiness
hope
joy
love
respect

**Negative feelings**

| | |
|---|---|
| alienation | helplessness |
| anger | hopelessness |
| disgust | hostility |
| distrust | insecurity |
| embarrassment | jealousy |
| envy | loneliness |
| fear | resentment |
| frustration | sadness |
| guilt | suspicion |

Emotions exist on a continuum that ranges from mild to extreme. For example, in its milder forms, anger may be expressed as annoyance or irritation. The moderate form of anger is expressed as being mad, progressing to the extremes of frustration and rage.

When stating problems that people have in the self-concept, it is helpful to focus on the patient and the feelings that he or she is experiencing. *That* is the problem that he or she is having at that particular time. The problem is defined as coping with feelings, such as the positive and negative feelings previously listed, but must be *shown* to be a problem that distresses the patient, interferes with his or her ability to cooperate with treatment, or creates obstacles for the nursing care. The second level assessment includes using anxiety and losses as stimuli that can be manipulated by the nurse to help change ineffective behaviors to reduce anxiety, and to promote the patient's comfort and adaptation.

## COPING MECHANISMS IN ILLNESS

People use many different kinds of coping mechanisms to reduce their anxiety. Coping mechanisms are patterns of behaving or responding to certain stimuli. A certain way of coping tends to be used over and over again when it has been proved to be useful in decreasing the discomforts of anxiety. Everyone uses one or another of the common coping mechanisms of eating, smoking, talking, sleeping, vigorous activity, laughing, crying, seeking the reassurance of touch or sound, or carrying out creative activities in the arts, music, crafts, and so on.

Patients who are sick in hospitals or in their homes are denied many of these common coping methods. Frequently, they are NPO or are placed on a restricted diet for diagnostic tests or as part of the medical treatment. Oral satisfaction is restricted when food is not available, and smoking may be prohibited. The need for bed rest limits one's participation in vigorous activities and in most creative outlets. Patients are often alone or must rely on care-givers who are usually strangers when they wish to talk or seek reassurance. Pain and discomfort often interfere with their sleep and rest. What coping mechanisms are left for them to use in reducing their anxiety?

Other coping mechanisms are used to deal with anxiety feelings. These mechanisms include repression of one's feelings, escaping temporarily from reality through daydreams or diversions such as watching television or reading, rationalization, projecting one's feelings onto others or onto objects, or regression to a level of functioning associated with an earlier stage of life that was more satisfying. Other forms of coping that are associated with aggression and feelings of anger include bossiness, negativism, acting superior to others, being uncooperative or not complying with treatment or regulations, and

taking out one's feelings on others. Many of these methods of coping require the use of more energy, and, although they do work to reduce anxiety, some are less effective than other means of coping and indicate the presence of problems.

The following case history illustrates how one patient tried to cope with her feelings about being ill and being in a strange environment.

Mary G. is a 70-year-old black woman who grew up on an Indian reservation. She has done manual labor, such as digging ditches, for most of her life. When hospitalized for a gastric disturbance and difficulty in swallowing, she saved all the uneaten food from her tray, despite the nurse's request not to do this. She hid bottles of juice, bread, cake, and puddings in her bedside stand and dresser drawer. Papers, straws, and ashes were strewn on the floor so the room always looked messy. She insisted on smoking but asked the nurses to hide the ashtrays before her doctor visited and requested everyone who entered the room to bring coffee to her. She states, "Everyone tells me what to do all day long. I get told not to smoke, not to drink, when to get up, when to take my bath...I get so mad I can't stand it!" "I don't hurt no one but me, so why can't they leave me be?" Then, as she looks around her room, she remarks, "This room is never clean like I keep it at home."

With a complete assessment of psychosocial functioning, the nurse is better able to identify how Mary G. sees herself, the values and beliefs that direct her behavior, and the stimuli causing her to act as she does. With this information, the nurse works with Mary G., forming a definite plan for reducing her anxieties and problems in coping with her feelings.

## COPING WITH LOSS

All of us have experienced potential or actual losses of some sort during our lives. Loss refers to the absence, deprivation, or disappearance of a valued person or object that gave us gratification. Some losses are minor and cause only a temporary state of regretting or grieving the loss, such as the loss of a baby tooth, the loss of a favorite book, or the loss of energy when running a temperature of 101° F., or 38.3° C., accompanied by a sore throat. Obvious losses are seen following the amputation of a limb, creation of a colostomy, and fracture of the hip. Other less obvious losses may involve highly valued parts or functions of the body and create an emotional crisis for the individual affected.

Nurses encounter a high incidence of problems that people have in dealing with their losses by the very nature of their contact with sick and troubled people. Early recognition of and intervention in coping with problems concerning loss should be given high priority in order to promote an adapted state as soon as possible.

## TYPES OF LOSSES

Loss is defined as being deprived of a valued object or person. What is valued varies widely and is highly individualistic. What is greatly treasured by one person may have little value or meaning for another person. However, losses can be generally classified into one of the following categories:

1. Loss of significant or valued person.
2. Loss of some aspect of the self.
3. Loss of some aspect of the developmental skills.
4. Loss of external objects.

**Loss of Valued Person.** The death of a parent, spouse, or child creates a severe loss that can be easily recognized as a cause of an emotional crisis. Although death represents a permanent absence, even temporary absence leads to missing a valued person and may be perceived as a loss. This occurs when a loved one has gone on an extended trip, is away at college, is serving at a military post, or has moved to a more distant locale. When the absence causes an interruption in one's routine activities and relationships of daily living, one becomes aware of how much one depended upon the missing person and experiences feelings of loss. Loss also occurs when one is no longer regarded as highly as one was previously, as happens when two lovers quarrel and part. The separation anxiety experienced by infants and small children when parted from their mothers is a form of loss because the mother is the center of their world.

**Loss of Part of the Self.** Losses involving some aspect of the self, whether real or perceived, are widespread and of prime importance to the nurse. Disease and injury cause physical damage to the body and result in changes in body function, altered body structure, lack of control over body functions, and deviation from normal appearance. Loss of health imposes many changes that the person must deal with when assuming the sick role, most of which are perceived as losses. For example, pain represents loss of comfort, and urinary incontinence results from loss of control of the bladder sphincter. Control over body functions is highly valued by our society and by most individuals. A temporary lapse of control generally causes feelings of shame, and prolonged or persistent loss of control causes low self esteem.

Many people value certain parts of their bodies more than other parts, and potential or actual loss of these valued parts has a greater impact and leads to more intense grieving. Typically, men place a higher value on the genital organs and their legs, whereas women are more concerned with losses that affect their face or figure, especially the breasts. When patients experience the loss of a highly valued body part or its function, they are more apt to have problems coping with their feelings than when the loss involves some other portion of their body.

Actual changes in the physical body produce changes in one's mental image of the body, feelings associated with its functions, such as pressure, pain, or even the beat of the heart, and emotional responses to these changes. For example, in the case study in Chapter Eighteen, Mr. Peters had decreased vision due to cataracts and a detached retina of the right eye. The diseases caused loss of function and changes in structure that decreased his visual field, produced sensations of flashing lights, and made the images blurred and fuzzy. Mr. Peters placed a high value on being well and able to see in order to care for his sick wife, to carry out his profession of teaching, and to be a good father to his young son. The way that he perceived the loss of his vision and the intense feelings that he had about his illness caused a disruption in the physical self of his self-concept.

**Loss of Developmental Skills.** During the childhood stages of life, children learn how to make appropriate responses to different situations that arise, how to control their emotions and feelings, and socially acceptable ways to relate to other people. Disturbances of one's personal self-concept occur when anxiety-provoking stimuli interfere with the normal growth and development of these social strategies, causing losses of identity, trust, self-confidence, control of situations and self, initiative, privacy, productivity, and so on. Losses occur as the individual moves from one stage of life to the next. The comfortable dependency of childhood is lost as one progresses to the teen-age years. The changes of puberty, menopause, and aging render individuals particularly vulnerable to feelings of loss.

Changes in the family and other developmental tasks cause losses associated with divorce, change of a job, and retirement.

**Loss of External Objects.** People attach a symbolic meaning to many objects that are used to carry out their roles in life. The term *object* is used in a broad sense to include people, material things, and abstract ideas. Objects such as an automobile, home, money, jewels, job, status, pets, rose garden, teddy bear, and a child's security blanket may produce an emotional crisis when lost.

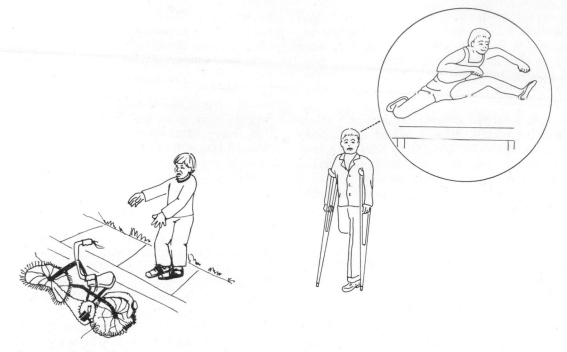

**Figure 19–1.**   Loss of a favorite toy and loss of a significant part of the body cause feelings of grief.

## REACTIONS TO LOSS

When people experience loss of any sort, they suffer feelings of sorrow, hurt, pain, and discomfort. Their state of well-being and effectiveness has been interrupted by the loss. They send out cries of help to others in an effort to overcome their feelings of helplessness, powerlessness, and anger about what has happened to them. They cope with the loss through grief and mourning.

**The Grieving Process.**   Grief is the emotional response that follows the loss of a valued person or object. Grieving responses include feelings of sorrow, loneliness, fears, and guilt as well as helplessness, powerlessness, and anger. Mourning is the total psychological process of adapting to the loss, loosening the ties with the lost object or person, and returning to one's usual activities of living. Engel, a psychiatrist who studied grief extensively, has compared loss and mourning with a wound and its healing. The loss is, in essence, a wound, and mourning is the process of healing, and grief is likened to the pain caused by the wound.

Grief is a normal, adaptive process that develops to resolve the pain associated with the loss. It is self-limiting and may last only a short time for less important or less valued objects. For major losses, such as the death of a loved one, the acute phase of grieving lasts from 2 weeks to 2 months, and it should be resolved in 1 year or less.

According to Engel, the stages of the grieving process consist of the shock and disbelief upon learning of the loss, the developing awareness that it really happened, the period of restitution, and finally, resolution. These stages, the time periods for each stage, and some characteristic types of behaviors are shown in Table 19–1.

People react differently to the same type of loss. Some people sit motionless, stunned, and in a daze as though the loss were unreal; others talk and act as though they accept the reality of the loss and make appropriate decisions or arrangements. They are able to block the full impact of the loss from penetrating their consciousness and causing anguish and pain. Although the loss is recognized, it is partially denied. People also go through the grieving process when distant events cause actual or potential loss of people or objects that have great symbolic value. In the spring of 1981, the assassination attempts on the lives of President Reagan and Pope John Paul II produced waves of shock and disbelief as millions of people watched televised reports of the actual events. In subsequent hours, days, and weeks, people worked through their feelings toward resolution as the victims recovered from their wounds.

**Table 19–1.  STAGES OF THE GRIEVING PROCESS**

| Stage | Time | Behavior |
|---|---|---|
| Shock and disbelief | Immediate | Surprise and denial<br>Intellectualization<br>"Oh no, it can't be!"<br>Routine, automatic actions |
| Developing awareness | Minutes to hours or days | Crying and anguish<br>Feelings of emptiness, failure, or guilt<br>Expressions of anger at others<br>Difficulty in making decisions to take action<br>Inward crying; suppression of tears |
| Restitution | Days to months | Ritualistic and symbolic actions, funerals, good-byes<br>Minimal use of aggression<br>Regression to an earlier pattern of behavior |
| Resolution, or recovery | Days to one year | Idealizes the lost person or object<br>Identifies with the lost person<br>Talks about memories, many reminders of the lost person<br>Increased body awareness after numbness passes<br>Dependent relations with others |

The intermediate stage of developing awareness occurs as the reality of the loss is recognized and is characterized by sadness. The behaviors of this stage reflect the painful nature of the loss and the anguish of feelings of emptiness, helplessness, hopelessness, and futility. Crying is common in this stage, although some people may cry only when alone or inwardly. The inability of the person to cry for a major loss often indicates highly ambivalent feelings of love and hate for the lost person or feelings of guilt.

The final stages of the grieving process are restitution and resolution, or recovery. In the final stages, the grieving person realizes that life and work go on, that one can deal with the reality of today, and that the absence of the loved object or person can be tolerated with less pain. Restitution is more rapid when the grieving person depends upon and adheres to old, established relationships to provide a continuity to life. A review of memories regarding the lost person or object helps to detach the loss from the present and to place it in the past. The successful accomplishment of the grieving stages leads to allowing joy and pleasure in one's life once again.

The experiences of Helen, who is a mother, aged 30 years, illustrates the stages of the grieving process.

Helen has just been informed that the pathology report of the biopsied lump from her breast indicated it was cancerous. Upon hearing the diagnosis, her first response was shock and disbelief.

Although she had intellectually considered such a possibility when she discovered the lump, the news is like a verdict of death. She is aware of a hollow feeling in the pit of her stomach and of thinking, "Oh no, it can't be happening to me. I'm too young to have cancer. I don't want to die now." It is as if it were the end of the world for her, and in a daze, she consents to surgery to remove the cancerous breast.

In the days following surgery, she was very quiet, made few, if any, requests for pain medication or help, and said that she was trying to be a "good patient." With growing awareness of her loss of the breast and the threat to her life, she was plagued with thoughts of "I've got cancer, and I'm afraid that I will die." Helen cried at night when she was alone and when others could not hear her. Slowly, the pain and anguish receded. She awakened day after day feeling stronger and recovering from the operation, and finally came the realization that "Yes, I have cancer, but today is another day to live." From day to day, her feelings continued to fluctuate, and, at times, she was particularly vulnerable to the painful realization of her loss, such as when dressing in street clothes, taking her child to the beach, or when she interpreted her husband's actions as being disinterested in her. Although the surgical wound has healed, the psychological wound heals more slowly.

**The Ultimate Loss – Death.**  People experience losses of some form from the time that they are born. The final loss is of one's mortal life—death. Death is the one universal event that everyone will experience, even though most people try to avoid thinking about it and have been sheltered from contact with dying people and actual death. Many attitudes about death have been obtained from books, newspapers, and television. With few exceptions, movies and television programs picture death in sudden, violent, and mutilative ways. Even the evening news programs on television highlight deaths of a violent nature — murders, suicides, accidents, and other types of disasters. Thus, the picture that most people have of death is so horrifying and painful that they push the thought of death and dying out of their minds. Death happens to other people but not to them. Through the use of denial, people can blot out the reality of death. However, denial exacts a high price in the energy needed to cope with feelings of anxiety, depression, anger, and other forms of violent behavior when the threat of death arises.

The belief that death is a violent experience is a gross distortion because most people die in bed. More than 80 per cent of all deaths in this country occur in hospitals and related health facilities. Nurses see more of death than do most people. The leading causes of death in the United States are heart disease, cancer, cardiovascular accident or stroke, accidents, and influenza and pneumonia. Millions of people who are suffering from these conditions are hospitalized each year. Nurses who care for patients in the terminal phase of their illness must deal with the feelings of the patients, their families, and the nurses themselves as they cope with the impending loss.

**The Stages of Dying.** When people such as Helen suspect or learn that they have a terminal illness, they are faced with the task of coping with their ultimate loss — life. For most people, death does not come immediately, and they continue to live for days, weeks, and months. Although they know that their lives are limited, they still have to live each day and cope with their feelings as they go through the grieving process.

The curtain of silence and denial that had surrounded those who were dying has been lifted by the research of Dr. Elisabeth Kubler-Ross. She interviewed countless dying people in her attempts to learn the meaning of death and to learn from dying people how to live until death occurs. A definite pattern of how the people coped with their feelings about dying began to emerge. This pattern has been described as the psychological stages of dying. (Table 19-2.) The feelings that are characteristic of the grieving process for the last crisis of life are also experienced by people who are mourning other types of losses.

These stages overlap and do not have a definite time schedule. Some people move back and forth between the stages; thus, at some time during the day, they may use bargaining for more time or to make things better, followed by anger because dying is happening to them. Some people may skip stages, others go rapidly through all stages to acceptance, whereas others never move beyond denial. The following comparison shows that the stages of dying are similar to the stages of grieving.

Nurses do not customarily inform patients or clients that they have a terminal illness such as cancer, nor do they tell them that they are dying. The nurse's role is to deal with the feelings that patients or clients have. When patients or their families use denial, nurses may acknowledge that they have the right to express their feelings and should not force people to move beyond that stage until they are able to tolerate the awareness of their impending loss. The use of denial to avoid psychological pain has been compared with the man who is unable to swim and clings to a rotten log after his boat sinks. Although a rotten log is not a substitute for a life jacket, one would not take the log away from the man because it is the only thing that is keeping him from drowning. Denial may serve the same purpose for some people.

**Children and the Dying Process.** The primary fear of children under the age of 4 years who are grieving and dying is separation from their parents. They view death as a temporary condition, or they may feel that death is a punishment for bad thoughts. The child who when angry yelled, "Momma, I wish you would drop dead," has enormous guilt if the mother dies, and believes that his wishes are extremely potent. When ill, young children have great fear of mutilation of their own bodies. Any intrusive procedure, such as injections, lumbar puncture, or catheter-

| Phase | Stages of Grieving | Stages of Dying |
|---|---|---|
| First | Shock and disbelief | Denial |
| Second | Developing awareness | Anger and rage |
| | | Bargaining |
| | | Depression |
| Third | Restitution and recovery | Acceptance |

**Table 19-2.** THE PSYCHOLOGICAL STAGES OF DYING

| Stage | Response | Behavior |
|---|---|---|
| Denial | "No, not me." | Rejects the information; cannot believe that it is happening to him or her or discounts the seriousness of the illness<br>Blots out information; forgets or distorts facts to ease discomfort |
| Anger and rage | "Why me?" | May cry or scream and express anger at the world in general; triggered by anybody<br>Complains a lot; is resentful toward staff or visitors who are peppy, active, and cheerful when his world is collapsing |
| Bargaining | "Yes, me, but —" | Seeks to temporize, gain more time<br>Has unfinished business to take care of; is unable to let go of roles or objects<br>Pleas to "make it better" |
| Depression | "Yes, me." | Withdraws more from contact with others; becomes quiet as mourns future losses<br>Needs to be allowed to cry but is often not allowed to by others |
| Acceptance | "Yes, me." | Not resignation or giving up but a feeling that it's all right<br>Needs one loving or caring person who can sit with him as he dies with peace and dignity. |

ization, is interpreted as damage to the body and is thought to result in one's insides leaking out or being "mooshed up."

Children between the ages of 5 and 10 years begin to develop thoughts and feelings similar to those of adults. Often, they know that they are sick and may die. Some children are able to draw pictures to illustrate what it is that concerns them. Kubler-Ross reports of the child who visioned his illness as a huge tank that was approaching him and that he was powerless to stop with his little "Stop" sign. Kubler-Ross cautions nurses not to treat children according to the way that they look. Although they seem small or physically weak, some children talk as maturely as wise adults and want to talk about dying. They need time to adapt to and to accept dying. With help in dealing with their fears, they too are able to reach the acceptance stage of grieving.

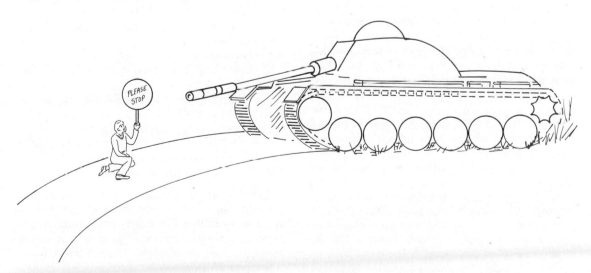

**Figure 19-2.** The threat of anxiety can overwhelm a person when the coping mechanism is not strong enough to conquer it.

When talking with people who are living with a terminal illness, it is important to use the language of the patient. Many people, including children who lack the vocabulary, use symbolic language. They may never use the words *death* or *dying*. Instead, they refer to *it* or use countless other ways to describe their experience.

**Grieving by the Families.**  The families of dying patients are faced with coping with their grief of losing a loved one. Problems occur when family members and the patient are in different stages of the grieving process. Communication and emotional support is lacking when they are out of synchronization. Family members have the following needs as they cope with the impending loss of a loved one:

1.  Need for adequate information.
2.  Need for relief of anxiety about their loved one.
3.  Need to stay with the patient.
4.  Need to do things for the patient and be helpful.
5.  Need for support from others and to express fears and feelings.

The time of dying and death is a reality, and family members can help dying adults to settle unfinished business and reassure them of their value. The lines of communication need to be kept open, and members of the family must recognize that they need to talk about their feelings about the impending loss of their loved one. Children especially need warm day-to-day relationships, although all dying persons need reassurance that they will not be deserted.

**What Has Been Learned from Dying Patients.**  The growing interest and research in the plight of dying patients has provided several insights into their fears and needs. With few exceptions, people should be told that they have a serious illness. The actual knowledge provides something tangible with which to work and is less terrifying than the dark, unspoken worries and fears that they had previously. Kubler-Ross found that chronically ill patients know that they are dying and that they know when they will die. When dying people have the need to talk to someone about their experience, they should be allowed to do so immediately; otherwise, it may be too late.

All dying people expressed the need for hope, although the focus of the hope changed. Hope provides the reason to live and takes them into tomorrow. The kind of hope changes for the fatally ill person. No longer is there the hope to see one's grandchildren grow up or the hope that medical therapy will arrest the disease for a period of time. Instead, there is the hope that one can eat a little more at the next meal or be free of pain for a few hours.

Many terminally ill patients stated that their fears were not of death but of being abandoned or deserted. They needed to know that others would "stick it out" with them and that pain or suffering would be relieved so that they could die in peace with dignity. Terminally ill patients need someone to be with them to relieve their fears, the loneliness, and the depression.

## PATHOLOGICAL GRIEVING

The outcome of the grieving process depends upon several factors, including the degree of dependency in the relationship of the grieving person and the lost person, ambivalent feelings between the two people, the age of the lost person, the age of the grieving person, and the number of meaningful relationships that remain to the grieving person. Losses have a cumulative effect; additional losses do not become easier to resolve. Although grievers may have had experiences with loss, the stress of additional losses may revive incompleted grieving from the past and cause more difficult coping problems.

People need help to cope when they reach an impasse in the grieving process and are unable to move through it to attain complete resolution. Pathological grieving is evidenced by loss of self-esteem, depression, excessively strong dependency needs, and ambivalent feelings for the lost person or object. Disruption in the grieving process is characterized by the following types of behavior:

1.  Excessive and disproportionate grieving in relation to the degree of the loss.
2.  Grieving that lasts longer than is expected for similar losses.
3.  Persistent feelings of hopelessness and irrational despair.
4.  Profound loss of personal identity.
5.  Belief that at no time in the future will the pain be healed.
6.  Feelings of guilt and belief that one was at fault for the death.
7.  Inability to give affection to others.
8.  Inability to transfer dependency needs from the lost person to another person.
9.  Periods of apathy or aimless hyperactivity.

Pathological grieving leads to problems in coping that can be stated according to the feelings and behaviors that one expresses. Feelings of depression, helplessness, and guilt are common manifestations of difficulties in coping with loss.

**Feelings of Depression.**  Everyone has experienced the blues at some time or has felt homesick when away from home for a period of time.

Both feelings are a form of depression. Depression ranges from being very mild to being severe and incapacitating and disrupting the person's life. Depression occurs when the loss of a valued person or when the threat to one's security overwhelms one's coping abilities, resulting in one's feeling powerless to remove the pain or the threat.

The grieving process is the normal, adaptive response used to cope with the loss of something or someone that is valued, whereas depression is the maladaptive response. Depression is characterized by *anger turned inward toward the self.* Table 19–3 shows the stages of depression and types of behavior associated with each stage. The process of depression differs from normal grieving in only one stage.

**Assessment of Depression.** Depression has many guises and is expressed in many different ways. It is one of the more common coping problems that the nurse encounters when caring for patients in clinical practice. Not all depressed people are gloomy, pessimistic, or withdrawn. Some may smile pleasantly while acting overdependent or suppressing feelings of fear and resentment, whereas others express angry, hostile, and aggressive feelings. Depressed people not only show a wide variety of feelings but also may have various physiological symptoms associated with depression. Some complain of lack of appetite, weight loss, headache, impotence, indigestion, backache, or chest pain. Although some of these physical signs are findings of organic illness, they may also have their origins in depression.

Depression results from low self-esteem. Typical behaviors include negativistic statements. Usually, depressed people do not want to talk or to discuss feelings; however, when they do, they say things, such as

"I don't see anything good in the future."
"I don't enjoy anything anymore."
"I'm a failure; my life is empty."
"I'm not good for anything."
"No one would miss me if anything happened."
"I'm just a burden to everyone."

Typically, behaviors of depression include lack of interest in other things, slowing of the thought process, impaired ability to concentrate, withdrawal from interpersonal contacts, and neglect of personal hygiene. Some depressed people increase their use of alcohol or drugs. They usually talk in a monotone, and speech shows a blocking of their train of thought, or their mind goes blank.

Second level assessment is carried out to identify the actual or perceived loss or the threat to one's security as being the focal stimulus. Influencing factors in depression include one's age or stage of life, previous experiences with losses, the way in which one meets one's self-expectations, reactions of acceptance or rejection by others, and one's perceptions of how others see one.

The case history of Mr. James illustrates how one man coped with numerous losses in his life.

Mr. James is a 48-year-old man, with bilateral amputation of the legs, who has been living in a

**Table 19–3.** STAGES OF DEPRESSION

| Stages | Behaviors |
|---|---|
| Shock and disbelief | Surprise and denial<br>Intellectualization<br>"Oh, no, it can't be!"<br>Routine, automatic actions |
| Developing awareness | Crying and anguish<br>Feelings of emptiness, failure, or guilt<br>Expressions of anger at others<br>Difficulty in making decisions to take action<br>Inward crying; suppression of tears |
| Anger turned inward | Blames self for the loss<br>Sense of worthlessness<br>May use self-punishing actions; suicide, deprivation |
| Recovery | Shifts anger from self to others<br>Critical and complaining<br>Blames others |

nursing home. A week ago, he was readmitted to the hospital with infection of wounds in the groin and the stump of the right leg. He is no longer on isolation precautions, but the wounds are irrigated and the dressings are changed every shift. He is occasionally incontinent of feces and urine, which soil the dressings; however, he pays no attention to them. He is regarded by the nursing staff as "confused" and "a pill" to take care of because he does not talk except to ask for a light for his cigarette or to beg for cigarettes when he does not have any. He sits up in bed watching television all day, smokes constantly, is unshaven with wisps of graying hair standing up on his balding head, and flicks ashes over the bedding and onto the floor. He has a dull expression on his face and shows no interest in people or what is happening around him.

After taking care of Mr. James for two days, the student nurse held a nursing care conference with staff nurses to share information and to devise a plan of care for his needs. After identifying some of his undesirable behaviors that were a source of irritation to the staff, the student nurse related the following information from her psychosocial assessment. The medical history on the chart merely stated that he was a bilateral amputee because of arteriosclerosis obliterans with a femoral popliteal bypass one year ago and revision of a below the knee amputation to an above the knee amputation of the right leg one month ago.

The next of kin was listed as the public guardian of the county who signed the consent forms for his treatment. Although Mr. Jones was reluctant to talk to any extent or to give more than a few details, the nurse obtained the following information. When asked what kind of work he had done, he replied that he worked for a national news magazine for 12 years and was chief of part of the advertising section. Then, he lived in a large metropolitan city, but he now lives in the nursing home. Additional comments were that he was not married, and when asked about his family, he replied that they were dead. He never volunteered information, but when asked if he had military service, he replied that he was a pilot in the Air Force and that he flew for 6 years. In regard to his illness, he said, in a detached, disinterested manner, that he had trouble walking about 4 years ago and that they took off his left leg and then the right one.

The nursing staff expressed surprise that he was a former pilot and that he had held a middle management position with the well-known magazine because, at this time, he looks more "like a bum from Skid Row." They discussed the qualifications that are needed for these jobs or roles in terms of education, health, and other abilities. The student nurse said that Mr. James must feel as though he is being reduced to nothing and is dying bit by bit. First, he had trouble walking, then they amputated the left leg. Problems with the right leg were not taken care of by the bypass

surgery; thus, the right leg was removed below the knee, and now, more of the right leg has been amputated. His body is failing him part by part, and now that he has the infection in the groin area, what will be the next part of his body to be lost to the surgeon's knife?

The nurses listed some of the losses (that they know about) that Mr. James has suffered in the past 4 years and concluded that he has been unable to complete the mourning of his losses. The nursing diagnosis was that he has feelings of severe depression because of the damage done to his self-image by his illness. The nurses researched some of the causes of his depression and listed interventions they could use to help him improve his feelings of self-esteem and deal with his feelings of grief.

## NURSING INTERVENTIONS FOR GRIEVING

The basic resource used by nurses to help patients and clients who are experiencing loss is an understanding of the grieving process and the use of the nursing process as the method of solving problems of coping. Coping problems are expressed in the behaviors of patients who are too quiet and withdrawn, angry, depressed, demanding, complaining, pessimistic, overly dependent, and so on. To understand the grieving process, nurses must come to grips with their own feelings about life and death, losses, dying, pain, helplessness, and hopelessness. Only by understanding their own attitudes toward grieving and death can they help others in an open and honest way.

Ujhely has described numerous strategies and therapeutic measures that the nurse can use to help patients through the grieving process.

1. *Use anticipatory guidance through the grieving process.* Explain that grieving is a normal process that consists of several phases, each with its characteristic feelings and behaviors. It is normal for grievers to cry and to be angry. The mother of a dying child said, "I just want to scream. I'm so angry at God for letting this happen to my child."

2. *Help the person to talk about the impending or actual loss and its meaning to him or her.* The psychosocial assessment paves the way for this. As one's losses are identified and information is gathered about how the person feels about his or her illness, the effect that it has had on daily living, and the changes in his or her physical self and personal self, it becomes easier to talk with and to understand the patient.

3. *Lessen the impact of the loss.* Explore and emphasize the remaining strengths and abilities that the person has. Use available resources from

the surroundings and seek ways to mobilize people and objects into a support system.

4. *Consider the mourner's value system and the meaning attached to the loss.* Avoid imposing your values if they contradict those of the patient —for example, wanting the patient to continue the struggle to live though he wants to die in peace.

5. *Allow sufficient time for the mourning process.* People vary in their ability to work through their feelings and to resolve their grief. Feelings of anger or bargaining in the restitution phase do not pass in one hour or one day but may recur as one idealizes the lost person or object, reviews memories, and copes with new feelings.

6. *Do not force an emotional response if it is lacking.* The lack of feelings about an actual or potential loss is denial of reality. It serves as a protective mechanism that should not be ruthlessly destroyed. Some patients refuse to hear or accept a diagnosis, such as cancer, and blot it out of their consciousness. They refuse to have the recommended surgery or chemotherapy. However, during the assessment of physical needs and developmental tasks, these patients often give clues—they can talk about their illness in terms of a growth or the symptoms it is causing, which may be as much reality about the impending loss that they can handle at that time.

Nursing interventions that are used to help the grieving person use his or her limited energies in constructive ways and to strengthen coping mechanisms in order to shorten the period of severe grief or acute depression include

1. *Be accepting of the griever's feelings and experiences.* They exist and are real for the person at that time.

2. *Encourage the griever to avoid making unnecessary or unreasonable demands on himself and to seek ways to reduce additional stresses.* The griever needs to be able to cope with the changes caused by the loss of the person or object before taking on other demands in order to prevent chaos and total breakdown of his or her coping mechanisms.

3. *Explore, with the griever, what it is that makes him or her feel that the situation is hopeless or irreparable or that he or she is worthless and life is not worth living, and search for ways to overcome these conclusions.* Because depression is anger turned inward, toward the self, outward expressions of anger are necessary to move toward resolution. People who suffer from depression are at risk fo being self destructive, such as by deliberately committing suicide or neglect-

ing to take of themselves in a normal way. It is best to face the issue and the person: "You mentioned dying and that life is not worth living now. Please explain what you mean by that."

4. *Protect and bolster the griever's self-esteem and self-confidence.* Treat the person with respect, provide privacy as needed, involve him or her in decision-making that concerns aspects of his or her life, as appropriate for that stage of life, and encourage purposeful activity. Give praise, or recognition, for achievements and progress toward adaptation and effective coping.

A nursing care plan for grieving patients often extends to include the family members. Such a plan provides family members with information, including the names of doctors or other caregivers, arrangements to talk by phone and to report on the patient's general condition, and clear and simple explanations of the patient's care. Some interventions meet the family members' needs to be with the patient and to be of help. These include providing a chair at the patient's bedside, arranging flexible visiting hours, providing an explanation whenever family members are asked to leave the bedside because of some aspect of patient care, and discussing ways in which they can assist the nurse in helping the patient. The nurse is able to provide support for family members by asking how they are holding up and coping with their feelings. By recognizing that they too are going through the grieving process, the nurse shows a better understanding of their anxieties and concerns.

## COPING WITH POWERLESSNESS

In our modern, complex society, people are often assailed with feelings of powerlessness, particularly when they are ill. Many stimuli and environmental factors pose threats to the self-concept; thus, feelings of powerlessness occur when discrepancies are perceived in one's ability to control the things that happen. To better understand powerlessness, one must understand the concept of power.

### TYPES OF POWER

Power represents the degree of mastery and control over one's life. The more power that one has, the more that one can control one's destiny and achieve desired goals. To utilize power, one must have a commitment to goal-directed actions, make an analysis of the situation, and be willing to take action to assume the power.

People exert power and achieve their goals by

using different types of power, which can be classified as follows:

- *Strength* — force applied by physical strength; the use of machines or technology, political laws and regulations, and size or mass of objects.
- *Command* — power derived by authority of one's birth or position or as a result of domination.
- *Reputation and prestige* — power accorded to individuals on the basis of their successes, accomplishments, or distinctions that set them apart from others.
- *Persuasion* — use of verbal and psychological methods to influence the thoughts, feelings, and beliefs of others.
- *Ability* — authority vested in experts or specialists through the acquisition of knowledge beyond that of other people.

Healthy people are those who grow and develop during the childhood stages of life and enter adulthood with mastery and control of motor activities and an integrated image of their identity. They are able to master their environment and to perceive the world and themselves in realistic terms and are adequate and effective in dealing with the changes that are constantly occurring. As people gain more control over objects in their environment, they incorporate this control, or power, into their self-image. The teen-ager who has learned to drive a car includes this ability in his or her self-concept, whereas an older person who has never driven a car excludes it from one's self-concept, feels powerless when near a car, and depends upon others to drive.

## DISCRIMINATION

People seem to have an inherent need to seek to dominate or to compete in order to influence others. They seek to retain their power, increase it, and demonstrate, or use it. To have or to exert power is to dominate some person or some object. Discrimination refers to one group having less power than another and, as a result, receiving less favorable treatment.

The group of people that is most discriminated against in most societies is the poverty group. People in this group have the least amount of control, or power, over events in their lives and even the type of health care that they receive. Other targets of discrimination include black Americans, the aged, women, people of Spanish descent, and Indians. When these people become ill, they often have feelings of powerlessness because most health professionals are from the upper-middle and middle classes who treat middle-class patients as equals, with similar amounts of power. As a result of segregation and discrimination, minorities are underrepresented in health care professions. Although blacks constitute 11 per cent of the population, less than 2 per cent of doctors or dentists are black, and even fewer are from the Spanish-speaking or Indian groups.

## POWERLESSNESS AND ALIENATION

Feelings of powerlessness arise from circumstances that occur in one's environment or as a result of actual or perceived threats to the personal self. Individuals with feelings of powerlessness believe or expect that certain goals or rewards are beyond their control and cannot be achieved through their own efforts or behaviors. These feelings represent a loss of control over the outcomes of behavior and an alienation from the self.

Melvin Seeman, a sociologist, has described powerlessness as one of the components of alienation. Alienated and powerless people have a decreased sense of control over their lives. Although they respond to events and changes in their lives, their efforts fail to achieve the goals that they desire, and they feel that the only way to get along is to conform. Conforming behavior is a form of self-estrangement in which they carry out the bidding, or directing, of powers outside the self. Alienated people do not see themselves as the center of their world or as the creation of their own actions. They see themselves as being dependent upon outside powers and manipulated by them.

Sometimes the terms *alienation* and *powerlessness* are used interchangeably, although *alienation* is more like a syndrome that has powerlessness, meaninglessness, and social isolation as major factors. Meaninglessness reduces one's understanding of events going on around one. One lacks sufficient information to see the issues clearly enough to make reasonable decisions or to predict the results of acting on any belief that one has. When one does not understand a hemoglobin of 11.5 gm or a statement in a foreign language, the information is meaningless and useless and serves to isolate or to make one dependent upon those who understand and control it. The meaninglessness has contributed to and increased one's feelings of powerlessness, or lack of control over one's life.

The case of Robella B. shows typical behaviors of powerlessness.

Robella B. is a black woman, aged 82 years, widowed, and hospitalized for the treatment of a

**Table 19–4.** SEEMAN'S THEORY OF ALIENATION

| Alienation Component | Behavioral Consequences | Opposite the Adaptation Component of |
|---|---|---|
| Powerlessness | Cannot control outcomes<br>The expectation or probability held by individuals that their own behavior cannot determine the outcomes or reinforcements they seek | Mastery and autonomy |
| Meaninglessness | Cannot predict behavioral outcome<br>The minimal standards for clarity in decision-making are not met, so individuals are unsure of what they ought to believe and are unable to predict future outcome of behavior | Insight and understanding |
| Normlessness | Individuals have high expectancy that socially unapproved behaviors must be used to achieve the given goals | Trust and order |
| Isolation | Individuals assign low values to goals or beliefs typically held in high value in the given society | Commitment and consensus |
| Self-estrangement | Individuals feel they are less than they might be if circumstances in society were otherwise | Integrity and involvement |

stasis ulcer of her leg and arteriosclerotic heart disease. Three weeks following surgery, she is quiet and withdrawn. In an apathetic manner, she states, "Nurse, you decide whenever you want to do my bath; it doesn't matter to me." When questioned about her illness, she was resigned, and she replied, "I know I have to stay in bed to get better, so I will. The doctor wanted to do the skin graft on my leg and put the pacemaker in my heart. I let him do it to make him happy." As a black woman growing up and living in a predominantly white culture, Robella has had to cope with discrimination and feelings of powerlessness throughout most of her life. Her illness is just another condition over which she feels she has no control and is powerless to influence in any way.

People who feel alienated and powerless — those who have little or no control over their fate, such as patients and prisoners — rely on the opinion of experts, look to the bureaucratic structure and authority for guidelines, and show a lack of community ties. When illness strikes, they do not seek information about their illness. They are not sensitive to cues in the environment because they believe that nothing they can do will change anything. They learn only when the learning will benefit them. They regard goal-directed activities as pointless when faced with powerful factors, such as luck, fate, the will of God, or "city hall."

## ASSESSMENT OF POWERLESSNESS

Powerlessness as a problem in coping is identified by obtaining information about how the

patient or client carries out the growth and developmental tasks for the appropriate stage of life. Behaviors associated with powerlessness show loss of control over some aspect of life or the lack of knowledge needed to be able to achieve the desired goals. People respond to their problems in coping with feelings of powerlessness with emotions and behaviors the same as those used to express anxiety or loss. First level assessment behaviors include

| | |
|---|---|
| anger | apathy |
| withdrawal | frustration |
| hostility | fatalism |
| resignation | indecision |
| lack of direction or motivation | low level of learning |
| feeling victimized | feeling frail or incapable |

Second level assessment of stimuli generally shows the focal stimulus to be the loss of control over something or the lack of knowledge about something. When people are sick and feeling powerless, the focal stimulus is the loss of health or the disease causing the illness. Other influencing factors include many that have already been discussed: age, personality, religion, occupation, educational level, income, social class, and the hospital setting. Factors that contribute to feelings of powerlessness when ill include physical changes as a result of the disease, pain, growth of tumors, bleeding, loss of physical functioning, lack of privacy, examinations, being asked very personal questions, and often being treated in a very depersonalized way, such as "the hernia in Room 206," or the "preop."

Other hospital customs that contribute to patients' feelings of powerlessness are restrictions on personal items, visiting hours and regulations, the need to change one's daily routine to fit the hospital's schedule, giving up much of one's personal decision-making, and assuming a dependent role, with others giving directions. Activities are limited to the bedside area or to one's room, and patients are not encouraged to explore or go where they wish in the hospital. Often medical equipment and machines, such as the IV standard, suction apparatus, or dressing packs, displace their own possessions at bedside. Patients may be unable to reach their own personal property or the call light to summon help when they need it.

## NURSING INTERVENTIONS

The goal of nursing actions is to reduce the patient's feelings of powerlessness about whatever is causing the loss of control or the lack of knowledge. The nursing interventions are directed toward changing the stimuli leading to the problem and increasing the patient's feeling of power. To gain power, the patient must have a commitment to a goal-directed action, sufficient information to analyze the situation, and a willingness to act. Nursing interventions focus on ways to help the patient gain control and to increase his or her knowledge through health-teaching.

- *Physiological control* — Keep the patient informed of his or her physical progress. Even no change represents a degree of control over bodily functions. Control may be measured by decrease in fever, gain in hemoglobin, or increased strength shown by sitting up 10 minutes longer.
- *Psychological control* — Increase verbalization to enable patient to discuss fears and concerns. Actively listen to the patient as a significant person and assist in planning, directing, and participating in portions of his or her care. Personalize the patient's care and address him or her by name. Give positive feedback to help improve the patient's self-esteem.
- *Environmental control* — Allow the patient to keep personal belongings at bedside. When possible, use flexibility in making changes in the schedule of daily activities, visiting, bedtime, location of furniture, and so on. Allow and encourage the patient to participate in making decisions about his or her care.
- *Increase knowledge base* — Keep the early explanations brief and simple and obtain feedback as to the patient's level of knowledge about the disease, treatment, progress, and home care.

With the highly alienated patient, the nurse may have to assume an active role for a prolonged period of time when the patient fails to act, even though he or she is physically capable of doing so. For example, the patient may be able to walk but refuse to do so. Some complicating factors that serve as barriers in reaching the nursing goal of reducing the patient's feelings of powerlessness include authoritarian behavior of others, discrimination toward the patient, the patient's failure to achieve the developmental tasks of childhood in a satisfying way, or the presence of mental illness or senility.

## COPING WITH FEELINGS OF SHAME AND GUILT

Everyone has had feelings of guilt or shame at some time in his life. Almost everyone can recall events that proved to be embarrassing or that caused him to have feelings of guilt. Both shame and guilt develop early in life as the child forms an image of the self and learns to function as a social being interacting with others. Guilt and shame are often linked together because they frequently overlap, but they are different from each other and are related to distinct parts of the self-concept. Shame and embarrassment involve the feelings of "What I am" compared with the beliefs of "What I am able to be." They signify a conflict between the image of the self and the self-ideal. On the other hand, guilt is associated with discrepancies between "What I do" and "What I should or ought to do," signifying a coping problem between the self and the moral-ethical self. Comparison of differences between feelings of shame and guilt are shown in Table 19–5.

Generally, the feelings of guilt and shame are regarded as negative in nature because they cause discomfort and pain to the person who is experiencing them. However, they do have a positive value and purpose. They provide a message about oneself and can lead to opportunities for further development of the self. Guilt and shame are signals, or warning devices, that one's behavior has or will fail to meet the standards of the self and may keep one from acting inappropriately. This happens frequently when people find themselves in strange or new situations. The stress of the first few days on a new job is related to the feelings of shame and guilt that one has when other workers say, "Who did this? That's not the way we do it here." The new employee sees himself or herself as being capable of doing the job but is embarrassed by not performing as well as expected. As a result, the new employee is more cau-

Table 19–5. COMPARISON OF DIFFERENCES BETWEEN
FEELINGS OF GUILT AND SHAME

| Guilt | Shame |
|---|---|
| 1. Conflict between self and moral-ethical self. | 1. Conflict between self and self-ideal. |
| 2. Occurs with failure to adhere to or conform to specific codes or laws. | 2. Occurs when ideal or goal is not reached and deficit is exposed to others. |
| 3. Concerns violations of social expectations of role function – the rules, the do's or don'ts, for behavior. | 3. Concerns basic and unchangeable aspects of the self compared with the ideals – the ought-to's and should's. |
| 4. The underlying threat is fear of retaliation and punishment. | 4. The underlying threat is fear of being abandoned, unworthy, or unloved. |
| 5. Results from what one has done – the bad things. | 5. Results from what one is – inadequate, imperfect, or weak-willed. |
| 6. Associated with feelings of wrongdoing toward a loved object; may include unconscious hostility. | 6. Associated with feelings of having loved the wrong person or being unworthy of the person one loves. |
| 7. To be guiltless is to be innocent or exonerated – good. | 7. To be shameless is to be insensitive to self and others; arrogant – bad. |
| 8. Predominately a reaction to verbal statements of accusation, denial, or demand. | 8. Predominately a reaction to visual exposure. |

Source: Laney, Hilda. Shame. *In* Carlson, Carolyn (ed.). Behavioral Concepts and Nursing Intervention. Philadelphia, J. B. Lippincott Co., 1970, p 71.

tious about checking out a procedure with others before undertaking it and making a fool of himself or herself. Student nurses often experience feelings of humiliation or embarrassment when they encounter new situations in the care of their patients. They often have high expectations of themselves as superior practitioners and feel ashamed to admit that they do not know how to perform a simple procedure or to do it skillfully.

Healthy, adapted people have feelings of guilt and shame; however, they cope with them effectively and use them as a means of evaluating their performance of "How am I doing?" Problems in coping with feelings of guilt and shame occur when they diminish the person's self-esteem, when they persist for a longer period of time than is warranted by the circumstances, when they are recalled or recur in response to other than the original situation, and when they influence the person's other behaviors. Feelings of guilt and shame can interfere with one's pattern of daily living by causing intense mental discomfort and distress. The loss of self-esteem may cause one to be regarded as a weakling, a square, a loser, or a sucker.

## FEELINGS OF SHAME

Anxiety that is generated by differences between the self and the self-ideal leads to specialized feelings of shame, embarrassment,

humiliation, or disgust. Shame occurs when a hidden or undesirable part of the self has been suddenly exposed to others. It is "loss of face," or like being seen by others from behind without anything to cover one's nakedness.

Feelings of shame are most often associated with child-rearing practices and are first seen in the second stage of life, as toddlers are faced with learning to control their bodies and to form a mental picture of themselves as an autonomous person. During this period, they must learn to perform motor skills involved in eating, walking, running, gaining control of bowel and bladder, and curbing impulsive or acting-out behavior. Toddlers strive to please the most important people in their lives – their parents – in order to keep their love and attention. Successful performance of these tasks leads to feelings of autonomy and pride in their abilities, whereas failure leads to shame, doubt, and embarrassment. Failure also carries with it the threat of being unloved or abandoned as being unworthy.

In the later stages of childhood, children venture away from the home and family to seek recognition and acceptance from peer groups. They take the risk of being rejected or ridiculed if not accepted and of coping with feelings of humiliation. Teen-agers often experience acute embarrassment from any perceived deviation in their physical appearance from the ideal image.

**Assessment of Shame.** Nurses should be aware

**Figure 19–3.** Parents frequently use shaming to teach children socially accepted behavior.

that many situations cause feelings of shame and embarrassment for people when they are ill and should recognize the characteristic body responses or behaviors that result from being observed by others. These behaviors include:

1. Withdrawal from visual contact by lowering the eyes, looking away, covering the face or part of the body.
2. Change in speech by stuttering, using a weak voice or a very soft tone, having a dry mouth, or being unable to speak at all.
3. Gestures that indicate nervousness, such as twisting or twiddling fingers, cracking knuckles, chewing fingernails, patting hair or clothing repeatedly, or having weak knees.
4. Skin color changes, resulting in paleness or flushing of face and neck.

Second level assessment of stimuli causing feelings of shame centers on those that affect body function and self-image. When people are ill, they are dependent upon others to take care of many of their most intimate body functions. This may create a conflict with their self-image of being independent, capable, and in control of them-

selves and their lives. Patients are especially vulnerable to feelings of embarrassment and shame in many common nursing situations, including

1. *Sense of modesty.*
   a. Lack of privacy.
   b. Exposure of the body.
   c. Reactions to elimination or loss of bowel or bladder control.
   d. Procedures involving the genitourinary organs.
2. *Loss of emotional control.*
   a. Outbursts of anger and hostility.
   b. Periods of crying.
   c. Inappropriate responses of swearing, ranting, and so on.
3. *Physiological illnesses or changes in self or loved one.*
   a. Amputation or disfigurement.
   b. Mental retardation or mental illness.
   c. Immobility or a physical handicap.
   d. Genitourinary conditions and venereal disease.
   e. Offensive odors, emesis, or drainage from wound.

**Nursing Interventions.** In addition to helping their patients deal effectively with feelings of shame, nurses may also be able to help parents deal effectively with feelings of shame in their children. The extensive damage of shaming to one's self-esteem can be avoided by parents who convey attitudes of respect and care for their children. Parents can be sincere and nurturing as they help their child to express and deal with feelings of shame and to cope with disappointment in positive ways, and provide sympathy and support. It is important that the dignity and self-esteem of children and all patients be maintained through the use of common courtesies, such as addressing people by name and treating each person as a unique and valuable individual.

Situations that lead to shame and embarrassment are generally handled by avoidance and correction. Whenever possible, the nurse should avoid subjecting the patient to situations that cause shame. This is accomplished by knocking on the door before entering the room, pulling curtains to screen the bed from others, draping patients during procedures to avoid unnecessary exposure of the body, asking or explaining that you would like to inspect dressings or wounds on the body, and so on. If situations occur that cause shame, they can be corrected. In some cases, the shamer apologizes and makes amends by helping the shamed person to regain face. For patients who are having problems coping with feelings of shame, the nurse uses insight therapy. Briefly, the steps of insight therapy are as follows:

1. Recognize that the patient has a problem in coping.
2. Assist the patient in acknowledging his or her feelings of shame.
3. Assist the patient in finding the reasons (stimuli) causing these feelings.
4. Re-evaluate the self-ideal for realistic goals.
5. Manipulate the external stimuli, if possible.
6. Support the patient's coping mechanisms.

## FEELINGS OF GUILT

Guilt is the result of conflicting views between what one does and what one ought to do, or in adaptation terms, between the self and the moral-ethical self. Guilt is the unpleasant feeling of self-criticism that results from acts, thoughts, or impulses that are contrary to one's conscience, or sense of right and wrong. The amount of guilt one feels does not necessarily reflect the amount of damage done by the individual who is feeling guilty. Guilt is related to violations of the social codes of behavior, the do's and don'ts, and is the reflection of what one has done.

The psychosocial task of the preschool stage of life is that of initiative versus guilt. Preschool children develop their personality during the third stage of life by learning to communicate through language, refine their motor skills, and expand the scope of their world. They learn to use initiative to take hold and to carry out purposeful activities to achieve goals that they set. Preschool children learn the social skills involved in making things in groups or alone and prepare for taking on additional roles in life through make-believe and play-acting. Successful accomplishment of these tasks leads to the control of impulses and the ability to tolerate some degree of frustration and delays in pleasure-seeking activities. Preschoolers begin to learn what they can and cannot do, what the parents allow, and the boundaries or limitations that are imposed. Feelings of guilt arise when children are made to feel that they are behaving without reason or logic or when they are ridiculed.

Children conform to the demands of the parents to gain their approval and to escape their fears of punishment or retaliation. Children will have greater problems with irrational guilt in later life if parents place unreasonable or excessive demands on them, coupled with threats of disgrace and withdrawal of affection. At puberty, teenagers are exposed to more intense guilt feelings as they attempt to cope with disapproval of their parents and other authority figures, problems of sexual curiosity, and the persistence of incestuous desires.

**Assessment of Guilt.** Guilt is the painful expression of anxiety that results from one's image of oneself as a moral and ethical person. Guilt is characterized by physiological responses of the autonomic nervous system and often involves elements of anger directed toward the person or object that aroused the guilt feelings. Severe and irrational guilt feelings may require referral for psychiatric care. Such guilt feelings are a prominent feature in depressions, suicides, and mental illnesses.

When nurses assess the growth and developmental tasks individuals carry out for their stage of life, the following behaviors may indicate problems in coping with feelings of guilt.

1. *Statement of guilt and apology for certain actions or events.* The patient with a colostomy who says, "I can't stand to look at that thing or change the bag. I'm sorry that you have to do it," is expressing feelings of guilt and shame.
2. *Rationalization, or seeking to explain actions as based on logical reasons.* "I couldn't study for the test because I had to go out of town to attend my cousin's wedding."

3. *Moving-away behaviors.* Withdrawal from others and trying to avoid expressing feelings. If forced to confront others or one's own painful feelings, the person usually becomes angry or hostile.

4. *Blaming self for events or actions, or being self-incriminating.* Makes statements such as, "If I hand't asked Johnnie to go to the store, he would never have had the accident and gotten hurt."

5. *Expressing feelings of unworthiness, of not being able to do anything right.* "My kids are nothing but trouble. I can't make them do good. They don't listen to me; just go around with that gang and run wild."

6. *Masochistic types of behavior.* Seems to invite disaster, unpredictable happenings, or maltreatment by others. The accident-prone person seems to seek out accidents as a way of coping with guilt feelings and is not happy unless he is suffering; the physiological pain is a method of reducing the psychological discomforts of anxiety and guilt.

7. *Defensive types of behavior.* May be overly sensitive to any criticisms or questioning of motives and may respond with outbursts of anger or by attacking. "What do you mean, did I eat food not on my diet? You're just like the day nurses; you take forever to come around when I'm having pain."

8. *Interference with sexual functioning.* Guilt feelings lead to problems such as impotence and lack of sexual pleasure and satisfaction.

The second level assessment is carried out to determine the cause of the guilt feelings and the problems in coping with these feelings. The focal stimulus generally concerns expectations — either the expectations of others concerning how one should behave or one's own expectations of how one should act. Guilt results from the differences between the actions that occurred and the actions that were expected, or should have happened. Behavior is expected to conform with the standards of right and wrong, the code of ethics, or the rules and regulations governing a particular society or culture. The dependency that results from illness causes some people to feel guilty when it conflicts with their expectation, which equates being independent with being good. Another example of guilt is running away from a situation that one is expected to face or abandoning someone who has depended upon one.

Other influencing factors in coping with problems of guilt include the person's age, stage of development, conditions affecting health, requirements for medical treatment, and the resources available. The amount of guilt experienced by the person depends upon the child-rearing practices of one's family and the way one was programmed in childhood to respond to pressures on one's moral-ethical self.

**Nursing Interventions.** The nurse manipulates the stimuli causing the guilt primarily by insight therapy and health-teaching. Insight therapy is used to help the patient identify the guilt feelings as the cause of distress and to research the causes of these feelings. Together, the nurse and client explore ways to achieve the desired goals and to avoid violating the moral codes, or rules. Through health-teaching, they explore other types of responses, or ways of coping. The nurse then helps the patient to feel more at ease with the coping actions to be used.

## APPLICATION TO CLINICAL PRACTICE

In most areas of clinical practice, nurses encounter many patients who have problems coping with feelings that affect their self-concept on a daily basis. Health problems and illness produce anxiety about the functions of one's body and force changes in one's self-image as one deals with losses. Perceptive and sensitive nurses recognize and treat the psychological discomfort, as well as the physiological disruption, of people in their care.

### EXPLORING YOUR FEELINGS ABOUT DEATH

Before you can understand and effectively help patients cope with losses and grieving, you need to understand your own feelings. If possible, join a discussion group to examine some of the following questions and issues.

The following situations are encountered by nurses in their practice and often pose dilemmas: "What should be done?" "What is right?" or "What do I believe?"

1. When should heroic measures that keep someone alive by mechanical means be discontinued? Who makes the decision of when to "pull the plug?"

2. Cardiopulmonary resuscitation should be given to every person suffering an arrest, including those dying of an incurable disease.

3. Infants born with little or no brain cortex should be allowed to die by withholding feedings.

4. The cost of keeping a brain-dead person alive should not be a factor for consideration when it comes to our moral responsibility to prolong life.

5. Life is sacred and must be maintained at any cost.

Consider your reaction to the following and complete the statement.

1. If I learned today that I have a fatal illness, I would probably _____

_____

2. I (would/would not) want my family to know I have a fatal illness because _____

_____

3. If I were dying, I would want to be certain that _____

_____

4. What bothers me the most in taking care of a dying patient is _____

_____

## EXPLORING THE PATIENT'S PROBLEMS IN COPING

As you provide care for patients in the clinical setting, continue to carry out the complete assessment of physiological need areas and the role performance of the growth and developmental tasks for their appropriate stage of life. Most people have a combination of different feelings over a period of time; however, it is possible to focus on certain feelings and to analyze one type at a time. During the second and third stages of illness, all hospitalized patients experience feelings related to coping with a loss — from feelings of powerlessness caused by restrictions imposed by the disease or care in the hospital setting to feelings of shame or guilt.

For your initial assessment of self-concept problems, focus on the assessment of losses. Loss is the most common problem because it is related to changes in the physical self-concept and is easy to observe in hospitalized patients. Consider the adaptive methods of coping as well as evidence that the coping might be ineffectual. Organize the information you have gathered from the patient, the chart, and other sources to answer these questions.

What losses has the client experienced? What part of the self-concept is involved?
How is the client responding? State some of the behaviors you have assessed.
What stage of grieving is the client in?
What method of coping is the patient utilizing?
If the patient is having a problem coping with his or her feelings, how would you state the problem?
What nursing interventions would you use to help the patient deal with these feelings?

In subsequent assessments, focus on assessing powerlessness and feelings of guilt or shame.

# REFERENCES

Aadalen, Sharon, and Stroebel-Kahn, Florence: Coping with quadreplegia. Am J Nurs, *81*:1471–1478, (August) 1981.

Beck, Aaron, and Kovacs, Maria: Depression. Psychology Today, 94–102, (January) 1977.

Breu, Christine, and Dracup, Kathleen: Helping the spouses of critically ill patients. Am J Nurs, *78*:50–53, (January) 1978.

Bunch, Barbara, and Zahra, Donna: Dealing with death: the unlearned role. Am J Nurs, *76*:1486–1492, (September) 1976.

Burnside, Irene: You will cope, of course. Am J Nurs, *71*:2354–2357, (December) 1971.

Byrne, Karin, et al.: Don't let me fall. Am J Nurs, *82*: 1242–1245, (August) 1982.

Carlson, Carolyn: Behavioral Concepts and Nursing Intervention. Philadelphia, J. B. Lippincott Co., 1970.

Craytor, Josephine: Talking with persons who have cancer. Am J Nurs, *69*:744–748, (April) 1969.

Diran, Margaret: You can prevent suicide. Nursing 76, *6*:60–64, (January) 1976.

Engel, George: Grief and grieving. Am J Nurs, *64*:94–98, (September) 1964.

Forsyth, Diane McNally: The hardest job of all. Nursing 82, *12*:86–91, (April) 1982.

Giacquinta, Barbara: Helping families face the crisis of cancer. Am J Nurs, *77*:1585–1588, (October) 1977.

Groff, Ben: Death and I. Am J Nurs, *82*:1080–1084, (July) 1982.

Guimond, Joyce: We knew our child was dying. Am J Nurs, *74*:248–249, (February) 1974.

Gyulay, Jo Eileen: The forgotten grievers. Am J Nurs, *75*:1476–1479, (September) 1975.

Johnson, Dorothy E.: Powerlessness: a significant determinant in patient behavior. J Nurs Ed, *6*:39–44, (April) 1967.

Kelly, Lucie Young: The power of powerlessness. Nurs Outlook, *26*:468, (July) 1978.

Kubler-Ross, Elisabeth: What it is like to be dying. Am J Nurs, *71*:54–62, (January) 1971.

Marks, Mary Jo: The grieving patient and family. Am J Nurs, *76*:1488–1491, (September) 1976.

Programmed Instruction. Helping depressed patients in general nursing practice. Am J Nurs, *77*:1–32, (June) 1977.

Quint, Jeanne: The dying patient: A difficult nursing problem. Nurs Clin North Am, *2*(4): 276, (December) 1977.

Raymond, Marsha C., and Laube, Jerri: Time to say good-bye. Am J Nurs, *82*:933–935, (June) 1982.

Roberts, Sharon: Behavioral Concepts and the Critically Ill Patient. Englewood Cliffs, Prentice-Hall, Inc., 1976.

Rosenbaum, Marily: Depression: what to do, what to say. Nursing 80, *10*(8):64–66, (August) 1980.

Seeman, Melvin: On the meaning of alienation. Am Sociol Rev, *XXIV*:783–791, (December) 1959.

Thaler, Otto: Grief and depression. Nurs Forum, *5*(2): 8–22, 1966.

Ujhely, Gertrude: Grief and depression—implications for preventive and therapeutic nursing care. Nurs Forum, *5*(2):22–35, 1966.

# The Interdependence Mode

## OBJECTIVES  Information in this chapter will help you to

1. State the basic underlying drives for dependent and independent behavior.
2. Define interdependence and trace its development through the various stages of life.
3. State the patterns of behavior that are used to cope with feelings of dependence and independence, and use these coping mechanisms as a framework for classifying the assessed behaviors of the client or patient.
4. Assess the interdependence mode of functioning by gathering information about how one carries out the growth and developmental tasks associated with one's primary role.
5. Identify the stimuli that affect interdependence functioning, with special emphasis on relationships with family members and significant others and with support systems available for use.
6. Indicate the problems of dysfunctional dependence or dysfunctional independence in coping with others.
7. Plan nursing interventions that include insight therapy, behavior modification, and manipulation of environmental factors.

## DEFINITION OF TERMS

**affection-seeking** — acting to obtain approval, praise, or emotional satisfaction from another.

**affiliation** — an attachment or relationship between two or more persons based on a shared belief, value, or feeling.

**aggression** — a response to stimuli that is characterized as energetic, vigorous, hostile, attacking, or belligerent.

**attention-seeking** — acting to gain notice and response from another.
**dependence** — behavior indicating feelings of love, of being nurtured, or caring derived from other people.
**independence** — behavior indicating feelings of self-reliance and satisfaction from achievements.
**initiative-taking** — beginning and working on a task by oneself.
**interdependence** — the comfortable balance between dependence and independence needs.
**obstacle-mastery** — completing tasks or overcoming barriers to achieve a goal by oneself.

To live successfully in the world, people must develop the ability to function and to get along with others in social ways. They must be able to trust others and to provide care as needed for the young, the weak, and the feeble. People must cooperate to construct buildings, erect cities, and maintain complex transportation and communication networks. They also compete with each other to see who can climb higher, run more swiftly, or make more money. In addition to developing into self-reliant and self-directing adults, everyone needs to know that he is loved and supported by others. People seek interactions with others that provide evidence that they are valued as individuals and are worthy of love and affection and that show that they can provide nurturing and support to others.

The underlying dependency needs to be loved and supported persist throughout all stages of life, even as people learn to carry out the independent tasks of living successfully. One's dependent and independent needs should become a comfortable balance of interdependence as one matures into adulthood, so that one is able to give and receive care from others as well as being able to master tasks in a self-reliant way. The interdependence mode emerges as one learns to relate to others in social ways. The social aspect of living requires that people acquire many complex skills, including learning to use language and communication skills, recognizing the feelings and attitudes of others, giving appropriate emotional feedback, initiating relationships, working with others, and working alone.

In this chapter, the interdependence mode is described as the development of a calm, untroubled balance between dependence and independence needs, as these two opposing needs are traced through the stages of life. The ways in which people respond to these needs provide patterns of coping that the nurse uses as a framework for classifying behaviors obtained during the assessment process. The behaviors used to carry out the developmental tasks for the patient's appropriate stage of life are assessed and compared with the social expectations for those roles. Behaviors outside the normal range are indicative of problems in coping with dependence or independence needs.

The second level assessment focuses on the patient's internal drives or needs for affection or achievement (the most common focal stimuli) and examines other influencing factors, including family relationships, child-rearing practices of one's parents, presence of significant others, and additional support systems that are available to the individual. Nursing interventions that may be used to help people with coping problems in the interdependence mode are discussed.

## THE THEORY OF INTERDEPENDENCE

The interdependence mode consists of a combination of dependent and independent behaviors that people use to demonstrate their adequacy as individuals and their social integrity. All human beings have a need to be loved and supported so that their lives and actions have meaning. Throughout each stage of life, people exhibit both dependent and independent needs, although at some times, one type of need may be more dominant and outweigh the other.

The key to the interdependence mode is the interaction that occurs. Whereas the physiological and self-concept modes focused on the specific individual, the interdependence mode features the interaction between the client and another person or object in the environment. It is a more complex mode because it includes the client's needs, expectations, and actions, as well as the needs, expectations, and response of another person. The behavior of one participant shapes and influences the behavior of the other (Patterson, 1971). Interdependence grows from relationships in which both participants are able to have their needs met in mutually satisfying ways. Much of one's social life is based on developing relationships with others to achieve these positive outcomes. Several times a day, one turns to others to receive some sign of affection, approval for what one does, or assistance in completing a task, and several times a day, one extends these same responses to other people.

## DEPENDENCE NEEDS

Dependent behaviors are learned and begin early in life as a result of interactions between the helpless, newborn infant and the mother. Initial responses to stimuli by the newborn include crying, mouthing, sucking, reflexive movements, gross clutching and grasping, and primitive reactions to sight, sound, and changes in position. The infant is dependent upon the mother, or care-giver, for meeting most basic needs for survival. The infant's biological need for food produces a state of tension, and the infant responds with the coping mechanisms available to him or her, such as crying and gross motor activity, alerting the mother to the need for care. The response of the mother is more complex than merely providing food for the infant. The interactions of the mother with the infant include picking up and cuddling the infant in her arms, the warmth of her body, the degree of tension in her muscles, and talking in soothing tones. The infant associates the total response of the mother with the feeding, bathing, dressing, or other activities involved in his or her physical care. The infant has learned the emotional responses that are connected with care.

In the interaction between the mother and the infant, both are influenced by the responses of the other. When the infant stops crying, eats eagerly, smiles and coos, the behavior is rewarded by the mother by touching, kissing and making comments, such as "That's my good baby." The mother is apt to respond differently if the infant continues to cry and spit out and push away food. Early feeding experiences have been found to affect the way in which the child relates to other people later in life. When the response of the mother is warm and loving, the infant develops feelings of security and trust in the mother that are extended to other people. Emotionally cold, anxious, or hostile mothers communicate these feelings to their children. These feelings interfere with the child's ability to successfully work through the developmental tasks of establishing trust, autonomy, and intimacy.

From this rudimentary beginning, dependent behaviors develop from the individual's psychological wish to be nurtured and ministered to, or taken care of, in the same comfortable and gratifying way as when one was a child. These affiliation needs are first met and dependent patterns of coping are established within the family. As one matures, people in the neighborhood, school, and community become increasingly important in meeting one's needs for affection, attention, and assistance.

During childhood, dependent behavior is encouraged as appropriate for one's specific stage

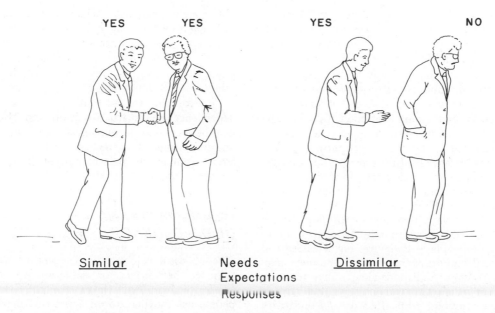

YES    YES                    YES                    NO

Similar              Needs              Dissimilar
              Expectations
              Responses

**Figure 20–1.** Interdependence needs are met when the needs, expectations, and responses of both parties are similar. Coping problems arise when the needs, expectations, and responses of both parties are dissimilar.

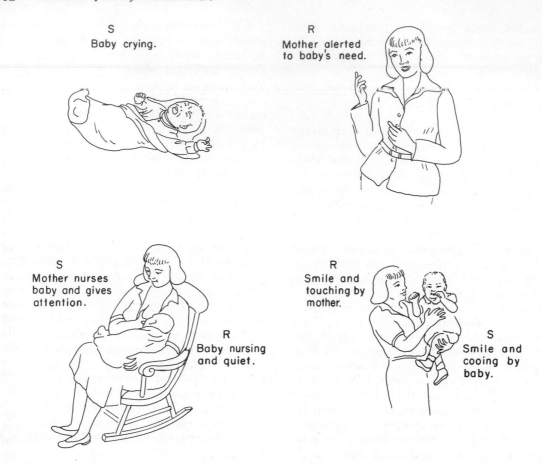

**Figure 20–2.** Development of dependency needs related to affection, attention, and assistance. (S = stimulus, R = response)

of growth and development. Young children are taught to curb their aggressive impulses to hit, kick, or bite anyone who challenges their desires. Parents caution active youngsters to stay in the yard when playing and not to run out in the street and prohibit activities that their children are too young to do safely. As children mature to adolescence and young adulthood, they become more skillful at meeting many of their physical and social needs. However, they continue to have the dependent needs of relating to others and the emotional needs for belonging and love.

Throughout their lives, adults who are in an adaptive state continue to exhibit dependent behaviors in ways that are appropriate for the situation. They turn to family members or other important people in their lives for affection and emotional support as they seek continuous validation of themselves as individuals. They relate to others in warm and trusting ways and rely on others to respond with affection and sensitivity to their needs. They view their relationships with others as satisfying and rewarding.

Although dependent behavior is appropriate and sanctioned during infancy and early childhood, it is commonly acceptable in other circumstances, such as old age, chronic illness, or when physically or mentally disabled. Dependence on others for assistance and care is appropriate behavior for the second stage of illness. Other dependence needs for attention and affection may be increased during illness, especially during hospitalization when medical treatment and isolation from family present barriers to one's fulfillment.

## COPING PATTERNS OF DEPENDENCY

People use a wide variety of coping mechanisms to meet their needs for affiliation with others and for getting along in the social world. Generally, people use moving-toward types of behavior to satisfy their needs for affection. They want to feel loved, wanted, worthy, and trusted by those with whom they have contact. They use the coping patterns of help-seeking, attention-seeking, and affection-seeking behaviors to achieve the desired results.

**Help-Seeking Behaviors.** The pattern of help-seeking behaviors is used to enable people to meet their physical and emotional needs for assistance or to aid in reaching a goal. The help may be sought or expected, even though the person appears to be physically able to carry out the activity alone. This pattern of behavior is observed in children who call out for help from the parent by crying, begging, or pleading. They look, point, and name objects that they would like to have. Children and adults alike may use inactivity as a means of obtaining help by waiting for others to offer assistance or to perform the activity without being asked. Another way of seeking assistance is by conforming and complying with the rules or expectations of others, which is, in effect, a way of saying "Tell me what you want me to do and I will do it."

During illness, people use many help-seeking behaviors to satisfy their increased needs for assistance, support, and security. During the second stage of illness, it is appropriate to be dependent upon the nurses and other care-givers, but the amount of dependent or help-seeking behaviors should be decreased as the patient moves through the convalescent stage.

Help-seeking behaviors associated with the sick role include

### Adaptive Behaviors

Seeks medical care by doctor
Agrees to hospitalization and treatment
Seeks relief from responsibilities
Follows instructions for medical and
 nursing care
Asks for advice and instructions in
 returning to former level of activities
Asks for help from nurse, spouse, or
 friends in resuming more activity

### Maladaptive Behaviors

Ignores condition and symptoms
Continues to carry out usual activities
 and responsibilities
Makes numerous complaints about
 hospital routine or care received
Makes no complaints; is quiet and
 withdrawn
Cries easily and often
Does not request help; does everything
 alone, or nothing at all

**Attention-Seeking Behaviors.** Individuals use attention-seeking behaviors to stimulate others to notice them and to respond to their presence. Everyone uses this coping pattern at some time. It is often seen in children as they engage in showing off, bragging about their exploits, talking loudly, hanging onto another person, or physically interrupting the activities of other people. Other methods used to attract attention include the use of bold make-up, wearing colorful clothing, adopting an unusual or dramatic style of dress, playing practical jokes, or talking persistently so that others find it difficult to interrupt or to join in the conversation.

Patients use a variety of attention-seeking behaviors—some less obvious than others. They gain attention from nurses, doctors, and family by asking for attention and by talking about their illness or operation. They make demands for care and services beyond those ordinarily needed by others with similar illnesses, or they give generous praise and gratitude for the care that they receive. Others gain attention and approval by being very sociable and carrying on an interesting conversation with everyone who enters the room. People who have problems coping with their feelings of dependence may express them in angry outbursts and by numerous complaints and show other types of moving-against behaviors that also attract attention.

Attention-seeking behaviors associated with the sick role include

### Adaptive Behaviors

Recounts symptoms and history of
 illness
Requests frequent visits from family
 and friends
Displays flowers, cards, and gifts
Talks of progress and of bodily
 functions
Greets others first and engages them
 in conversation

### Maladaptive Behaviors

Hides all symptoms or worries
Exaggerates symptoms
Seductive behavior toward staff and
 medical personnel of opposite sex
Turns on call light and makes many
 demands
Complains constantly of pain or other
 symptoms
Expresses anger without apparent cause
Is defiant and resistant to following rules

**Affection-Seeking Behaviors.** This type of coping occurs when one person stimulates another to care, comfort, console, and protect him or her. The purpose of affection-seeking behavior is to establish a relationship with a significant other that provides recognition, praise, love, and approval. Socialization begins during childhood, with the accomplishment of the developmental tasks by which one learns how to gain emotional pleasure and satisfaction from close contact with another person. It begins with the trust relationship established between the mother and the infant that grows and changes to the love and intimacy that is found in the marriage of caring adults.

Affection-seeking behaviors include greeting or saying good-bye to relatives or friends by hugging or kissing them, using good manners to insure the good will of others, complimenting others about how nice they look or how well they are doing something, and giving gifts. Although each of these actions is a display of affection, it is also an invitation to be given affection in return for being nice. When Jane asks her friend Maria, "How do you like my dress?" she is seeking Maria's approval. By offering to help her mother, she may be seeking praise or recognition. Reaching out and touching someone are significant forms of affection-seeking behaviors.

Affection-seeking behaviors associated with the sick role include

### Adaptive Behaviors

Reaches out and holds onto the nurse's hand

Says to the doctor and nurse, "Tell me what you want me to do, and I'll do it if I can"

States, "All you nurses are so wonderful and take such good care of me"

Comments, "Aren't those gorgeous flowers? The people in the office where I work sent them to me"

### Maladaptive Behaviors

States that the nurses spend all their time with the other patient and never answer his or her call light

Asks the nurse for a kiss; makes other verbal advances with sexual overtones

Talks continuously, and makes numerous demands so that the nurse is unable to leave the room without being rude

States that he or she loves everybody

States that the nurses are so busy that they should not bother doing anything for him or her

## INDEPENDENCE NEEDS

Independence needs are goal-directed and achievement-oriented and emerge slowly. They are motivated by the needs for achievement and separateness. The dependent young child develops a gradual awareness of the satisfaction and gratification that comes from being apart from the mother and from doing things alone. Through self-reliant and self-assertive behavior, the child meets the independence needs of feeding himself and exploring other rooms of the house and, thus, seeks nurturing from others less frequently. The goal of independence is to reach adulthood as an individual who is self-reliant and able to take care of oneself and others. Adults spend much of their time acting in assertive ways that are directed toward achieving goals. They work at jobs, raise families, and provide nurturing and emotional support to others.

The basic drive behind independence needs is thought to be aggression, and Ellison (1976) is credited with developing this concept within the adaptation model of nursing. The purpose of the aggressive drive is to make contact with objects in one's environment and to gain control over them. Individuals become less dependent upon others as they learn to control their body functions and emotions and become free to compete more successfully in the world. In the example of dependent behavior given previously, the infant makes contact with the mother by the independent actions of crying and squirming body movements. He or she gains control when these behaviors resulting in being fed and the disappearance of the discomfort causing the initial arousal.

Through the years of maturation and development, children experiment with different methods of achieving self-control and self-reliance in addition to the pleasure gained from accomplishing a task. They learn to control their aggressive drives and to express them in socially acceptable ways. Aggression has the potential for leading to personal or social harm when it is expressed in angry, hostile, or combative behaviors, or it may be the basis for independent action that is constructive, creative, and goal-directed. Positive expressions of aggression are described by terms such as dynamic, energetic, enterprising, and adventuresome types of behavior. Lack of control over aggressive impulses turns other people away and deprives one of achieving goals that one is striving to reach or of having one's dependency needs for love and support satisfied.

## COPING PATTERNS OF INDEPENDENCE

People use the moving-against pattern of behavior most frequently when they initiate actions to achieve a goal, or work to accomplish a desired outcome. The specific coping patterns associated with independence are initiative-taking and obstacle-mastery behaviors.

**Initiative-Taking Behaviors.** This pattern of coping is used by people who decide to work on a problem or task by themselves. They recognize the circumstances that indicate that something needs to be done, make the decision to undertake the job, and begin working on the project. Independent individuals enjoy doing some things alone, and carrying out the steps of the task in their own way without the advice or interference of others. All independent and goal-directed activity requires initiative-taking to begin the task or to initiate some response.

Initiative-taking behaviors of 18-year-old Mike, who is preparing to go to college, might include

### Adaptive Behaviors

Fills out the application form for
the college he prefers to attend
Reads catalog and determines the
courses he will have to take
Gets a part-time job to help pay
some of his expenses

### Maladaptive Behaviors

Relies on parents to make arrangements for
enrollment and dormitory reservations
States that he does not know what major
or classes he wants to take
Asks parents for money whenever he needs
it or has spent all his allowance

Usually, maladaptive behaviors, or behaviors that fall outside the adapted range for independent coping, are those that indicate dependent patterns of functioning.

**Obstacle-Mastery Behaviors.** People cope with stimuli that present obstacles in their lives by overcoming them, or mastering them. They act to solve problems and to complete the work that is to be done. Initiating actions is not enough. Follow-through must occur in terms of analyzing the problem, using logic and reason to reduce or change the stimuli causing the problem, and persevering to the end so that the problem is resolved, or the task accomplished.

Consider some obstacles that nursing students must overcome to become licensed nurses. They have to learn the skills and expectations of the new role, study difficult science courses, pass examinations that measure their understanding of diseases, master skills involved in patient care, use medical terminology, and administer medications. Each task must be approached head-on; actions must be taken to begin working on the task; and one must persevere until the task is completed successfully. Some nursing students may need to study harder than others, seek clarification from the instructor, rewrite lecture notes, and outline readings to overcome obstacles that may prevent them from achieving their goal of becoming a nurse.

Obstacle-mastery behaviors of June S., who is coping with changes that diabetes has caused in her life, include

### Adaptive Behaviors

Refers to diet instructions and exchange
lists when preparing meals
Draws up accurate dose of insulin in
syringe
Injects insulin properly and rotates the
site
Tests her urine for glucose 4 times a day,
using urine sticks

### Maladaptive Behaviors

Ignores diet restrictions when dining out with
husband once or twice a week
Refuses to learn how to give her own injections;
insists that her husband do it
Snacks on candy and chips during the day while
watching television
Does not recognize difference between symptoms
of hypoglycemia and hyperglycemia

## DEVELOPMENT OF INTERDEPENDENCE

Interdependence is more characteristic of adulthood than childhood and represents a comfortable balance between the dependence needs of nurturing and affection and the independent needs of being self-sufficient. The childhood stages of life are dedicated to learning behaviors and skills that decrease the degree of one's physical, emotional, environmental, and social dependence upon others. The degree of independence that individuals achieve in each of these areas varies. One's goal is not to be totally independent of others but to live successfully in a social world by giving and receiving affection and support. The various steps in the development of dependent and independent tasks for each stage of life are shown in Table 20–1.

**Physical Independence.** The ability to care for one's own basic physical needs and to gain control of certain body functions leads to physical independence and freedom to engage in other activities. From birth, infants are able to meet several basic needs. They are able to breathe and obtain the oxygen that is essential for survival, move about, make primitive noises and sounds, respond to noxious stimuli by reflexive actions, and excrete waste products from the body. They must rely on others to provide all other needs, including food, fluids, sensory stimulation, safety, security, comfort, love, belonging, shelter, warmth, cleanliness, and care.

By the time children are at the school-age stage, they should be able to care for most of their physical needs. They show independence and increasing autonomy in feeding and bathing themselves, controlling bowel and bladder functions, brushing their teeth, and dressing without assist-

ance, although tying shoelaces may still be troublesome for some.

**Emotional Independence.** Autonomy of emotions emerges slowly from the engulfing self-centeredness of toddlers and preschool children as they learn to consider other people who are close to them. They soon see and recognize different emotional responses of the parents and seek ways to gain their approval. Approval is expressed by smiling, by warm and caring actions, and in other ways that provide pleasurable feelings. Disapproval is shown through harsh and scolding tones of the voice, by anger, and by actual physical restraint or punishment. Independence is achieved through the control of emotions; thus, the temper tantrums of the two-year-old child fade away as the school-aged child learns to verbalize feelings of anger and to control impulsive behavior through logic and reason. Teen-agers seek to resolve their conflict between striving to be independent as emerging adults and the familiar comfort of dependence on parents. This is made more difficult in the American culture, which places emphasis on college education as preparation for many occu-

**Table 20–1.** THE DEVELOPMENT OF INTERDEPENDENCE OVER THE LIFE SPAN, WITH SELECTED CHARACTERISTICS OF DEPENDENT AND INDEPENDENT BEHAVIOR FOR EACH STAGE OF LIFE

| Stage of Life | Significant Relationships | Development of Interdependence |
|---|---|---|
| Infancy | Mother | **Dependence:** Total reliance on care-giver for physical and emotional support. Reflexive actions, and primitive reactions to sight, sound, movement, and vocalization. Mistrust leads to anxiety.<br>**Independence:** Establishes trust in mother, and organizes sensory perceptions. Can see close objects; holds up head at 1 month; crawls at 5 months; sits up alone by 7 months; and reaches or grasps with hands. Many other independent behaviors by end of first year. |
| Toddler | Parents | **Dependence:** Physically and emotionally dependent upon parents. Has shame and embarrassment when unable to do what parents expect. Displays attention-seeking behavior, and by age 2 years tends to be stubborn and negative and have temper tantrums.<br>**Independence:** Gains autonomy through control of motor activity and control of bowel and bladder. Separates self from mother, and expands world from playpen to rooms in the house and the yard. Learns to walk, run, and climb, and experiments with activities in a trial and error fashion. Beginning to talk. |
| Preschool | Basic family | **Dependence:** Physically and emotionally dependent upon family. Develops feelings of guilt when violating parents' rules of right and wrong. Verbalizes anger and frustrations, and seeks affection from parents and others.<br>**Independence:** Learns to take initiative and decides to act or carry out tasks. Spends much time in |

**Table 20–1.** *Continued*

| Stage of Life | Significant Relationships | Development of Interdependence |
|---|---|---|
| | | play with other children by age 4 years, and is very competitive by age 5 years. Refines motor skills so can swerve, change directions, do two things at a time, catch a ball, dress self, and perform most of own personal care. Communicates more needs and thoughts as vocabulary increases from about 600 to 2000 words. Can handle classification of things, see relationships, and use numbers, but more in an intuitive way of thinking. Learning skills to prepare for school. |
| School-age | Family; peers; teacher | **Dependence:** Relies on family for emotional support, and seeks support from friends. If rebuffed or rejected, has feelings of inferiority. From ages 6 years to 9 or 10 years, tends to have poor manners, and is inconsistent in social skills.<br>**Independence:** Learns industrious skills of recognizing the task to be done, planning what to do, and carrying out the activity to completion to achieve the goal. Develops logical and concrete ways of thinking. Begins to see that adults make mistakes, and questions parental authority by ages 10 to 12 years. Shows loyalty to members of group or gang. |
| Adolescent | Family; in-groups; out-groups; peers | **Dependence:** The physical and hormonal changes in the body at puberty upset the stable self-concept of the previous stage and causes confusion in one's identity. Emotional instability leads to daydreaming and hostility. Many conflicts between parent and teen-ager who seeks acceptance and emotional support from peers. Much ambivalence about growing independence.<br>**Independence:** Achieves own identity and sexual identity. Group and peer pressures guide social behavior; accepts more responsibilities for own life, and adopts a moral code, usually resembling that of the parents. A time for experimenting with ideas and activities and learning social skills for adult living. Seeks friends of opposite sex, and begins dating. |
| Young Adult | Partners in friendship, marriage, work, cooperation or competition | **Dependence:** Inability to share one's self and feelings with another leads to isolation and loneliness. Retains close ties with family. Forms strong affectional bond with potential marriage partner or with friends, professional colleagues, or other relatives.<br>**Independence:** Ability to give love or be caring with others. Socially, economically, and emotionally independent of parents. Has self-direction. |
| Generative Adult | Spouse; family; coworkers; community | **Dependence:** Changes in family, menopause, and aging require reworking identity of self and of spouse, relationships with grown children, and with aging parents. Poor coping leads to depression or self-absorption and self-centeredness.<br>**Independence:** Expansion of the self continues to show mastery of the world, obtaining material gains, and approval of others until some point determined to be enough. Contributes to the well-being of others and carries out work of society. |
| Mature Adult | Family; "my kind"; mankind | **Dependence:** Avoids despair over increasing losses of strength, vigor, health, and loved ones, and accepts help. Looks to family for emotional support and help. Retirement from work; decreased income.<br>**Independence:** Maintains integrity as person. Compensates for losses through increased skill. Retains physical and economical security, and remains active to find purpose in life. |

pations and makes young people financially dependent upon their parents for a longer period of time. Teen-agers must resolve their ambivalent feelings about their parents. Teen-agers are emotionally independent when they are able to listen, reason, question, and treat parents with esteem and respect. Excessive emotional dependence leads to maladaptive behaviors, such as anxiety, conflict, rigidity, and self-defensiveness, and one finds it difficult to learn, think, solve problems, or give and receive affection, respect, and esteem.

The comfortable balance of interdependence is achieved when one can say, "I can stand alone, but I choose to share my feelings and myself with another." Interdependence is one of the most important developmental tasks, and it may be the most difficult to achieve. It is more important for one to be self-reliant than to be self-sufficient. The self-reliant person is able to give, receive, and share love; the capacity to love someone else is a basic part of emotional interdependence.

**Environmental Independence.** Everyone must learn ways to control the environment. Today, children become quite sophisticated at an early age. They learn to turn on lights, obtain food from the refrigerator, operate water faucets, select channels on the television, use a tape recorder, and play records. They ride bicycles, learn to cope with automobile traffic on busy streets, and learn how to travel from place to place by different means. They learn how to use money to obtain material objects that they need or want and get jobs so that they can earn money.

Modern technology provides greater control over nature and other environmental forces. Governmental agencies and groups of people join together to accomplish what one person might not be able to do alone to control the environment. In this way, dams are built to prevent flooding, canals are dug for irrigating purposes, buildings are air-conditioned, an air travel system is developed for covering great distances rapidly, and other systems are devised to insure stability of working places and on-the-job safety. The

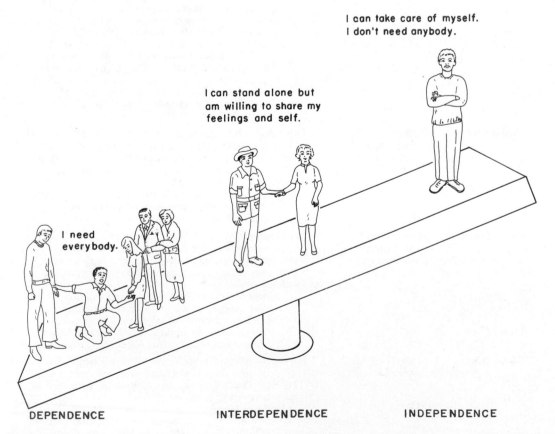

**Figure 20–3.**  Interdependence is the comfortable balance between depending on others and being self-sufficient to the degree of shutting others out.

more that people can do to regulate the environment and to reduce unpredictable occurrences, the more independent and successful they become.

**Social Independence.** Probably there is no such thing as social independence but rather the condition of social interdependence because people always have needs to be nurtured and supported. It is the form and the nature of the nurturing that changes as one grows and develops. The first step toward social independence occurs when the child is able to separate himself or herself from the mother and begins to develop a self-concept. In learning the skills of how to get along with others, preschool children identify with adults whom they admire and imitate their responses to different situations. During the school-age years, children learn social skills through their play and make-believe activities. They learn the expectations and requirements of roles that they will carry out in adulthood by playing house or school or by acting like Superman, a cowboy, a singing star, an athlete, or a space traveler.

Social independence is characterized by being able to function as a mature adult and successfully carrying out one's various roles in life. Other people provide expressions of approval and recognition that meet one's needs for affection and belonging. People who have difficulty carrying out their primary and secondary roles and who fail to meet the expectations of society face problems of disapproval, isolation, and low self-esteem.

## ASSESSMENT OF INTERDEPENDENCE

### *FIRST LEVEL ASSESSMENT*

Interdependence mode functioning is determined by assessing the way that the individual carries out the developmental tasks for his or her appropriate stage of life. The information gathered by the nurse concerning the way that the roles are performed gives evidence about the person's social integrity. The data are classified according to the dependent and independent coping patterns observed. (See the sample format in Application to Clinical Practice, at the end of this chapter.)

Coping patterns help to show where imbalances exist and the individual's needs and point to actual or potential problems in coping with relationships with other people and objects in one's life. When behaviors fall within the normal range, or within the expectations of the role, the person

is adapted and deals successfully with the social world.

Social interactions involve not only the patient or client but also the significant other and the interaction itself. The nurse includes these in the assessment and obtains sufficient information on which to base decisions. Particular attention is given to the family, significant others, and other support systems.

**The Family.** The family is the link between past generations and the future generation. Through its structure, the family accomplishes these tasks of society: (1) procreation and rearing of the next generation, (2) nurturing its members, and (3) providing learning for its members to function successfully in the social world. The family is a complex structure of interactions, each member striving to accomplish his or her own developmental tasks while also trying to meet family goals.

The magnitude of parental influence on the growth and development of their children cannot be overemphasized. Throughout much of the first years of life, children are physically, emotionally, and environmentally dependent upon their parents. Although the dominant features of one's personality are present by the age of 5 years, the task of learning to give love and support to others continues throughout one's life. During the childhood years, children learn to cope with problems, frustrations, and changes in life in much the same way that their parents cope. Their attitudes, values, and concepts of right and wrong are, in large part, a heritage of their parents. Socialization begins in the shelter of the family, and only after acquiring basic skills and control do children move outside the family into the neighborhood and the larger community to form ties with other people. Membership in the family also determines the race, ethnic origin, social class, and, generally, the religious beliefs of the child.

The nurse gathers information about the family from the patient or client, from other family members, and from personal observations of interactions among the individuals. The first level assessment should provide data that answer the following questions and concerns:

1. Who are the members of the family?
2. How are they carrying out their developmental tasks?
3. How are rules and decisions made in the family?
4. Who makes the decisions and enforces the rules?
5. Effectiveness of communications among family members.
6. Type of parent-child relationship.

Members of the nuclear family consist of parents and children living in the same household, whereas the extended family includes children living away from home and other persons related by marriage or kinship. Authority in the family may be exercised by the father or the mother, shared by the parents, or extended democratically to include the children in the decision-making process. Communications among family members are effective when the messages are clear, direct, congruent, relevant, and honest.

The type of parent-child relationship that exists indicates how the parent relates to the child and the type of discipline that is used. Kaluger (1974) describes the democratic home life as being based on parental involvement, warmth of feelings, tolerance, and flexibility that leads to the development of a child who is active, aggressive, playful, curious, and nonconforming. The controlled home life is characterized by authoritarian parents who tend to be strict, detached, intolerant, and cold in their relationship with their children. Children brought up in such homes are quiet, well-mannered, and non-aggressive but also may show intolerance to change, have blunted curiosity, and give way to impulsive acts. Parents with many children often have a controlled type of authority to maintain some degree of order.

**Significant Others**. Not all adults marry or have children; many people in our society live alone. During early adulthood, many young people move away from home and live far from their families or relatives. Others choose not to maintain a close relationship with their families. Some adults remain single and live contented lives without forming family units of their own. Others marry and are unable to have children or choose not to have any. Married people who lose their spouse through death or divorce must cope with changes in the family structure. When lacking close ties with family members, they form relationships with others who assume a significant place in their lives.

As social beings, we all need to have someone who cares about us and with whom we can share our thoughts, hopes, and fears. The role of the significant other is often filled by a friend, a roommate, a coworker, or the next-door neighbor when a loved one or family member is not available. For some people, a pet may serve as the significant other in their lives. As part of the assessment of the significant other as a support system, the nurse seeks information concerning the importance attached to the person by the client, whether or not the feelings of closeness are reciprocated by the other person, and the degree to which the significant other is available for interaction and support.

**Other Support Systems**. Social interactions among people also involve factors in the environment that contribute to their interdependence needs, and these factors are included in the nurse's assessment. Many of the secondary roles used to carry out developmental tasks are the result of people coping with factors such as culture, religious beliefs, social class, government, technology, and economic conditions. Social class is a complex social concept that is associated with the individual's educational background, type of occupation, and level of income. All these factors influence the values and beliefs of the social group, their lifestyle, the way that they perform their roles, and even the neighborhood where they live. Belonging to various interest groups provides the members with means of meeting their interdependence needs for affection, attention, and assistance, while providing a means for carrying out other goals of the group.

In addition to assessing the support systems used by individuals as they cope with the social world in their everyday lives, it is important to assess the support systems that are essential during illness. These support systems include an income that is adequate to cover the living expenses of the family or to maintain a home, health insurance or eligibility for state and federal programs that provide medical services, and the availability of help from others, when needed. Some communities have programs and organizations that provide services, such as homemaker services, Meals on Wheels, counselling centers, crisis intervention clinics, and rehabilitation clinics.

The first level assessment focuses on the client's behaviors that are used to carry out his or her developmental tasks and the presence of social factors that serve as support systems. The following case history illustrates how the assessment of the family, significant others, and support systems provides information about the ways in which an individual meets his or her interdependence needs.

Nettie M. is a 77-year-old black woman who is being treated for cancer of the colon with complications following her colostomy. She is dependent upon nurses for irrigating the colostomy, for changing dressings on an infected wound, and for controlling the pain in her back. The first level assessment revealed that she has been a widow for 22 years and that she has one married daughter and two grandchildren who are in school. The daughter stops by to see her mother each day on her way home from work or telephones her to find out how she is. Three close woman friends visit her each day. They help to maintain her house and lawn and have been her next-door neighbors for more than 40 years. The pastor of her church and other members of the congregation come to see her frequently. They sing favorite hymns in harmony and pray together for her recovery. The second level assessment shows that her family, cultural group, close neighbors, church membership, participation in church activities, home, and eligibility for Medicare benefits are all important support systems that help her to meet most of her interdependence needs in an adapted way.

## SECOND LEVEL ASSESSMENT

Various factors influence the expression of dependent and independent needs. The focal stimulus generally is the individual's internal need or drive for affiliation with others in ways to resolve dependency needs or to gain control over the environment and to achieve goals. People have certain expectations and desires that are brought to interactions with others, and the other participant has his or her own expectations and desires. When the expectations and desires are congruent, the responses provide mutual satisfaction for the participants. However, when the expectations, needs, or responses differ, the interaction leads to negative consequences for one or both parties because their needs for love, support, or achievement are not met. In interactions, responses that are defensive and ineffective in gaining desired goals lead to problems in coping with interdependence needs.

The following factors influence behavioral responses to interdependence needs. (Not all these stimuli need be involved at the same time when coping problems exist.)

1. *Presence of a care-giver.* Assess for the presence of family members and significant others.

2. *Support systems.* Include economic factors, such as occupation, health insurance, and interest groups in your assessment.

3. *Primary role of age and sex.* Indicates the maturation level and gives a measure of the criteria used to judge the observed behaviors. The style of dress chosen by a 5-year-old girl differs from that expected for an 18-year-old girl or a 75-year-old woman.

4. *Child-rearing practices of parents.* Dynamics of the home life are important in forming the child's coping patterns. Continued frustration creates high dependency, dominance by one parent leads to submissiveness because this is rewarded, whereas a permissive home allows the child to try new ideas and responses.

5. *Level of learning.* One's ability to reason and control internal drives and emotions is related in part to learning. A third grader's ability to use

language and abstract concepts differs from that of a high-school teacher.

6. *Availability of rewards or sanctions related to the behavior.* The child who whines, fusses, and procrastinates when told to go to bed is rewarded by the parent's attention, even though the parent does not approve of the behavior.

7. *Illness.* The presence of illness and restrictions imposed by medical treatment may limit the use of previous patterns of coping that were effective in meeting interdependence needs. The business person who manages and directs other employees finds it difficult to adjust to bed rest and to follow instructions of the doctor and nurse during an illness.

8. *Environmental factors.* Include available time, space, geographical location, and weather.

9. *Intrinsic factors.* Include the individual's values, feelings, ideas, or beliefs that influence the way one's needs are met.

## PROBLEMS OF INTERDEPENDENCE

Problems related to the interdependence mode result when the balance between dependence and independence is not maintained or is not appropriate to the specific stage of life. The maladaptive behaviors fall outside the normal range of behaviors that are socially acceptable for the roles that are undertaken or the developmental tasks to be accomplished. The coping problem is then expressed through dependent or independent behaviors that are excessive, too few, or too infrequent in occurrence or that are inappropriate or ineffective. At the present time, these problems are referred to as dysfunctional dependence and dysfunctional independence.

## DYSFUNCTIONAL DEPENDENCE

Coping problems of dysfunctional dependence use dependent behaviors to the detriment of one's well-being. Help-seeking, attention-seeking, and affection-seeking behaviors that interfere with movement toward maturity and being well are observed. The assessment reveals a conflict between the person's dependence needs and the demands for independence made by the health-illness situation. This conflict is frequently seen in the third stage of illness in patients who cry easily and complain bitterly of being weak or tired when asked by the nurse to take part of their bath or to sit in the chair. Their behavior is often found to be related to unmet dependence needs. The patient's problem might be defined as "Patient has dysfunctional dependence due to excessive help-seeking behaviors." This statement of the problem includes the internal drive, or focal stimulus, that is causing the problem.

Some coping mechanisms that people use to meet dependence needs are less effective or are inappropriate and may lead to behavior patterns such as the following:

1. *Overeating syndrome* — food has become a symbol of love and gratification that is substituted when dependence needs for attention, affection, or assistance are not met.

2. *Substance abuse* — use of drugs or alcohol to disguise or lessen the discomfort of unmet needs.

3. *Hypochondriasis* — individual reacts to natural bodily function or to mild physical discomforts with complaints and with the fussiness of a baby and expects to be cared for by others.

4. *Compliant personality* — basic need to feel safety by belonging; requires help, guidance, and continual approval from others; avoids any action that might lead to loss of support from others.

5. *Passive-aggressive personality* — anger and hostility; based on experiences of frustration in meeting dependence needs in infancy and early childhood.

6. *Narcissism* — one finds the external world so cold and hostile that one turns to oneself for gratification; he feels that one can depend only upon oneself.

7. *Loneliness* — an extremely unpleasant feeling resulting from the lack of a significant other and other intimate interpersonal contacts; loneliness can exist even though one is surrounded by people because it is traced to one's inability to enter into meaningful contact with others.

8. *Separation anxiety* — the condition that exists when a child lacks a warm, intimate, and continuous relationship with the mother, in which both find satisfaction and enjoyment; often seen in the sick and in the hospitalized child.

The separation anxiety experienced by infants and young children when deprived of their mother's or care-giver's presence causes mild to moderate disturbance of behavior. However, in prolonged or severe deprivation, such anxiety may lead to death. The child's behaviors are characteristic of three distinct stages: protest, despair, and denial. The behaviors range from vigorous crying when left by the mother, calling for her, and reacting negatively to other adults to showing regression, such as returning to the bottle or sucking the thumb. The child loses weight and may ignore the mother or respond passively when she visits. Such disturbed behavior may persist for days to several months after the child is reunited with the mother (Johnson, 1966).

## DYSFUNCTIONAL INDEPENDENCE

The aggressive drive is the motivation for independence. It is the force that stimulates individuals to make contact with their environment and to seek to gain control over it. The aggressive drive arouses some type of motor response ranging from speech to finely coordinated body movements. It motivates people to explore their surroundings, seek out new tasks and experiences, and derive satisfaction from being alone and apart from others at times. Dysfunctional independence occurs when individuals are not able to achieve these independence needs. Their behavioral responses to aggression interfere with their social adaptation.

The behaviors associated with the aggressive drive range from energetic, purposeful, and dynamic activities to the more violent and destructive displays of anger, frustration, kicking, hitting, or fighting. An important task of childhood is to learn how to control aggressive drives and to express them within the limits defined by society. Dysfunctional independence is seen in initiative-taking and obstacle-mastery behaviors that indicate undercontrol or overcontrol of aggression and that fall outside the socially acceptable range. Undercontrol is inadequate restraint; thus, the negative behaviors of anger, hostility, frustration, and rage are expressed. Lack of sufficient control of aggression in adults leads to social problems, such as child abuse, wife beating, and temper tantrums. Overcontrol of the aggressive drive can be seen in individuals who are reluctant to explore their environment, who tend to avoid displays of anger, even when provoked and appropriate, who become passive or inactive, and who withdraw from close contact with others. The perfectionist is an example of overcontrol of the aggressive drive. The individual attempts to gain control over all aspects of life.

During illness, people experience many situations in which they lack control over what is happening to them, which is a loss of their ability to meet independence needs. The lack of control poses a threat to their self-concept, causing feelings of anxiety. The nurse may have to consider both the illness and the lack of control in order to help the patient regain an adapted state. At times, the difference between the two problems is very fine and it may be difficult to distinguish which is the presenting problem. The following case history illustrates this point.

Millie P. is a 42-year-old woman who is hospitalized for treatment of an intestinal obstruction. She makes numerous complaints about the hospital and the care she receives and has frequent outbursts of anger. She is easily frustrated when trying to carry out her own activities of daily living, such as moving up in the bed. She is obese and becomes very upset when being positioned on the bedpan. She lashes out at the nurse, "Why can't you get it right the first time?" Other frequent complaints include, "The nursing care is lousy. No one ever answers my light. It's at least an hour before anyone comes"; "I'm so sick of this tube in my nose. One of these days I'm just going to rip it out"; and "I don't see why you have to starve me. I'm not vomiting anymore, and I want some food. Everyone else can eat, but you don't bring me anything." She pushes the nurse away, slaps at her hand, and turns her head away with a look of disgust.

In this example, the nurse treats the patient's behavior as a problem of dysfunctional independence by focusing on the interactions between Millie P. and other people. If the focus is on behaviors that involve the patient's inner thoughts, ideas, and feelings, the problem could be expressed as one related to the self-concept. Some nurses may feel more comfortable handling problems related to the interactions of interdependence, whereas others are more at ease dealing with problems related to feelings and the self-concept. Interventions for both modes are similar, utilizing insight therapy or behavior modification and the manipulation of the causative stimuli.

## NURSING INTERVENTIONS

The basic principle in planning interventions for problems in the interdependence mode is that the dependence needs must be met before the individual can move successfully into independent functioning. The deprivation of love and caring relationships or abandonment during infancy frequently leads to inadequate control of aggressive drives in later life and interferes with development of independence. When subsequent needs arise for attention, affection, or support and fulfillment is not forthcoming, the individual responds in a dysfunctional way that interferes with health care or social adaptation.

The plan of nursing care for problems of interdependence include interventions to provide for dependence needs, manipulation of the environmental stimuli, and the utilization of communication skills to alter the individual's internal drives or motivations. The individual's coping behaviors are changed by insight therapy or behavior modification.

## INSIGHT THERAPY

Insight therapy is described in Chapter Seven as a method used to reduce anxiety and to change behavior. It is also equally effective in dealing with other problems in coping with changes in the social world. It is an intervention used to explore the way that the individual perceives and mentally structures the situation. When using insight therapy, the nurse and the client follow these three steps: (1) recognize that the client is experiencing some unmet need for attention, affection, support, control of the environment or aggressive impulses, (2) examine the scope of the problem in terms of how the client perceives it and what is causing it, and (3) help the client to change either the stimuli that are causing the problem or his response to the stimuli.

## BEHAVIOR MODIFICATION

People teach other people how to act, and much of one's behavior is the result of parental approval of some behaviors and disapproval of others. Children soon learn which behaviors please the parents and repeat these and avoid those that are frowned upon; thus, the basis for behavior modification, which is discussed in greater detail in Chapter Six.

When using behavior modification as an intervention for problems of interdependence, the nurse identifies the behavior to be changed and counts the number of times it occurs. The basic principle of behavior modification is followed which states behavior that is reinforced will be repeated; behavior that is not reinforced tends to fade and not recur. Social reinforcers can be a smile, attention, recognition, or praise. The nurse then recognizes and reinforces the desired behavior when it does occur and does not reinforce undesired behaviors. Behavior modification is more successful when other members of the nursing team and the family are consistent in the use of reinforcers for the desired behavior.

## MANIPULATION OF THE ENVIRONMENT

Whenever possible, the nurse manipulates stimuli in the environment that cause or influence the client's problem in interdependence. Some environmental stimuli are easier to modify or change than others. The nurse can change the arrangement of furniture in a room, reduce the noise level in nursing units at night, and schedule tests or baths at a more convenient time. Family and friends can be involved in planning ways to meet the patient's interdependence needs for nurturing or achievement.

Other stimuli may be more difficult to manipulate, but the nurse helps the patient to find alternative methods of coping, to plan strategies for meeting needs, and to contact special programs or organizations that provide needed services. This category includes stimuli that limit one's access to resources and reduce one's chances of learning how to use aggressive energy and to channel it in constructive ways. Nurses who work in community health centers work with many people who are deprived or affected by social stimuli that are beyond the control of the individual. Factors that deprive people include poverty, inadequate materials or opportunities, social isolation, long periods of hospitalization or illness, and prison or other forms of institutional life. Other forms of environmental stimuli that influence behavior and present a challenge to the nurse in planning interventions include loss of a job, lack of money, severe weather conditions, and political or social actions that are beyond the individual's control.

## APPLICATION TO CLINICAL PRACTICE

As you provide nursing care for patients in the clinical setting or for clients in the community, continue to do a complete assessment of physiological and psychosocial functioning so that any problem areas can be identified early and potential problems may be averted.

Information about the interdependence mode is obtained in the same manner as the data for the self-concept mode. Briefly, the steps include identifying the individual's primary role and stage of life, listing the developmental tasks for that period of life, stating the roles that the person uses to carry out these tasks, and gathering information about the role performance. Process this information according to the coping patterns associated with dependence and independence needs. The following is a sample of this format.

**Primary role**_____    **Stage of life**_____
**Developmental tasks**                 **Roles**

_____            _____
_____            _____
_____            _____
_____            _____
_____            _____


**Dependent behaviors**                 **Independent behaviors**
Help-seeking_____         Initiative-taking_____

_____            _____
Attention-seeking_____     Obstacle-mastery_____

_____            _____
Affection-seeking_____

_____

# REFERENCES

Burgess, Ann Wolbert: Psychiatric Nursing in the Hospital and the Community, 3rd ed. Englewood Cliffs, Prentice-Hall, Inc., 1981.

Diebert, Alvin, and Harmon, Alice: New Tools for Changing Behavior. Champaign, Illinois, Research Press, 1973.

Dennis, Lorraine B.: Psychology of Human Behavior for Nurses, 3rd ed. Philadelphia, W. B. Saunders Company, 1967.

Ellison, Edythe: Problem of interdependence: aggression. *In* Roy, Sister Callista (ed.): Introduction to Nursing: An Adaptation Model. Englewood Cliffs, NJ, Prentice-Hall, Inc., 1976, pp. 330–341.

Erikson, E. H.: Childhood and Society, 2nd ed. New York, W. W. Norton and Co., Inc., 1963.

Johnson, Dorothy: The meaning of maternal deprivation and separation anxiety for nursing practice. *In* Bullough and Bullough (eds.): Issues in Nursing. New York, Springer Publishing Co., Inc., 1966, p. 249.

Johnson, Linda: Sharon wanted more than we could give. Nursing 81, *11*(4):96–99, (April) 1981.

Kaluger, George, and Kaluger, Meriem: Human Development: The Span of Life. St. Louis, The C. V. Mosby Co., 1974.

Kastenbaum, Robert: Humans Developing: A Lifespan Perspective. Boston, Allyn and Bacon, Inc., 1979.

Patterson, George: Families: Application of Social Learning to Family Life. Champaign, Illinois, Research Press, 1971.

Poush, Mary: Interdependence mode. Unpublished notes. Los Angeles, Mount St. Mary's College, Revised January 1981.

Robbins, Margaret, and Schacht, Thomas: Family hierarchies. Am J Nurs, *82*:284–286, (February) 1982.

Roberts, Sharon L.: Behavioral Concepts and the Critically Ill Patient. Englewood Cliffs, Prentice-Hall, Inc., 1976.

Sternback, Richard: Principles of Psychophysiology. New York, Academic Press, Inc., 1966.

# COMMON INFLUENCING FACTORS FOR COPING PROBLEMS

What are the influencing factors that affect behavior? Many focal and contextual stimuli have been mentioned that influence patients' responses and that have an effect on the problems in coping with changes in patients' lives. Although each problem generally has one focal stimulus, many other factors impose an effect on either the way that the problem is perceived or the responses to it that make it unique to the person experiencing it. Although it is easy to see the relationship between contextual stimuli such as the type of diet and the problem of inadequate nutrition or bed rest or traction for problems of immobility, the relationships of other common influencing factors may be less apparent, such as the effects of aging, the role of cultural values and beliefs, and poverty as well as various types of crisis events that occur throughout life.

Age is one of the most significant influencing factors to be considered by the nurse in planning nursing care. In Chapter Twenty-one, the normal changes produced by the aging process are described, and these provide the standard for comparing behaviors observed in elderly persons. Gerontology is a relatively new field of study, with little research having been done before 1950. Only in this century have increases in the standard of living and advances in medical science greatly increased one's life span. Now, millions of people can expect to live into their seventies and eighties. Nurses need to know what changes are normal as people age and which changes are due to disease processes or to a breakdown in coping.

People learn to respond to situations in life in ways that are consistent with their cultural values and beliefs. Although not every person in the culture holds exactly the same belief, certain general beliefs and attitudes bind the members together and give them an identity and a sense of belonging. These beliefs provide a measure of stability and predictability, enabling the nurse to anticipate certain behavioral responses to health or coping problems. Poverty is a condition of life that exerts a tremendous influence on values, beliefs, and behavior. Poverty narrows one's choices in life, limiting one's alternatives and opportunities. People's values and beliefs about life and the world must be revised according to the realities imposed upon them by poverty. Poverty is a potent contextual stimulus that influences the way that poor people utilize health services and their health practices and must be considered by the nurse when planning health-teaching and other nursing interventions.

Almost any event in life is capable of producing a crisis, from developmental changes in the various stages of life to the external situations involving other people or the physical environment. Crisis results from a highly emotional upheaval in which one is unable to cope and resolve the problem without help and feels cast aside with nothing to hold on to for support. Loss is generally the basis for a crisis problem in coping. In Chapter Twenty-four, several types of losses, such as those involving pregnancy, illness, sexual abuse, and suicide, are presented, as well as the stresses associated with nursing that may cause a coping crisis.

# Adaptation in Old Age

**OBJECTIVES**   Information in this chapter will help you to

1. Define terms related to the aging process.
2. Discuss the increase in the aged population of American society and characteristics of this group.
3. Explain the various theories that are being advanced to explain the aging process.
4. State the normal physiological changes in aging that have few or mild consequences for the health of the older adult.
5. Discuss time-related pathophysiological changes that have more severe consequences for health and their implications for nursing care.
6. Explain psychological changes and common personality characteristics of the aged population.
7. Discuss cultural and social changes that the aged adult must adapt to in terms of
   a. changes in family structure
   b. changes in economic status
   c. retirement
   d. housing and transportation

## DEFINITION OF TERMS

**aging** – regular behavioral changes that occur in mature adults as they advance in chronological age.

**cohort** – any group or company.

**geriatrics** the study of diseases of the aged.

**gerontology** – the science of aging.

**old age** – arbitrarily designated, for economic reasons, as beginning at age 65 years, though some authorities believe it should be based on life cycle standards instead of chronological age.

**presbycusis** – loss of hearing caused by the aging process.

**presbyopia** – visual impairment consisting of hyperopia and loss of accommodation caused by the aging process.

**senescence** – the process of growing old.

**senility** – physical and mental deterioration in aged people with abnormal loss of physical, mental, or emotional control.

Growing old is a universal trait that begins with birth. Today, an increasing number of people are living many years longer than previously. Society's major concern is that the years of longer life should be satisfying and meaningful, not simply the extension of life processes. Often, younger people have a stereotypical view of old age as the time of life when older people become "senile" and revert to an earlier time, known as "second childhood." They see the elderly as ill, obsolete, depressed, dissatisfied and unhappy with their lives, unable to take care of their own business, and even dependent upon others for their daily needs and care. This description does indeed pose a grim picture of old age, leading one to view it as a time of life to be avoided or approached with a sense of dread.

Fortunately, this view of old age does not apply to the majority of people in this stage of life. Healthy, middle-aged adults move into old age over a period of time, which allows for adjustments that compensate for losses to be made along the way. In spite of losses, the elderly continue to have a sense of optimism, adapt to environmental changes, and derive satisfaction from life. With aging, people experience problems, and one of the most difficult is contending with the rigid and unsympathetic attitudes of younger people about aging.

People over the age of 65 years are in the most rapidly growing segment of the population in the United States, and this segment will continue to expand well into the twenty-first century. This growth is a rapid and dramatic change in our society that makes it necessary to reorder fundamental priorities and services. The health and social needs of a country with an increasingly

large number of aged citizens are vastly different from those of a country with a population whose median age is 20 years. In this chapter, the "graying of America" is examined in terms of the increasing size of the group over age 65 years and its outstanding characteristics. Various theories of aging are presented to illustrate the variety of approaches being used to explain the complex adaptation to physical, psychological, and social changes encountered in advanced maturity. The changes that universally accompany aging but that pose no serious threat to health are described, as well as the time-related pathophysiological changes that with stress or illness cause more serious consequences. Methods the individual may use for adjustment and nursing interventions are suggested.

Not only does aging affect the physical functioning of the body but, in time, it alters brain functions. The accumulation of developmental stresses and maladaptive coping responses in the earlier stages of life poses a higher risk for adapting well in later life. Many support systems used earlier in life are no longer available to the elderly; thus, one's self-esteem is more easily damaged and emotional distress is increased. Although the aged are not a homogeneous group, certain emotional characteristics and changes in psychological functioning are common. These characteristics and changes as well as brain failure are discussed in this chapter, and nursing interventions are indicated.

Aging represents a continuous interaction with the social environment as people change and modify their behaviors along the course of life. They adapt to lost or changing roles and to other changes that influence the way they live. In this chapter, some of these changes are examined, including the structure of the family, the economic status of the elderly, retirement, and housing and transportation.

## WHY STUDY THE AGED AND AGING?

The assessment of adaptation requires that nurses assess the behaviors of the client or patient and make judgments about those behaviors that constitute a problem and should be changed. To avoid making rash and arbitrary decisions, nurses are guided by the norms, or standards, for primary role performance. Although aged people have been a part of every society since ancient times, until now they have been relatively few in number, and little has been known about their role norms or expectations. Only since the middle of this century have studies been made of this group.

It is important that nurses learn more about the aging process, especially in the last stage of life. The majority of nurses have limited firsthand knowledge of who the elderly are and how they live. Most nurses are in the young adult or generative stage of life and have had no personal experience with the problems with which the elderly must cope. In contrast, all nurses can relate to the growth and development that occurs in the childhood years because they, too, have lived through those years and experiences. Old age is still in the future and known only through anticipation. Nurses' understanding of the aged person tends to be narrow and limited when their only contact with older people is an infrequent visit with grandparents, fleeting encounters at social gatherings, or caring for the elderly sick person. It is hoped that further study of aging will increase nurses' knowledge and understanding of the needs of this rapidly expanding segment of the population.

Knowledge of aging expands the nurse's assessment skills. For the first level assessment, the nurse needs to know whether the observed behavior in one individual is representative of how aging affects all people or whether it is a sign of disease. Many older people either love to eat sugar or sweets or completely lose their craving for them because of the progressive loss of sweet taste buds in aging. On the other hand, impaired mental function and gross memory deficits are more pronounced in people who have hypertension than in those with normal blood pressure (Wilkie and Eisdorfer, 1971).

Age is an extremely important factor in the second level assessment because it influences behavioral responses and indicates the appropriate stage of life and its associated develop-

mental tasks. With a knowledge of aging changes and characteristics, the nurse is able to compare the assessed information with the norm for that group. Without this knowledge, it may be difficult to know what information to gather, or the nurse may compare it with standards for the wrong age group. For example, Mr. W. is 77 years old and is being followed in the clinic for treatment of a cardiovascular disease. Information about the population over the age of 65 years provides the nurse with this basic data: most elderly men are married and live with their wives; since 1970, less than 10 per cent of the elderly are foreign-born; and by 1970, about 44 per cent of the people over 65 years had completed a high school education. Although Social Security is a primary source of income, many people have other economic resources, including pensions from their place of employment. All these factors may serve as contextual stimuli for problems that Mr. W. may encounter in understanding his health problems and in complying with treatment.

## GROWTH OF THE AGED POPULATION

Older people in any society should be viewed as survivors. They have outlived the weak and sickly, avoided fatal accidents and disasters, and have handled personal and environmental stresses in an adequate way. Because of a variety of reasons, more and more people in the United States are living longer, and their numbers have increased dramatically in the twentieth century.

The elderly people in our society are a heterogeneous group. They have had a wide variety of life experiences, developed different personalities, and formed their own patterns of coping with problems encountered in life. Even among those of the same chronological age, great differences can be seen. Some people at the advanced ages of 80 and 90 years seem much younger than their age implies. They have smooth skin, bright eyes, and a zest for living. Others at much younger chronological ages may increasingly exhibit signs of senility.

Approximately 4000 persons reach the age of 65 years each day and join the segment of the population designated as the elderly. Each group, or cohort, moving into the final stage of life differs from preceding groups. The size and composition of groups change as new groups enter and replace those who have died. According to Uhlenberg (1977), "This process allows for quite rapid change in the character of the older population, because over a decade there is about a 60 per cent change in the individuals who comprise the population aged 65 and over." He

**Table 21–1.** THE POPULATION OF THE UNITED STATES AND THE MEDIAN AGE FROM 1790 to 1979

| Year | U.S. Population (in 1000s) | Median Age |
|------|---------------------------|------------|
| 1790 | 3,929 | not available |
| 1800 | 5,308 | 16* |
| 1850 | 23,192 | 18.9 |
| 1900 | 75,994 | 22.9 |
| 1950 | 150,697 | 30.2 |
| 1975 | 213,051 | 28.8 |
| 1979 | 220,099 | 30.0 |

*White only

Sources: Statistical Abstract of the United States, 1980, 101st ed. No. 31. Washington, D.C., Bureau of the Census, 1980; *and* Historical Statistics, Colonial Times to 1970. Series B, 76–91, p. 24, Washington, D.C., Bureau of the Census, 1975.

points out that each cohort begins at a different time and experiences different historical conditions or events.

## SIZE OF THE AGED GROUP

Until the middle of the twentieth century, the United States had been a nation of young people. Immense growth in the population resulted from the flow of young immigrants from Europe and from high birth rates, which led to large families. Families with 8, 10, or even 12 children were not uncommon. People who were willing to travel to the United States to make a new life for themselves tended to be younger adults, not the older generations. The first census in 1790 enumerated about 4 million people, and the population grew by leaps and bounds, resulting in 76 million people by 1900. Since that time, the rate of growth has slowed as the birth rate has fallen and immigration has been limited by quotas that have been imposed on those seeking to enter the country. However, Table 21–1 shows that the United States population doubled in less than 50 years; thus, more than 150 million people lived in this country by 1950. By 1979, the population reached more than 220 million people.

Growth alone in the size of the population is not evidence of an increase in the size of the aged population. However, national statistics indicate that people over the age of 65 years are increasing at an unprecedented rate. The median age of the United States population has been rising since the first records in 1800 showed half the population to be under the age of 16 years until the present time, when the average age is 30 years. Table 21–2 shows that the group of people over the age of 65 years numbered no more than 3 million people in 1900, or just 4 per cent of the total population. By 1979, this group accounted for 11.2 per cent of the population and numbered more than 24.7 million people. By the year 2000, it is projected that there will be more than 31 million people, or about 12.2 per cent of the total population, in this age group.

Among the aged group, the fastest growing segment includes people who are older than 80 years. In 1960, 2.5 million people were over age 80 years, and less than 20 years later, there were 5.1 million people in that age group. By the year 2000, about 8 million people will be 80 years old or older. That figure represents a 300 per cent increase in 100 years. The health and social needs of this group of citizens will become increasingly important as its size increases.

**Table 21–2.** POPULATION 65 YEARS OLD AND OVER FROM 1900 to 1979, AND PROJECTIONS TO THE YEAR 2000

| | Population (in millions) | | | | | | | |
|---|---|---|---|---|---|---|---|---|
| | 1900 | 1960 | 1970 | 1975 | 1979 | 1985* | 1990* | 2000* |
| U.S. population | 76 | 178 | 203 | 213 | 220 | 233 | 244 | 260 |
| 65 years and over | 3 | 16.7 | 20.1 | 22.4 | 24.7 | 27.3 | 29.8 | 31.8 |
| 65–69 years | not available | 6.3 | 7.0 | 8.1 | 8.7 | 9.2 | 10.0 | 9.2 |
| 70–74 years | not available | 4.8 | 5.5 | 5.8 | 6.6 | 7.3 | 7.8 | 8.2 |
| 75–79 years | not available | 3.1 | 3.9 | 4.0 | 4.3 | 5.1 | 5.5 | 6.4 |
| 80–84 years | not available | 1.6 | 2.3 | 2.7 | 2.8 | 3.1 | 3.6 | 4.2 |
| 85 years and over | not available | 0.9 | 1.4 | 1.9 | 2.3 | 2.6 | 2.9 | 3.8 |
| Percentage 65 years and over | 4 | 9.2 | 9.8 | 10.5 | 11.2 | 11.7 | 12.2 | 12.2 |

*Projected numbers in this table are the same for Series I, II, and III; projected percentages of total population are for Series II. Base year for projections is 1976.

Source. Statistical Abstract of the United States 1980, 101st ed. Nos. 31 and 542. Washington, D.C., Bureau of the Census, 1980.

## AVERAGE LIFE EXPECTANCY

In any population, as more people reach old age, a longer life expectancy is anticipated for every child from birth. With each successive birthday, one can expect to live beyond the average life span. For example, if one's life expectancy at birth is 70 years, by age 30 years it would be 43 more years, and by age 70 years, one could look forward to approximately 11 more years. Table 21–3 shows that in the United States, life expectancy has increased from an average of 39 years in 1850 to 73.3 years in 1978.

Differences exist between the sexes; since the turn of the century, men have a somewhat shorter life span than do women. Although the life expectancy for men has increased slowly during the past decades, the life expectancy for women has increased more rapidly, and the difference between the sexes has widened. Women now tend to live approximately 8 years longer than men.

Although the United States enjoys one of the highest standards of living in the world, its people do not have the longest life span. Table 21–4 shows that people who live in 10 other nations of the world have a longer average life expectancy, led by those living in Iceland and Norway. In 1972, Canadians had a life expectancy of 72.85 years, whereas the life expectancy of people in the United States was 72.6 in 1975. Many nations of the Third World have a very low life expectancy (see Table 21–4). On the whole, these tend to be poorer nations that are less

**Table 21–3.  LIFE EXPECTANCY BY GENDER FOR SELECTED YEARS FROM 1850 TO 1978**

| Year | Life Expectancy at Birth | |
|------|-----|-------|
| | Men | Women |
| 1850 | 38* | 40* |
| 1900 | 48 | 51 |
| 1920 | 53.6 | 54.6 |
| 1940 | 60.8 | 65.2 |
| 1960 | 66.6 | 73.1 |
| 1978 | 69.5 | 77.2 |

*In Massachusetts
Sources: Statistical Abstract of the United States 1980, 101st ed. No. 106. Washington, D.C., Bureau of the Census, 1980; *and* Historical Statistics, Colonial Times to 1970. Series B, 76–91, p. 24, Washington, D.C., Bureau of the Census, 1975.

**Table 21–4.  LIFE EXPECTANCY FOR VARIOUS COUNTRIES IN THE WORLD ACCORDING TO GENDER, AND PERCENTAGE OF THE POPULATION OVER THE AGE OF 65 YEARS**

| Country | Life Expectancy at Birth (in yr) | | | Year | Per Cent over Age 65 yr |
|---------|---------|------|--------|------|------|
| | Average | Male | Female | | |
| Iceland | 76.1 | 73.0 | 79.2 | 1976 | 12.6 |
| Norway | 74.98 | 71.85 | 78.12 | 1976 | 18.8 |
| Sweden | 74.87 | 72.1 | 77.65 | 1976 | 20.5 |
| Japan | 74.75 | 72.15 | 77.35 | 1972 | 16.1 |
| Netherlands | 74.2 | 71.2 | 77.2 | 1975 | 14.7 |
| Denmark | 73.95 | 71.1 | 76.8 | 1977 | 18.1 |
| Switzerland | 73.25 | 70.29 | 76.22 | 1976 | 17.1 |
| France | 72.9 | 69.0 | 76.9 | 1974 | 18.7 |
| Canada | 72.85 | 69.34 | 76.36 | 1972 | not available |
| Great Britain | 72.72 | 69.62 | 75.82 | 1976 | 19.3 |
| United States | 72.6 | 68.7 | 76.5 | 1975 | 10.5 |
| Israel | 72.1 | 70.3 | 73.9 | 1976 | 11.4 |
| Italy | 71.92 | 68.97 | 74.88 | 1972 | 16.1 |
| Finland | 71.65 | 67.38 | 75.93 | 1975 | 14.7 |
| West Germany | 71.6 | 68.3 | 74.8 | 1976 | 19.7 |
| Nations with low life expectancy | | | | | |
| Chad | 32 | 29 | 35 | 1964 | 4.0 |
| Bangladesh | 35.8 | 35.8 | 35.8 | 1975 | not available |
| Angola | 38.55 | 37 | 40.1 | 1975 | not available |
| Niger | 38.55 | 37 | 40.1 | 1975 | 4.7 |
| Afghanistan | 40.3 | 39.9 | 40.7 | 1975 | not available |
| Guinea | 40.9 | 39.4 | 42 | 1975 | 9.3 |
| India | 41.22 | 41.89 | 40.55 | 1960 | 5.3 |
| Ghana | 43.5 | 41.9 | 45.1 | 1975 | 10 |
| Saudi Arabia | 45.35 | 44.2 | 46.5 | 1975 | not available |
| Bolivia | 46.5 | 45.1 | 47.9 | 1975 | 5.4 |

Source: The World Almanac and Book of Facts, 1980. New York, Newspaper Enterprise Association, Inc., 1980.

industrialized or modernized and that have high birthrates. Because so many people die at younger ages, the number of aged is small. Chad and Niger are among the African nations with very short life expectancies, due in part to severe famines and high infant mortality rates.

## COMPOSITION OF THE AGED GROUP

Other differences among members of a group, or cohort, entering the aged segment include the ratio of men to women and ethnic origin. Women outnumber men because they live an average of 8 years longer than do men. This results in 3 women for every 2 men over the age of 65 years. The increase in the number of women over the age of 80 years has been even more marked. In less than 20 years, the number has more than doubled, while the number of men over the age of 80 years has increased by more than two thirds. The following figures show the increases.

| Year | Men (aged 80 yr and over) | Women (aged 80 yr and over) |
|---|---|---|
| 1960 | 1,059,972 | 1,455,872 |
| 1979 | 1,712,096 | 3,392,730 |
| % of change | 61% | 133% |

When race is considered, the ratio of men to women is 68 men to 100 women for whites, 71 men to 100 women for blacks, and 86 men to 100 women for Spanish-speaking groups. These figures should be used with caution because they do not indicate that black men and men with Spanish surnames live longer than white men—quite the contrary. Black people and people of Spanish-speaking origin have a lower life expectancy rate for both men and women and higher death rates for all ages. It may well be that in the survival of the fittest, the difference between the sexes has been reduced.

The black population of this country has grown from one million in 1800 to 25.8 million in 1979. The size of the black population is about the same as the size of the elderly population: 11.8 per cent black, 11.2 per cent elderly. The number of blacks in the elderly group is slowly increasing. The life expectancy for both black men and women has averaged about 10 years less than for whites; however, in recent years, the gap has been closing. By 1978, black men lived an average of 65 years, and black women lived about 73.6 years.

## OTHER SOCIAL CHARACTERISTICS OF THE AGED GROUP

Several other characteristics often attributed to the aged are not really signs of aging but are social and cultural factors of the specific group moving into old age. In addition to race and the ratio of men to women, factors that reflect changes in the society are whether one is native or foreign-born and lives in a rural or an urban area and one's level of education.

**Native or Foreign-Born.** The New World has been populated largely by immigrants and their descendants. The largest flow of immigrants entering the United States occurred during the latter part of the 1800s and the early 1900s. Since World War I, the sharp decline in immigration has been due to restricted quotas that currently allow the entry of approximately 400,000 persons annually.

People who immigrated to this country were usually young people, and often they had no skills with which to make their way in the new land. They arrived with little or no money and, with difficulty, found a place in the economy. Their problems of mastering a new language and adjusting to a new culture were magnified. Those who tended to cling to the familiar ways of the "old country" encountered greater problems in coping with changes when they moved into old age because they were less familiar with the entire pattern of the new social system. Prior to 1950, more than one fourth to one third of the aged segment of the population were foreign-born, but, since that time, the percentage has been declining. From now through the end of the century, the number of foreign-born aged citizens will average between 5 and 8 per cent.

**Urbanization.** Modern nations are characterized by industrialization and the growth of cities as more people settle in urban areas to work in the plants and businesses located there. The United States has changed from a rural society with about 50 per cent of the population living on farms in 1900 to an urban society with less than 5 per cent of the population now living on farms. For the aged, urban life requires more social adjustments than are needed in rural areas. More stress is encountered when living in contact with large numbers of people and confronting the problems of traffic, pollution, and crime that plague city dwellers. Favorable results of urbanization include the high standards of living, the high levels of sanitation and public health, and the availability of governmental programs and voluntary organizations to provide services.

**Level of Education.** In the past, the aged as a group have always been disadvantaged because their children and the younger population had more education than they did. Less education also means fewer opportunities in a highly technical society and a lower economic status. The aged with less education have less power and less prestige. However, major changes are taking place in the educational status of people who are entering old age. In 1970, less than 3 per cent of the people over 65 years were illiterate (unable to read or write in any language); by the year 2000, more than 70 per cent of the people over 65 years will have a high school education. The aged who have less education are more apt to be among the foreign-born or the poor, or to be black or another minority. The increased educational level of the aged more closely parallels that of other adults and may be the basis for improved social position for the aged in the future.

## CAUSES FOR INCREASED LONGEVITY

The increase in the life span and the number of people reaching old age may be attributed to the population explosion. The magnitude of the increase in the population is due to one or more of these circumstances: an increase in the birthrate, increased in-migration, or a decrease in the death rate. The world population has grown very rapidly in the past 300 years, even though the birthrate has remained fairly stable. North and South America gained people through massive in-migration during this time, but the tremendous surge in population of all countries is due primarily to a decline in the death rate.

Although one is tempted to consider the declining death rates as the result of medical advances and technology, Marshall (1972) points out that the population explosion began in Europe in about 1650 and until 1930 was seen primarily among the Caucasian nations of Europe, North America, and Latin America. More than half the growth took place before 1800, long before the advent of improvement in sanitation and public health, medical cures for infectious diseases, and the discovery of miracle drugs, such as antibiotics. Insulin was first used to treat diabetes in 1928, and penicillin was introduced in 1944. The critical factor in this immense population growth seems to be improved nutrition of the people. With even a slight improvement in nutrition, people are healthier and are better able to resist disease, produce healthier babies, and raise their standard of living. Since 1930, better nutrition in the nations of Africa, Asia, and South

America where the average age is less than 20 years, has had a pronounced effect on the population which can double in one generation.

The death rate in the United States continues to fall slowly as medical care and treatment help to extend the lives of those who become ill. In 1960, the death rate was 954.7 per 100,000 persons, and in 1978, it was 883.4 per 100,000 persons; thus, in 1978, more than 71 of every 100,000 persons were living longer than in previous years.

## THEORIES OF AGING

Aging is generally viewed as an involuntary process that produces changes in the systems of the body because of the passage of time. The process occurs in all levels of the human experience: anatomical changes on the cellular and tissue level, biochemical changes that affect body functions, psychological aging in terms of changes in intellectual skills and memory, and behaviorally, in the ways that people cope with their changing world.

Little is actually known of what causes aging or what can be done to retard it. Researchers are seeking an explanation of aging that will (1) describe the changes that occur at all levels, (2) explain why these changes or events occur, (3) predict the results when certain conditions exist, and (4) in time, gain control of the aging process by retarding or eliminating the changes it causes. No comprehensive theory of aging exists at this time, although a number of theories have been proposed that investigate aging on one of the levels. Eventually, all, none, or a combination of these theories may provide the answers to questions about aging. A summary of some representative theories of aging follows.

## BIOLOGICAL THEORIES

Biological theories of aging focus on the molecule and the cell to explain the loss and decline seen in physiological functioning. The premise is that aging is an involuntary process and the result of wear and tear produced by time that leads to the accumulation of wastes in the cells.

Researchers now theorize that life is finite, based on evidence showing that human cells in tissue cultures have a life span of 50, plus or minus 10, passages. Wallace (1977) states that if all diseases could be cured, the best that we could hope for would be a life span where "everyone would drop dead at midnight of their ninetieth birthday." Extensions of the life span beyond that limit may be achieved by manipulating factors such as nutrition, immunological function, lowering the core temperature of the body two to four degrees and use of pharmaceutical products and by reinstituting the repressed functions of the genes. Such procedures might extend the life span to 150 to 200 years.

The following theories are representative of the directions being undertaken by biological research but do not include all the theories. Considerable overlapping exists among them.

1. *Genetic theory of mutation of chromosomes or DNA.*
   a. The change may be programmed by some force in the universe or may occur randomly.
   b. The DNA fails to replicate or to translate accurately or transcribes errors.
   c. Aging is intrinsic to every cell and is a degenerative and deteriorating process.
   d. Evidence is seen in the decrease in hormones, renal cells, gastric acidity, and many other cellular functions in aging.
   *Weakness of the theory:* A large number of cells and their functions remain intact in aging with little or no deficit in their functions.
2. *Autoimmunity theory.*
   a. Tissue in the body is changed by some unknown mechanism.
   b. The immune system attacks the changed tissue as being foreign to the body.
   c. Changes may be initiated by a virus, heredity, or other factors.
   *Weakness of the theory:* Not all human beings acquire autoantibodies as they age. Plants and invertebrates have no immune systems, yet they undergo the aging process.
3. *Free radical theory of autointoxication.*
   a. Free radicals are substances released by polyunsaturated fats.
   b. Changes are caused by an increase in the unstable free radicals in the body, and the cells are unable to get rid of the accumulated wastes.
   c. Changes include chromosome damage, accumulation of lipofuscin pigments within the cells, and alterations in the large molecules, such as those found in collagens.
   *Weakness of the theory:* Eighty years of study have failed to show a relationship between the accumulated lipofuscin pigments and the deleterious effects of aging.
4. *Virus theory.* (The most recent theory.)
   a. Linked to the transmission of a virus vertically from the molecular to the cellular tissue level and horizontally from person to person or from mother to child.
   b. The implicated virus is the RNA tumor virus, identified in 12 species and possibly present in man, that is capable of making proteins, including two antigens.
   c. The role of the RNA tumor virus is expressed in the fetus and depressed at birth.
   d. If the RNA tumor virus is activated by environmental stress, hormones, or another viral infection, it can cause the cell to make an oncogene (cancer transforming protein) or an age-producing protein.
   e. The RNA tumor virus is implicated in cancer, in certain autoimmune diseases, and in viral diseases such as amyotrophic lateral sclerosis.
   *Weakness of the theory:* Conclusions are based on animal research, and the presence of the virus in humans has not been verified but is thought to be probable.

## SOCIOLOGICAL THEORIES

The cultural values of the United States and other modern nations often stress the roles and skills related to youth and productivity to the detriment of the elderly. These values are not held by just the young people, but pervade all age groups, including the aged themselves. However, as people age, these are precisely the attributes and skills that are most readily lost. Older people are given less value by society and are more vulnerable to damage to their self-esteem as they become less productive. Although vulnerable, they are able to modify their activities and make adjustments to compensate for the lost skills; thus, not all the effects of aging are negative.

The social theories of aging center on how people adapt to their changing roles and circumstances. As in the biological theories, considerable overlapping exists in the social theories. The following theories are among those described by Hendricks and Hendricks (1979):

1. *Disengagement theory of Cummings and Henry.*
   a. First introduced in 1961, but now largely discredited. However, it was important in stimulating research in this area and in formulating other theories.
   b. Disengagement was seen as inevitable and as a universal process.
   c. Represents the mutual withdrawal between the aging person and others in his or her society.

d. A continuous shrinkage of interactional opportunities for the aged.

e. The process may be initiated by the person or by society, and societal needs take precedence if it is necessary to remove the older person to make way for younger people.

f. Re-engagement occurs only if the aging person develops new skills that are valued.

*Weakness of the theory:* Assumptions that the process was inevitable and universal were criticized in addition to the lack of consideration of personality factors and their effect on social interactions. The emphasis was on social equilibrium and pressures imposed on the elderly to withdraw from previously held roles.

2. *Developmental approach by Neugarten, Henry, and others.*

a. Personality is seen as continually evolving and adjusting to each successive stage of life.

b. The individual utilizes the coping strategies of earlier age periods, as well as current environmental factors.

c. In aging, there is more of a turning toward greater interiority.

d. The degree of interiority and the nature of the coping mechanisms determine the amount of disengagement or engagement during the later stages of life.

3. *Activity theory.*

a. In aging, people experience a reduction of their activity level that narrows their social realm and leads to a loss of the sense of who they are.

b. People compensate through restitution of activities that lead to keeping fit and having higher morale.

c. The following assumptions are made regarding the theory:

1. The greater the role loss, the less participation in activities.

2. High level of activity allows greater support for the roles the people claim.

3. The stability of role insures a stable self-concept.

4. The more positive the self-concept, the greater is the individual's satisfaction with life.

*Weakness of the theory:* The nature of the compensatory activities has not been explored because not all types provide nurturing to the self-concept but may constitute a meaningless busy type of work or activity. However, many studies have found a positive association among activity level, personal adjustment, and morale.

4. *Theory of a subculture of the aged.*

a. A subculture is formed when one category of people interact more among themselves than with people from other categories.

b. The members form a sense of identity with the group and adjust better to aging.

c. The new involvement gains more importance than previous role interactions and statuses.

d. Good health and physical mobility confer greater status among the aged, whereas education, occupation, or economic prestige is less influential.

*Weakness of the theory:* Not all aged people have a sense of group identity with other elderly people, although there is growing evidence of retirement communities, retirement policies that block avenues for the elderly to integrate with the larger society, increased participation in senior citizen centers and organizations and formation of a voting bloc that suggests the emergence of a subculture.

The social theories of disengagement, activity, and subculture have not proved to be predictive of how people adjust to old age, but they do have value in furthering the investigation of the process, according to Hendricks and Hendricks (1979). They also point to the emergence of the following theories of social gerontology that stress the interaction between role alternatives and individual adjustment.

5. *Theory of rebalancing exchange relationships.*

a. All parties in an interaction maximize the rewards and satisfactions to be gained while minimizing the costs of the interaction.

b. The shrinking social network of the aged is due to the fading influence they are able to exert over their environment.

c. The aged person is more often the recipient rather than the initiator of the social interaction and the formation of personal bonds.

d. Older people use compliance to gain acceptance and support from others.

6. *Theory of social breakdown.*

a. Assesses the interdependence of older people and their social world.

b. In aging, the increasing loss of roles, the ambiguous standards for behavior, and the loss of reference groups lead to susceptibility to psychological problems. The aged look to society for cues to follow.

c. The societal view of those seeking cues is that they are incompetent and obsolete. This view leads to negative labelling of the person.

d. The individual adopts negative views when unable to keep up with the skills, productivity, and activity levels formerly achieved.

e. The societal negative view is reinforced as the behavior resembles what it was labelled.

7. *Theory of age stratification.*

a. Society is arranged in a hierarchy of age, with the obligations and expectations assigned to its members as they move from one level to the next.

b. Social roles shape the individual, but the role parameters are formed by the environment and the forces impinging on the person.

c. Each stratum of age differs from the others.

d. The distribution and patterning of social roles are according to age strata and are only accessible to people within a certain time frame.

e. As people age, they adopt and abandon a sequence of roles.

## PSYCHOLOGICAL THEORIES

Many people who study social aging believe that no one theory explains successful patterns of aging. People have developed distinctive patterns of personality as they cope with the tasks of living, and these patterns tend to persist into old age. Developed during middle-age, these personality patterns are dynamic and always evolving and the coping patterns that were successful in the past are used again and again.

Researchers have sought to classify the types of personalities that represent different ways of coping with the changes of age. One analysis yielded five types of older men, described as mature, rocking-chair, or armored types, who were more successful in adjusting to the changes of aging, and the angry and self-hater types, who were less successful. Another group of researchers found four personality types for both men and women that they characterized as integrated, armored-defended, passive-dependent, and unintegrated in terms of life satisfaction. No psychological theory of aging has gained widespread acceptance at this time.

## PHYSIOLOGICAL CHANGES IN AGING

As people move into old age, they must work through and resolve the developmental tasks for that period of life. They have to cope with de-

creasing strength and stamina, as well as with other changes in the body. Some changes are the effects of normal aging that are observed in all older people, whereas other alterations involve pathophysiological changes that have a far more serious impact on health.

Normal signs of aging include the more benign occurrences of developing wrinkles, hair turning gray, and decrease in the fatty layer under the skin. The pathophysiological changes do not necessarily occur in everyone, but the incidence increases in proportion to advancing age, and the consequences are more serious. For example, cataracts may occur in any age group, but they are much more prevalent in each progressively older group. Decrease in renal and heart function in aging significantly reduces the reserves needed when ill or when under emotional stress. Normal and time-related pathophysiological changes are summarized in the following sections.

## NORMAL CHANGES

As people move into the aged group, an increasing number of changes occur in their bodily appearance, structure, and function. These changes do not occur uniformly at a specific age because individuals differ widely in the rate at which they age. Some people in their seventies continue to have smooth skin and natural color to their hair, whereas other people in their forties have wrinkles, lose increasing amounts of hair, or have gray hair. However, if people live long enough, they will exhibit the following changes, with few, if any, exceptions.

1. *Changes in the skin and subcutaneous tissue.* The skin becomes dry, inelastic, and lacks springiness as aging progresses. A decrease in the amount of collagen and elastic fibers occurs. Wrinkles develop as the tissues begin to sag. This is most prominent in the ear lobes — in some people, they dangle like pendants. The atrophy of subcutaneous tissue leads to a myriad of fine wrinkles, with the appearance of crinkled paper, around the eyes, mouth, and in the neck. The skin under the chin sags to form two or three layers of skin that resembles a dewlap.

The skin of the aged shows thinning of the epithelial and subcutaneous fatty layers as well as a decrease in sebaceous and sweat glands. As a result, the aged often feel cold, have difficulty controlling body temperature in adjusting to extremes of environmental temperatures, and, with the prominence of bony areas, are more susceptible to trauma from pressure. The loss of pigmentation causes the hair to turn gray, and, with fewer melanocytes, the skin loses its ruddy hue and becomes even whiter in Caucasians. There is loss of hair, causing hair to become quite sparse over the scalp, the extremities, and the axillary and pubic areas. However, women may experience a growth of hair on the face as hormone levels change with age.

The implications of these skin changes for nurses include protecting the skin from the trauma of pressure, oiling dry skin and avoiding too frequent contact with soap and water, controlling the temperature to avoid extremes, and providing extra clothing, blankets, or warmth as may be needed.

2. *Musculoskeletal changes.*

By the sixth decade of life, the muscles become smaller and stringier. They contain more connective tissue and fatty cells, whereas the bones become lighter in weight and show a loss of the calcified matrix. Both muscles and bones are less strong, so older people have decreased body strength and endurance. Approximately ½ inch of height is lost at about the ages of 50 to 55 years because of shrinkage of the invertebral discs of the spine. Among people over the age of 75 years, as much as 2 to 4 inches of height is lost as a result of bowing of the thoracic spine and changes caused by osteoporosis.

3. *Changes in organs and functions.*

Beginning in the third decade of life, the size of the various organs, such as the heart, liver, kidney, pancreas, and brain, begins to decrease. The shrinkage is most marked past the age of 50 years. Muscles, organs, and other lean tissues make up the functioning mass of the body, or the lean body mass. The size of these tissues is measured by isotope counting of potassium. The lean body mass has an appreciable amount of potassium, whereas fat cells do not.

The brain is estimated to undergo a cellular loss of 50 to 100 thousand cells per day from the age of the midtwenties. The cell loss leads to a gradual decrease in the total weight (because brain cells do not regenerate), flattening of the gyri and the sulci structures, and increase in the space occupied by the ventricles. Even with this degree of neuron loss, the brain still contains billions of functioning cells, many of which have no known function but may be available for use, if needed. Changes in functions of the brain are described in the section that describes psychological changes.

The functions of the heart and lungs remain sufficient for normal activities but show a decrease with the added stress of activity or disease. The kidneys show the following declines in people from age 20 to 90 years: the blood flow through the kidney diminishes by 53 per cent, and the filtration rate decreases by 47 per cent.

The organs of the digestive system age better than those in some other systems. The amount of hydrochloric acid produced decreases, but other enzymes provide back-up assistance in the digestion of proteins. However, appetite may be decreased, and the tone of the large intestine may be diminished.

4. *Neurological changes.*

In the nervous system aging produces several significant changes. A slowing of the transmission of the impulse occurs, especially at the synapses; thus, it takes longer to respond to incoming stimuli. The nerve tissue requires a longer refractory time all along the central nervous system, so that fewer messages are transmitted. As a result of these alterations, older people have decreased perceptions of physical pain. They may suffer severe burns from hot objects, such as a hot water bottle, before feeling any discomfort. They can have actual tissue damage from wearing tight shoes or from an ill-fitting brace causing pressure before they are aware of anything wrong. The pain, cold, and heat stimuli must be more intense for older people to feel them. They are less able to discriminate between temperatures in the middle ranges and often complain of being cold, even in balmy summer weather with temperatures in the 80° range.

5. *Changes in sensory organs and perception.*

Several changes in the structures of the eyes are characteristically found among the older population; however, these changes vary in the time of their onset. Older people who wear glasses also are troubled by dryness of the eyes due to a decrease in the production of tears, and the eyes lack their usual luster. White deposits of fatty material around the cornea form a whitish arc or circle called arcus senilis. This is often seen among the aged and generally has no effect on vision. Other structural changes involve the sagging of eyelids and pupils that become smaller and irregular in size.

The sense of smell becomes less acute with age, and the decrease is most pronounced after the age of 70 years. Older people may not be able to detect the smell of burning food or smoke from a fire in the same building. They are also not as likely to detect bad breath or body odors they may have. Some older women use perfume and colognes too liberally because a stronger stimulus is required to activate the olfactory cells that also adapt rapidly to the scent; thus, they no longer smell it, although others still would.

The sense of taste is altered in aging and begins to degenerate after the age of 45 years. One has less sensitivity to sweet and salty tastes, although the taste buds responsible for sour and bitter tastes continue to function well. The sweet taste buds are the most numerous and are located on the anterior surfaces of the tongue, the sour taste buds are on the lateral edges of the tongue, the bitter taste buds are at the back of the tongue where they serve to protect one from swallowing noxious or poisonous plants, and the salt taste buds are present all over the tongue. With the actual loss of the number of sweet taste buds, it is not uncommon for some older people to put three, four, or five spoons of sugar in their coffee to make it taste as sweet as they remember it to be. They crave and eat more candy or sweet desserts than usual in the attempt to regain the sweet taste.

Changes in proprioception occur, with a gradual decline in the sense of balance. Aging produces changes in the vestibular apparatus of the ear, conduction of motor impulses is slowed, and, when looking upward, the neck is hyperextended with a decrease in the blood flow through the vessels, reducing circulation to the brain. As a result, when older people lose their balance and begin to fall, they continue to fall rather than being able to recover their balance. They also become insecure when situations demand a rapid change of position or adjustment, such as is needed to avoid a swinging door or when approaching a steep decline.

6. *Dental changes.*

Loss of teeth is associated with aging. This is often due to the reabsorption of bone around the teeth, leading to recession of gums and gum disease. The remaining teeth appear to be longer as the supporting tissues shrink back. This bony reabsorption leads to a shorter distance from the nose to the lower mandible and an inward pulling or inversion of the lips. The retraction of tissues makes it more difficult to adjust to dentures, as the cushioning layer over the bone becomes increasingly thin. The retention of one's natural teeth through old age helps to reduce the bony reabsorption, although the surfaces of the teeth flatten out because of years of use.

7. *Hormonal changes.*

As the aging process progresses, the metabolic rate slows. This may be due to atrophy of the thyroid gland. Women begin menopausal changes usually sometime during their forties, and the ovarian follicles cease to function within 10 to 15 years, inevitably by age 60 years. The reduction of estrogen may be as much as 90 per cent in some women and may lead to distressing symptoms, such as hot flashes, osteoporosis, or senile vaginitis. The life span of the testes is greater than that of the ovaries, but men show a decrease in testosterone levels by age 60 years. Typically, men in their seventies have decreased sexual energy and decreased viable sperm.

## TIME-RELATED PATHOPHYSIOLOGICAL CHANGES

Some conditions that accompany biological aging are deviations in the aging process and pathophysiological changes that have more serious consequences for body functions. Some deviations in the aging process, such as loss of accommodation and lowered diffusion of gases in the lungs, tend to be seen in most, if not all, the aging population, whereas others, such as cataracts, occur with greater frequency at each successive age. Pathophysiological changes increase one's susceptibility to more serious symptoms and complications during illness and may, in fact, lead to medical disruption of the body system.

Several time-related pathophysiological changes follow. The diseases seen most frequently in old age and the implications for nursing care are presented.

**Cardiorespiratory Changes.** Typical changes occur in the heart function of older people. The cardiac reserve is diminished, and the heart reacts poorly to sudden stress. The valve tissue shows a thickening that distorts the valve edges and leads to incomplete closing. This leads to increased workload for the heart and development of congestive heart failure. The presence of arteriosclerosis and atherosclerosis increases with age. Both conditions are associated with type of diet, hypercholesterol levels in the blood, gender, and hypertension. The changes produced by arteriosclerosis are not universal, and great selectivity exists concerning the sites where it occurs. The build-up of plaque is more common where arteries divide or branch off and where they are curved or twisted.

Other changes in the heart increase the possibility of arrhythmias. Medications and varying degrees of heart block are associated with sinus bradycardia, with the heart rate falling to as low as 30 per minute; however, slow heart rates are more often the result of pathological changes than of deviations in the aging process. Tachycardia is also a compensatory mechanism in which the fast heart rate should return to normal when the workload on the heart is reduced; however, prolonged tachycardia may be life threatening to patients, regardless of age.

The lungs show a decrease in their elasticity because of the increase in the amount of connective tissue and the changes it undergoes in aging. The lung volume is less because the lungs are unable to expand to their previous size, and the amount of residual air increases. The pulmonary blood vessels become more fibrotic, and in old age are able to expand only 50 per cent. As less air is inspired, the diffusion of gases is reduced about 8 per cent for each decade of life beyond middle-age.

Major disruptions associated with age include coronary artery disease, valvular diseases, hypertension, arrhythmias, pneumonia, lung cancer, bronchitis, and emphysema. The implication for nursing care is that nurses must recognize age as a stimulus or an influencing factor in the treatment of these conditions. The nursing plan of care should emphasize the following types of interventions:

1. Measures to conserve energy and decrease cardiac workload.
2. Close monitoring of blood gases and fluid balance.
3. Protection from even moderate levels of stress.
4. Prompt recognition and treatment of arrhythmias, including tachycardias and bradycardias.

**Changes in Renal Function.** By the seventh decade, the aging kidney loses one third to one half the number of glomeruli that existed in early adult life. The bulk of the nephrons has been reduced by arteriosclerotic changes and persistent vasoconstriction. Like most glandular organs, the concern is not the loss of functioning units but rather the miracle that there is so much kidney reserve left. More than two thirds of people over the age of 65 years have normal glomerular function in spite of gradual losses. Changes in the lower urinary tract involve voiding, control of sphincters, and the role of the bladder.

The disruptions in renal function encountered with age usually result from diseases that arise in other systems, such as congestive heart failure, or from dehydration, excessive use of diuretics and hemorrhage, and these conditions have a profound effect on the kidneys. Diseases of the kidney itself include acute or chronic pyelonephritis, glomerulonephritis, renal calculi, and uremia. Other conditions include bladder infections, enlarged prostate, incontinence, retention, and impotence.

When caring for older people with decreased renal function, the following principles have significant nursing implications:

1. Older patients have little tolerance for changes in fluid and electrolyte levels.
2. Inability of kidneys to remove excess fluids leads to interstitial and pulmonary edema.
3. With decreased urinary output from the kidneys, the skin becomes a more active vehicle for the excretion of fluids and wastes.
4. Oral and IV fluids may need to be limited.

5. Caution must be used in the medications prescribed because most are excreted by the kidneys, and, with impaired function, toxic levels of the drug may build up in the blood.
6. Hypertension develops in patients with renal failure as a consequence of the obstructed blood flow through the kidneys or as a response to regulating enzymes.
7. Dietary regulation of the amounts of potassium, sodium, and protein may be necessary. The normal intake of 60 to 80 grams of protein may be reduced to the minimum requirements of 10 to 20 grams.

**Changes in the Digestive System.** Aging and pathological events occurring in the digestive system are primarily due to changes in the nervous system and to some alteration of the structures of the gastrointestinal tract. As a result, between the ages of 20 and 90 years, a 30 per cent decrease occurs in the sensory conduction speed versus a 15 per cent reduction in motor nerve conduction. This results in less motility of the entire tract, a delay in feedback mechanisms, diminished response to pain and other sensations, and a decreased vasomotor response to digestion and/or emotions.

In addition to decreased peristaltic movement, a decrease occurs in the secretion of hydrochloric acid, mucin, and gastric juices. The hypoacidity of the stomach contents alters the actions of drugs, and there is less tolerance for fats. With less hydrochloric acid, people over age 70 years need twice as long to digest and to absorb fats— 7 hours as opposed to 3 hours for younger adults. The amount of trypsin produced by the pancreas diminishes after age 40 years, affecting the digestion of proteins. These changes also alter the bacterial flora of the intestines. Any one of these events may cause a ripple effect or slow the digestive process.

Medical conditions that involve the gastrointestinal tract and that are seen increasingly with age include cancer, obstruction, malabsorption, ulcers, hiatus hernia, gastritis, diverticulitis, constipation, and fecal incontinence. Nursing implications for aged persons with problems of the gastrointestinal tract include scrupulous attention to

1. Assessment of nutritional needs and the elimination of solids.
2. The altered effect of drugs in circumstances in which some are absorbed more quickly in an alkaline stomach and cause damage to the stomach lining.
3. Reduced awareness of acute pain usually associated with perforation. Older people may complain only of discomfort radiating to the

back, but the discomfort may be accompanied by abdominal tenderness and rigidity.

4. The person often being emotionally anxious or depressed by his or her condition.

**Muscular and Skeletal Changes.** The normal changes of aging lead to atrophy of muscles and decrease in strength and produce a picture of flexion in many aged people. The stronger flexor muscles gradually overpower the weaker extensor groups; thus, older people have more difficulty standing straight but continue to have a degree of flexion in their knees and hips. Beyond the age of 40 years, the incidence of osteoarthritis increases. Various joints of the body are involved and show a deterioration of the articular cartilage with the proliferation of new bony deposits. In women, the distal joints of the fingers are often involved and are characterized by the thickening of the joints, which are called Heberden's nodes. Involvement of the hips and knees is important clinically because the pain and limitation of motion can be relieved by surgical intervention to replace the diseased joints. Arthritis of the spine is more often seen in elderly men, whereas kyphosis caused by osteoporosis is seen in women who have decreased levels of estrogen.

Other pathophysiological changes include an increase in muscle cramps and tingling or numbness of the legs, which is thought to be related to circulatory changes. The incidence of Dupuytren's contracture is 10 per cent or higher among the aged population. The fascia in the palms of the hands becomes fibrosed, making full extension of the fingers difficult or impossible; this is treated surgically to remove the contracture. Carpal tunnel syndrome, a condition in which the compression of the median nerve causes pain, numbness, and tingling of the fingers, is more common among middle-aged women and is usually treated medically.

Disease conditions affecting the musculoskeletal system that occur more frequently among the older age group are fracture of the hip, more common in women than in men, osteoarthritis, rheumatoid arthritis, gout, osteoporosis, and knee or hip joint replacements.

An important implication for nursing care is to *help the patient to help himself.* Restoring the patient's abilities for mobility and encouraging older people to use their existing abilities are vital interventions. The nursing care focuses on interventions that lead to rehabilitation.

1. Establish a regular regimen for taking drugs, such as the salicylates to control the pain and discomfort of arthritis.

2. Consider the type of packaging of medica-

tions. Arthritic hands lack the strength to open many types of child-proof caps on bottles.

3. Schedule rest and activity periods geared to the acute or chronic phase of the disease, medical restrictions, and the individual's abilities.

4. Proper use of splints, braces, walking frames, and other supportive devices.

5. Modify the environment for additional safety and protection. Examples of ways to help elderly people adapt to decreased abilities and mobility include ramps for wheelchairs, avoiding high curbs, elevating toilet seats, removing slippery scatter rugs on floors, and installing handrails in halls or bathrooms.

**Changes in Sensory Perception.** Normal changes in taste, smell, and the structure of the eye have been described, but other changes in the sensory organs have more serious consequences. Decrease in visual acuity and in ability to hear interferes in the way older people perceive what is happening in the world and in how they communicate with others.

With advancing age, almost all people show some signs of discriminative hearing loss called presbycusis. The signs begin at about the age of 35 years and are progressive, with greater loss for the high tones than for the lower ones. Presbycusis is due to the slowing of the organ of Corti fibers' ability to vibrate rapidly to produce the cycles needed to create the higher sounds and may also involve a decrease in nerve conduction. A greater hearing loss results for consonants than for vowels, and more difficulty is found when using the more guttural languages of English and German than when using those with more vowels, such as Spanish and Hawaiian. The consonants most affected are B, D, G, P, and T and the group of L, M, and N. As part of the consonant blends into the vowel sound of *ee,* it is increasingly difficult to distinguish between similar sounding words, such as *bare, dare, mare,* or *pair.* With aging, people are less able to hear these sounds clearly. The announcement "It's time to eat" often sounds more like "Iss eye oo eee." Anyone who hears this would think the speaker was talking gibberish if hearing losses associated with presbycusis were not understood.

Hearing loss leading to conduction deafness affects one of three persons by the age of 70 years but is more common in men than in women. In people past the age of 50 years, the problems of hearing sounds are magnified when the background consists of many different conversations or competing noises. The additional sounds distort the speech and make it more difficult to understand.

For most people, visual acuity declines with

aging. The eye decreases in size, and changes in the retina cause decreases in visual perception. Near and far vision lead to the need for glasses to correct the focus of the image. By age 45 years, almost 90 per cent of the people in the United States wear glasses. The lens of the eye gradually loses its elasticity by that age and is unable to accommodate or bring images into bright focus, regardless of the distance of the object. People experiencing difficulty in accommodation often remark, "My arms aren't long enough for me to read that." Bifocal glasses aid in seeing near and far objects more clearly. Not only does the lens lose its elasticity, but it becomes cloudy and opaque, forming senile cataracts to some degree in more than 95 per cent of people over the age of 65 years. However, only a small percentage of these people have a significant reduction in vision requiring surgical removal of the lens and use of corrective lens.

Through middle-age and in old age, the decrease in visual acuity makes it imperative to have increased light in order to see as well to read, sew, or carry out similar activities. Although individuals differ, it may be necessary to double the candlepower of lights for each additional 12 to 13 years of age. Studies further indicate that loss of color discrimination occurs, especially toward the blue end of the color spectrum, and difficulties exist in distinguishing among shades of blacks, blues and greens, and whites.

The major types of disruptions related to changes in sensory perception in the aged include cataracts, glaucoma, deafness, disorientation, withdrawal, and sensory deprivation.

When planning care for older people, nurses must assess their sensory perceptions and take steps to avoid sensory deprivation. The following actions can be used to intervene in some problems related to decreased hearing and poor vision.

1. Provide adequate lighting for activities, avoid glaring lights, and eliminate night driving, if possible.
2. For people who are visually impaired, use talking-book records, large-print books, and magazines.
3. Describe the location of furniture, foods, and so on for those with poor vision.
4. Speak to the blind, introduce yourself, use touch, and face the person when talking.
5. For the hearing impaired, speak slowly and distinctly. People with presbycusis are not hard of hearing, so it is not necessary to speak louder, but it may be necessary to rephrase sentences if they have difficulty understanding some words.
6. Screen out extraneous noises by turning down the volume of radios or televisions or by reducing the competition from other conversations.

## PSYCHOLOGICAL ASPECTS OF AGING

The stereotype of old age that younger people have is of senile people in their second childhood who spend most of their time sitting in a rocking chair or staring off into space. Although a small percentage of people may fit this picture, the majority of older people remain physically and intellectually active until the end of their lives. The psychological changes associated with aging begin much earlier in life and occur gradually during the years. When there is a rapid decline in the mental abilities or a sudden change in the personality of the older person, the change is due to disease, a preclinical condition, or increased stress rather than aging. The longer these conditions are allowed to go untreated, and lacking some type of support system for the older person, the more damage occurs to one's self-esteem. This reduces one's ability to recover former levels of intellectual activity.

The psychological task facing aged people is to achieve and maintain their integrity and to avoid despair and disgust in the final stage of life. As they carry out social developmental tasks, they can promote integrity by focusing on the positive aspects of the tasks, or develop low morale with despair, depression, and disgust by emphasizing or concentrating on the negative side. In coping with the task of adjusting to declining strength, some positive aspects that contribute to high morale include being free not to work, being excused from strenuous work, being able to sit back and observe rather than compete, being able to choose to do what one wants to do, and being able to refuse others without feeling guilty. Some negative aspects of the task which lead to low morale are prolonged mourning of lost abilities, comparing present performance in an unfavorable light to past achievements, or complaining about the unfairness if it is necessary to continue competing with younger workers.

Changes in psychological functioning that occur among the aged include normal alterations in intellectual skills that are time-related, common personality attributes, and changes seen in brain failure in acute or chronic conditions.

### NORMAL CHANGES

Individuals differ in the ways they adapt to old age depending upon their personality, the mental abilities they have developed during their lifetime, and their general health. However, certain psychological functions can be identified that are general characteristics of the aged population in the United States. Nurses tend to conclude that "all old people are senile" and that they have mental deterioration when they see mainly sick older people. In fact, less than 5 per cent of people over the age of 65 years live in institutions such as hospitals, nursing homes, or similar types of long-term care facilities. More than 95 per cent of the old people live in the community, taking care of their own needs and pursuing their interests. They continue to retain brain functions and mental skills related to cognition and intelligence. Cognition includes the mental processes needed to learn and to know—namely, acquiring information, processing it, storing or remembering it, evaluating it, synthesizing it, and using it to reason. A popular myth is that people lose these abilities as they age, but this is not necessarily so. Although some skills decline with age, other mental abilities remain intact, and some may even show gains.

**Stable Mental Skills.** Intelligence as measured by IQ tests has been shown to increase during childhood until the age of 20 years when it levels off and remains quite stable until late in life. However, it is possible to "teach an old dog new tricks," and older people are able to learn. Some older people may experience difficulty in unlearning a well-established way of doing something, but they are constantly learning new ways to adapt to a changing environment with fluctuating interest and inflation rates, budgeting their resources, monitoring the political climate, and making decisions about personal and social issues. In recent years, intelligence has been thought to be a complex interweaving of abilities, some declining with age from the teen years onward and others increasing with age because of experience.

Intellectual skills that remain stable or show an increase are related to oral expression and the use of language, whereas skills that tend to deteriorate or decline are those requiring psychomotor responses. Judgment, accuracy, and general knowledge are categories that tend to increase. Adequate educational levels tend to increase one's ability to use intellectual skills in processing information, comprehending new material, and learning vocabulary. The most recently acquired material is the first to be lost and the earliest learned is the last to disappear. In old age, people who are foreign-born tend to have increased difficulty in understanding English and revert to their native language.

**Declines in Mental Skills.** Any rapid change or decline in mental skills is associated with moderate or severe health problems. However, age-related, gradual declines occur in some skills and involve a slower overall reaction time, pacing, load-shedding (selecting some information as relevant and dropping off, ignoring, or reducing the number of other details to be considered), problem-solving, increased coding and sequencing, and short-term memory loss.

Beginning at about age 45 years, a reduction in the speed of response occurs, even though the strength or intensity of the stimulus is increased. The slower response is thought to be due to the changes affecting the nervous system and neural transmission. Older people take longer to respond in all spheres: verbally, motor activity, or reaching decisions. However, when older people are given more time, they do as well as younger people. The response time is increased when there are several choices to be considered, and nurses may consider limiting the options when it is necessary to make effective use of time. The slower response of older people is often seen as cautiousness and a reluctance to take risks. They may proceed more cautiously, using more accuracy and reducing risk and uncertainty. Pacing refers to the speed at which new information is learned or tasks are performed. Older people perform better when working at their own pace than when being rushed. Although older people as a group perform at a slower pace, individual differences do exist, with some older people responding faster than some younger people.

Older people have a decreased need to achieve. This may be a factor in the slower response time; however, this is a speculative area and one that needs further research. Interest and motivation are highest when people are learning something, and most adults reach a peak in their knowledge and skills between the ages of 35 and 40 years, although they continue to gain experience after that time. Experience and practice in solving familiar problems or in performing their work makes people more efficient and effective. Then they are able to increase the amount of coding and sequencing of information and to do more load-shedding. Coding and sequencing involve classifying information into usable categories; however, problems are encountered because of the tendency to generalize and to lump things together that have a few similarities, although they are not truly alike. Sequencing is the method of arranging events logically so that certain deductions can be made. For example, based on prior knowledge of similar events, the older person hears that cold weather has hit the Florida citrus belt and deduces that a shortage of oranges will follow and that the price of oranges will be increased. This may, in fact, occur unless other vital facts have been shed, or not taken into consideration, such as the actual temperature, the length of the cold spell, the effectiveness of smudge pots to warm the air, or the stage of growth of the fruit. Older people do more load-shedding than do younger people. It enables more efficient decision-making for familiar problems; however, inaccurate or ineffective decisions result if relevant facts have been omitted or if the information is incomplete.

Studies of the decision-making and problem-solving methods of older people show that older people are efficient and make good decisions when they have had previous experience in solving similar problems. The disadvantages of most older people have to do with new information and unusual problems. Often, essential details are ignored and stereotyped methods of problem-solving are used that were effective in the past but are not relevant to the current problem. Part of the difficulty is that many people among the present aged group had a limited educational background that focused on concrete terms and did not teach any problem-solving methods. Consequently, they have trouble identifying essential and relevant data, setting goals, or arriving at creative solutions to problems.

People experience increased memory loss with the passing years. Memory consists of three mental processes: obtaining, storing, and recalling information. Recall is the retrieval of information that may be stored for minutes, hours, or years. As they grow older, people have more difficulty learning new material and recalling it; part of the problem may be due to interference caused by competition with other information learned in the past. Consider the older person who meets someone named John White. In order to remember his name, that information has to compete with all the other Johns he has met or known. The ability to remember is increased when older people are provided with additional visual or verbal cues. Visual aids are especially helpful because recognition aids remembering more effectively than the free recall of information presented verbally.

The greatest memory deficit is in the short-term memory, or the inability to recall the most recently acquired information. People tend to remember occurrences that happened when they were in control of their lives, most productive, most satisfied, and most respected. Events that are repetitive or lead to feelings of disappointment, failure, anxiety, or frustration are blocked, repressed, and forgotten. Older people can describe vividly the events that happened when they were younger, even when they have difficulty remembering recent experiences. Memories of early events are retained longer because the events are recalled frequently, reviewed, compared with others, and tend to be associated with feelings of satisfaction. Short-term memory is greatly disturbed by illness, even a slight decline in health causes more of a greater deficit. To older people, sickness represents a serious threat and produces high levels of anxiety that interfere with learning and the ability to recall names, dates, facts, and recent experiences. When nurses assess the nutritional intake of older patients, it is not uncommon for the patients to forget that

Frame of reference:

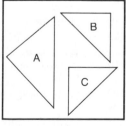

(1) Familiar problem

Frame of reference:

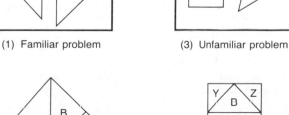

(3) Unfamiliar problem

**Figure 21–1.** Decision-making for elderly persons is easier when dealing with familiar problems with all details falling within their frame of reference or range of knowledge (1) and leading to a familiar solution (2). Solutions to unfamiliar problems (4) are influenced by relevant details outside their frame of reference (3).

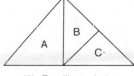

(2) Familiar solution

(4) Unfamiliar or unusual solution

they have eaten or precisely what they had eaten an hour or two earlier. If they are 70 years of age, they have eaten meals for more than 25,000 days, and the last one was probably similar to thousands of others they have eaten and was not particularly memorable.

## COMMON PERSONALITY CHARACTERISTICS

As mentioned previously, any serious change in the personalities of older people is less a result of aging than a consequence of poor health. The personality characteristics described here are present in all age groups. They are not unique to the older population, even though they may seem to occur more frequently or be more visible in this age group.

Older people are unique because they have lived so long. Butler (1977) points out the following traits that are characteristic of old age:

1. *A sense of fulfillment or satisfaction with life.* More people are satisfied with how their lives turned out than is popularly believed. Most people have a sense of contentment and serenity about their lives. This is not the same as being successful in the normal sense of the word nor is it saying that all old people gained fame or fortune. Rather, the satisfaction comes from knowing that they have done their best, that they have handled challenges, and that they have survived hardships.

2. *A sense of having gained wisdom in living and a desire to leave a legacy to the younger generations that follow.* They have developed a concept of life from birth to death with continuity from generation to generation and want to serve, guide, counsel, and pass on something of themselves that they value. The legacy they leave can be of any form, from their children to works of art to material possessions or even to donating organs for transplantation.

·3. *Change in the sense of time.* Time seems to pass faster for older people. They no longer are as concerned as middle-aged adults with the number of years left to live. Their focus is now on the present and on the need to live for the moment. As time becomes more precious, they place more value on the intangible and elementary things in life, such as their children, peace, plants, color, warmth, and comfort.

4. *A close attachment to familiar objects.* Older people form an emotional attachment to familiar surroundings and belongings. The years of living in their home, with furniture, pictures, keepsakes, and pets provide a sense of continuity, familiarity,

security, and comfort, as well as helping their memory. When forced to part with these familiar objects, they go through the painful process of grieving.

Older people are more susceptible to problems in coping with accumulating numbers of losses and changes associated with aging. Burnside (1981) lists the common emotional problems of anxiety, grief, loneliness, and paranoia and describes nursing interventions aimed at improving the mental health of the elderly.

**Anxiety.** There are many causes of anxiety for aged people. Anxiety is related to feelings of insecurity, to threats involving their physical and mental integrity, the increased isolation from their support systems, and their decreasing ability to control the environment and events in their lives. They are further battered with the realization that there is little hope that things will get much better for them. The methods used by the elderly to cope with feelings of anxiety include the following:

1. *Physical complaints.* Many older people disguise their anxiety or other concerns by complaining about normal functions of the body, such as feeling cold, having gas pains, and hearing a loud heart beat.

2. *Isolation.* Many older people hide their anxiety by escaping the attention of and contact with other people. They lie or sit motionless with minimal or no talking.

3. *Being stoic and not complaining about their troubles or problems.* Many older people are not accustomed to expressing their feelings to others and keep their feelings hidden.

4. *Behavioral signs.* Many behaviors provide clues that people are anxious, such as excessive talking, hand-twitching, clenching of fists, wringing of hands, pacing, chain-smoking, and increased agitation.

5. *Physiological signs.* Body responses to anxiety are of the autonomic nervous system and include increased pulse rate, elevated blood pressure, frequent urination, insomnia, and increased muscular tension.

Nursing interventions for reducing anxiety include the presence of a warm, caring person, the use of touch, and attentive listening. Insight therapy is used to help older people identify that they are anxious, express the cause or the threat that they perceive, and learn more effective ways of coping with it.

**Grief.** Older people take longer to resolve their grief after suffering a loss. As a person ages, the number of losses that one experiences increases and the effects are cumulative when previous grieving was not completed. Grieving occurs over the loss of a spouse, of family members, of health, of eyesight, of one's home, of a pet, or of anything that has value to oneself. The usual period of time for the acute stage of grief for a loved one is 4 to 6 weeks, but it lasts longer in older people who lose a spouse. Many of them have been married for 40 or 50 years or longer, and the death of a spouse is like having part of oneself die.

Nursing interventions focus on assisting people through the grieving process, encouraging them to cry and to examine any feelings of guilt and hostility, and taking measures to prevent suicide for those who feel there is no further reason for living.

**Loneliness.** Older people experience increasing loneliness as they continue to experience many kinds of losses, changes in their roles, and fewer meaningful interactions with other people. They are less able to recruit replacements for lost loved ones, and their children often live far away or have few personal contacts with them. Their circle of friends is diminished by illness and death, and they have few, if any, ties with their former area of employment. Loneliness is the fear of emotional isolation, and people can be lonely even though surrounded by other people. Feelings of loneliness are banished only by warm and friendly relationships with others, which serve as sources of nourishment for the self-esteem.

Nursing interventions for loneliness are challenging and take time and patience. Listening to the lonely person and devising interactions with other people who will treat the lonely person in a warm and caring way are important.

**Paranoia.** In normal aging, older people experience a decrease in sensory input, and when the decline is significant, they have a different view of their environment. People who have loss of vision and loss of hearing are especially vulnerable to misperceiving the real world because they are unable to see clearly or to hear what others say. Paranoid ideas are formed when they blame others for their difficulties. They become angry at those they believe are doing them wrong and see the world as a hostile and unfriendly place. They make paranoid accusations, such as that someone is stealing their property or that they are being poisoned.

Nursing interventions for paranoia focus on accurately assessing the sensory deficits and modifying the environment and compensating for the losses by utilizing methods described in Chapter Fourteen. Medications, as ordered by the physician, are also used.

## MENTAL PROBLEMS COMMON TO AGING

Problems encountered by nurses caring for older people in mental health settings are primarily depression and brain failure. The term brain failure is relatively new in nursing literature, but, according to Yurick et al (1980), it is helpful to the nurse because "it incorporates conditions which may be acute or chronic, reversible, or irreversible." It relieves the nurse of problems caused by the misuse of diagnostic terms, such as dementia, senile dementia, acute brain syndrome, and chronic brain syndrome. The medical profession is inconsistent in using diagnostic terms, since sometimes symptoms displayed by one patient are not distinguished in any way from another patient with a different diagnosis.

**The Incidence of Mental Illness in the Elderly.** The number of people over the age of 65 years who are hospitalized for brain impairment has risen sharply and accounts for most of the nearly one million people now residing in institutions, or about 5 per cent of all the elderly. Of those in mental institutions, one third of the elderly patients were admitted when they were young and grew old there. The remaining two thirds were admitted in old age with pronounced impairment of brain function.

The hospitalization care of the elderly who have mental problems of depression or brain failure needs to be improved. Many conditions can be corrected and mental functioning can be improved for elderly patients by focusing nursing actions on reducing anxiety, modifying environmental factors, providing a support system, and using techniques to enhance the patients' self-esteem. Too often, however, care is of the custodial type, providing only the bare essentials of shelter, food, and clothing. During the 1960s a transfer of aged patients out of the institutions and back into the community occurred, but, unfortunately, this move did not improve their plight. Rather than being given help to solve their fundamental problems of living, they were often merely kept quiet and peaceful through the use of tranquilizers. Although estimates vary, about 50 per cent of organic brain disease may be reversible and due to treatable causes such as malnutrition, infections, drug reactions, or congestive heart failure. Depressions can be treated and the condition reversed when treatment is initiated without undue delay.

**Depression.** One of the most common emotional conditions among the aged population is depression; however, the condition is often undetected, undiagnosed, and untreated. Depression is a morbidly sad or dejected state that is excessive for the degree of loss, as distinguished from grief that is realistic and proportionate to the loss. Older people are extremely vulnerable to depression in a society that views them as being "over the hill," having low value, and obstructing the way for younger people to move ahead. They are faced with numerous losses, including their own declining health and eventual death, the death of a spouse, children leaving home, lowered income, loss of power or prestige, and a feeling that time is running out for them. When trying to cope with the feelings aroused by losses, assault, and lower self-esteem, depression results. The most common feelings are helplessness, powerlessness, apathy, and anger turned inward toward the self.

Depression has many faces, and some depressed people are adept at hiding their feelings. However, common behaviors associated with the condition include apathy, staring off into space in a preoccupied way, lack of interest in surroundings or events, physical inactivity, inability to sleep, weight loss, feelings of hopelessness and unworthiness, and thoughts of self-injury or destruction. Suicide rates are sharply higher among the aged, particularly for older men. Even so, the rates do not reflect the more subtle ways older people may use to commit suicide, such as their refusal to eat, continuing to drive when unable to do so safely, and excessive use of alcohol. Every suicide gesture and attempt should be taken seriously by the nurse, even when the gesture is a statement to the effect "I'll never get well and I can't live like this. No one would miss me around here, anyway."

Nursing interventions for depression involve helping depressed patients deal with their painful feelings and work through their sadness and grief. They need to talk about these feelings, interact with the nurse and others who demonstrate that they care about the depressed person, and develop ways in which to gain control over their lives again. Particular attention should be directed toward identifying and treating illness and health problems in depressed individuals. Some researchers have concluded that older people adapt better to the loss of loved objects or prestige than they do to losses in their physical health, and, by preventing health problems, the incidence of depression could also be reduced (Busse and Pfeiffer, 1973).

**Brain Failure.** The function of the brain depends upon not only its physiology and anatomical structure but also the personality mode and resources of the individual and the general resources in the environment that help the individual to resist the effects of stress and anxiety.

(See Chapter One.) Brain failure occurs when people have disturbances of essential mental abilities that interfere with their abilities to cope with changes in their lives. The term is not used to refer to the common and normal changes associated with aging, although sometimes the line between normal changes and failure is very fine.

The behaviors signifying brain failure can be arranged on a continuum that ranges from the very mild forms that are not significantly different from normal aging to moderate disturbances to severe disability. Behaviors significant of moderate and severe impairment are not difficult to identify. The condition may have a rapid onset and be due to acute or chronic causes or may be gradual, extending over a period of months or years before signs of brain impairment are recognized. Generally, brain failure is not total or complete except in cases of brain injury or coma. Most older people experience disturbed functions that are most clearly seen in these five areas: judgment, dulling of affect, memory deficits, increased confusion, and problems of orientation to reality.

Commonly, mental impairment follows the principle that the most recent learning is lost first, and what was learned first is the last to be lost. This applies both to memory and to the higher levels of intellectual functioning. As brain failure continues, those afflicted show less ability to think in abstract terms, to analyze material, to synthesize new approaches for solving problems, to discriminate accurately, and to make good decisions or judgments. A backward progression results, from the cognitive skills learned and refined in adulthood to those of the teen-age years to school-age abilities to early childhood, when children learned to tell time, control their bowel and bladder, and perform other psychomotor activities. In severe brain failure, one is both mentally and physically incapacitated to the extent of needing assistance in meeting most physiological and hygiene needs.

Memory loss of more recent events is commonly seen in people who have brain failure. In mild impairment, it resembles memory loss of normal aging; however, there exists a greater degree of indecision, vagueness, and the need to be reminded about doing usual tasks. With increasing memory deficit, many elderly people become frightened that they are losing their minds and will be institutionalized. This creates a vicious circle, making it more difficult for them to learn and recall information. The problems of remembering cause misinterpretation of reality, disorientation, and confusion. Behavior of confused people appears disjointed, irrelevant, and unpredictable to those observing it, although the behavior has meaning for those using it. Confused patients often pace, become agitated, and wander away in their attempts to cope with a reality that differs from that experienced by others. The degree of confusion varies: at times the person is completely oriented but may be confused upon waking, when tired, or in the evening.

It is important for the nurse to attempt to find out the meaning of the confused patient's behavior in order to change it to adaptive behavior. One elderly woman was considered confused by the nursing staff because she kept talking about bananas and saying that she needed to get them but refused bananas whenever they were offered to her. As the days passed, she became more agitated and vehement about getting the bananas. The nurses tried using pictures, putting bananas in milk shakes, on puddings, and leaving them at her bedside; however, all this was to no avail. Finally, the problem was solved by the social worker who had gone to her home to take care of some details. On the kitchen windowsill were several smelly, decomposed, and fly-infested bananas. The patient had been worried about the spoiled bananas at home and had assumed that others knew what she was talking about, but when they did not, she was labelled as confused. As this process continues, one's contact with reality is reduced and confusion increases.

In this country, the medical profession continues to consider brain failure to be caused by organic brain changes. This diagnostic approach fails to take into account the differences in personality and the environmental resources that people use in meeting the challenges of daily living. Organic brain changes are classified as acute brain syndromes, which are usually reversible with treatment, and chronic brain syndromes, which are regarded as progressive in nature, irreversible, and having a poor prognosis.

Acute brain syndromes are caused by medication reactions, metabolic disturbances, electrolyte imbalance, malnutrition, anemia, tumors, cirrhosis or hepatitis, and circulatory and vascular conditions, such as strokes, infections, fevers, and changes in arterial blood gases of hypoxia or hypercapnia. Chronic brain syndromes are conditions resulting from arteriosclerotic changes that reduce the blood flow to parts or all the brain or the formation of senile plaques in the brain tissue that leads to senile dementia. Researchers have attempted to diagnose chronic brain syndromes according to anatomical differences; however, post mortem examinations show an inconclusive relationship between these changes and the diagnosis. The condition of the brain tissue also failed to show a correlation with the mental state and behavior exhibited by the patient. The brains of elderly patients with severe brain failure often showed fewer senile plaques or less arteriosclerotic change in blood vessels than did those of patients with normal behavior and functioning.

The prognosis for patients with chronic brain syndrome is not as bleak as it once was, when the diagnostic approach overemphasized the organic changes as the cause and when no treatment was available to reduce the arteriosclerosis or the senile plaques. Now, endarterectomy, drugs and various psychosocial approaches offer greater hope for the elderly to regain their ability to once again function and care for their own needs.

## SOCIOLOGICAL ADJUSTMENTS IN AGING

As people move into old age, unique changes occur as they carry out the developmental tasks for the last stage of life. The way that people adjust to these age-specific expectations varies widely from culture to culture and, even, from group to group, but the tasks they must achieve are fairly universal. The developmental tasks are a measure of how they get along in the social system, whereas how they feel about these interactions is part of their self-concept. In review, the tasks are:

1. Adjusting to decreasing physical strength and declining health.
2. Coping with retirement and a changed financial status.
3. Maintaining satisfactory living arrangements.
4. Reworking relationships with grown children, relatives, and others of one's own age group.
5. Adjusting to the death of a spouse and the losses of significant others.
6. Assuming a new pattern of social and civic responsibilities.

Socially, aging is characterized by the change and loss of roles and the lack of defined norms or expectations of how the aged should act or expect others to respond in certain situations. The sudden increase in the aged population literally took this country by surprise; thus, generally accepted answers for the following questions are unavailable: Are children in this country abandoning their aged parents? Should older single individuals live alone? Should adult children be required to assume financial responsibility for aged parents and relatives? Should elderly people live in retirement communities or be integrated into the general population? What are the expectations or norms for the relationship between an older woman and a younger man? Should the retirement age for Social Security benefits be raised now that more people are living longer?

From these representative questions, it is apparent that the issues confronting aging and society are numerous and complex. Among the issues are how these changes are affecting older people in terms of family structure, economic status, retirement, housing, and transportation.

## FAMILY STRUCTURE

More than 90 per cent of the people over the age of 65 years either are or have been married, and more than 80 per cent of them have living children. One of the first changes in the family occurred as the children became adults and left home. The last child usually leaves home when the mother is between the ages of 50 and 55 years. The woman's role as a mother then changes. Some women have difficulty adjusting to the new role after devoting all their energies to the family, and they experience intense feelings of grief for that void in their life.

Many elderly married couples continue to live in their own homes. Three out of four men over the age of 65 years are married and live with their wives; however, only one of three elderly women are married and living with their spouses. Most are widows who live alone or with one of their children, usually a daughter. During the earlier stages of life, women who were widowed were in the minority, compared with those who were married, but in old age, they become the majority because women live longer than men.

Because many women live several years in old age as a widow, they not only have lost a familiar loved one but also a social partner. The death of a spouse alters relationships with other couples who have been friends of both the husband and wife. The surviving widow no longer fits in easily with the social activities of other couples. She finds it necessary to develop other friendships, usually with other widows and single people. Not all people have a happy marriage, and the death of a spouse may represent release from an unsatisfying marriage and a new kind of freedom.

Table 21–5. MARITAL STATUS OF
MEN AND WOMEN OVER THE AGE OF
65 YEARS, IN 1979

|  | Age 65 yr and over | |
|---|---|---|
|  | Males | Females |
| Per cent married | 77.1 | 36.5 |
| Per cent widowed | 14.1 | 52.2 |

Source: Statistical Abstracts of the United States 1980, 101st ed. No. 39. Washington D.C., Bureau of the Census, 1980.

Investigators have noted that after a period of mourning, most people who have lost a spouse settle into a lifestyle that is satisfying to them.

Growing evidence indicates that aged parents and their children maintain close ties. Because the children often live at great distances from their parents and there is less frequent personal contact, phone calls, letters, and vacation visits are relied on for communication. More than two thirds of older parents see their children or grandchildren at least weekly. When the elderly parents need help, the children and members of the extended family shoulder their traditional obligations for them. The myth that most children neglect or abandon their aged parents may stem from professionals who work with the aged and tend to see those without family support.

The response of aged people to many losses are generally believed to be negative, and not enough attention has been given to the positive aspect. Compensations exist for some of the losses. The modifications in parent roles provide a relief from responsibilities for grown children and from the daily mini-crises of life. They are able to assume the new roles of grandparent and great-grandparent which allows them to form close relationships with grandchildren based more on fun and enjoyment rather than on authority or discipline. Perhaps the greatest advantage of the modification in the parent roles is the increase in personal freedom. Older people are released from confining activities, the need to work and to obey the rules and regulations associated with it. Less need arises to be agreeable to everyone, and more freedom exists to be creative or the kind of person they want to be. For some, the adjustment to losses may mean an escape from an unhappy situation involving the children or the spouse.

## ECONOMIC STATUS

For successful psychosocial aging, people need an income that is adequate for their needs. Not only should they have enough money for food, shelter, clothing, heat, and medical expenses but also to provide for transportation, entertainment, travel, and interests. Some elderly people continue to work beyond the age of 65 as either a matter of choice or of necessity when the earnings are vital for those who are poor. The majority of elderly people do not work but live on income derived from one or more of the following sources: Social Security benefits, private or government pensions, public assistance programs, personal investments, or savings. About 75 per cent of retired workers have some type of private pension income. However, many of these sources of income pay small monthly amounts and stop when the worker dies, leaving the surviving spouse without that income. Another 25 per cent of older people participate in government pension plans resulting from either civilian or military service. These plans provide a more generous income and have provisions for paying lesser amounts to survivors following the death of the worker. The fixed income of a private pension plan is more subject to the pressures of inflation whereas government pensions generally provide for cost-of-living increases at intervals.

The primary source of income for most elderly people is the Social Security program. The Social Security program was passed by Congress in 1935, and its original purpose was to provide additional income for retired workers. It was not intended to be the only source of retirement income, although many people rely solely upon it. As one of the major social programs resulting from the depression of 1929, it has been expanded extensively during the years to serve as a "social safety net" for millions of workers, their families, and survivors. Money is paid into the fund by workers and employers based on the worker's earnings, and benefits are paid after one reaches age 65 years and retires from the work force or is unable to work at any age because of prolonged or continuous disability. The benefits include payments to the spouse and minor children of workers who are disabled or die, regardless of one's age or whether one is retired. In recent years, the Social Security program has encountered financial difficulties because the number of recipients has greatly increased, the costs have skyrocketed, and the ratio of workers to recipients has declined from 16 to 1 in 1935 to 3 to 1 at present. Substantial changes in the program are expected to be made by Congress in the coming years in order to continue providing Social Security benefits for elderly people.

The number of poor among the elderly population has been declining during the past 20 years as more people reach old age with a higher level of education, and fewer older people are foreign-born. Foreign-born people have more difficulties in adjusting to a new culture. More education is associated with obtaining better jobs, having a higher income, and acquiring more financial assets such as a home, stocks, bonds, or other valuables, and better medical treatment. Although the majority of elderly people have adequate financial resources, they are unsure of how much of these resources will be eaten away by inflation or whether they will live longer than their money will last. In 1959, poor people over 65 years of age numbered 5.4 million, or 35 per cent of all persons over 65. In 1978, the number of older poor people had dropped to 3.2 million, or 14 per cent of this age group, according to government figures. Although the number of elderly poor people has declined, the rate for elderly poor people is higher than the 11.4 per cent rate for the nation as a whole.

Elderly poor people are most commonly white, women, and widowed, although the poorest of poor people is the black woman who is old and widowed. Less than 1 million of the 3.2 million elderly poor people are men, and most of those men are single or living alone. Women who depended upon husbands for their support are more apt to have meager incomes when the spouse dies because private pension income usually stops and the survivor's benefit from Social Security is the only income. In 1979, the income that was considered to be the poverty level for a couple aged 65 years was $4,394. For the single or widowed woman, it was $3,469, or less than $300 per month. Elderly single men do not fare much better, but they average a few dollars more per month on which to subsist. Many elderly poor

**Table 21–6.** INCIDENCE OF POVERTY AMONG PEOPLE
65 YEARS AND OVER IN 1960 AND 1979, ACCORDING TO
GENDER AND STATUS OF HEAD OF HOUSEHOLD

| Characteristics of People 65 yr and over | 1960 | | 1979 | |
|---|---|---|---|---|
| | Male | Female | Male | Female |
| Households at or below poverty level (per cent) | | | | |
|   Head of family | 28.7 | 31.5 | 7.7 | 12.2 |
|   Unrelated person | 58.8 | 69.1 | 20.7 | 28.8 |
| Median income | | | | |
|   Head of family | $2,831 (all) | | $10,197 | $9,513 |
|   Unrelated person | $1,006 (all) | | $4,893 | $4,160 |
| Poverty level income | | | | |
|   Head of family | $1,762 | $1,752 | $4,394 | $4,362 |
|   Unrelated person | $1,409 | $1,391 | $3,515 | $3,469 |

Source: Statistical Abstracts of the United States 1980, 101st ed. No. 39 and 769, Washington, D.C., Bureau of the Census, 1980.

people live in tenements or cheap apartments in the central portions of cities.

People who have always been poor continue to be poor in old age, whereas others become poor when they retire from the work force and their income drops or is depleted by such things as high medical expenses. Poverty also follows racial lines. White elderly people account for 22 million of the 24.6 million people over the age of 65 years, and 2.5 million of them are poor. They far outnumber the 2 million elderly black people; however, one of every three black people is poor. Even now, more than 24 per cent of black elderly women have incomes less than $2,000 a year, and many of them continue to work as domestics or at other low-paying jobs to survive. A truism states that people who are poor tend to have more health problems and serious illnesses than people who are not poor, and that serious illness can cause poverty.

## RETIREMENT

With the significant increase in the life span during this century, many more people are spending 10 to 20 years or longer in the retirement stage of life. Older people look forward to retiring from the work force, and increasing numbers of them are retiring at an earlier age. They look forward to the well-earned freedom to do as they want with their lives.

Retirement is a complex social process: It is a phase in an occupation or career when the worker is entitled to an income without the responsibilities or expectations of producing further work for it. It is also a role that specifies expectations, rights, and relationships of the retiree in the social structure. To carry out the retirement role, people must have good health, financial security, and personal adaptability. This phase of life ends when the retiree becomes sick or disabled and is no longer able to carry out the role or when he or she dies.

The retirement role carries with it certain expectations. Retired people are expected to exhibit the same personality and behavior as they did when working. The job role is more than just performing certain skills; it includes one's way of thinking, certain mannerisms, and predictable ways of interacting with other people, which are expected to carry over into retirement living. Retirees are expected to manage their own lives and to have decision-making responsibilities in all spheres of their lives. Previously, the employer set down conditions such as the days and hours of work, the type of activities required by the job, appropriate dress and appearance, times for meals, when to take vacations, and even the privi-

leges and benefits, such as health care insurance. In retirement, less structure is involved in relationships with other people and in one's use of time and space. For some workers, severing ties with coworkers leaves them extremely isolated from other people unless they are able to form new social contacts. Finally, retired people are expected to live within their means and to avoid becoming dependent upon their children or the community.

Workers who retire generally have been working for 40 years or longer. Most of them are men because most elderly women have been housewives much of their lives. Retirement represents a drastic change in the lives of most men, whereas housewives continue to carry out the same activities of cooking, cleaning, and shopping as they did at earlier stages. Women adapt better to retirement, but those who have had careers or who have worked outside the home may encounter problems adapting to retirement as do some working men.

Successful retirement is a period of having good morale, being contented with life, and being able to deal with changes in a comfortable or satisfying way. Retirees who succeed are those who are involved in a wide range of activities and who have developed leisure time skills. In addition, they are more likely to have planned for their retirement years and voluntarily decided when to retire. Those who retire involuntarily as a result of poor health or because of age tend to have more difficulty adjusting to the changes. People go through certain stages in retirement that are similar to the phases seen in "culture shock." These stages have been described as follows:

1. Honeymoon phase
2. Disenchantment phase
3. Reorientation phase
4. Stability phase
5. Termination phase

Not all people go through all the different stages or spend the same amount of time in each stage. The honeymood phase is usually a busy time filled with many activities as the newly retired person savors his or her new freedom by attempting to do "all the things I never had time to do before." This phase may last for years if the person is able to afford the activities and if resources are available. Few people can keep up a hectic pace indefinitely, so they settle into a more routine way of life. The disenchantment phase results from the emotional letdown of those who have few alternatives, little money, poor health, or other losses. People in this phase have feelings of emptiness, much self-pity, and depression. The reorientation phase begins when the person finds it necessary to "pull himself together" and restructure his life by exploring new alternatives or by getting involved in a senior center, a church, or community activities. The stability stage is characterized by self-reliant retirees who manage their own affairs without being overly dependent upon others. The termination phase occurs gradually for most elderly people as they are forced by age to increasing dependence. They have to relinquish the activities of the retirement role and take on more of the sick and disabled role.

Some problems in adapting to retirement can be associated with jobs that demanded the total energies of the worker. Physically demanding jobs, such as mining, steel mill, foundry, and high-pressure jobs in competitive industries, leave workers with less time for themselves or for preparing for retirement. Other jobs result in poverty in retirement. Such jobs pay low wages and have poor, if any, pension plans. Because an average drop of about 50 per cent in income results when one retires, workers in such jobs are poor when they enter old age and can no longer work.

Many nurses have a negative view of retirement because they tend to see older, retired people only when they are ill or hospitalized. When illness strikes, older people are in the process of giving up the independence of their retirement role for the dependence of the sick role. Nurses are more apt to see older people during the disillusioned phase of retirement when they are emotionally depressed and are expressing negative views. Some elderly people may develop psychosomatic illnesses in order to avoid the responsibilities of this stage of life. Before they can recover, they must be helped to find a more positive and meaningful concept of the retirement years.

## HOUSING AND TRANSPORTATION

One of the persistent myths about aging is that most elderly people are sick and live in nursing homes, hospitals, and similar institutions. In fact, 95 per cent of people over age 65 years are healthy enough to live in the community and manage most of their affairs, whereas only 5 per cent live in institutions. More than 70 per cent of elderly people live with a spouse or other family members, but one of four lives alone. Significant differences exist between men and women who live alone. In 1979, only 15 per cent of elderly men lived by themselves, whereas 41 per cent of elderly women lived alone. Most elderly people treasure their independence, and only 19 per cent of them live with one of their children, usually a daughter. Men do not live as

long as women; thus, most of them live their lives with wife and family. After the death of the husband, the wife generally lives alone. It is ironic that the largest number of people who live alone are the most frail people: those in their late seventies or eighties who are widowed or single women. More elderly black women live with relatives or friends than do white women. This may be for financial reasons rather than a desire to avoid social isolation.

The housing of elderly people is only slightly less modest than for the general population, even though most elderly people live on a fixed income and 14 per cent have incomes below the poverty level. Those with ample income live in homes that they own, and some have migrated to comfortable retirement communities usually located near large cities in the sun-belt states. Others seek more affordable housing in mobile homes and low rent public housing and the cheaper rentals in the central areas of cities. Struyk (1977) reported on the findings of the Annual Housing Survey in 1973 regarding housing for elderly citizens. It was found that a majority of them, 55 per cent, lived in large metropolitan areas, 40 per cent lived in smaller communities, and only 5 per cent lived on farms. More elderly people own their own homes than do other segments of the population, but the homes are smaller and more modest. They have fewer bedrooms and bathrooms and are of an older vintage. Elderly people living in more rural areas and numbering about 30 per cent of households age 65 years or over have larger homes but these have a striking lack of basic services, such as hot and cold running water, complete kitchens, indoor bathrooms, and central heating. Those living in central parts of cities reported the major problem of housing to be the poor neighborhood. Elderly couples tend to have the best housing, followed by individuals living alone.

Geographically, 45 per cent of all elderly people live in seven states. They tend to remain in the same general area where they lived most of their adult lives. Less than 2 per cent move out of the state. In 1979, the states with the largest number of people over the age of 65 years were:

| California | 2.3 million |
| New York | 1.2 million |
| Florida | 1.6 million |
| Pennsylvania | 1.5 million |
| Texas | 1.3 million |
| Illinois | 1.2 million |
| Ohio | 1.1 million |

Nearly one of every 11 people over the age of 65 years lives in California. Elderly blacks live mainly in New York, Texas, California, North Carolina, and Georgia.

Older people take much longer to adjust when they move from one location to another, whether the move is from one state to another, to a different home, or to another room or nursing unit in the hospital. When sick, aged people are far less able to adjust to changes in their environment. Some authorities have reported that changing their location or residence leads to higher mortality rates, greater stress, more illness, and increased dependence. Admission to a nursing home is often a crisis event for elderly people who are forced to give up the independence of retirement because of illness or debility of aging. Too many nursing homes do not provide good care geared to needs, but rather provide custodial services with few, if any, activities. To older people, nursing homes represent the "end of the line," a place to go and wait to die. During the period following admission, they go through the greiving process for their bleak future, the separation from their home and familiar objects, and the decreased contact with families or relatives.

Transportation and mobility among elderly people are related to their state of health. The greater the impairment of health, the less mobile they are. Healthy and active people continue to drive their own cars until they are well into their eighties. Although their responses are slower than those of young adults, older drivers compensate by driving slower and by more carefully observing traffic laws. Some older people may continue to drive even though decreases in their visual acuity and hearing have reduced their ability to drive safely. Some people enjoy travelling during their retirement years. They continue to travel as long as they are healthy and able to get around and can afford to do so. Many people enjoy travelling around the country in recreational vehicles and campers, and a large number of the people who take tours abroad are senior citizens.

Older people commonly experience increasing difficulty in ambulating with the passing years. Because of decreasing strength and arthritic and other aging changes, they have less ability to climb stairs, to negotiate steps when climbing aboard buses or going into buildings, or to walk more than a block or two without resting. Increasingly, they must rely on public transportation, such as buses or taxi cabs, or rides from their relatives or friends in order to go from place to place and to handle their affairs.

## APPLICATION TO CLINICAL PRACTICE

As you take care of older clients in the community or older patients in the clinical setting, make an assessment of the changes associated with aging. Your observations should include normal aging, time-related pathophysiological changes, and psychological ways in which the clients or patients adapt to retirement or carry out their developmental tasks. The following report shows some observations made by a nursing student about the effects of aging. Such an assessment may help to sharpen your awareness of some of the changes that have been presented in this chapter.

"Mrs. Ruth K., age 83 years, manifests almost all the time-related physiological changes of the aging process, in addition to many social and mental changes.

*Normal aging:* Ruth states that she has shrunk from 5'3" to 5'2". She gets cold very easily because she has little fatty layer to provide insulation and asks for blankets constantly. Her skin is very dry with poor turgor. Her hair is thin and gray. Her gums are receding. She complains of "tasteless" food and finds a mechanical bland diet easier to eat and digest. She also does not notice her own body odor.

*Time-related pathophysiological changes:* (Cardiovascular) Ruth's blood pressure is 160 over 90, and she complains of being very tired and weak after using the bathroom, siting in a chair, or moving in bed. She states, "I can't catch my breath" after any exertion. (Renal) She has urinary frequency and nocturia, and a history of hydronephrosis. (Digestive) She refuses bacon for breakfast and states, "Fatty foods don't agree with me." (Musculoskeletal) She complains of arthritis in the left shoulder and is unsteady on her feet. (Sensory organs) Ruth states that she cannot read even with her glasses, but she can see the television just fine. She often thinks that a nurse has said something different from what was really said. She has some difficulty hearing unless the words are spoken in a low tone of voice and pronounced distinctly.

*Social changes:* Ruth has experienced the loss of many of her roles. She has been a widow for 35 years, and her son recently placed her in an "old ladies' home." She never worked but states that she was always "well off" on her husband's salary (he was a builder). Now she lives solely on his Social Security and finds herself unable even to pay for a taxi or bus. Most of her friends have died, her grandchildren never visit her, and she calls her roommate at the home "crazy" and "a thief." She is having difficulty with a lack of norms for her age. She expects her family and acquaintances to pay more attention to her than they do.

*Mental changes:* Ruth responds to questions very slowly and usually answers a yes/no question with a resounding "NO!" She forgets who she last spoke to or what she ate but tells vivid stories of her childhood in Canada. Her stories also seem to wander from point to point because she has difficulty following one idea to its conclusion. For example, she starts talking about her "tasteless food" and wanders to planting tomatoes, and then to how her husband liked to garden, without ever really explaining which food was tasteless or what could be changed. She also expresses feelings of anger and says that she feels lonely because her family and friends neglect to visit her.

# REFERENCES

Bergman, Moe, et al.: Age-related decrement in hearing for speech. J Gerontol, *31*(5):533–583, (September) 1976.

Botwinick, Jack: Aging and Behavior: A Comprehensive Integration of Research Findings, New York, Springer Publishing Co., Inc., 1973.

Bozian, Marguerite, and Clark, Helen M.: Counteracting sensory changes in the aging. Am J Nurs, *80*:473–476, (March) 1980.

Brotman, Hermann: Population projections: part I. Tomorrow's older population (to 2000). Gerontologist, *17*(3):203–209, (June) 1977.

Bureau of the Census. Statistical Abstract of the United States 1980, 101st ed. Washington, D.C., 1980.

Burnside, Irene M.: Nursing and the Aged, 2nd ed. New York, McGraw-Hill, Inc., 1981.

Burnside, Irene M.: Recognizing and reducing emotional problems in the aged. Nursing 77, *7*(3):56–59, (March) 1977.

Busse, Ewald, and Pfeiffer, Eric (eds.): Mental Illness in Later Life. American Psychiatric Association, Washington, D.C., 1973.

Butler, Robert, and Lewis, Myrna: Aging and Mental Health: Positive Psychosocial Approaches, 2nd ed. St. Louis, The C. V. Mosby Co., 1977.

Harris, Raymond: Cardiopathy of aging: are the changes related to congestive failure? Geriatrics, *32*(2):42–46, 1977.

Hendricks, Jon, and Hendricks, C. Davis: Dimension of Aging: Readings. Cambridge, Mass., Winthrop Publishers, Inc., 1979.

Hirschfeld, Miriam J.: The cognitively impaired older adult. Am J Nurs, *76*:1981–1984, (December) 1976.

Kaluger, George, and Kaluger, Meriem: Human Development: The Span of Life. St. Louis, The C. V. Mosby Co., 1974.

Lowenthal, Marjorie F., Thernher, Majda, and Chiriboga, David: Four Stages of Life. San Francisco, Jossey-Bass Inc., Publishers, 1975.

Marshall, Carter: Dynamics of Health and Disease. New York, Appleton-Century-Crofts, 1972.

Programmed Instruction. Sensory changes in the elderly. Am J Nurs, *81*(10): 1851–1880, (October) 1981.

Shore, Herbert: Designing a training program for understanding sensory losses in aging. Gerontologist, *16*: 157–165, (April) 1976.

Struyk, Raymond: The housing situation of elderly Americans. Gerontologist, *17*(2):130–139, (April) 1977.

The World Almanac and Book of Facts 1980. New York, Newspaper Enterprise Association, 1980.

Uhlenberg, Peter: Changing structure of the older population of the USA during the twentieth century. Gerontologist, *17*(3):197–202, (June) 1977.

U. S. Dept. of Health, Education and Welfare. Almost 65; Baseline Data from the Retirement History Study. Social Security Administration. Office of Research and Statistics. Washington, D.C., U. S. Government Printing Office. Res. Rep. No. 49, 1976.

Wallace, Daniel J.: The biology of aging. J Am Geriatr Soc, *25*(3):104–111, 1977. *In* Hendricks, Jon, and Hendricks, C. Davis: Dimensions of Aging: Readings. Cambridge, Mass., Winthrop Publishers, Inc. 1979.

Wilkie, Frances L., and Eisdorfer, Carl: Intelligence and blood pressure in the aged. Science, *172*:957–962, (May) 1971.

Yurick, Ann G., et al.: The Aged Person and the Nursing Process. New York, Appleton-Century-Crofts, 1980.

# Chapter TWENTY-TWO

# Adaptation and Cultural Diversity

## OBJECTIVES   Information in this chapter will help you to

1. Define the terms associated with cultural beliefs and practices.
2. State some of the common middle-class American values shared by most nurses and discuss ways that these values may influence the nursing care of patients from another cultural background.
3. Define the stages of culture shock and list some behaviors that are characteristic of each stage.
4. Compare the experience of hospitalization with that of culture shock.
5. State some variations seen in different ethnic groups that may require different or modified nursing interventions.
6. Carry out a cultural assessment that focuses on values and beliefs regarding family relationships, personality traits, material goods, time, religious beliefs, respect and authority, and health practices.

## DEFINITION OF TERMS

**culture** — the prescribed values, beliefs, knowledge, symbols, and patterns of behavior of a social group that are passed on to each succeeding generation.

**discrimination** — the result of one group having less power in relation to another, and thus, receiving less favorable treatment.

**ethnic group** — a group of people who have a common and distinctive culture through their race or historical ties.

**ethnocentricity** — the belief that one's way of life is the preferred, or best, one.

**folk medicine** — health practices that are part of the culture and consist of the caring and protective activities that are valued by the people, although some have no known scientific basis for being effective.

**matriarchy** — a family dominated by the mother.

**patriarchy** — a family dominated by the father.

**shaman** — a medicine man; one who works with magic or the supernatural forces.

**subculture** — a social group within the larger group that does not subscribe to all beliefs of the culture or modifies them.

The focus of the adaptation approach to nursing is on how people think and behave as they respond to changes in their world and daily lives. A common myth is that all people are alike and that they think and act alike. In reality, many differences can be found in the way people respond as a result of factors such as biological inheritance, effects of the physical environment, and unique social experiences. All these factors influence the attitudes, values, beliefs, and prescribed ways of carrying out roles that are passed on from one generation to the next as the cultural inheritance. People fashion and mold the pattern of their lives, the way they act, and the way they feel about things according to their culture.

Nurses who use the adaptation approach to nursing must regard culture as a major stimulus that influences the way patients from a different cultural background think and behave when ill. The ineffective or disruptive behavior that causes a problem in coping may well be the result of cultural values and beliefs that differ from those who are providing the health care. Most doctors and nurses in this country tend to hold the values and beliefs of middle-class white Americans, whereas many patients come from minority or other ethnic backgrounds. In recent years, greater efforts have been made to recruit members from other cultural groups into the health care professions.

The study of culture is important as a means of increasing nurses' awareness of the diversity of values and beliefs among the various social groups. It also provides the nurses with norms, or standards, to use when determining whether or not observed behaviors are adaptive. When behavior is adaptive in the person's native culture, it is necessary for nurses to ask themselves the question, "Do I have the right to judge this behavior as maladaptive and seek to change the behavior? Am I forcing my values on this person?" Cultural values and beliefs tend to be quite resistant to

change; thus, the patient's problems in coping are apt to persist unless the cultural effects are taken into consideration.

In this chapter, some of the concepts related to cultural theory will be explored and the values and beliefs of the dominant cultural groups in this country will be examined. The process of adapting to a new culture is described as the stages of culture shock and is related to the experience of patients when confined to the unfamiliar stresses of the hospital setting. One method of assessing cultural background as a stimulus for behavior involves exploring the attitudes and beliefs in several categories related to the individual and the social group to which he or she belongs. Finally, four different cultural groups are compared to provide a basic framework from which to better understand individuals who have similar values and beliefs.

## THE NATURE OF CULTURE

Culture is defined as the prescribed values, beliefs, knowledge, symbols, and patterns of behavior of a social group that are passed on from one generation to another. Culture provides the framework for learning this information in terms of when the learning takes place, those who impart the knowledge, the rate of learning, and the sanctions or rewards attached to it. Although culture is passed on from parents to their children, the existence and continuity of cultural values do not depend upon particular individuals. Children without parents acquire the same knowledge and skills from other people in their social group (grandparents, relatives, or other care-givers) as they would had their own parents taught them.

### COMPONENTS OF CULTURE

The concept of culture embraces all facets of living and beliefs that are held by a social group concerning how that life should be lived. The nurse's assessment of culture focuses on ways in which different cultures influence the way people carry out their roles in life. Components that have great importance include

1. Communication and use of language.
2. Lifestyle of individuals and family relationships.
3. The way in which one views one's world.
4. Practices regarding health and illness.
5. Beliefs, myths, and taboos held within the group.

Communication takes many forms, from verbal use of language to nonverbal gestures, silence, eye contact, forms of touching, and music. Members of the same cultural group share a common language based on their mutual understanding of words and symbols. Through their use of language, they learn the fine nuances of their culture, the expression of emotions and feelings, ways of relating to the world of nature, and the concepts of time and space.

Problems of communication arise when members of different cultural or subcultural groups do not speak the same language or are less fluent in expressing themselves in the language used by the dominant society. English is the dominant language of the United States, and few doctors, nurses, or other health care providers speak another language. Even when people speak the same language, misunderstandings can occur because words may have different meanings in other areas of the country or to those who belong to other subcultural groups. For example, young members of street or neighborhood gangs use many slang terms and give common words unusual meanings known by insiders but confusing to others. For the large Spanish-speaking population, the American Indians, and other ethnic groups, English is a second language, and their degree of fluency in expressing themselves varies greatly. Those who are bilingual may be reluctant to use what English they do know, especially during times of stress, illness, or high anxiety when a tendency exists to revert to the language used during childhood.

Interpreters may be needed when nurses take care of clients or patients from a different cultural background who do not speak the same language. Often a member of the family or a close friend who speaks English can serve as interpreter so that the client can make his needs known and the nurse can obtain information needed to provide an individual plan of care.

Many variations are found in the lifestyles and family relationships, views of the world, attitudes and practices in health and illness, and the beliefs, myths, and taboos of different cultures. Although it would be difficult for nurses to know about every culture, they can begin by focusing on one individual or culture that is different from their own and examine these areas in more depth. In this chapter, several different cultures that illustrate variations in these cultural components are described.

## TYPES OF CULTURES

Major cultures of the world are composed of populations bound together by a common language, customs, religious beliefs, and a characteristic pattern of life. These cultures are named on the basis of nationality or the country of origin and are referred to, for example, as English, Greek, Japanese, Mexican, or Swahili cultures.

In the United States, between 150 and 200 cultural groups exist, as well as many additional subcultures. Members of a major cultural group may belong to several subcultural groups that advocate beliefs and practices that they accept and embrace. Groups that have similar values and beliefs on the basis of their nationality or native country are called ethnic groups. They may also be referred to as minority groups when they differ from the dominant culture. In this country, minority groups are frequently classified by race, color, or creed, but any subcultural group holding opposing views to those of the major culture can be classified as a minority.

The economic status of people often has a greater influence on their culture than does nationality, color, or race. The values of the large middle-class are predominant in our culture. People who belong to different social classes tend to have more variations in their values and lifestyles, whereas those from different backgrounds who belong to the same social class tend to have more similar values and lifestyles. One example of this is the culture of poverty. (See Chapter Twenty-three.) Poverty is more than a lack of money. It constitutes a way of life that allows the poor to carry on and to survive. It provides defense mechanisms, a view of the world, and the values that provide stability and set it aside from other social classes.

People belong to various subcultural groups, which deal with particular segments of life or specific beliefs that are important to the individual. Thus, subcultures are formed by occupational, religious, and other interest groups. Members of occupational groups tend to gravitate toward each other and to form subcultures of nurses, insurance clerks, math teachers, lumberjacks, or

**Figure 22–1.** The United States is a "melting pot" with its citizens coming from different cultures all over the world. Although these people may acquire similar lifestyles after living in this country for years or even generations, they also retain some of their former values and beliefs.

bank tellers. They share a technical language, follow the same practices and customs, and have similar experiences in their work lives. Similar religious beliefs form the basis for other subcultural groups, such as Jewish, Mormon, Amish, Methodist, Catholic, or Muslim. Various interest groups lead to other subcultural groups when people associate with others who have similar attitudes and beliefs. Examples of interest groups include political parties, coin collectors, "Save the Whales" workers, members of the American Heart Association, art and music devotees, Girl Scouts, and Little League baseball players.

## PROBLEMS OF CULTURE

When the attitudes, values, and beliefs of one cultural group conflict or differ from those of another, the people involved in the interaction may be confronted with several problems. People who belong to a minority group often receive different and discriminating treatment and respond with feelings of anger or powerlessness or act in noncompliant ways. Both groups of participants may experience cultural blindness, ethnocentricity, or cultural conflict. People who enter a new culture may undergo some degree of

"culture shock" as they learn new ways of adapting to a different culture.

**Discrimination.** The practice of discrimination occurs when one group in society has less power than another and, as a result, receives less favorable treatment. Members of minorities and ethnic groups, including blacks, Indians, those from Spanish-speaking countries, women, the aged, the lower classes, and especially the poor, are frequent targets of discrimination. Discrimination occurs when people move from one social role to another and find that they are at a disadvantage in respect to others in a similar role. For example, in a group of working women, the housewife may receive discriminatory treatment when others fail to listen to her suggestions or encourage her participation. In a similar manner, the female executive is a minority and at a disadvantage in most meetings with male executives. Naturalized citizens encounter discrimination practices as they seek to understand customs and regulations, acquire and use new language, and find jobs to provide for their economic security.

Discriminatory practices result in barriers to health care for those who are targets for unequal treatment. The health field is dominated by members of the white middle-class, who follow their practices and beliefs of cleanliness, punctuality, and so on. Middle-class patients are treated as equals because they have the same cultural values and similar amounts of power as those dominating the health field, while others with less power must wait longer or receive less service or courtesy. As a result of discrimination, poor people make fewer visits to doctors or dentists, going only when they are in pain or acutely ill. Even when cost is not a factor, they make less use of health services and pay less attention to preventive health measures, such as immunizing their children against childhood diseases and polio.

People who are discriminated against respond to their feelings of powerlessness in a variety of ways. They use the coping patterns of moving-toward, moving-away, or moving-against behavior and suppress or express their feelings of anger. Many people cope with the discriminating practices by conforming in a pleasing and cooperative manner as they wait their turn or accept less courteous service or experience other inconveniences. They are passively agreeable and "don't want to rock the boat" for fear that they will be ignored or receive even worse treatment. Those who cope by moving-away behaviors avoid confrontations or contact with the dominant cultural group or withdraw by being quiet or not making eye contact or seeking out attention. The feelings of anger and powerlessness provoked by discrimination are often expressed in moving-against behaviors that are antagonistic and uncooperative. The degree to which anger is allowed to be expressed differs among the various cultural groups and is suppressed when people suspect or know that it will lead to denial or withdrawal of needed services or to some form of punishment. An increase of anger and frustration within a cultural group may lead to increases in crimes, such as assaults, battering, robberies, muggings, rapes, and homicides. Less overt signs of suppressed anger may include behaviors by nurses such as slowing down their rate of work, slowness in answering the patient's call light, or looking away and not answering when others speak.

**Cultural Blindness.** When people associate only with people in their own social group, they develop cultural blindness and fail to see or appreciate differences between themselves and others. The only people they know are those who share their language, values, attitudes, and beliefs and who live in similar environments. Lacking contact with people who have differing points of view, they develop the conviction that everyone thinks, acts, and believes as they do. Even when meeting others from a different cultural background, they are unable to see or comprehend that they might have dissimilar values or beliefs about life and the world.

Actions that demonstrate caring about and using touch are given a high value by middle-class white nurses in this country, but to patients from other cultures, these behaviors may be regarded as intrusive, aggressive, and having sexual overtones. Arab patients regard a biopsychosocial assessment as an intrusion into their personal lives and expect doctors and nurses to be expert in providing highly technical medical care that will lead to a cure (Meleis, 1981). That which is highly valued in one culture may be seen in a very different light by those in another culture. The young student nurse with light blond hair had trouble persuading her patient to let her give him his bath. The older, black male patient repeatedly refused in a quiet and dignified way. Both the nurse and the patient were allowing cultural values and beliefs to blind them to the differences each placed on providing nursing care. The nurse expected the patient to accept her nursing care as readily as did the majority of her patients, whereas the black man showed embarrassment and indicated that it was not appropriate for her to provide such personal care.

**Ethnocentricity.** Ethnocentric people believe that the values, beliefs, and practices of their culture are the best and should be given preference over those of other cultures. They are convinced that "the way we do things is the best way" and that others should be willing to change to this superior way. They attempt to impose their standards on people from other cultures and judge other peoples' cultural beliefs or ways to be inferior. Although a certain amount of ethnocentricity is necessary for the survival of the culture, nurses should seek to understand cultural differences of their patients and consider these differences when planning their nursing care. Nursing interventions that conflict with cultural or religious beliefs will be less acceptable to the patient and may lead to rejection of care, noncompliance with the treatment, or problems in coping with feelings of anxiety, anger, or guilt.

**Cultural Conflict.** Conflict occurs when the values of one cultural group are not held or practiced in the same way by another culture. Conflicting values and misunderstandngs are increased as nurses care for patients from different minority groups or ethnic backgrounds and even from different parts of the country. Nurses who do not consider cultural differences are more apt to be critical of behavior that does not conform to their own beliefs or is different from their expectations. Conflicting views interfere with the nurse-patient relationship, the care the patient receives, and the rate of recovery or return to an adapted state.

In the field of health care, one common area where conflict causes problems is the way different cultural groups respond to pain. The typical middle-class American attitude is that the person should be a "good scout," control the expressions of pain, and be noncomplaining. The person who has severe pain wants to be left alone but also looks for relief of the pain. Nurses tend to expect all patients to tolerate a certain amount of pain, and they imply that they are reluctant to give pain medications when they ask, "Are you sure you're having pain and need something now?" Two studies showed that doctors and nurses who were in close contact with patients in pain tended to underestimate the severity of the pain when their ratings were compared with ratings by patients themselves. They also rated patients' pain as less severe than did social workers, teachers, and nurses from other countries (McCaffery, 1980; Davitz, 1976). The implication for nursing practice is that doctors frequently fail to prescribe medication to relieve the pain, and patients may be made to wait too long between doses of the drugs.

Patients from other cultural backgrounds have different responses to pain. Jewish people have a low tolerance for pain, and they describe pain in great detail as being terrible and unbearable. They do not want to be left alone and they cry aloud or moan to mobilize those around them to help. They also insist on knowing the diagnosis or cause of the pain and being cured. Italians are another group who have a low tolerance for pain. They become depressed when pain causes a loss of energy and interferes with their ability to enjoy life. They want relief immediately and are not concerned with the reason for the pain. On the other hand, the Irish withdraw from others when they have pain and place a high cultural value on remaining calm and unemotional. They do not share information about their pain experience easily with health professionals (Zborowski, 1969).

Other conflicts arise when nurses and patients have differing values and beliefs regarding family relationships and health practices. Many ethnic groups, including blacks, American Indians, Samoans, and gypsies, place a high value on the presence of their family for emotional support when they are ill. As many as 10 to 20 members of their extended family may come to the hospital to see the patient and may plan to stay indefinitely. This distresses nurses who follow hospital policies that limit the number of visitors to two

persons at a time and to members of the immediate family and that only allow visitors during specific visiting hours.

**Culture Shock.** The concept of culture shock originally referred to the feelings of people who moved from their native country to a new and unfamiliar country. Brink (1976) points out that numerous other situations cause reactions identical to culture shock. Such situations cause stress in people who are trying to adapt to foreign environments where their usual coping mechanisms are less effective and cues for appropriate behavior may be missing or unknown.

Culture shock produces a stress syndrome that has several distinct stages. Basic stress results from the abrupt transition from familiar surroundings to a new environment with alterations in one's lifestyle that are both positive and negative. Other sources of stress include differences in communication, new ways of dealing with the mechanics of living, isolation from friends and familiar objects, adjusting to different customs, and learning about the attitudes and beliefs of the people in the new location. One's ability to cope with or adjust to the new culture is greatly impaired when one does not speak the same language as the people who are already living or working there. Even if they speak the same language, each locale has a different way of speaking; words are given slightly different meanings, and slang terms are used differently. Problems in communication reduce the verbal feedback needed by the newcomer for giving and receiving clues for appropriate behavior. Newcomers must adapt to changes in ways of travel, maintaining a house or home, obtaining services, and such common things as different types of foods, taste of the water, and unfamiliar government or legal regulations that affect their daily lives.

When people move to a different community, state, or foreign country, they are isolated from familiar people, practices, and surroundings. Customs vary, and they must be learned, as well as the attitudes and beliefs associated with roles for parents, children, and spouse. One must learn ways to act in reciprocal roles, such as the expectations and etiquette in the roles between coworkers and employer or between the mother of the school child and the child's teacher.

The following four phases are involved in adjusting to a new culture.

*Phase 1* — The "honeymoon phase" is characterized by newcomers' excitement and eagerness to explore and become acquainted with their new surroundings. Each experience is new, different, and exhilarating whether it be the student going away to college for the first time or the immigrants coming to a new land. Both sightsee, look forward to and enjoy work, and settle into their new homes.

*Phase 2* — The "disenchantment phase" begins after the initial newness and excitement wear off. People examine their new surroundings and begin to see imperfections and the inefficiency of different agencies, and they rebel because of the amount of time spent doing just the ordinary activities of life, because these activities have to be done in ways with which the newcomer is not familiar. Newcomers have to give up their belief that "the way I do things is right" and must do things as required by the new culture. The "disenchantment phase" is a difficult period to live through, and many people would give up and return home if they were able to or were given the choice.

*Phase 3* — The beginning of the "resolution phase" occurs as newcomers begin to adjust to the host culture, feel more comfortable, form friendships, and find that life has become easier. Often they have contact with later arrivals who are worse off, are trying to cope with the disenchantment phase, and need their help in learning how to adapt to the new ways.

*Phase 4* — The "effective functioning phase" finds newcomers adjusting to their new surroundings and living as comfortably as they had been in their old cultural setting. They have made the host culture their own and may experience culture shock upon return to their original surroundings.

**Hospitalization and Culture Shock.**  For many people, hospitalization is a stressful experience, similar to the culture shock people experience when moving from one country to another (Brink, 1976). The degree to which hospitalization resembles culture shock depends upon to what extent the following factors are present:

1. The hospital environment is an unfamiliar setting for the individual.

2. Other environmental stressors exist that influence the individual's adaptation to the hospital setting.

3. The transition from the individual's home to the hospital setting was abrupt, not gradual.

4. The stay in the new setting requires planning for the future, whether the hospital stay is for days, weeks, or longer.

When people become ill and are hospitalized, they frequently encounter environmental stressors, including communications, mechanical differences in daily living, customs, isolation, and attitudes and beliefs, that tax their coping abilities.

- *Communications.* A different language is spoken by personnel in hospitals, even though the patient and health care providers both speak English. Doctors, nurses, and technicians use medical terminology, many abbreviations, and unfamiliar terms. Patients often have difficulty understanding what is meant by the nurse who states, "You're going to be NPO after midnight for GI studies in the morning. Has the IV nurse come to insert your heparin lock?" Even common terms, such as bed rest, partial bath, and bathroom privileges, have meanings that may vary from one institution to another.

- *Mechanical differences in daily living.* Patients and personnel must learn how to operate the equipment and machines found in the hospital setting that are used in the care of various medical conditions. Patients must learn how to summon help from the nurses, operate the controls to raise or lower the head or foot of the bed, find the bathroom, and remember the location of furniture in the room. Patients' activity and exercise are curtailed and restricted by casts, traction, IV lines, and so on. Lights may interfere with their sleep at night, and strange sounds may cause fear. Even the food tastes different, and it is served at unaccustomed times and eaten while one is lying or sitting in bed.

- *Customs.* When people become ill and assume the sick role, they are required to act in different ways, and, often, they lack information and cues for what they are expected to do. The hospital routine varies from the usual pattern of their lives, with patients being awakened early in the day, baths given in the morning, lack of privacy about their bodies and functions, and, often, a continuing stream of strangers entering the room for one reason or another. Patients must depend upon others for their care and carry out the instructions of nurses, who are, in most cases, women. For some men this causes a conflict when their role places a high value on men being strong, in control, the decision-maker, and dominant over women.

- *Isolation.* In the hospital, patients are isolated from family and friends by visiting hours that allow only two visitors at a time and restrict the daily visitation time to certain hours. A hospitalized patient is in a strange bed in an unfamiliar room and is surrounded by strangers who minister to his needs. Often a patient is forced to share a room with another sick person who may not be friendly, may have upsetting personal habits, or require medical and nursing care for distressing physical conditions.

*Attitudes and beliefs.* Members of the hospital staff tend to impose their values, attitudes, and beliefs on patients. They expect patients to be quiet, undemanding, cooperative, and grateful for their care. Patients expect to be informed about their illness and progress, but often feel that "the patient is the last to know." Nurses may withhold information or use the excuse that "this is what the doctor ordered." When patients' expectations differ from the attitudes and beliefs of the staff, the patients suffer disillusionment and discontent with the hospital experience.

Culture shock occurs when these stressors upset the patient's usual coping mechanisms, causing them to be ineffective in handling the anxiety provoked by the illness and hospitalization. In the hospital setting, all familiar belongings are taken away, leaving one with only a few toilet articles, a robe, and slippers. Nurses can help patients cope with the strangeness of the hospital environment by regarding these stressors as stimuli, by manipulating them, and by reducing their effects. Methods used include better communication with patients, an orientation to hospital services and the patient unit, explanation of the daily routine, explanations of procedures, and effective health-teaching.

## ASSESSMENT OF CULTURE

Nurses learn about cultures by focusing on one culture that is different from their own and by continuing to learn about additional cultures as the opportunity arises. Gathering information about the beliefs of a cultural or subcultural group is easier when the client and the nurse speak the same language. When the patient or client speaks a different language, the assessment of values and beliefs becomes more difficult. It is then necessary to read about the culture or ask someone who speaks the language to interpret. Although young children may be bilingual, efforts should be made to secure the services of a teenager or an adult who is more apt to understand and be able to explain health concepts and complex ideas.

The cultural assessment extends the information gathering process by noting how the patient or client carries out his or her developmental tasks.

It also includes the values, expectations, and preferences that are acceptable in the culture of one's origin. Children adapt more easily to the new culture than do their parents or other older adults because the old ways of doing things and the old beliefs were not as firmly ingrained. As children grow older, they tend to have more values and attitudes associated with the dominant culture but also cling to some beliefs of their parents. To identify cultural influences on patients' behavior, the nursing assessment includes characteristics of the individual or the self, family and kinship relationships, time orientation, religious beliefs, attitudes toward respect and authority, material goods or property, and health practices and beliefs (Leininger, 1981).

Information about the self includes personality attributes promoted by the cultural group, including values such as individual autonomy, passiveness, trust, modesty, competitiveness, decision-making, stubbornness, perseverance, and "saving face." Family and kinship relationships focus on whether the family is patriarchal, matriarchal, or egalitarian in the way it is governed. In some cultures, family includes many other relatives. In some cultures, the grandmother is the pivotal member and the decision-maker for the entire extended family, whereas in Mexican-American families, the husband makes all decisions concerning family members. In all cultures, family and kinship ties are important, but significant differences are found. In the middle-class American culture, nurses expect young unwed mothers to give up their babies for adoption or to take care of the babies themselves. However, in many lower social class subcultures, the child of an unwed mother is reared by the maternal grandmother. Family relationships also are affected by values and beliefs associated with pregnancy, giving birth, and rearing children.

People in different cultures do not always have the same perception of time. Many people focus on the present and have little or no concept of the future. They do not plan for tomorrow but deal with each day is it comes; they have a relaxed concept of time and are not governed by a clock. They consider people who time their activities as lacking manners and gentility, whereas people with a keen sense of time are frustrated when workers fail to arrive on the day or at the time they said they would.

Religious beliefs should be explored in the nursing assessment because they often extend to all areas of one's life and provide a framework for the way people regard themselves and their world. When sick, many people seek spiritual comfort from their religious practices or customs.

People of the Catholic faith take communion and receive solace from the annointing of the sick; the Muslim kneels toward Mecca and prays five times a day; and the Indian receives comfort from the "sing" ceremony.

One's attitudes about respect and authority indicate one's beliefs about right and wrong, fairness, justice, and the form of government of one's family, community, or society. When people are sick, the same attitudes may influence the degree of trust or suspicion toward others in authority, including doctors or nurses who exercise some power over their lives. The health practices and beliefs of a particular culture influence the manner in which the people of that culture accept help and from whom. Illness is regarded in many different ways: the will of God, punishment for sins, the natural order of things, or fate, or one's destiny. Health practices are frequently determined by a mixture of beliefs about scientific medicine and folk medicine. Assessment of material goods and property provides a measure of the resources available for living, including rural or urban society, type of housing, distribution of foods and goods, availability of electricity, water supply, sanitation, and methods of transportation. People's attitudes and feelings about material goods vary from societies that regard everything owned as communal property to societies that regard property as private and belonging to an individual.

## THE DOMINANT CULTURAL VALUES IN THE UNITED STATES

The dominant culture of the United States is composed of white, middle-class people with Protestant backgrounds. Many members of this cultural group are descendants of the early settlers who arrived from Europe in the seventeenth century and who settled in the states along the Atlantic seaboard. Many came from England, France, and the Netherlands to escape religious persecution and brought their beliefs and cultural values with them. People who arrived in this country later were expected to adopt these values and practices if they wanted to belong to the dominant group who had the most influence and power.

The values of white, middle-class Americans have persisted for generations and provide the framework for the American way of life. Values derived from a Puritan heritage emphasize individual freedoms, family ties, cleanliness, orderliness, and achievement. The assessment categories described previously can be used to classify the dominant characteristics of the American culture.

*Self.* Great emphasis is placed on the value of each individual's life and each person's autonomy. People have the freedom to speak, act, and worship as they wish. They are highly competitive and are achievement-oriented. A high value is placed on having a youthful and attractive appearance. A preoccupation with cleanliness prompts the frequent use of deodorants, mouthwashes, lotions, showers, and washing. Both the people and their surroundings are scrubbed and washed to a degree that some other cultures view as bordering on neurotic behavior.

*Family.* The nuclear family is most important, and family activities center around it. Families are very mobile, and grown children often live far from their parents and other relatives. However, grandparents and other members of the extended family are included in some activities when they live within the same community. Children are highly valued as sources of emotional gratification, and the relationships between parents and children tend to be democratic and egalitarian. Mothers are expected to rear the children according to the latest techniques rather than follow the methods used by the grandmothers.

*Time orientation.* White, middle-class Americans live by the clock. They rush to get things done and place a high value on being prompt, businesslike, and not wasting time. They are also future-oriented. They plan extensively for the future and are often able to delay gratification of their desires.

*Religious beliefs.* Most white, middle-class Americans have a Protestant background, although not everyone practices his religion. Their concept of right and wrong is based on biblical teachings and the Ten Commandments, and they believe in the punishment of sins and the concept of heaven and hell.

*Respect and authority.* Members of this group believe in justice and in fair play. They have respect for laws and private property and abide by rules and regulations. They respect their parents and people in positions of authority. Patriotism and love of country are highly valued characteristics of this group.

*Material goods.* Achievement is important to this group. They place great emphasis on technological progress, advanced technology, and the scientific approach to solving problems. Education is highly valued as a means of obtaining the material goods necessary for achieving "the good life."

*Health practices.* White, middle-class Americans have a high regard for good health and spend a lot of money on achieving and maintaining it. Americans believe in the germ theory and rely on medical science and technology to find cures for diseases. Their children are immunized; they use preventive measures; and they have health insurance to help defray costs of treating illnesses. Health facilities are convenient for their use, and their needs dictate the types of services that are provided.

These characteristics represent many values, attitudes, and beliefs of the middle-class American culture as well as those of people from other minority, ethnic, or social class groups. Not all members of this cultural group are WASP (white, Anglo-Saxon, and Protestant), although they do constitute the majority.

## COMPARISONS OF DIFFERENT CULTURES

The study of cultures is appropriate for nurses because they provide care for patients and clients from diverse backgrounds. Knowledge of cultural beliefs is useful when dealing with ethnic groups in our society who, for one reason or another, have not assumed the values of white, middle-class Americans. Other subcultures have many of these values but still retain some of their old cultural ways and beliefs. Knowing how people meet their basic needs, such as eating, sleeping, working, playing, and relating to others, reduces barriers and misunderstandings when planning their care.

### THE BLACK AMERICAN CULTURE

No single, typical black American culture exists; rather, there are several different cultures that trace their heritage back to the Negro tribes of Africa. The first blacks to come to this country arrived here more than 300 years ago, and, by 1790, they accounted for nearly 20 per cent of the United States population. By 1979, the black American population had grown to nearly 26 million people and constituted approximately 12 per cent of the population. (See Table 22–1.)

Black culture is not simply a black version of white American culture. The first black people to arrive in this country were taken from their native lands and brought here to be sold as slaves to work on plantations in the southern states. Although a few blacks lived in the northern states following the Civil War, the majority of them stayed in rural areas of the South until after World War I. Many blacks then migrated to industrial cities in the North and, in later decades, moved west to California. The states with the highest percentage of blacks are the southern

**Table 22–1.** GROWTH OF THE BLACK POPULATION IN AMERICA FROM 1790 TO 1979

| Year | Number | Percentage of Total Population |
|------|--------|-------------------------------|
| 1790 | 757,000 | 19.3 |
| 1850 | 3,639,000 | 15.7 |
| 1900 | 8,834,000 | 11.6 |
| 1950 | 15,045,000 | 10.0 |
| 1979 | 25,863,000 | 11.8 |

Source: Statistical Abstract of the United States 1980, 101st ed. No. 31. Washington, D.C., Bureau of the Census, 1980.

states, but the northern and western states have the greatest numbers of blacks. (See Table 22–2.)

Slavery had a profound effect on the black culture in this country. During slavery, family members were often sold to different owners, marriage was forbidden, use of their native language was forbidden, and slaves were required by their owners to observe Christian beliefs. Although slavery was abolished more than a century ago, some white people still regard blacks as inferior people. As a result, blacks have been segregated from whites, have received less education, and have been targets for political and economic discrimination. With less education and fewer opportunities, they qualified for mainly low-paying and menial jobs and were among the first people to lose jobs during difficult times. In 1979, according to the Bureau of the Census statistics approximately 30 per cent of blacks' incomes were below the poverty level. Black male workers tend to earn an average of $5,000 a year less than their white counterparts, although black women earn only about $400 a year less than white women. Black families tend to be larger than white families, and larger families are more apt to be poor. The birth rate for black women is about 50 per cent higher than that for white women. Although life expectancy has recently increased for black people, white men live 5 years longer than black men, and white women live 4 years longer than black women.

**Table 22–2.** LOCATION OF BLACK POPULATION IN THE UNITED STATES

| States | Percentage of State Population | States | Population (millions) |
|--------|-------------------------------|--------|----------------------|
| Mississippi | 33.9 | New York | 2.2 |
| Georgia | 26.0 | Illinois | 1.7 |
| Alabama | 25.3 | California | 1.6 |
| Louisiana | 23.7 | Texas | 1.4 |
| Florida | 14.8 | Georgia | 1.3 |

The cultural values of black Americans incorporate both their African heritage and the values and beliefs acquired during their experiences in America. A summary of cultural characteristics of blacks follows.

**Beliefs about the Self.** Part of a person's self-concept is formed from how others respond to him or her. Although black children are affected by other factors, parental attitudes and views of life are the most influential factors. Black parents teach their children control over body functions and emotions. Obedience is a very important characteristic. Black parents tend to use physical punishment to discipline their children more often than they use verbal abuse; however, the discipline is balanced with a great deal of love for their children.

**Family and Kinship Ties.** Some blacks live in extended families that consist of relatives by blood and marriage or augmented families that include friends or boarders. Interaction and involvement with kin are frequent and intense in the black culture. Family members provide mutual support, both emotionally and economically. Black parents pride themselves on their children. The parents have flexible roles in the rearing of their children. Some black children are cared for by extended family members. In many families, both parents must work, so other family members, such as the grandmother, an aunt, or older sister cares for the children.

The history of slavery and its effects on black culture have produced several myths about the disorganization, instability, and matriarchal tendency of the black family. Many research studies overlooked the inherent strengths of black families as they focused on families headed by women whose husbands were missing, the large number of illegitimate births, the economic dependence of black men, the degree of poverty, and lack of motivation. These characteristics are usually associated with poverty rather than being unique to the black culture (Willis, 1978). Lower-class black families, like lower-class white families, are more apt to be one-parent households. There has been an increase in the number of black single-parent families — the Washington Post reported that 50 per cent of all black babies born in 1976 were to unmarried mothers. Among middle-class black families generally one parent is a college graduate.

**Time Orientation.** Emphasis on time in the black culture varies, depending upon social class. People in the lower class and those who retain their African heritage tend to be present-oriented, rather than being future-oriented. They may be fatalistic owing to the influences of poverty, slavery, and discrimination.

**Material Goods.** Achievement is important to black people. They want to have comfortable homes and furnishings, stylish clothing, and nice cars. Even when they lack money to buy what they want, some black people use credit and, because they are a poor credit risk, they pay much more for their credit. Those who live in poverty with few material goods have fewer aspirations for their children, and are segregated into black neighborhoods or ghettos. The extremely poor have been in a subordinate position in society for generations, and the stresses for survival are so great that they do not see education as an effective way for them to escape from poverty and the ghetto. Middle-class blacks regard education as a means for getting better jobs, living in better neighborhoods, and becoming integrated into the mainstream of American culture.

**Religious Beliefs.** Religion plays an important part in the lives of most black people. Their beliefs are a combination of traditional African beliefs and Christian influences. The majority of blacks in this country follow Protestant faiths of the Baptist and Methodist churches, and many blacks are of the Muslim faith. Through the church, blacks participate in community activities and gain a sense of recognition.

**Respect and Authority.** As a result of discrimination and injustice for generations, many blacks developed fear and contempt for white American justice, for police, and for other institutions that they believe have kept them at a disadvantage. Until recent years, blacks did not join political organizations, were not active in community activities, and did not vote. They felt powerless to change the system; thus, they retreated from it. Although changes *are* taking place, black men are frequently "hassled" by police when a crime occurs. Black youths from ghetto neighborhoods are often involved in street gangs, criminal activities, and violence. Among black youths aged 15 to 19 years, homicide is the second leading cause of death; accidents are the major cause.

**Health Beliefs and Practices.** Social class influences health beliefs and practices in the black culture. Lower-class blacks retain the belief from their African heritage that diseases have natural and unnatural causes. Their religious beliefs are closely allied with the belief that natural events are predictable, whereas unnatural occurrences are out of harmony and are a punishment for a sin or for lack of faith. Some black subcultures are convinced that unnatural illnesses are caused by witchcraft, voodoo, or hexes. Cures for such illnesses require the services of people who possess supernatural powers.

Both the high cost of health care and the fact that one third of all blacks live in poverty compound the health problems of blacks and cause delay in the treatment for disease until it is advanced. Blacks tend to continue working as long as possible and refer to pain as "a misery," often denying pain when a plausible medical reason exists for having it. The special health problems of black Americans include hypertension, which occurs at an epidemic rate, higher infant and maternal deaths than among whites, and a high incidence of pneumonia, influenza, tuberculosis, strokes, and deaths due to homicide. Other health problems particular to this ethnic group include sickle cell anemia (a hereditary disease of red blood cells), inflammation of hair follicles, and keloid formation (the excessive growth of scar tissue).

## THE MEXICAN AMERICAN CULTURE

More than 12 million people in the United States are among Spanish-speaking ethnic groups. Those who originally came from Mexico constitute more than 7 million of these people, although the number may be much higher because many Mexican Americans entered the country illegally and avoided being counted in the census. Another 3 million people arrived here from Cuba and Central and South America, and the remainder are Puerto Ricans. Most Mexican Americans have a Spanish and Indian heritage, are called Chicanos or Latinos, and live in the southwestern states. Hispanics are citizens who are descendants of the early Spanish settlers and American Indians and who live primarily in New Mexico and Colorado. Those who came from Puerto Rico have a Spanish and black bloodline and live on the East Coast, with a high concentration living in New York City. Spanish-speaking neighborhoods in cities are called barrios.

In the United States, census statistics show that more than 85 per cent of all Spanish-speaking people live in cities. Only two of every five Mexican Americans have a high school education; thus, they have fewer job skills and must take lower-paying jobs. They tend to have large families, and more than half this ethnic group is under the age of 21 years. The poverty rate varies among the Puerto Ricans, Mexican Americans, and those from other Spanish-speaking countries; however, overall, it is less than the rate for black Americans. Among Puerto Ricans, nearly 40 per cent have an income at or below the poverty level, whereas only 18 per cent of Mexican Americans and 13 per cent of people from other

Spanish-speaking countries are at or below the poverty level.

Although each subculture has different values and beliefs, the three groups have some values and beliefs in common. Because Mexican Americans constitute the largest Spanish-speaking group, this assessment focuses on their culture.

**Beliefs about the Self.** Although the concepts of *La Raza* and *machismo* were once values held by Mexican American men, today, their values are more closely aligned with those of white men. La Raza referred to the race of people who were united in language and in cultural and spiritual bonds with God. They had a strong sense of fatalism and believed that good or bad luck was predestined and therefore should be accepted. They believed "What will be, will be." They did not see themselves as making mistakes or committing sins. They viewed such occurrences as external happenings over which they had no control or as simply adverse circumstances. If members of La Raza had more material possessions than their friends, it aroused envy among members of the group.

Machismo refers to the sense of manliness and defines what was once the ideal Mexican American male role. Mexican Americans do not like to be indebted to anyone; thus, they are reluctant to seek help from charities or other institutions. They would be humiliated and feel that they were compromising their honor. Honor requires that Mexican American men avoid being wrong, so they often delay making a statement or decision until they are sure of the outcome. Today, although Mexican American men are still very much in authority, many changes are taking place. The roles of Mexican American women have changed also. They are no longer regarded as weak and submissive and are now treated with respect. Men recognize their need to be productive and to have a feeling of self-worth.

**Family and Kinship Ties.** Marriages endure because these vows are taken in church and are seen as sacred. Divorce is considered sinful. The family is very important in the Mexican American culture and is headed by the father or oldest male relative who defends its honor. The family extends to grandparents, aunts, uncles, and so on, and demands that each member act as a symbol of the family. To bring shame to the family is unforgivable. Families tend to be patriarchal; however, early in life, Mexican American children learn that their mothers can influence their fathers in subtle ways. Mexican American children are taught to respect older people and to be polite.

Parents give their children responsibilities at an early age. Both husband and wife are usually involved in raising their children. Mexican American children may have problems in school owing to their different cultural and linguistic background.

**Time Orientation.** Most Mexican Americans live for the present. They lack the future orientation of white Americans because they believe that God, rather than men, controls the events in their lives.

**Material Goods.** The values of Mexican Americans depend upon social class pressures and the exposure to white influences, such as the length of time they have lived in this country. They see the United States as the land of opportunity and wealth of which they thought they could never be a part. Lower-class Mexican Americans regard money as a means for enjoying themselves, not as a means for changing their position in life. They tend to be suspicious of people outside the family, so often do not join labor unions, trade organizations, political groups, and so on. Folk custom dictates that people do not strive to outdo their relatives or friends in success or to arouse their envy by having better material possessions, such as a house, car, or clothing.

**Religious Beliefs.** Most Mexican Americans are Catholic. The religion of the lower classes includes superstitions from their Indian heritage. They often have a family altar with pictures of saints and their deceased relatives. They believe in curanderos and faith healers to cure them of supernatural diseases.

**Respect and Authority.** Mexican Americans show respect to all family members, young and old. Men are considered the head of the household; they see themselves as protectors of the family. They tolerate no offense to the family, maintain its public image, and assume no obligations that would conflict with their familial roles.

**Health Beliefs and Practices.** Mexican Americans' understanding of illness depends upon how closely they identify with their ethnic traditions and the amount of contact with white culture. For most, their knowledge of illness and its treatment comes from (1) folk medicine, (2) American-Indian folk medicine, and (3) scientific medical sources. Some believe that illness is subject to God's will and that, therefore, little can be done about it.

Diseases are classified according to causes rather than symptoms. There are good, or natural diseases that upset the balance of the natural world and bewitchments, caused by people using demonic powers. Natural diseases include the medically recognized such as pneumonia, colds, diabetes, and stroke. Bewitchments are folk diseases treated at home by the curanderos and faith healers. Folk beliefs are combined with scientific medicine with the gradual merging of Mexican and white cultures. Some folk beliefs

include treating "hot" diseases with cold remedies or foods and "cold" diseases with hot foods or remedies. The condition of "evil eye" (mal ojo) is believed to be caused by people with a strong gaze who admire or envy one's good fortune or children and who try to cause bad luck or emotionally upset them. *Susto* and *espanto* are diseases that may result from a frightening experience. Fright caused by natural occurrences, such as a narrow escape from an auto accident is susto. Fright caused by supernatural encounter with spirits or ghosts is espanto. "Fallen fontanels" is one of the most common folk ailments of infants. School-age children are likely to suffer from *empacho,* a form of indigestion. Most folk remedies rely on herbs, teas, prayers, massage, and manipulation of parts of the body by the parent or curandero.

Many Mexican Americans who cling to their ethnic beliefs mistrust American physicians. Although most know of the germ theory, they reject it as a cause of disease. Because many have a limited English vocabulary, they find the doctor's explanations difficult to understand. Even with the help of an interpreter, they may not understand the concepts of preventive medicine or the need for hospitalization. In general, like other cultures, their health conditions reflect their socioeconomic status. People in the lower-class have a higher rate of illness and illnesses of a more serious nature than do people in the middle-class.

## THE AMERICAN INDIAN CULTURE

According to the U. S. Census of 1970, approximately 800,000 American Indians live in the United States. Many continue to live on reservations in traditional ways. They belong to different tribes, each having different values, beliefs, and languages. Some Indians living on reservations may have limited experience speaking English. Indians have often been described as overly shy, owing to their manner of assessing each situation before they commit themselves and become involved. They prefer to be called by their tribal name — Hopi, Navajo, Cherokee, Sioux, and so on rather than to be called "Indian." In 1970, the state with the highest population of Indians was Oklahoma with 98,500 people, followed by Arizona, California, New Mexico, Washington, and South Dakota.

**Beliefs about the Self.** Some Indians have values and lifestyles that are in sharp contrast with white society's competitive and materialistic values. Status in the white American culture results from accumulating money, possessions, and power as well as from one's work; however, in

Indian communities, status is achieved through generosity and sharing with others. In this way, they take care of each other. Those who cannot work, the elderly, and others who have less are provided for. They are a noncompetitive group and believe that being is more fundamental than achieving.

Indians have a strong and close relationship with nature. The concept of the supernatural is a common belief in Indian families. Indians believe that they are guests on earth and that they must walk carefully so as not to upset the balance of nature for all living things. Individual freedom and independence are highly valued, as well as their adherence to the principle of noninterference. They do not try to change anyone's style of living and resent health care professionals who try to coerce, manipulate, or force on them health practices that they do not understand or want to accept. When spoken to, Indians often respond with downcast eyes and avoid making eye contact. Looking into another person's eyes is considered to be an invasion of one's privacy and is thought of as being impolite. Some Indians regard a firm handshake as a display of aggression and back away slightly from the vigorous hand-shaker.

**Family and Kinship Ties.** In the Indian world, the family and tribe are most highly valued. The extended family includes distant relatives as well as close friends. Children are treasured and encouraged to be independent from an early age. Parents rarely tell children what they can or cannot do. However, children are told the consequences so they learn and live by their decisions. Parents are skilled in using nonverbal language to control their children's behavior in public. Indians regard all people as being related and consider being truly poor as being without relatives. Older people in the tribe are respected and revered for their knowledge and wisdom.

**Time Orientation.** Indians live in the present and take life one day at a time. They view time as a continuum with no beginning or end. Their attitude toward time is very casual and relative to what needs to be done. They observe few set routines; for example, Indian children eat when they are hungry and sleep when they are tired. They may eat two meals today because they were busy at some other activity, but they may eat four meals tomorrow because there was less to do.

**Material Goods.** Wealth and material goods are not highly valued by Indians. They revere the land and regard the earth like a mother and all animals as brothers. If they have the bare essentials, Indian families do not strive to accumulate

material things or to "better" themselves. This may be due in part to their social class expectations. Indians are among the poorest of the poor. Among the reservation Indians, the annual income is about one half the poverty level income of the country as a whole, and unemployment is 30 per cent or higher (Bullough, 1972). Many Indians who leave the reservations go to the cities full of hope but become trapped in poverty when they find that they are unskilled and undereducated for the available jobs.

**Religious Beliefs.** Indians believe in a "spirit power" that controls the earth and nature and influences medicine and religion. Some methods of practicing medicine involve ceremonies and rituals performed by the medicine man. They do not believe in life after death as a reward for one's good deeds. Death is viewed as part of the life cycle, the time when one goes to join the world of one's ancestors. Funerals usually take place in the home, with large feasts and gift-giving to relatives and friends of the deceased.

**Respect and Authority.** Older members of the tribe are respected and revered for their wisdom and counsel. Indians are intimidated by competitive people, especially the white man. They are proud, but passive and noncompetitive. They believe that one does not embarrass one's friends by beating them in competition. Instead, they often let the other person win.

**Health Beliefs and Practices.** Health is seen as the result of a harmonious balance with nature, whereas illness represents a wrong attitude about life. Indians have no concept of the germ theory. They believe in the practice of folk medicine, which is intricately interwoven with the religious beliefs in which rituals, ceremonial dances, and "sings" are performed for the ill person, with herbs and plants used as medicines.

During illness, many relatives arrive at the hospital to provide support and comfort to the sick Indian, usually to the dismay of nurses, doctors, and hospital officials. Relatives may hold healing rituals that include sprinkling cornmeal around the patient's bed or placing an item with special curative powers on the patient or at the bedside. Corn is usually regarded as having sacred properties, and removal of the cornmeal without their permission causes mental distress.

One of the biggest barriers to health care in the Indian culture is the Indians' lack of trust in the available health care. Further, their health problems are aggravated by their poverty. Life expectancy on an Indian reservation is about 44 years. The infant mortality rate is three times the national average. Other major health problems include tuberculosis, malnutrition, hypertension, alcoholism, and suicide.

## APPLICATION TO CLINICAL PRACTICE

When caring for patients from a different ethnic background, the assessment of psychosocial adaptations should consider the effects of culture and its influence on the values and beliefs held by the patient. Nurses may have cultural blindness and may not be aware that differences exist unless they make a conscientious effort to learn more about other cultures. Begin by studying one culture different from your own and read at least one article about it. Several articles are listed in the references. Write some values and beliefs of the culture or subculture in terms of

Beliefs about the self                Religious beliefs
Family and kinship ties            Respect and authority
Time orientation                       Health practices
Material goods

Attention should also be given to ways to modify interventions and nursing care in order to reduce conflicts with the patient's beliefs and practices.

Information about cultural values helps nurses using the adaptation approach to evaluate patients' health practices, including the expectations and role performances in their own culture, rather than imposing on them nurses' value systems.

## REFERENCES

### General

Brink, Pamela (ed.): Transcultural Nursing. A Book of Readings. Englewood Cliffs, New Jersey, Prentice-Hall, Inc., 1976.

Bullough, Bonnie, and Bullough, Vern: Poverty, Ethnic Identity, and Health Care. New York, Appleton-Century-Crofts, 1972.

Davitz, Lois, Davitz, Joel, and Sameshimo, Yasuko: Suffering as viewed in six different cultures. Am J Nurs, 76:1296–1297, (August) 1976.

Leininger, Madeline: Transcultural Nursing, Concepts, Theories, and Practices. New York, John Wiley & Sons, Inc., 1978.

Leininger, Madeline: Transcultural Nursing Workshop. Golden West College, Huntington Beach, CA, February 20–21, 1981.

MacGregor, Frances: Uncooperative patients: some cultural interpretations. Am J Nurs, 67:81–91, (January) 1967.

McCaffery, Margo: Understanding your patient's pain. Nursing 80, 10:26–31, (September) 1980.

McMahon, Margaret, and Miller, Sister Patricia: Pain responses: the influence of psychosocial-cultural factors. Nurs Forum, 17:58–71, (November) 1978.

Statistical Abstract of the United States 1980, 101st ed. Washington, D. C., Bureau of the Census, 1980.

Symposium on cultural & biological diversity and health care. Nurs Clin North Am, 12(1):1–86, (March) 1977.

Taylor, Carol: The nurse and cultural barriers. In Hymovich, Debra, and Barnard, Martha (eds.): Family Health Care. New York, McGraw-Hill, Inc., 1973.

Zborowski, Mark: People in Pain. San Francisco, Jossey-Bass, Inc., Publishers, 1969.

### Black American Culture

Banks, James, and Grambs, Jean: Black Self Concept. New York, McGraw-Hill, Inc., 1972.

Bartz, Karen, and LeVine, Elaine. Childrearing by black parents: a description and comparison to Anglo and Chicano parents. Journal of Marriage and the Family, 40(4):709–719, (November) 1978.

Black skin problems. Am J Nurs, 79:1092–1094, (June) 1979.

Branch, Marie, and Paxton, Phyllis: Providing Safe Nursing Care for Ethnic People of Color. New York, Appleton-Century-Crofts, 1976.

Clark, Ann L.: Culture and Child-Rearing, Philadelphia, F. A. Davis Company, 1981.

Davis, Mardell: Getting to the root of the problem. Nursing 77, 7(1):60–65, (January) 1977.

Grier, William, and Cobbs, Price: Black Rage. New York, Basic Books, Inc., Publishers, 1968.

James, Sybil: When your patient is black West Indian. Am J Nurs, 78:1908–1909, (November) 1978.

Lunkraft, Dorothy (ed.): Black Awareness: Implications for Black Patient Care. New York, American Journal of Nursing Publishing Co., 1976.

Nobles, Wade: Toward an empirical and theoretical framework for defining black families. Journal of Marriage and the Family, 40(4):679–687, (November) 1978.

Roach, Lora: Color changes in dark skin. Nursing 77, 7(1):48–51, (January) 1977.

Willie, Charles, and Greenblatt, Susan: Four "classic" studies of power relationships in black families: a review and look to the future. Journal of Marriage and the Family, 40(4):691–694, (November) 1978.

### Spanish-Speaking Culture

Baca, Josephine: Some health beliefs of the Spanish speaking. Am J Nurs, 69:2172–2176, (October) 1969.

Clark, Margaret: Health in the Mexican-American Culture. University of California Press, Berkeley and Los Angeles, 1970.

Gonzales, Hector: Health Care Needs of the Mexican-American. New York, National League for Nursing Publication, 1976.

Johnson, Carmen: Nursing and Mexican-American folk medicine. Nurs Forum, 3(2):104–112, 1964.

Madsen, William: The Mexican Americans of South Texas. New York, Holt, Rinehart and Winston, 1973.

## American Indian Culture

Adaire, J., and Deuschle, K.: The People's Health: Medicine and Anthropology in a Navajo Community. New York, Appleton-Century-Crofts, 1970.

Burkhardt, Margaret: Nursing the Navajo. Am J Nurs, 77:95–96, (January) 1977.

Debo, Angie: A History of the Indians of the United States. Norman, The University of Oklahoma Press, 1970.

Farris, L. Sanders: Approaches to caring for the American Indian maternity patient. Matern Child Nurs J, 1(2):80–87, (March/April) 1976.

Kniep-Hardy, Mary, and Burkhardt, Margaret: Nursing the Navajo. Am J Nurs, 77:95–96, (January) 1977.

Mealey, Shirley: Factors that influence Navajo patients to keep appointments. Nurs Pract, 1:18–22, (March/April) 1977.

Primeaux, Martha: Caring for the American Indian patient. Am J Nurs, 77:91–94, (January) 1977.

Rosenblum, Estelle: Conversation with a Navajo nurse. Am J Nurs, 80:1459–1461, (August) 1980.

Spector, Rachel: Health and illness among ethnic people of color. Nurse Educator, 2:10–13, (May/June) 1977.

Stuckey, William: Navajo medicine men. Science Digest, 78:35, (December) 1975.

Wallace, Louella: Patient is an American Indian. Supervisor Nurse, 32–33, (May) 1977.

## Other Cultures

Anderson, Gwen, and Tighe, Bridget: Gypsy culture and health care. Am J Nurs, 73:282–285, (February) 1973.

Campbell, Teresa, and Chang, Betty: Health care of Chinese in America. Nurs Outlook, 21:245–249, (April) 1973.

DeGracia, Rosario T.: Filipino cultural influences. Am J Nurs, 79:1412–1414, (August) 1979.

Gordon, Verona, Matousek, Irene, and Lang, Theresa: Southeast Asian refugees: life in America. Am J Nurs, 80:2031–2036, (November) 1980.

Gropper, R. C.: Gypsies in the City. New Jersey, The Darwin Press, Inc., 1975.

Meleis, Afaf: The Arab American in the health care system. Am J Nurs, 81:1180–1183, (June) 1981.

# Chapter TWENTY-THREE
# Poverty and Adaptation

## OBJECTIVES   Information in this chapter will help you to

1. Define poverty in terms of level of income and incidence in the United States.
2. Explain the causes of poverty and the people most at risk of being or becoming poor.
3. Describe the values, attitudes, and lifestyle of people with low incomes.
4. State the health beliefs and health practices of people in the lower socioeconomic group.
5. Discuss common health problems of poor people and the barriers they encounter when seeking health care.
6. List some federal programs and community resources available to help poor people.
7. Assess patients from low income groups for the influence of poverty on their lifestyle and their health practices.

## DEFINITION OF TERMS

**adaptational perspective of poverty** — the view of the poor as a special subgroup of society responding to a social system that makes it impossible for them to achieve the values and practices of the dominant cultural group.

**alienation** — feelings of estrangement from the rest of society.

**barrios** — city neighborhoods of Spanish-speaking people.

**culture of poverty** — a view of poverty as a subculture with its own set of values and behaviors that differ from the nonpoor and are passed on from generation to generation. The attitudes and values transcend ethnic and regional boundaries.

**poverty** — lack of income and resources needed to provide for all one's basic needs and comforts.

Poverty is an important determinant that influences how people live their lives and affects their attitudes and practices related to health. Most members of the middle-class have little or no experience with poverty and have limited contact with those who are poor. Some middle-class people believe that poor people somehow deserve their fate and that if they had enough ambition they could rise above poverty. However, nursing care is provided to all people in a nondiscriminating way, regardless of age, gender, race, color, creed, or income. When nurses from middle-class backgrounds see the poor as inferior, socially flawed, and lacking the will or determination to improve their condition, discriminatory practices may result. Lack of understanding interferes with the quality of nursing care and leads to avoidance and withdrawal by the client or patient.

In the adaptation approach to nursing care, poverty is an important stimulus that influences how people respond to social conditions that are depressive and often demoralizing. People with low incomes have needs, desires, and aspirations similar to nonpoor people; however, poor people must spend a greater percentage of their money on survival needs. In this chapter, the causes of poverty, the people most likely to be poor, how poverty affects coping and one's lifestyle, health problems associated with being poor, and some resources and programs that provide assistance to poverty groups will be examined.

## POVERTY IN THE UNITED STATES

People of other countries see the United States as a country of great hope and opportunity and as having one of the highest standards of living in the world. Yet, with all its affluence, one of ten United States citizens lives in poverty. Although poverty in this country is not on the same scale as poverty in Chad, Bangladesh, and other poor nations, poverty does exist. Poverty not only is the lack of money but also is the fear and dread of being in want of necessities.

### WHAT IT MEANS TO BE POOR

To live in poverty is to live miserably without being able to change the conditions, to have the dread of hunger, and to work hard but not gain any advantage. Most people who are poor live in run-down, miserable homes in dismal neighborhoods where most middle-class people do not go or in crowded tenement buildings in the slums of large cities. They buy cheap food of inferior quality and eat unbalanced diets that often lead to numerous health problems. Poor people have to accept handouts and assistance, which robs them of their dignity. Despite efforts to eradicate poverty, many people have not shared in the wealth and increased standard of living while others have prospered and gained a home in the suburbs, a late model car, or annual vacation trips.

With few exceptions, people who are poor live in substandard housing with numerous defects. Lack of repairs and defects, such as leaking roofs, broken windows, frayed electrical wiring, broken steps or railings, and nonfunctioning or nonexistent plumbing, and rats or cockroaches can be found in the rural farmhouse as well as in the apartment in the slums. Bullough (1972) described the problem of rats that she encountered as a public health nurse giving follow-up care to William Henry.

"William Henry's mother and four siblings lived in a dug-out basement under a dilapidated row house in Chicago during the 1950s. Mrs. Henry was awakened one night by the cries of her baby, and found two huge gray rats on top of him. When she snatched William up, his hand was a bleeding mass of mangled flesh. She took her baby to Cook County Hospital for emergency care. However, Cook County was more than an hour away by bus. In order to get there, she had to borrow money from her neighbors to take a taxi. Because she was afraid to leave her other four children alone at home, she took all of them with her, and they spent the night in the emergency room waiting for the baby to be treated and admitted. Most of the hand could be saved, although he lost the distal part of three fingers.

Several families in the area had built heavy screen cages over their children's beds, and sometimes at night they would hear rats gnawing on the screens. Mrs. Henry, however lacked money to buy screens and had little talent as a carpenter. After the baby came home from the hospital, she tried staying awake at night to protect the baby, but became exhausted. In a desperate attempt, she got two half-grown cats. Before the week was out, the rats had eaten the cats."*

A slum clearance project was found to be a major factor in the problem people were having with the rats. Tenement buildings were torn down to make way for new rat-proof, high-rise buildings; thus, displaced rats invaded the existing slums. When food from the uncollected garbage was not sufficient for the increased rat population, they began to attack infants.

---

*Reprinted by permission. Bullough, Bonnie, and Bullough, Vern: Poverty, Ethnic Identity, and Health Care. New York, Appleton-Century-Crofts, 1972, pp. 2–4.

People living in poverty are often referred to as the "invisible poor" because they are congregated in poor sections of cities or in rural areas and are often difficult to distinguish from the nonpoor by their attire alone. Some poor people appear well dressed, even though their clothes are cheap copies of current fashions. Through television, Americans are trained to want things and to spend money on consumer items in order to win the respect of others and to maintain their self-respect. Many poor people buy on credit and pay higher interest rates because they are poorer credit risks.

## CAUSES OF POVERTY

Throughout the history of the world, most people were born poor and remained poor all their lives. In the United States, fewer people are poor, as a result of concerted efforts to eliminate poverty. However, poverty is a complex problem that requires many different approaches and solutions. Poverty is caused by a mixture of social and economic circumstances that are not easily corrected or changed. Among the causes are

- Racial discrimination
- Limited education
- Limited job opportunities
- Resources of the geographical area where one lives
- Illness or physical handicap
- Being too old or too young to work
- Lack of skills
- Broken family through death or separation of wage earner

The prevalence of discrimination is one of the disadvantages of a diverse society such as the United States, with its many cultural groups. At some time, everyone is a member of a minority group and subject to the discriminatory practices of people who have more power. Most discrimination today is related to social and economic decisions in which the disadvantaged people become a source of cheap labor. Immigrants from Puerto Rico, Mexico, and other Central American countries, as well as American Indians and blacks, are victims of racial discrimination. Such discrimination restricts their job opportunities, increases the price they must pay for goods and services, determines the type of education they receive, and narrows their choices in every aspect of life. They are most susceptible to changes in the labor market and, in any downswing in business, are among the first people to lose their jobs. Discrimination produces feelings of powerlessness, alienation, and hopelessness that are manifested in a wide array of social and health problems.

Limited education is another major cause of poverty. Lack of education limits job opportunities. During the past few decades, there has been a drastic decline in the number of unskilled jobs and an increase in technical and skilled jobs that require preparation at the college level. Although public school education has no tuition fee, it does cost money to send children to school. Children need to have adequate clothing and school supplies and to have a place to study in the often crowded and noisy home. They have more difficulty learning if they have a poor or unbalanced diet or go to school hungry. Homes of poor people often lack books, magazines, and other learning materials frequently found in middle-class homes. Children of poor parents who had little education often lack encouragement and motivation from their parents. Although many parents express the wish that their children graduate from high school and go to college, the realities of poverty make the achievement of these goals unlikely. Poor people may lack the skills that are required for the labor market. For example, many black youths excel in sports, but keen competition and few job opportunities for professional athletes leaves most of these youths with a skill that is unsalable.

Poverty is not confined to any one location. It is found in all areas of the United States, although people who live in some parts of the country are more apt to be poor than people who live in other parts. Much poverty is found among the white people living in Appalachia and in the northern parts of Michigan, Wisconsin, and Minnesota where the natural resources have been exhausted or, at best, produce a marginal existence. Following World War I, the extreme poverty on the small farms of the South caused a mass migration of black families to the industrial cities of the North and Midwest. In the future, the concentration of poverty is expected to be greatest in urban areas. Poor people have been moving to the cities to seek a better life. With little education and few skills, they are ill-equipped to find jobs that will help them escape poverty.

Poverty is common among people who have mental or physical illness or handicaps and are usually unable to obtain steady employment and among the young children and older people who are unable to support themselves. Elderly people are unable to perform the physical labors required in most unskilled jobs. Families often become poor upon the death or departure of the wage earner through divorce or imprisonment or other reasons. Some men voluntarily leave their families so that the wife will qualify for financial assistance. Regulations of most welfare and assistance programs prohibit benefits to families headed by men, even though these men are unable to obtain regular employment.

## WHO ARE THE POOR?

Just as poverty has many causes, it also involves people from many different groups. Many poor people have been poor all their lives and their parents also were poor. Others became poor because circumstances in their lives changed. People with the following characteristics tend to be poor: the unemployed, people with less than a high school education, the ill and handicapped, elderly people over the age of 65 years, families headed by women, families with six or more children under the age of 18 years, people living in rural areas or on small farms, and some people from black, American Indian, or Spanish-speaking cultures.

Black people are more likely to be poor than are white people. According to the Bureau of Census information for 1979, 31 per cent of all black people were living in poverty, and another 40 per cent were in the "near poverty" level with incomes that were up to 25 per cent higher than the poverty level. Fewer black people than white people complete high school. Unemployment is twice as high among black men as it is for white men, and black men earn an average of $5,000 a year less. Black families have tended to be larger than white families, and, although black women state they would like to have fewer children, their lack of education and inadequate incomes often pose barriers to effective family planning. Only 7 per cent of black families headed by a man were below the poverty level, whereas 32 per cent of black families headed by a woman were poor, including 48 per cent of those with children under the age of 18 years.

Although a higher percentage of black people are poor, the largest number of people living below the poverty level are white people. (See Table 23-1.) More than 16.7 million white people were poor, but this number constituted only 9 per cent of the white population. This number includes many elderly people who have a longer life expectancy than do their black counterparts. The federal government War on Poverty campaign that began in 1964 has been effective in reduc-

**Figure 23-1.** Those people most apt to be among the poor are young black males, children, families headed by women, the aged, and the sick or handicapped.

ing the number of poor whites by 58 per cent whereas the impact on blacks was only a 30 per cent reduction in the number of poor people.

The Spanish-speaking people in the United States have a lower poverty rate than do black people although the poverty rate for immigrants from Puerto Rico is approximately 40 per cent according to census statistics for 1979. The pride of most Mexican American men motivates them to seek and find jobs, even though many lack a high school education and the skills necessary for better paying jobs. Immigrants from Mexico were originally recruited to work in agriculture, but, with a lesser demand for farm laborers, more of them have settled in barrios, or Spanish-speaking neighborhoods in larger cities. Because many entered the country illegally, they face discrimination by employers who exploit them by paying low wages with the threat of exposing them to the authorities. Language is a further barrier; children from the barrios must learn English as well as Spanish, making school more difficult for all but the very dedicated students.

Among the poorest of the poor people are American Indians who live on reservations. They have the lowest average income, live in traditional ways in close harmony with nature, and speak their own tribal language. Those who migrate to cities to earn more money find that they are disadvantaged by their inferior education, different cultural values, and lack of job skills and that their degree of poverty becomes even greater.

People who have one or more of the following characteristics tend to be poor:

1. Nonwhite
2. Family has no wage earners
3. Family consists of more than six children under age 18 years
4. Family is headed by a woman
5. Between 14 and 25 years or over 65 years
6. Less than an eighth grade education
7. Lives in rural area or on a farm
8. Lives in the South

## THE NUMBER OF POOR

The number of poor people has been declining in the last two decades as the social programs that were begun under President Kennedy and President Johnson expanded services and assistance to the poor and needy. In 1959, more than one of five Americans was poor, but by 1979 this number had been reduced to one of ten by the War on Poverty campaign. The measure of poverty used by the government is the income needed to provide for the basic necessities for a nonrural family of four people. This figure varies from year to year according to the rate of inflation and the cost of the necessities.

In 1960, approximately 40 million people, or 22 per cent of the total population, were poor, with an income of slightly more than $3,000 per year. (See Table 23-2.) The median family income for all families was about $5,400 per year. By 1978, 11.4 per cent of the population was poor, a total of 24.5 million people, with an income for a family of four of $6,662. However, the median family income for all families has risen more than threefold to $17,640 in the same span of time. The number of poor and near-poor people (those with incomes of 125 per cent of the poverty level) approached 55 million people, or 16.3 per cent of the total population. Although some progress has been made in reducing the number of poor people, many people continue to be trapped in the devastating conditions of poverty.

## THE COSTS OF POVERTY

The costs of poverty not only fall on people who are poor but also fall on society as a whole.

**Table 23-1.** POPULATION AND PERCENTAGE OF WHITE AND BLACK PEOPLE IN THE UNITED STATES WITH INCOMES AT OR BELOW THE LEVEL OF POVERTY FROM THE 1950s THROUGH THE 1970s

| Year | White Poor Population (in millions) | Per cent | Black Poor Population (in millions) | Per cent |
|---|---|---|---|---|
| 1959 | 28.5 | 18.1 | 11.0 | 56.2 |
| 1969 | 16.7 | 9.5 | 7.1 | 32.2 |
| 1979 | 16.7 | 8.9 | 7.8 | 30.9 |

Source: Statistical Abstract of the United States 1980, 101st ed. No. 773. Washington D.C., Bureau of the Census, 1980.

**Table 23–2.** POPULATION AND PERCENTAGE OF PEOPLE
IN THE UNITED STATES WITH INCOMES AT OR BELOW
POVERTY LEVEL FROM THE 1960s THROUGH 1978
WITH THE CUTOFF INCOME OF THE POOR COMPARED
WITH THE MEDIAN INCOME OF NONPOOR FAMILIES

| Year | Below Poverty Level *Population (in millions)* | *Per cent* | Average Income Cutoff for Nonfarm Family of 4 | Median Family Income for All Families |
|---|---|---|---|---|
| 1960 | 39.9 | 22.2 | $3,022 | $5,417 |
| 1965 | 33.2 | 17.3 | $3,223 | $6,957 |
| 1970 | 25.4 | 12.6 | $3,968 | $9,867 |
| 1975* | 25.9 | 12.3 | $5,500 | $13,719 |
| 1978* | 24.5 | 11.4 | $6,662 | $17,640 |

*Not exactly comparable with previous years due to revised procedures.
Source: Statistical Abstract of the United States 1980, 101st ed. No. 771.
Washington, D.C., Bureau of the Census, 1980.

By products of poverty are increased disease, crime, delinquency, ignorance, and irresponsibility. People who are poor are deprived of material comforts, dignity, and fulfillment as human beings. High rates of unemployment lead to increased welfare costs and are often associated with broken homes, alcoholism, malnutrition, high school dropouts, and so on. Poverty breeds slums in cities that become the breeding ground for street gangs, juvenile delinquency, and crime. Drug-dealing and gambling may provide a high payoff for some people who, because of their success, may be seen as role models by young people.

Poverty extracts a high cost from individuals and from society in terms of health. The stresses of poverty leave people with feelings of insecurity, powerlessness, and alienation. Many poor people are lonely because inadequate resources do not draw people together but tend to separate them. When people have difficulty obtaining enough food for the next meal, they do not invite guests to dinner. They are also more likely to develop health problems from malnutrition, ignorance, and the inability to afford medical care. When sick, they must travel to the doctor's office, clinic, or hospital emergency room. Like William Henry's mother, they may need to take their other children with them if they are unable to afford to pay a babysitter.

Most poor people are without medical insurance and rely on government assistance for medical care. They utilize public health services and well-baby clinics for preventive health care, such as immunizations, but, when sick, they must receive care at tax-supported county hospitals. These hospitals are often overburdened, and care is fragmented. With few exceptions, interns and residents provide the medical care with poor people serving as learning models in the clinic. The barriers to health care are sufficient to keep poor people from obtaining proper health care until they are seriously ill and their diseases are far advanced.

## CHARACTERISTICS OF LOW-INCOME PEOPLE

In the past, much was written about the "culture of poverty" and the idea that behaviors among people in the lower socioeconomic class were passed from generation to generation. Mason (1981) points out that the culture of poverty represents a racist stereotype associated with blacks, and proposes an adaptational perspective for nursing because it views one's behavior as an interaction with one's environment. Poor people have to alter, or modify middle-class values to avoid continual feelings of failure, hopelessness, and frustration. These changes in one's values represent a means of adapting to environmental changes and effects on their lives. Although many of the ways that poor people alter their values and practices are positive and adaptive, others conflict with middle-class expectations and are viewed as being negative.

People living in poverty have learned to cope with their situation and not succumb to hopelessness. Their hopes are different from those of people in the middle-class. Middle-class people expect the poor to be sober, thrifty, and industrious enough to move into the middle-class and assume their values and attitudes. However, even with an adequate or comfortable income, those who have been poor live in fear of want and cling to their own value system. Any increase in money is seen as a means for gaining more material goods, making life easier, and allowing them to live in a better neighborhood. Those who remain poor pass on to their children ways of coping with the stresses of poverty. Now, second and third generations of poor families are seen by welfare workers.

People in low-income and poverty groups are characterized by several distinct themes that influence their lives and the way they behave. The themes that recur include fatalism, a present rather than a future orientation, reliance on authoritarian approaches in decision-making, and concreteness in terms of tangible results rather than intellectual pursuits. These elements can be seen in the common characteristics associated with low-income and poor people as described by both Irelan (1968) and Riessman (1965). Although the following characteristics are not unique to people in the lower socio-economic group, they are far more prevalent in this group than in any other social class.

## CHARACTERISTICS OF THE SELF

Poor and underprivileged people may hold the world responsible for their misfortunes and see their problems as being caused by external forces. Such attitudes provoke feelings of powerlessness and alienation from society that are expressed as frustration and antagonism toward those who have a better life. Poor people cling to traditional attitudes about morality, punishment, the role of women, proper education, and government, and these attitudes are not open to discussion or change. Their approach to problems is a practical one based on the conviction that life is the best teacher and that end results are those that count.

Among the poor, physical strength is highly valued because strength is needed for many jobs that are available to them. Emotional strength is also necessary to work and carry out their daily activities. The male role is sometimes more highly valued than the female role. Objects of admiration include those with strength and great endurance, such as sports stars and prizefighters, and activities featuring physical skills or contact.

The underprivileged tend to be poorly informed about many subjects, may be ineffective readers, and are susceptible to being taken advantage of by others. Poor people usually follow authoritarian approaches and attitudes rather than using reason and tend to be more prejudiced and intolerant in their views than others who have had more education. They regard themselves as equals of other people and often treat others in outspoken and informal ways.

## FAMILY AND KINSHIP TIES

Lower-class families tend to be patriarchal, with major decisions made by the husband or male head of household. Tension often arises because the men are dominant and free to come and go as they wish whereas the women often feel downtrodden in their roles of housekeeper and mother. In many families, the men earn the money and the women manage and spend it. In many underprivileged families, a brittle, emotional distance exists between the husband and wife. Both seek satisfaction of emotional needs from friends and relatives. Courtship may be short, and young couples often marry because of proximity to each other or because "it just seemed to happen."

More sexual promiscuity and a higher rate of illegitimate births have been associated with lower-class people but these may also be due to revised values caused by poverty. Low-income women state that they want to be married before they have babies, but their boyfriends did not have a job or ran away from the responsibility of a family. Sex is often regarded as one of the few free things left in life. Many single-parent families are found among poor people because of the death of a spouse, separation, divorce, or imprisonment. Often families are headed by an unmarried mother. From an early age, children are reared to take care of themselves and to be obedient. Because many poor peoples' homes are crowded, children often play and spend their time in the streets and the neighborhood.

## TIME ORIENTATION

Limited resources contribute to feelings of fatalism, because little is left for tomorrow. Poor people believe that whatever happens does so because they are unable to save and provide some protection from the stresses of life. They are caught in the present and live one day at a time. Children learn in terms of immediate reward or punishment and follow the pleasure principle of seeking gratification now and not depriving themselves in the present for some future reward. If poor people have extra money today, they spend it for things they want because they cannot count on tomorrow.

## MATERIAL GOODS

The emphasis of poor people's lives is more to "get by" than to "get ahead." They have the same wants and desires as middle-class people — namely, a nice home in the suburbs, a car, clothes, a new television set, and labor-saving appliances. All Americans have been taught to be consumers of infinite capacity, and the poor are no exception. They like news stories and gossip. New gadgets add excitement to their humdrum daily lives. Poor people prefer jobs with security rather than those associated with more risk. Young people tend to choose occupations that provide more in monetary returns rather than occupations that yield intellectual or emotional rewards. They are more apt to work for the paycheck than for the satisfaction derived from the work itself. Their homes contain few books, magazines, or educational toys.

## RELIGIOUS BELIEFS

Women tend to be more religious than men; however, both white and black deprived people are more likely to enjoy the physical expression of their emotions through singing, hand clapping, and swaying. They often find more solace in religions with these practices rather than those with dignified sermons and services. Pomp and pageantry help to brighten their otherwise drab and bleak lives. Many black people in the poverty group continue to have superstitious beliefs they observe for fear of dreadful things that might happen to them if they did not.

## RESPECT AND AUTHORITY

Poor people tend to be hostile toward authorities and institutions, yet at the same time, they rely on authority as the basis for decision-making. They learn at an early age that strength is the source of power and that the existing system is "right." They seldom enter into politics and many do not vote in elections. Few poor people belong to community organizations; however, they may belong to a labor union. Many have traditional attitudes about punishment. They dislike Communism intensely, but have inconsistent views of democracy.

## HEALTH PRACTICES

Poor health is more prevalent among underprivileged people and those living in poverty than among the middle class for several reasons. They are more likely to be undernourished or to eat unbalanced meals. Lack of education results in their ignorance of good health practices, and poverty means that they lack the money to obtain better health care. The following are influencing factors in the health beliefs and practices of poor people:

1. Lack of information about health and illness.

2. Definition of illness. Physical discomfort is not considered a signal of disease or illness. Illness means that one is incapacitated and unable to carry out one's daily work or responsibilities.

3. Preventive measures are less apt to be taken, and they delay longer in seeking health care. Unskilled jobs seldom provide sick leave benefits or health insurance.

4. Increased health hazards both in their immediate environment and in their place of employment (usually in a menial, unskilled job requiring physical strength). Slum neighborhoods tend to be rundown and hostile and have higher crime rates.

5. Health is low on their priority list of values. Higher priority is given to improving their lives, such as finding a better place to live, replacing wornout furniture, buying needed appliances or even some luxuries, and fixing the car so that it will run.

6. Little participation in community health programs and more reliance on self-medication or folk medicine practices.

## HEALTH PROBLEMS OF THE POOR

People who are less able to afford health services often have greater need for them and receive less health care than others, despite governmental programs designed to meet their needs. Sickness is more prevalent among poor people than among middle-class people, and, by the time the poor seek professional help, it can be of a serious nature.

## BARRIERS TO HEALTH CARE

When underprivileged people are sick, many obstacles confront them and deter them from obtaining health care. A visit to the doctor or a clinic means taking the day off from work and losing a day's pay. Their low-paying jobs fail to provide sick leave benefits or health insurance coverage associated with better-paying jobs. Clinics are usually overcrowded; thus, they must arrive early in the morning in order to sign in or get a low number so that they can be seen by the doctor before noon. Those who arrive later in the morning may have to wait hours before seeing the doctor and then wait additional hours for laboratory work and x-rays to be completed.

The poor are likely to be victims of discrimination and depersonalized care. In clinics, they are required to fill out numerous applications and forms, are called by number rather than addressed by name, and suffer from the bureaucratic inefficiency and application of rules and regulations. If they are late arriving for an appointment, it may be cancelled and they will have to make another appointment for a future date, take more time off from work, and hope that nothing interferes with keeping the new appointment. They may be treated by several doctors because interns and residents have rotating assignments through the clinics and hospital services. Poor people often complain about being treated like "guinea pigs" by doctors who are learning clinical medicine and gaining experience before going into private practice. Their care may be fragmented, and it is not uncommon for a person with several health problems to be scheduled in many different clinics.

A lack of communication and trust exists between poor people who feel alienated and health care providers who come from a middle-class background and have middle-class values and beliefs. Although people with financial power in the community provide health services for the poor, the recipients are seldom consulted about their wishes and needs. The health care is planned more for the convenience of the middle-class workers who provide the service than for the poor people. The workers determine the hours of operation and the amount of manpower and other resources to be committed for this purpose. Few clinics and hospitals are located in neighborhoods where poor people live, because health providers do not want to work in undesirable or slum areas. Often, those poor people who are sick must travel miles for their health care, using public transportation.

Lack of communication and trust leads to care that poor people view as being insensitive and callous; they feel powerless to change it but respond with anger or apathy. This is illustrated by the case of an elderly man who had a serious eye infection that produced much purulent drainage. He lives in a nursing home, and an appointment was made for him to be seen at the eye clinic of the county hospital. He dressed carefully in clean clothes and arrived at the clinic where he waited to see the doctor. Later, the intern called his number, and, when he saw the patient, said, "Send this man back, and don't reschedule him until someone cleans him up. I won't examine anyone with such a dirty face." Such remarks show a lack of understanding that the disease was the cause of the drainage that soiled the man's face and are damaging to the self-esteem.

As a result of many barriers, poor people make fewer visits to doctors and dentists. They avoid seeking health care until they are acutely ill or suffering from pain. Even when cost is not a factor, they make less use of available services. Many poor children do not receive vaccines to protect them from childhood diseases until they go to school and receive them there, even though immunizations are available in many public health centers in the community.

As the result of the civil rights movement and federal health programs, some progress has been made in reducing discrimination and making health care more available to the elderly and the disadvantaged, but many changes need to be implemented.

## TYPES OF HEALTH PROBLEMS

The United States is a society composed of several social classes. Some health problems and diseases are seldom seen among people in the upper class, whereas the incidence of these diseases may increase among the lower social classes. Although medical science has found cures for many diseases, and early treatment provides cures for many conditions, many indigent people have higher rates of illness as a result of their health practices, the way they define illness, the cost of health care, their feelings of fatalism, and ignorance of signs and symptoms of disease.

The poverty group includes various subgroups of people. Some health problems are more prevalent in one group than another. Overall, the lower classes have the highest rates for such diseases as cervical cancer (a disease that is curable when diagnosed in the early stages), schizophrenia, diabetes, and heart disease. As a group, poor people have four times as many limited days of activity because of chronic disease, especially among those over the age of 45 years, and they have a longer length of stay when hospitalized than any other group. The major causes of limited activity are diseases of the heart, arthritis, rheumatism, and orthopedic conditions. Mental illness is seldom treated in the early stages, and, when the condition is finally diagnosed, the individual may be psychotic and require hospitalization (HEW, 1967).

Compared with the white population, blacks, American Indians, Asians and Hawaiians have a life expectancy that is 5 years shorter for men and 4 years shorter for women, a maternal death rate that is 4 times higher, and an infant mortality rate that is 2 times higher (Bureau of Census, 1980). The incidence of cardiovascular disease is higher than among other cultural groups, with hypertension occurring at nearly epidemic proportions. Other diseases that are most prominent among black people in the poverty level are strokes, diabetes, cancer, pneumonia, and tuberculosis. The nonwhite population also has much higher rates of alcoholism, drug abuse, accidents, suicides, homicides, and cirrhosis of the liver than the white population (Bullough, 1972).

Significant health problems found among poor Spanish-speaking people include pneumonia, respiratory diseases, rheumatic fever, and a high incidence of diabetes. However, their rate of cardiovascular disease is lower than among the white population. Special health problems of American Indians include tuberculosis, pneumonia, dysentery, cirrhosis of the liver, alcoholism, and suicide. Even when health services are available, these groups have a higher incidence of certain diseases than the general population. This is thought to be due to the effect of poverty and to their particular lifestyle.

## RESOURCES FOR THE WAR ON POVERTY

In order to help clients who are poor, nurses need to know the resources that are available in their community and the type of assistance that is provided. Many poor people are already obtaining money and services, whereas others get by on their meager earnings but need help to meet the cost of medical care when ill.

### OBJECTIVES OF ANTI POVERTY PROGRAMS

Many citizens support community efforts and voluntary organizations to help the poor and less fortunate people. Through charitable efforts, they provide food and shelter. In spite of the efforts of local groups of people, poverty remains. Federal legislation and programs to eliminate the multiple causes of poverty seek to meet the following objectives:

1.  To provide employment for all citizens.
2.  To increase job opportunities for young adults and youths.
3.  To eliminate discrimination.
4.  To assist aged and disabled people.
5.  To improve the health care of citizens.
6.  To expand educational opportunities for disadvantaged people.
7.  To improve the economy of poorer regions of the country.
8.  To rehabilitate run-down urban areas and rural communities.

### ANTIPOVERTY PROGRAMS

Many programs enacted by the federal government meet more than one objective for eliminating poverty. In the past, important landmarks in the War on Poverty resulted from legislation to protect workers. Child labor laws prohibited employment of children and freed them from exploitation and lives of misery. Minimum wage and hour laws protected all workers and set standards for health and safety to be observed by employers in all work settings. Unemployment benefits help those who have lost their jobs and workers' compensation and accident insurance were established to protect workers from losses due to injury on the job.

The Social Security program was enacted in 1934 to provide supplemental benefits for workers and their families when the worker became too old to work or became disabled. The amount of the benefit was based on a percentage of one's total earnings, and payment began at age 65 years. At that time, the average life expectancy was approximately 60 years, compared with 71 years at present. Today, more people are living longer and, thus, collect benefits from this program. During the years, Social Security benefits have increased, and the program has expanded to include payments not only to the worker and to the worker's spouse but also to disabled workers of any age, to minor children of deceased workers, and others. In 1965, the Medicare program was added to the Social Security program. This provides medical care for people over 65 years. Under the provisions of Medicaid, each state is required to provide medical services to the poor of any age.

During the 1960s, many social programs were enacted by the government in a concerted effort to fight poverty. Two of the most significant programs were the Civil Rights Act and the Economic Opportunity Act, both passed in 1964. The Civil Rights Act is an important poverty program because it protects minority groups from discrimination in the areas of equal access to jobs, housing, and education. The Economic Opportunity Act established the Office of Equal Opportunity (OEO) and incorporated many programs aimed at helping the poor to help themselves to share in the prosperity of the country. It set up the Job Corps for training young adults in job skills and the Community Action programs through which the poor are urged to participate in their local communities, thinking of ways to end poverty, applying for funds, and carrying out projects. VISTA is the volunteer program in which people work directly with the indigent and help them to identify their needs and to take action. Public assistance is available to the poor in the form of general welfare. Women who are heads of families receive Aid to Dependent Children. Other specialized forms of assistance are available, such as the Crippled Children's programs and Aid to the Needy Blind.

Although these programs help alleviate the stresses produced by low incomes, poverty has not been eliminated, despite vigorous efforts. The social and health costs of poverty are still very much in evidence.

## APPLICATION TO CLINICAL PRACTICE

It is important for nurses using the adaptation approach to nursing to understand the effects of poverty on patients' values, beliefs, and behavior. Poverty is a powerful stimulus for behavior and, thus, is part of the second level assessment. The way people cope with the effects of poverty can be assessed with the same format that is used to assess cultural diversity. To enlarge your understanding of antipoverty programs, select one type of program offered in your community and gather more information about its requirements and the amount of assistance provided for indigent beneficiaries. If possible, interview one recipient of that program and determine the benefits to the individual and the deficits that still exist.

When caring for poor patients in the clinical setting, assess the effects of poverty on the patients' ways of life. Compare the patients' behaviors and values with those of the middle-class and identify those that are different. Describe how poor people have altered their expectations, values, and behavioral responses as a result of the stresses produced by poverty.

## REFERENCES

Brickner, Philip, et al.: Outreach to welfare hotels, the homebound, the frail. Am J Nurs, *76*:762–764, (May) 1976.

Bullough, Bonnie, and Bullough, Vern: Poverty, Ethnic Identity, and Health Care. New York, Appleton-Century-Crofts, 1972.

Delivery of Health Services for the Poor. Human Investment Programs, U. S. Department of Health, Education, and Welfare, (December) 1967.

Herzog, Elizabeth: Facts and fiction about the poor. *In* James Scoville (ed.): Perspectives on Poverty and Income Distribution. Lexington, Mass., D. C. Heath and Co., 1971, pp. 100–112.

Hollingshead, August, and Redlich, Fredrick: Social Class and Mental Illness. New York, John Wiley & Sons, Inc., 1953.

Irelan, Lola (ed.): Low Income Life Styles. U.S. Department of Health, Education, and Welfare, Publication No. 14, Welfare Administration, Washington, D.C., 1968.

Leinwand, Gerald, (ed.): Poverty and the Poor. New York, Washington Square Press, Inc., 1968.

Mason, Diana: Perspectives on poverty. IMAGE, Official Journal of Sigma Theta Tau, *13*(3):82–85, (October) 1981.

Riessman, Frank: A portrait of the underprivileged. *In* Will, Robert, and Vatter, Harold (eds.): Poverty in Affluence. New York, Harcourt Brace & World, Inc., 1965.

Savage, James, Adair, Alvis, and Friedman, Philip: Community-social variables related to black parent-absent families. Journal of Marriage and the Family, *40*:4, (November) 1978.

Scoville, James G.: Perspectives on Poverty and Income Distribution. Lexington, Mass., D. C. Heath and Co., 1971.

Statistical Abstract of the United States 1980, 101st ed. Washington, D. C., Bureau of the Census, 1980.

Strasser, Judith: Urban transient women. Am J Nurs, *78*:2076–2079, (December) 1978.

Will, Robert E., and Vatter, Harold (eds.): Poverty in Affluence. New York, Harcourt Brace & World, Inc., 1965.

# Chapter TWENTY-FOUR
# Life Crisis Events

## OBJECTIVES   Information in this chapter will help you to

1. Define a crisis as an event in life that disrupts adaptation in any mode and leaves the person unable to cope with the problem without assistance.
2. Relate social and environmental changes in life that produce varying amounts of disruption in lives and increase the possibility of developing a serious illness.
3. Compare the usual crisis intervention with the nursing process used in the adaptation approach to nursing.
4. Describe developmental and situational events that become stimuli for coping problems for people in a crisis period.
5. Discuss interventions that the nurse can use to help the client or patient resolve a crisis.

Most people go through life at a fairly even pace, maintaining an adapted state until something unexpected occurs that proves to be a hazard or a threat to them. They then become frightened, disorganized, and emotionally upset, and these feelings increase when they find that their usual coping mechanisms are no longer effective in reducing the threat. The responses they used in the past have little or no influence on the present situation but leave them feeling increasingly frustrated and helpless.

The number of people experiencing emotional distress associated with crisis events has been increasing and is considered to be a side effect of the stresses of contemporary life in the United States. Today, most people live in large urban areas and in nuclear families consisting of parents and minor children and are isolated from other relatives. They are extremely mobile and have a rapid turnover among their friends and business associates. They meet many people daily, but the relationships tend to be superficial or short-lived as those associated with tertiary roles. People lack the stability and warm personal relationships found in the past among large families living in the same rural community. Someone was always available that one could talk to about one's problems with whom one shared strong emotional ties and a sense of responsibility and loyalty. With isolation from extended family members, people become overwhelmed by problems created by a complex urbanized life and feel incapable of solving them. The breakdown in one's coping mechanisms leads to a period of crisis.

Nurses see many people who are in crisis. Illness is a common cause of crises because it produces a threat to one's being and interferes with coping mechanisms that one uses to reduce one's anxieties, such as physical exercise, eating, or drinking, or other activities. Patients trying to cope with their feelings about their disease and the losses they have suffered are often in a crisis state and need help in resolving their problems. Without help, ineffective coping measures have a negative impact and the emotionally upset state continues, delaying adaptation.

Through the adaptation approach and the nursing process, nurses are better able to identify clients and patients at risk of having coping problems, prevent breakdown of coping mechanisms or identify the crisis in the earlier stages, and intervene effectively.

In this chapter, the crisis theory will be examined, as well as the types of crisis events that can disrupt adaptation in any mode: physiological, role-function, self-concept, or interdependence. Through assessment, nurses identify the threat that is causing the psychological and emotional distress and use interventions that will reduce the causative stimuli, provide an adequate support system, or enhance effective coping mechanisms.

## CRISES OF LIFE

Nurses see many people during crisis periods in their lives and have the potential to help them regain an adapted state. Crises occur when people face problems that they cannot solve with their customary coping mechanisms. This failure of the coping mechanisms to bring about the desired solution produces high levels of anxiety, disorganized behavior, and inability to function adequately. The crisis state in individuals can be compared with a raft that is caught in the rapids and is tossed and turned at the mercy of the rushing waters.

### THE THEORY OF CRISIS

A crisis situation results from one's emotional response to loss, which involves the self-concept. The person dealing with the loss, whatever it may be, is in an acute, distressful emotional state. Crisis theory evolved from the attempts of those working in the field of psychiatry to deal with people who were unable to cope with changes in their lives and whose mental health was impaired by ineffective responses to the crisis event.

Mental health is the state of adapting to the psychosocial aspects of life. People who have good mental health act, or behave, in ways that indicate a healthy personality. Characteristics of good mental health include

1  Self understanding and acceptance of one's self. Possesses insight and has an understanding of his or her motives, strengths, and weaknesses.

2. Using reason to solve problems. Is able to make decisions and take responsibility for them.
3. Possession of worthwhile values or a code of ethics.
4. Control of emotions. Avoids being a slave to any of the passions.
5. A social conscience and a degree of unselfishness. Shows concern for others.
6. Continuous search for truth and wisdom. Is able to understand the relativity of truth and facts — what was once known can be outdated by new knowledge, discoveries, or situations.
7. Ability to be happy.

Mental health is impaired by emotional distress generated by the threats or hazards of anxiety. The distress is compounded by the inability to cope with changes in life and can be visualized as a continuum that ranges from mild tension at one end, to a transient problem in coping, to the acute distress of crisis at the other end in which one is unable to function in an effective way. People who have problems in coping with their feelings and changes in their lives such as those described in previous chapters, may still be able to function adequately in some areas, whereas in other areas they may be in crisis and unable to find ways to reduce their upset emotional state. A fine line exists between people who have a problem in coping but can function and people who are in a crisis state and cannot function. It can be said that anyone who needs help in finding ways to cope effectively is in a state of crisis. The coping mechanisms people use are generally those that have been effective in the past in reducing their stress but are now ineffective and do not work. Some responses may be partially effective in reducing the particular threat but have other undesired consequences that become a further source of anxiety. Examples of this type of coping mechanism are those associated with the social problems of alcohol abuse, drug abuse, child or wife battering, rape, sexual molestation of children, homicide, or suicide. People who attempt to cope with their feelings of threat to their self-concept with such responses have to cope with additional difficulties that result from these behaviors.

The acute turmoil of crisis is self-limiting and usually lasts from 4 to 6 weeks. By that time, the hazard to the person has generally been reduced, some form of coping has been found to be effective to decrease the emotional upset, or the person has adjusted to the new unresolved situation. Because crisis periods usually are not long in duration, people need help immediately. Crisis intervention can be carried out by professionals in the psychiatric field, by nurses, and by nonprofessionals who have had some training in the methods. Many volunteers answer "hot lines," taking phone calls from troubled people who have problems that range from sexual identity, strict parents, and drug habits, to attempted suicide.

## TYPES OF CRISES

Two major categories of crises exist: developmental and environmental. Developmental crises occur at times of changes in one's life and at various maturation points. They are expected, must be adjusted to, and can be predicted with reasonable accuracy. Some examples of developmental crises points include birth, puberty, start or end of school, death in the family, marriage, menopause or climacteric, and old age. For example, many teen-agers go through a crisis when they believe their appearance does not measure up to what they see the ideal to be. An outbreak of pimples before an important school or social function can be devastating to young people who are unable to cope or function in their usual way. Other causes of crisis include failure to make an expected grade in a course or failure to make a sports team. Adjusting to the loss of a spouse or member of the family is stressful and may lead to a crisis. For some people, a crisis period may be associated with adjusting to the losses of aging, such as the loss of strength, the loss of job (with retirement), loss of vigor, loss of prestige or status, and loss of beauty or good looks.

Environmental crises are situational and relate to losses that involve illness, drug use, divorce, unemployment, promotions, accidents, disasters, relocating to a different home or community, changes in roles or status, and conditions such as war, riots, or even premature birth. Nurses may find themselves in crises from working in intensive care units, coronary care units, or oncology or in other high stress areas of nursing.

Environmental or situational stresses have been classified as stresses caused by family dismemberment, accession, demoralizing factors or a combination of these stresses (Hill, 1965). Family dismemberment stresses occur when members of the family are alienated by divorce, wartime separation, wife-beating, or child abuse. Accession stresses are caused by additions to the family through birth, adoption of a child, or new members by marriage. Demoralizing factors include those associated with being fired, being unemployed, nonsupport of the family, alcoholism, drug abuse, imprisonment, stressful work situations, and conditions leading to discrimination or powerlessness. The fourth type is a combination of any or all the other stresses.

Second level assessment focuses on the identification of events that have caused the crisis. It is crucial to identify the threat or hazard to the person, but this is not always as easy as it may seem. Many people find it difficult to face the cause of their painful emotions; thus, they may not be aware of the cause, use denial of the event or its significance, or direct attention elsewhere to hide or mask their inner conflicts. The focal stimulus for the coping problem is the threat causing it. Contextual stimuli that influence or affect responses to crises include differing cultural values and expectations regarding the family, age, sex, occupation, education, religion, and social class. Other important contextual stimuli are the situational resources available, the family support system, and attitudes regarding mental health.

## DISRUPTION OF MODES

Losses can affect function in the physiological, self-concept, role-function, or interdependence mode, so any of these may be disrupted by a crisis. Mitchell (1977) states that crisis commonly affects one of the human need areas, and she describes those that are most commonly jeopardized as narcissism or self-esteem, libidinal, dependence or nurturing, and biological needs.

- *Self-esteem is a function of the self-concept.* Needs are met by successful experiences in carrying out one's social roles. Jeopardy occurs when one is unsuccessful and fails to meet the expectations of others or oneself. Lack of resources available also leads to low self-esteem. The need area is the answer to "How and what I think of myself." It is composed of all one's feelings about what one is like (self-consistency), what one would like to be (self-ideal), and what one ought to be (moral-ethical self). Crisis occurs when any of these areas are threatened or when loss occurs in the physical self.

- *Libidinal needs are fulfilled through sexual role mastery or carrying out the appropriate developmental tasks for one's stage of life.* Vocational roles, sexual identity, heterosexual relationships, or parenting roles are commonly accepted ways of meeting these needs. Crises occur frequently during puberty and adolescence, and, unless resolved in healthy, adapted ways can lead to further disruptions during adulthood.

- *Dependence or nurturing needs are those of interdependence in which the goal is a comfortable balance between dependence and independence.* One needs to be supported and cared for as well as needing to be competitive or self-reliant. Crises occur when these needs are thwarted.

- *Biological needs are the physiological areas that must be satisfied to support life.* Illness is one of the most common causes of crisis and the one most frequently seen by nurses.

The first level assessment provides information that the nurse uses to determine whether the client or patient is having a problem in coping with changes or is in crisis and is not able to cope effectively. The nurse looks for behaviors that indicate a realistic perception of the event, the presence of situational supports, and the adequacy of the coping mechanisms. Behaviors that provide clues that a person is in crisis include the following:

1. *A breakdown in the person's familiar coping patterns.* Even though the coping response does not lead to the desired outcome, it is used again and again. New methods of coping that are inappropriate may be tried, or there may be regression to behaviors that were used and that led to satisfaction at an earlier stage of life. An example of regression is a 49-year-old woman, coping with the recent death of her husband, who begins to use baby talk and to say things like "Me don't want to go now. Me tired."

2. *A preoccupation with the events that led to the crisis, and being unable to attend to other matters.* Memories of past events that are linked to the present one suddenly emerge in statements such as "It's just like it was when Uncle Charley died." The assessment of Esther R. illustrates this point. She was an elderly woman treated for complications following cataract surgery. She complained that her family was ignoring her and just waiting for her to die, that her children and grandchildren failed to visit her each day and that they looked for excuses to avoid staying with her, leaving after spending just a few minutes with her. In addition, she complained that the nurses did not answer her call light and refused to do anything for her but gave the other woman in the room all their attention and service. "It is just as bad as the last time I was in the hospital when I had that cancer operation," she said. The threat posed by her present illness is compared with the one in the past and is severe enough to put her into crisis as indicated by her restricted perception of reality and ineffective coping mechanisms.

3. *An immediate connection between the present problem in coping and the event causing it.* Once the threat is perceived, an immediate response of anxiety emerges that persists when coping is inadequate to reduce the threat. Usually the cause of the threat has occurred within a two-week period from the onset of the crisis and the call for help. Assessing activities and events during that time should lead the nurse to the threat producing the crisis.

Behavioral responses to losses that constitute the threat of the crisis are those of the grieving process as described in Chapter Nineteen. The distinct stages of the grieving process are (1) shock, denial, and disbelief, (2) anger, (3) bargaining, (4) depression, and (5) resolution or acceptance of the loss. People in crisis exhibit behaviors that are disorganized and chaotic and show inability to concentrate, decreased reasoning ability, impaired judgments and decision-making, and inadequate methods of coping. Frequent and prolonged anxiety produces predictable physiological changes related to preparing the body for "fight or flight," including increases in systolic blood pressure, pulse rate, and respirations and dilated pupils, copious perspiration, and release of the antidiuretic hormone. Slower acting parasympathetic responses are also seen in increased secretion of nasal and digestive glands, increased peristalsis in the intestinal tract, and copious output of urine.

After processing the information obtained by the first level assessment, the nurse carries out the second level assessment to determine the cause of the threat or the hazardous event and other influencing factors. From this information, the statement of the individual's problem is made in terms of the feelings being expressed, such as "Person has feelings of (anger, fear, or depression) about the threat of _____." The goal is then formulated, and interventions are planned by which the various stimuli are manipulated to change the behavioral response to the adapted range.

## CRISIS INTERVENTIONS

Interventions in crisis are based on the principles that responses to loss involve working through the grieving process and result in certain patterns of behavior. People go through the stages of grieving when adjusting to a loss, regardless of the type of loss—whether of a loved one, removal of a part of the body, decreased control over one's life, or damage to the self-esteem. The goal is to reduce the threat by focusing on promoting a realistic perception of the event, providing adequate support in the situation, and using adequate coping mechanisms. The interventions are in the "here and now" rather than exploring the individual's past development except when the past provides clues for understanding the present crisis.

Interventions include the use of insight therapy to help people see the relationship between the way they are feeling and the problem or situation that is causing the distress. Many people do not see the relationship and often attribute their feelings to vague or superficial causes. It is essential to help people express feelings that may have been repressed or hidden. If suicidal or homicidal feelings are expressed, further assessment should be made to ascertain whether the person is only talking about such actions or whether specific plans have been made to carry them out because professional psychiatric help may be needed. After exploring the person's feelings, examine the coping mechanisms that have been used in the past with similar problems and, with the person, try to identify why these coping mechanisms are not working in the present situation. When the usual coping mechanisms are not achieving the desired goal, alternative ways to respond should be considered and tried. As progress is made in reducing the threat of the crisis situation, the nurse gives guidance by reinforcing the person's use of positive coping mechanisms and points out improvements that have been made. Repeopling the person's world can be highly effective for those who have suffered the loss of a loved one; the introduction of new people can help fill the void in their social world. Ways of making new friends, establishing meaningful relationships, and using available friends and relatives as support systems are other techniques that can be incorporated into the nursing care plan for the person in crisis.

The final step of the nursing process is the evaluation phase, in which the nurse assesses the changes in behavior in the direction of adaptation and achieving the goal.

## COMMON CRISIS EVENTS

Crisis can be caused by anything that represents the loss of a familiar or valued object. The loss may be taking away the accustomed or adding something that is unfamiliar. Life is a tapestry of changes that are potential points of crisis when people lack the ability to cope with them. Some life events associated with crisis are illness, pregnancy, prematurity, sexual abuse, suicide attempts, and the personal vulnerability of the nurse in stressful work situations. The crisis of

death and dying is discussed in Chapter Nineteen as one of the significant problems of the self-concept.

## THE CRISIS OF ILLNESS

One of the puzzles confronting people in the field of health is the occurrence of illness. Why does a person become ill at a particular time? Why now? What causes the person to become ill from a cold, diabetes, or congestive heart failure or to suffer some injury? To find the answer, researchers studied sick people and learned that the events of ordinary life help to trigger a physical illness. The effort required to cope with the demands of a new job, moving to a new home, or having a baby uses additional energy and weakens resistance to disease. Although life events do not cause the disease, the changes are thought necessary to strain the coping mechanisms so that illness occurs. Holmes and Masuda (1972) identified events in life that have been known to precede an illness. (See Table 24–1.) They asked subjects to rate these events as requiring more or less adjustment than marriage, which was given an arbitrary value of 50. The ratings show the most stressful events were the death of a spouse, divorce, marital separation, and jail term. The least stressful events were minor violations of the law, Christmas, and vacations.

Studies of stresses caused by life events, cited by Holmes (1972), indicate that the presence of several changes is associated with increased risk of developing a physical illness. The accumulation of stress caused by changes can lead to a life crisis, and the higher the number of units of stress for life events, the more serious the disease. The scale below shows the relationship between the number of units and the incidence of illness within a one-year period in several studies.

Other researchers are more reluctant to attribute illness to changes caused by life events and point out that many other variables can be identified that cloud the issue. Miller (1981) cites differences in the abilities of individuals to cope with change as one of the variables that is difficult to both measure and control in research studies.

Patients with serious illnesses are in a potential crisis situation because of the psychological threat associated with loss of bodily function or control, disturbed social relationships, restricted availability of coping mechanisms, and potential

150–199 units — mild crisis.    About one in three had a mild illness.
200–299 units — moderate crisis.    About 50 per cent had health changes.
300 and over — severe crisis.    More than four of five were ill and had
    more serious illnesses.

Table 24–1.   THE SOCIAL-READJUSTMENT
RATING SCALE

| Rank | Life Events | Mean Value |
|------|-------------|------------|
| 1 | Death of spouse | 100 |
| 2 | Divorce | 73 |
| 3 | Marital separation | 65 |
| 4 | Jail term | 63 |
| 5 | Death of close family member | 63 |
| 6 | Personal injury or illness | 53 |
| 7 | Marriage | 50 |
| 8 | Fired at work | 47 |
| 9 | Marital reconciliation | 45 |
| 10 | Retirement | 45 |
| 11 | Change in health of family member | 44 |
| 12 | Pregnancy | 40 |
| 13 | Sex difficulties | 39 |
| 14 | Gain of new family member | 39 |
| 15 | Business readjustment | 39 |
| 16 | Change in financial state | 38 |
| 17 | Death of close friend | 37 |
| 18 | Change to different line of work | 36 |
| 19 | Change in number of arguments with spouse | 35 |
| 20 | Mortgage over $10,000 | 31 |
| 21 | Foreclosure of mortgage or loan | 30 |
| 22 | Change in responsibilities at work | 29 |
| 23 | Son or daughter leaving home | 29 |
| 24 | Trouble with in-laws | 29 |
| 25 | Outstanding personal achievement | 28 |
| 26 | Spouse begins or stops work | 26 |
| 27 | Begin or end school | 26 |
| 28 | Change in living conditions | 25 |
| 29 | Revision of personal habits | 24 |
| 30 | Trouble with boss | 23 |
| 31 | Change in work hours or conditions | 20 |
| 32 | Change in residence | 20 |
| 33 | Change in schools | 20 |
| 34 | Change in recreation | 19 |
| 35 | Change in church activities | 19 |
| 36 | Change in social activities | 18 |
| 37 | Mortgage or loan less than $10,000 | 17 |
| 38 | Change in sleeping habits | 16 |
| 39 | Change in number of family get-togethers | 15 |
| 40 | Change in eating habits | 15 |
| 41 | Vacation | 13 |
| 42 | Christmas | 12 |
| 43 | Minor violations of the law | 11 |

Source: Holmes, Thomas, and Masuda, Minoru: Psychosomatic syndrome. Psychology Today, 6(4):106, (April) 1972. Reprinted from Psychology Today Magazine. Copyright ©1972. Ziff-Davis Publishing Company.

loss of life. Patients in acute care settings, such as coronary care, intensive care, oncology, and emergency rooms, are particularly at risk of being in crisis. Other stimuli include potential hazards created by strange noises, lights, equipment, and procedures in the acute care setting, as well as being able to see other seriously ill patients whose condition may become worse or who may die.

While the patient is dealing with several losses during illness, the family also faces hazards to their emotional integrity. They may be in the grieving process, too, and at different stages at different times. Some threatening situations for family members include nearly total isolation from their loved ones, loss of control over factors such as visiting hours, feelings of helplessness in not being able to help the patient, and lack of information about what is happening, the degree of progress, or other details about the illness. They may also be buffeted by stresses outside the hospital that strain their coping abilities.

**Interventions.** The adaptation approach to nursing helps to identify difficulties in coping with losses in the early stage so that actions can be taken. When caring for seriously ill patients, nurses can use the crisis theory as a preventive measure. Interventions include the following:

1. Establish communications between nurse and patient and between nurse and family.
2. Give patient and family frequent reports of the health status and progress. Explanations should be given for procedures, routines, and other examinations.
3. Continuously orient the patient to time, place, and person during the waking hours. Be honest in answering questions and promote a trust relationship.
4. Use insight therapy to discuss concerns of patient and/or family.
5. Screen patient from more seriously ill patients and show respect for the patient's need for privacy.
6. Assess family members for their coping behaviors. It is helpful to know who makes the decisions in the family and for the patient.

## THE CRISIS OF PREGNANCY

Pregnancy is a time not only for thinking about cute, cuddly babies, but also of many changes for the childbearing woman, and, for some, it is a period of crisis. Pregnancy may represent a loss of independence and a slim figure, may interfere with what the woman wants to do, and may lead to strained relationships with the baby's father. The nurse must assess all modes to ascertain any hazard to coping, with special emphasis on the self-concept and interdependence modes.

An increasing number of pregnancies occur among unmarried teen-agers, and the number of unwanted pregnancies ending in abortion for all age groups is about one million annually. Among teen-agers who become pregnant, Curtis (1974) indicated that many of them had a childhood characterized by a broken home, unstable family relationships, and being abandoned by the parents. Few of the girls had a hobby or engaged in sports or other activities. They spent their leisure time watching television or sleeping. With their constricted interests, they viewed pregnancy as an escape from their home problems. Crisis is apt to occur when a conflict develops between dependence needs and the desire to be independent, with a home of one's own. However, young unmarried mothers tend to live in poverty, resulting in more stresses in their lives.

Another crisis that may result from pregnancy is the birth of a premature baby. Parents are then faced with several events that can strain their coping abilities to the point of crisis, including

separation from the infant until the infant gains weight and matures enough to be discharged from the hospital, possible death of the infant due to immaturity, the expense of prolonged hospital care, feelings of failure by the mother to carry the infant to full-term, and the added responsibility to provide special care for the infant's needs and growth patterns. Weil (1981) points out that families during high-risk pregnancies face similar marital and emotional problems.

Although most attention is focused on the mother-to-be, some expectant fathers find pregnancy a stressful time and find themselves in a crisis state as their anxiety levels increase. Men becoming fathers for the first, and even up to the fifth, time are subject to feelings of conflict about their sexual role. Their anxiety is generally expressed in the form of physical complaints of nausea, vomiting, indigestion, abdominal bloating, and backache. A significant number of expectant fathers develop abdominal cramps that are similar to their wives' labor pains, a neurotic and ritualistic syndrome called couvade.

According to Hott (1976), other studies have shown that anxiety in expectant fathers increases their antisocial behavior. An increase in the number of sexually deviant behaviors exist among men whose wives are pregnant or have just delivered a child, and more men desert their families during this time. Sexually deviant actions during this time include rape, child molestation, exhibitionism, homosexual acts, and obscene phone calls. Also at risk of crisis are men who have their dependence needs met by "mothering" wives and who find that these needs are neglected during pregnancy when they are expected to "mother" their wives.

The termination of a pregnancy by abortion is another stressful situation and often a crisis period for the pregnant woman and her family. Since the United States Supreme Court ruling in 1973 that a state could not intervene in the abortion decisions of the woman and her physician during the first trimester, abortions have been used as a method of birth control. Some authorities believed that the rate of illegitimate births would decline when abortion was available for single women who became pregnant. However, the number of illegitimate births has increased greatly, whereas married women in their twenties have more abortions. The emotional responses of women to an abortion depends upon the circumstances surrounding it and the individual's resources for coping. Women who wanted their babies but suffered a spontaneous abortion go through the grieving process; those who underwent a therapeutic abortion for health reasons may have mixed feelings; and those who chose abortion to rid themselves of an unwanted pregnancy may have feelings ranging from guilt to relief, depending upon their moral-ethical beliefs.

Fischman (1975) reported that a Baltimore study of unwed black teen-agers showed significant differences between girls who chose to have an abortion and those who delivered their babies. Those who elected to abort were from a higher socioeconomic status, remained in school, were better students, and had a shorter and less stable relationship with their boyfriends than those who delivered their babies. They reported less favorable relationships with their mothers and more of them had fathers who had died. The girls in this group were more interested in self-improvement and upward mobility. On the other hand, those who had their babies were doing poorly or had dropped out of school before they became pregnant, and more of them lived in a household already receiving welfare support. They had closer relationships with their mothers and received emotional support from their fathers who lived elsewhere. These girls had stable relationships with their boyfriends, and they stated that they were happy to be pregnant and to have a baby. The investigators speculated that having a baby was one of the few things that an undereducated girl from a welfare family could accomplish successfully.

**Interventions.** When crisis is related to pregnancy, the nursing assessment must lead to the identification of the threat to the individual. Because other people are involved in the relationship, the pregnancy may be a threat to the expectant father, to the parents of an unwed woman, and to others in the family. Crisis intervention is carried out by establishing lines of communication, making a realistic examination of the relationships between the pregnant woman and her spouse, sex partner, or family, and setting achievable goals. When dealing with pregnant teen-agers, it is necessary to support their dependence needs for attention, affection, and help-seeking. When these have been met, they can be encouraged to work toward self-reliance and independence goals. Whenever possible, the expectant father should be included in the planning and interventions because he may also have dependence needs and anxieties related to changes made by the baby's impending arrival.

## THE CRISIS OF SEXUAL ABUSE

The incidence of sexual abuse and trauma is more widespread than indicated by the number of reported cases of rape, sexual assault, and molesting of children. In all but a minor percentage of cases, the offender is a man, and the victims are women and children. These maladaptive and assaultive behaviors are used by men in attempts to reduce their feelings of anxiety, insecurity, powerlessness, and fear resulting from perceived threats to their sexual role mastery.

More than half the children who are victims of sexual abuse know the offender, who often is a member of the family. Sometimes, these male offenders have assumed the role of father in the family and have access to the child because their presence as stepfather or the mother's boyfriend is not questioned. In such cases, the children are unable to protest. They may also be pressured into sexual activity by men who give them gifts of money or candy, who misrepresent the moral standards and assure the child that the activity is all right, or by those who prey on the child's need for human contact and love. Children are then sworn to secrecy about the events by instilling fear of punishment if they tell others or threatening that the children will be abandoned or rejected by the family or that no one will believe anything that they say. Most children are silent and do not report sexual abuse owing to fear. Occasionally, some children gain pleasure from their sexual encounters and use their charm to seduce the offender and gain rewards. The first level assessment of children who have been sexually molested shows a change in their behavior patterns, such as being silent, trying to avoid contact with the offender, or having nightmares. They may have unexplained bruises on their bodies or suddenly have more money, toys, or other benefits.

Rape is a crime of violence against women that is being reported more frequently and with more rapists being prosecuted since women began asserting their rights more vigorously. Women rape victims are now encouraged to report the crime and to receive medical treatment. Most victims have suffered physical as well as psychological trauma, and lacerations and bruises are found on gynecological examination. Medical treatment in the hospital emergency room includes obtaining specimens of semen for evidence, examination for sexually transmitted diseases, and treatment to guard against pregnancy. In the immediate postrape period, most women are in the shock and denial stage of grieving. They are shocked that this could happen to them but believe that they can handle it and cope; thus, the emotional trauma and crisis of rape may not be seen until days or weeks later.

**Interventions.** When sexual abuse has occurred, it is essential that the nurse establish communication with the victim. Children should be encouraged to talk about the events and their feelings. When young children lack the language to describe what has happened, they can be asked to draw a picture. Whenever possible, the parents should be involved in counselling because the way that the child interprets the event will greatly depend upon the way the parents respond.

When the rape victim comes for medical treatment, nurses can be very supportive by providing her with an opportunity to talk about the crime and by avoiding judgmental statements or manners. Nurses can insure that she is treated without delay and prepared emotionally and physically, with skill and understanding, for the pelvic examination. She should be afforded privacy for medical and police interviews. In addition, nurses can provide for her comfort by supplying mouthwash, soap and towels, a place for her to bathe, safety pins, needle or thread to repair torn clothing, or tissues. Finally, the rape victim should be referred to a counselling service for follow-up care, and her family or friends should be contacted for transportation home and emotional support.

## THE CRISIS OF SUICIDE

Throughout the world, the number of suicides is increasing, according to World Health Organization statistics (Los Angeles Times, 1977) with more than 1000 people taking their own lives each day and 10 times that number making a suicide attempt. Developed countries with the highest suicide deaths per 100,000 population include Hungary, with 37; Denmark, with 24; and Finland, with 23.5. The United States has a rate of 12.5 per 100,000 population, and, although the rate is relatively unchanged, the number of attempts among youths is increasing. Most care-givers regard a suicide attempt as a cry for help when confronted with a crisis situation when coping mechanisms are impaired or ineffective and supportive resources are inadequate. Suicide is a greater risk among people who are experiencing deep feelings of depression, isolation, and hopelessness. Other high risk factors include past suicide attempts, alcohol or drug abuse, isolation and withdrawal from meaningful relations with others, disoriented and disorganized behavior, and hostility.

Of particular concern to health professionals is the rise in teen-age suicide, which is now the second leading cause of death (preceded by accidents) in this age group. Adolescence is a time of many biological and chemical changes in the body as the child matures. Feelings about sexuality reach a fever pitch, with intensified interest in members of the opposite sex and great importance placed on gaining acceptance by peers of both sexes. Introspection is magnified so that all

happenings in life are forecast in terms of what they mean to the individual and his or her values and beliefs. In addition, there are feelings of loss as the teen-ager cuts ties with parents. Thus, there may be a period of mourning, or of wishing that things could be the same as they were previously. Depression is a common response when teen-agers' dependence needs are unmet or when they perceive threats to their self-concept. In periods of crisis, they may consider suicide as the way to end their agony.

One study of girls who attempted suicide pinpointed the focal stimulus as rejection by a boyfriend or lover (Schrut, 1968). Other characteristics included having an unstable or stormy family life, strong feelings of ambivalence toward their parents, and frequent threats of suicide by parents. Other stimuli leading to teen-age suicides include

*Conflicting values.* Victims have difficulty resolving the differences between what they believe as their emerging philosophy of life and what they see in the real world.

*Lack of communication.* The attempt at suicide is a plea for help. Victims are often described as quiet people. Others may come from families in which members talk, shout, and argue but fail to communicate in meaningful and constructive ways.

*Overprotectiveness.* Young people who have been shielded by their parents from all difficulties in life become self-indulgent and lack the confidence to face problems on their own.

*Competitiveness of schools.* The middle-class values of competition and achievement place great stress on teen-agers to succeed. For many, this means attending prestigious colleges where the emphasis is on achievement rather than on self-acceptance and self-growth.

The problems of young people that may cause attempts of suicide as a solution to their crisis situation include

1. Absence or loss of a significant personal relationship. It is said that "the death of love evokes death."
2. Use of drugs or alcohol, which impairs judgment and may increase the probability of suicide.
3. Communication problems at home, and feeling that their parents do not understand them.
4. Sudden change in personality. Behaviors may change or persist, and several behaviors may occur at the same time. For example, a person may become withdrawn, secretive, spend time alone in his or her room and may receive lower grades in schoolwork.

Although suicides are an important cause of

death among young people, the largest number of suicides occur among men in the 35- to 50-year-old group (Hatton, 1977). The other group at risk and having a high death rate from suicide is men over the age of 65 years, especially those who have a physical or mental health problem, are isolated or alienated from others, or do not have an adequate support system.

**Interventions.** It is important for people contemplating suicide to establish communications with someone. Approximately 200 suicide prevention centers and mental health clinics exist in this country where those in crisis can phone for help. Nurses who come in contact with people threatening to take their lives must intervene to help meet the immediate crisis needs. Interventions are geared to insight therapy and manipulation of the causative stimuli, focusing on

1. Assessing the current crisis and the threat causing it.
2. Helping the client to gain a clear idea of the problem and its cause.
3. Reducing the immediate danger. Encourage the client to give up any method planned to carry out the suicidal plan and to make a verbal contract not to take such action.
4. Evaluating the need for medication, hospitalization, or the presence of someone who will help protect the client from self-destructive impulses.
5. Helping the client to return to a climate of being worthy, wanted, and cared for by others. When possible, involve family members and activate other supportive resources.

## THE CRISIS OF STRESS IN NURSING

Studies have concluded that nursing is a stressful occupation that creates high levels of anxiety. Nurses are susceptible to more stressful factors in their occupation than are doctors, lawyers, clerks, and teachers. Nurses carry out tasks that many people regard as disgusting, disagreeable, frightening, or associated with pain and discomfort. They work in highly charged emotional atmospheres in which patients may be in crisis, trying to cope with the threat produced by their illness. Numerous demands are made on nurses by patients, patients' families, doctors, hospital administrators, and other staff members. These stresses may generate strong feelings, but the role of the nurse does not provide for expression of negative feelings and, therefore, anxiety results.

The first level assessment of stress in nurses focuses both on the individual and on the group (nursing unit). Individual behaviors of stress are typically those associated with anxiety, including tachycardia, blushing, high blood pressure, muscular tension and aches, lethargy, headache, increased perspiration, urinary frequency, nausea, and nervousness. Mentally, the nurse may experience irritability, inability to concentrate, feelings of anger and frustration, disorganization, apathy, or depression. Professional and emotional burnout may be a prelude to crisis. Stresses in nurses involved in group interactions are more somatic in nature and also include lack of communication with others, rivalry between shifts, paranoia, and a high rate of turnover of personnel.

The types of stresses in nursing can be classified into four groups: patient care, outside forces acting on the nurse, tensions among the staff, and unrealistic self-expectations. Nurses working with critically ill patients in various settings, such as intensive care, oncology units, and burn units, are vulnerable to high levels of stress. Not all nurses working in intensive care or coronary care have difficulty dealing with the stresses of the "life or death" types of emergencies; some have a high level of morale. Characteristics associated with high morale and low morale include

**High Morale**
Involved in saving lives
Sees self as an "elite" nurse
Sees patients as medically interesting
Close relationship with staff
Challenging work

**Low Morale**
Sees many critically ill and dying patients
Little good news for the family
Complexity of equipment
Limited working space
Traffic and congestion in the unit
Demanding and constant responsibility

Staff nurses identify the bureaucratic structure of the hospital setting and conflicts of the nurse's role as other job-related stresses. These outside forces involve the amount of support from hospital and nursing administration. The bureaucratic structure of the hospital may cause stresses in nurses who wish to carry out comprehensive nursing care and make professional decisions about the quality of care, in contrast with the business goals of the institution. Other features of hospital bureaucracy involve the nurse as an employee: responsibilities are defined in a job description, performance is based on routine procedures and policies, and communications and orders follow a set chain of command. Stress is increased when therapeutic goals for the patient conflict with hospital goals and when little or no room is left for the nurse to use professional judgment or exercise autonomy. Other factors outside the control of the nurse include shortages of nurses, lack of support from hospital and nursing administration, and expecting nurses to perform non-nursing duties or to cover for lack of other supportive services, such as filling in for the absent ward clerk and taking calls at the telephone switchboard at night.

Tensions among members of the nursing staff increase when politics produce power struggles. Dissatisfied staff members spread discontent among others; low morale infects the whole group. Physicians are a source of stress when they regard nurses as inferiors, ignore their suggestions and recommendations about patients, expect nurses to wait on them, and demand immediate attention to their requests or orders rather than treating nurses as colleagues. Many nurses have a "super nurse" complex and have unrealistic expectations that they should know everything, be able to do everything, be able to meet all the patient's needs, be all things to all people, and be able to keep a firm control on their emotions so that they never become angry or irritated. Idealism, competence, and knowledge are certainly needed in giving quality nursing care but not to the point of wasting time and energy in chastizing themselves for failing to achieve perfection. It is much healthier to accept the reality that no nurse is able to help every individual in every situation, that other alternatives can be found, and that others may be more effective in remedying the problem.

**Interventions.** It is important to recognize stress in oneself or in members of the nursing staff. Although some behaviors are obscure, responses to stress should be identified and a notation should be made of their occurrence, followed by a search for their causes. After completing the first and second level assessments, plan to reduce the stresses by manipulating the stimuli producing these effects. A variety of interventions can be used to reduce stresses produced by patient care situations. The adaptation approach helps nurses to identify problems in coping and anxiety in patients who are withdrawn, angry, or depressed or who have been labelled as "complainers," "crocks," or "difficult" patients. Insight therapy, health-teaching, and

guidance through the grieving process are effective interventions that help restore patients to an adaptive state. Other measures that may reduce stress for the nurse include changing his or her assignment to another nursing unit, conferring with other staff members and working together to solve stressful problems, organizing to gain power to make changes in the work setting, or, if necessary, seeking a different job. Nursing covers a wide spectrum; some types of nursing are much less stressful than others.

It is best to avoid the crisis stage and to prevent burnout, which Storlie (1979) has likened to "literal collapse of the human spirit." Measures that are effective in reducing stress include

*Relaxation techniques.* Even on the most hectic and busy day, the nurse should schedule a period of relaxation. For example, lunch should be eaten away from the nursing unit rather than be rushed between answering lights and administering medications.

*Decompensation routines.* Soaking in a hot tub, listening to favorite music, reading, or other activities that allow quiet time for one's self help to decrease tension.

*Physical coping mechanisms.* Exercise is healthy and directs energy outward in such activities as jogging, cleaning closets, dancing, playing tennis, or gardening.

*Reviewing one's philosophy of life.* Develop assertive skills, be able to say "no" and feel comfortable about doing so, and be aware that life is unfinished and goes on in spite of what one does. Before assuming additional tasks or hurrying one's work in ways that increase stress, ask "Must I do this now?" "Will it make a difference to anyone 5 years from now?"

*Develop other aspects of the self.* Avoid concentrating only on the professional life. Engage in other activities, expand other interests, and, above all, keep a sense of humor. Finding satisfactions from other areas of life helps to reduce tensions associated with nursing.

Through the early detection of stresses in the nurse, steps can be taken to reduce the anxiety they produce and problems that result from them. Intervention techniques help to foster the nurse's inner strengths, support belief in one's self, and contribute to high morale and satisfaction in one's profession.

## APPLICATION TO CLINICAL PRACTICE

Crisis theory and intervention is a way of interacting with patients, patient's families, and staff members who are under stress and helping them regain an adapted state. For most nurses who are beginning their nursing practice, the challenge of nursing is gaining skill and expertise in working with sophisticated equipment and in understanding the pathophysiology of seriously ill patients. Yet the most fulfilling challenge is actively helping reduce the emotional trauma of patients and families in crisis.

In the clinical setting, identify factors that produce stress for patients and identify responses made to those stresses. Does illness pose a crisis for the patient? Within the past year, has the patient been subject to any stresses that have required additional energy for coping?

Use the Social-Readjustment Rating Scale on page 378 to determine the numerical value for changes that have occurred in your life during the past year. The higher the mean scores, the greater the chances that you will have a change in your health status. Examine your working situation and identify possible stressors in regard to (1) patient care and condition, (2) outside factors, (3) sources of tension among staff members, and (4) the personal expectations of the nurse. What are some possible interventions that could be used to reduce these stresses?

## REFERENCES

Aguilera, Donna, and Messick, Janice: Crisis Intervention: Theory and Methodology, 3rd ed.: St. Louis, The C. V. Mosby Co., 1978.

Baha, Robert: The potential for suicide. Am J Nurs, 75: 1782–1788, (October) 1975.

Burgess, Ann, and Holmstrom, Lynda: The rape victim in the emergency room. Am J Nurs, 73:1741–1745, (October) 1973.

Burgess, Ann, and Holmstrom, Lynda: Sexual trauma of children and adolescents: pressure, sex, and secrecy. Nurs Clin North Am, 10(3):551–563, (September) 1975.

Curtis, Frances: Observations of unwed pregnant adolescents. Am J Nurs, 74:100–102, (January) 1974.

Davis, Marcella: Socioemotional component of coronary care. Am J Nurs, 72:705–709, (April) 1972.

Fischman, Susan: The pregnancy-resolution decisions of unwed adolescents. Nurs Clin North Am, 10(2):217–227, (June) 1975.

Frye, Barbara, and Barham, Barbara: Reaching out to pregnant adolescents. Am J Nurs, 75:1502–1504, (September) 1975.

Hatton, Corrine, Valente, Sharon, and Rink, Alice: Suicide Assessment and Intervention. New York: Appleton-Century-Crofts, 1977.

Hill, Reuben: Generic features of families under stress. In Crisis Intervention: Selected Readings. Parad, H. J. (ed.). New York, Family Service Association of America, 1965, p. 38.

Hitchcock, Janice: Crisis intervention: the pebble in the pool. Am J Nurs, 73:1388–1389, (August) 1973.

Holmes, Thomas, and Masuda, Minoru: Psychosomatic syndrome. Psychology Today, 6(4):160, (April) 1972.

Hott, Jacquiline: The crisis of expectant fatherhood. Am J Nurs, 76:1436–1440, (September) 1976.

Kandell, Netta: The unwed adolescent pregnancy: an accident? Am J Nurs, 79:2112–2114, (December) 1979.

Kramer, Marlene: Reality Shock: Why Nurses Leave Nursing, St. Louis, The C. V. Mosby Co., 1974.

Kuenzi, Sandra, and Fenton, Mary: Crisis intervention in acute care areas. Am J Nurs, 75:830–834, (May) 1975.

Leaman, Karen: The sexually abused child. Nursing 77, 7(5):68–72, (May) 1977.

Los Angeles Times: Experts to meet in effort to curb suicide rate. June 19, 1977, Part 1, p. 9.

Michaels, Davida: Too much in need of support to give any? Am J Nurs, 71:1932–1935, (October) 1971.

Miller, Thomas W.: Life events scaling: clinical methodological issues. NR, 30:316–320, (September/October) 1981.

Mitchell, Carol: Identifying the hazard: the key to crisis intervention. Am J Nurs, 77:1194–1196, (July) 1977.

Oberst, Marily: The crisis-prone staff nurse. Am J Nurs, 73:1917–1921, (November) 1973.

Olson, Robert J.: Index of suspicion: screening for child abusers. Am J Nurs, 76:108–110, (January) 1976.

Salerno, Elizabeth: A family in crisis. Am J Nurs, 73: 100–103, (January) 1973.

Schrut, Albert: Some typical patterns in the behavior and background of adolescent girls who attempt suicide. Am J Psychiatry, 125:69–74, (July) 1968.

Scully, Rosemary: Stress in the nurse. Am J Nurs, 80: 911–914, (May) 1980.

Seiden, Richard: The problem of suicide on college campuses, J of School Health, 41(5):243–248, 1971.

Shubin, S.: Burnout: the professional hazard you face in nursing. Nursing 78, 8(8):22–27, (July) 1978.

Smith, Peggy, Mumford, D., and Hamner, Elinor: Child-rearing attitudes of single teen-age mothers. Am J Nurs, 79:2115–2116, (December) 1979.

Storlie, Frances: Burnout: the elaboration of a concept. Am J Nurs, 79:2108–2111, (December) 1979.

Symposium. Crisis intervention. Nurs Clin North Am, 9(1):5–96, (March) 1974.

Tierney, Mary Jo, and Strom, Lani: Type A behavior in the nurse. Am J Nurs, 80:915–918, (May) 1980.

Vollen, Karen and Watson, Charles: Suicide in relation to time of day and day of week. Am J Nurs, 75:263, (February) 1975.

Wandelt, Mabel, Pierce, Patricia, and Widdowson, Robert: Why nurses leave nursing and what can be done about it. Am J Nurs, 8:72–77, (January) 1977.

Weil, Susan: The unspoken needs of high-risk pregnant families. Am J Nurs, 81:2047–2049, (November) 1981.

Westercamp, Twlla M.: Suicide. Am J Nurs, 75:260–262, (February) 1975.

# Appendix A _____

## Adaptation Assessment Form

The assessment form consists of all the various behaviors related to the physiological need areas and the growth and developmental tasks for the primary role of the person being assessed. The assessment tool helps to organize data and indicates normal behaviors. When nearly all behavior falls in the normal column, or indicates adaptive behavior, the patient may need minimal nursing assistance to carry out the basic needs. However, behaviors that are observed to be unusual or outside the normal range are generally related to the medical problem or indicate the patient's difficulty in meeting these needs. At a glance, the assessment form can be used to indicate the assistance needed by the patient, and it can also be used as a guide for charting nursing care, as well as the foundation for the nursing care plan.

The assessment tool has been found to be useful in recording observations and information about patients and their progress. It provides an organized method of charting that reduces the chances of omitting useful information about the patient's condition and, at the same time, avoids duplication. The topics can be reduced to a manageable number and can include the need areas of oxygenation, fluids and electrolytes, nutrition, general hygiene and care of skin, rest and activity, and elimination and a category for other observations that contains information about special treatments, equipment, dressings, monitors, health-teaching, and any psychosocial problems in coping. When these labels are used as headings, it is easy for anyone to locate specific information. Charting should be accurate, brief, and complete. Objective behaviors observed by the nurse and subjective information provided by the patient give a meaningful description of the patient's condition.

Charting the specific behaviors of the patient is much more meaningful than recording statements of assumptions or conclusions made by the nurse. For example, many nurses record "Poor appetite" which gives a general idea but in no way indicates whether the person ate anything from the tray, ate everything but without enthusiasm, or merely nibbled. When patients have a problem in the nutritional area, it is advisable to list specific behaviors that show that nutritional needs are being met or the extent of the deficit. An entry that the patient has a beginning decubitus on the sacrum is very general; a better description is "Has reddened area on sacrum, 1½ inch in diameter." This should be followed by interventions used to reduce the effects of pressure: "Back rub given, area gently massaged, patient turned from side to side each hour." First, the need is described in behavioral terms; then, the nursing actions are stated. The nurse selects the pertinent information that is to be charted from the assessment. Not every behavior is included because this would result in lengthy nursing notes that no one would have time to read. A charting system based on the need areas helps to eliminate duplication of such behaviors as "Up to bathroom and voided" in several separate entries. In one entry, under the elimination heading, it can be stated as "Up to bathroom and voided x 3 since 0700."

Name_____
Patient's initials_____
Date_____

| Normal or Expected Behaviors | Unusual or Maladaptive Behaviors |
|---|---|
| *Oxygenation* | |
| Awake; alert; asleep | Lethargic; nonresponsive; comatose<br>Minimal response to verbal, touch, or movement |
| Oriented to reality: time, person, and place | Confused; hallucinating<br>Irrational; irrelevant; memory loss<br>Unusual irritability; headache<br>Apprehension; agitation; restlessness |
| Usual degree of visual acuity | Sudden visual blurring, dimming, or seeing spots |
| Vital signs within normal range:<br>  B/P (lying) _____<br>  B/P (sitting) _____<br>  Pulse _____<br>  Respirations _____ | Vital signs outside normal range:<br>  B/P ↑ in early acute hypoxia<br>  B/P ↓ in progressive or severe hypoxia |
| Pulse—regular and full<br>No pulse deficit | Pulse—rapid, weak, thready<br>Arrhythmia; pulse deficit of _____ |
| Respirations—rhythmic and effortless<br>  Normal chest movement<br>  No complaints of shortness of breath | Respirations—rapid, labored, shallow<br>  Intercostal or substernal retractions<br>  Excessive use of scalenus or abdominal muscles<br>  Barrel-shaped chest<br>  Complains of shortness of breath; chest pain; dilated nostrils<br>  $O_2$ at _____ L/min. |
| Clear unobstructed airway | Wheezing, audible rales, or rhonchi<br>Excessive mucus or secretions<br>Worried, apprehensive facial expression |
| Skin—cool to warm<br>  Pink healthy color of mucous membrane and skin | Skin—clammy, perspiring<br>  Pale, gray, or blue-tinged skin<br>  Reddened areas over bony prominences |
| | **Laboratory findings** |
| RBC   M = 4.8 to 5.5 million/mm³<br>      F = 4.5 to 5.0 million/mm³<br>Hgb   M = 14.5 to 16.5 gm/dl<br>      F = 13.0 to 15.5 gm/dl<br>$PaO_2$      80 to 100 mm Hg<br>$PaCO_2$    35 to 45 mm Hg | RBC _____<br><br>Hgb _____<br><br>$PaO_2$ _____<br>$PaCO_2$ _____ |
| *Fluids and Electrolytes* | |
| Daily<br>  Intake _____ ml<br>  Output _____ ml | Increased intake; decreased intake<br>Increased output; decreased output |
| Urine—normal color and constituents | Urine—concentrated, contains sugar, blood, proteins, or has ammonia odor |
| No abnormal fluid loss through:<br>  Nasogastric suctioning<br>  Vomiting<br>  Profuse perspiration<br>  Wound drainage<br>  Hemorrhage<br>  Diarrhea<br>  Serous fluid loss in burns | Loss of body fluids<br>  Type _____<br>  Amount _____ |
| No use of tubes | Use of IV, hyperalimentation, catheters, suction, or drainage tubes |
| No unusual retention of fluid | Edema of feet, ankles, hands, eyelids, or sacrum<br>Ascites, gurgling rales |
| Maintains usual weight | Gain or loss of more than ½ lb/day |
| Neck veins fill in supine position | Neck veins fill in sitting position;<br>Veins flat when lying down |

| Normal or Expected Behaviors | Unusual or Maladaptive Behaviors |
|---|---|

*Fluids and Electrolytes (Continued)*

| | |
|---|---|
| Pink, moist mucous membranes | Dry mouth and mucous membranes<br>Thirsty |
| Skin—warm, dry, good turgor | Skin—cool, cold, clammy, hot, poor turgor |
| No unusual impairment of muscles, brain function | Examples of imbalances:<br>  Loss of K: large muscles soft and flaccid, extreme weakness, abdomen distended<br>  Loss of Na: dizziness, abdominal cramps, weakness, loss of fluid<br>  Loss of Ca: muscle twitching, muscle and abdominal cramps |

**Laboratory findings**

Hct _____

K   _____

Na  _____

Ca  _____

*Nutrition*

| | |
|---|---|
| Weight in normal range for age and height<br>  Current weight _____<br>  Ideal weight _____ | Overweight _____ lbs<br>Underweight _____ lbs |
| Maintains usual body weight | Loss or gain of _____ lbs<br>  in period of _____ |
| Basal needs _____ cal<br>Activity needs _____ cal<br>Metabolic needs _____ cal<br>Total needs _____ cal | Fever of _____°<br>  Metabolic rate—increased; decreased |
| Consumes foods to meet caloric needs | Food intake lacks _____ calories |
| No restriction of foods | Special diet<br>  Type _____<br>  NPO |
| Eats normally and retains foods | Nausea and vomiting |
| Chews and swallows food easily | Lacks teeth to chew<br>Difficulty swallowing; chokes easily |
| Eats balanced diet of four food groups | Food dislikes _____ |

| | Excess or Lack |
|---|---|
| Protein | _____ |
| Fats | _____ |
| Carbohydrates | _____ |
| Minerals | _____ |
| Vitamins | _____ |

| | |
|---|---|
| Energetic, vigorous | Feels "tired," "nervous," or "weak" |
| Blood glucose—65 to 120 mg/dl | Outside the normal range<br>Blood glucose—_____ mg/dl |
| Hunger before eating<br>Good appetite | No hunger or appetite |
| Skin—pink, firm, moist | Skin—dry, pale, flaky |
| Skeleton—well formed | Skeleton—bowed legs, deformed rib cage |
| Abdomen—flat | Abdomen—protruding, swollen, distended |
| Hair—shiny, springy | Hair—dry, brittle, lifeless |
| Teeth and gums strong and smooth | Dental caries, swollen gums |

*Continued on next page.*

| Normal or Expected Behaviors | Unusual or Maladaptive Behaviors |
| --- | --- |
| *Elimination* | |
| *Urine Elimination* | |
| _____ ml/24 hr | Less than 25 to 30 ml/hr/day<br>Oliguria, anuria<br>Less than 100 ml per voiding |
| Normal characteristics: clear, aromatic, yellow to amber in color | Contains glucose, blood, protein, acetone, sediment<br>Other _____ |
| Continent, control of sphincter<br>Can stop and start urine stream | Loss of control; dribbling<br>Incontinence<br>Retention of urine |
| Voids easily<br>No pain or discomfort | Pain; bladder spasms; urgency; burning; frequency; or bladder distention |
| Voids normally through urethra | Altered means of voiding:<br>    Use of catheter, ureterostomy tube, or urinary diversion |
| *Elimination by Skin* | |
| Dry skin, no visible perspiration | Visible sweating, profuse diaphoresis |
| Normal body temperature | Elevated temperature of _____ ° |
| *Bowel Elimination* | |
| Has regular bowel movement every 1–3 days | Irregular elimination; no bowel movement for _____ days |
| Brown color, moderate amount, and formed stool | Black and tarry appearance; bloody; clay-colored; mucoid<br>Small, hard particles<br>Liquid stool<br>Other _____ |
| Voluntary control, able to initiate or suppress urge | Incontinent, loss of control<br>Leaking of liquid brown stool |
| Abdomen soft<br>Passes flatus<br>Active bowel sounds | Abdomen distended, tympanitic<br>"Gas pains," cramping<br>No bowel sounds |
| Normal defecation through anus | Altered means requiring use of laxatives, cathartics, stool softener, enema, suppositories, or has colostomy or ileostomy |
| *Activity and Sleep Needs* | |
| Body parts present and in good proportion | Amputation of _____<br>Curvature of spine, hump back |
| Good muscle size, definition, and tone | Atrophy of muscles; hypertrophy |
| Smooth, coordinated movement, deliberate and purposeful | Jerky; uncoordinated; tremors; constant motion; very fast; very slow |
| Unrestricted movement of joints | Limited movement; flexion contracture of _____<br>_____; pain on movement; foot drop |
| Good strength; moves independently; overcomes some resistance | Weak grip of right, left, or both hands<br>Requires support; needs assistance; tires easily |
| Good balance; holds head up; bears weight on both feet | Unstable; unable to bear weight; unsteady; wobbles; sways |
| Turns over; changes position; sits up without assistance | Requires help to turn, change position or sit up |
| Carries out activities of daily living— dresses self, feeds self, washes or bathes self, grooms self, controls elimination functions | Requires assistance to dress, undress, cut food, feed self, bathe<br>Unable to shave, comb hair, go to bathroom use toilet or bedpan without assistance |
| Ambulates without assistance; is steady; has normal gait | Unstable; shuffles feet, short or tottering steps; difficulty climbing steps |
| 7–8½ hours of bed rest or as appropriate for age | Bed rest _____ hrs: (less than 7 hrs or more than 8½ hrs<br>Naps—morning, afternoon |
| Usual bedtime _____<br>Usual rising time _____ | Too few, too many hours of sleep |

| Normal or Expected Behaviors | Unusual or Maladaptive Behaviors |
|---|---|
| *Activity and Sleep Needs (Continued)* | |
| No interruptions of sleep, but may awaken at end of sleep cycles as appropriate for age | Interrupted sleep for treatment _____ times Unable to fall back to sleep easily Voids _____ times/night |
| Awakens well rested, refreshed | Awakens tired; yawning; difficult to concentrate |
| Falls asleep easily | Use of sedatives, other drugs, or alcohol to promote sleep |
| *Sensory Regulation* | |
| **Vision**—able to see near and far objects | Wears glasses or lenses Unable to see near or far objects; blurring of images; distortion; blind |
| Appropriate size, color and shape of eyes Sclera white | Skin discolored, lids swollen Sclera red; tearing; drainage |
| Pupils react promptly and are equal in size Eye movements parallel and in unison | Pupils unequal in size Squint; "crossed eyes"; irregular movements; nystagmus Cataracts; removal of lens |
| Identifies different colors | Unable to see certain colors Sees only grays, light, and dark |
| **Hearing**  hears voices within normal range | Uses hearing aid Ringing in ears; sounds merge as noise |
| Hears sounds ranging from high to low tones | Loss of high frequency sounds Makes errors between words beginning with b, d, p, etc. |
| **Speech Formation and Perception**— speaks clearly, initiates and understands language | Mumbles; slurs words; stutters; talks irrelevantly; rambles; uses nonsensical words |
| Speaks dominant language | Speaks _____ language |
| **Sense of Touch**  distinguishes size, shape, or texture of objects | Makes errors in identifying objects by touch |
| At ease; comfortable | Pain Location _____ Pattern _____ Type—itching; numbness; tingling; sharp; stabbing; burning; dull; aching; severe |
| Temperature in normal range—37° C, 98.6° F (± 1°) | Elevated temperature _____° Increased pulse; respirations; skin warm; malaise; headache; delirium, convulsions Hypothermia Skin cold; numbness and loss of feeling; shivering; lethargy |
| Intact, healthy skin | Reddened; damaged; bruised; discolored (ecchymosis), or rash Broken area; surgical incision; decubitus; ulcer; wound |
| **Gustatory**—identifies sweet, sour, salt, or bitter tastes, and combination | Loss of taste for sweets or salt Metallic or abnormal taste sensations |
| **Olfactory**—identifies different odors | Unable to discriminate odors; abnormal odor sensations |
| *Endocrine Regulation* | |
| Normal body growth and development | Stunted growth; excessive size |

Primary Role _____   Stage of life _____

| *Growth and Developmental Tasks* | *Roles* |
|---|---|
| | |
| | |
| | |
| | |
| | |
| | |
| | |

# Appendix B _____

## Sample Nursing Care Plans

Two examples of nursing care plans are presented here. In the case of Mary O'Neil, the assessment data are presented in a narrative form, and a nursing care plan is formulated from the information. Note that a brief history of her illness is stated in the care plan and that her symptoms are aligned with the medical treatment and the related nursing actions to show the logical sequence and relationship among the three sections. Although there may appear to be some overlap or duplication between her medical history of weight loss and the problem of inadequate caloric intake, it is significant that the physician did not take any steps other than to order the low salt diet. It is the concern of the nurse to see that the patient meets her needs in this area and eats the food provided. Only four problems are listed on the care plan, although there may be others that could be identified. When more problems are included they may indicate that the person is completely helpless in meeting most basic needs or that a problem has been broken down into several component parts (each behavior treated as a separate problem) rather than handled as a whole. When several problems are listed, they should be given a priority rating so that the most pressing ones are handled first.

The second nursing care plan gives a descriptive picture of the patient (D. M.) with severe congestive heart failure, her medical treatment, and nursing problems. The nurse observes the patient carefully for complications of her disease in the medical portion of the care plan and, as part of the nursing actions, carries out health-teaching for management of her diabetes and obesity. Almost all patients with a serious health problem have some nursing problems; if they do not, they are undoubtedly in the third stage of illness and ready to be discharged from the hospital. The most common nursing problems include limitation of one's activities, disruption in nutrition, and feelings related to anxiety. D. M. has two of these problems as she attempts to cope with her illness.

With practice, the information from the nursing assessment can be transformed into a written nursing care plan in approximately 30 minutes to one hour.

### CASE OF MRS. MARY O'NEIL

Mrs. Mary O'Neil, age 45 years, was admitted to the oncology unit with metastatic cancer of the breast with lymph node involvement. At age 43 years, she had a left mastectomy with radiation and chemotherapy. She now complains of pain in the chest, nausea, and weight loss.

### *NURSING ASSESSMENT INFORMATION*

Mrs. O'Neil is lying on her left side in a curled up, fetal position with the head of the bed elevated at about 40°. She is wearing a hospital gown, no make-up, and her hair is tousled. She has a worried look on her face, seems tense, and changes her position frequently. Her vital signs are: temperature—98.4, pulse—92, respiration—18, blood pressure—144/90.

The nursing staff describes Mrs. O'Neil as a "complainer," "whiner," and a difficult patient. During the past 4 days, she has complained a great deal and cries much of the time when the nurses are giving her care. She states the low salt diet does not appeal to her or taste any good, so she eats very little food. The odor of the foods make her nauseated. When she does eat, she complains of a catching pain in her right side that she believes is caused by adhesions between her right chest and the liver. She also says that the lymph drainage tubes inside her left chest cause severe pain that bothers her day and night. She asks for pain medication every 3–3½ hours.

For several nights, Mrs. O'Neil has been incontinent of urine and has wet her bed or made puddles on the floor as she hurried to the bathroom. She cries that she has to void every half hour and that she cannot hold her urine. She also complains about the "spots on her lungs," frequent dizziness, loss of weight, a "moon face" as a result of the cortisone she has been taking, and large lumps on her forehead, right knee, and in the clavicular area which have appeared within the past year. Mrs. O'Neil is 5' 3" tall and weighs 112 lbs. She has lost 9 pounds in the past 5 weeks. Yesterday, her fluid intake was 1000 ml, and she did not eat any breakfast this morning.

According to the Kardex, the orders for Mrs. O'Neil include

Up ad lib, and bathroom privileges (BRP).
Low sodium diet.
Routine vital signs.
Darvon 65 mg PO, q 3–4 h, prn for pain.
Demerol 75 mg q 3 h, prn, if pain not relieved by Darvon.
Colace 300 mg daily.
Dalmane 30 mg hs, prn.
2 units of packed cells this pm.
Tests and examinations have included electrocardiogram, AP and lateral chest x-rays, skeletal bone survey, CAT scan of the brain, intravenous pyelogram, CBC, urinalysis, and blood chemistries including Na, Cl, P, K, BUN, and $CO_2$.

The soft tissue lumps and lymph nodes were not biopsied, but the laboratory tests and examinations, including the chest x-ray and IVP, were reported as essentially negative, or within normal limits, except for a mild anemia. The hemoglobin was 10.2 gm with a hematocrit of 37 percent.

## PSYCHOSOCIAL ASSESSMENT

Mrs. O'Neil's husband, son, and daughter visit her every day and phone her often, as do her close friends and neighbors. Her son Patrick is 14 years old and in the ninth grade. Ellen, her daughter, is 18 years old and is to be married in 3 months to a young man the family knows and likes very much. Ellen's mother cries that she may not be alive to see Ellen married and that she does not want to miss her only daughter's wedding. Her husband has just recently been promoted to department manager in a local lumber company. He is concerned about his wife's condition. The whole family seems to be close to one another. Both children helped their mother with the housework and cooking when she was sick at home and are now helping their father to keep the home running in her absence.

Since her surgery 2 years ago, Mrs. O'Neil has been taking numerous medications daily. These have included iron tablets, vitamins, cortisone, Darvon, and aspirin with codeine. "I've taken mountains of pills, but they haven't helped. They didn't make me well," she stated. She wants "medical science" to cure her and rid her of all the pain. Her husband later told the nurse that his wife changes doctors frequently, usually every 3 to 6 months, looking for one who would cure her cancer.

Mrs. O'Neil was born in New York and was of the Greek Orthodox faith until she converted to the Roman Catholic faith shortly after her marriage. She stated that she has not been very religious since she became ill because she has been so unhappy and in such severe pain. It has been more than a year since she has been to Mass or confession. Mary dropped out of school when she was in the eleventh grade. For a number of years, she has been working as a clerk in the lingerie department of a large store. Medical insurance coverage is provided by the company, and she has been on sick leave for more than a month now. She has no interests outside her family and job and does not have any special hobbies or belong to clubs or organizations.

At frequent intervals during the interview, Mrs. O'Neil mentions with tears that even with chemotherapy, the doctors tell her that she only has a 50–50 chance of living. She said that it was not fair for her to get cancer because she tried so hard to live a good life. She did not smoke, drink, or even nurse her babies. Even so, she got cancer and lost her breast.

Based on this information, fill out the medical portion of the nursing care plan, then identify problems that Mary O'Neil has in (1) meeting her basic needs, and (2) coping with her feelings and changes in her life, so that the nurse can help her move toward adaptation.

## SAMPLE NURSING CARE PLAN

Medical Diagnosis

Primary   Metastatic Cancer of Breast

Secondary   Anemia

Patient's Initials   (Mary O'Neil)

Primary Role   45-year-old woman

Secondary Roles   wife, mother of two, sales clerk, Roman Catholic, friend

| Medical Problems | Medical Treatment | Nursing Actions |
| --- | --- | --- |
| **Metastatic Cancer of the Breast.** Two years ago, she had left mastectomy followed by chemotherapy, including hormones and steroids. | Up ad lib, BRP | Encourage activity within her abilities. Take own bath, hygiene, but assist if needed. |
| | Low salt diet | Assess actual food intake and caloric needs. Determine food likes/dislikes; give small frequent feedings. Fluids to 2000 ml daily. |
| Now admitted with complaints of recent weight loss of 9 lbs nausea and vomiting pains in chest frequent dizziness urinary frequency and incontinence at night lumps on forehead, right knee, and clavicular area which have appeared in the past year. | Routine vital signs | Check vital signs at least bid. Check for cardiorespiratory complications. |
| | Darvon 65 mg PO, q 3–4 h, prn, for pain | Assess pain location, duration, cause. Position for comfort, give back rub, and provide diversion when pain controlled. Observe the 5 rights, and response to drugs. |
| | Demerol 75 mg q 3 h, prn for pain, if not relieved by Darvon Colace 300 mg daily Dalmane 30 mg hs, prn | |
| Diagnostic work-up included ECG, IVP, CBC, skeletal bone survey, chest x-rays, CAT scan, blood chemistries, and urinalysis. Lab tests, chest x-ray, and IVP were normal except for Hgb 10.2 gm. | 2 units of packed cells this PM | Observe for adverse effects, site of the needle, and rate of flow. |

| Nursing Problems Manifested by Stated Behaviors | Stimuli—Focal (F) and Contextual (C) | Goal and Nursing Interventions |
| --- | --- | --- |
| 1. **Patient has inadequate caloric intake to maintain body weight.** —states the odor of food makes her nauseated. —says the low salt diet doesn't taste good or appeal to her. —eats only a few bites of food from the tray. —has lost 9 lbs. in past 5 weeks, now weighs 112 lbs. —says, "What's the use? I'm afraid I'm going to die anyway." | F—Metastatic cancer of breast C—anxiety re health C—low salt diet C—pain in chest (pulling of drain) C—pain medications C—height 5' 3" C—nausea | **Patient will eat sufficient calories to maintain body weight.** —assist in selecting balanced meals with foods she likes. —provide nourishment between meals. —control pain by giving medication prior to meals or activities. —have her reduce movement when nauseated. —weigh daily each morning at 7 AM. —obtain order for antiemetic if nausea persists. —insight therapy for anxiety: identify the threat, strengthen her coping mechanisms. |

| Nursing Problems Manifested by Stated Behaviors | Stimuli—Focal (F) and Contextual (C) | Goal and Nursing Interventions |
|---|---|---|
| 2. **Patient has frequent urinary incontinence, especially at night.**<br>—complains she cannot hold her urine. When she has the urge, she cannot wait at all.<br>—has to void about every half hour during the day.<br>—cries because she has wet her bed the past two nights and makes puddles on the way to the bathroom. She said the nurses scolded her.<br>—takes sleeping pill and often a hypo for pain at bedtime. | F—Metastatic cancer of breast<br>C—sleeping medication<br>C—reduced fluid intake<br>C—anxiety<br>C—age 45 yr<br>C—pain in chest | **Patient will regain control over urine elimination.**<br>—schedule intake of 1500–2000 ml:<br>  7:00 AM – 3:00 PM –1000–1250<br>  3:00 AM – 11:00 PM – 500– 650<br>  11:00 PM – 7:00 AM—minimal<br>—provide bedpan for use at night, place it on chair or nearby so she can easily reach it.<br>—offer bedpan or assistance to bathroom at frequent intervals day and night. |

*Self-Concept Mode*

| Nursing Problems Manifested by Stated Behaviors | Stimuli—Focal (F) and Contextual (C) | Goal and Nursing Interventions |
|---|---|---|
| 3. **Patient has depression and fears of dying.**<br>—wants doctors and medical science to cure her and rid her of pain "once and for all."<br>changes doctors frequently<br>states she has taken a mountain of pills and they have not helped.<br>—states her chest pain is caused by lymph drainage tubes and adhesions to the liver.<br>—cries frequently during day when talking to staff, family, or others.<br>—states she's afraid she will not live to see her daughter married in 3 months. | F—Metastatic cancer of breast<br>C—knowledge of body function and disease<br>C—no external evidence of lymph drainage tubes<br>C—expected a cure of disease<br>C—has 2 teen-age children<br>C—spread of disease in past year; nausea; lumps; weight loss<br>C—anxiety<br>C—age 45 yr | **Patient will have decreased depression and fears of dying.**<br>—use insight therapy for her anxiety:<br>  identify the anxiety and threat;<br>  help her to identify it and the stressors;<br>  develop alternative ways to cope, and<br>    strengthen effective coping mechanisms.<br>—give accurate health information about disease, function of body, and treatment.<br>—help her to set achievable short-term goals.<br>—encourage family members and friends to provide emotional support by visits, phone calls, etc. |
| 4. **Patient has feelings of guilt that she is being punished for past sins.**<br>—stated she tried to live the good life; did not smoke, drink, or nurse her babies, but still got cancer.<br>—has not attended Mass or confession for more than a year.<br>—stated she would like to see a priest when it was suggested by nurse. | F—expectation that if you follow the rules, you will be rewarded<br>C—health habits<br>C—knowledge of body and disease<br>C—raised as Greek Orthodox<br>C—converted to Catholicism | **Patient will have decreased feelings of guilt.**<br>—arrange for priest to visit.<br>—accept her feelings and explore them using insight therapy.<br>—provide health-teaching about disease, functions of the body, etc. |

## SAMPLE NURSING CARE PLAN

| Medical Diagnosis | Patient's Initials   D. M. |
|---|---|
| Primary   Congestive heart failure | Primary Role   54-year old woman |
| Secondary   Hypertension, chronic thrombophlebitis, | Secondary Roles   mother of 2, renter, |
|    diabetes, poliomyelitis |    church member, separated, Girl Scout |
|  |    leader |

| Medical Problems | Medical Treatment | Nursing Actions |
|---|---|---|
| Has a history of CHF for 2 yr, with high blood pressure. | Bed rest, BRP as tolerated | Elevate head of bed 30°. |
| Has become worse in past 2 months. |  | Support arms on pillows or rest on overbed table. |
| She has progressive swelling of legs and 30 lb weight gain in past 6 months. | Vital signs q 4 h | Monitor more frequently if needed. |
| On admission she had |  | Be alert for tachycardia, rales, and signs of complications. |
| —inability to speak except when sitting upright. | O₂ at 2 L/min prn | Observe for signs of respiratory distress, dyspnea, and anxiety. |
| —severe dyspnea on exertion accompanied by anxiety. |  | Check respiration and pulse rates for tolerance for activities. Provide rest periods frequently. |
| —severe generalized edema of the legs. |  |  |
| —paralysis of right leg following polio at age 27 yr. | Lasix, 40 mg, IV, q 12 h Intake and output | Check heparin lock, urine output, and fluid balance. |
| —ulcers of right and left leg, 1 cm in in diameter, tender. | Elevate feet | Elevate legs when in bed, avoid crossing legs. Check for signs of thrombosis, emboli. Care of skin. |
| **Diabetes Mellitus** |  |  |
| Has family history of diabetes, and has required insulin for years. | NPH pork insulin, 20 u, subcutaneous, q AM | Rotate sites. Use medicine at room temperature and check dosage. |
| Obese, is 5′ 2″ and weighs 195 lb. | Test urine for sugar and acetone qid | Collect second voided specimen. Record results. |
| Fasting blood sugar—212 mg on second hospital day. | 2 gm Na, 1000 cal ADA diet | Make sure diet is eaten, no salt is added. Health-teaching about diet, skin care, and managing health problems. |
|  | Weigh daily | Use same scale, weigh at same time and same conditions each morning. |
| **Chronic Thrombophlebitis** |  |  |
| Has had recurrent thrombophlebitis and leg ulcers for 24 yr. Skin of legs is thick and lichenized. | Heparin 5000 u (H) q 12 h | Rotate sites on abdomen. Do not aspirate or massage site. Check for bleeding at site, gums, gastrointestinal tract, renal, etc. |
| Has taken heparin 5000 u (H) for 12 yr. |  |  |

| Nursing Problems Manifested by Stated Behaviors | Stimuli—Focal (F) and Contextual (C) | Goal and Nursing Interventions |
|---|---|---|
| 1. **Patient has decreased ability to carry out her own ADLs.** | F—Congestive heart failure | **Patient will carry out own ADLs as tolerated and without dyspnea.** |
|    —is in bed approximately 23 hr/day, as opposed to usual 7 hr/night at home. | C—polio with paralysis of right leg | Conserve energy by |
|    —gets up only to ambulate to the bathroom with assistance. | C—Diabetes for 8 yr | —providing assistance with bath, hygiene, ambulation, and other activities. Anticipate other needs. |
|    —is able to wash hands and face, but not to bathe the rest of her body. | C—severe edema of legs C—age 54 yr | —pacing activities to allow rest after each. |
|    —after moving about or ambulating, she complains of dyspnea, and has deep cyanosis around the mouth. | C—obesity C—diuretic medication C—bed rest with BRP | —giving O₂ before and during activities. Provide long tubing so patient can ambulate with it. |
|    —uses O₂ intermittently during the day. | C—O₂ prn | —when decreasing O₂, allow time to adjust to room air before exertion. |
|    —complains that she cannot catch her breath when lying down, but continues to sit at the side of the bed with feet hanging down. |  | Provide support when ambulating by —leaving call bell so nurse can be summoned. |
|    —gets up to go to the bathroom frequently and 2–3 times during the night to void large amounts of urine. |  | —obtaining cane or walker and instruct in its use. |
|    —walks with difficulty because right leg is paralyzed, and needs support when ambulating. |  | —bedside commode or bedpan can be used when frequent voiding leads to prolonged fatigue and shortness of breath. |

| Nursing Problems Manifested by Stated Behaviors | Stimuli—Focal (F) and Contextual (C) | Goal and Nursing Interventions |
|---|---|---|
| 2. **Patient has feelings of anxiety and fear about her health problems.**<br>—talks almost continually when anyone is in the room.<br>—cries intermittently when talking about all the problems she has.<br>—states she overeats to make herself feel better and calmer.<br>—she is 5′ 2″ tall, and weighs 195 lb.<br>—states she is afraid of the possibility of heart surgery (mitral commissurotomy) and that it might fail.<br>—she said the doctor told her how dangerous the operation could be for her because of the diabetes, clotting, and her weight problems.<br>—states that she is separated from her husband but that she has a son and a 20-year-old daughter who help her. She worries about the daughter, who is unmarried but will have a baby in a couple of weeks.<br>—states that she cannot do anything anymore, she is so disabled. She used to work as a bookkeeper, was a Girl Scout leader, and loved to dress up in a formal gown to attend dinners at a women's club. | F—Congestive heart failure<br>C—Diabetes mellitus<br>C—Thrombophlebitis of legs<br>C—Heparin treatment—12 yr<br>C—paralyzed right leg<br>C—obesity<br>C—age 54 yr<br>C—former bookkeeper | **Patient will have decreased feelings of anxiety and fear.**<br>Use insight therapy to<br>—provide opportunity to talk of her worries and anxieties.<br>—help her to identify the threat and some of its causes.<br>—use open-ended questions.<br>—assist to change or strengthen her coping mechanisms (change from overeating).<br>Provide health-teaching as needed.<br>—diabetic diet and salt restrictions.<br>—pre- and post-operative instructions.<br>—management of medications and treatment needed for chronic illnesses. Signs and symptoms of hyperglycemia, other complications.<br>Provide information about social services, such as community counselling centers for family and/or personal problems. |

## EVALUATION

After 10 days of diuresis, treatment, and tests, Mrs. M. was discharged. She had lost 13 lb, no longer required oxygen, had minimal dyspnea when ambulating, eating, or moving slowly. She was far less anxious and seemed more at ease. Following the angiogram, the doctor informed her that the risk of surgery far outweighed the benefits at this time but could be reconsidered when she weighed about 140 lb.

# Index

Page numbers in *italics* refer to illustrations; page numbers
followed by (t) refer to tables.